# Evidence-Based Crime Prevention

Crime prevention policy and practice is often far from objective. Instead of being based on scientific evidence the crime policy agenda is sometimes driven by political ideology, anecdotal evidence and program favorites of the month. *Evidence-Based Crime Prevention* seeks to change this by comprehensively and rigorously assessing the existing scientific knowledge on the effectiveness of crime prevention programs internationally.

Reviewing more than 600 scientific evaluations of programs intended to prevent crime in settings such as families, schools, labor markets, places and communities, this book grades programs on their validity using "the scientific methods scale." This collection, which brings together contributions from leading researchers in the field of crime prevention, will provide policy-makers, researchers and community leaders with an understandable source of information about what works, what does not work and what is promising in preventing crime.

**Lawrence W. Sherman** is Albert M. Greenfield Professor of Human Relations in the Department of Sociology and Director of the Jerry Lee Center of Criminology and Fels Center of Government, University of Pennsylvania. **David P. Farrington** is Professor of Psychological Criminology in the Institute of Criminology, University of Cambridge. **Brandon C. Welsh** is Assistant Professor in the Department of Criminal Justice, University of Massachusetts Lowell. **Doris Layton MacKenzie** is Professor in the Department of Criminology and Criminal Justice, University of Maryland.

# Evidence-Based Crime Prevention

Edited by Lawrence W. Sherman,
David P. Farrington,
Brandon C. Welsh and
Doris Layton MacKenzie

WITHDRAWN

London and New York

First published 2002 by Routledge
11 New Fetter Lane, London EC4P 4EE

Simultaneously published in the USA and Canada
by Routledge
29 West 35th Street, New York, NY 10001

Transferred to Digital Printing 2003

*Routledge is an imprint of the Taylor & Francis Group*

© 2002 Editorial matter and selection, Lawrence W. Sherman,
David P. Farrington, Brandon C. Welsh and Doris Layton
MacKenzie; individual chapters, the contributors

Typeset in Baskerville by Wearset Ltd, Boldon, Tyne and Wear
Printed and bound in Great Britain by
TJI Digital, Padstow, Cornwall

*British Library Cataloguing in Publication Data*
A catalogue record for this book is available from the British Library

*Library of Congress Cataloging in Publication Data*
Evidence-based crime prevention/edited by Lawrence W. Sherman
... [et al.].
    p.cm.
  Includes bibliographical references and index.
  1. Crime prevention.  I. Sherman, Lawrence W.
HV7431 .E98 2002
364.4–dc21
                                              2001048447

ISBN 0-415-27047-2

# Contents

# Tables

# Contributors

**Shawn D. Bushway** is an Assistant Professor in the Department of Criminology and Criminal Justice, University of Maryland (College Park, Maryland).

**John E. Eck** is an Associate Professor in the Division of Criminal Justice, University of Cincinnati (Cincinnati, Ohio).

**David P. Farrington** is Professor of Psychological Criminology in the Institute of Criminology, University of Cambridge (Cambridge, England), and Jerry Lee Research Professor of Criminology in the Department of Criminology and Criminal Justice, University of Maryland (College Park, Maryland).

**Denise C. Gottfredson** is a Professor in the Department of Criminology and Criminal Justice, University of Maryland (College Park, Maryland).

**Akemi Hoshi** is a graduate student in the Department of Criminal Justice, University of Massachusetts Lowell (Lowell, Massachusetts).

**Doris Layton MacKenzie** is a Professor in the Department of Criminology and Criminal Justice, University of Maryland (College Park, Maryland).

**Stacy Skroban Najaka** is a Faculty Research Assistant in the Department of Criminology and Criminal Justice, University of Maryland (College Park, Maryland).

**Peter Reuter** is a Professor in the School of Public Affairs and the Department of Criminology and Criminal Justice, University of Maryland (College Park, Maryland).

**Lawrence W. Sherman** is Albert M. Greenfield Professor of Human Relations in the Department of Sociology and Director of the Jerry Lee Center of Criminology and the Fels Center of Government, University of Pennsylvania (Philadelphia, Pennsylvania).

**Brandon C. Welsh** is an Assistant Professor in the Department of Criminal Justice, University of Massachusetts Lowell (Lowell, Massachusetts).

**David B. Wilson** is an Assistant Professor in the Administration of Justice, George Mason University (Washington, DC).

# Foreword

You may wonder why someone from the broadcast industry is writing the foreword to this book. It can be answered in one word: *research*. I use research to produce ground-breaking changes in my industry. Research is routinely used as the springboard for success in the business world and it's high time research became a routine springboard for success in public policy. Research is simply information and information is essential for success. You may not always get the right answers immediately, but research can show you the right questions.

I've been fortunate in being involved in a number of philanthropic endeavors, particularly in the areas of crime prevention, education and community development in America's inner cities. I know how important it is to empower our public and private sector leaders with information about what works and what doesn't to make our communities safe and more thriving.

Back in 1997, I was surfing the Internet and found a just-released report, *Preventing Crime: What Works, What Doesn't, What's Promising*. I called the senior author, Lawrence Sherman, and arranged to meet him at the University of Maryland. Here was research used to tell us about the widely varying rates of success in our nation's many crime prevention efforts. The report was justifiably hailed by the *New York Times* as "the most comprehensive study ever of crime prevention."

Since then I have had the chance to work closely with Lawrence Sherman and his co-authors. In forming the Consortium for Building a Safer Society (CBASS), we've been able to bring together researchers at the University of Pennsylvania, the University of Maryland, and Cambridge University to broaden the base of knowledge in criminal justice and connect this information to the public.

CBASS has brought together policy leaders, the media, and the worlds of business, philanthropy, and academe. The report's authors have presented their findings to the US Congress, federal agencies, state legislatures, foreign governments, and universities throughout the world. A web site, www.preventingcrime.org, has been launched to make findings available as fast as possible.

*Evidence-Based Crime Prevention* is an outstanding new study which continues to answer those three basic questions – what works, what doesn't, and what's promising. It shows that crime prevention means more than just cops on the beat or locks on your door. We are beginning to see the connections with areas such as communities, corrections, labor markets, premises and places, policing and schools. We thank the authors for broadening the definitions and strengthening our knowledge base of the origins and spread of crime.

But while it gives many answers, *Evidence-Based Crime Prevention* also raises many questions. As you embark upon this historic study, view it not as the last word on crime prevention, but rather the first. I hope it will be viewed as the beginning of a long journey toward a deeper understanding of the causes and prevention of crime, leading to policies and programs based not on rhetoric but on research and results.

Jerry Lee
President
Radio Station WBEB 101.1FM
President
Jerry Lee Foundation
Founder
Jerry Lee Center of Criminology
University of Pennsylvania

# Preface

Effective public policy and practice needs to be based on scientific evidence. This is the approach taken in medicine and other fields dedicated to the betterment of society. This is not, however, the standard usually adopted in crime prevention and criminal justice. Anecdotal evidence, program favorites of the month and political ideology seemingly drive much of the crime policy agenda. This book aims to change this by assessing the existing scientific knowledge on the effectiveness of crime prevention programs. It shows what works, what does not work and what is promising in preventing crime, reviewing programs as diverse as training parents in child rearing techniques, preschool intellectual enrichment programs, drug abuse resistance education (DARE) in schools, CCTV and improved street lighting, targeted police activities at crime hot spots, and juvenile boot camps.

This book presents the most up-to-date, comprehensive and rigorous assessment of the scientific evidence on the effectiveness of preventing crime in the United States, the United Kingdom and internationally. It reviews more than 600 scientific evaluations of programs intended to prevent crime in seven settings in which crime prevention takes place: families, schools, communities, labor markets, places (e.g. urban centers, homes), police and courts/corrections. Programs are evaluated on the "scientific methods scale," which ranks scientific studies from 1 (weakest) to 5 (strongest) on overall internal validity. This scale is not only important scientifically, but it also helps more effectively to communicate science to policymakers, practitioners, the media and the general public.

This book updates and substantially revises the 1997 report *Preventing Crime: What Works, What Doesn't, What's Promising*, by Lawrence Sherman and his colleagues at the University of Maryland. This report was commissioned by the United States Congress as an independent, scientifically rigorous assessment of more than $4 billion worth of federally-sponsored crime prevention programs. The *New York Times* called *Preventing Crime* "the most comprehensive study ever of crime prevention." It is our hope that the present volume will deserve a similar accolade and, more importantly, lead to more effective public policy in preventing crime and building safer communities.

This book is a publication of the Jerry Lee Center of Crimology at the University of Pennsylvania, in collaboration with the University of Maryland and the University of Cambridge.

The development of this book, and its contribution to the field, was the result of many dedicated and visionary individuals and funding organizations. Jerry Lee, President of the Jerry Lee Foundation and Philadelphia radio station WBEB-101.1, provided the initial inspiration for this project and continues to be one of its most important benefactors. Funding was also provided by an anonymous foundation and the National Institute of Justice. The authors, of course, take sole responsibility for the work.

Lawrence W. Sherman
David P. Farrington
Brandon C. Welsh
Doris Layton MacKenzie

# 1 Preventing crime

*Lawrence W. Sherman, David P. Farrington,*
*Brandon C. Welsh and Doris Layton MacKenzie*

Unfortunately, "crime prevention today as in the past has a tendency to be driven more by rhetoric than reality" (Visher and Weisburd, 1998, p. 238). Effective public policy and practice needs to be based on scientific evidence. This is an approach that has garnered much support in medicine (Millenson, 1997) and other fields dedicated to the betterment of society. It is not, however, the standard usually adopted in crime prevention and criminal justice. Anecdotal evidence, program favorites of the month, and political ideology seemingly drive much of the crime policy agenda. As a result, we are left with a patchwork of programs that are of unknown potential in preventing crime. Crime prevention programs may or may not work – or, worse yet, may produce harmful or iatrogenic results. We are not suggesting that the public is being intentionally misled by lawmakers and policymakers who are funding programs with no scientific evidence of effectiveness, but rather that lawmakers and policymakers are shirking their responsibility to the taxpaying public by not giving funding priority to those programs with evidence of effectiveness in preventing crime.

In writing on the subject of evidence-based policing, Sherman (1998, p. 6; see also Sherman and Eck, Chapter 8, this volume) notes that: "Most police practice, like medical practice, is still shaped by local custom, opinions, theories, and subjective impressions." But "[e]vidence-based policing challenges those principles of decision making and creates systematic feedback to provide continuous quality improvement in the achievement of police objectives" (Sherman, 1998, p. 6). This is equally applicable to the larger field of crime prevention, whether it be for police, courts or corrections, or alternative, non-criminal justice approaches, such as violence prevention programs in schools or gang intervention programs in communities.

By assessing existing scientific knowledge on the effectiveness of crime prevention programs and presenting this information in an understandable form for decision-makers, the present volume aims to change how national, state, and local crime policies and practices are shaped. The more difficult task, one that this book does not pretend to solve fully, is how to change the mindset of decision-makers to utilize scientific knowledge – to subscribe to the evidence-based approach to preventing crime and building safer communities.

This chapter presents an overall framework for understanding the evidence-based approach to preventing crime. It is divided into six sections. The first provides a brief history of the research project that led to the development of this book's predecessor, *Preventing Crime*, by Lawrence Sherman and his colleagues (1997), which inspired the present volume. The second and third sections deal with important theoretical and organizational features of crime prevention, as used throughout this volume. The fourth section presents key elements contributing to a science of crime prevention. The fifth section summarizes the research methods employed in the collection, review, and analysis of crime prevention programs reported in Chapters 3 to 9, and the sixth and final section describes the key aims and the layout of this book.

## History of project

In 1996, a federal law required the US Attorney General to provide the US Congress with an independent review of the effectiveness of state and local crime prevention assistance programs funded by the US Department of Justice, "with special emphasis on factors that relate to juvenile crime and the effect of these programs on youth violence." The law required that the review "employ rigorous and scientifically recognized standards and methodologies." Framers of the law expected that the evaluation would measure three important aspects of crime prevention programs:

1   reductions in delinquency, juvenile crime, youth gang activity, youth substance abuse, and other high-risk factors;
2   reductions in the risk factors in the community, school, and family environments that contribute to juvenile violence; and
3   increases in the protective factors that reduce the likelihood of delinquency and criminal behavior.[1]

After an external, peer-reviewed competition, the National Institute of Justice (NIJ) selected the proposal of a group from the University of Maryland's Department of Criminology and Criminal Justice to perform the review. With only 6 months to complete the review, the authors achieved something just short of a miracle in social science research: they reviewed just over 500 crime prevention programs and produced a 565-page report. The report, authored by Lawrence Sherman and his colleagues and released in 1997, was entitled *Preventing Crime: What Works, What Doesn't, What's Promising*.[2] The *New York Times* called *Preventing Crime* "[t]he most comprehensive study ever of crime prevention" (Butterfield, 1997, p.A20).

Following the release of the report, the University of Maryland's Department of Criminology and Criminal Justice established a Crime Prevention Effectiveness Program with the support of gifts and grants from private foundations and donors. The Program had two goals: to better inform policymakers on the importance of basing crime prevention programs on scientific evidence; and to advance the body of knowledge upon which sound crime prevention decisions can be made.

The *Preventing Crime* report has been the subject of four US Congressional hearings, and its authors have been invited on a number of occasions to brief policymakers and other criminal justice leaders throughout the US and internationally. The report's largest impact, however, has been evident in the

United Kingdom, where it greatly influenced the Home Office report on *Reducing Offending* (Nuttall, Goldblatt and Lewis, 1998). This led to the £250 million, 3-year Home Office "Crime Reduction Programme" initiated by Home Secretary Jack Straw in April 1999.

## Key concepts in crime prevention

Crime prevention is widely misunderstood. In the US, for example, the national debate over crime often treats "prevention" and "punishment" as mutually exclusive concepts, polar opposites on a continuum of "soft" versus "tough" responses to crime: peer mentoring versus juvenile boot camps, for example. The science of criminology, however, contains no such dichotomy. It is as if public debate over physics had drawn a dichotomy between flame and matches. Flame is a result. Matches are only one tool for achieving that result. Other tools besides matches are well known to cause fuel to ignite into flame, from magnifying glasses to tinder boxes.

Similarly, crime prevention is a result, while punishment is only one possible tool for achieving that result. Both peer mentoring and juvenile boot camps may logically succeed or fail in achieving the scientific definition of crime prevention: any policy which causes a lower number of crimes to occur in the future than would have occurred without that policy.[3] Some kinds of punishment for some kinds of offenders may be preventive, while others may be "criminogenic" or crime-causing, and still others may have no effect at all. Exactly the same may also be true of other programs that do not consist of legally imposed punishment, but which are justified by the goal of preventing crime.

Crime prevention is therefore defined not by its intentions, but by its consequences. These consequences can be assessed in at least two ways: the number of criminal events; and the number of criminal offenders (Hirschi, 1986). Some would also assess them by the amount of harm prevented (Reiss and Roth, 1993, pp.59–61) or by the number of victims harmed or harmed repeatedly (Farrell, 1995). What all of these definitions have in common is their focus on observed effects, and not the "hard" or "soft" content, of a program.

Which definition of crime prevention ultimately dominates public discourse is a critically important factor in political and public understanding of the issues. If the crime prevention debate is framed solely in terms of the symbolic labels of punishment versus prevention, policy choices may be made more on the basis of emotional appeal than on solid evidence of effectiveness. By employing the scientific definition of crime prevention as a consequence, this book is in keeping with the Congressional mandate of the 1997 report: "to employ rigorous and scientifically recognized standards and methodologies." It broadens the debate to encompass the entire range of policies we can pursue to build a safer society. A rigorously empirical perspective on what works best is defined by the data from research findings, not from ideologically driven assumptions about human nature.

The value of a broad framework for analyzing crime prevention policies is its focus on the whole forest rather than on each tree. Most debates about crime prevention address one policy at a time. Few debates, either in politics or criminology, consider the relative value of all prevention programs competing for funding. While scientific evidence may show that two different programs both "work" to prevent crime, one may be far more cost-effective than the other. One may have a stronger effect, cutting criminal events by 50 percent, while the other cuts crimes by only 20 percent; or one may have a longer duration, reducing crimes among younger people whose average remaining lifetime is 50 years, compared to a program treating older people with an average remaining life of 20 years. A fully informed debate about crime prevention policy choices requires performance measures combining duration and strength of program effect. While such accurate measures of "profitability" and "payback" periods are a standard tool in business investment decisions, they have been entirely lacking in crime prevention policy debates (but see Aos *et al.*, 2001).

Yet comparative measurement is not enough. Simply comparing the return on investment in each crime prevention policy to its alternatives can mask another key issue: the possible interdependency between policies, or the economic and social conditions required for a specific policy to be effective. Crime prevention programs are not delivered in a vacuum. A Head Start program may fail to prevent crime in a community where children grow up with daily gunfire. A chain gang may have little deterrent effect in a community with 75 percent unemployment. It may be necessary to mount programs in several institutional settings simultaneously – such as labor markets, families, and police – in order to find programs effective in each setting.

One theory is that the effectiveness of crime prevention in each of the seven institutional settings depends heavily on local conditions in other institutions. Put another way, the necessary condition for successful crime prevention practices in one setting is adequate support for the practice in related settings. Schools cannot succeed without supportive families; families cannot succeed without supportive labor markets; labor markets cannot succeed without well-policed safe streets; and police cannot succeed without community participation in the labor market. These and other examples are an extension of the "conditional deterrence" theory in criminology (Tittle and Logan, 1973; Williams and Hawkins, 1986), which claims that legal punishment and its threat can only be effective at preventing crime if reinforced by the informal social controls of other institutions. The conditional nature of legal deterrence may apply to other crime prevention strategies as well. Just as exercise can only work properly on a well-fed body, crime prevention of all kinds may only be effective when the institutional context is strong enough to support it.

By suggesting that the effectiveness of some crime prevention efforts may depend upon their institutional contexts, we do not present a pessimistic vision of the future. While some might say that no program can work until the "root causes" of crime are cured, we find no scientific basis for that conclusion – and substantial evidence against it. What this book documents is the potential for something much more precise and useful, based on a more open view of the role of scientific evaluation in crime prevention: a future in which program evaluations carefully measure, and systematically vary, the institutional context of each program. That strategy is essential for a body of scientific knowledge to be developed about the exact connections between institutional context and program effectiveness.

We expect that greater attention to the interdependency of institutions may help us discover how to shape many institutional factors simultaneously to prevent crime more successfully than we have been able to do thus far. The apparent failure of a few efforts to prevent crime does not mean that we should give up our work to prevent crime. Such failures marked the early stages of almost all major advances in science, from the invention of the light bulb to the development of the polio vaccine. The fact that our review finds crime prevention successes in all seven of the institutional settings (see Chapters 3 to 9) suggests that even more trial and error could pay off handsomely. In the US, the national investment in research and development for crime prevention to date has been trivial (Reiss and Roth, 1993; Blumstein and Petersilia, 1995), especially in relation to the level of public concern about the problem. Attacking the crime problem on many institutional fronts at once should offer more, not fewer, opportunities for success.

Defining crime prevention by results, rather than program intent or content, focuses scientific analysis on three crucial questions:

1  What is the independent effect of each program or practice on a specific measure of crime?
2  What is the comparative return on investment for each program or practice, using a common metric of cost and crimes prevented? (For recent research on this question, see Welsh and Farrington, 2000; Welsh, Farrington and Sherman, 2001.)
3  What conditions in other institutional settings are required for a crime prevention program or practice to be effective, or to increase or reduce that effectiveness?

The current state of science barely allows us to address the first question, and it tells us very little about the second or third questions. Just framing the questions, however, reveals the potential contribution that government support for crime prevention evaluations could offer. That potential may depend, in turn, on a clear understanding of the location of every crime prevention practice or program in a broad network of social institutions.

## Settings, practices and programs

Crime prevention is a result of everyday practices concentrated in different institutional settings. A "setting" is a social stage for playing out various roles, such as parent, child, neighbor, employer, teacher, and church leader. There are many ways to define these settings, and their boundaries are necessarily arbitrary. Yet much of the crime prevention literature fits quite neatly into seven major institutional settings: (1) families, (2) schools, (3) communities, (4) labor markets, (5) places, (6) police agencies and (7) courts and corrections. The definitions of these settings for crime prevention are rather broad, and sometimes they overlap. But as a framework for organizing research findings on crime prevention effectiveness, they are quite workable.

Crime prevention research examines two basic types of efforts in these seven settings. One type is a "practice," defined as an ongoing routine activity that is well established in that setting, even if it is far from universal. Most parents make children come home at night, most schools have established starting times, most stores try to catch shoplifters, most police departments answer emergency calls. Some of these practices have been tested for their effects on crime prevention. Most have not. Some of them (such as police patrols and school teacher salaries) are funded in part by government programs. Most are not. Regardless of the source of funding, we define a practice as an activity that may change naturally over time, but which would continue in the absence of specific new government policies to change or restrict it.

A "program," in contrast, is a focused effort to change, restrict or create a routine practice in a crime prevention setting. Many, but far from all, programs are funded by governments. Churches may adopt programs to discourage parents from spanking children or letting children watch violent television shows and movies. Universities may adopt programs to escort students from the library to their cars in the hours after midnight. Shopping malls may ban juveniles unescorted by their parents on weekend evenings, and police may initiate programs to enforce long-ignored curfew or truancy laws. In time, some programs may turn into practices, with few people remembering the time before the program was introduced.

Perhaps the clearest distinction between programs and practices is found among those programs requiring additional resources. The disciplinary practices of parents, for example, and the hiring practices of employers are largely independent of tax revenue. But calling battered women to notify them of their assailant's imminent release from prison may be a practice that only a government funded program can both start and keep going. Whether government resources are required is of course a matter of local funding decisions. But in many jurisdictions, practices begun under government programs might die out in the absence of continued government funding.

These distinctions are important to crime prevention for reasons of evidence: newly funded programs are more likely to be subjected to scientific evaluations than long-standing practices. The modern trend towards demanding accountability for public expenditures has made program evaluations increasingly common, at least in the United States and United Kingdom. Paradoxically, we probably know more about potentially marginal new ideas than we do about the mainstream practices of the major crime prevention institutions. Police DARE (Drug Abuse Resistance Education) programs, for example, have been subjected to more numerous evaluations than the far more widespread practice of police patrol (Sherman and Weisburd, 1995). Similarly, neighborhood watch programs (Hope, 1995) have been subjected to far more extensive evaluation than the pervasive role of zoning practices in physically separating commercial and residential life in communities, reducing face-to-face contact among neighbors who used to see each other at the corner grocery store.

The availability of evidence on crime prevention is itself a major issue for a national policy debate. Where expenditures are high but evidence is weak or non-existent, the need for evaluation research is great. Even where expenditures are low, practices or programs that provide good reason to conclude that they are causing or preventing crime should merit a high priority for research. In order to identify the key gaps in our knowledge, however, we must start not with the available evidence, but with an inventory of crime prevention programs and practices in each institutional setting. Throughout this book, this inventory guides our review of what works, what does not work, what is promising, and what we need to know a lot more about.

## The science of crime prevention

To most practitioners, crime prevention is an art. But the art of crime prevention (like the art of medicine) can be evaluated and guided by the science of measuring program effects. Scientific evaluations of crime prevention have both limitations and strengths. The major limitation is that scientific knowledge is provisional. This is because the accuracy of generalizations to all programs drawn from one or even several tests of specific programs is always uncertain. The major strength of scientific evaluations is that rules of science provide a consistent and reasonably objective way to draw conclusions about cause and effect.

### Scientific knowledge is provisional

The most important limitation of science is that the knowledge it produces is always becoming more refined, and therefore no conclusion is permanent. As the US Supreme Court noted in its analysis of scientific evidence in the 1993 case of *Daubet vs. Merrell Dow*,[4] no theory (or program) of cause and effect can ever be *proved* to be true. It can only be disproved. Every test of a theory provides an opportunity to disprove it. The stronger the test and the more tests each theory survives, the more confidence we may have that the theory is true. But all theories can be disproved or, more likely, revised by new findings.

### Generalizations are uncertain

The rules of science are relatively clear about the way to test cause and effect in any given study – a concept known as "internal validity." The rules are far less clear, especially in social sciences, about the way to judge how widely the results of any study may be generalized – a concept known as "external validity." For example, the results of a very strong, internally valid test of how to reduce child abuse among rural, white teenage mothers may or may not generalize to a population of inner-city African American teenage mothers. The two populations are clearly different, but the question of whether those differences change the effects of the program can best be answered by testing the program in both populations.

We cannot assess the strength of external validity using standard scientific methods and rules in the same way that we can assess internal validity (see Chapter 2). The test of the external validity or generalizability of internally valid results of an evaluation is continued testing, that is, replication. Until replications become far more common in crime prevention evaluations, the field will continue to suffer from the uncertain external validity of both positive and negative findings.

### Rules for assessing cause and effect

The strength of the scientific method is that there are widely agreed-upon rules for assessing the level of certainty that a conclusion in any one test is correct. These rules are presented in detail in standard texts, notably Cook and Campbell (1979). In Chapters 3 to 9, programs are evaluated on the "scientific methods scale," a shorthand means of summarizing these rules that was developed by Lawrence Sherman and his colleagues at the University of Maryland and first used in *Preventing Crime* (Sherman *et al.*, 1997). The scientific methods scale ranks evaluation reports from 1 (weakest) to 5 (highest) on overall internal validity (for more details on the scale, see Chapter 2). This scale is important not only scientifically; it also helps to communicate science more effectively to policymakers, practitioners, and the general public.

## Research methods

As noted above, the present volume updates and substantially revises the report by Sherman and his colleagues (1997). In producing the most up-to-date scientific conclusions about what works, what does not work, and what is promising in preventing crime across the seven diverse institutional settings in which crime prevention takes place, the present volume (Chapters 3 to 9) follows, as closely as possible, a standard methodology.

### The search for new studies

Shortly following the release of the 1997 report, with funding provided principally by the Jerry Lee Foundation, updates of the chapters on the seven crime prevention settings were commissioned of the original and some new authors. Unlike the research for the 1997 report, the research for the present volume was not subject to similar time constraints, thus enabling the present authors to be even more thorough. For some chapters, where secondary sources (e.g. reviews of the literature) were previously used, primary sources were collected and analyzed. For all of the chapters in the present volume, the authors initiated new searches, computer and/or manual, to identify new programs or more recent follow-ups of existing programs. Chapters were written mainly in 2000 and therefore cover material up to the end of 1999. As reported below, this resulted in more than 100 new studies that evaluated the effectiveness of crime prevention programs.

### A focus on impact

The primary factor used to select evaluations of crime prevention programs for review was evidence (positive or negative) about their impact on crime. The majority of evaluations of crime prevention programs are "process" evaluations that describe what was done, rather than "impact" evaluations that assess what effect the program had on crime. While process evaluations can produce much valuable data on the implementation of programs and the logic of their strategies, they cannot offer evidence as to whether the programs "work" to prevent crime. Evaluations containing both process and impact measures provide the most information, but they are rarely funded or reported.

### A focus on crime

The focus of the present volume is on crime impacts; that is, knowing if crime went down, went up, or remained unchanged as a result of the program. In addition to focusing on crime outcomes, some chapters report on programs that measured risk factors for crime (e.g. disruptive child behavior, unemployment, school drop-out) or related problem behavior outcomes such as antisocial behavior and alcohol or other drug use. Where outcomes other than crime are measured, this is clearly noted.

### Scientific methods scale

As noted above, the present volume (Chapters 3 to 9) uses the scientific methods scale to assess the methodological quality of crime prevention programs (for more details on the scale, see Chapter 2). This book has updated the scientific methods scale to address some of the inconsistencies across the different chapters in the report by Sherman *et al.* (1997). It also provides more information about the scale to allow policymakers, researchers, students, and others to test its reliability and utilize it in their work.

### Assessing effectiveness

The "bottom line" of this book is what works, what does not work, and what is promising in preventing crime. For each of the seven institutional settings in which crime prevention takes place (families, schools, communities, labor markets, places, police, and courts/corrections; Chapters 3 to 9, respectively), the authors present their findings for what works, what does not work, and what is promising, as well as for what is unknown. These findings are guided by a set of rules that, importantly, take account of the existing state of scientific evidence on crime prevention (see below). These rules, first established by Sherman and his colleagues (1997), and used in the present volume, are as follows.

### What works

These are programs that we are reasonably certain prevent crime or reduce risk factors for crime in the kinds of social contexts in which they have been evaluated and for which the findings can be generalized to similar settings in other places and times. For a program to be classified as "working," there must be at least two level 3 (minimum) studies with significance tests demonstrating effectiveness and the preponderance of evidence in support of the same conclusion.

*What does not work*

These are programs that we are reasonably certain fail to prevent crime or reduce risk factors for crime, using the identical scientific criteria used for deciding what works. For the classification of "not working," there must be at least two level 3 (minimum) studies with significance tests showing ineffectiveness and the preponderance of evidence in the same direction.

*What is promising*

These are programs for which the level of certainty from available evidence is too low to support generalizable conclusions, but for which there is some empirical basis for predicting that further research could support such conclusions. For the classification of "promising," one level 3 (minimum) study is required with significance tests showing effectiveness and the preponderance of evidence in support of the same conclusion.

*What is unknown*

Any program not classified in one of the three above categories is defined as having "unknown" effects.

Important consideration is given to the existing state of scientific knowledge in the first three categories by making evaluation studies reaching at least level 3 on the scientific methods score the minimum cut-off point for inclusion. Here we are faced, however, with a dilemma: How high should the threshold of scientific evidence be for determining program effectiveness? A very conservative approach might require at least two level 5 studies showing that a program is effective (or ineffective), with the preponderance of the remaining evidence in favor of the same conclusion. Employing a threshold that high, however, would leave very little to say about crime prevention, based on the existing science. There is a clear trade-off between the level of certainty in the answers that can be given on program effectiveness and the level of useful information that can be gleaned from the available science. The present volume takes the middle road between reaching very few conclusions with great certainty and reaching very many conclusions with very little certainty. This is a dilemma that also faces other social science disciplines, such as education and social work.

## Aims and organization of the book

This book has four key aims:

1    to update and substantially revise the report, *Preventing Crime* (Sherman *et al.*, 1997);
2    to provide the most up-to-date, comprehensive, and rigorous assessment of the scientific evidence on the effectiveness of preventing crime in the United States, the United Kingdom, and internationally;
3    to clarify the scientific methods scale; and
4    to provide policymakers, researchers, and community leaders in the

United Kingdom, United States, and other Western nations with an understandable source of information on what works, what does not work, and what is promising in preventing crime.

This book is divided into ten chapters. Chapter 2 discusses in detail the scientific methods scale that has been used throughout the present volume to assess the methodological rigor of evaluations of crime prevention programs.

Chapters 3 through 9 review the existing evidence on the effectiveness of preventing crime in seven institutional settings in which crime prevention takes place: families, schools, communities, labor markets, places, policing, and courts/corrections, respectively. Each of these seven chapters follows a consistent style of introducing and discussing key elements of the setting under study, reviewing crime prevention programs that fall within each setting, and presenting scientific conclusions on what works, what does not work, and what is promising in preventing crime.

Chapter 10, the final chapter, summarizes the findings of crime prevention effectiveness in the seven settings and brings together the main conclusions. In this chapter we also explore the evidence-based crime prevention ideal: conclusions about crime prevention effectiveness based on the highest quality science being used by policymakers as the basis of local, state, and national policies on preventing crime.

## Notes

1    104th Congress, 1st Session, House of Representatives, Report 104–378.
2    Subsequent to this 1997 report, a NIJ *Research in Brief* of the same title was prepared (Sherman *et al.*, 1998), which summarized its findings.
3    Some developmental criminologists distinguish factors and programs that help stop people from ever becoming offenders from those which help prevent further offenses after a first offense (e.g. Tremblay and Craig, 1995).
4    *Daubet vs. Merrell Dow* (1993), US Sup. Ct. No. 92–102, June 28, 1993 [509 US 579].

## References

Aos, S., Phipps., P., Barnoski, R. and Lieb, R. (2001) The comparative costs and benefits of programs to reduce crime: A review of research findings with implications for Washington State. In B.C. Welsh, D.P. Farrington and L.W. Sherman (eds), *Costs and benefits of preventing crime.* Boulder, CO: Westview Press, 149–75.

Blumstein, A. and Petersilia, J. (1995) Investing in criminal justice research. In J.Q. Wilson and J. Petersilia (eds), *Crime.* San Francisco, CA: ICS Press, 465–87.

Butterfield, F. (1997) Most efforts to stop crime fall short, study finds. *New York Times,* April 16, A20.

Cook, T.D. and Campbell, D.T. (1979) *Quasi-experimentation: Design and analysis issues for field settings.* Chicago, IL: Rand McNally.

Farrell, G. (1995) Preventing repeat victimization. In M. Tonry and D.P. Farrington (eds), *Building a safer society: Strategic approaches to crime prevention: Vol. 19. Crime and justice: A Review of research.* Chicago, IL: University of Chicago Press, 469–534.

Hirschi, T. (1986) On the compatibility of rational choice and social control theories of crime. In D.B. Cornish and R.V. Clarke (eds), *The reasoning criminal: Rational choice perspectives on offending.* New York: Springer-Verlag, 105–18.

Hope, T. (1995) Community crime prevention. In M. Tonry and D.P. Farrington (eds), *Building a safer society: Strategic approaches to crime prevention: Vol. 19. Crime and justice: A Review of research.* Chicago, IL: University of Chicago Press, 21–89.

Millenson, M.L. (1997) *Demanding medical excellence: Doctors and accountability in the information age.* Chicago, IL: University of Chicago Press.

Nuttall, C., Goldblatt, P. and Lewis, C. (eds) (1998) *Reducing offending: An assessment of research evidence on ways of dealing with offending behaviour.* London, UK: Home Office Research and Statistics Directorate.

Reiss, A.J., Jr. and Roth, J.A. (eds) (1993) *Understanding and preventing violence.* Washington, DC: National Academy Press.

Sherman, L.W. (1998) Evidence-based policing. *Ideas in American Policing,* July. Washington, DC: Police Foundation.

Sherman, L.W., Gottfredson, D.C., MacKenzie, D.L., Eck, J., Reuter, P. and Bushway, S.D. (1997) *Preventing crime: What works, what doesn't, what's promising.* Washington, DC: National Institute of Justice, US Department of Justice.

Sherman, L.W., Gottfredson, D.C., MacKenzie, D.L., Eck, J., Reuter, P. and Bushway, S.D. (1998) Preventing crime: What works, what doesn't, what's promising. *Research in Brief,* July. Washington, DC: National Institute of Justice, US Department of Justice.

Sherman, L.W. and Weisburd, D.L. (1995) General deterrent effects of police patrol in crime "hot spots": A randomized, controlled trial. *Justice Quarterly,* 12, 625–48.

Tittle, C. and Logan, C.H. (1973) Sanctions and deviance: Evidence and remaining questions. *Law and Society Review,* 7, 371–9.

Tremblay, R.E. and Craig, W.M. (1995) Developmental crime prevention. In M. Tonry and D.P. Farrington (eds), *Building a safer society: Strategic approaches to crime prevention: Vol. 19. Crime and justice: A Review of research.* Chicago, IL: University of Chicago Press, 151–236.

Visher, C.A. and Weisburd, D.L. (1998) Identifying what works: Recent trends in crime prevention strategies. *Crime, Law and Social Change,* 28, 223–42.

Welsh, B.C. and Farrington, D.P. (2000) Monetary costs and benefits of crime prevention programs. In M. Tonry (ed.), *Crime and justice: A review of research: Vol. 27.* Chicago, IL: University of Chicago Press, 305–61.

Welsh, B.C., Farrington, D.P. and Sherman, L.W. (eds) (2001) *Costs and benefits of preventing crime.* Boulder, CO: Westview Press.

Williams, K.R. and Hawkins, R. (1986) Perceptual research on general deterrence: A critical review. *Law and Society Review,* 20, 545–72.

# 2   The Maryland Scientific Methods Scale

*David P. Farrington, Denise C. Gottfredson,*
*Lawrence W. Sherman and Brandon C. Welsh*

The main aim of the Maryland Scientific Methods Scale (SMS) is to communicate to scholars, policymakers and practitioners in the simplest possible way that studies evaluating the effects of criminological interventions differ in methodological quality. The scale is largely based on the classic book by Cook and Campbell (1979).

As an example, imagine that the following research hypothesis is to be tested: "Closed circuit television (CCTV) causes a decrease in crime." This hypothesis could be tested by investigating whether areas with CCTV have lower crime rates than areas without CCTV. However, assuming that this result was obtained, this essentially correlational design would not prove unambiguously that the research hypothesis was correct. Just to highlight one obvious problem, areas without CCTV could differ in numerous other ways from areas with CCTV, and the differences in crime rates could be attributable to one or more of these differences in extraneous variables.

An experimental design, in which the presence or absence of CCTV is deliberately manipulated, produces less ambiguous results. For example, the research hypothesis could be tested by investigating whether the crime rate decreased in an area after CCTV was installed, compared with before. However, again, this design is relatively weak because it does not exclude numerous plausible alternative explanations of the results. Perhaps the crime rate decreased because of some other change in the area (e.g. more intensive police patrolling), perhaps the decrease was merely the continuation of a prior trend, perhaps the decrease was artefactual because police methods of recording crimes changed, or perhaps the CCTV was installed just after an unusually high crime period which was then followed by a "normal" downward fluctuation. The problem is to disentangle the effects of CCTV from these other possibilities. In order to test these kinds of alternative explanations, some kind of control condition is needed which does not receive the experimental intervention (the CCTV).

The randomized experiment is usually considered to be the strongest or most compelling experimental design for testing causal hypotheses, because it makes possible the exclusion of the largest number of plausible alternative hypotheses. For example, the research hypothesis could be tested by randomly assigning city blocks to have CCTV surveillance or not, and investigating whether crime rates decreased after installation for the experimental blocks compared with the control blocks. This design controls whether or not each block has CCTV installed or not, and it controls extraneous influences on crime rates (since these are, on average, equal in experimental and control conditions).

These ideas underlie the Maryland SMS, which is a simple five-point scale of methodological quality. On this scale, the cross-sectional design would score 1, the simple before-and-after design would score 2, and the randomized experiment would score 5. The remainder of this chapter explains the SMS in more detail.

## Testing causal hypotheses

If it is suggested that some factor X causes some factor Y, what this means is that a change in X is (probabilistically) followed by a change in Y. Thus, the research hypothesis discussed above suggests that a change in CCTV (from absent to present) causes a decrease in crime rates. Causal hypotheses in social sciences are probabilistic rather than deterministic because there are numerous causes and numerous effects. There is no single cause of crime, for example. In an experiment, X is deliberately manipulated by an experimenter, whereas a quasi-experimental analysis attempts to draw causal conclusions by observing naturally varying Xs and Ys and analysing them as though X had been experimentally manipulated. Therefore, causal hypotheses can be tested more convincingly in experimental than in quasi-experimental research.

Cook and Campbell (1979) distinguished four types of validity, each with associated threats. "Validity" here refers to the truth or falsity of statements about cause and effect. *Statistical conclusion validity* refers to the truth of the question: "Are X and Y related?" Conclusions may be drawn about the size of the relationship between X and Y and its associated 95 percent confidence interval and statistical significance. The main threats to this type of validity arise from the insufficient statistical power of studies to detect effects (e.g. because of small sample size) and the use of inappropriate statistical techniques (e.g. where the data violate the underlying assumptions of the test).

*Internal validity* refers to the truth of the key question: "Does a change in X cause a change in Y?" In investigating this question, some kind of control condition is essential in order to estimate what would have happened to the experimental units (e.g. people or areas) if the intervention had not been applied to them. One problem is that the control units rarely receive no treatment, but instead typically receive the more usual treatment or some kind of treatment that is different from the experimental intervention.

The main threats to internal validity are selection (pre-existing differences between experimental and control conditions), history (some change in the experimental condition other than X has an effect on Y), maturation or a continuation of pre-existing trends, changes in measurement or instrumentation, testing effects, statistical regression to the mean, and mortality or differential attrition (Cook and Campbell, 1979; Farrington, 1977, 1987). Other threats center on the direction of causal influence of X on Y, and on various types of contamination of the control units by the experimental intervention (e.g. if treatment professionals or subjects know about the experimental design).

In principle, a randomized experiment has the highest possible internal validity because it can rule out all threats to internal validity, although in practice differential attrition and contamination may still be problematic.

The conclusion that $X$ causes $Y$ is not necessarily the final conclusion. It is desirable to go beyond this and investigate links in the causal chain ("media-tors" according to Baron and Kenny, 1986) between $X$ and $Y$ and the dose–response relationship between $X$ and $Y$.

*Construct validity* refers to the adequacy of the operational definition and measurement of the theoretical constructs that underlie the empirical vari-ables $X$ and $Y$. Threats center on the extent to which the experimental inter-vention succeeded in changing what it was intended to change (e.g. whether there was treatment fidelity or implementation failure) and on the validity and reliability of outcome measures (e.g. how adequately the empirical vari-able of reconviction measures the theoretical construct of reoffending). Interaction effects between different treatments on $Y$ should be investigated.

*External validity* refers to the generalizability of causal relationships across different persons, places, times, and operational definitions of interventions and outcomes. It is important to investigate interaction effects between these factors (boundary conditions or moderators) and the effect size. Unfortu-nately, many projects provide insufficiently detailed information about either the intervention or the context.

## Scales of methodological quality

There have been many prior attempts to devise scales of methodological quality, especially in the medical sciences. Moher *et al.* (1995) identified 25 scales devised up to 1993 for assessing the quality of clinical trials. The first of these was constructed by Chalmers *et al.* (1981), and it included 30 items each scored from 0 to 10, designed to produce a total quality score out of 100. The items with the highest weightings focused on how far the study was a double-blind trial (i.e. how far the subjects and treatment professionals knew or did not know about the aims of the study). Unfortunately, with this kind of scale, it is hard to know what meaning to attach to any score, and the same score can be achieved in many different ways.

Juni *et al.* (1999) compared these 25 scales. Interestingly, inter-rater relia-bility was excellent for most scales, and agreement between the 25 scales was considerable ($r = .72$). The authors of sixteen scales defined a threshold for high quality, with the median threshold corresponding to 60 percent of the maximum quality score. However, the relationship between methodological quality and effect size varied considerably over the 25 scales. Juni *et al.* (1999) concluded that this was because some of these scales gave more weight to the quality of reporting, ethical issues or the interpretation of results rather than to internal validity. Methodological quality scales can be used in systematic reviews to determine the criteria for inclusion of studies in the review. Alter-natively, they can be used in trying to explain differences in results between different evaluation studies. Juni *et al.* (1999) carried out a meta-analysis in which they correlated quality scores with effect sizes, but these were not significantly related in their study.

As an example of a methodological quality scale developed in the social sci-ences, Gibbs (1989) constructed a scale for assessing social work evaluation studies. This was based on fourteen items which, when added up, produced a score from 0 to 100. Some of the items referred to the completeness of reporting of the study, while others (e.g. randomization, a no-treatment control group, sample sizes, construct validity of outcome, reliability of outcome measure, tests of statistical significance) referred to methodological features.

In developing the Scientific Methods Scale, the Maryland researchers were particularly influenced by the methodological quality scale developed by Brounstein *et al.* (1997) in the National Structured Evaluation of Alcohol and Other Drug Abuse Prevention. These researchers rated each prevention program evaluation on ten criteria using a scale from 0 to 5: adequacy of sampling, adequacy of sample size, pretreatment measures of outcomes, adequacy of comparison groups, controls for prior group differences, adequacy of measurement of variables, attrition, post-intervention measurement, adequacy of statistical analyses, and testing of alternative explanations. They also gave each program evaluation an overall rating from 0 (no confidence in results) to 5 (high confidence in results), with 3 indicating the minimum degree of methodological rigor for the reviewers to have confidence that the results were reasonably accurate. Only 30 percent out of 440 evaluations received a score of 3–5.

Brounstein *et al.* (1997) found that the inter-rater reliability of the overall quality score was high (.85), while the reliabilities for the ten criteria ranged from .56 (testing of alternative explanations) to .89 (adequacy of sample size). A principal component analysis of the ten criteria revealed a single factor reflecting methodological quality. The weightings of the items on this dimension ranged from .44 (adequacy of sample size) to .84 (adequacy of statistical analyses). In attempting to improve future evaluations, they recommended random assignment, appropriate comparison groups, pre- and post-measures, the analysis of attrition and assessing levels of dosage received by each participant.

## The Scientific Methods Scale

In constructing the SMS, the main aim was to devise a simple scale measuring internal validity that could easily be communicated to scholars, policymakers and practitioners. Thus, a simple 5-point scale was used rather than a summation of scores (e.g. from 0–100) on a number of specific criteria. It was intended that each point on the scale should be understandable, and the scale is as follows (see Sherman *et al.*, 1998):

> *Level 1:*  Correlation between a prevention program and a measure of crime at one point in time (e.g. "areas with CCTV have lower crime rates than areas without CCTV").

This design fails to rule out many threats to internal validity and also fails to establish causal order.

> *Level 2:*  Measures of crime before and after the program, with no comparable control condition (e.g. "crime decreased after CCTV was installed in an area").

This design establishes causal order but fails to rule out many threats to internal validity. Level 1 and level 2 designs were considered inadequate and uninterpretable by Cook and Campbell (1979).

*Level 3:*   Measures of crime before and after the program in experimental and comparable control conditions (e.g. "crime decreased after CCTV was installed in an experimental area, but there was no decrease in crime in a comparable control area").

This was considered to be the minimum interpretable design by Cook and Campbell (1979), and it is also regarded in this book as the minimum design that is adequate for drawing conclusions about what works. It rules out many threats to internal validity, including history, maturation/trends, instrumentation, testing and mortality. Its main problems center on selection effects and regression to the mean (because of the non-equivalence of the experimental and control conditions).

*Level 4:*   Measures of crime before and after the program in multiple experimental and control units, controlling for other variables that influence crime (e.g. "victimization of premises under CCTV surveillance decreased compared to victimization of control premises, after controlling for features of premises that influenced their victimization").

This design has better statistical control of extraneous influences on the outcome and hence deals with selection and regression threats more adequately.

*Level 5:*   Random assignment of program and control conditions to units (e.g. "victimization of premises randomly assigned to have CCTV surveillance decreased compared to victimization of control premises").

Providing that a sufficiently large number of units are randomly assigned, those in the experimental condition will be equivalent (within the limits of statistical fluctuation) to those in the control condition on all possible extraneous variables that influence the outcome. Hence, this design deals with selection and regression problems and has the highest possible internal validity.

While randomized experiments in principle have the highest internal validity, in practice they are relatively uncommon in criminology and also often have implementation problems. In light of the fact that the SMS as defined above focuses only on internal validity, all evaluation projects were also rated additionally on statistical conclusion validity and on construct validity. Specifically, the following four aspects of each study were rated as follows.

*Statistical conclusion validity*

a   Was the statistical analysis appropriate?
b   Did the study have low statistical power to detect effects because of small samples?
c   Was there a low response rate or differential attrition?

*Construct validity*

d    What was the reliability and validity of measurement of the outcome?

If there was a serious problem in any of these areas, the SMS might be downgraded by 1 point. For example, a randomized experiment with serious implementation problems (e.g. high attrition) might receive a rating of level 4 rather than level 5. The justification for this was that the implementation problems had reduced the comparability of the experimental and control units and hence had reduced the internal validity.

External validity was addressed to some extent in the rules for accumulating evidence from different evaluation studies. The over-riding aim was again simplicity of communication of findings to scholars, policymakers and practitioners. The aim was to classify all programs into one of four categories: what works, what does not, what is promising, and what is unknown.

### What works

These are programs that prevent crime in the kinds of social contexts in which they have been evaluated. Programs coded as working must have at least two level 3–5 evaluations showing statistically significant and desirable results and the preponderance of all available evidence showing effectiveness.

### What does not work

These are programs that fail to prevent crime. Programs coded as not working must have at least two level 3–5 evaluations with statistical significance tests showing ineffectiveness and the preponderance of all available evidence supporting the same conclusion.

### What is promising

These are programs where the level of certainty from available evidence is too low to support generalizable conclusions, but where there is some empirical basis for predicting that further research could support such conclusions. Programs are coded as promising if they were found to be effective in significance tests in one level 3–5 evaluation and in the preponderance of the remaining evidence.

### What is unknown

Any program not classified in one of the three above categories is defined as having unknown effects.

The SMS criteria are not too dissimilar to the methodological criteria adopted by the Center for the Study and Prevention of Violence at the University of Colorado in developing Blueprints for exemplary violence prevention programs (see <http://www.colorado.edu/cspv/blueprints>). Eleven violence prevention programs have been identified as the basis for a national violence prevention initiative because they meet very high scientific stand-ards of program effectiveness, defined as follows:

a   *a strong research design*, defined as a randomized experiment with low attrition and reliable and valid outcome measures;
b   *significant prevention effects* for violence, or for arrests, delinquency, crime or drug use;
c   *replication* in at least one additional site with experimental design and significant effects;
d   *sustained effects* for at least 1 year after the treatment.

Other programs were identified as promising if they had significant preven-tion effects on violence, delinquency, crime, drug use or predelinquent aggression (e.g. conduct disorder) in one site with a good experimental or quasi-experimental (with a control group) design. Promising programs did not necessarily have to demonstrate sustained effects.

## Improving the SMS

In discussing the SMS, it is desirable to distinguish (a) the 5-point SMS scale of internal validity, (b) the system of downgrading scores to take account of statis-tical conclusion validity and construct validity, and (c) the method of drawing conclusions about effectiveness, which attempts to address external validity. Because of the over-riding aim of devising a scale which is simple to communic-ate to scholars, policymakers and practitioners, all of these aspects are vulner-able to criticism. Unfortunately, all methods of improving the SMS would make it more complicated, less meaningful, and less easy to communicate.

One problem with the 5-point scale is that it is designed to apply equally to all experimental units, whether people, schools, prisons, communities, etc. The example given above, of the effects of CCTV, generally involves areas as the experimental units to be compared. Unfortunately, it is difficult to carry out a randomized experiment based on areas, or at least difficult to randomly assign a sufficiently large number of areas to achieve the prime advantage of randomization in equating areas on extraneous variables within the limits of statistical fluctuation (Farrington, 1997). In practice, many good area-based evaluations have measures of crime rates before and after an intervention in one experimental area and one control area: level 3 on the SMS. Therefore, it might be argued that one SMS is needed for evaluation studies based on indi-viduals and a different SMS is needed for evaluation studies based on larger units such as areas (see Chapter 5 by Welsh and Hoshi).

Many researchers try to avoid the problems created by larger units by basing analyses on individuals. For example, ten schools might be randomly assigned to experimental or control conditions and 5,000 children in these ten schools might be analyzed. Unfortunately, the unit of analysis should be the unit of assignment (the school in this case). Designs based on mixed units require special analytic methods such as hierarchical linear modeling.

Another problem with the 5-point scale is that it does not explicitly encompass all possible designs. In particular, time series designs (regression-discontinuity designs according to Cook and Campbell, 1979) are not incorporated explicitly, although they are clearly superior to designs with only one pre-test and one post-test measure of the outcome. For example, consider a comparison of a time series of crime rates in an experimental area (with an intervention in the middle) compared with a time series of crime rates in a control area. This would be classified as level 3 on the SMS. However, it clearly deals with threats to internal validity (e.g. history, maturation/trends, regression to the mean) more adequately than the pre-test/post-test, experimental-control design. In principle, this time series design can also address the neglected issue of the time lag between cause and effect, as well as the persistence or "wearing-off" of the effects of the intervention over time.

The downgrading procedure can be criticized as arbitrary and likely to impair the clearness and meaningfulness of the 5-point score. It is also likely to introduce unreliability into the scoring system. A further problem is that it was not carefully explained by Sherman *et al.* (1997, 1998), causing problems of replicability.

The method of drawing conclusions about what works and so on can be criticized because it focuses on statistical significance rather than on effect size. Statistical significance depends partly on effect size and partly on sample size. Thus, a given $p$ value can reflect either a large effect in a small sample or a small effect in a large sample. Meta-analysts argue that effect size is more important than statistical significance, and they have developed sophisticated methods of combining and summarizing effect sizes obtained in a number of evaluation studies (see Lipsey and Wilson, 2001). Whereas all the chapters in this book classify studies according to the SMS, only the chapter by Gottfredson, Wilson and Najaka additionally reports effect size in each study. Arguably, it is more meaningful to scholars, policymakers and practitioners to report that 75 percent of studies found that an intervention was significantly effective than to report that the mean effect size (Cohen's $d$) is .15. However, it would be essential to use effect size in investigating the dose–response relationship between interventions and outcomes. Cost–benefit analyses would also be useful in measuring the effectiveness of prevention studies.

The SMS also focuses on the effect of $X$ on $Y$ and neglects links in the causal chain between $X$ and $Y$. Nor does it systematically attempt to investigate how the effect varies across different persons, places, times and operational definitions of interventions and outcomes.

One possibility would be to develop a new methodological quality scale based on the summation of scores on a number of subscales. For example, following Cook and Campbell (1979), four subscales could be developed for statistical conclusion validity, internal validity, construct validity and external validity. It might also be desirable to develop a fifth subscale describing the quality and completeness of the reporting of the study. Each subscale could be scored from 0 to 20 (based on scores for explicit diagnostic criteria, after the fashion of Chalmers *et al.*, 1981), yielding a total methodological quality score from 0 to 100. Alternatively, some subscales (e.g. internal validity) could be given greater weightings than others.

In many ways, this system would be more defensible than the SMS. However, it would also be less meaningful, more difficult to use in practice, and harder to communicate to the field. This is why, at the present time, this book is based on the SMS.

## Conclusions

The Maryland SMS is a simple 5-point scale of methodological quality that is used throughout this book. The simple system of classifying what works, what does not, what is promising and what is unknown is also used. These classification systems make it possible to compare the effectiveness of programs in different settings.

As explained, the SMS can be criticized, but it has the virtue of simplicity. It can be improved, but at the cost of simplicity. What is essential is to use some kind of methodological quality scale in order to communicate to scholars, policymakers and practitioners that not all research is of the same quality, and that more weight should be given to higher quality evaluation studies. Indeed, the same also applies to explanatory studies attempting to draw conclusions about the causes of offending rather than evaluating the impact of interventions.

## References

Baron, R.M. and Kenny, D.A. (1986) The moderator–mediator variable distinction in social psychology research: Conceptual, strategic and statistical considerations. *Journal of Personality and Social Psychology*, 51, 1173–82.

Brounstein, P.J., Emshoff, J.G., Hill, G. and Stoil, M.J. (1997) Assessment of methodological practices in the evaluation of alcohol and other drug (AOD) abuse prevention. *Journal of Health and Social Policy*, 9, 1–19.

Chalmers, T.C., Smith, H., Blackburn, B., Silverman, B., Schroeder, B., Reitman, D. and Ambroz, A. (1981) A method for assessing the quality of a randomized control trial. *Controlled Clinical Trials*, 2, 31–49.

Cook, T.D. and Campbell, D.T. (1979) *Quasi-experimentation: Design and analysis issues for field settings*. Chicago: Rand McNally.

Farrington, D.P. (1977) The effects of public labelling. *British Journal of Criminology*, 17, 112–25.

Farrington, D.P. (1987) Evaluating area-based changes in policing strategies and laws. *Police Studies*, 10, 67–71.

Farrington, D.P. (1997) Evaluating a community crime prevention program. *Evaluation*, 3, 157–73.

Gibbs, L.E. (1989) Quality of study rating form: An instrument for synthesizing evaluation studies. *Journal of Social Work Education*, 25, 55–66.

Juni, P., Witschi, A., Bloch, R. and Egger, M. (1999) The hazards of scoring the quality of clinical trials for meta-analysis. *Journal of the American Medical Association*, 282, 1054–60.

Lipsey, M.W. and Wilson, D.B. (2001) *Practical Meta-Analysis*. Thousand Oaks, CA: Sage.

Moher, D., Jadad, A.R., Nichol, G., Penman, M., Tugwell, P. and Walsh, S. (1995) Assessing the quality of randomized controlled trials. *Controlled Clinical Trials*, 16, 62–73.

Sherman, L.W., Gottfredson, D.C., MacKenzie, D.L., Eck, J., Reuter, P. and Bushway, S.D. (1997) *Preventing crime: What works, what doesn't, what's promising*. Washington, DC: National Institute of Justice, US Department of Justice.

Sherman, L.W., Gottfredson, D.C., MacKenzie, D.L., Eck, J., Reuter, P. and Bushway, S.D. (1998) Preventing crime: What works, what doesn't, what's promising. *Research in Brief*, July. Washington, DC: National Institute of Justice, US Department of Justice.

# 3 Family-based crime prevention

*David P. Farrington and Brandon C. Welsh*[1]

The aim of this chapter is to review current knowledge about the effectiveness of family-based crime prevention programs. Such programs typically target family risk factors such as poor child-rearing, poor supervision, or inconsistent or harsh discipline; for recent reviews of such risk factors, see Farrington (1998) and Hawkins *et al.* (1998). Family-based programs delivered by psychologists are often classified into parent management training, functional family therapy, or family preservation (see Wasserman and Miller, 1998, pp. 199–201). Typically, these programs attempt to change social contingencies in the family environment so that children are rewarded in some way for appropriate or prosocial behaviors and punished in some way for inappropriate or antisocial behaviors. Family-based programs delivered by other health professionals (e.g. nurses) are typically less behavioral, mainly focusing on advice and guidance to parents.

This chapter is not a meta-analysis of all available family-based programs, but rather a review of what we consider to be the most important family-based programs, according to specified criteria. A major problem is that many programs are multi-modal, including many different elements, making it difficult to assess the distinctive effect of any particular (family or non-family) element.

A main aim is to update Sherman's (1997) review, which – because of shortage of time – was largely based on secondary sources (Yoshikawa, 1994; Tremblay and Craig, 1995; Wasserman and Miller, 1998). This chapter takes Sherman's (1997) review as a starting point but aims to stand alone, representing a new review based on our previous research on family-based delinquency and crime prevention (for more details, see Farrington and Welsh, 1999).[2]

The chapter describes programs which aim to influence family risk factors for delinquency and later offending. In an influential classification scheme for crime prevention strategies (Tonry and Farrington, 1995), these would be included under the heading of developmental prevention. Excluded are programs which can only be classified under the other headings of situational, community or criminal justice prevention. Thus, we focus on programs intended to improve child-rearing rather than programs intended to prevent violence between spouses.

Programs have been grouped into one of six categories: home visitation, parent education plus day care/preschool, clinic-based parent training plus child training, school-based child training plus parent training, home/

community parent training, and multisystemic therapy. These categories were chosen on the basis of the studies we identified for this review. Only programs including outcome measures of delinquency, antisocial behavior, or disruptive child behavior are included; a program would be excluded if it only had outcome measures of risk factors such as IQ or poor parenting.

## Methodology

Faced with a short time-frame for new programs to have appeared in the published literature since Sherman's (1997) comprehensive review, we employed the following search strategies to discover new programs and more recent follow-ups of ongoing longitudinal intervention experiments:

1 we studied recent reviews of the literature on family-based interventions (e.g. Barlow, 1997; Kazdin, 1997) and early interventions in general (e.g. Tremblay and Craig, 1995; Utting, 1997; Wasserman and Miller, 1998; Tremblay, LeMarquand and Vitaro, 1999);
2 we searched selected criminological journals in 1997–99; and
3 we contacted leading researchers in the field to solicit recently published or in-press papers.[3]

   In selecting programs for inclusion, we used the following criteria:
   a The family (parent/guardian and/or child) was the focus of the intervention(s). Programs targeted only on the child (e.g. skills training) were excluded.
   b There was an outcome measure of offending, antisocial behavior, or disruptive child behavior. Many of the programs did not have a direct measure of offending, because that would have required a long-term follow-up. However, there is considerable continuity between disruptive child behavior and offending (see, for example, Farrington, 1998). Therefore, programs that have immediate effects on disruptive child behavior are likely to have long-term effects on offending.
   c The evaluation design was of high quality methodologically: a randomized experiment or an experiment with a matched control group (a scientific methods score of 4 or 5; see below).
   d The original sample size (treatment and control groups combined) was at least 50 individuals. A minimum of 100 would have been preferable, but this would have resulted in the loss of one-third of the programs included (11 out of 34). Even by using 50 as our minimum, a number of well known family-based intervention programs were excluded (e.g. the Yale Child Welfare Research Program of Seitz, Rosenbaum and Apfel, 1985).

Tables 3.1 to 3.6 summarize key features of the 34 included family-based intervention experiments. The columns of the tables set out these features as follows.

*Study author, name and location*   The authors and dates of the most relevant works are listed here, together with the name of the project, if it has a recognized name and its location (where specified). The studies have been listed in chronological order, according to the date of publication.

*Age at treatment*    This refers to the initial age of the child or young person.

*Type*    Programs were classified as universal, selective or indicated. A universal program is one applied to a complete population, as in primary prevention. A selective program is one applied to a high-risk subgroup of the population, as in secondary prevention. An indicated program is one applied to identified cases, such as disruptive children, as in tertiary prevention. Unfortunately, these terms are not used consistently in the literature. In particular, for a program targeted on children living in a high-crime area, Wasserman and Miller (1998, p. 199) would term this "universal," whereas Tremblay and Craig (1995, p. 167) would term this "selective." Wasserman and Miller restrict the term "selective" to programs where children are individually identified as high-risk (e.g. possessing some combination of risk factors). Thus, targeting children according to family poverty would constitute a selective program in Wasserman and Miller's terms, but not targeting children according to area poverty. We prefer the Tremblay and Craig usage, since children living in low-income areas are just as clearly high-risk as a group as are children living in low-income families; we have defined all these types of programs as "selective," restricting the term "universal" to programs targeted at fairly representative samples of the general population. Actually, there are very few truly universal programs in this sense. Most programs aim to reserve scarce resources for children and families in greatest need, and these inevitably tend to be the high-risk children and families.

*Risk factors manipulated*    These are rarely specified explicitly. Ideally, they should be not only specified but also measured in a risk–needs assessment, so that there is only an attempt to improve a family (e.g. parenting) if there is some kind of inadequacy present. There may be little point in applying parent training where the existing parenting is perfectly satisfactory.

*Context of intervention*    This is defined as the physical setting in which the intervention took place. Because many interventions were multi-modal, it was common for treatments to be implemented both in the home and in some kind of facility (day care, preschool, community center, clinic, etc.)

*Treatment type*    Key features of the treatment program are listed here. Where applicable, different treatment conditions are described. Where the control group received some kind of special intervention (other than the usually available resources of the community), this is also described.

*Sample size and retention*    The figures listed here are initial sample sizes at the start of treatment or in some kind of pre-test assessment, and the percentage and number of the initial sample remaining at the latest follow-up. Since low retention (or high attrition) can pose a considerable threat to internal and external validity, we have taken this into account in assessing the methodological quality of studies (see Chapter 2).

*Duration of treatment* Ideally, the number of contacts should be noted, as the intensity of treatment depends both on its duration and on the number and intensity (e.g. length) of contacts. It would be desirable to quantify the "dose" of treatment received by each family and to relate this to measures of treatment success (taking account of treatment need). However, this is rarely possible on the basis of published studies.

*Follow-up and results* The follow-up period is the length of time after the program ended at which outcome measures were taken. Often, program effects were assessed both immediately (that is, at the end of treatment) and after some follow-up period. Where there were more than two post-intervention assessments, we have reported in the tables on the earliest (e.g. immediate outcome) and latest. In summarizing results, the focus was on the most relevant outcomes for this review (e.g. child behavior problems, delinquency) and comparisons between treatment and control groups. Following Sherman (1997), the focus was also on reporting results of significance tests rather than trying to develop and summarize measures of effect size. The problem with significance tests is that they depend partly on sample size and partly on strength of effect. A significant result in a large sample could correspond to a rather small effect size, and conversely a large effect size in a small sample may not be statistically significant. Nevertheless, it is important to know whether or not there are significant differences between treatment and control groups, and this is why these are summarized in the tables.

*Scientific methods score* We have used the scientific methods scale developed by Sherman *et al.* (1997), which ranks studies from level 1 (weakest) to level 5 (strongest) on overall internal validity (see Chapter 2). Level 5 is widely recognized as the "gold standard" of evaluation design and seems unambiguous. However, the randomized experiment is only the gold standard if a sufficiently large number of units are randomly assigned to ensure that the program group is equivalent to the control group on all possible extraneous variables. As a rule of thumb, at least 50 in both categories are needed (Farrington, 1997) to ensure equivalence within a narrow range of statistical fluctuation. This number is relatively easy to achieve with individuals but very difficult to achieve with larger units, such as schools or areas. Thus, a randomized experiment based on a small number of units (e.g. ten areas) should in our view be classified as level 4, because there is only some control of extraneous variables.

*Other dimensions* Treatment programs differ on many different dimensions, and it is impossible to include more than a few in summary tables such as ours. An important question raised by Sherman (1997) was how far the effectiveness of treatment depended on the neighborhood and community context. It is difficult to investigate this, because often such contexts are not measured adequately or reported in evaluation papers. It would be possible in principle for researchers to study whether there are interactions between types of families (parents and/or children) and types of treatment effects, but this is rarely attempted. It is more common for researchers to demonstrate that their effects are stronger in certain subgroups of the sample (e.g.

unmarried, low socioeconomic status (SES), teenage mothers; see Olds *et al.*, 1997), but such subgroups are often chosen with hindsight (after the fact) and not always justified satisfactorily. The greatest need is probably for a system of classifying elements of the treatment so that it is possible to specify and compare treatments more satisfactorily.

The following six sections review family-based crime prevention programs grouped according to the categories noted above. For each category we summarize and present in tabular form the key features of the programs, describe in detail selected programs, and discuss why some programs did or did not work in preventing child aggressive behavior, delinquency, or other related outcomes. The next section classifies the program categories under one of three headings: working, not working or promising, using the standards set by Sherman *et al.* (1997). The last section identifies gaps in knowledge and priorities for research in the area of family-based interventions.

## Home visitation programs

Table 3.1 summarizes the key features of five home visitation programs. All were carried out in the United States except the Montreal experiment of Larson (1980). All were based on selective samples (at-risk parents and/or children). The direct target of the intervention could be the parent (usually the mother), the child or both.

Three of the five programs (Strayhorn and Weidman, 1991; Kitzman *et al.*, 1997; Olds *et al.*, 1997) targeted parenting directly, and four of the five programs implemented a parent education intervention; the program by Strayhorn and Weidman (1991) used group parent training. The Elmira Prenatal/Early Infancy Project (PEIP; Olds *et al.*, 1997) and its urban replication in Memphis (Kitzman *et al.*, 1997) supplemented parent education with parent support, community support and family planning.

Sample size varied considerably across the five programs, from a high of 1,139 persons in the experiment by Kitzman and her colleagues to a low of 65 in Barth, Hacking and Ash (1988). There was a modestly high sample retention rate among the programs, with the experiment by Olds *et al.* retaining just over four-fifths (81.0 percent; 324 of 400) of its initial sample at a 13-year post-intervention follow-up. Treatment duration varied from 5 months to 2 years, and the length of follow-up varied from immediate outcome measures to the previously noted 13 years for the Elmira PEIP.

In all of the cases, subjects were randomly assigned to treatment or control groups, and hence most studies had a scientific methods score (SMS) of 5. The one exception was the program by Larson (1980), which we deemed to have a SMS of 4. This was because subjects were randomly assigned to one treatment group (prenatal visits only) or to the control group, but were not randomly assigned to the other treatment group (prenatal and postnatal visits). Both treatment conditions were included in the analysis of the program's effects on child injuries.

Each of the five programs produced desirable results for outcomes of interest. Lower rates of child injuries, child abuse and neglect, and self-reported arrests (for children and mothers) were some of the desirable results achieved by the home visitation programs. Results from the Elmira program are particularly noteworthy. At the completion of the program – immediate outcome – a substantial reduction in child abuse and neglect was evidenced for high-risk[4] program mothers compared to their control counterparts (4 percent vs. 19 percent). Thirteen years after the completion of the program, fewer program compared to control mothers in the sample as a whole were identified as perpetrators of child abuse and neglect (29 percent vs. 54 percent). At the age of 15, children of the higher-risk mothers who received the program reported fewer arrests than their control counterparts.

The Elmira PEIP, started in 1980, was designed with three broad objectives:

> (1) to improve the outcomes of pregnancy; (2) to improve the quality of care that parents provide to their children (and their children's subsequent health and development); and (3) to improve the women's own personal life-course development (completing their education, finding work, and planning future pregnancies).
>
> (Olds *et al.*, 1993, p. 158)

The program enrolled 400 at-risk women (see note 4) prior to their thirtieth week of pregnancy. Women were randomly assigned to one of four treatment or control conditions. In the first control condition (N = 90) no services were provided during pregnancy. Screening for sensory and developmental problems took place at ages 1 and 2, and was provided for all four conditions. Women in the second control condition (N = 94) were provided with transportation vouchers to attend regular prenatal and child visits to physicians. Women in the first treatment condition (N = 100), in addition to the free transportation, received nurse home visits during pregnancy on average once every 2 weeks, and those in the second treatment condition (N = 116) received the same services as those in the first, but as well received continued nurse home visits until the children reached the age of 2 years. Three major activities were carried out during the home visits: "(1) parent education about influences on fetal and infant development; (2) the involvement of family members and friends in the pregnancy, birth, early care of the child, and in the support of the mother; and (3) the linkage of family members with other health and human services" (Olds *et al.*, 1993, p. 158).

Analyses of treatment effects focused on comparisons between combined conditions one and two (control group) and treatment condition two (program group). Control conditions one and two (not visited by a nurse during pregnancy or infancy) were grouped together because no differences between the two groups were observed in the use of the free transportation service for prenatal and child visits to physicians. Treatment condition one was excluded, as few lasting benefits were observed for nurse home visits during pregnancy relative to visits during infancy (treatment condition two).

Trying to isolate the key features that make home visitation programs a successful early intervention for the prevention of child aggression and later antisocial behavior problems is no easy task. This is because these programs are invariably multi-dimensional; that is, there is a combination of interventions which are in operation either simultaneously or one after the other. It may be that the success of these programs lies not in one particular programmatic

Table 3.1 Home visitation programs

| Study author, name, and location | Age at treatment | Type | Risk factors manipulated | Context of intervention | Treatment type | Sample size and retention[a] | Duration of treatment | Follow-up[b] and results[c] | Scientific methods score[d] |
|---|---|---|---|---|---|---|---|---|---|
| Larson (1980), Montreal, Canada | Prenatal | Selective (low SES mothers) | Social environment | Home | T1 and T2 = parent education, parent support (only T1 received a prenatal home visit and postpartum hospital visit) | Initial: 115 mother-infant pairs: T1 = 35, T2 = 36, C = 44 Follow-up: 78.3%, 90 (T1 = 26, T2 = 27, C = 37) | 1.5 years | Immediate outcome (T1 vs T2, C); child injuries + | 4 (random assign. to T1 and C; T2 subjects added until a predetermined date) |
| Olds et al. (1986, 1997, 1998), Prenatal/Early Infancy Project, Elmira, NY | Prenatal | Selective (mothers had at least 1 socio-demographic risk factor) | Parenting, family planning | Home | T1 = parent education, community support, family planning; T2 = T1 minus postnatal home visits; C = 2 conditions not receiving home visits (screening services and free transport to clinic) | Initial: 400 mothers: T1 = 116, T2 = 100, C = 184 Follow-up: 81.0%, 324 (T1 = 97, T2 = 79, C = 148) | 2 years | Immediate outcome (T1 vs C): high-risk mothers: child abuse and neglect + 13 years (T1 vs C): mothers: child abuse and neglect +; high-risk mothers: arrests and convictions +; children (of high-risk mothers): arrests + | 5 (random assign. to 2 Ts and 2 Cs of varying intensity) |
| Barth et al. (1988), Child Parent Enrichment Project, USA | Prenatal | Selective (mothers identified as at-risk of abusing child) | Social support | Home | Parent education, parent support | Initial: 65 mothers[e]: T = 29, C = 36 Follow-up: 76.9%, 50 (T = 24, C = 26) | 6 months | Immediate outcome: child temperament +, child abuse +[f] | 5 (random assign. to T and C) |

| Strayhorn and Weidman (1991), USA | 3.7 years (average) | Selective (low SES and at least 1 behavioral or emotional problem in child) | Parenting | Home | T = group parent training; C = parenting information | Initial: 98 parents: T = 50, C = 48; 105 children: T = n.a., C = n.a. Follow-up: parents: 78.6%, 77 (T = 40, C = 37); children: 80.0%, 84 (T = 45, C = 39) | 5 months | 1 year (approximately): hyperactivity + | 5 (random assign. to T and C) |
| Kitzman et al. (1997), replication of the Prenatal/Early Infancy Project, Memphis, TN | Prenatal | Selective (mothers had at least 2 socio-demographic risk factors) | Parenting, family planning | Home | T = parent education, parent support, community support, family planning; C = free transport conditions (postnatal 2 conditions excluded) and child screening | Initial: 1,139 mothers: T = 228, C = 515 Follow-up: 90.8%, 675 (T = 208, C = 467)[g] | 2 years | Immediate outcome: child injuries and ingestions +, child behavioral problems 0 | 5 (random assign. to 2 Ts and 2 Cs of varying intensity) |

Notes

T = treatment group; C = control group; n.a. = not available.

a  Percentage and number of initial sample remaining at latest follow-up.
b  Period of time in which program effects are evaluated once program has ended.
c  "0" = no treatment effects; "+" = desirable treatment effects; "–" = undesirable treatment effects.
d  5 = highest; 1 = lowest.
e  Each mother had at least one child. No information was provided on number of children in treatment and control groups.
f  Did not reach statistical significance.
g  Taken from number of home assessments completed at the 2-year period. Only one assessment could be completed per mother.

feature, but rather in the interaction of the package of measures and the targeted population. In each one of the five programs reviewed here the targeted mothers had some pre-existing disadvantage (e.g. low SES), which can further exacerbate the difficult situation of raising a newborn. By providing generic services (e.g. links to community resources) to help mothers improve their life course development and providing them with basic information on parenting, some of the hardships can be alleviated. This may translate into improved care and attention for the child, both at a physical and socio-emotional level.

Several economic analyses show that the monetary benefits of the Elmira PEIP outweighed its costs for the lower-class unmarried mothers. The most important are by Karoly *et al.* (1998) and Aos *et al.* (1999). However, both measured only a limited range of benefits. Karoly *et al.* measured only benefits to the government or taxpayer (welfare, education, employment, and criminal justice), not benefits to crime victims consequent upon reduced crimes. Aos *et al.* measured only tangible benefits to crime victims and criminal justice savings. Nevertheless, both reported that the benefits of this program outweighed its costs; the benefit–cost ratio was 4.1 according to Karoly *et al.* and 1.5 according to Aos *et al.* (For more details about cost–benefit analyses, see Welsh and Farrington, 2000; Welsh, Farrington and Sherman, 2001.)

It would of course be desirable to know more about the long-term effects of home visitation programs beyond the Elmira program. Three of the five programs (Larson, 1980; Barth, Hacking and Ash, 1988; Kitzman *et al.*, 1997) reported on treatment effects at immediate outcome, and the program by Strayhorn and Weidman (1991) had a 1-year follow-up. Whether the benefits of these programs persist beyond these short-term time horizons will be of great value to policy development in this area. The continued follow-up of the Memphis program offers to address this important question.

### Parent education plus day care/preschool programs

Table 3.2 summarizes the key elements of six programs that have the combined components of parent education and day care/preschool. All programs were carried out in the United States. At the start of treatment, the age of the subjects ranged from birth to around 4 years. All of the programs were based on selective samples. All of the evaluations used relatively large samples, ranging from a high of 985 individuals to a low of 123. Sample retention was moderate; however, considering that the mean average length of follow-up across the six programs was around 8 years, this is not surprising. All of the programs used parent education and four used parent training in some form or another (e.g. parent management training, problem-solving training) to intervene at the family level. The most common child-focused interventions were intellectual enrichment and skills training.

The methodological strength of the research designs to evaluate the effects of the six programs was moderately high. Four of the programs used randomized experiments. A matched control group was used by Lally, Mangione and Honig (1988) in the Syracuse Family Development Research Program. Webster-Stratton (1998) randomly assigned nine Head Start centers to treatment or control groups, but not individual subjects. Because the number of randomized units was not large enough to ensure that experimental and control subjects were equivalent on all extraneous variables, this was given a SMS of 4.

All six of the programs showed desirable treatment effects in favor of the experimentals compared to the controls at some follow-up. Schweinhart, Barnes and Weikart (1993), Johnson and Walker (1987), Lally, Mangione and Honig (1988) and Webster-Stratton (1998) found desirable effects, and these effects were often maintained over long time periods (8 years in the Houston project; 10 years in the Syracuse project; and 22 years in the Perry Preschool project). The Infant Health and Development Program (IHDP; McCarton *et al.*, 1997) and Stone, Bendell and Field (1988) found immediate beneficial effects which then disappeared in the longer term.

The success of the Perry preschool project is especially noteworthy. This was essentially a Head Start program targeted on disadvantaged African American children, who were allocated approximately randomly to experimental and control groups. The experimental children attended a daily preschool program, backed up by weekly home visits. The preschool program was designed to increase thinking and reasoning abilities and school achievement. By age 27, the experimental group had accumulated only half as many arrests as the controls (Schweinhart, Barnes and Weikart, 1993). Also, they were more likely to have graduated from high school, had significantly higher earnings, and were more likely to be home owners. For every $1 spent on the program, $7 were saved in the long run (Barnett, 1993).

The absence of long-term beneficial effects in the IHDP is perhaps the most troubling result in Table 3.2. This was a large-scale, well funded randomized experiment, involving 985 low-birth-weight infants in eight sites across the United States. The intervention included home visits, parent group meetings, and attendance at specially designed child development centers. Home visits occurred weekly in the first year and bi-weekly in the second and third years. Parent group meetings were held four times per year. The day care was for an average of 267 full days per year. The average program cost was $15,000 per child per year, although about one-third of this was for transportation to the child development centers.

Mostly encouraging messages can be drawn from the findings of these six parent education plus day care/preschool programs. Most importantly, each produced a desirable effect on outcomes of interest to this review at some follow-up. On the other hand, the passage of time resulted in the decay of beneficial effects for two programs. Again, the multi-dimensional nature of these programs makes it difficult to say with any certainty what the key elements are that make a successful or unsuccessful program.

## Clinic-based parent training plus child training programs

The key features of seven clinic-based parent training plus child training programs are summarized in Table 3.3. Again, all of the programs were carried out in the United States. The age of the children at the start of treatment varied considerably, from 2 to 14 years. Programs were based on selective

Table 3.2 Parent education plus day care/preschool programs

| Study author, name, and location | Age at treatment | Type | Risk factors manipulated | Context of intervention | Treatment type and retention | Sample size[a] | Duration of treatment | Follow-up[b] and results[c] | Scientific methods score[d] |
|---|---|---|---|---|---|---|---|---|---|
| Schweinhart and Weikart (1980), Schweinhart et al. (1993), Perry Preschool Project, Ypsilanti, MI | 3–4 years | Selective (low SES and children at-risk for school failure) | Cognitive development | Preschool, home | Preschool intellectual enrichment, parent education | Initial: 123 children (72 boys, 51 girls): T=58, C=65 Follow-up: 95.1%, 117 (T=56, C=61) | 1–2 years | 9–10 years (ages 14–15): delinquency + 22 years (age 27): police arrests + | 5 (stratified random assign. to T and C) |
| Field et al. (1980), Stone et al. (1988), Mailman Center for Child Development, USA | Birth | Selective (very low SES mothers) | Parenting, SES | Home, nursery school | Parent education, parent training, employment | Initial: 131 children and mothers: T=58, C=73 Follow-up: 46.6%, 61 (T=31, C=30) | 6 months | Immediate outcome (approximate): child temperament + 4–7 years (ages 5–8): child behavior problems 0 | 5 (random assign. to 2 Ts and C) |
| Johnson and Breckenridge (1982), Johnson and Walker (1987), Houston Parent-Child Development Center, TX | 1–3 years | Selective (low SES) | Parenting, cognitive development | Home, day care | Parent training, parent education | Initial: 458 families: T=214, C=244 Follow-up: 57.2%, 262 (T=111, C=151)[f] | 2 years | 1–4 years: child destructive behavior + 5–8 years: child anti-social behavior + | 5 (random assign. to T and C at yearly intervals for 5 years) |

| Study | Age at start | Sample type | Focus | Setting | Program components | Sample | Outcome period[b] | Design[d] |
|---|---|---|---|---|---|---|---|---|
| Lally et al. (1988) Syracuse University Family Development Research Project, NY | Birth | Selective (mothers had low SES and other socio-demographic risk factors) | Education, nutrition, family environment | Home, day care | Parent training, children: education, nutrition, health and safety, mother–child relationship | *Initial:* 182 children: T = 108, C = 74[a] *Follow-up:* 65.4%, 119 (T = 65, C = 54) | 5 years Immediate outcome: social-emotional functioning + 10 years (age 15): delinquency + | 4 (matched C – time lag recruitment) |
| IHDP (1990) McCarton et al. (1997), IHDP, USA | Birth | Selective (low birth weight and premature) | Parenting, cognitive development | Home, child development center | Child care, parent education, parent support | *Initial:* 985 children in 8 sites: T = 377, C = 608 *Follow-up:* 88.7%, 874 (T = 336, C = 538) | 3 years Immediate outcome (age 3): behavior problems + 5 years (age 8): behavior problems 0 | 5 (stratified random assign. to T and C) |
| Webster-Stratton (1998), PARTNERS, USA | 4.7 years (mean) | Selective (above average risk for developing conduct problems) | Parenting, academic skills | Classroom (Head Start centers) | T = Head Start (academic skills) plus parent training and teacher training; C = Head Start | *Initial:* 426 families: T = 296, C = 130 *Follow-up:* 69.5%, 296 (T = 189, C = 107) | 8–9 weeks Immediate outcome: child behavior problems at home (observed only) and school + 1 year: child behavior problems (observed only) + | 4 (random assign. of 9 Head Start centers [64 classes] to T and C) |

Notes

T = treatment group; C = control group; IHDP = Infant Health and Development Program; n.a. = not available.

a Percentage and number of initial sample remaining at latest follow-up.

b Period of time in which program effects are evaluated once program has ended.

c "0" = no treatment effects; "+" = desirable treatment effects; "–" = undesirable treatment effects.

d 5 = highest; 1 = lowest.

e Represents two combined treatment conditions. Of the sample for the 4–7 year follow-up (N = 61), 31 received treatment and of these 12 received the home-based intervention (parent training and education) and 19 received the nursery-based intervention (parent training and education plus employment). At immediate outcome, treatment effects were stronger for mothers in the nursery-based intervention than the home-based on outcomes of child temperament and mothers' return to work or school and repeated pregnancy. At the most recent follow-up, no differences were found between the two intervention groups.

f Represents sample retention at the end of treatment. Insufficient information was provided to enable the calculation of sample sizes at either follow-up.

g Represents those controls that remained in the sample up to immediate outcome. Information was not provided on the initial number of controls.

and indicated samples. Sample size was quite similar across the seven programs, ranging from a high of 119 to a low of 52 children/young people, and sample retention was moderately high; however, in three cases (Kazdin, Siegel and Bass, 1992; Long *et al.*, 1994; Dishion and Andrews, 1995) sample retention could not be accurately determined.

For only three programs (Szapocznik *et al.*, 1989; Long *et al.*, 1994; Dishion and Andrews, 1995) did the length of follow-up to assess treatment effects continue beyond the assessment at the time of program completion (immediate outcome). This, however, has much to do with three programs (Webster-Stratton, Kolpacoff and Hollinsworth, 1988; Spaccarelli, Cotler and Penman, 1992; Webster-Stratton and Hammond, 1997) employing a wait-list control group which received a delayed intervention. Treatment duration was rather short, with no intervention lasting for more than 6 to 8 months. Many different types of parent and child training were used, including videotape modeling by Webster-Stratton, Kolpacoff and Hollinsworth (1988) and problem-solving skills training by Kazdin, Siegel and Bass (1992), as well as structural family and individual psychodynamic child therapy by Szapocznik *et al.* (1989).

Five programs randomly assigned subjects to treatment or control groups or, in the case of Kazdin, Siegel and Bass (1992), multiple treatment conditions. A time-lag recruited matched control group was used by Long *et al.* (1994). The study by Dishion and Andrews (1995) added, as part of a later follow-up, a quasi-experimental, no-treatment control group to its initial randomized-controlled design, which reduced its SMS from a level 5 to a level 4.

Four out of the six clinic-based programs which used a control group (i.e. all except Kazdin, Siegel and Bass, 1992) showed desirable treatment effects in favor of the experimentals compared to the controls at some follow-up. Webster-Stratton and Hammond (1997) assessed the effectiveness of parent and child training for children with early-onset conduct problems, and Webster-Stratton, Kolpacoff and Hollinsworth (1988) compared different parent training interventions based on videotape modeling and group discussion. Both programs demonstrated desirable treatment effects at immediate outcome for the individual treatment conditions compared to the no-treatment, wait-list control condition on child behavior problems and other outcomes. Spaccarelli, Cotler and Penman (1992) also reported beneficial results at immediate outcome on child behavior problems, while Dishion, Patterson and Kavanagh (1992) and Dishion and Andrews (1995) reported that initial desirable treatment effects on child behavior problems wore off, from the time of the completion of the intervention to 1 year later.

Long *et al.* (1994) found no long-term differences between their treated clinic sample and their matched control sample, and Szapocznik *et al.* (1989) found no program effect at a 6-month post-intervention follow-up on the outcome of child behavioral and emotional problems for the two treatment groups (structural family therapy and individual psychodynamic child therapy) compared to the control group (recreation services).

The program by Kazdin, Siegel and Bass (1992) compared the combined intervention of parent management training (PMT) plus problem-solving skills training (PSST) to the individual components for children exhibiting severe antisocial behavior. This was done to test the hypothesis that a package of interventions would be more effective than its individual parts. They found that PMT plus PSST showed statistically significant improvements over the single treatment conditions of PMT and PSST for conduct problems at immediate outcome. Desirable but not significant improvements were found for delinquency and aggression at the immediate outcome follow-up.

Why did most clinic-based programs work, while some did not? Focusing on treatment duration seems like a good starting point in trying to answer this question, since across the seven programs treatment duration was low, at least, in relation to the other categories of family interventions reviewed in this chapter. This might partially explain why the program by Long *et al.* (1994), which was a highly structured, clearly specified, well developed behavioral parent training program, did not show any desirable benefits. Although precise information on treatment duration in hours or days was not provided, each program participant received only eight to ten sessions. However, the same number of treatment sessions were administered to participants in one of the treatment conditions in the program by Spaccarelli, Cotler and Penman (1992) and, at immediate outcome, desirable benefits were achieved for the experimental compared to the control group. It is likely that more might be gleaned from an assessment of treatment intensity, but few of the programs provided this information.

Another possible avenue to pursue in attempting to uncover answers to this important question is the match between the treated sample and the intervention; that is, does this high-risk population require a more comprehensive treatment package? From the findings of these seven programs it would appear that, on the whole, there is a good fit between the interventions and the population. It would appear, however, that more research is needed to address these and other important issues in understanding what makes clinic-based family interventions effective in reducing child aggression and later antisocial behavior problems.

## School-based child training plus parent training programs

Table 3.4 summarizes the key elements of six school-based child training plus parent training programs. Three programs were carried out in the United States, two in Canada (Pepler *et al.*, 1995; Tremblay *et al.*, 1995), and one in England (Kolvin *et al.*, 1981). At the start of treatment, the age of the subjects ranged from 5 to 6 (grade 1 age) to around 12 years. Programs were based on universal, selective, or indicated samples. The programs targeted a wide range of risk factors for antisocial behavior and later delinquency, including parenting, behavioral and social-cognitive functioning, and attachment to family and school.

Sample size varied considerably across the six school-based programs, ranging from a high of 2,181 to a low of 74 individuals, with the majority having sample sizes in the hundreds. Sample retention was reasonably high for five of the six programs for which it could be measured. Treatment duration ranged from 10 weeks to 6 years. For four of the programs, the follow-up period to assess treatment effects went beyond immediate outcome, and one program – the Earlscourt Social Skills Group Program in Toronto (Pepler *et*

*Table 3.3* Clinic-based parent training plus child training programs

| Study author, name, and location | Age at treatment | Type | Risk factors manipulated | Context of intervention | Treatment type | Sample size and retention[a] | Duration of treatment | Follow-up[b] and results[c] | Scientific methods score[d] |
|---|---|---|---|---|---|---|---|---|---|
| Webster-Stratton et al. (1988), USA | 3–8 years (mean = 4.5 years) | Indicated (child misconduct) | Parenting | Clinic | T1 = IVM, T2 = GDVM, T3 = GD (all different versions of parent training) C = 48 | *Initial:* 114 children and 194 parents: T1 = 49, T2 = 48, T3 = 47, C = 50 *Follow-up:* 91.8%, 178 (T1 = 45, T2 = 47, T3 = 38, C = 48) | 10–12 weeks | Immediate outcome (T1, T2, T3 vs C): child behavior problems + | 5 (random assign. to 3 Ts and wait-list C) |
| Szapocznik et al. (1989), USA | 6–12 years (mean = 9.2 years) | Indicated (children recruited with behavioral and emotional problems) | Parenting, behavioral and social-cognitive functioning | Clinic | T1 = SFT, T2 = IPCT, C = recreation | *Initial:* 69 boys: T1 = 26, T2 = 26, C = 17 *Follow-up:* 84.1%, 58 (T1 = 23, T2 = 21, C = 14) | 6 months (max.) with 12–24 (min./max.) contact hours | Immediate outcome (T1, T2 vs C): child behavioral and emotional problems 0 6 months (T1, T2 vs C): child behavioral and emotional problems 0 | 5 (random assign. to 2 Ts and C) |
| Dishion et al. (1992) Dishion and Andrews (1995), Adolescent Transitions Program, USA | 10–14 years | Selective (high risk) | Parenting, self-control | Clinic | T = parent training, child self-regulation and pro-social behavior C = no parent training (at follow-up information only) | *Initial:* 119 families and children: T = 56, C = 63 *Follow-up:* (C = 39 added): 158 families and children[e]: T = 90, C = 68[f] | 12 weeks | Immediate outcome: child antisocial behavior +[g] 1 year: child behavior problems (mother reports) 0 | 4 (addition of quasi-experimental C to random exp.- assign. to T and C) |

| Study | Age | Prevention type (focus) | Program focus | Setting | Conditions | Sample[a] | Program duration | Follow-up / Outcome[b] | Outcome[c] | Design rating[d] |
|---|---|---|---|---|---|---|---|---|---|---|
| Kazdin et al. (1992), USA | 7–13 years (mean = 10.3) | Indicated (children referred for severe anti-social behavior) | Parenting, problem-solving | Clinic | T1 = PSST, T2 = PMT, T3 = PSST/PMT | Initial: 97 children: T1 = 29, T2 = 31, T3 = 37 Follow-up: 78.4%, 76 (T1 = 25, T2 = 22, T3 = 29) | 6–8 months (mean = 7.1) | Immediate outcome (T3 vs T1, T2): conduct problems + | 3 Ts) | 5 (random assign. to 3 Ts) |
| Spaccarelli et al. (1992), USA | 6.1 years (mean) | Selective (self-referral and concern with child behavior problems) | Parenting | Clinic | T1 = PT/PS, T2 = PT/D | Initial: 53 parents and children: T1 = 21, T2 = 16, C = 16 Follow-up: 84.9%, 45 (T1 = 14, T2 = n.a.) | 16 hours (T1 = 8 two hour sessions; child behavior problems + | Immediate outcome (T1, T2 vs C): child behavior problems + | list C) | 5 (random assign. to 2 Ts and wait-list C) |
| Long et al. (1994), USA | 2.3–7.8 years | Selective (non-compliant behavior) | Parenting | Parent training | T = 26 (from original 47 children), C = 26[h] | 52 young adults: T = 26 (from original 47 children), C = 26 | n.a. (8–10 sessions) | 14 years (approximately): delinquency 0 | recruitment) | 4 (matched C – time lag recruitment) |
| Webster-Stratton and Hammond (1997), USA | 4–8 years (mean = 68.9 months) | Indicated (child misconduct) | Parenting | Clinic | T1 = PT, T2 = CT, T3 = CT/PT, C | 97 children and 166 parents: T1 = 26 and 43, T2 = 27 and 47, T3 = 22 and 36, C = 22 and 40[i] | 22–24 weeks | Immediate outcome (T1, T2, T3 vs C): child behavior problems + | list C) | 5 (random assign. to 3 Ts and wait-list C) |

Notes

T = treatment group; C = control group; CT = child training; PT = parent training; CT/PT = child training + parent training; PSST = problem-solving skills training; IVM = individually administered videotape modeling; GDVM = group discussion videotape modeling; GD = group discussion; PT/PS = parent training + problem-solving training; PT/D = parent training + extra discussion; SFT = structural family therapy; IPCT = individual psychodynamic child therapy; n.a. = not available.

a   Percentage and number of initial sample remaining at latest follow-up.
b   Period of time in which program effects are evaluated once program has ended.
c   "0" = no treatment effects; "+" = desirable treatment effects; "−" = undesirable treatment effects.
d   5 = highest; 1 = lowest.
e   There may be one more or one less person in T or C, as N = 157 according to Table 1 in Dishion and Andrews (1995, p.541).
f   Sample retention could not be calculated because of the addition of 39 controls at follow-up.
g   Did not reach statistical significance.
h   Sample retention could not be calculated fully because a new control group was set up at follow-up.
i   Information was not provided to enable the calculation of sample retention.

*Table 3.4* School-based child training plus parent training programs

| Study author, name, and location | Age at treatment | Type | Risk factors manipulated | Context of intervention | Treatment type | Sample size and retention[a] | Duration of treatment | Follow-up[b] and results[c] | Scientific methods score[d] |
|---|---|---|---|---|---|---|---|---|---|
| Kolvin et al. (1981), Newcastle upon Tyne and Gateshead, England | Junior: 7–8 years; Senior: 11–12 years | Indicated (junior: signs of social or psychiatric disturbance or learning problems; senior: psychiatric disturbance) | Academic training, parenting | School | Junior: T1 = PC, T2 = GT, T3 = NW; Senior: T1 = PC, T2 = GT, T3 = BM | Initial: 592 children: junior: 270: T1 = 69, T2 = 74, T3 = 60, C = 67; senior: 322: T1 = 83, T2 = 73, T3 = 74, C = 92 Follow-up: junior: 86.3%, 233 senior: 89.8%, 289 | 3–15 months (1–5 school terms) | 20–32 months: junior: antisocial behavior (T1, T2, T3 vs C) 0 senior: antisocial behavior (T1, T2, T3 vs C) + | 5 (random assign. by school class to 3 Ts and C) |
| Hawkins et al. (1992, 1999), Seattle Social Development Project, WA | 6 years | Selective (high crime areas) | Family and school attachment | School | Modified classroom teaching practices, parent training, child social skills training | 1–4 years: 1,053 children: T = n.a., C = n.a. 5–6 years: 177 children (high risk): T = 102, C = 75[e] | 4–6 years (grades 1 through 6) | 5 months after 4 years of treatment: delinquency + 6 years follow-up after treatment: delinquency (violence) + | 4 (addition of quasi-experimental T after end of 4 year treatment to random exp. – assign. to T and C classrooms) |
| Tremblay et al. (1992, 1995), Montreal Longitudinal Experimental Study, Canada | 7 years (average) | Indicated (disruptive boys, low SES families) | Social behavior, parenting | School | Parent training, social skills training | Initial: 166 boys: T = 43, C = 41, Observation (O) = 82 Follow-up: 99.4%, 165 (T = 43, C = 41, O = 81) | 2 school years (20 months) | Immediate outcome (T vs C/O): aggressive behavior + 6 years (T vs C/O): delinquency + | 5 (random assign. to T, C and O) |

| Study | Age | Type[d] | Focus | Setting | Intervention components | Sample[a] | Duration[b] | Outcome[c] | Design[d] |
|---|---|---|---|---|---|---|---|---|---|
| Pepler et al. (1995), Earlscourt Social Skills Group Program, Toronto, Canada | 6–12 years (mean = 9.2 years) | Selective (aggressive and social-cognitive problems) | Behavioral and social-cognitive functioning | School | Social skills training, parent groups | Initial: 74 children: T = 40, C = 34. Follow-up: 97.3%, 72 (T = n.a., C = n.a.) | 12 to 15 weeks | Immediate outcome: externalizing behavior assign. to T and wait-list (teacher rating) + | 5 (random assign. to T and wait-list C) |
| Eron et al. (2000), Metropolitan Area Child Study, Chicago and Aurora, IL | Grades 2–3 to 5–6 | Selective (aggressive behavior) | Social cognitive development, social environment (school, peers, family) | School | T1 = GECI T2 = GECI + SGPST T3 = GECI + SGPST + FI | Initial: 2,181 children Follow-up: 70.0% 1,518 | 2 years | Immediate outcome (T3 vs C): early intervention cohort (grades 2–3): aggression +; late intervention cohort (grades 5–6): aggression 0; early intervention cohort: aggression + plus late intervention cohort: aggression + | 4 (16 schools block [4 schools] 4 groups of [4 schools] randomly assign. to 3 Ts and C) |
| Reid et al. (1999), Linking the Interests of Families and Teachers Program, USA | Grades 1 and 5 | Universal | Parenting, social environment (school, peers, family) | School | Group parent training, child social and problem-solving skills training | Initial: 671 children and families: T = 382, C = 289 Follow-up: 88.0%, 590 (T = n.a., C = n.a.)[f] | 10 weeks | Immediate outcome: child physical aggression (playground) + 1 year: child behavior problems (classroom) + | 4 (12 schools randomly assigned in 3 one-year waves to T, C and alternate) |

Notes

T = treatment group; C = control group; GECI = general enhancement classroom intervention; GT = group therapy; NW = nurture work; BM = behavior modification; n.a. = not available.
counseling–teacher consultation; SGPST = small group peer-skills training; FI = family intervention; PC = parent

a Percentage and number of initial sample remaining at latest follow-up.
b Period of time in which program effects are evaluated once program has ended.
c "0" = no treatment effects; "+" = desirable treatment effects; "–" = undesirable treatment effects.
d 5 = highest; 1 = lowest.
e Sample retention could not be calculated because of the addition of a second treatment and control group.
f Sample retention is based on the number of children who were rated by teachers at 1 year follow-up.

*al.*, 1995) – used a wait-list control group, which received a delayed intervention that did not permit future follow-ups comparing the treatment and control groups.

The methodological rating of the six experiments was reasonably high. Five of the six programs used random assignment to experimental and control conditions; however, for two of these programs (Reid *et al.*, 1999; Eron *et al.*, 2000), the unit of assignment was the school and the unit of analysis was the individual. (This issue is addressed in the concluding section of this chapter, "Gaps in knowledge and priorities for research.") For the sixth program – the Seattle Social Development Project (SSDP) of Hawkins *et al.* (1999) – we rated it as a level 4, because it introduced a quasi-experimental treatment condition towards the end of the full intervention cycle (4 years) – the original design being a randomized experiment involving school classrooms.[5]

All six of the programs showed desirable treatment effects in favor of the experimentals compared to the controls for at least one comparison at some follow-up. In the case of the program by Kolvin and his colleagues (1981), desirable benefits were found for the senior cohort on the outcome measure of antisocial behavior, but not for the junior cohort.

The Montreal Longitudinal-Experimental Study of Tremblay *et al.* (1995) targeted disruptive boys from low SES neighborhoods. The program lasted for 2 years and had two components: home-based parent training and school-based social skills training. The parent training component was based on social learning principles and involved training parents on how to provide positive reinforcement for desirable behavior, use non-punitive and consistent discipline practices, and develop family crisis management techniques. Social skills training for the children was focused predominantly on improving child-peer interaction. At the latest follow-up, 6 years post-intervention, in contrast to the controls, program members showed many desirable effects, including lower rates of self-reported delinquency.

The SSDP (Hawkins *et al.*, 1999), which included modified classroom teaching practices, parent training and child social skills training, showed substantial improvement from immediate outcome to follow-up (6 years). The parents were trained to notice and reinforce their children's socially desirable behavior in a program called "Catch them being good." At immediate outcome after 6 years of intervention, treatment effects on delinquency and academic achievement varied by gender; no effect on delinquency was found for girls, but a desirable effect was found for boys (not shown in Table 3.4). At the 6-year follow-up period, the full intervention group admitted less violence, less alcohol abuse, and fewer sexual partners than the controls. The benefit–cost ratio of this program according to Aos *et al.* (1999) was 1.8.

The largest program reported here, the Metropolitan Area Child Study (MACS; Eron *et al.*, 2000), which tested the effectiveness of three different treatments (general enhancement classroom intervention (GECI); GECI plus small group peer-skills training (SGCPST); and GECI plus SGCPST plus family intervention (FI)) compared to a no-treatment control group, found varied effects as a function of the time of intervention and school resource level. Just focusing on the comparison between the most intensive intervention (GECI plus SGCPST plus FI) and the control group, in the early

(grades 2–3) and early plus late (grades 2–3 and 5–6, respectively) intervention cohorts, aggression was found to be lower for the treatment group,
while for the late intervention cohort, the program showed no effect on
aggression. In addition to these largely beneficial results, Eron *et al.* (2000,
p. 2) report that "Iatrogenic effects on aggression were noted for younger
children in low resource schools receiving the most intensive intervention as
well as for older children receiving classroom plus small group training
regardless of school resource level" (not shown in Table 3.4).

Overall, these six school-based programs were of very high quality conceptually, methodologically and in delivery. It is more than likely that the success
of these programs has a great deal to do with these qualities. Indeed, the provision of child training in the school environment in a non-stigmatizing
manner combined with high quality parent training were special features of
these programs.

## Home/community parent training programs

Table 3.5 summarizes the key features of five home/community parent training programs. Four of the programs were carried out in the United States
and one in Dublin, Ireland (Mullin, Quigley and Glanville, 1994). At the
start of treatment, the age of the subjects ranged from 3 months to 17 years.
Programs were based on universal, selective or indicated samples. A number
of risk factors were targeted by the programs, including parenting and social
environment.

Two programs used very large samples: 671 young people in Harrell,
Cavanagh and Sridharan (1999) and 650 boys in McCord (1978). Sample
retention was very high for three (Bank *et al.*, 1991; Mullin, Quigley and
Glanville, 1994; Harrell, Cavanagh and Sridharan, 1999) of the four programs for which it could be calculated. Length of follow-up was low, with the
exception of the study by McCord (1978) which had a 30-year follow-up. The
duration of treatment varied considerably, but two programs (Chamberlain
and Reid, 1998; Mullin, Quigley and Glanville, 1994) did not report this
information.

All of the programs used very high quality research designs to assess treatment effects: four used randomized experiments and the program by Mullin,
Quigley and Glanville (1994) used what Barlow (1997) has called a sequential randomized experiment,[6] but, in our view, sequential assignment of subjects to experimental and control units does not have the same power as
random assignment to control for extraneous variables.

Three (McCord, 1978; Bank *et al.*, 1991; Mullin, Quigley and Glanville,
1994) of the five home/community parent training programs failed to show
desirable effects on outcome measures of child behavior problems and official and unofficial delinquency. The most noteworthy finding comes from
the Cambridge–Somerville Youth Study (McCord, 1978), which found that
after 30 years those boys who received academic tutoring, counseling or
other interventions were worse off than the boys that did not participate in
the program. Harmful or iatrogenic treatment effects were evidenced in such
areas as recidivism, dying early, serious mental illness, alcohol use, and stress-
related disease (i.e. high blood pressure and heart problems). It is important

*Table 3.5* Home/community parent training programs

| Study author, name, and location | Age at treatment | Type | Risk factors manipulated | Context of intervention | Treatment type | Sample size and retention[a] | Duration of treatment | Follow-up[b] and results[c] | Scientific methods score[d] |
|---|---|---|---|---|---|---|---|---|---|
| McCord (1978), Cambridge-Somerville Youth Study, MA | 5–13 years | Selective (rated as "difficult" and "average") | Social support | Community, home | Academic, tutoring, counseling, medical assistance, parent training, recreation | *Initial:* 650 boys; T = 325, C = 325 *Follow-up:* 36.2%, 235 (T = 113, C = 122) | 5.5 years (average) | 30 years: criminal behavior (self-reported and police arrests) | 5 (random assign. to T and C) |
| Bank et al. (1991), USA | 13.8 years (mean) | Indicated (at least 2 arrests) | Social environment, home | Community center, home | T = parent training, family therapy; C = court mandated family therapy, group therapy; drug therapy; drug counseling (in community) | *Initial:* 55 parents and youths; T = 28, C = 27 *Follow-up:* (youths): 98.2%, 54 (T = 28, C = 26) | T = 44.8 hours (average), C > 50 hours (average), 6 months after intake for both | Immediate outcome: police arrests (total rate) 0 3 years: police arrest (total rate) 0 | 5 (random assign. to T and C) |
| Mullin et al. (1994), Eastern Health Board, Dublin, Ireland | 3 months–14 years | Universal | Parenting | Community | Parent training, behavior mod., self-management skills | *Initial:* 79 mothers and children; T = 39, C = 40 *Follow-up:* 98.7%, 78 (T = n.a. C = n.a.) | n.a. | Immediate outcome: behavior problems 0 | 4 (sequential assign. to T and wait-list C) |

| Harrell et al. (1997, 1999), Children At Risk Program, USA | 12.4 years (mean) | Indicated (high risk in multiple domains: personal, family, school) | Multiple individual, community, family, and peer group | Community, home | Parenting skills training, case management, education, mentoring[e] | Initial: 671 youths in 5 cities: T = 338, C = 333 Follow-up: 74.5%, 500 (T = 264, C = 236) | 2 years | Immediate outcome: delinquency (all measures) 0 1 year: delinquency same neighbor-hood offenses 0 | 5 (random assign. to T and C in same neighbor-hood) |
|---|---|---|---|---|---|---|---|---|---|
| Chamberlain and Reid (1998), USA | 12–17 years (mean = 14.9 years) | Indicated (history of serious and chronic offending) | Social environment | Community (alternative family homes) | T = MTFC (individual therapy [e.g. skill building in problem-solving], family therapy [e.g. PMT]), C = GC | Initial: 79 youths (male) and parents: T = 37, C = 42 Follow-up: n.a. | n.a. | 1 year: police arrests + | 5 (random assign. to T and C) |

Notes

T = treatment group; C = control group; GC = group care (group, individual, and family therapy); MTFC = multidimensional treatment foster care; PMT = parent management training; n.a. = not available.

a Percentage and number of initial sample remaining at latest follow-up.

b Period of time in which program effects are evaluated once program has ended.

c "0" = no treatment effects; "+" = desirable treatment effects; "–" = undesirable treatment effects.

d 5 = highest; 1 = lowest.

e Other treatments included: multiple family services (e.g. counseling), after-school and summer activities, and criminal justice.

to point out that, for the most part, the package of interventions was divided up among treatment group members.

> Family problems became the focus of attention for approximately one third of the treatment group. Over half of the boys were tutored in academic subjects; over 100 received medical attention; one fourth were sent to summer camps; and most were brought in contact with the Boy Scouts, the YMCA, and other community organizations.
>
> (McCord, 1978, p. 284)

The Urban Institute's Children At Risk (CAR) program targeted high risk youths (average age 12.4) in poor neighborhoods of five cities across the United States (Harrell, Cavanagh and Sridharan, 1999). Eligible youths were identified in schools and randomly assigned to experimental or control groups. The program was a comprehensive community-based prevention strategy targeting risk factors for delinquency, including case management and family counseling, family skills training, tutoring, mentoring, afterschool activities, and community policing. The program was different in each neighborhood.

The initial results were disappointing, but a 1-year follow-up showed that (according to self-reports) experimental youths were less likely to have committed violent crimes and used or sold drugs (Harrell, Cavanagh and Sridharan, 1999). The process evaluation showed that the greatest change was in peer risk factors. Experimental youths associated less often with delinquent peers, felt less peer pressure to engage in delinquency, and had more positive peer support. In contrast, there were few changes in individual, family or community risk factors, possibly linked to the low participation of parents in parent training and of youths in mentoring and tutoring. The implementation problems of the program were related to the serious and multiple needs and problems of the families.

The multidimensional treatment foster care (MTFC) program by Chamberlain and Reid (1998) also produced desirable benefits. Participants (young males with a history of serious and chronic offending and their parents) in the MTFC program received individual (e.g. skill building in problem solving) and family (e.g. parent management training) therapy, while controls received what the authors refer to as group care (GC), which involved variations on group, individual, and family therapy. One year after the completion of the program, MTFC members were less likely than GC members to have engaged in further criminal activity, as measured by police arrests.

It is not altogether clear why three of the programs failed to show desirable benefits. In the case of the program by Bank *et al.* (1991), one possible explanation has to do with the "control" group receiving more hours of treatment than the "treatment" group. This is an unusual circumstance and one that the researchers had no control over, as the interventions received by the control group were mandated by court. The program by Mullin, Quigley and Glanville (1994) perhaps suffered from its non-targeted approach, although no information was provided on the duration of treatment, which could have also contributed to the program producing no effect. With respect to the

McCord (1978) program, questions can be raised about the quality and dosage of the interventions received by the treatment group; it appears that most of the interventions were rather insubstantial and not clearly based on theory.

## Multisystemic therapy programs

Table 3.6 summarizes the key elements of five multisystemic therapy (MST) programs, all conducted in the United States, and each one based on a different sample of adjudicated youths or youths approved for emergency psychiatric hospitalization. At the start of treatment, the average age of participants was between 13 and 15 years. The home, school or community (e.g. recreation center) were the main settings for the interventions. Sample size ranged from 84 to 176 individuals, and sample retention was very high for three of the five programs (Borduin et al., 1995; Henggeler et al., 1997, 1999) for which it could be accurately calculated. The length of follow-up (post-intervention) to assess treatment effects ranged from 6 months to 4 years. Treatment duration was quite consistent across the five programs.

The MST approach to treating serious antisocial behavior in youth focuses on intrapersonal (e.g. cognitive) and systemic (family, peers, school) factors associated with antisocial behavior (Henggeler et al., 1998). In all of the programs the control group also received some type of intervention, which was, in the case of the programs for adjudicated youths, often the usual services provided to youths in custody or on probation (e.g. substance abuse treatment). In the program by Borduin et al. (1995), the "control" group received more hours of treatment than the "treatment" group. All of the programs used a randomized experimental design to test the effectiveness of treatment, and hence had a scientific methods score of 5.

In each of the five trials of MST, desirable effects favoring the experimental group were shown on the outcomes of interest to this review and other outcomes. At 4 years after the completion of treatment, Borduin et al. (1995) found statistically significant reductions in recidivism (police arrests) and in the severity of offenses for the experimental group that received MST compared to the control group that received individual therapy, which focused on personal, family and academic issues. Henggeler et al. (1993) also found significant reductions in recidivism at just over 2 years follow-up. In a more recent trial of MST (Henggeler et al., 1997), statistically significant findings favoring the treatment group were found for youth behavior problems at immediate outcome, but not for delinquency at 1.7 years follow-up (the outcome measure of youth behavior problems was not assessed at this follow-up). The treatment group did, however, show lower annualized rates of re-arrest (25.8 percent lower) and days incarcerated (47.2 percent lower) compared to the control group at 1.7 years follow-up. For three of the programs (Borduin et al., 1995; Henggeler et al., 1993, 1999), improvements were also found in the functioning of the family unit as a whole, as measured by the outcome of family cohesion (not shown in Table 3.6).

The MST approach to treating serious antisocial behavior in youth provides strong evidence of effectiveness. Ongoing testing of MST (Henggeler,

*Table 3.6* Multisystemic therapy programs

| Study author, name, and location | Age at treatment | Type | Risk factors manipulated | Context of intervention | Treatment type | Sample size and retention[a] | Duration of treatment | Follow-up[b] and results[c] | Scientific methods score[d] |
|---|---|---|---|---|---|---|---|---|---|
| Henggeler et al. (1992, 1993), USA | 15.2 years (mean) | Indicated (history of serious offending) | Intrapersonal (e.g. cognitive), systemic (family, peers, school) | Home, school, community (e.g. recreation center, project office) | T = MST (focus on intra-personal and systemic factors), C = DYS (court ordered services and mental health) | Initial: 84 parents and youths (average), T = 43, C = 41 Follow-up: n.a. | T = 13.4 weeks (average), C = n.a. | Immediate outcome: police arrests + 2.1 years: police arrests + | 5 (random assign. to T and C) |
| Borduin et al. (1995), Missouri Delinquency Project, USA | 14.8 years (mean) | Indicated (at least 2 arrests) | Intra-personal, systemic | Home, school, community | T = MST C = IT (focus on personal, family, and academic issues) | Initial: 176 parents and youths: T = 92, C = 84 Follow-up: 71.6%, 126 (T = 70, C = 56) | T = 23.9 hours (mean), C = 28.6 hours (mean) (not given in, e.g., weeks, months) | Immediate outcome: behavior problems (mother reports) + 4 years: police arrests + | 5 (random assign. to T and C) |
| Schoenwald et al. (1996), USA | 15.7 years (mean) | Indicated (offending and substance abuse or dependence) | Intra-personal, systemic | Home, school, community | T = MST, C = US (probation with substance abuse treatment) | Initial: 118 families and youths: T = 59, C = 59 Follow-up: n.a. | T = 130 days (average), C = n.a. | 6 months: institution time +[e] | 5 (random assign. to T and C as part of an earlier study) |

| Henggeler et al. (1997), USA | 10.4–17.6 years (mean = 15.2 years) | Indicated (history of violent or chronic offending) | Intra-personal, systemic | Home, school, community | T = MST, primary caregivers and youths: T = 82, C = 73 *Follow-up:* 90.3%, 140 (T = 75, C = 65) | C = US (probation conditions, e.g., drug counseling) | *Initial:* 155 | T = 116.6–122.6 days, C = 6 months (min.) | Immediate outcome: behavior problems + and C delinquency 0 | 5 (random assign. to T and C) |
|---|---|---|---|---|---|---|---|---|---|---|
| Henggeler et al. (1999), USA | 13.0 years (mean) | Indicated (approved for emergency psychiatric hospitalization) | Intra-personal, systemic | Home | T = MST (44% also received hospitalization), C = psychiatric hospitalization[f] | *Initial:* 116 families and youths: T = 57, C = 59 *Follow-up:* 97.4%, 113 (for initial hospitalization) (T = 57, C = 56) | T = 123 days (average), C = n.a. | Immediate outcome: behavior problems (caregiver and teacher reports) +, police arrests 0 | 5 (random assign. to T and C) |

Notes

T = treatment group; C = control group; MST = multisystemic therapy; IT = individual therapy; DYS = Department of Youth Services (in South Carolina); US = usual services provided to youth offenders in the South Carolina Department of Juvenile Justice; n.a. = not available.

a Percentage and number of initial sample remaining at latest follow-up.

b Period of time in which program effects are evaluated once the program has ended.

c "0" = no treatment effects; "+" = desirable treatment effects; "–" = undesirable treatment effects.

d 5 = highest; 1 = lowest.

e It was not reported if this finding achieved statistical significance.

f "Forty-two of the 56 youths received community-based treatment (home-based, office-based, clinical day programming) ... for an average of 8.5 hours" (Henggeler et al., 1999, p.1334).

1998) offers to provide an even stronger evidentiary base to contribute to policy and legislation for this important subgroup of the offending population.

## Conclusions: assessing program effectiveness

This section classifies the six identified categories of family-based prevention programs under one of three headings: working, not working or promising, using the standards set by Sherman *et al.* (1997). For a program category to be classified as "working" there must be a minimum of two level 3 studies with significance tests demonstrating effectiveness and the preponderance of evidence in support of the same conclusion. For the classification of "not working" there must be a minimum of two level 3 studies with significance tests showing ineffectiveness and the preponderance of evidence in the same direction. The classification of "promising" is given to "programs for which the level of certainty from available evidence is too low to support generalizable conclusions, but for which there is some empirical basis for predicting that further research could support such conclusions" (Sherman *et al.*, 1998, p.6). For the classification of "promising," at least one level 3 study is required with significance tests showing effectiveness and the preponderance of evidence in support of the same conclusion.

### What works

We found that four of the six categories of family-based prevention programs were effective in preventing child behavior problems, delinquency, and other related outcomes: (1) home visitation; (2) parent education plus day care/preschool; (3) school-based child training plus parent training; and (4) multisystemic therapy. Programs in these four areas were of the highest quality methodologically, conceptually, and in delivery. Not only were these categories of family-based programs extremely effective in reducing aggression, delinquency, and other types of childhood antisocial behavior, but they also produced other beneficial outcomes.

Our confidence in these conclusions is strengthened somewhat by a similar effort, being led by Delbert Elliott at the Center for the Study and Prevention of Violence at the University of Colorado at Boulder, to identify and transmit for wider use in the United States the most effective[7] violence prevention programs. Known as "Blueprints for Violence Prevention," this program of research has also identified, among its eleven prevention programs – not all family-based – deemed to be the most effective, the home visitation program developed by David Olds and the multisystemic therapy program developed by Scott Henggeler.

### What does not work

The family-based program category of home/community parent training was judged to be ineffective. With the exception of two of the five reviewed programs in this category, all reported either no effects for the outcomes of interest or, in the case of the program by McCord (1978), harmful or iatrogenic effects (see also Dishion, McCord and Poulin, 1999) for experimental compared to control participants. Interestingly, one (Chamberlain and Reid, 1998) of the two programs that did show desirable effects is one of the eleven Blueprint programs. Although this does not necessarily pose a problem to our present rating of this category of programs, it does suggest that home/community parent training programs should not be discarded altogether. More experimentation with these programs will be required to address this important matter.

### What is promising

One of the six program categories was judged to be promising: clinic-based child training plus parent training. Mixed results from the seven programs coupled with, for the most part, very little follow-up to assess the effects of treatment led to our decision to rate this category of family-based programs as promising. However, these programs are, in our view, much closer to the high end of the promising classification, largely because of the successes achieved by the high quality parent training interventions developed by Carolyn Webster-Stratton.

## Gaps in knowledge and priorities for research

This chapter reviewed family-based studies of only the highest quality methodologically: 29 of the 34 studies used randomized experimental designs to assess the effectiveness of the interventions. Similarly, using the scientific methods score developed by Sherman *et al.* (1997) to assess the quality of evaluation designs, 25 programs were judged to be a level 5, the gold standard of evaluation design.

Three of the 28 programs that employed randomized experimental designs but did not receive a level 5 rating involved large units (e.g. schools, classrooms). The difficulty stems primarily from the need to randomize a large enough number of units – minimum 50 in total – to "gain the benefits of randomization in equating experimental and control communities [or other units] on all possible extraneous variables" (Farrington, 1997, p. 160). It is common to overlook this issue, which invariably leads to mixed units of analysis. This occurs when the unit of analysis differs from the unit of assignment; for example, if the school is the unit that is assigned to experimental or control conditions, it follows that the school should be the unit of analysis in assessing the impact of the intervention. (See Chapter 5 for a discussion of this issue.) It would be desirable to test the effects of family-based crime prevention programs by randomly assigning large numbers of schools or classrooms to treatment and control conditions, but the costs may be too prohibitive.

Another issue deserving of attention in the use of randomized experiments, at least from the perspective of long-term follow-up, is the use of wait-list control groups. In all of the programs that we reviewed that employed wait-list control groups, each received a delayed intervention prior to any follow-up beyond immediate outcome. This eliminated any chance of comparing longer-term effects of experimental and (no-treatment) control conditions. There are of course many virtues to wait-list controls, one of which is to circumvent a common ethical concern about withholding treatment from others who could benefit. Many programs adopt this design feature to address a policy of "treat all," but it would be desirable either to delay intervention for the wait-list controls until a later point in time or, where sample size is large enough, to treat only a portion of the wait-list control group, thus enabling longer-term comparisons between the experimental and control groups.

Research is also needed to help identify the active ingredients of successful (and promising) family-based prevention programs. Most delinquency and crime prevention programs are multi-dimensional (see Tremblay and Craig, 1995), which makes it difficult to isolate the independent effects of the different components. Future experiments are needed which attempt to disentangle the different elements of successful programs, especially: (1) the home visitation program of Olds *et al.* (1997), (2) the day care/preschool plus home visitation program of Schweinhart, Barnes and Weikart (1993), (3) the school-based child training plus parent training program of Tremblay *et al.* (1995), and (4) the school-based child training plus parent training program of Hawkins *et al.* (1999). A program of replication and follow-up experiments is needed. This should lead to more specific and cumulative knowledge about what are the effective elements of family-based crime prevention programs.

## Notes

1   We are grateful to Lawrence Sherman and Denise Gottfredson for helpful comments on an earlier draft of this chapter.
2   We do not restrict ourselves only to reports that have appeared since the Sherman (1997) review, but include all relevant reports, based on information from the original sources (see methodology section).
3   For helpful responses, we are very grateful to Jeanne Brooks-Gunn, Marion Forgatch, Deborah Gorman-Smith, Adele Harrell, David Hawkins, Scott Henggeler, David Olds, Gerald Patterson, John Reid, Patrick Tolan, Richard Tremblay and Carolyn Webster-Stratton.
4   Women were recruited for the program if they had no previous live births and had at least one of the following characteristics prone to health and developmental problems in infancy (85 percent had at least one of the characteristics): under 19 years of age, unmarried, or low socioeconomic status. High-risk women are those who were both unmarried and from households of low SES at the time of program enrollment.
5   We disagree with Gottfredson, Wilson and Skroban Najaka's (Chapter 4, this volume) coding of this program as a level 2 on the Scientific Methods Scale.
6   As described by Mullin and her colleagues (1994, p. 170), sequential assignment to the treatment and control group went as follows: "Thirty-nine mothers [were] in the Experimental group which was formed from the top thirty-nine mothers on the course waiting list. The next forty on the list were assigned to the Control group."
7   To be judged effective programs had to have: "(1) an experimental design, (2) evidence of a statistically significant deterrent (or marginally deterrent) effect, (3) replication at multiple sites with demonstrated effects, and (4) evidence that the deterrent effect was sustained for at least one year post-treatment" (Elliott, 1998, p. xv).

# References

Aos, S., Phipps, P., Barnoski, R. and Lieb, R. (1999) *The comparative costs and benefits of programs to reduce crime: A review of national research findings with implications for Washington State: Version 3.0.* Olympia, WA: Washington State Institute for Public Policy.

Bank, L., Marlowe, J.H., Reid, J.B., Patterson, G.R. and Weinrott, M.R. (1991) A comparative evaluation of parent-training interventions for families of chronic delinquents. *Journal of Abnormal Child Psychology,* 19, 15–33.

Barlow, J. (1997) *Systematic review of the effectiveness of parent-training programmes in improving behaviour problems in children aged 3–10 years: A review of the literature on parent-training programmes and child behaviour outcome measures.* Oxford, England: Health Services Research Unit, Department of Public Health, University of Oxford.

Barnett, W.S. (1993) Cost–benefit analysis. In L.J. Schweinhart, H.V. Barnes and D.P. Weikart. *Significant benefits: The High/Scope Perry preschool study through age 27.* Ypsilanti, MI: High/Scope Press, 142–73.

Barth, R.P., Hacking, S. and Ash, J.R. (1988) Preventing child abuse: An experimental evaluation of the Child Parent Enrichment Project. *Journal of Primary Prevention,* 8, 201–17.

Borduin, C.M., Mann, B.J., Cone, L.T., Henggeler, S.W., Fucci, B.R., Blaske, D.M. and Williams, R.A. (1995) Multisystemic treatment of serious juvenile offenders: Long-term prevention of criminality and violence. *Journal of Consulting and Clinical Psychology,* 63, 569–87.

Chamberlain, P. and Reid, J.B. (1998) Comparison of two community alternatives to incarceration for chronic juvenile offenders. *Journal of Consulting and Clinical Psychology,* 66, 624–33.

Dishion, T.J. and Andrews, D.W. (1995) Preventing escalation in problem behaviors with high-risk young adolescents: Immediate and 1-year outcomes. *Journal of Consulting and Clinical Psychology,* 63, 538–48.

Dishion, T.J., McCord, J. and Poulin, F. (1999) When intervention harms: Peer groups and problem behavior. *American Psychologist,* 54, 755–64.

Dishion, T.J., Patterson, G.R. and Kavanagh, K.A. (1992) An experimental test of the coercion model: Linking theory, measurement and intervention. In J. McCord and R.E. Tremblay (eds), *Preventing antisocial behavior: Interventions from birth through adolescence.* New York: Guilford, 253–82.

Elliott, D.S. (1998) Editor's introduction. In S.W. Henggeler (ed.), *Blueprints for violence prevention: Multisystemic therapy: Book 6.* Denver, CO: C&M Press, xi–xxiii.

Eron, L.D., Guerra, N.G., Henry, D., Huesmann, L.R., Spindler, A., Tolan, P.H. and Van Acker, R. (2000) A cognitive-ecological approach to preventing aggression in urban settings: Initial outcomes for high-risk children. Manuscript under review.

Farrington, D.P. (1997) Evaluating a community crime prevention program. *Evaluation,* 3, 157–73.

Farrington, D.P. (1998) Youth crime and antisocial behaviour. In A. Campbell and S. Muncer (eds), *The social child.* Hove, East Sussex, England: Psychology Press, 353–92.

Farrington, D.P. and Welsh, B.C. (1999) Delinquency prevention using family-based interventions. *Children and Society,* 13, 287–303.

Field, T.M., Widmayer, S.M., Stringer, S. and Ignatoff, E. (1980) Teenage, lower-class black mothers and their preterm infants: An intervention and developmental follow-up. *Child Development,* 51, 426–36.

Harrell, A.V., Cavanagh, S.E., Harmon, M.A., Koper, C.S. and Sridharan, S. (1997) *Impact of the Children At Risk Program: Comprehensive final report: Vol. 1.* Washington, DC: The Urban Institute.

Harrell, A.V., Cavanagh, S.E. and Sridharan, S. (1999) Evaluation of the Children At Risk Program: Results 1 year after the end of the program. *Research in Brief,* November. Washington, DC: National Institute of Justice, US Department of Justice.

Hawkins, J.D., Catalano, R.F., Morrison, D.M., O'Donnell, J., Abbott, R.D. and Day, L.E. (1992) The Seattle Social Development Project: Effects of the first four years on protective factors and problem behaviors. In J. McCord and R.E. Tremblay (eds), *Preventing antisocial behavior: Interventions from birth through adolescence.* New York: Guilford, 139–61.

Hawkins, J.D., Catalano, R.F., Kosterman, R., Abbott, R. and Hill, K.G. (1999) Preventing adolescent health-risk behaviors by strengthening protection during childhood. *Archives of Pediatrics and Adolescent Medicine,* 153, 226–34.

Hawkins, J.D., Herrenkohl, T., Farrington, D.P., Brewer, D., Catalano, R.F. and Harachi, T.W. (1998) A review of predictors of youth violence. In R. Loeber and D.P. Farrington (eds), *Serious and violent juvenile offenders: Risk factors and successful interventions.* Thousand Oaks, CA: Sage, 106–46.

Henggeler, S.W. (1998) *Blueprints for violence prevention: Multisystemic therapy: Book 6.* Denver, CO: C&M Press.

Henggeler, S.W., Melton, G.B., Brondino, M.J. and Schere, D.G. (1997) Multisystemic therapy with violent and chronic juvenile offenders and their families: The role of treatment fidelity in successful dissemination. *Journal of Consulting and Clinical Psychology,* 65, 821–33.

Henggeler, S.W., Melton, G.B. and Smith, L.A. (1992) Family preservation using multisystemic therapy: An effective alternative to incarcerating serious juvenile offenders. *Journal of Consulting and Clinical Psychology,* 60, 953–61.

Henggeler, S.W., Melton, G.B., Smith, L.A., Schoenwald, S.K. and Hanley, J.H. (1993) Family preservation using multisystemic treatment: Long-term follow-up to a clinical trial with serious juvenile offenders. *Journal of Child and Family Studies,* 2, 283–93.

Henggeler, S.W., Rowland, M.D., Randall, J., Ward, D.W., Pickrel, S.G., Cunningham, P.B., Miller, S.L., Edwards, J., Zealberg, J.J., Hand, L.D. and Santos, A.B. (1999) Home-based multisystemic therapy as an alternative to the hospitalization of youths in psychiatric crisis: Clinical outcomes. *Journal of the American Academy of Child and Adolescent Psychiatry,* 38, 1331–9.

Henggeler, S.W., Schoenwald, S.K., Borduin, C.M., Rowland, M.D. and Cunningham, P.B. (1998) *Multisystemic treatment of antisocial behavior in children and adolescents.* New York: Guilford.

IHDP (Infant Health and Development Program) (1990) Enhancing the outcomes of low-birth-weight, premature infants: A multi-site, randomized trial. *Journal of the American Medical Association,* 263, 3035–42.

Johnson, D.L. and Breckenridge, J.N. (1982) The Houston Parent-Child Development Center and the primary prevention of behavior problems in young children. *American Journal of Community Psychology,* 10, 305–16.

Johnson, D.L. and Walker, T. (1987) Primary prevention of behavior problems in Mexican-American children. *American Journal of Community Psychology,* 15, 375–85.

Karoly, L.A., Greenwood, P.W., Everingham, S.S., Houbé, J., Kilburn, M.R., Rydell, C.P., Sanders, M. and Chiesa, J. (1998) *Investing in our children: What we know and don't know about the costs and benefits of early childhood interventions.* Santa Monica, CA: RAND.

Kazdin, A.E. (1997) Parent management training: Evidence, outcomes and issues. *Journal of the American Academy of Child and Adolescent Psychiatry,* 36, 1349–56.

Kazdin, A.E., Siegel, T.C. and Bass, D. (1992) Cognitive problem-solving skills training and parent management training in the treatment of antisocial behavior in children. *Journal of Consulting and Clinical Psychology,* 60, 733–47.

Kitzman, H., Olds, D.L., Henderson, C.R., Hanks, C., Cole, R., Tatelbaum, R., McConnochie, K.M., Sidora, K., Luckey, D.W., Shaver, D., Engelhardt, K., James, D. and Barnard, K. (1997) Effect of prenatal and infancy home visitation by nurses on pregnancy outcomes, childhood injuries and repeated childbearing: A randomized controlled trial. *Journal of the American Medical Association*, 278, 644–52.

Kolvin, I., Garside, R.F., Nicol, A.R., MacMillan, A., Wolstenholme, F. and Leitch, I.M. (1981) *Help starts here: The maladjusted child in the ordinary school*. London, England: Tavistock.

Lally, J.R., Mangione, P.L. and Honig, A.S. (1988) The Syracuse University Family Development Research Program: Long-range impact of an early intervention with low-income children and their families. In D.R. Powell (ed.), *Parent education as early childhood intervention: Emerging directions in theory, research and practice*. Norwood, NJ: Ablex, 79–104.

Larson, C.P. (1980) Efficacy of prenatal and postpartum home visits on child health and development. *Pediatrics*, 66, 191–7.

Long, P., Forehand, R., Wierson, M. and Morgan, A. (1994) Does parent training with young noncompliant children have long-term effects? *Behavior Research Therapy*, 32, 101–7.

McCarton, C.M., Brooks-Gunn, J., Wallace, I.F., Bauer, C.R., Bennett, F.C., Bernbaum, J.C., Broyles, R.S., Casey, P.H., McCormick, M.C., Scott, D.T., Tyson, J., Tonascia, J. and Meinert, C.L. (1997) Results at age 8 years of early intervention for low-birth-weight premature infants: The Infant Health and Development Program. *Journal of the American Medical Association*, 277, 126–32.

McCord, J. (1978) A thirty-year follow-up of treatment effects. *American Psychologist*, 33, 284–9.

Mullin, E., Quigley, K. and Glanville, B. (1994) A controlled evaluation of the impact of a parent training programme on child behaviour and mothers' general well-being. *Counseling Psychology Quarterly*, 7, 167–79.

Olds, D.L., Eckenrode, J., Henderson, C.R., Kitzman, H., Powers, J., Cole, R., Sidora, K., Morris, P., Pettitt, L.M. and Luckey, D. (1997) Long-term effects of home visitation on maternal life course and child abuse and neglect: Fifteen-year follow-up of a randomized trial. *Journal of the American Medical Association*, 278, 637–43.

Olds, D.L., Henderson, C.R, Chamberlin, R. and Tatelbaum, R. (1986) Preventing child abuse and neglect: A randomized trial of nurse home visitation. *Pediatrics*, 78, 65–78.

Olds, D.L., Henderson, C.R., Cole, R., Eckenrode, J., Kitzman, H., Luckey, D., Pettitt, L., Sidora, K., Morris, P. and Powers, J. (1998) Long-term effects of nurse home visitation on children's criminal and antisocial behavior: 15-year follow-up of a randomized controlled trial. *Journal of the American Medical Association*, 280, 1238–44.

Olds, D.L., Henderson, C.R., Phelps, C., Kitzman, H. and Hanks, C. (1993) Effects of prenatal and infancy nurse home visitation on government spending. *Medical Care*, 31, 155–74.

Pepler, D.J., King, G., Craig, W., Byrd, B. and Bream, L. (1995) The development and evaluation of a multisystem social skills group training program for aggressive children. *Child & Youth Care Forum*, 24, 297–313.

Reid, J.B., Eddy, J.M., Fetrow, R.A. and Stoolmiller, M. (1999) Description and immediate impacts of a preventive intervention for conduct problems. *American Journal of Community Psychology*, 27, 483–517.

Schoenwald, S.K., Ward, D.M., Henggeler, S.W., Pickrel, S.G. and Patel, H. (1996) Multisystemic therapy treatment of substance abusing or dependent adolescent offenders: Costs of reducing incarceration, inpatient and residential placement. *Journal of Child and Family Studies*, 5, 431–44.

Schweinhart, L.J., Barnes, H.V. and Weikart, D.P. (1993) *Significant benefits: The High/Scope Perry preschool study through age 27.* Ypsilanti, MI: High/Scope Press.

Schweinhart, L.J. and Weikart, D.P. (1980) *Young children grow up: The effects of the Perry preschool program on youths through age 15.* Ypsilanti, MI: High/Scope Press.

Seitz, V., Rosenbaum, L.K. and Apfel, N.H. (1985) Effects of family support intervention: A ten-year follow-up. *Child Development,* 56, 376–91.

Sherman, L.W. (1997) Family-based crime prevention. In L.W. Sherman, D.C. Gottfredson, D.L. MacKenzie, J. Eck, P. Reuter and S.D. Bushway. *Preventing crime: What works, what doesn't, what's promising.* Washington, DC: National Institute of Justice, US Department of Justice, 4-1 to 4-42.

Sherman, L.W., Gottfredson, D.C., MacKenzie, D.L., Eck, J., Reuter, P. and Bushway, S.D. (1997) *Preventing crime: What works, what doesn't, what's promising.* Washington, DC: National Institute of Justice, US Department of Justice.

Sherman, L.W., Gottfredson, D.C., MacKenzie, D.L., Eck, J., Reuter, P. and Bushway, S.D. (1998) Preventing crime: What works, what doesn't, what's promising. *Research in Brief,* July. Washington, DC: National Institute of Justice, US Department of Justice.

Spaccarelli, S., Cotler, S. and Penman, D. (1992) Problem-solving skills training as a supplement to behavioral parent-training. *Cognitive Therapy and Research,* 16, 1–18.

Stone, W.L., Bendell, R.D. and Field, T.M. (1988) The impact of socioeconomic status on teenage mothers and children who received early intervention. *Journal of Applied Developmental Psychology,* 9, 391–408.

Strayhorn, J.M. and Weidman, C.S. (1991) Follow-up one year after parent-child interaction training: Effects on behavior of preschool children. *Journal of the American Academy of Child and Adolescent Psychiatry,* 30, 138–43.

Szapocznik, J., Rio, A., Murray, E., Cohen, R., Scopetta, M., Rivas-Vazquez, A., Hervis, O., Posada, V. and Kurtines, W. (1989) Structural family versus psychodynamic child therapy for problematic Hispanic boys. *Journal of Consulting and Clinical Psychology,* 57, 571–8.

Tonry, M. and Farrington, D.P. (1995) Strategic approaches to crime prevention. In M. Tonry and D.P. Farrington (eds), *Building a safer society: Strategic approaches to crime prevention: Vol. 19. Crime and justice: A Review of research.* Chicago, IL: University of Chicago Press, 1–20.

Tremblay, R.E. and Craig, W.M. (1995) Developmental crime prevention. In M. Tonry and D.P. Farrington (eds), *Building a safer society: Strategic approaches to crime prevention: Vol. 19. Crime and justice: A Review of research.* Chicago, IL: University of Chicago Press, 151–236.

Tremblay, R.E., LeMarquand, D. and Vitaro, F. (1999) The prevention of Oppositional Defiant Disorder and Conduct Disorder. In H.C. Quay and A.E. Hogan (eds), *Handbook of disruptive behavior disorders.* New York: Plenum, 525–55.

Tremblay, R.E., Pagani-Kurtz, L., Mâsse, L.C., Vitaro, F. and Pihl, R.O. (1995) A bimodal preventive intervention for disruptive kindergarten boys: Its impact through mid-adolescence. *Journal of Consulting and Clinical Psychology,* 63, 560–8.

Tremblay, R.E., Vitaro, F., Bertrand, L., LeBlanc, M., Beauchesne, H., Boileau, H. and David, L. (1992) Parent and child training to prevent early onset of delinquency: The Montréal Longitudinal-Experimental Study. In J. McCord and R.E. Tremblay (eds), *Preventing antisocial behavior: Interventions from birth through adolescence.* New York: Guilford, 117–38.

Utting, D. (1997) *Reducing criminality among young people: A sample of relevant programmes in the United Kingdom.* London, England: Research and Statistics Directorate, Home Office.

Wasserman, G.A. and Miller, L.S. (1998) The prevention of serious and violent juvenile offending. In R. Loeber and D.P. Farrington (eds), *Serious and violent juvenile offenders: Risk factors and successful interventions.* Thousand Oaks, CA: Sage, 197–247.

Webster-Stratton, C. (1998) Preventing conduct problems in Head Start children: Strengthening parenting competencies. *Journal of Consulting and Clinical Psychology,* 66, 715–30.

Webster-Stratton, C. and Hammond, M. (1997) Treating children with early-onset conduct problems: A comparison of child and parent training interventions. *Journal of Consulting and Clinical Psychology,* 65, 93–109.

Webster-Stratton, C., Kolpacoff, M. and Hollinsworth, T. (1988) Self-administered videotape therapy for families with conduct-problem children: Comparison with two cost-effective treatments and a control group. *Journal of Consulting and Clinical Psychology,* 56, 558–66.

Welsh, B.C. and Farrington, D.P. (2000) Monetary costs and benefits of crime prevention programs. In M. Tonry (ed.), *Crime and justice: A review of research: Vol. 27.* Chicago, IL: University of Chicago Press, 305–61.

Welsh, B.C., Farrington, D.P. and Sherman, L.W. (eds) (2001) *Costs and benefits of preventing crime.* Boulder, CO: Westview Press.

Yoshikawa, H. (1994) Prevention as cumulative protection: Effects of early family support and education on chronic delinquency and its risks. *Psychological Bulletin,* 115, 28–54.

# 4   School-based crime prevention

*Denise C. Gottfredson, David B. Wilson and Stacy Skroban Najaka*[1]

Schools have great potential as a locus for crime prevention. They provide regular access to students throughout the developmental years, and perhaps the only consistent access to large numbers of the most crime-prone young children in the early school years; they are staffed with individuals paid to help youth develop as healthy, happy, productive citizens; and the community usually supports schools' efforts to socialize youth. Many of the precursors of delinquent behavior are school-related and therefore likely to be amenable to change through school-based intervention.

Figure 4.1 shows several school-related precursors to delinquency identified by research. These factors include characteristics of school and classroom environments as well as individual-level school-related experiences and attitudes, peer group experiences, and personal values, attitudes and beliefs. School environment factors related to delinquency include availability of drugs, alcohol and other criminogenic commodities such as weapons; characteristics of the classroom and school social organization, such as strong academic mission and administrative leadership; and a climate of emotional support. School-related experiences and attitudes which often precede delinquency include poor school performance and attendance, low attachment to school, and low commitment to schooling. Peer-related experiences, many of which are school-centered, include rejection by peers and association with delinquent peers. And individual factors include early problem behavior, impulsiveness or low levels of self-control, rebellious attitudes, beliefs favoring law violation, and low levels of social competency skills, such as identifying likely consequences of actions and alternative solutions to problems, taking the perspective of others, and correctly interpreting social cues. Several recent reviews summarize the research literature linking these factors with crime (Lipsey and Derzon, 1998; Gottfredson, Sealock and Koper, 1996; Hawkins, Catalano and Miller, 1992; Howell *et al.*, 1995).

Figure 4.1 also draws attention to the fact that schools operate in larger contexts which influence their functioning as well as their outcomes. By far the strongest correlates of school disorder are characteristics of the population and community contexts in which schools are located. Despite the substantial national interest in the rare but shocking school shootings that have occurred over the past few years in suburban and rural settings, the fact remains that schools in urban, poor, disorganized communities experience more disorder than other schools (Gottfredson and Gottfredson, 1985).

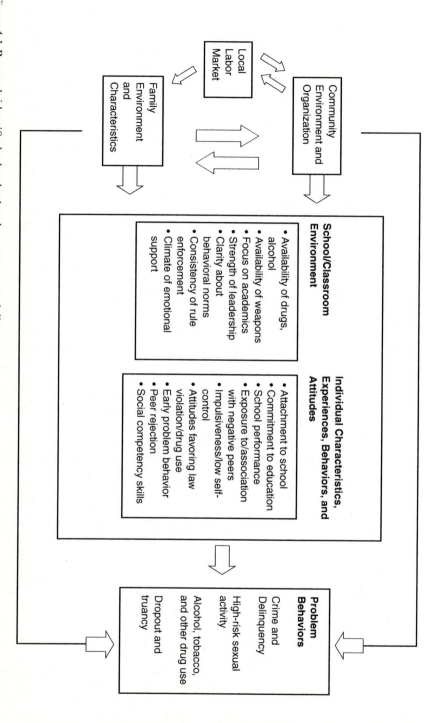

*Figure 4.1* Research identified school-related precursors to delinquency

Research has also suggested that the human resources needed to implement and sustain school improvement efforts – leadership, teacher morale, teacher mastery, school climate, and resources – are found less often in urban than in other schools (Gottfredson, Fink *et al.*, 1997; Gottfredson, 2001). Although schools cannot be expected to reverse their communities' problems, they can influence their own rates of disorder. Controlling on relevant characteristics of the larger community, characteristics of schools and the way they are run explain significant amounts of variation in school rates of disorderly behavior (Gottfredson and Gottfredson, 1985).

National priorities for children focus on schools as a locus for the prevention of diverse social problems including crime. The Department of Health and Human Services' *Healthy People 2000* goals include increasing high school graduation rates and reducing physical fighting, weapon-carrying, substance use and pregnancy among adolescents. National Education Goal 6 states that every school will be free of drugs, violence, and the unauthorized presence of firearms and alcohol, and will offer a disciplined environment conducive to learning by the year 2000. The 1986 Drug-Free Schools and Communities Act legislation provided substantial funds to states to develop and operate school-based drug prevention programs. In 1994 this legislation was modified to authorize expenditures on school-based violence prevention programs as well.

This substantial national interest in schools as a prevention tool is not matched by federal expenditures in this area. Table 4.1 shows that federal expenditures on school-based substance abuse and crime prevention efforts are modest,[2] particularly when compared with federal expenditures on control strategies such as policing and prison construction.[3] Perhaps more troubling, the meager federal expenditures on school-based prevention are not well spent. The single largest federal expenditure on school-based prevention (Safe and Drug-Free Schools and Communities monies administered by the US Department of Education) funds a relatively narrow range of intervention strategies, many of which have been shown either not to work (e.g. counseling) or to have only small effects (e.g. drug instruction).

This chapter is intended to provide information for use in setting research agendas and guiding funding decisions about what works, what does not work, what is promising, and how delinquency prevention efforts can be strengthened. It begins by clarifying the outcomes sought in school-based prevention programs. It then classifies school-based prevention activities within two broad approaches – environmental- and individual-focused – into more specific program types. Next it reviews research related to each type of activity, comments on the quality of the available information about the efficacy of each type of activity, and summarizes knowledge about what works, what does not work, and what is promising. It ends with a summary of findings and recommendations for funding of school-based prevention interventions and further research.

*Table 4.1* Partial list of federal expenditures on school-based prevention

| Federal program | Agency | Funding level | Strategies |
|---|---|---|---|
| Safe and Drug-Free Schools and Communities Program[a] | DOE[b] | FY95: 467M<br>FY96: 466M<br>FY97: 556M<br>FY98: 556M<br>FY99: 566M | State and local education agency programs: instruction, student assistance programs, teachers and staff training, curriculum development and acquisition; red-ribbon week; before- after-school programs and community service.<br>Governor's state and local programs: instruction, replication of other drug education programs, high-risk youth programs. |
| High-Risk Youth Demonstration Program | DHHS[c] [CSAP][d] | FY95: 65.2M<br><br>Discontinued after FY95 | Various. In-school and after-school programs; violence and drug prevention. |
| Youth Violence Prevention Program | DHHS[c] [CDC][e] | FY95: 10.7M | Various. Projects include instruction (violence prevention, self-control, social competency; cognitive behavioral methods, tutoring, mentoring, recreation, campaigns to change norms, peer mediation and conflict resolution, changes in school management processes, parent training). |
| Community Schools Youth Services and Supervision Program | DHHS[c] [ACF][f] | FY95: 10M<br>FY96: no new appropriation<br>FY97: 12.8M<br>FY98: no reauthorization | Various. Prevention and academic achievement enhancement during non-school hours. |
| Learn and Serve America Program | Corporation for National Service | FY95: 32M<br>FY96: 32M<br>FY99: 37.5M | Community service tied to the school curriculum. Attempt to engage youths in school to prevent drop-out. Character education. |
| DARE (Drug Abuse Resistance Education) | DOJ[g]/DOI[h] [BJA][i] | FY95: 1.75M<br>FY96: 1.75M<br>FY97: 1.75M<br>FY98: 1.75M<br>FY99: 1.75M<br>Plus annual funds from Byrne Block Grant | To DARE America: Instruction (core program and booster lessons), a recent extension of the program (DARE + PLUS – Play and Learn Under Supervision), and an after-school program. |
| GREAT (Gang Resistance Education and Training) | DOJ[g]/ TREAS[j] [ATF[k]/ NIJ[l]] | FY95: 16.2M<br>Plus 300K (evaluation) | Instruction |
| CIS (Cities in Schools) | DOJ[g] [OJJDP][m] | FY95: 592K<br>FY96: 340K<br>FY00: 340K | School-based supportive services for at-risk students and their families |
| JUMP (Juvenile Mentoring Program) | DOJ[g] [OJJDP][m] | FY96: 15M<br>FY00: 13.5M | Mentoring |
| LRE (Law-related education) | DOJ[g] [OJJDP][m] | FY95: 2.7M<br>FY96: 1.2M<br>FY98: 1M<br>FY99: 1.5M<br>FY00: 1.9M | Instruction, character education |

Notes

M = million; K = thousand; both represent US$.

a Prior to 1994, this program funded drug programs in schools. The 1994 legislation authorized expenditures on violence prevention programs and curricula as well.

b Department of Education.

c Department of Health and Human Services.

d Center for Substance Abuse Prevention.

e Center for Disease Control.

f Administration for Children and Families.

g Department of Justice.

h Department of the Interior.

i Bureau of Justice Assistance.

j Treasury Department.

k Alcohol, Tobacco, and Firearms.

l National Institute of Justice.

m Office of Juvenile Justice and Delinquency Prevention.

# The nature of school-based prevention

## *Measures of effectiveness*

School-based prevention programs include interventions to prevent a variety of forms of "problem behavior," including theft, violence, illegal acts of aggression, alcohol or other drug use, rebellious behavior, antisocial behavior, aggressive behavior, defiance of authority and disrespect for others. These different forms of delinquent behavior are highly correlated and share common causes. Many of the programs considered in this chapter were not specifically designed to prevent the problem behaviors, but instead to affect presumed causal factors, such as school drop-out, truancy, or other correlates which are expected to increase protection against or decrease risk towards engaging in problem behaviors at some later date. This focus on non-crime program outcomes is entirely appropriate given the young ages of many of the targeted students. Different outcomes have different saliencies for different age groups. Positive program effects on reading skills for 6-year-old children may be as important in terms of later crime prevented as reducing marijuana use for 16-year-old youth. Many prevention researchers and practitioners also assume a link between less serious problem behaviors and later, more serious crime. They are satisfied when their interventions demonstrate effects on the early forms of problem behavior. This developmental perspective underlies many school-based prevention efforts today and may explain the wide variety of outcome measures used to assess the effectiveness of these programs, some of which are summarized in Box 4.1.

---

**Box 4.1**

**Alcohol and other drug use (AOD)** Ingestion of alcoholic beverages and ingestion of any illicit drug are considered substance use. Dimensions of use that are often measured distinctly in evaluations of prevention programs include age of first use (age at onset); status as having used alcohol or other drugs at least once; and current use, including frequency of use and amount typically used. Substance use is most often measured using youth self-reports in evaluations of school-based prevention programs.

**Delinquent and criminal behavior** Delinquent or criminal behavior is any behavior which is against the law. Delinquency is criminal behavior committed by a young person. Laws, and therefore the precise definition of behaviors in violation of the law, vary slightly from state to state. Crime and delinquency includes the full range of acts for which individuals could be arrested. It includes crimes against persons, ranging in seriousness from murder to robbery to minor assault. It includes an array of crimes against property ranging from arson to felony theft to joyriding. Crime and delinquency also includes possession, use and selling of drugs. For juveniles, it includes status offenses, such as running away. Dimensions of crime that are often measured distinctly in evaluations include age of first involvement, status as a delinquent ever in one's life, current criminal activity and frequency of delinquent involvement. Delinquency is more often measured using youth self-reports than official records of arrest or conviction in evaluations of school-based prevention programs.

**Withdrawal from school** Leaving school prior to graduation from the twelfth grade and truancy are often used in measuring success in prevention programs. The precise definition of truancy differs according to location. For practical purposes it is often measured as the number of days absent from school.

**Conduct problems, low self-control, aggression** These characteristics are so highly related to delinquent behavior that they may be considered proxies for it. Studies of school-based prevention often measure these characteristics in addition to or in lieu of actual delinquent behavior because (1) the subjects are too young to have initiated delinquent behavior, (2) the questions are less controversial because they are not self-incriminating, or (3) teachers and parents are more able to rate youth on these characteristics than on actual delinquent behavior, which is often covert. Conduct problem behavior subsumes a variety of behaviors: defiance, disrespect, rebelliousness, hitting, stealing, lying, fighting, talking back to persons in authority, etc. Low self-control is a disposition to behave impulsively, and aggression involves committing acts of hostility and violating the rights of others.

**Risk and protective factors** As noted in the text, the effectiveness of prevention programs is often assessed by examining program effects of a variety of factors which are known to elevate or reduce risk for delinquent involvement at a later date. These factors are discussed above and shown in Figure 4.1.

Studies of the effects of school-based prevention on serious violent crime are rare. Of the 178 studies examined for this review, only thirteen measured program outcomes on murder, rape, robbery or aggravated assault. Only eighteen measured outcomes on serious property crimes such as burglary, larceny-theft and motor vehicle theft. Only 39 measured any type of criminal behavior. Far more common are studies assessing program effects on alcohol, tobacco or other drug use (77 studies) and other less serious forms of rebellious, antisocial, aggressive or defiant behaviors (102 studies). Most studies measure the risk or protective factors directly targeted by the program (e.g. academic achievement, social competency skills).

In this chapter, prevention effects on crime, delinquency, alcohol or other drug use, and other forms of antisocial behavior[4] are highlighted. Effects on school-related problem behaviors (truancy and drop-out) are also shown. A distinction between substance use (including alcohol, marijuana and harder drug use), school-related problem behaviors, antisocial behavior or other conduct problems, and actual crime is maintained throughout the report. Programs are considered to influence one of these outcomes if their evaluations demonstrate effects on any measure of each outcome, regardless of its type or seriousness level.

## Categories of school-based prevention

Programs included in this chapter are located primarily in school buildings (even if outside of school hours) or are implemented by school staff or under school or school system auspices. Programs targeting all grade levels – kindergarten, elementary and secondary – are included.

*Table 4.2* Percentage of studies including each intervention strategy

| Program strategy | Percentage of studies including |
|---|---|
| Instructing students | 81 |
| Managing classrooms | 75 |
| Teaching thinking strategies and using behavioral modification | 64 |
| Establishing norms or expectations for behavior | 30 |
| Counseling and social work | 17 |
| Mentoring, tutoring and work-study | 16 |
| Managing schools and discipline | 12 |
| Providing recreational, enrichment and leisure activities | 11 |
| Regrouping students | 5 |

Box 4.2 describes four categories of school-based prevention focusing on altering school or classroom environments, and Box 4.3 describes five categories of school-based prevention focusing on changing the behaviors, knowledge, skills, attitudes or beliefs of individual students.[5] Classifying any particular school-based prevention activity is a difficult task because most school-based prevention programs contain a mix of different types of activities. In the 178 studies examined for this review, most (94 percent) contained multiple components (i.e. components falling into more than one of the major categories of program activity shown in the figures). Forty-one percent of the studies contained components in four or more different categories. Table 4.2 shows the major types of activities and the percentage of studies whose evaluated programs contained each type of activity. It shows that the school-based programs described in most studies include an instructional component and a component intended to alter classroom management strategies. These common strategies are often combined with attempts to teach students cognitive skills that will help them deal better with potential social problems, and behavior modification programs.

---

**Box 4.2**

**Managing schools and discipline** This category includes interventions to change the decision-making processes or authority structures to enhance the general capacity of the school. These interventions often involve teams of staff and (sometimes) parents, students, and community members engaged in planning and carrying out activities to improve the school. They often diagnose school problems, formulate school goals and objectives, design potential solutions, monitor progress, and evaluate the efforts. Activities aimed at enhancing the administrative capability of the school by increasing communication and cooperation among members of the school community are also included. Often, these interventions also include efforts to establish or clarify school rules or discipline codes and mechanisms for the enforcement of school rules.

**Establishing norms for behavior** School-wide efforts to redefine norms for behavior and signal appropriate behavior. It includes activities such as newsletters, posters, ceremonies during which students declare their intention to remain drug-free, and displaying symbols of appropriate behavior. Some well-known interventions in this category are "red ribbon week" sponsored through the Department of Education's Safe and Drug-Free Schools and Communities program and school-wide campaigns against bullying.

**Managing classes** Using instructional methods designed to increase student engagement in the learning process and hence increase their academic performance and bonding to the school (e.g. cooperative learning techniques and "experiential learning" strategies); and classroom organization and management strategies. The latter include activities to establish and enforce classroom rules, uses of rewards and punishments, management of time to reduce "down-time," strategies for grouping students within the class, and use of external resources such as parent volunteers, police officers, or professional consultants as instructors or aides.

**Regrouping students** Reorganizing classes or grades to create smaller units, continuing interaction, or different mixes of students, or to provide greater flexibility in instruction. It includes changes to school schedule (e.g. block scheduling, scheduling more periods in the day, changes in the lengths of instructional periods); adoption of schools-within-schools or similar arrangements; tracking into classes by ability, achievement, effort, or conduct; formation of grade level "houses" or "teams;" and decreasing class size.

**Box 4.3**

**Instructing students** The most common strategy used in schools. These interventions provide instruction to students to teach them factual information, increase their awareness of social influences to engage in misbehavior, expand their repertoires for recognizing and appropriately responding to risky or potentially harmful situations, increase their appreciation for diversity in society, improve their moral character, etc. Well-known examples include Drug Abuse Resistance Education (DARE), Life Skills Training (LST), Law-related Education (LRE), and Gang Resistance Education and Training (GREAT).

**Behavior modification and teaching thinking strategies** Behavior modification strategies focus directly on changing behaviors and involve timely tracking of specific behaviors over time, behavioral goals, and use feedback or positive or negative reinforcement to change behavior. These strategies rely on reinforcers external to the student to shape student behavior. Larger or more robust effects on behavior might be obtained by teaching students to modify their own behavior using a range of cognitive strategies research has found lacking in delinquent youth. Efforts to teach students "thinking strategies" (known in the scientific literature as cognitive-behavioral strategies) involve modeling or demonstrating behaviors and providing rehearsal and coaching in the display of new skills. Students are taught, for example, to recognize the physiological cues experienced in risky situations. They rehearse this skill and practice stopping rather than acting impulsively in such situations. Students are taught and rehearsed in such skills as suggesting alternative activities when friends propose engaging in a risky activity. And they are taught to use prompts or cues to remember to engage in behavior.

**Counseling and social work** Individual counseling, substance abuse treatment, case management and similar group-based interventions, including peer counseling are included in this category.

**Mentoring, tutoring, and work-study experiences** Mentoring is one-on-one interaction between an adult, usually a lay person rather than a trained counselor, and the student. Mentoring is distinguished from counseling also because it is not necessarily guided by a structured approach. Tutoring and apprenticeship or work-study experiences are also included in this category of "individual attention" strategies.

**Providing recreational, community service, and leisure activities** Activities intended to provide constructive or fun alternatives to delinquent behavior. Drop-in recreation centers, after-school and week-end programs, dances, community service activities, and other events are offered in these programs as alternatives to the more dangerous activities. The popular "Midnight Basketball" is included here.

The multi-component nature of the interventions in studies of school-based prevention is perfectly reasonable given the nested nature of the schooling experience and the multiple routes to problem behavior. Student behavior is most directly influenced by the attitudes, beliefs and characteristics of the student and his or her peers. Individually targeted interventions, such as instructional or behavior modification techniques that teach students new ways of thinking and acting, may be effective in changing these individual factors. But several of these individual factors (e.g. low self-control, academic failure experiences, and attitudes favorable to drug use) are likely causes of problem behavior and are best targeted through a set of inter-related program components rather than through a single intervention. Moreover, students interact in the context of classrooms, each of which has its own normative climate encouraging or discouraging certain behaviors. And classrooms exist in school environments which establish larger contexts for all activities in the school. An instructional program teaching students to resolve conflicts non-violently is not likely to be as effective for reducing violence in a school or classroom setting in which fights are regularly ignored as in one which immediately responds to such incidents. The interconnections among different prevention components and the interdependence of different contexts should be considered in the design of prevention programs (Elias *et al.*, 1994).

Most recent reviews of school-based prevention are organized by developmental level (e.g. elementary, junior high, senior high) rather than by program type. Despite the difficulties inherent in classifying prevention activities, it is nevertheless a useful activity because only by disaggregating different sets of activities into their major parts can we (a) describe the activities; (b) describe how the mix of activities varies across location (e.g. urban, suburban, rural) and developmental level; and (c) design evaluations of specific constellations of components. Also, several evaluations of relatively narrow programs are available and can provide information about the potential of each activity as a piece of a larger, more potent, prevention strategy. Other research (Gottfredson and Gottfredson, 1996) has cross-classified program types by developmental level and school location, providing a more comprehensive picture of which school-based prevention activities are used, in which locations, and for which grade levels.

## Methods

### Inclusion criteria and search for relevant studies

To be included in this review, a study had to meet the following criteria:

a   it evaluated an intervention, that is, a distinct program or procedure intended to reduce problem behaviors among children and youth, that was school-based, that is, the intervention took place in a school building or was implemented by school staff or under school or school system auspices;
b   it used a comparison group evaluation methodology, including non-equivalent comparison group research designs; and
c   it measured at least one outcome of interest to this review.

Outcomes of interest included indicators of:

a   crime, delinquency, theft, violence, illegal acts of aggression;
b   alcohol and other drug use, excluding cigarette and smokeless tobacco use;
c   withdrawal from school, school drop-out, truancy, or school tardiness; and,
d   rebellious behavior, antisocial behavior, aggressive behavior, defiance of authority, disrespect for others, suspension/expulsion, or other acting out behavior.

Potentially relevant studies were identified through searches of computer bibliographic databases (e.g. PsychLit, ERIC, and Sociological Abstracts) and through an examination of recent reviews of prevention programs (Botvin, 1990; Botvin, Schinke and Orlandi, 1995; Dryfoos, 1990; Durlak, 1995; Hansen, 1992; Hawkins, Arthur and Catalano, 1995; Institute of Medicine, 1994; Tobler, 1986, 1992; Tremblay and Craig, 1995). This list was augmented with additional studies already known to the first author. In all, 178 eligible studies from 228 documents were determined eligible for this review and coded.

### Coding unit: treatment-comparison contrasts

It was common for studies to report on multiple treatment-comparison contrasts or to otherwise report data in a disaggregated way that represented a meaningful distinction for the purpose of this review. Examples include two distinct interventions compared to a single control group, the same intervention applied to distinct age groups, and an intervention examined after differing amounts of treatment (e.g. 1-year of program, 2-years of program, full-program plus booster, etc.). In this last scenario, the same program students may have been represented in the different treatment-comparison contrasts, that is, the data for the treatment-comparison contrast without the booster may be based on the same students as the treatment-comparison contrasts with the booster. Each treatment-comparison contrast that represented a distinct intervention or a distinct student population, even if two or more contrasts shared some or all of the students, was coded separately, as detailed below. Although this introduced statistical dependencies in the data, this was balanced against the potential benefit of examining these programs in a more differentiated fashion. The 178 studies produced 266 treatment-comparison contrasts of interest.

### Coding of study characteristics

A code book similar to a survey form was developed to capture information regarding the specific nature of the intervention, characteristics of the student population, research methodology, measures of problem behaviors, and observed effects on these measures at all measurement points. Studies were coded by trained graduate students who met weekly to discuss coding decisions. All studies were coded by at least two coders and all coding discrepancies were discussed and resolved. Aspects of the coding protocol relevant to this report are discussed below. A copy of the code book can be obtained from the authors.

### Program categories

A major challenge in reviewing a vast literature of this nature is grouping the interventions into conceptually meaningful categories. The program categories we used in this chapter are based on a similar classification developed for a National Study of Delinquency Prevention in Schools (Gottfredson and Gottfredson, 1996). The categories were refined through our interaction with the studies, and we believe they represent a reasonable and meaningful categorization. Each treatment program was assessed for the presence or absence of seventeen treatment components or activities (e.g. instruction, cognitive-behavioral or behavioral modeling, reorganization of grades). If a treatment component was present, a judgment was made as to whether it was a major or minor component of that intervention. Each of these seventeen components had sub-elements that detailed the specific activities associated with that intervention. After all studies were coded, an iterative process was undertaken using these codes to group programs into mutually exclusive program categories, resulting in eleven program categories (see Table 4.3). Although other categorizations of these programs are possible, we believe that this categorization is both conceptually meaningful and consistent with the actual practices of school-based prevention programs.

### Students

The nature of the student population participating in the school-based prevention program was captured by a set of items addressing the age and grade

*Table 4.3* Methods scores by program strategy

| Program strategy | Scientific Methods Score[a] | | |
|---|---|---|---|
| | Mean | SD | N |
| **Environmentally focused programs** | **3.26** | **0.98** | **69** |
| School and discipline management interventions | 3.27 | 0.90 | 11 |
| Interventions to establish norms or expectations for behavior | 2.92 | 1.26 | 25 |
| Classroom or instructional management | 3.55 | 0.64 | 27 |
| Reorganization of grades or classes | 3.33 | 0.82 | 6 |
| **Individually focused programs** | **3.44** | **1.10** | **197** |
| Self-control or social competency instruction using cognitive-behavioral or behavioral instructional methods | 3.71 | 0.81 | 77 |
| Self-control or social competency instruction without cognitive-behavioral or behavioral instructional methods | 2.67 | 1.32 | 42 |
| Other instructional programs | 3.25 | 1.00 | 16 |
| Cognitive behavioral, behavioral modeling, or behavior modification interventions | 3.88 | 0.91 | 32 |
| Counseling, social work, and other therapeutic interventions | 2.88 | 1.55 | 8 |
| Mentoring, tutoring, and work study | 3.63 | 0.96 | 16 |
| Recreation, community service, enrichment, and leisure activities | 3.83 | 0.41 | 6 |

Note
a  Mean methods rating varies by program category ($p < .01$).

range and gender and racial distribution represented in the study. The coding protocol also captured a written description of the student sample, often taken verbatim from the written report or published document.

### Coding of scientific rigor

In evaluating the evidence for the effectiveness of a school-based prevention approach, it is critical to assess the soundness of the empirical evidence. In this review, this was accomplished through seven items in the coding protocol that assessed the methodological rigor of the research study. These items addressed assignment to conditions (e.g. random assignment to conditions), unit-of-assignment (e.g. student, class, school), unit-of-analysis, use of control variables in analyses to adjust for initial group differences, rating of initial group similarity, attrition, and an overall five-point evaluation of methodological quality. This latter item, called the Scientific Methods Score, was informed by answers to the method rigor items and had the following anchors to assist the coders in making consistent ratings: level 1, no reliance or confidence should be placed on the results of this evaluation because of the number and type of serious shortcomings in the methodology employed; level 3, methodology rigorous in some respects, weak in others; and level 5, methodology rigorous in almost all respects. The double coding of these items by two graduate students and discussion of discrepancies helped improve the reliability of the final score assigned to a study. This Scientific Methods Score is a prominent feature of the tables in this chapter.

The modal Scientific Methods Score for the 266 modules was 4, with 47 percent of the modules receiving this rating. Only 26 (10 percent) received the highest rating of 5, suggesting that there is much room for improvement in the quality of evaluations of school-based prevention strategies. Also, the rigor of the evaluations varied by program category. Table 4.3 shows the average methods ratings for all studies in each program category. Studies of recreation, enrichment and leisure activities (of which there are only six), and the more numerous studies of behavior modification and teaching cognitive self-management skills have been studied most rigorously. Studies of counseling, social work, and other therapeutic interventions and self-control or social competency instruction without cognitive-behavioral or behavioral instructional methods interventions have been studied least rigorously. Strategies whose research is of poorer quality have a lower probability of being identified as effective simply because confidence cannot be placed in the results of the research. On the other hand, the type of prevention interventions that can be studied most rigorously may have only limited generalizability to natural settings.

### Coding of study effects

The first task in capturing the study effects was to identify and code the characteristics of all dependent measures of problem-behavior. These included measures of criminal and delinquent behavior, alcohol and other drug use, drop-out and truancy rates, and other antisocial and aggressive behaviors (see Box 4.1 for more detail). Next, the direction of the effect (i.e. favored the treatment group, favored the control group, or no difference), the statistical significance of the effect, and an effect size were coded for each dependent measure of interest at each measurement point (pretest, post-test, first follow-up, etc.). Specific aspects of this coding are discussed below.

#### Direction of effect and statistical significance

The tables presented in this chapter report three indicators of program effectiveness for each treatment-control comparison: (1) the direction of the difference between the treatment and comparison group, (2) whether or not that difference was found to be significantly different from zero, and (3) the effect size. Direction is reported for all treatment-comparison group contrasts for which the direction could be determined either from the authors' reports or by viewing the tables provided. Thirteen studies involving 35 contrasts were omitted from the tables because the direction of the difference reported could not be ascertained. The statistical significance for each contrast generally reflects the report of the original authors: if they indicated that a contrast was significant, regardless of whether their report is based on a one-tailed or two-tailed test, it is so reported on our tables. However, our report of significance for a particular contrast sometimes differs from the original authors' reports because we sometimes combined subgroups (e.g. males and females, low- and high-implementation sites, groups differing on initial level of drug use) and recalculated the significance based on the total sample. Also, if the contrast reported by the original author was not the treatment-control contrast at post-test, we calculated the significance level for the contrast relevant to this study. In a few cases, significance test results reported by the authors were simply incorrect. We corrected these. In several cases, the effect size we calculated was statistically significant, even though the test the original author reported was not. In such cases, we reported the contrast as significant. Our calculations use a two-tailed test at the $p < .05$ level.

## Effect size

The magnitude of the program effect is expressed whenever possible as a standardized mean difference effect size (*ES*), a measure of the difference between the program and comparison groups relative to the standard deviation of the measure employed. Whenever possible, the post-treatment or follow-up mean difference was adjusted for any pre-test mean difference on that measure. The standardization of the program and comparison difference by use of the *ES* allows for the direct comparison of effects across studies and outcomes. Furthermore, the standardized mean difference effect size can be computed from a wide variety of data configurations reported by the primary studies (Lipsey and Wilson, 2001). *ES*s typically range from negative 1, indicating that the treatment group performed one standard deviation lower than the comparison group, to positive 1, indicating that the treatment group performed one standard deviation higher than the comparison group, although the *ES* is not constrained by positive and negative 1 and larger absolute values do occur. Rosenthal and Rubin (1982) showed that the *ES* can be translated into success rate differentials between the program and comparison groups, greatly facilitating the interpretation of the *ES*. For example, an *ES* of 0.50 translates into a success rate of 62 percent for the program group and 38 percent for the comparison group; a success rate differential of 24 percent. This is based on the assumption of an overall success rate of 50 percent. Lipsey and Wilson (1993), summarizing effect sizes from 302 reviews of psychological, behavioral, and educational interventions, reported an average of the average effect sizes across these reviews of 0.50. Thus, consistent with Cohen's (1962) original rule-of-thumb for interpreting effect size magnitudes, an effect size of 0.50 is a moderate or typical effect for social interventions. By comparison, Lipsey (1992) showed the average effect size across 397 delinquency treatment and prevention evaluations was 0.17. Delinquent behavior appears more difficult to change than more conventional behaviors. Furthermore, the difficulty in reliably measuring delinquent behavior attenuates the observed effects (Hunter and Schmidt, 1990). The practical significance of an effect size depends largely on the seriousness of the outcome for the population and the effort needed to produce the effect. Lipsey argues that even a small effect (e.g. an $ES = 0.10$) for serious criminal behavior has practical significance.

Tables in this chapter report average effect sizes across all measures of each of the four problem behavior outcomes. Note that effect sizes can be computed only for a subset of the treatment-control contrasts included on the tables due to many studies reporting insufficient statistical information. Of the 1,010 post-intervention treatment-versus-control effects of interest to this review, we were able to determine the direction for 891 effects, and we were able to compute an *ES* for 594 of these 891 effects, or 67 percent. These 891 effects and 594 *ES*s are summarized in the tables below.

### Determination of what works, what is promising, and what does not work

The criteria used for judging whether each category of programs ("works," "does not work," or is "promising") were the same criteria used in the 1997 Report to Congress (Sherman *et al.*, 1997). A category is said to work if at least two different studies with methodological rigor greater than or equal to 3 found "significant" effects on a given outcome measure. If an effect was reported as statistically significant in the original report, or if our recalculation of the effect was statistically significant at the $p < .05$ level, the effect was considered to be significant. To be placed in this category, the preponderance of evidence from all studies in the category had to support the efficacy of the approach. This requirement was most often operationalized in this chapter as the absence of significant negative findings. However, if the average effect size across all studies in the category was positive and significant, the preponderance criterion was met even if some individual effects were significantly negative.

A category is said to not work if at least two different studies with methodological rigor greater than or equal to 3 found null or negative effects on a given outcome measure, and if the preponderance of evidence from all studies in the category supported the conclusion. This requirement was generally operationalized as the absence of significant positive findings, but a single significant positive finding was accepted if the clear pattern of effects was negative.

A category is said to be promising if only one study with methodological rigor greater than or equal to 3 found "significant" effects on a given outcome measure and the preponderance of the evidence favors the program. As above, if an effect was reported as statistically significant in the original report, or if our recalculation of the effect was statistically significant at the $p < .05$ level, the effect was considered to be significant. The preponderance requirement was operationalized as above.

Categories and outcomes whose results fit none of the above criterion were classified as "do not know." These categories contained studies whose results were mixed. The determination of which categories of programs work, do not work, or are promising was made separately for each of the four outcomes examined in this report.

## Studies of school-based prevention

This section summarizes evidence from 178 empirical studies on what works in school-based crime prevention. It first reviews the evidence on the four environmental change strategies described earlier, and then on the seven individually-targeted strategies. A summary table is provided for each of the eleven sections. These tables show the citation for each study relevant to the program type,[6] the characteristics of the students included in the study, the methods rating, and the number of months elapsed between the end of the intervention and the follow-up data collection. When studies reported effects for more than one group of students (and they could not be combined after-the-fact), or for different versions of the program (e.g. with and without a "booster" session), multiple entries appear on the table. For each of the four categories of outcome measures (crime; alcohol and other drug use; drop-out and truancy; and antisocial or other conduct problems) the table reports the number of outcomes reported for which the program group out-performed the comparison group (positive effects), or the comparison group out-performed the program group (negative effects). Statistically significant differences are reflected in the left-most ("−*") and right-most ("+*") columns on the table. Statistically non-significant outcomes and those outcomes for which only the direction of the effect could be determined are reflected in the columns headed ("−") and ("+"). Finally, the mean effect size and the number of outcomes included in the mean are provided. These means are based only on those outcomes for which an effect size could be calculated from the available information and may be less than the number for which direction and/or significance could be determined.

Some studies are not included in the tables. Table 4.4 shows the number of studies and treatment-comparison contrasts omitted because the direction of the effects could not be determined or because the methods used in the study did not fall above the cut-off point selected for inclusion. Studies whose methods score was less than 3[7] were omitted from the tables because their results do not contribute to the overall determination of what works, does not work, or is promising.

### Changing school and classroom environments

Correlational evidence suggests that the way schools are run predicts the level of disorder they experience. Schools in which the administration and faculty communicate and work together to plan for change and solve problems have higher teacher morale and less disorder. These schools can presumably absorb change. Schools in which students notice clear school rules and reward structures and unambiguous sanctions also experience less disorder. These schools are likely to signal appropriate behavior for students (D.C. Gottfredson, 1987; Gottfredson and Gottfredson, 1985; Gottfredson, Gottfredson and Hybl, 1993). Schools governed by a system of shared values and expectations for behavior, in which meaningful social interactions occur, and in which students feel that they belong and that people in the school

*Table 4.4* Studies and treatment-comparison contrasts omitted from tables

| Reason dropped | Studies | Treatment-comparison contrasts |
|---|---|---|
| Missing direction | 14 | 36 |
| Method score less than 3 | 31 | 50 |
| Either of above | 43 | 78 |
| Number remaining | 135 | 188 |

Note
There were a total of 178 unique studies from 228 documents. These 178 unique studies reported on the results from 266 treatment-comparison contrasts.

care about them, also experience less disorder (Duke, 1989). These "communal" (Bryk and Driscoll, 1988) schools are probably better at controlling behavior informally. Intervention studies have tested for a causal association between each of these factors and delinquency or substance use among students. Evidence related to the four major strategies for changing school and classroom environments are summarized below:

1    building school capacity to manage itself effectively and to manage discipline by establishing and enforcing school rules, policies, or regulations;
2    establishing norms or expectations for behavior;
3    changing classroom instructional and management practices to enhance classroom climate or improve educational processes; and
4    grouping students in different ways to achieve smaller, less alienating or otherwise more suitable micro-climates within the school.

*Building school capacity to manage itself or to manage discipline*

As noted above, correlational research has repeatedly found that schools with more favorable student outcomes generally have stronger administrative capability. Not surprisingly, the management of discipline is also more effective in these schools. A constellation of discipline management-related variables – clarity about behavioral norms, predictability, consistency and fairness in applying consequences for behaviors – are inversely related to rates of teacher and student victimization in schools. What the correlational evidence does not tell us, however, is whether altering the capability of the school to manage itself and, more specifically, its discipline systems, results in a reduction in crime, drug use, and other problem behaviors. The correlations might simply reflect assignment of better administrators to the better schools. Seven[8] reasonably rigorous studies have attempted to manipulate school and discipline management practices. They are summarized in Table 4.5 and discussed below.

Several of the studies in this category use a school-team approach (Program Development Evaluation (PDE); Gottfredson, 1984a; Gottfredson, Rickert *et al.*, 1984) to facilitate local involvement in planning for and implementing changes related to school safety and discipline. PDE is a structured organizational development method developed to help organizations plan, initiate, and sustain needed changes. Researchers and practitioners collaborate to develop and implement programs using specific steps spelled out in the program materials. A spiral of improvement is created as researchers continuously provide data feedback during the implementation phase to the practitioners and work with them to identify and overcome obstacles to strong program implementation. The method, first developed for use with schools participating in an Office of Juvenile Justice and Delinquency Prevention (OJJDP) funded alternative education initiative, was intended to solve the problem that evaluations up until that time had found few efficacious delinquency prevention models. The developer assumed that the poor showing was due to weak evaluations, failure to inform program design with research knowledge and social science theory, and weak program implementation.

PDE was used in a comprehensive school improvement intervention, project PATHE, that altered the organization and management structures in seven secondary schools between 1981 and 1983 as part of OJJDP's alternative education initiative (Gottfredson, 1986; methods rating = 4). District-level administrators used PDE to develop a general plan for all seven schools, and then used PDE to structure specific school-level planning interventions. These efforts increased staff and student participation in planning for and implementing school improvement efforts. Changes resulting from the planning activity included efforts to increase clarity of rules and consistency of rule enforcement and activities to increase students' success experiences and feelings of belonging. These activities targeted the entire population in each school.

The evaluation of the project compared change on an array of measures from the year prior to the treatment to 1 year (for four high schools) and 2 years (for five middle schools) into the intervention. One school at each level was a comparison school selected from among the non-participating schools to match the treatment schools as closely as possible. The students in the participating high schools reported significantly less delinquent behavior and drug use, and fewer school punishments after the first year of the program. Students in the comparison high school did not change significantly on these outcomes. A similar pattern was observed for the middle schools after 2 years. As serious delinquency increased significantly in the comparison school, it decreased (nonsignificantly) in the program middle schools. Changes in drug use and school punishments also favored the program schools. Several indicators of the school climate directly targeted by the program (e.g. safety, staff morale, clarity of school rules and effectiveness of the school administration) also increased significantly in the program schools.

D.C. Gottfredson (1987; methods rating = 3 or 4, depending on contrast) reported the results of a similar effort in a difficult Baltimore City junior high school, called The Effective Schools Project. PDE was used with a team of school and district-level educators to plan and implement changes to instructional and discipline practices. School-wide and classroom-level changes were made to the disciplinary procedures to increase the clarity and consistency of rule enforcement, and to substitute positive reinforcement strategies for strategies that relied solely on punishment. Instructional innovations including cooperative learning and frequent monitoring of classwork and homework were put in place, an expanded extracurricular activities program was added, and a career exploration program, which exposed youth to positive role models in the community, took them on career-related field trips, and provided instruction on career-related topics, was undertaken.

The evaluation of the project involved a comparison of pre-treatment measures to post-treatment measures taken 2 years later for the one treatment school and a second school which was intended to receive the program but instead chose to develop a school improvement plan with minimal assistance from the researchers. Significant reductions from pre- to post-treatment on delinquency and increases in classroom orderliness were observed for the treatment school. A reduction in student reports of rebellious behavior in the

*Table 4.5* School and discipline management interventions

| Program name and citation | Students | Method rating |
|---|---|---|
| **High school grades** | | |
| Classroom Change Promoting Achievement through Cooperative Learning (PACT)<br>*Weinstein et al., 1991* | 312 students in grade 9; students assigned to the lowest track of English class in a mid-sized urban high school | 3 |
| Project Pathe (schoolwide intervention)<br>*Gottfredson, 1986; Gottfredson, 1990* | 1548 students in grades 9–12; Charleston County, SC | 4 |
| School Safety Program<br>*Kenney and Watson, 1996* | 451 students in grade 11; 2 schools in Charlotte, NC | 3 |
| **Middle/junior high school grades** | | |
| Multiyear, multischool program to reduce misbehavior<br>*Gottfredson et al., 1993* | 5719 students in grades 6–8; Charleston, SC | 4 |
| Project CARE<br>*Gottfredson, D.C. 1987* | 1157 students in grades 7–8; predominantly African-American students from impoverished communities in Baltimore (internal control group) | 3 |
| Project CARE<br>*Gottfredson, D.C. 1987* | 1873 students in grades 7–8; predominantly African-American students from impoverished communities in Baltimore (external control group) | 4 |
| Project Pathe (schoolwide intervention)<br>*Gottfredson, 1986; Gottfredson, 1990* | 1467 students in grades 6–8; Charleston County, SC | 4 |
| **Elementary school grades** | | |
| Comer School Development Program<br>*Cook et al., 1998* | 1685 students in grades 5–8; inner city Chicago schools | 4 |
| Comer School Development Program (SDP)<br>*Comer et al., 1989* | 267 students in grades 3–5; black students attending schools in low socioeconomic areas | 3 |

Notes

a  Frequency distribution represents the number of outcomes for which the program group out-performed the comparison group (positive effects) or the comparison group out-performed the program group (negative effects). Statistically significant positive and negative outcomes are reflected in the columns "+*" and "−*" respectively. Statistically nonsignificant effects or outcomes for which only the direction of effect was known are in the "+" and "−" columns.

treatment school was observed (not significant) while a significant increase was observed in the comparison school. The contrast between the treatment and comparison schools favored the treatment schools and was significant for both delinquency and rebellious behavior. In a second (and less rigorous) analysis which used an earlier cohort in the treatment school as a comparison group, the experimental students also reported less delinquent and rebellious behavior than the comparison student, although these differences were not significant and of a smaller magnitude.

| Follow-up (months) | Outcome | Frequency distribution[a] | | | | | Effect size[b] | |
|---|---|---|---|---|---|---|---|---|
| | | −* | − | 0 | + | +* | | |
| 12 | Drop-out/Truancy | 1 | 0 | 0 | 1 | 0 | | |
| | Anti-Soc./Aggr. | 0 | 0 | 0 | 1 | 0 | .30 | (1) |
| 0 | Crime | 0 | 0 | 0 | 1 | 0 | .15* | (1) |
| | AOD | 0 | 0 | 0 | 1 | 0 | .15* | (1) |
| | Drop-out/Truancy | 0 | 1 | 0 | 0 | 0 | −.10 | (1) |
| | Anti-Soc./Aggr. | 0 | 0 | 0 | 1 | 0 | .21* | (1) |
| 0 | Crime | 0 | 0 | 0 | 0 | 1 | .65* | (1) |
| 0 | Anti-Soc./Aggr. | 1 | 2 | 1 | 1 | 0 | −.03 | (3) |
| 0 | Crime | 0 | 0 | 0 | 1 | 0 | .12 | (1) |
| | Anti-Soc./Aggr. | 0 | 0 | 0 | 1 | 0 | .11 | (1) |
| 0 | Crime | 0 | 0 | 0 | 0 | 1 | .31* | (1) |
| | Anti-Soc./Aggr. | 0 | 0 | 0 | 1 | 1 | .18* | (1) |
| 0 | Crime | 0 | 0 | 0 | 0 | 1 | .31* | (1) |
| | AOD | 0 | 0 | 0 | 0 | 1 | .33* | (1) |
| | Drop-out/Truancy | 0 | 0 | 1 | 0 | 0 | .00 | (1) |
| | Anti-Soc./Aggr. | 0 | 0 | 0 | 0 | 1 | .16* | (1) |
| 0 | AOD | 0 | 0 | 0 | 0 | 1 | | |
| | Anti-Soc./Aggr. | 0 | 0 | 0 | 0 | 1 | | |
| 0 | Drop-out/Truancy | 0 | 0 | 0 | 0 | 1 | | |

b The mean effect size is based only on those outcomes for which an effect size could be calculated. This may be fewer than the number of effects represented in the frequency distribution. Significance is based on the observed effect size data and may disagree with the frequency distribution if the authors performed a different test or used a different criterion, such as a one-tail test.

Kenney and Watson (1996; methods rating = 3) report on an intervention to empower students to improve safety in schools. This study involved 11th grade students (N's range from 372 to 451) in the application of a problem-solving technique to reduce problems of crime, disorder and fear on the school campus. As part of their government and history class, students implemented a four-step problem-solving method commonly used in problem-oriented policing interventions to identify problems, analyze possible solutions, formulate and implement a strategy, and evaluate the outcomes of the intervention. The investigators anticipated that empowering students to serve as change agents in the school would produce safer schools. Among the problems selected by the students were streamlining lunch-room procedures and monitoring the restrooms.

Change over a 1-year period was examined for the treatment and one comparison school. The study found that students in the treatment school reported significantly less fighting and less teacher victimization, and were less fearful about being in certain places in the school at the end of the intervention period compared with their baseline. Students in the comparison school did not change on these outcomes.

Another effort to alter school capacity for self-management is Comer's School Development Program (SDP; Comer, 1985; Comer, Haynes and Hamilton-Lee, 1989; Haynes, 1994). It is the only model that has been tested in elementary schools. SDP is a comprehensive school organization development intervention seeking to broaden the involvement in school management of stake-holders in the school. The program creates a representative governance and management team composed of school administrators, teachers, support staff and parents that assesses school problems and opportunities, identifies social and academic goals for the school, plans activities to address the goals, monitors activities, and takes corrective action to keep the activities on track. This team oversees other program components, which include:

1    a social calendar that integrates arts and athletic programs into school activities;
2    a parent program in support of academic activities and extracurricular activities which fosters interaction among parents, teachers, and school staff by paying parents to work in classrooms, encouraging them to volunteer in the school, and having them serve on the School Advisory Council; and
3    a multidisciplinary health team that works on global school climate issues, provides direct services to students, and provides consultation to individual teachers in managing student behavior problems.

The program, designed to enhance urban elementary schools, had been implemented in more than 550 schools and 80 school districts as of 1995.

Early evaluations of the model conducted by Comer and his associates generally lacked the methodological rigor necessary to support strong conclusions about the effectiveness of the model, and most failed to measure the program's effects on problem behavior outcomes. However, one study (Comer, Haynes and Hamilton-Lee, 1989, methods rating = 3) compared 176 elementary students who attended SDP schools with 130 who did not on measures of perceptions of the classroom and school climate, attendance, and classroom grades. Generally, children in the SDP schools showed larger changes in the positive direction than students in the control schools. The outcome of interest to this review, attendance, improved significantly for the treatment students relative to the comparison students.

A more rigorous study was recently conducted by researchers at the Institute for Policy Research at Northwestern University. Cook, Hunt and Murphy

(1998; methods rating = 4) evaluated SDP in ten inner city Chicago schools over a 4-year period. These schools were compared with nine randomly selected no-treatment comparison schools. Student ratings (but not teacher ratings) of the schools' social climate improved significantly. Both teachers' and students' perceptions of the academic climate improved significantly. Students' rate of increase in reports of acting out (measured by an 11-item scale of mischievous and delinquent behaviors) and substance use were significantly lower in the SDP than in the comparison schools.

SUMMARY

The studies summarized in this section most often combine efforts to improve school-wide discipline policies and practices, school social climate and the school's general management capability. The studies most often involve school teams and a structured organization development method designed to focus a school's attention on identifying its problems, developing strategies to overcome these problems, and using data feedback to guide the implementation of these plans over a several-year period. These programs often also focus on clarifying expectations for behavior, monitoring and providing consequences for behavior, and especially providing positive reinforcement for desired behavior. They sometimes involve training school staff in behavioral principals and techniques, and the establishment of school-wide systems to clarify expectations, monitor behavior and reward compliance. Taken as a set, these school-wide management strategies are effective for reducing crime (D.C. Gottfredson, 1986; 1987; Kenney and Watson, 1996; = 0.27, $p < .05$), substance use (Cook, Hunt and Murphy, 1998; Gottfredson, 1986; = 0.24, $p < .05$), and antisocial/aggressive behavior (Cook, Hunt and Murphy, 1998; D.C. Gottfredson, 1986, 1987; = 0.13, $p > .05$). Truancy and drop-out were measured in only three studies (Comer, Haynes and Hamilton-Lee, 1989; Gottfredson, 1986; Weinstein *et al.*, 1991) and the results were mixed. The studies also demonstrate effectiveness at all levels of schooling.

*Establishing norms or expectations for behavior*

The previous section demonstrated that efforts to clarify school rules and provide consistent enforcement of those rules improves student behavior. Studies in this section demonstrate that other methods for establishing and communicating expectations for behavior are also effective. The studies summarized below have in common a focus on clarifying behavioral norms. Some attempt to establish or change school norms using campaigns, ceremonies or similar techniques. Others involve students in activities aimed at increasing their exposure to pro-social beliefs and attitudes, or correcting misperceptions about the prevalence of illegal or harmful behaviors. The lion's share of the studies summarized here have tested normative change programs that are part of a junior high school substance abuse prevention program. These are primarily instructional in nature, and the norm-change "lessons" are most often integrated with lessons aimed at teaching social competency skills. In only one study (Hansen and Graham, 1991) are the normative and resistance skill components studied separately. Table 4.6 shows the results of the studies summarized below.

Among the six reasonably rigorous studies of normative education which include a major curricular component, all find significant positive effects on student behavior. None of the few negative effects were statistically significant. Four of the six studies assessed program effects only on substance use outcomes.

Probably the best known of the normative education programs is the Midwestern Prevention Project (MPP; Johnson *et al.*, 1990; MacKinnon *et al.*, 1991; Pentz, Dwyer *et al.*, 1989; Pentz, MacKinnon *et al.*, 1989; Pentz *et al.*, 1990; methods rating = 4). MPP is a comprehensive, community-based, multifaceted program aimed at reducing adolescent substance use. It includes five components: mass media programming, a school program with continuing boosters, a parent education and organization program, community organizing and training, and local policy change. It attempts to inoculate the population against drug use directly by training adolescents to improve their skills for resisting drugs and indirectly by providing complementary training for parents and teachers to support these skills; increase anti-drug community norms through a media campaign and family-support; reduce drug availability by tightening local ordinances restricting cigarette smoking; and institutionalize the program by creating and maintaining a coalition of key community leaders to support, plan and implement prevention services. Although the program is community-based, it is summarized in this chapter because its centerpiece is a school curriculum. Also, the community-wide elements affected the comparison as well as the MPP schools, so the evaluations do not capture their effects.

The school program is initiated in grade 6 or 7; it is delivered by trained teachers and facilitated by peer leaders who are nominated by each class and trained by the teacher. The ten sessions focus on increasing skills to resist pressures to use drugs, and on changing norms about the acceptability of drug use. A five-session booster is provided during the next school year. Homework assignments are designed to involve family members. The parent program involves a parent–principal committee that meets to review school drug policy and also includes parent–child communications skills training. The remaining components are designed to reinforce the non-drug use norm and are phased in over a 6-year period.

Testing of MPP began in 1984 in Kansas City. The initial evaluation compared schools within communities assigned to intervention or delayed intervention conditions. Results indicated a reduction (relative to students in the comparison schools) from baseline to 1-year follow-up in the use of cigarettes, alcohol, and marijuana for students in the treatment schools (Pentz, Dwyer *et al.*, 1989). As the students entered high school in the third year of the program, positive effects were found only for cigarette and marijuana use. The reductions in alcohol use were not sustained (Johnson *et al.*, 1990). Significant reductions in both cigarette smoking and marijuana use were equivalent for both low- and high-risk adolescents after 3 years, suggesting community-wide prevention programs can have similar influence on those at greatest risk for drug use as well as those at low risk (Johnson *et al.*, 1990).

The curriculum used in the MPP is typical of a class of such curricula that combine a focus on social competency skill development and normative redefinition. Such curricula often include portrayals of drug use as socially unacceptable, identification of short-term negative consequences of drug use, presentation of evidence that drug use is less prevalent among peers than children may think, encouragement for children to make public commitments to remain drug-free, and the use of peer leaders to teach the curriculum (Institute of Medicine [IOM], 1994, p. 264). These activities are present in 29 percent of drug prevention curricula (Hansen, 1992), but always in conjunction with other components such as conveying information about risks related to drug use and resistance skills training. Norm-setting and public pledges to remain drug-free are usually elements of the most effective drug education curricula, but meta-analyses have not been able to disentangle the effects of the various components. In a study designed to do just that, Hansen and Graham (1991; methods rating = 4) found that positive effects on marijuana use and alcohol use were attributable more to a normative education than to a resistance skills training component. Schools were randomly assigned to receive either resistance skills training only, normative education only, both resistance skills training and normative education, or a placebo condition. The normative education program corrected erroneous perceptions of the prevalence and acceptability of alcohol and drug use among peers and established conservative norms regarding substance use. The resistance skills program taught adolescents to identify and resist peer and advertising pressure to use alcohol and other substances. Significant main effects were found only for the normative education program.

Positive effects of normative education have also been demonstrated on non-substance use outcomes. Foshee *et al.* (1998; methods rating = 5) provide evidence that a school- and community-based program aimed at changing norms for dating violence can also be effective. The school activities in the Safe Dates Program include a theater production performed by peers, a ten-session curriculum, addressing dating violence norms, gender stereotyping and conflict management skills, and a poster contest. The community activities include special services for adolescents in abusive relationships and community service provider training. The program was tested with 8th and 9th graders in fourteen schools in a rural county. Results varied somewhat by whether the adolescent had ever been a victim or perpetrator of dating violence, but the results for the full sample showed that the students in the treatment schools reported significantly less psychological abuse and violence perpetrated against the current dating partner than the students in the control schools. Most of these effects explained by changes in dating violence norms, gender stereotyping and awareness of services.

Each of the programs discussed so far includes a major curricular intervention, although some of the curricula are designed to involve a minimum of didactic information. Rather, they involve youths in interactive activities, such as interviewing others about their opinions about substance use, discussing survey results showing the prevalence of substance use in the school, or incorporating anti-drug messages in raps.

Several programs have involved minimal or no curricular components and instead have focused on school-wide activities to establish norms. Olweus reports on one such intervention designed to limit conflict in schools

*Table 4.6* Interventions to establish norms or expectations for behavior

| Program name and citation | Students | Method rating |
|---|---|---|
| **Includes a major instructional component** | | |
| **Middle/junior high and high school grades** | | |
| Safe Dates Program<br>*Foshee et al., 1998; Foshee et al., 1996* | 2344 students in grades 8–9; 14 public schools in a rural county in North Carolina | 5 |
| **Middle/junior high school grades** | | |
| Here's Looking at You, 2000 (curriculum and community activities)<br>*Stevens et al., 1996* | 581 students in grades 5–7; children from rural farm or rural non-farm towns in New Hampshire from 4 school districts | 4 |
| Highly Role Specified Alcohol Prevention Program (HRS)<br>*Wilhelmsen et al., 1994* | 637 students in grade 7; Bergen, Norway | 4 |
| Less Role Specified Alcohol Prevention Program (LRS)<br>*Wilhelmsen et al., 1994* | 637 students in grade 7; Bergen, Norway | 4 |
| Midwestern Prevention Project<br>*Johnson et al., 1990; Pentz et al., 1990; Pentz, Dwyer et al., 1989; MacKinnon et al., 1991* | 1608 students in grades 6–7; adolescents in 8 Kansas City schools, predominantly white | 4 |
| Midwestern Prevention Project<br>*MacKinnon et al., 1991; Pentz, Dwyer et al., 1989; Pentz, MacKinnon et al., 1989; Pentz et al., 1990* | 5065 students in grades 6–7; 42 schools in the Kansas City area | 4 |
| Project Model Health (PMH)<br>*Moberg and Piper, 1990)* | 265 students in grade 8; in or near suburban Madison area in Wisconsin | 4 |
| Resistance Training and Normative Education<br>*Hansen and Graham, 1991* | 1480 students in grade 7; Los Angeles and Orange Counties, California | 4 |
| **Does not include a major instructional component** | | |
| **Middle/junior high school grades** | | |
| Normative Education<br>*Hansen and Graham, 1991* | 1506 students in grade 7; Los Angeles and Orange Counties, California | 4 |
| Project Northland<br>*Perry et al., 1996* | 2351 students in grades 6–8; 24 rural, lower-middle to middle-class districts | 3 |
| Start Taking Alcohol Risks Seriously (STARS) (after peer consultation)<br>*Werch et al., 1996* | 104 students in grades 6–8; inner-city public school in Jacksonville, Florida | 5 |
| **Elementary school grades** | | |
| Bullying Prevention<br>*Olweus and Alsaker, 1991; Olweus, 1991; Olweus, 1992* | 2500 students in grades 5–7; Bergen, Norway | 3 |
| PeaceBuilders<br>*Krug et al., 1997* | 3899 students in grades K-5; 9 schools selected because of high rates of crime in their catchment areas | 4 |

Notes

a  Frequency distribution represents the number of outcomes for which the program group out-performed the comparison group (positive effects) or the comparison group out-performed the program group (negative effects). Statistically significant positive and negative outcomes are reflected in the columns "+*" and "−*" respectively. Statistically nonsignificant effects or outcomes for which only the direction of effect was known are in the "+" and "−" columns.

| Follow-up (months) | Outcome | Frequency distribution[a] | | | | | Effect size[b] | |
|---|---|---|---|---|---|---|---|---|
| | | −* | − | 0 | + | +* | | |
| 1 | Crime | 0 | 0 | 0 | 2 | 1 | | |
| 27 | AOD | 0 | 0 | 0 | 1 | 1 | | |
| 1 | AOD | 0 | 0 | 0 | 0 | 1 | .17* | (1) |
| 1 | AOD | 0 | 1 | 0 | 0 | 0 | −.13 | (1) |
| 27 | AOD | 0 | 1 | 0 | 0 | 1 | .17* | (2) |
| 3 | AOD | 0 | 0 | 0 | 0 | 2 | .22* | (2) |
| 15.5 | AOD | 0 | 0 | 0 | 2 | 1 | .25 | (3) |
| 12 | AOD | 0 | 0 | 0 | 2 | 0 | .16 | (2) |
| | Anti-Soc./Aggr. | 0 | 0 | 0 | 0 | 1 | .57* | (1) |
| 12 | AOD | 0 | 0 | 0 | 0 | 2 | .31* | (2) |
| | Anti-Soc./Aggr. | 0 | 0 | 0 | 0 | 1 | .57* | (1) |
| 0 | AOD | 0 | 0 | 0 | 1 | 2 | .18* | (3) |
| 1 | AOD | 0 | 0 | 1 | 3 | 2 | .24 | (6) |
| 0 | Crime | 0 | 0 | 0 | 1 | 0 | | |
| | Anti-Soc./Aggr. | 0 | 0 | 0 | 1 | 0 | | |
| 0 | Anti-Soc./Aggr. | 0 | 0 | 0 | 0 | 1 | | |

b The mean effect size is based only on those outcomes for which an effect size could be calculated. This may be fewer than the number of effects represented in the frequency distribution. Significance is based on the observed effect size data and may disagree with the frequency distribution if the authors performed a different test or used a different criterion, such as a one-tail test.

undertaken in Norway (Olweus, 1991, 1992; Olweus and Alsaker, 1991; methods rating = 3). This work suggests that school-wide efforts to redefine norms for behavior reduce delinquency. Olweus noted that certain adolescents, i.e. "bullies," repeatedly victimized other adolescents. This harassment was usually ignored by adults who failed to actively intervene and thus provided tacit acceptance of the bullying. A program was devised to alter environmental norms regarding bullying. A campaign directed communication to redefining the behavior as wrong. A booklet was directed to school personnel, defining the problem and spelling out ways to counteract it. Parents were sent a booklet of advice. A video illustrating the problem was made available. Surveys to collect information and register the level of the problem were fielded. Information was fed back to personnel in 42 schools in Bergen, Norway. Among the recommended strategies to reduce bullying were: establishing clear class rules against bullying; contingent responses (praise and sanctions); regular class meetings to clarify norms against bullying; improved supervision of the playground; and teacher involvement in the development of a positive school climate.

The program was evaluated using data from approximately 2,500 students (aged 11 to 14) belonging to 112 classes in 42 primary and secondary schools in Bergen. The results indicated that bullying decreased by 50 percent. Program effects were also observed on self-reports of delinquent behavior, including truancy, vandalism and theft. Effects were observed for boys and girls and for students in all grades included in the study. Also, a dosage-response relationship was observed, with the largest effects emerging after 2 years of the program.

A more recent study of the PeaceBuilders program (Krug *et al.*, 1997; methods rating = 4) also demonstrated a positive effect on fighting from a program that fostered pro-social behavior not by teaching children skills or providing information, but by altering the nature of day-to-day interactions among all members of the school community. The program, in effect, floods the school environment with activities, actions and words that emphasize rewards, praise and pro-social behavior. The program is organized around five principles: praise people, avoid put-downs, seek wise people as advisors and friends, notice and correct hurts, and right wrongs. But children are not taught these principles as part of an isolated curriculum. Instead, all members of the school staff have roles in modeling and reinforcing these principles. For example, teachers greet children using a cue to help children think about how he or she will be a "PeaceBuilder" that day. The principal reads over the public address system the names of children who have exhibited positive behaviors that day. Teachers incorporate into their story-telling times questions or comments on how the characters modeled peace-building behaviors. Notes are sent home reporting positive behaviors to parents, and parents are encouraged to praise their children for these behaviors. Through these multiple and reinforcing activities, a definite norm favoring positive social behavior and discouraging hurtful behavior is established.

The initial evaluation of the program compared changes in the rate of nurse visits from baseline till the end of the first intervention year in nine schools that had been randomly assigned to receive the program or not. Visits to the nurse as well as injury-related visits to the nurse declined significantly in the treatment as compared with the control schools.

SUMMARY

Programs aimed at establishing norms or expectations for behavior have been demonstrated in several studies of reasonable methodological rigor to reduce alcohol and marijuana use (Johnson *et al.*, 1990; Hansen and Graham, 1991; Moberg and Piper, 1990; Pentz *et al.*, 1990; Perry *et al.*, 1996; Stevens *et al.*, 1996; Werch *et al.*, 1996; Wilhelmsen *et al.*, 1994), delinquency (Foshee *et al.*, 1998; Olweus, 1991, 1992; Olweus and Alsaker, 1991) and anti-social or other aggressive behaviors (Krug *et al.*, 1997; Olweus, 1991, 1992; Olweus and Alsaker, 1991). The mean effect size for alcohol and marijuana use across all twelve treatment-comparison contrasts with available data was 0.09 ($p > .05$). Restricting this analysis to those 9 contrasts (7 studies) with a methods rating greater than 2 produces a mean effect size of 0.17 ($p < .05$), nearly double in size and statistically significant. Effects on truancy and school withdrawal have not been assessed. While most of the studies have involved curricular interventions aimed at altering perceptions of norms about substance use (and most of these have confounded the effect of social competency skill development with normative education), positive effects have also been demonstrated for programs that focus directly on altering the school environment without directly teaching students any skills. Additionally, the Hansen and Graham (1991) study provides evidence that the normative change elements contribute more to the reduction in substance use than the social competency elements of the curricula. Additional tests of this type of intervention should be conducted to shore up the relatively thin findings for outcomes other than substance use.

*Managing classes*

Most of students' time in school is spent in classrooms. How these micro-environments are organized and managed may influence not only the amount of disorderly behavior that occurs in the class but also important precursors of delinquency and drug use, including academic performance, attachment and commitment to school, and association with delinquent peers.

---

**Box 4.4**

- Smaller kindergarten and first grade classrooms
- Within-class and between-grade ability grouping in elementary grades
- Non-graded elementary schools
- Behavioral techniques for classroom management
- Continuous progress instruction (e.g. instruction in which students advance through a defined hierarchy of skills after being tested for mastery at each level usually with teachers providing instruction to groups of students at the same instructional level)
- Computer-assisted instruction
- Tutoring
- Cooperative learning

---

Classroom organization and management strategies are found in three-fourths of the studies of school-based prevention. They are usually incorporated into both the school-wide interventions summarized above and (less often) into the instructional interventions described later. For example, cooperative learning strategies were used in Project PATHE (Gottfredson, 1986), the Effective Schools Project (D.C. Gottfredson, 1987) and Project STATUS (Gottfredson, 1990), all of which demonstrated reductions in delinquent behavior. Classroom management techniques were used in Project BASIS (Gottfredson, Gottfredson and Hybl, 1993). In all of these projects, the classroom instruction and management strategies were elements of broader, school-wide organization development or discipline management projects (or in the case of STATUS, a law-related education curricular intervention), thus making it impossible to isolate the effects of the classroom strategies. Classroom management innovations constitute the major intervention in the studies summarized in this section, although even in these studies the classroom management strategies are combined with either a curriculum or some other strategy.

The literature on effective instructional processes is vast. Most of this literature assesses effectiveness on academic outcomes rather than on behavioral outcomes. Brewer *et al.* (1995) summarize existing meta-analyses of instructional strategies and conclude that the strategies shown in Box 4.4 increase academic performance, which is related to delinquency and drug use. These instructional strategies should be considered promising elements of prevention efforts at the classroom level, although their effects on delinquency and substance use have, for the most part, not been demonstrated.

Table 4.7 summarizes evidence from several interventions intended to test the efficacy of upgrading classroom instructional and management methods on subsequent problem behavior. Note that strictly *behavioral* classroom management strategies are not included in this set of studies. The studies on the table are separated according to whether or not they combine classroom management strategies with a major emphasis on teaching self-control or social competency skills. Results are generally positive for the studies containing such a focus, but it is difficult to disentangle the effects of the management strategies from those of the curriculum. (As we will see below, curricular interventions with self-control or social competency content, when used without the instructional or classroom management strategies, are effective for reducing problem behaviors.) The results are more mixed in studies of classroom management strategies used without a self-control or social competency skill focus.

The earliest studies of altering classroom and instructional management strategies were conducted in a series of studies known as the "Napa" studies. Several studies were conducted in elementary school, testing a variety of strategies: Effective Classroom Management (ECM), Magic Circle and Cooperative Learning.[9] Schaps *et al.* (1984; methods rating = 4) reported on an in-service course in which fourth through sixth grade teachers were taught communication skills (e.g. tailored feedback, "I-Messages," clarifying responses, reflecting feelings, reflecting content), problem-solving (e.g. creating problem statements, brainstorming, evaluating alternative solutions, Force Field Analysis, developing an action plan), and self-esteem enhancement techniques (e.g. techniques that create opportunities to describe and receive recognition for a positive trait, skill or experience) for use in their classrooms. In another in-service training workshop (Moskowitz, Schaps and Malvin, 1982; methods rating = 4), third grade teachers were trained to lead structured small-group discussions ("Magic Circle" classroom meetings) about a variety of interpersonal and intrapersonal topics. Each of these teacher training activities was intended to make the classroom environment more responsive to students' affective and cognitive needs in order to eventually reduce students' acceptance and use of drugs. The programs were expected to operate indirectly by changing students' attitudes, behaviors, and perceptions of norms.

In each study, schools were randomly assigned to treatment and control conditions. Teachers in the experimental schools were invited to participate in the training sessions, but not all teachers agreed. Analyses were generally conducted at the classroom and the individual levels, comparing immediate outcomes for all students in the classrooms of all treatment and control teachers, controlling for any pre-existing differences between the groups. When high percentages of teachers failed to participate, additional analyses compared only the participating teachers with the control teachers.

Table 4.7 shows the results from the studies. The preponderance of evidence suggests that the training activities had no positive effect on measures of problem behavior. Teacher ratings of misbehavior significantly favored the Magic Circle control group. Measures of involvement with substances (not shown on the table because they include peer use and intentions to use in addition to actual use) showed some positive effects, but they were inconsistent across level of analysis and gender groups.

Malvin *et al.* (1984; methods rating = 4) report on the ECM teacher training intervention described above but implemented with junior high school teachers. Table 4.7 shows a positive effect for this program: boys in the program had significantly fewer unexcused absences from school. No effects were found for girls. Not shown on the table are negative effects for reported involvement with substances; when pre-treatment differences were statistically controlled, males in the treatment school reported significantly *more* drug and alcohol involvement, attitudes more favorable to substance use and more negative attitudes towards school. The authors attributed the negative effects of the program to differential attrition, and concluded the program had no effect on any of the targeted outcomes.

One of the Napa studies (Moskowitz *et al.*, 1984; Moskowitz *et al.*, 1983) combined the ECM classroom management strategies with a drug education curriculum. ECM was as described above. The curriculum covered decision-making skills, goal-setting, social influences, alternatives to drug use and assertiveness skills. These two strategies were tested on a population of 552 male and female seventh graders, but only the results for the males are included in Table 4.7. As above, substance use measures included intentions and peer use, and for measures of non-substance-related outcomes the direction of the differences could not be ascertained for females. However, no significant differences in self-reports of alcohol or marijuana involvement were reported between participants and non-participants. Female participants reported less drug involvement among their peers and less cigarette use

*Table 4.7* Classroom or instructional management

| Program name and citation | Students | Method rating |
|---|---|---|
| *Includes focus on self-control or social competency* | | |
| **High school grades** | | |
| Teams-Games-Tournaments (TGT) Wodarski, 1987a; Wodarski, 1987b | 981 students in grades 9–12; 5 Georgia school systems | 3 |
| **Middle/junior high school grades** | | |
| Effective Classroom Management (ECM) and Drug Education Moskowitz et al., 1984; Moskowitz et al., 1983 | 348 students in grade 7; male students in 2 schools in a middle-class suburban public school system | 4 |
| **Elementary school grades** | | |
| Seattle Social Development Program (2 years of intervention) 1991; Hawkins et al., 1992; Hawkins et al., 1999 | 458 students in grades 1–2; 8 Seattle schools | 3 |
| Seattle Social Development Program (at least 1 semester of intervention while in grades 1–4) Hawkins et al., 1992; Hawkins et al., 1991; Hawkins et al., 1999 | 908 students in grades 1–4; 18 Seattle schools | 2 |
| Seattle Social Development Program (full intervention across grades 1–6) Hawkins et al., 1992; Hawkins et al., 1991; Hawkins et al., 1999 | 643 students in grades 1–6; 18 Seattle schools | 2 |
| *Does not include focus on self-control or social competency* | | |
| **Middle/junior high school grades** | | |
| Effective Classroom Management (ECM) Malvin et al., 1984 | 134 students in grades 7–9; male students in a predominantly white, middle-class suburban school system | 4 |
| Law-Related Education (LRE) Johnson and Hunter, 1985 | 296 students in grade 9; students in 1 school | 4 |
| Seattle Social Development Program (7th grade component only) Hawkins et al., 1988 | 160 students in grade 7; low math achievers from 5 middle schools in Seattle | 4 |
| **Elementary school grades** | | |
| Child Development Project Battistich et al., 1996 | 1600 students in grades 5–6; 24 geographically diverse schools | 3 |
| Classroom Meetings Sorsdahl and Sanche, 1985 | 91 students in grade 4; Saskatoon, Saskatchewan, Canada | 3 |
| ClassWide Peer Tutoring (CWPT) Greenwood et al., 1993; Greenwood et al., 1989 | 296 students in grades 1–4; low SES at-risk students in Chapter 1 schools | 4 |
| Effective Classroom Management (ECM) Sharps et al., 1984 | 997 students in grades 4–6; predominantly white, middle-class suburban public school system | 4 |
| Law-Related Education (LRE) Johnson and Hunter, 1985 | 561 students in grades K–12; students in 7 schools | 3 |
| Magic Circle Moskowitz et al., 1982 | 233 students in grade 3; males in 13 schools in a predominantly white middle-class suburban public school system | 4 |
| Program to Enhance Prosocial Development Battistich et al., 1989; Solomon et al., 1988 | 350 students in grades K–4; 6 elementary schools | 4 |
| Social Problem Solving Training (Study 1) Nelson and Carson, 1988 | 101 students in grades 3–4; mostly white students from schools with a high proportion of children with special needs | 3 |
| Success for All Jones et al., 1997 | 172 students in grade 1; predominantly black students in 2 schools in Charleston, SC. | 3 |

Notes

a Frequency distribution represents the number of outcomes for which the program group out-performed the comparison group (positive effects) or the comparison group out-performed the program group (negative effects). Statistically significant positive and negative outcomes are reflected in the columns "+*" and "−*" respectively. Statistically nonsignificant effects or outcomes for which only the direction of effect was known are in the "+" and "−" columns.

| Follow-up (months) | Outcome | Frequency distribution[a] | | | | | Effect size[b] | |
|---|---|---|---|---|---|---|---|---|
| | | −* | − | 0 | + | +* | | |
| 24 | AOD | 0 | 0 | 0 | 0 | 3 | | |
| 0 | Drop-out/Truancy | 0 | 0 | 0 | 0 | 1 | .32* | (1) |
| 0 | Anti-Soc./Aggr. | 0 | 0 | 0 | 1 | 1 | .29* | (1) |
| 0 | Crime | 0 | 0 | 0 | 1 | 0 | .18 | (1) |
| | AOD | 0 | 0 | 0 | 0 | 1 | .22 | (1) |
| | Anti-Soc./Aggr. | 0 | 1 | 0 | 0 | 0 | −.12 | (1) |
| 72 | Crime | 0 | 0 | 0 | 3 | 1 | .18 | (4) |
| | AOD | 0 | 0 | 2 | 1 | 0 | .03 | (3) |
| | Drop-out/Truancy | 0 | 0 | 0 | 0 | 1 | .26* | (1) |
| | Anti-Soc./Aggr. | 0 | 0 | 0 | 2 | 1 | .25 | (2) |
| 0 | Drop-out/Truancy | 0 | 0 | 0 | 0 | 1 | | |
| 0 | Crime | 0 | 0 | 0 | 2 | 0 | .20 | (1) |
| | AOD | 0 | 0 | 0 | 0 | 1 | .25 | (1) |
| | Anti-Soc./Aggr. | 0 | 0 | 0 | 0 | 1 | .45* | (1) |
| 0 | Crime | 0 | 3 | 0 | 0 | 0 | −.16 | (3) |
| | AOD | 0 | 0 | 0 | 1 | 0 | .04 | (1) |
| | Anti-Soc./Aggr. | 0 | 0 | 0 | 0 | 1 | .23 | (1) |
| 0 | Crime | 0 | 1 | 0 | 4 | 2 | .27* | (7) |
| | AOD | 0 | 0 | 0 | 0 | 2 | .19* | (2) |
| | Drop-out/Truancy | 0 | 0 | 0 | 1 | 0 | .13 | (1) |
| | Anti-Soc./Aggr. | 0 | 0 | 2 | 0 | 0 | .00 | (2) |
| 0 | Anti-Soc./Aggr. | 0 | 0 | 0 | 0 | 2 | | |
| 24 | Anti-Soc./Aggr. | 0 | 0 | 1 | 1 | 0 | .09 | (2) |
| 0 | Drop-out/Truancy | 0 | 0 | 1 | 1 | 0 | .05 | (2) |
| | Anti-Soc./Aggr. | 1 | 0 | 1 | 0 | 0 | −.11 | (2) |
| 0 | Crime | 0 | 1 | 0 | 5 | 0 | | |
| | AOD | 0 | 1 | 0 | 0 | 0 | | |
| | Anti-Soc./Aggr. | 0 | 0 | 0 | 1 | 0 | | |
| 0 | Anti-Soc./Aggr. | 1 | 0 | 0 | 0 | 0 | −.86* | (1) |
| 0 | Anti-Soc./Aggr. | 0 | 1 | 0 | 0 | 0 | | |
| 6 | Anti-Soc./Aggr. | 0 | 1 | 0 | 1 | 0 | −.05 | (2) |
| 0 | Anti-Soc./Aggr. | 0 | 1 | 0 | 0 | 0 | −.23 | (1) |

b  The mean effect size is based only on those outcomes for which an effect size could be calculated. This may be fewer than the number of effects represented in the frequency distribution. Significance is based on the observed effect size data and may disagree with the frequency distribution if the authors performed a different test or used a different criterion, such as a one-tail test.

than female non-participants, but these results were not observed for males. Male participants reported more drug knowledge and had fewer unexcused absences than male non-participants, but these results were not replicated for females.

The Napa studies, taken together, demonstrated mixed effects on measures of problem behavior for classroom and instructional management practices. The evidence suggests a positive effect on school attendance, no effects on involvement with substances and a negative effect on other problem behaviors.

A second major classroom intervention (CDP, the Child Development Project) was conducted with several cohorts of elementary school students in twelve elementary schools for 2 consecutive years beginning in 1992 (Battistich *et al.*, 1996; methods rating = 3). It included the following components:

- "cooperative learning" activities intended to encourage student discussion, comparison of ideas, and mutual challenging of ideas on academic and social topics;
- a "values-rich" literature-based reading and language arts program intended to foster understanding of diversity;
- "developmental discipline," a positive approach to classroom management that stresses teaching appropriate behavior rather than punishment, involving students in classroom management, and helping them to learn behavior management and conflict resolution skills;
- "community-building" activities aimed at increasing appreciation for diversity or students' sense of communal involvement and responsibility; and
- "home-school" activities to foster parent involvement in their children's education.

A similar program (labeled "Program to Enhance Prosocial Development" on Table 4.7) was conducted in three elementary schools for 5 consecutive years beginning in 1982 (Battistich *et al.*, 1989; Solomon *et al.*, 1988; methods rating = 4). The evidence from evaluations of this earlier effort is also summarized in Table 4.7. The earlier program increased pro-social behaviors but did not decrease negative behavior among students in grades K through 4. In the Child Development Project (Battistich *et al.*, 1996), significant positive effects were found on measures of delinquency, marijuana and alcohol use.

The Seattle Social Development Project (Hawkins *et al.*, 1988, 1991, 1999; Hawkins, Catalano, Morrison *et al.*, 1992; O'Donnell *et al.*, 1995) used cooperative learning strategies, proactive classroom management and interactive teaching. The full version of the program also provided cognitive-based social competence training in the first grade, using Shure and Spivak's (1979, 1980, 1982) ICPS model which is described later in this chapter. Proactive classroom management consisted of establishing expectations for classroom behavior, using methods of maintaining classroom order that minimize interruptions to instruction, and giving frequent specific contingent praise and encouragement for student progress and effort. Interactive teaching involved several instructional practices generally accepted as effective (e.g. frequent assessment, clear objectives, checking for understanding, remediation). Cooperative learning used small heterogeneous learning groups to reinforce and practice what the teacher taught. Recognition and team rewards were provided to the teams, contingent on demonstrated improvement. Parent training in family management practices was also provided. This program was implemented continually from first through sixth grades in several elementary schools beginning in 1981. In addition, the classroom management strategies were implemented without the parent training or the social competency training in a 1-year study of seventh graders (Hawkins, Doueck and Lishner, 1988).

Several of the project reports are summarized in Table 4.7. The evaluations demonstrated consistent significant positive effects on attachment and commitment to school, and the absence of such effects on belief in moral order and attitudes about substance use. The strongest evidence for the program comes from the earliest report from the study (Hawkins, Von Cleve and Catalano, 1991; methods rating = 3) which showed results for subjects who had been randomly assigned to treatment and control conditions. In this report, measures of self-destructive behavior (and measures of aggressive behavior, but only for males) favored the treatment group in second grade. After this point, the study was expanded and random assignment was abandoned. The later reports are based on a quasi-experimental design, and showed that students exposed to the intervention for at least one semester during grades 1 through 4 reported less substance use than students not so exposed[10] (Hawkins, Catalano, Morrison *et al.*, 1992; methods rating = 2). A measure of delinquency initiation also favored the treatment group, although the difference is not statistically significant. For low-achieving seventh graders who received the classroom portion of the program with no parent training, no significant effects were observed on measures of delinquency and drug use, although the treatment group had significantly fewer suspensions from school (Hawkins, Doueck and Lishner, 1988; methods rating = 4). The most recent report from the study (Hawkins *et al.*, 1999; methods rating = 2) compares participants who received the program in grades 1 through 6 and those who received it later (in grades 5 and 6) with students who did not receive it at all. The report found that students who received the full intervention (e.g. beginning in grade 1) reported significantly less school misbehavior, lower prevalence of violent delinquent behavior and less frequent alcohol consumption than students not receiving the intervention. Students receiving the intervention in grades 5 and 6 were no different from the control group. Because our meta-analysis could not handle the complexity of redefining the experimental groups, the effect sizes for this follow-up in Table 4.7 are based on our recalculation of the results using the same groups reported in the earlier studies (e.g. only the students who received the full intervention are considered in the treatment group; others are considered as comparison students). In this re-analysis, one significant difference remains on the outcomes examined in this chapter: those students receiving the intervention were significantly less likely than the comparison students to have dropped out of school. This recalculation of effects may underestimate true program effects to the extent that the group receiving the program late benefited from the program. In summary, the

SSDP produced positive effects on antisocial behavior. It also registered effects on crime, substance use, and school drop-out, but these results are more tenuous than the results from the more conclusive early comparison of randomly assigned treatment and control students. At any rate, positive effects are observed only for the full intervention condition delivered beginning in grade 1 and continuing through their elementary school years.

Other studies have also suggested that the combination of a curricular component with improved classroom instructional and management strategies may produce positive effects on problem behaviors. The national evaluation of Law-Related Education (LRE; Johnson and Hunter, 1985) studied the effects of a LRE curriculum combined with classroom instructional management strategies. LRE curricula are designed to familiarize youths with the country's laws, develop appreciation of the legal process, encourage responsible political participation, develop moral and ethical values, and develop analytical skills. Lack of knowledge about the law, citizenship skills, and positive attitudes about the law and the role of the government are cited in LRE materials as causes of juvenile crime. Uniformed police officers assist teachers in implementing the curriculum, usually taught as a half-year unit in a Law and Government course. A variety of activities intended to engage students, including mock trials, police ride-alongs, home security audits, and students taking the role of police and other professionals in the justice system augmented the curriculum.

The report on the national evaluation of LRE (Johnson and Hunter, 1985; methods rating = 3 for the entire study) summarized the results for the strongest implementation year (1983) comparing outcomes, separately by teacher, for students in twenty-one LRE classes and fourteen comparison classes (most of which were non-randomly assigned). These classrooms included all school levels: elementary, junior high and senior high schools. Out of 132 effects reported for the eleven delinquency items, fifteen showed a significant effect (thirteen would have been expected by chance using the one-tailed test of significance reported). Nine of these differences favored the LRE students, and six favored the comparison students. Significant program effects on attitudes towards deviance and violence favored the comparison students. When the results for the groups are pooled across school level and the means combined (see Table 4.7), the direction of the effect favors the LRE group for five of the six delinquency measures and a measure of school rule infractions. The direction of the effect favors the control students on one measure of delinquency and a measure of substance use. Many positive effects were found for outcomes measuring knowledge about the law. In summary, the national evaluation of the LRE curriculum by itself showed clear program effects on law-related factual knowledge, but effects on other outcomes were mixed.

The authors noted, however, that effects were stronger in a site that had implemented the program particularly well. In this site, the LRE intervention included a large dose of general instructional and classroom management training for teachers in addition to law-related activities. Teachers in this site had been trained in techniques to promote high student involvement and interaction, mastery learning, and cooperative learning. Johnson and Hunter (1985; methods rating = 4 for these classes) focused on the nine LRE classes in this one site in which randomization to treatment and control conditions was also obtained. They showed that the nine LRE classes fared significantly better than the two control classes on more than half of the 41 possible measures. Three of the eleven items measuring delinquency and substance use were reported as significantly favoring the LRE group for one or more classes. Our recalculation of effect sizes based on data presented in Johnson and Hunter (1985) showed significant effects for rule infractions, and effects favoring the LRE group (although they are not significantly different from zero) for substance use and delinquency.

SUMMARY

The set of studies included in this category suggest that changing classroom instructional and management strategies produce positive effects on measures of crime initiation ($\overline{ES} = 0.18$, $p < .05$), but among comparisons with rigor ratings of three or higher, only one of 3 studies (Battistich *et al.*, 1996) found significant positive effects. Significant positive effects have been found on measures of substance use (Battistich *et al.*, 1996; Wodarski, 1987a, 1987b, $\overline{ES} = 0.17$, $p < .05$). Significant positive effects are found on measures of antisocial behavior and aggression in three of the higher quality studies (Hawkins, Von Cleve and Catalano, 1991; Johnson and Hunter, 1985; Sorsdahl and Sanche, 1985; $\overline{ES} = 0.05$, $p > .05$), but seven studies also fail to find significant effects, and two high-quality studies reported significant negative effects (Moskowitz, Schaps and Malvin, 1982; Schaps *et al.*, 1984). These studies seldom examine effects on school attendance and withdrawal, but significant positive effects have been found in two studies with methods scores of 3 or higher (Malvin *et al.*, 1984; Moskowitz *et al.*, 1984; $\overline{ES} = 0.15$, $p < .05$), and the preponderance of evidence is positive. The evidence therefore suggests that efforts to improve instructional and classroom management are promising for preventing crime initiation, and work to decrease substance use and to increase attendance and school persistence. However, the inconsistency of the findings, especially with respect to measures of antisocial behavior, is troubling and suggests that the group of studies included in this set are fairly heterogeneous. Several ingredients are combined in the studies summarized here: the programs with the most positive effects tend to be of longer duration and tend to combine classroom and instructional management strategies with some other major ingredient (e.g. parent training or social skills instruction). Further research is needed to disentangle the various elements included in these interventions.

*Reorganization of grades or classes*

Five reasonably rigorous studies have examined interventions which group students to create more supportive or challenging environments for high-risk youths. These studies are all conducted within a regular school setting; that is, they group disruptive students within the regular school setting for at least part of the school day but do not completely remove the students to an alternative school setting. Most involve senior high school students. Felner, Ginter and Primavera (1982) and Felner and Adan (1988; both methods rating = 4) studied the School Transitional Environmental Project (STEP), a 1-year program for students making the transition to high school.[11] Incoming students were assigned to small "schools within the school" consisting of 65 to 100 students. Students remained in intact small groups for their home room period and their academic subjects. These classrooms also were physically close together. The role of the home room teacher was redefined so as to include more responsibility for meeting the administrative, counseling, and guidance needs of the students. Reyes and Jason (1991; methods rating = 4) implemented a similar program which also contained an attendance monitoring component. Trice, Parker and Safer (1982; methods rating = 3) reported on a self-contained classroom for disruptive tenth graders that combined behavioral discipline management strategies with an off-campus apprenticeship experience. The class contained only eighteen students. In this study, disruptive students were grouped together for their major subject instruction (four periods). Behavior modification techniques were used to reward students for being prepared for class, remaining on task and completing work. Daily progress reports were sent home to parents, and sometimes these reports were used to support a home-based reinforcement program. Students received vocational training in the afternoons, for which they received pay. Gottfredson (1990; methods rating = 4) studied another school-within-a-school intervention: Student Training Through Urban Strategies (STATUS). This program grouped high-risk youths to receive an integrated social studies and English program which involved a law-related education curriculum and used instructional methods emphasizing active student participation. Students stayed together for 2 hours each day. STATUS was similar in content and process to the LRE program described in the preceding section, except for the addition of an explicit regrouping component. Hausman, Pierce and Briggs (1996; methods rating = 3) reported on a violence prevention curriculum delivered to a small group of students participating in a pilot project called the Fenway Project. Class sizes were smaller than typical and students remained with their classes during participation in the project. The pilot project emphasized community-building and involved a great deal of contact with the students' families. The violence prevention curriculum taught students factual information regarding violence as well as skills for choosing alternatives to fighting. These studies are summarized in Table 4.8.

STEP had consistent positive effects over a 5-year period on school achievement, attendance and persistence in school. By the end of high school, STEP students' drop-out rate was about half that of the comparison group. Felner *et al.*'s (1993) downward extension into grades 6 and 7 did find significant effects on behavior problem and acting out but, as noted in note 10, these differences cannot be reliably attributed to the STEP program. Reyes and Jason (1991), in another high school study, found no significant differences in school attendance between the regrouped and comparison students. The students in Trice, Parker and Safer (1982) self-contained classroom fared no better than the comparison "mainstreamed" students in terms of their attendance and persistence in school. Students in Hausman, Pierce and Briggs (1996) self-contained violence prevention curriculum had significantly fewer suspensions than students in the comparison group.

Finally, STATUS reduced delinquency and drug use, and changed in the desired direction several risk and protective factors related to delinquency. STATUS involved innovative teaching methods (many of which are reviewed in the classroom management section above), a law-related education curriculum, and the innovative school-within-a-school scheduling. It is not possible to disentangle the effects of these components. However, the major intermediate outcome through which the law-related education curriculum was expected to reduce delinquency – belief in the validity of laws – was the only outcome that did not favor the treatment group. It is unlikely, therefore, that the positive effects found in the STATUS program were due solely to the law-related education curriculum. Also, because the STATUS effects are larger and more consistent than the LRE effects described above, it is likely that the unique element introduced in STATUS, the innovative group-ing and scheduling, was beneficial.

SUMMARY

Programs which group high-risk students to create smaller, more tightly knit units for instruction show promise for reducing delinquency and drug use, but only one study of reasonable methodological rigor has reported effects on these outcomes (Gottfredson, 1990). Two reasonably rigorous studies have demonstrated significant positive effects on conduct problems (Hausman, Pierce and Briggs, 1996; Gottfredson, 1990; $ES = 0.23$, $p < .05$). And two studies (Felner, Ginter and Primavera, 1982; Felner and Adan, 1988; Gottfredson, 1990) report positive effects for school non-attendance ($ES = 0.16$, $p > .05$). Programs which group high-risk students together are risky in light of other research that shows negative effects of grouping high-risk youths for peer counseling or other therapeutic services (to be reviewed shortly); however, the studies summarized in this section suggest that it may be beneficial to group high-risk students for instruction in the context of "schools-within-schools" which offer a strong academic program, use effective instruction and classroom management strategies, and supportive staff. Replications are needed in this area.

### A note on alternative schools

Several of the programs described above grouped disruptive students together within the regular school setting. A few studies have examined interventions which completely remove such students from the regular school setting. Two such studies are summarized in this report (Gottfredson, 1990, see Table 4.13; and Gold and Mann, 1984, see Table 4.11). Because so few studies of alternative schools have been conducted, and because the interventions delivered in these settings are so heterogeneous, we chose to classify the studies according to their major intervention strategy rather than according to their structural arrangement. Elsewhere (D.C. Gottfredson, 2001; G.D. Gottfredson, 1987) we have concluded that alternative schools are far too variable in nature, student composition, structure and purpose to warrant any blanket statement about their effectiveness. G.D. Gottfredson (1987) reviews two alternative school models: one based on a theory that

*Table 4.8* Reorganization of grades or classes

| Program name and citation | Students | Method rating |
|---|---|---|
| **High school grades** | | |
| Dropout Prevention Program *Reyes and Jason, 1991* | 154 students in grade 9; a large urban school with a high drop-out rate; predominantly Hispanic, low-income population | 4 |
| School Transitional Environment Program (STEP) *Felner and Adan, 1988; Felner et al., 1982; Felner et al., 1993* | 185 students in grade 9; a large urban school from primarily low socioeconomic and minority backgrounds | 4 |
| Self-Contained Program *Trice et al., 1982* | 44 students in grade 10; disruptive students | 3 |
| Violence Prevention Curriculum for Adolescents (In-Class Program) *Hausman et al., 1996* | 313 students in grade 10; Boston | 3 |
| **Middle/junior high and high school grades** | | |
| Project STATUS (Student Training Through Urban Strategies) *Gottfredson, 1990* | 247 students in grades 7–9; high-risk students in 2 schools in Pasadena, CA | 4 |

Notes
a  Frequency distribution represents the number of outcomes for which the program group out-performed the comparison group (positive effects) or the comparison group out-performed the program group (negative effects). Statistically significant positive and negative outcomes are reflected in the columns "+*" and "−*" respectively. Statistically nonsignificant effects or outcomes for which only the direction of effect was known are in the "+" and "−" columns.

intense personal involvement of the educators with the youth would reduce delinquency through increased bonding, and the other based on the theory that rigorous discipline and behavior modification techniques would result in decreased delinquency. The evaluation of the first program found remarkable improvements in several risk factors for delinquency, including commitment to school, attachment to school and belief in rules. It also found significantly less self-reported drug use (but not self-reported delinquency or arrest records) among alternative school students than among controls. The evaluation of the second alternative school implied that the program was effective for increasing several measures of academic persistence, but that students liked school less and reported significantly more delinquent behavior than the comparison students. The varied models employed in alternative schools suggest that the question, "Are alternative schools effective?" is too simplistic. The components of the interventions involved in alternative schools must be disentangled in future evaluations.

### Individual-change strategies

The prevention strategies discussed above focused on changing the school or classroom environment in order to produce subsequent reductions in

| Follow-up (months) | Outcome | Frequency distribution[a] | | | | | Effect size[b] | |
|---|---|---|---|---|---|---|---|---|
| | | −* | − | 0 | + | +* | | |
| 0 | Drop-out/Truancy | 0 | 2 | 1 | 0 | 0 | −.07 | (3) |
| 36 | Drop-out/Truancy | 0 | 0 | 0 | 1 | 7 | .38* | (5) |
| 24 | Drop-out/Truancy | 0 | 2 | 0 | 2 | 0 | .07 | (3) |
| 0 | Anti-Soc./Aggr. | 0 | 0 | 0 | 0 | 1 | | |
| 0 | Crime | 0 | 0 | 0 | 1 | 1 | .36* | (2) |
| | AOD | 0 | 0 | 0 | 0 | 1 | .40* | (1) |
| | Drop-out/Truancy | 0 | 0 | 0 | 2 | 1 | .24 | (3) |
| | Anti-Soc./Aggr. | 0 | 1 | 0 | 1 | 1 | .23 | (3) |

b  The mean effect size is based only on those outcomes for which an effect size could be calculated. This may be fewer than the number of effects represented in the frequency distribution. Significance is based on the observed effect size data and may disagree with the frequency distribution if the authors performed a different test or used a different criterion, such as a one-tail test.

problem behaviors and increases in pro-social behaviors. The prevention strategies summarized below have in common the focus on changing knowledge, attitudes, beliefs, behaviors or skills of individual students. These strategies include instruction with specific content expected to reduce delinquency or drug use; strategies aimed at changing thinking processes (cognitive or cognitive-behavioral training); behavior modification; counseling and social work; mentoring, tutoring, and work-study experiences; and providing recreational, community service, or leisure activities.

### Instructing students

The most common school-based prevention strategy is instruction. Most schools provide instruction aimed at reducing drug use or delinquency, often in the form of the programs like Drug Abuse Resistance Education (DARE) and Gang Resistance Education and Training (GREAT), which enjoy substantial federal subsidy. The content of interventions that provide instruction to students is varied. Box 4.5 shows some of the topics covered in instructional programs.

---

**Box 4.5**

- General health or safety
- Alcohol, tobacco, and other drugs: information about and consequences of use
- Violence prevention
- Character/moral development
- Law
- Recognizing and resisting social influences to engage in misbehavior and risky situations, being assertive
- Identifying problem situations, generating alternative solutions, evaluating consequences
- Setting personal goals, self-monitoring, self-reinforcement, self-punishment
- Attributing the cause of events or circumstances to one's own behavior
- Interpreting and processing social cues, understanding non-verbal communication, negotiating, managing anger, controlling stress, anticipating the perspectives or reactions of others

---

The following pages summarize what is known about the effectiveness of instructional programs relating to drug and alcohol use, violence, and other problem behaviors. The most common type of prevention curricula to be studied is drug prevention. Often studies of such curricular programs assess only substance use outcomes. Occasionally, effects on crime and other conduct problems are also examined. Studies of these programs are presented in Tables 4.9–4.11 along with the less common studies of violence prevention programs and programs aimed at enhancing social competencies in general. The studies are organized by two dimensions which have been highlighted in prior reviews and meta-analyses: (1) the extent to which the instructional program focuses on social competency or resistance skills, and (2) the extent to which the instructional program makes use of cognitive behavioral or behavioral methods.

Several meta-analyses and reviews of the effectiveness of school-based drug prevention instruction have been conducted (Botvin, 1990; Botvin, Schinke and Orlandi, 1995; Dryfoos, 1990; Durlak, 1995; Hansen, 1992; Hawkins, Arthur and Catalano, 1995; Institute of Medicine, 1994; Tobler, 1986, 1992). Botvin (1990) traced the historical development of these programs and showed that "information dissemination" approaches which teach primarily about drugs and their effects, "fear arousal" approaches that emphasize the risks associated with tobacco, alcohol, or drug use, "moral appeal" approaches which teach students about the evils of use, and "affective education" programs which focus on building self-esteem, responsible decision-making, and interpersonal growth are largely *ineffective* for reducing substance use. In contrast, approaches which include resistance-skills training to teach students about social influences to engage in substance use and specific skills for effectively resisting these pressures, alone or in combination with broader-based life-skills training, do reduce substance use. Box 4.6 shows the typical content of these instructional programs. Curricula which focus on general life-skills are typically longer than those which focus only on social resistance skills.

---

**Box 4.6**

Components of social resistance skills instruction:

- Increasing student awareness of the social influences promoting substance use
- Teaching skills for resisting social influences from peers and the media
- Correcting normative expectations concerning the use of substances

Additional skills targeted in life-skills instruction:

- Problem-solving and decision-making
- Self-control or self-esteem
- Adaptive coping strategies for relieving stress or anxiety
- Interpersonal skills
- Assertiveness

---

The most recent meta-analysis of school-based drug prevention programs (Tobler and Stratton, 1997) examined 120 published and unpublished studies of school-based drug prevention programs appearing between 1978 and 1990. The main conclusion of the study was that "interactive" programs (e.g. those affording much opportunity for interaction among the adolescents) were more effective than "non-interactive" programs (e.g. didactic presentations). This analysis showed that program content categories (e.g. social influence, information only, affective) are correlated with mode of delivery (interactive vs. non-interactive), and suggested that some of the positive effect previously attributed to program content may in fact be due to the delivery method. However, multivariate analyses showed that content focusing on interpersonal competence was a necessary factor in the success of drug prevention curricula. Programs including interactive delivery methods but focusing on such intrapersonal factors as self-esteem or personal values were ineffective.

Tobler applied the name "interactive" to programs that make use of methods such as behavioral models (peers or videotapes) to demonstrate new skills, role-playing, rehearsal and practice. Programs using these methods rely less on lecture and individual seat work, and appear more interactive. These programs, according to our classification scheme, rely on cognitive-behavioral and behavioral methods, such as modeling behaviors, providing opportunity for practice of behaviors, giving specific and frequent feedback about new behaviors, providing cues to prompt the behavior, and using techniques to generalize the new behavior to different settings. Programs that use these techniques tend also to be interactive. Prior summaries of this literature therefore imply that effective instructional programs will contain (a) substantive content related to social competency skills, and (b) use cognitive-behavioral or behavioral modeling methods of instruction. We have organized the instructional programs according to these dimensions. Most programs that make use of cognitive-behavioral and behavioral methods also have content focusing on social competency skill development. These are contained in Table 4.9. Table 4.10 contains those programs which teach about social competency or resistance skills, but rely more on traditional didactic approaches to teaching. Table 4.11 contains "other" instructional programs which have neither a major focus on social competency development nor a reliance on cognitive-behavioral or behavioral methods of teaching.

### INSTRUCTIONAL PROGRAMS FOCUSING ON SOCIAL COMPETENCY SKILL DEVELOPMENT AND USING COGNITIVE-BEHAVIORAL OR BEHAVIORAL METHODS

Seven different studies of reasonably high methodological rigor reported on the effects of such programs on crime (see Table 4.9). Three of these studies reported positive effects on crime that were significantly different from zero, and for one of these (the Montreal Longitudinal Experimental Study), the average effect size for measures of crime was 0.24. No significant negative effects were reported.

In the Montreal Longitudinal Experimental Study (Tremblay *et al.*, 1991; Tremblay *et al.*, 1992; Tremblay *et al.*, 1994; Tremblay *et al.*, 1995; McCord *et al.*, 1994; methods rating = 5), low-SES, disruptive boys were randomly assigned to receive a preventive intervention or to be part of an attention control group or a no-contact control group. Disruptive boys for the pool were identified through kindergarten teacher ratings. The intervention began in the second grade (when the boys were 7 years old) and continued for 2 years. The program combined a successful model of parent training in family management (developed by the Oregon Social Learning Center; Patterson, 1982) with a social skills training program delivered by professionals in the schools. Approximately seventeen home visits per family were conducted over the 2-year period. These sessions focused on teaching parents to monitor their son's behavior, reinforce positive behavior, punish negative behavior without being abusive, and manage family crises. Parents were also given a reading program. The social skills sessions (nineteen over the 2-year period) grouped the disruptive boys with pro-social peers for sessions which focused on pro-social skills and self-control. Effective cognitive-behavioral strategies (e.g. coaching, peer modeling, self-instruction, behavioral rehearsal and reinforcement contingencies) were used during the sessions. The study followed the boys for 6 years after the end of the treatment.

Many different measures of antisocial and criminal behavior were taken between the end of the intervention and the final follow-up 6 years after treatment. Several different sources of data were examined. The preponderance of results support a positive effect of the 2-year early intervention, but some apparently negative effects were reported by the mothers of the boys. The average effect size across measures of crime is 0.24, indicating that boys in the treatment fared approximately one quarter of one standard deviation better on minor delinquent activities, such as fighting and stealing. But the average effect size across measures of antisocial behavior, primarily teacher and parent ratings of disruptive behavior, is −0.21. This negative effect is due to a significant negative effect on mother reports of disruption immediately after the treatment. The apparently contradictory mother reports may reflect a positive effect on the mothers' awareness of and sensitivity to the boys' negative behaviors, rather than an actual increase in negative behaviors.

Arbuthnot and Gordon (1986) and Arbuthnot (1992; both methods rating = 4) tested an intervention aimed at accelerating moral reasoning development in boys and girls (mostly in grades 8 and 9) who had been nominated by their teachers as behaviorally disordered. The intervention consisted of small discussion groups (size ranging from five to eight students) held weekly for one class period for 16 to 20 weeks. Researchers led the groups. Most of the discussions were "guided moral dilemma" discussions. Role playing of moral dilemmas was also used. Moral reasoning and perspective taking were the main foci of the discussions, although a couple of sessions were spent developing specific listening and communication skills deemed necessary for effective discussion. Problem solving skills (generation of alternatives, consideration of consequences, choice and action) were practiced throughout the intervention, and consideration of the rights, perspectives and obligations of the characters involved in the dilemmas was encouraged. The program contained content related to the development of social competency skills and used cognitive/behavioral methods, such as behavioral modeling and role-playing.

Subjects (n = 48) were randomly assigned to treatment and control groups. Treatment subjects' moral reasoning improved significantly (relative to control subjects) during the intervention. Official measures on misconduct and delinquency (office referrals and police contacts) also improved for the treatment subjects. Teacher evaluations of student misbehavior were not affected by the treatment. Grades in some classes and a measure of tardiness (but not absenteeism) also improved significantly during the period for the treatment subjects relative to the controls. Twelve months following the end of the treatment, positive effects on moral reasoning, certain grades, tardiness and absenteeism, and disciplinary referrals were still evident, although the police contact data converged for the two groups. The study was weakened, however, by severe attrition. Fewer than half of the subjects were measured at the 1-year follow-up, and there was a considerable problem with missing data at both the pre-test and the measurement immediately following the treatment.

Compared with the sparse evaluations of the effectiveness of instructional programs for reducing crime and violence, such evaluations of effects on substance use are plentiful and generally show positive effects on measures of substance use. Table 4.9 shows 32 different tests of the effectiveness of such curricula. Two of the better known instructional prevention programs which have been scrutinized using especially rigorous methods are ALERT (Bell, Ellickson and Harrison, 1993; Ellickson and Bell, 1990; Ellickson, Bell and McGuigan, 1993) and Life Skills Training (LST; Botvin, Baker, Botvin *et al.*, 1984; Botvin, Baker, Renick *et al.*, 1984; Botvin, Batson *et al.*, 1989; Botvin, Baker, Filazzola and Botvin, 1990; Botvin, Baker, Dusenbury, Botvin and Diaz, 1995) and are included in this table. ALERT is essentially a social resistance-skill curriculum consisting of eight lessons taught a week apart in the seventh grade, followed by three eighth grade "booster" lessons. LST is a more comprehensive program focusing on resistance skills training as well as the general life skills mentioned above. This program consists of sixteen sessions delivered to seventh grade students followed by eight session "boosters" in grades 8 and 9.

*Table 4.9* Self-control or social competency instruction using cognitive-behavioral or behavioral instructional methods

| Program name and citation | Students | Method rating |
|---|---|---|
| **High school grades** | | |
| Alcohol Misuse Prevention Study (AMPS) <br> *Shope, Copeland, Maharg and Dielman, 1996* | 2357 students in grade 10; 4 southeastern Michigan school districts | 4 |
| Cognitive and Social Skills Training <br> *Sarason and Sarason, 1981* | 127 students in grade 9; an urban, multi-ethnic school; low achievers | 3 |
| Drug Resistance Strategies Project (Film Group Only) <br> *Hecht et al., 1993* | 181 students in grades 9–12; a southwestern US community | 4 |
| Drug Resistance Strategies Project (Film Performance with discussion) <br> *Hecht et al., 1993* | 188 students in grades 9–12; a southwestern US community | 4 |
| Drug Resistance Strategies Project (Live Performance with discussion) <br> *Hecht et al., 1993* | 181 students in grades 9–12; a southwestern US community | 4 |
| PASS (Plan a Safe Strategy) <br> *Sheehan et al., 1996* | 2833 students in grade 10; Australia | 4 |
| Reconnecting Youth: Interpersonal Relations <br> *Eggert et al., 1990* | 264 students in grades 9–12; high-risk predominantly white, middle-class students in a northwest US urban high school | 3 |
| Reconnecting Youth: Personal Growth Class (I) <br> *Eggert et al., 1994* | 322 students in grades 9–12; high-risk youth identified as actual or potential drop-outs | 3 |
| Reconnecting Youth: Personal Growth Class I (5 month intervention) <br> *Eggert et al., 1995* | 97 students in grades 9–12; high-risk youths identified as at risk of suicide | 4 |
| Reconnecting Youth: Personal Growth Class II (10 month intervention) <br> *Eggert et al., 1995* | 88 students in grades 9–12; high-risk youths identified as at risk of suicide | 4 |
| Resisting Pressures to Drink and Drive <br> *Newman et al., 1992* | 3500 students in grade 9; students in Nebraska in 9 schools | 4 |
| Violence Prevention Curriculum for Adolescents (School-wide Program) <br> *Hausman et al., 1996* | 682 students in grade 10; Boston | 3 |
| **Middle/junior high and high school grades** | | |
| Project PATH (Programs to Advance Teen Health) <br> *Severson et al., 1991* | 2552 students in grades 7–10; rural and urban areas | 4 |
| Sociomoral Reasoning Development Program <br> *Arbuthnot, 1992; Arbuthnot and Gordon, 1986* | 48 students in grades 7–10; nominated by teachers as "seriously behavior disordered"; Appalachian Ohio | 4 |
| **Middle/junior high school grades** | | |
| Alcohol Misuse Prevention Study (AMPS) <br> *Shope et al., 1992; Dielman et al., 1986; Dielman, Shope, Butchart et al., 1989; Dielman, Shope, Leech et al., 1989; Campanelli et al., 1989* | 2670 students in grade 6; 6 school districts in southeastern Michigan | 4 |
| Alcohol Misuse Prevention Study (AMPS) <br> *Shope et al., 1994* | 3989 students in grades 6–8; 35 elementary and middle schools in 7 southeastern Michigan districts | 4 |
| Alert (adult health educator and teen leader) <br> *Ellickson and Bell, 1990; Bell et al., 1993; Ellickson et al., 1993* | 4352 students in grade 7; a wide range of environments, racial and ethnic groups, and socioeconomic levels, 30 schools | 4 |
| Alert (adult health educator and teen | 4352 students in grades 7–8; a wide | 4 |

| Follow-up (months) | Outcome | Frequency distribution[a] | | | | | Effect size[b] | |
|---|---|---|---|---|---|---|---|---|
| | | −* | − | 0 | + | +* | | |
| 26 | Crime | 0 | 1 | 0 | 1 | 0 | .00 | (2) |
| | AOD | 0 | 1 | 0 | 2 | 1 | .06 | (4) |
| 12 | Drop-out/Truancy | 0 | 0 | 0 | 1 | 1 | | |
| | Anti-Soc./Aggr. | 0 | 0 | 0 | 0 | 1 | | |
| 1 | AOD | 0 | 0 | 0 | 1 | 0 | | |
| 1 | AOD | 0 | 0 | 0 | 0 | 1 | | |
| 1 | AOD | 0 | 0 | 0 | 0 | 1 | | |
| 36 | Crime | 0 | 1 | 0 | 0 | 0 | −.10 | (1) |
| | AOD | 1 | 0 | 0 | 0 | 0 | −.21* | (1) |
| 0 | Drop-out/Truancy | 0 | 0 | 0 | 0 | 2 | .36 | (1) |
| 6 | AOD | 0 | 0 | 0 | 1 | 1 | .22 | (2) |
| | Drop-out/Truancy | 0 | 0 | 0 | 2 | 0 | .17 | (2) |
| 5 | Anti-Soc./Aggr. | 0 | 0 | 0 | 1 | 1 | .33 | (2) |
| 0 | Anti-Soc./Aggr. | 0 | 1 | 0 | 0 | 0 | −.37 | (1) |
| 13.5 | AOD | 0 | 2 | 0 | 4 | 0 | −.02 | (2) |
| 0 | Anti-Soc./Aggr. | 0 | 0 | 0 | 1 | 0 | | |
| 12 | AOD | 0 | 0 | 0 | 0 | 1 | | |
| 13 | Crime | 0 | 0 | 1 | 0 | 1 | .00 | (1) |
| | Drop-out/Truancy | 0 | 0 | 0 | 1 | 3 | | |
| | Anti-Soc./Aggr. | 0 | 0 | 0 | 0 | 2 | | |
| 26 | AOD | 0 | 0 | 1 | 5 | 0 | .05 | (6) |
| 2 | AOD | 0 | 0 | 1 | 1 | 0 | .03 | (2) |
| 9 | AOD | 0 | 1 | 0 | 2 | 1 | .06 | (4) |
| 45 | AOD | 0 | 1 | 4 | 1 | 0 | .01 | (6) |

*Table 4.9* Continued

| Program name and citation | Students | Method rating |
|---|---|---|
| leader with booster)<br>*Ellickson and Bell, 1990; Bell et al., 1993;*<br>*Ellickson et al., 1993* | range of environments, racial and ethnic groups, and socioeconomic levels, 30 schools | |
| Alert (adult health educator only)<br>*Ellickson and Bell, 1990; Bell et al., 1993;*<br>*Ellickson et al., 1993* | 4352 students in grade 7; a wide range of environments, racial and ethnic groups, and socioeconomic levels, 30 schools | 4 |
| Alert (adult health educator only with booster)<br>*Ellickson and Bell, 1990; Bell et al.,*<br>*1993; Ellickson et al., 1993* | 4352 students in grades 7–8; a wide range of environments, racial and ethnic groups, and socioeconomic levels, 30 schools | 4 |
| Anger Control Training<br>*Feindler et al., 1984* | 36 students in middle school; disruptive students suspended at least twice in the previous year; a metropolitan area | 4 |
| Culturally Focused Intervention (CFI)<br>*Botvin, Schinke et al., 1995* | 527 students in grades 7–8; inner city, minority adolescents | 4 |
| Generic Skills Intervention/Life Skills Training (GSI)<br>*Botvin, Schinke et al., 1995* | 377 students in grades 7–8; inner city, minority adolescents | 4 |
| Life Skills Training (LST)<br>*Botvin, Baker, Botvin et al., 1984* | 239 students in grade 7; 2 New York City schools | 4 |
| Life Skills Training (LST) (peer led)<br>*Botvin et al., 1990; Botvin, Baker,*<br>*Renick et al., 1984* | 524 students in grade 7; predominantly white, middle-class, suburban students | 4 |
| Life Skills Training (LST) (peer led with booster)<br>*Botvin et al., 1990; Botvin, Baker,*<br>*Renick et al., 1984* | 524 students in grades 7–8; predominantly white, middle-class, suburban students | 4 |
| Life Skills Training (LST) (teacher led)<br>*Botvin et al., 1990; Botvin, Baker,*<br>*Renick et al., 1984* | 524 students in grade 7; predominantly white, middle-class, suburban students | 4 |
| Life Skills Training (LST) (teacher led with booster)<br>*Botvin et al., 1990; Botvin, Baker,*<br>*Renick et al., 1984* | 524 students in grades 7–8; predominantly white, middle-class, suburban students | 4 |
| Life Skills Training (LST): Teachers given training workshop and feedback<br>*Botvin, Baker et al., 1995* | 3755 students in grades 7–9; predominantly white, middle-class suburban and rural schools | 5 |
| Life Skills Training (LST): Teachers trained via videotape with no feedback<br>*Botvin, Baker et al., 1995* | 4095 students in grades 7–9; predominantly white, middle-class suburban and rural schools | 5 |
| Project SMART: Social Curriculum<br>*Hansen, Johnson et al., 1988;*<br>*Graham et al., 1990* | 2055 students in grade 7; ethnically diverse students from Los Angeles | 4 |
| Resistance Training<br>*Hansen and Graham, 1991* | 1659 students in grade 7; Los Angeles and Orange Counties, California | 4 |
| Responding in Peaceful and Positive Ways<br>*Farrell and Meyer, 1997* | 1274 students in grade 6; predominantly African-American in Richmond Public Schools | 4 |
| Second Step: A Violence Prevention Curriculum<br>*Orpinas et al., 1995* | 212 students in grade 6; 4 schools | 3 |
| Second Step: A Violence Prevention Curriculum<br>*Orpinas et al., 1995* | 159 students in grade 6; 4 schools | 3 |
| Smoking Deserves a Smart Answer<br>*Kaufman et al., 1994* | 276 students in grades 6–7; predominantly black neighborhoods | 4 |

| Follow-up (months) | Outcome | Frequency distribution[a] | | | | | Effect size[b] | |
|---|---|---|---|---|---|---|---|---|
| | | −* | − | 0 | + | +* | | |
| 9 | AOD | 0 | 0 | 0 | 3 | 1 | .08 | (4) |
| 45 | AOD | 1 | 1 | 1 | 2 | 1 | .01 | (6) |
| 1.25 | Anti-Soc./Aggr. | 0 | 0 | 0 | 1 | 3 | 1.39* | (4) |
| 19 | AOD | 0 | 2 | 0 | 4 | 0 | .20 | (2) |
| 19 | AOD | 0 | 0 | 0 | 6 | 0 | .10 | (2) |
| 6 | AOD | 1 | 1 | 0 | 1 | 3 | −.11 | (6) |
| 12 | AOD | 0 | 4 | 0 | 6 | 3 | .22 | (8) |
| 7 | AOD | 0 | 2 | 0 | 4 | 4 | .29* | (6) |
| 12 | AOD | 0 | 4 | 4 | 4 | 0 | .03 | (9) |
| 7 | AOD | 3 | 6 | 0 | 1 | 0 | −.24 | (6) |
| 36 | AOD | 0 | 1 | 1 | 3 | 1 | .07 | (6) |
| 36 | AOD | 0 | 0 | 0 | 5 | 1 | .13 | (6) |
| 19.5 | AOD | 0 | 0 | 0 | 3 | 0 | | |
| 12 | AOD | 0 | 1 | 0 | 1 | 0 | −.04 | (2) |
| | Anti-Soc./Aggr. | 0 | 0 | 0 | 1 | 0 | .13 | (1) |
| 0 | Crime | 0 | 0 | 0 | 2 | 0 | .05 | (2) |
| | AOD | 0 | 0 | 0 | 1 | 0 | .08 | (1) |
| 3 | Anti-Soc./Aggr. | 0 | 2 | 0 | 0 | 0 | | |
| 3 | Anti-Soc./Aggr. | 0 | 0 | 0 | 2 | 0 | | |
| 6 | AOD | 0 | 0 | 0 | 2 | 2 | .23 | (4) |

*Table 4.9* Continued

| Program name and citation | Students | Method rating |
|---|---|---|
| Social Competence Promotion (SCP) *Weissberg and Caplan, 1994* | 421 students in grades 5–8; 4 urban multi-ethnic schools | 4 |
| Substance Abuse Prevention Program *Shope, Copeland, Marcoux and Kamp, 1996* | 442 students in grades 6–7 | 3 |
| The Positive Youth Development Program *Caplan et al., 1992* | 282 students in grades 6–7; an inner-city and a suburban school in south-central Connecticut | 4 |
| **Elementary school grades** | | |
| Alcohol Misuse Prevention Study (AMPS) *Shope et al., 1992; Dielman et al., 1986; Dielman, Shope, Butchart et al., 1989; Dielman, Shope, Leech et al., 1989; Campanelli et al., 1989* | 1840 students in grade 5; 6 school districts in southeastern Michigan | 4 |
| Alcohol Misuse Prevention Study (AMPS) *Shope et al., 1992; Dielman et al., 1986; Dielman, Shope, Butchart et al., 1989; Dielman, Shope, Leech et al., 1989; Campanelli et al., 1989* | 1699 students in grades 5–6; 6 school districts in southeastern Michigan | 4 |
| BrainPower Program *Hudley, 1994* | 48 students in grades 4–6; "aggressive," African-American boys from urban, lower middle SES schools in Los Angeles | 5 |
| Children of Divorce Intervention Program (CODIP) *Pedro-Carroll and Alpert-Gillis, 1997* | 63 students in grades K-1; 4 suburban and 1 rural school in the Rochester, NY area with parental separation | 5 |
| Children of Divorce Intervention Program (CODIP) *Pedro-Carroll and Cowen, 1985* | 75 students in grades 3–6; white, middle-class children of divorce | 5 |
| Children of Divorce Intervention Program (CODIP) *Pedro-Carroll et al., 1986* | 132 students in grades 4–6; predominantly white, middle-class children of divorce | 3 |
| Cognitive Restructuring *Forman, 1980* | 13 students in grades 3–5; referred to school psychologist for aggressive behavior (inner-city school) | 4 |
| Earlscourt Social Skills Group Program (ESSGP) *Pepler et al., 1991* | 40 students in grades 2–6; students referred by teachers as aggressive, disruptive, and noncompliant | 3 |
| Fast Track *Conduct Problems Prevention Research Group, 1997; Coie, 1997* | 898 students in grades 1–4; children who demonstrated very high levels of conduct problem behaviors | 4 |
| Montreal Longitudinal Study *Tremblay et al., 1995; Tremblay et al., 1994; Tremblay et al., 1991; Tremblay et al., 1992; McCord et al., 1994* | 319 students in grades 2–3; disruptive boys from low socioeconomic neighborhood schools | 5 |
| Multicomponent Cognitive-Behavioral Intervention *Bloomquist et al., 1991* | 36 students in grades 1–4; students with mild to moderately severe ADHD from 3 suburban schools | 4 |
| PATHS – Promoting Alternative Thinking Strategies *Greenberg et al., 1995; Greenberg, 1996* | 286 students in grades 2–3; students in regular education classrooms | 4 |
| PATHS – Promoting Alternative Thinking Strategies *Greenberg et al., 1995; Greenberg, 1996* | 140 students in grades 1–3; at-risk students in special needs classrooms | 4 |

| Follow-up (months) | Outcome | Frequency distribution[a] | | | | | Effect size[b] | |
|---|---|---|---|---|---|---|---|---|
| | | −* | − | 0 | + | +* | | |
| 0 | AOD | 0 | 0 | 0 | 1 | 0 | .04 | (1) |
| | Anti-Soc./Aggr. | 0 | 0 | 0 | 0 | 1 | .20 | (1) |
| 0 | AOD | 0 | 0 | 0 | 1 | 4 | .26* | (5) |
| 0 | AOD | 0 | 0 | 0 | 0 | 3 | .37* | (3) |
| 26 | AOD | 1 | 3 | 1 | 1 | 0 | −.06 | (6) |
| 14.25 | AOD | 2 | 2 | 0 | 0 | 0 | −.11 | (4) |
| 3 | Anti-Soc./Aggr. | 0 | 0 | 0 | 1 | 2 | | |
| .5 | Anti-Soc./Aggr. | 0 | 0 | 0 | 1 | 0 | .30 | (1) |
| .5 | Anti-Soc./Aggr. | 0 | 0 | 0 | 1 | 0 | .25 | (1) |
| .5 | Anti-Soc./Aggr. | 0 | 0 | 0 | 2 | 0 | .05 | (2) |
| 0 | Anti-Soc./Aggr. | 0 | 0 | 0 | 4 | 1 | | |
| 0 | Anti-Soc./Aggr. | 0 | 0 | 0 | 0 | 1 | | |
| 0 | Anti-Soc./Aggr. | 0 | 0 | 0 | 0 | 1 | .28* | (1) |
| 72 | Crime | 0 | 3 | 0 | 1 | 9 | .24 | (7) |
| | Anti-Soc./Aggr. | 1 | 3 | 1 | 4 | 0 | −.21 | (2) |
| 1.5 | Anti-Soc./Aggr. | 0 | 1 | 0 | 3 | 0 | .23 | (2) |
| 24 | Anti-Soc./Aggr. | 0 | 0 | 0 | 1 | 3 | | |
| 24 | Anti-Soc./Aggr. | 0 | 0 | 0 | 2 | 1 | | |

*Table 4.9 Continued*

| Program name and citation | Students | Method rating |
|---|---|---|
| Peacemakers Program, Year II<br>*Shapiro and Paulson, 1998* | 2000 students in grades 4–8; Cleveland public schools | 3 |
| Planned Short-Term Intervention (PSI)<br>*Elkin et al., 1988* | 96 students in grades 2–5; urban and suburban Rochester, NY schools with no long-standing severe problems | 4 |
| Problem Solving<br>*Olexa and Forman, 1984* | 32 students in grades 4–5; students enrolled in Title I programs, 3 southeast schools | 3 |
| Problem Solving and Response Cost<br>*Olexa and Forman, 1984* | 32 students in grades 4–5; students enrolled in Title I programs, 3 southeast schools | 3 |
| Relaxation Training<br>*Amerikaner and Summerlin, 1982* | 31 students in grades 1–2; learning disabled students with no physical handicaps or extreme cultural or SES disadvantages | 4 |
| Second Step<br>*Grossman et al., 1997* | 790 students in grades 2–3; students in 12 urban and suburban schools in the state of Washington | 4 |
| Social Problem Solving Skills (full curricula)<br>*Gesten et al., 1982; Gesten et al., 1979* | 133 students in grades 2–3; suburban, lower middle-class, predominantly white schools (3 schools) | 3 |
| Social Problem Solving Skills (videotape curricula)<br>*Gesten et al., 1982; Gesten et al., 1979* | 133 students in grade 3; suburban, lower middle-class, predominantly white schools (3 schools) | 3 |
| Social Problem Solving (SPS)<br>*Weissberg, Gesten, Carnrike et al., 1981* | 563 students in grades 2–4; suburban and urban | 4 |
| Social Problem Solving Training<br>*Weissberg, Gesten, Rapkin et al., 1981* | 243 students in grade 3; 2 suburban schools | 3 |
| Social Relations Training Program<br>*Coie et al., 1991* | 49 students in grade 4; nominated by their peers as aggressive, rejected | 4 |
| Social Skills Group<br>*Amerikaner and Summerlin, 1982* | 31 students in grades 1–2; learning disabled students with no physical handicaps or extreme cultural or SES disadvantages | 4 |
| **Preschool and kindergarten** | | |
| Interpersonal Cognitive Problem Solving (ICPS)<br>*Shure and Spivack, 1982; Shure and Spivack, 1979; Shure and Spivack, 1980* | 110 students in grades Pre-K-K; black inner city children trained in nursery school and kindergarten | 4 |
| Interpersonal Cognitive Problem Solving (ICPS)<br>*Shure and Spivack, 1982; Shure and Spivack, 1979; Shure and Spivack, 1980* | 155 students in grades Pre-K-K; black inner city children trained in nursery school or kindergarten | 4 |

Notes

a  Frequency distribution represents the number of outcomes for which the program group out-performed the comparison group (positive effects) or the comparison group out-performed the program group (negative effects). Statistically significant positive and negative outcomes are reflected in the columns "+*" and "−*" respectively. Statistically nonsignificant effects or outcomes for which only the direction of effect was known are in the "+" and "−" columns.

| Follow-up (months) | Outcome | Frequency distribution[a] | | | | | Effect size[b] | |
|---|---|---|---|---|---|---|---|---|
| | | −* | − | 0 | + | +* | | |
| 0 | Crime | 0 | 0 | 0 | 0 | 1 | | |
| | Anti-Soc./Aggr. | 0 | 0 | 0 | 0 | 4 | | |
| 1.5 | Anti-Soc./Aggr. | 0 | 0 | 0 | 0 | 2 | .45 | (2) |
| 1.25 | Anti-Soc./Aggr. | 3 | 2 | 0 | 1 | 2 | .18 | (8) |
| 1.25 | Anti-Soc./Aggr. | 1 | 3 | 2 | 0 | 2 | .64 | (8) |
| .5 | Anti-Soc./Aggr. | 0 | 0 | 0 | 0 | 1 | 1.12* | (1) |
| 6 | Crime | 0 | 2 | 0 | 0 | 0 | −.05 | (2) |
| | Anti-Soc./Aggr. | 0 | 4 | 0 | 2 | 0 | −.02 | (4) |
| 12 | Anti-Soc./Aggr. | 0 | 1 | 0 | 0 | 1 | .17 | (2) |
| 12 | Anti-Soc./Aggr. | 0 | 1 | 0 | 0 | 1 | .42 | (2) |
| 1.5 | Anti-Soc./Aggr. | 0 | 0 | 1 | 0 | 0 | .00 | (1) |
| 1.5 | Anti-Soc./Aggr. | 0 | 0 | 0 | 0 | 1 | .40* | (1) |
| 12 | Anti-Soc./Aggr. | 0 | 0 | 0 | 2 | 0 | | |
| .5 | Anti-Soc./Aggr. | 0 | 1 | 0 | 0 | 0 | −.02 | (1) |
| 0 | Anti-Soc./Aggr. | 0 | 0 | 0 | 0 | 1 | 1.62* | (1) |
| 0 | Anti-Soc./Aggr. | 0 | 0 | 0 | 0 | 1 | 1.43* | (1) |

b The mean effect size is based only on those outcomes for which an effect size could be calculated. This may be fewer than the number of effects represented in the frequency distribution. Significance is based on the observed effect size data and may disagree with the frequency distribution if the authors performed a different test or used a different criterion, such as a one-tail test.

The ALERT study (methods rating = 4) was a multi-site experiment involving the entire seventh grade cohort of 30 junior high schools drawn from eight urban, suburban, and rural communities in California and Oregon. These 30 schools were randomly assigned to treatment and control conditions. Results are reported using individuals as the unit of analysis, although the investigators reported that results from school-level analyses supported the same conclusions with more positive results. Program effects were assessed directly after the seventh grade programs as well as before and directly after the eighth grade booster. Students were followed up again when they were in ninth, tenth, and twelfth grades. The program had positive effects for both low- and high-risk students and was equally effective in schools with high and low minority enrollment. The program's most consistent effects were found for marijuana use. It reduced the use of marijuana among students at each risk level, with the strongest effects for the lowest-risk group: those students who had not initiated either cigarette or marijuana use at the time of the baseline measurement. In this group, 8.3 percent of the ALERT students compared with 12.1 percent of the control students had initiated marijuana use by the end of the eighth grade booster. Small but statistically significant positive effects on the amount of marijuana used were observed for students who had previously initiated marijuana use after the seventh grade sessions, but these effects were no longer statistically significant (and were not practically meaningful) by the end of the booster session. For all groups, small positive program effects were initially observed for alcohol use, but they too eroded by grade 8, and one measure significantly favored the control group. The follow-up studies showed that once the lessons stop, so did the program's effects on drug use. Although some effects on cognitive risk factors persisted through grade 10, they were not sufficient to produce reductions in drug or alcohol use. In short, the program had significant positive effects, but the magnitude of these effects was small (e.g. they range from $-0.08$ to $+0.16$), most fail to reach nominal levels of statistical significance, and one is significant in the negative direction.

LST has also undergone rigorous tests in an ongoing series of studies first published in 1980, conducted by Botvin and his colleagues. The more recent studies examined the effect of the program on alcohol and marijuana use (in addition to cigarette use) and tracked long-term program effects. Botvin, Baker, Renick, Filazzola and Botvin (1984; methods rating = 4) examined the effectiveness of a 20-session course delivered to seventh graders from ten suburban New York junior high schools. The subjects were primarily white, from middle-class families. Schools were randomly assigned to receive the program as implemented by older students, by regular classroom teachers, or to serve as controls. All analyses were reported using individuals as the unit of analysis. Results measured immediately after the program showed that program students compared with control students were significantly less likely to report using marijuana and engage in excessive drinking, but these positive effects were found only for the peer-led condition. Botvin, Baker, Filazzola and Botvin (1990; methods rating = 4) reported on the 1-year follow-up of this study. This study contrasts not only the teacher- and peer-led conditions, but also the presence or absence of a ten-session booster course delivered during eighth grade. As with the ALERT study, the results showed that the effects of the program diminished without the booster. In the peer-led condition with the booster session, significant effects were maintained at the end of the eighth grade on the amount of alcohol and marijuana use. Again, positive effects were found only for the peer-led condition. In the peer-led condition with the booster, the average effect size was +0.29 ($p<.05$) for all measures of substance use. However, some significant negative effects were found in the teacher-led condition with the booster, and the average effect size across all substance use measures was −0.24.

In a larger study involving 56 public schools, the same twenty-session seventh grade program, ten-session booster session in eighth grade, and an additional five-session booster in the ninth grade was studied for long-term effects on substance use at twelfth grade (Botvin, Baker, Dusenbury, Botvin and Diaz, 1995; methods rating = 5). In this study, the 56 schools (serving mainly white, middle-class populations) were stratified according to baseline levels of cigarette smoking and geographic location and randomly assigned to experimental conditions. All results were reported using individual students as the level of analysis. This study involved only teacher-led classrooms. The twelfth grade results for the full sample of 3,597 subjects revealed significant positive effects on the prevalence of drunkenness, but not for other measures of alcohol use. Significant effects were not reported for marijuana use, although the effect sizes for marijuana use are often larger than the effect sizes for alcohol use. The lower base rate for marijuana use reduces the likelihood of finding statistically significant results for this outcome. When only subjects who received a reasonably complete version of the program were examined, the results were more positive. Additional research (Botvin, Batson *et al.*, 1989; Botvin, Dusenbury *et al.*, 1989) showed that the positive effects generalize to African American and Hispanic American populations.

Some curricula focus on social competency development and use cognitive-behavioral teaching methods, but do not emphasize substance abuse. Weissberg's social competence promotion program, for example, covers the entire array of social competency skills without tying them directly to any specific problem behavior. Problem-specific modules aimed at preventing antisocial and aggressive behavior, substance use, and high-risk sexual behavior are available. The program ranges in length from 16 to 29 sessions, depending on the version. Caplan *et al.* (1992; methods rating = 4) studied the effect of a twenty-session version of Weissberg's social competence promotion program aimed at stress management, self-esteem, problem-solving, substances and health information, assertiveness and social networks on 282 sixth and seventh graders in an inner-city and a suburban middle school in Connecticut. Classrooms were randomly assigned to receive the program or not. Results were reported using individuals as the unit of analysis. Students in program classes improved relative to students in the control classrooms on measures of problem-solving ability and stress management. Teacher ratings of the participating students improved relative to the controls on measures of conflict resolution with peers and impulse control, both important protective factors for later delinquency and popularity. Effects on self-reports of intentions to drink alcohol and use drugs were mixed. No significant difference was found for a self-report measure of *frequency* of cigarette, alcohol and marijuana use, but program students reported significantly less *excessive* drinking than controls (*ES*s range from 0.27 to 0.51). The program was as effective for students in the inner-city and the suburban schools.

In another study involving 447 students from twenty classes in four urban, multi-ethnic schools, Weissberg and Caplan (1994; methods rating = 4) evaluated a similar sixteen-session social competence promotion program for students in grades 5 through 8. This version of the program did not include lessons on substance use. It focused on teaching students: (a) impulse-control and stress-management skills, (b) thinking skills for identifying problem situations and associated feelings, (c) establishing positive pro-social goals, and (d) generating alternative solutions to social problems, anticipating the likely consequences of different actions, choosing the best course of action, and successfully enacting the solution. Random assignment to treatment and control conditions was not accomplished in this study. Program students improved more than controls on problem-solving abilities and pro-social attitudes towards conflict resolution. Teacher ratings indicated that the training improved impulse control, problem-solving and academic motivation, and decreased teasing of peers, important risk and protective factors for later delinquency. Self-reported delinquency of a relatively minor form (stealing, starting fights, vandalism, skipping school, etc.) also increased less for the program participants (2.8 percent increase) than for comparison students (36.8 percent increase) between the beginning and the end of the program. No significant effects were observed for self-reports of substance use in this study. Weissberg and Greenberg (1998) summarize another study which shows that the positive effects of the program are maintained in the year after the program only when the training is continued into the second year.

These examples show that social competency skill curricula utilizing cognitive-behavioral methods can be effective. Most effects are positive, but some are not. Certain programs (e.g. the Alcohol Misuse Prevention Study when delivered to fifth grade students and Plan A Safe Strategy) have uniformly negative effects. Some generally effective programs are effective only under certain conditions (e.g. with boosters or peer-led). Table 4.9 shows also that even when the programs are effective, the effects are generally small.

Positive effects of social competency skill curricula utilizing cognitive-behavioral methods are of a larger magnitude when drop-out, attendance and forms of antisocial behavior other than crime and drug use are the outcome variables. Only four studies have examined effects on school attendance and persistence, but all four have reported positive results, and three of the four have reported positive results that are statistically significant. One of these programs (Arbuthnot's Moral Reasoning Development Program) has already been discussed. Another is Sarason and Sarason's (1981; methods rating = 3) study of a program which relied on modeling and role-playing to teach cognitive and social skills to the general population of high school students. Different topics (e.g. cutting class, getting along with parents, getting along with a boss) were introduced during a semester-long class and students enacted desirable and undesirable ways of handling them.

Results showed that students' problem-solving skills improved. During the year after the intervention, participating students had lower rates of tardiness to school and referrals to the office for behavior problems.

Eggert's "Reconnecting Youth" program (the "Personal Growth Class" reported in Eggert *et al.*, 1994, and its predecessor, the "Interpersonal Relations" intervention reported in Eggert, Seyl and Nicholas, 1990; both methods rating = 3) provided interesting combinations of counseling and cognitive-behavioral skills training to high school students at-risk for drug use and school drop-out. The semester-long class focuses on group support and life skills training in a small-group setting. One trial of this intervention demonstrated a significant positive effect on truancy. Results from a second study were in the desirable direction, but did not reach statistical significance.

Table 4.9 reports on 37 different tests of the effectiveness of social competency curricula using cognitive behavioral methods on antisocial or aggressive behavior. The results, some of which have already been discussed, are generally positive. Spivak and Shure's Interpersonal Problem-Solving Skills (ICPS) program was one of the earliest attempts to apply cognitive training to very young children. This program helps children learn to generate alternative solutions to problems, become aware of the steps required to achieve a certain goal, consider consequences of actions, understand how events are causally related, and become more sensitive to interpersonal problems. The program is designed for use with children as young as 4 years old. More sophisticated skills are taught to children in the early elementary school grades. Using the program, teachers work with small groups of children for about 20 minutes per day, using scripts prepared for each lesson. The intervention lasts approximately 3 months.

Shure and Spivak (1979, 1980, 1982; methods rating = 4) tested the program with 219 inner-city African American nursery school children. One hundred thirteen of these subjects continued with the study through kindergarten. Some children received the training in nursery school only, others in kindergarten only, and others in both years. A fourth group received no training. The investigators measured both the specific interpersonal cognitive problem-solving skills targeted by the program and teachers' ratings of overt behavioral problems. Results showed that (a) students trained in nursery school improved significantly more than controls both on measures of ICPS skills and behavioral adjustment; (b) these improvements were still evident a year following training, even when no additional training was provided; (c) students trained for the first time in kindergarten improved significantly more than controls both on measures of ICPS skills and behavioral adjustment; and (d) students trained for 2 consecutive years scored higher than any other group on measures of ICPS, but a second year of training made no difference in terms of behavioral ratings (i.e. one year of training was sufficient and equally effective either year).

Feindler, Marriott and Iwata (1984; methods rating = 4) studied an anger control training program delivered to junior high school boys who were participating in an existing program for disruptive youths. These students had been suspended for offenses other than smoking or truancy at least twice during the previous year. The thirty-six most disruptive of these youths were selected and randomly assigned to receive anger management training or not. The program consisted of ten 50-minute sessions delivered by a trained therapist over a fairly brief (7 week) period. The sessions taught (in small groups of six youths) both behavioral and cognitive controls. Students were taught to analyze the components of the provocation cycle – the antecedent anger cues, aggressive responses, and consequent events – using self monitoring and written logs. They learned to impose their own time out responses and to relax themselves. They learned to replace aggressive responses (e.g. threatening gestures, harsh tones) with appropriate assertive verbal and non-verbal responses. They learned specific cognitive behaviors, including self-instructions (e.g. thinking, "I'm going to ignore this guy and keep cool"), reinterpretation of potentially aggression-eliciting situations, self-evaluation during conflict situations (e.g. thinking "How did I handle myself?"), and thinking ahead. They also learned a sequence of problem-solving steps to take in difficult situations instead of reacting impulsively. The therapist relied almost entirely on behavioral modeling, role-playing, rehearsal, cues and other cognitive-behavioral strategies to teach the new skills. Participants also received immediate reinforcers (e.g. Coke and snacks, activities) for participation.

The experimental students improved more than controls on an interview measure of problem-solving skills and on teacher ratings of self-control. Daily records of "fines" for misbehavior (a measure both of the student behavior and the staff's recording practices) were collected for 6 weeks prior to, 7 weeks during, and 5 weeks following the intervention. They showed a significant positive treatment effect on the more frequent category of fines for mild verbal and physical misbehaviors, such as cursing, arguing, shoving and throwing small objects. For more serious infractions, the trend favored the treatment subjects but the differences were not statistically significant, perhaps due to the relative infrequency of these behaviors, the short duration of the experiment, and the small number of subjects.

Amerikaner and Summerlin (1982; methods rating = 4) contrasted the effects of a relaxation training and a personal/social skills training intervention on the classroom behavior of learning disabled children. Relaxation training consisted of twelve 30-minute sessions of listening to prerecorded relaxation tapes and participating in exercises designed to help the children identify tension, learn to relax and practice relaxing. The personal/social skills sessions consisted of twelve 30-minute sessions designed to help the children understand themselves, learn to cope with feelings and learn to relate to peers in appropriate ways. Most of the sessions focused on helping children to understand why they are special, different and important. The personal-social skills group improved significantly in their comfort and self-acceptance in social situations. The relaxation training group, however, improved substantially on teacher reports of acting out behavior in the classroom.

The most ambitious school-based prevention effort aimed at young school children to date is FAST Track (Families and Schools Together; Conduct Problems Prevention Research Group, 1992, 1997; Coie, 1997; Dodge and Conduct Problems Prevention Research Group, 1993; methods rating = 4). The program was developed by a consortium of social scientists on the basis of developmental theory about the causes of conduct disorder in children and previous evaluations of specific, theory-based program components. It integrates five intervention components designed to promote competence in the family, child and school, and thus prevent conduct problems, poor social relations and school failure, all precursors of subsequent criminal behavior, during the elementary school years. The program involves training for parents in family management practices; frequent home visits by program staff to reinforce skills learned in the training, promote parental feelings of efficacy and enhance family organization; social skills coaching for children delivered by program staff and based on effective models described earlier; academic tutoring for children three times per week; and a classroom instructional program focusing on social competency skills coupled with classroom management strategies for the teacher. The program therefore includes several of the most effective school-based strategies summarized earlier as well as the most effective strategies from the family domain.

The participating schools and families work closely with the research team to implement the program in a strong fashion and support its evaluation. After 1 year of this intensive program, clear positive effects were evident on several of the intermediate behaviors targeted by the program (e.g. parent involvement in the child's education and child social-cognitive skills) and significantly less problem behavior was recorded by trained observers for the treatment than for the comparison children. Linear Growth Curve modeling of the data through the end of grade 3 shows that the treatment and control groups, initially equivalent on measures of conduct problems and behavioral adjustment, gradually diverged over the 3-year period following baseline. Teacher ratings showed increasing problems for the control, but not for the experimental group. Parent ratings showed decreasing problems for both groups, but more so for the treatment group. The intervention's significant effects on teacher-rated conduct problems were mediated in part by measures taken at the end of grades 2 and 3 of peer acceptance, non-hostile attributions and reading comprehension. Peer acceptance and positive changes in parent discipline and support partially mediated the positive effects on parent ratings of conduct problems. By grade 4, thirty-seven and forty-eight percent of the treatment and control students had received Individualized Education Plans, which are based primarily on diagnoses of Behavioral Disorder by school psychologists. These positive results for such a difficult population are encouraging and attest to the need for more comprehensive, theory-based, preventive interventions implemented with careful attention to strength and fidelity. The cost of such high-quality program development is high compared with typical expenditures on program development and evaluation: FAST Track's budget exceeds $1 million per year for each of the four program sites.

SUMMARY

The evidence suggests that instructional interventions that focus on social skill development and makes use of high levels of modeling and practice, provide specific and frequent feedback about new behaviors, provide cues to prompt the behavior, and use techniques to generalize the new behavior to different settings work to reduce crime (Arbuthnot and Gordon, 1986; Arbuthnot, 1992; Shapiro and Paulson, 1998; Tremblay *et al.*, 1991; Tremblay *et al.*, 1992; Tremblay *et al.*, 1994; Tremblay *et al.*, 1995; McCord *et al.*, 1994; average effect size = 0.08, $p > .05$). These interventions work to reduce substance use (several studies show significant positive effects.) Those with effect sizes greater than 0.10 are Kaufman *et al.*, 1994; Botvin *et al.*, 1990; Botvin, Baker, Renick *et al.*, 1984; Botvin, Baker *et al.*, 1995; Shope, Copeland, Marcoux and Kamp, 1996; Caplan *et al.*, 1992; average effect size for all studies = 0.05, $p < .05$), but their effects are small and sometimes moderated by other features of the study, such as who delivers the instruction. These interventions work to reduce school drop-out and truancy (Arbuthnot and Gordon, 1986; Arbuthnot, 1992; Sarason and Sarason, 1981; Eggert, Seyl and Nicholas, 1990; average effect size = 0.23, $p < .05$). And they work to reduce antisocial behavior and other conduct problems (several studies show significant positive effects). Those with the largest and most consistent effects are Amerikaner and Summerlin's (1982) relaxation training; Elkin *et al.* (1988); Feindler, Marriott and Iwata (1984); Conduct Problems Prevention Research Group (1997); Coie (1997); Shure and Spivak (1982, 1979, 1980); Weissberg and Caplan (1994). The average effect size for this outcome is .30, $p < .05$. These interventions can be tailored to any developmental stage. They have been shown to be effective with pre-school (Shure and Spivak, 1982, 1979, 1980), elementary (Amerikaner and Summerlin, 1982; Conduct Problems Prevention Research Group, 1997; Coie, 1997; Elkin *et al.*, 1988; Gesten *et al.*, 1982; Gesten *et al.*, 1979; Greenberg *et al.*, 1995; Hudley, 1994; Pepler, King and Byrd, 1991; Weissberg, Gesten, Rapkin *et al.*, 1981), junior high (Botvin *et al.*, 1990; Botvin, Baker, Renick *et al.*, 1984; Botvin, Baker *et al.*, 1995; Ellickson and Bell, 1990; Ellickson, Bell and McGuigan, 1993; Kaufman *et al.*, 1994; Shope, Copeland, Marcoux and Kamp, 1996; Caplan *et al.*, 1992; Feindler, Marriott and Iwata, 1984; Weissburg and Caplan, 1994) and senior high (Arbuthnot and Gordon, 1986; Arbuthnot, 1992; Hecht, Corman and Miller-Rassulo, 1993; Sarason and Sarason, 1981; Eggert, Seyl and Nicholas, 1990; Severson *et al.*, 1991; Shope, Copeland, Maharg and Dielman, 1996) levels.

## SOCIAL COMPETENCY SKILLS CURRICULUM WITHOUT COGNITIVE-BEHAVIORAL METHODS

The studies of instructional programs described so far have combined a substantive focus related to social competency skills with the use of cognitive-behavioral or behavioral modeling methods of instruction. Several programs focus on social competency skill instruction similar to the focus in the studies described previously, but they depend more on traditional methods of instruction – workbooks, lectures and some class discussion – than on utilizing more effective strategies including the use of cues, feedback, rehearsal, role-playing and so on. Studies of these programs are shown on Table 4.10.

Several studies in this category lacked the required level of methodological rigor to be included on the table. Eight different studies of DARE and one study of GREAT were among those excluded from the table due to low methods ratings. Of the remaining studies, only one included a measure of crime: Lindstrom (1996; methods rating = 4) found a negative effect (not significant) of DARE on crime. Two studies assessed effects on drop-out or truancy. Neither reported positive effects and a significant negative effect was found in one study (Gottfredson, Gottfredson and Skroban, 1996; methods rating = 4). Three different studies reported effects on antisocial behavior or other conduct problem (excluding substance use and crime). None reported significant positive effects and Gottfredson, Gottfredson and Skroban (1996; methods rating = 4) reported significant negative effects. The others (all studies of DARE) found non-significant effects favoring both the participants and the comparison groups. The preponderance of the evidence cannot support the effectiveness of these strategies for reducing crime, and the evidence suggests that such strategies *do not work* for reducing drop-out or truancy, or other conduct problems.

Many more of the studies measured effects on substance use. Because half of these are studies of DARE, it will be highlighted.[12] Developed in 1983 by the Los Angeles Police Department and the Los Angeles Unified School District, DARE is now the most frequently used substance use education curriculum in the United States. According to DARE America (Law Enforcement News, 1996), the program is now used by 70 percent of the nation's school districts and was projected to reach 25 million students in 1996. About 25,000 police officers are trained to teach DARE. It is also popular in other countries, forty-four of which have DARE programs. The complete array of DARE activities currently on the market includes "visitation" lessons in which police officers visit students in kindergarten through fourth grade for brief lessons on topics such as obeying laws, personal safety, and the helpful and harmful uses of medicines and drugs; a 17-week core curriculum for fifth or sixth graders (to be described shortly); a 10-week junior high school program focusing on resisting peer pressure, making choices, managing feelings of anger and aggression, and resolving conflicts; and a 10-week senior high program (co-taught with the teacher) on making choices and managing anger. In addition, DARE offers an after-school program for middle-school-aged students, called DARE + PLUS (Play and Learn Under Supervision). This provides a variety of fun activities for students during the after-school hours. Programs for parents and special education populations are also available.

The core 17-lesson curriculum delivered to students in grades 5 or 6 has always been the most frequently used form of the program. The great majority (81 percent) of school districts with DARE implement the core curriculum, while 33 percent use the visitations, 22 percent the junior high, 6 percent the senior high and 5 percent the parent curriculum (Ringwalt *et al.*, 1994). The core curriculum is the only part of the program that has undergone rigorous outcome evaluation.

The core DARE program is taught by a uniformed law enforcement officer. The original 17-lesson core curriculum focuses on teaching pupils the skills needed to recognize and resist social pressures to use drugs. It also contains lessons about drugs and their consequences, decision-making skills, self-esteem, and alternatives to drugs. Teaching techniques include lectures, group discussions, question and answer sessions, audiovisual materials, workbook exercises, and role-playing. The curriculum was revised in 1993 to substitute a lesson on conflict resolution and anger management skills for one on building support systems.

*Table 4.10* Self-control or social competency instruction without cognitive-behavioral or behavioral instructional methods

| Program name and citation | Students | Method rating |
|---|---|---|
| **Middle/junior high and high school grades** | | |
| Positive Alternatives for Youth (PAY)<br>*Cook et al., 1984* | 154 students in middle and high school; Milwaukee public schools | 4 |
| **Middle/junior high school grades** | | |
| Adolescent Decision-Making (ADM) Program<br>*Snow et al., 1992; Gersick et al., 1988* | 1372 students in grade 6; public school in two southern New England towns | 3 |
| DARE<br>*Clayton, Cattarello and Walden, 1991; Clayton, Cattarello, Day and Walden, 1991; Clayton et al., 1996* | 2071 students in grade 6; 31 schools in Lexington, KY | 4 |
| DARE<br>*Ennett et al., 1994* | 36 schools, grades 5–6; students reporting no lifetime alcohol use at pre-test | 4 |
| DARE<br>*Ennett et al., 1994* | 36 schools, grades 5–6; students reporting no current (past 30 day) alcohol use at pre-test | 4 |
| DARE<br>*Ennett et al., 1994* | 36 schools, grades 5–6; students reporting current (past 30 day) alcohol use at pre-test | 4 |
| DARE<br>*Lindstrom, 1996* | 1830 students in grade 7; students in 26 schools in Sweden | 4 |
| Iowa Strengthening Families Program (ISFP)<br>*Spoth et al., 1999* | 846 students in grade 6; 22 rural schools in a midwestern state | 4 |
| Project PRIDE (Positive Results in Drug Education)<br>*LoSciuto and Ausetts, 1988* | 1084 students in grades 6–7; Philadelphia School System | 3 |
| Project SMART: Affective Curriculum<br>*Hansen et al., 1988; Graham et al., 1990* | 2022 students in grade 7; ethnically diverse students from Los Angeles | 5 |
| Social Competency Promotion Program<br>*Gottfredson et al., 1996; Skroban et al., 1999* | 1450 students in grades 7–8; 92/93 cohort, predominantly residential areas | 4 |
| Social Competency Promotion Program<br>*Gottfredson et al., 1996; Skroban et al., 1999* | 1500 students in grades 7–8; 93/94 cohort, predominantly residential areas | 4 |
| Social Competency Promotion Program<br>*Gottfredson et al., 1996; Skroban et al., 1999* | 1473 students in grades 7–8; 94/95 cohort, predominantly residential areas | 4 |
| World Health Organization (WHO) Alcohol Education: Peer Led<br>*Perry et al., 1989* | 1572 students in grades 8–9; Australia, Chile, Norway, and Swaziland | 4 |
| World Health Organization (WHO) Alcohol Education: Teacher Led<br>*Perry et al., 1989* | 1474 students in grades 8–9; Australia, Chile, Norway, and Swaziland | 4 |
| **Elementary school grades** | | |
| DARE<br>*Becker et al., 1992* | 3109 students in grade 5; 63 schools representing a diversity of racial and ethnic backgrounds | 3 |
| DARE<br>*Harmon, 1993* | 708 students in grade 5; students from 11 elementary schools in Charleston County, South Carolina | 3 |
| DARE<br>*Ringwalt et al., 1991* | 1270 students in grades 5–6; 16 urban and 4 rural North Carolina schools | 4 |
| DARE<br>*Rosenbaum et al., 1994* | 1800 students in grades 5–6; 36 urban, suburban and rural schools | 4 |

Notes

a  Frequency distribution represents the number of outcomes for which the program group out-performed the comparison group (positive effects) or the comparison group out-performed the program group (negative effects). Statistically significant positive and negative outcomes are reflected in the columns "+*" and "−*" respectively. Statistically nonsignificant effects or outcomes for which only the direction of effect was known are in the "+" and "−" columns.

| Follow-up (months) | Outcome | Frequency distribution[a] | | | | | Effect size[b] | |
|---|---|---|---|---|---|---|---|---|
| | | −* | − | 0 | + | +* | | |
| 0 | AOD | 0 | 0 | 0 | 0 | 1 | | |
| 24 | AOD | 1 | 1 | 0 | 3 | 0 | −.02 | (5) |
| 48 | AOD | 1 | 1 | 1 | 4 | 1 | | |
| 19.5 | AOD | 0 | 2 | 0 | 4 | 0 | | |
| 19.5 | AOD | 0 | 4 | 0 | 2 | 0 | | |
| 19.5 | AOD | 0 | 1 | 0 | 2 | 0 | | |
| 0 | Crime | 0 | 1 | 0 | 0 | 0 | | |
| | AOD | 0 | 1 | 1 | 0 | 0 | −.02 | (2) |
| | Anti-Soc./Aggr. | 0 | 0 | 0 | 1 | 0 | .09 | (1) |
| 44 | AOD | 0 | 0 | 0 | 6 | 1 | | |
| 0 | AOD | 0 | 0 | 0 | 0 | 1 | | |
| 19.5 | AOD | 4 | 0 | 0 | 0 | 0 | | |
| 0 | AOD | 0 | 2 | 0 | 0 | 0 | | |
| | Drop-out/Truancy | 1 | 0 | 0 | 0 | 0 | | |
| | Anti-Soc./Aggr. | 1 | 1 | 0 | 0 | 0 | | |
| 0 | AOD | 0 | 2 | 0 | 0 | 0 | | |
| | Drop-out/Truancy | 0 | 1 | 0 | 0 | 0 | | |
| | Anti-Soc./Aggr. | 0 | 1 | 0 | 1 | 0 | | |
| 0 | AOD | 0 | 2 | 0 | 0 | 0 | −.07 | (2) |
| | Drop-out/Truancy | 1 | 0 | 0 | 0 | 0 | −.12* | (1) |
| | Anti-Soc./Aggr. | 3 | 0 | 0 | 0 | 0 | −.24* | (3) |
| 1 | AOD | 0 | 0 | 0 | 0 | 1 | | |
| 1 | AOD | 0 | 0 | 1 | 0 | 0 | .00 | (1) |
| 0 | AOD | 0 | 2 | 0 | 7 | 0 | | |
| 0 | AOD | 0 | 0 | 0 | 3 | 1 | .10 | (4) |
| | Anti-Soc./Aggr. | 0 | 0 | 0 | 1 | 0 | .08 | (1) |
| 0 | AOD | 0 | 0 | 0 | 2 | 0 | .11 | (2) |
| 12 | AOD | 0 | 1 | 0 | 0 | 0 | −.10 | (1) |
| | Drop-out/Truancy | 0 | 1 | 0 | 0 | 0 | | |
| | Anti-Soc./Aggr. | 0 | 1 | 0 | 0 | 0 | | |

b  The mean effect size is based only on those outcomes for which an effect size could be calculated. This may be fewer than the number of effects represented in the frequency distribution. Significance is based on the observed effect size data and may disagree with the frequency distribution if the authors performed a different test or used a different criterion, such as a one-tail test.

Several evaluations of the original 17-lesson core have been conducted. Those with acceptable methodological rigor are shown on Table 4.10. These studies provide 41 different measures of the effects of DARE on substance use. Of these, two (exactly the number that would be expected by chance if in fact the program had no effect) reach conventional levels of statistical significance favoring the DARE participants. One of the measures reaches conventional levels of statistical significance favoring the control students. Among the nonsignificant results, twice as many favor the participants as the non-participants. Looking at all studies of DARE (including those with low methodological rigor), the average effect size on measures of alcohol and other drug use is 0.02. Although DARE has a non-zero effect on measures of substance use, it is a trivial effect.

But do the non-DARE studies in this category do any better? Of the seven studies, four find significant positive effects favoring the program participants, and two find significant effects favoring the comparison group. Those finding positive effects included a "Positive Alternatives for Youth" class (Cook *et al.*, 1984; methods rating = 4), the Iowa Strengthening Families Program (Spoth, Redmond and Shin, 1999; methods rating = 4), Project PRIDE (LoSciuto and Ausetts, 1988; methods rating = 3), and the World Health Organization Alcohol Education program peer-led condition (Perry *et al.*, 1989; methods rating = 4). The Adolescent Decision-Making Program (Snow *et al.*, 1992; Gersick, Grady and Snow, 1988; methods rating = 3) found mixed results, one of which significantly favored the comparison group. And the affective curriculum[13] used for comparison with Project SMART (Hansen, Johnson *et al.*, 1988; Graham *et al.*, 1990; methods rating = 5) found four significant negative effects. Unfortunately, effect sizes cannot be computed from these studies so it is not possible to directly compare the magnitude of their effects against DARE's .02 effect, but the pattern of results seems only slightly more favorable than that of DARE.

Programs in this category appear relatively heterogeneous in their effects on substance use. Some apparently positive effects are deceptive. For example, Cook *et al.* (1984) reported on a semester-long "alternatives" class provided as part of the regular school curriculum in five public schools. The class focused on communication skills, self-concept, coping with stress and depression, and teaching students about healthy alternatives to drug use. In the first year of the program, hard liquor use declined for the experimental students and increased for the control students ($p < .01$), but no significant differences were observed for nine other drugs or for the overall drug use scale. Only the alcohol finding is displayed on Table 4.10 because the direction of the effects could not be ascertained for the other outcomes. The second year evaluation of the program produced no significant differences between the treatment and control subjects on any measures of substance use. Therefore, although the only result displayed in the table is a positive finding, the preponderance of evidence from this study suggests no effect.

Interestingly, two of the other studies in this category reporting positive effects (Spoth, Redmond and Shin, 1999; LoSciuto and Ausetts, 1988) combine a skill-training curriculum for adolescents with a parent training component. The Iowa Strengthening Families Program (ISFP; Spoth, Redmond and Shin, 1999) is unlike most other programs summarized in this chapter in that it emphasizes parenting skills at least as much as it does the skills of the child. It involves seven sessions in which parents learn family management skills and children learn social skills. Such programs are usually considered in the family domain, but this one was delivered in a school building and so is considered a school program. Similarly, the Project PRIDE evaluation (LoSciuto and Ausetts, 1988) included, in addition to twelve weekly small-group sessions for students focusing on developing a variety of social skills as well as "affective education," a parenting skills component of unknown intensity. Another program demonstrated positive effects on substance use only when it was delivered by peers as opposed to teachers (Perry *et al.*, 1989). Other non-DARE studies in this category (Snow *et al.*, 1992; Gersick, Grady and Snow, 1988; Hansen *et al.*, 1988; Gottfredson, Gottfredson and Skroban, 1996; Skroban, Gottfredson and Gottfredson, 1999) produced a range of effects, some negative. For example, a twelve-session cognitive skill development curriculum delivered to sixth grade students (Gersick, Grady and Snow, 1988) produced improvements in decision-making skills but not in substance use. In fact, more experimental (54 percent) than control students (48 percent) reported experimenting with alcohol immediately after the intervention, and this negative effect was also observed 2 years later when the students were in eighth grade.

We must conclude that the evidence regarding an effect of these programs on substance use is mixed. About as many negative as positive findings are found. The presence of both significant negative and significant positive effects suggests that more research is needed to better understand the active ingredients in these programs. Several variables might account for the heterogeneity of effects observed for studies in this category, including the age of the target population, specific content of the program, who delivers it, the extent to which it involves parents in the intervention, and how long it lasts. It is beyond the scope of this report to attempt to disentangle these possible explanations.

Table 4.17 shows that the average effect sizes across all outcomes examined and all studies in this category never exceeds 0.07 and is never significantly different from zero, despite the relatively large number of studies found in the category. The evidence suggests that these programs do not work to reduce attendance or conduct problems (Gottfredson, Gottfredson and Skroban, 1996; Skroban, Gottfredson and Gottfredson, 1999; Rosenbaum *et al.*, 1994), that the evidence for effects on crime are unknown and that the evidence for effects on substance use is mixed.

"OTHER" INSTRUCTIONAL PROGRAMS

Table 4.11 shows results for the final set of instructional programs – a residual category that could not be classified into the two major categories described above. These studies are conducted on an extremely heterogeneous group of programs. They have in common only that they do not focus on social competency promotion and they do not make heavy use of cognitive-behavioral teaching methods. Most of the studies show no effects. Among the few that show significant effects favoring the participants are two interventions conducted in residential or alternative school settings. These studies show significant positive effects for conduct problems within the alternative-school setting, but no evidence supports a generalization of those effects outside the restrictive setting.

The other two studies on the table showing significant effects include two drug education courses. Stuart (1974; methods rating = 4) randomly assigned junior high school students to an experimental drug education course or a control group. The experimental group received ten sessions of fact-oriented drug education. The method included lectures by teachers and presentations by students designed to communicate facts about the physiology and pharmacology of drug use and its legal, social, and psychological ramifications. The

*Table 4.11* Other instructional programs

| Program name and citation | Students | Method rating |
| --- | --- | --- |
| **High school grades** | | |
| Adolescents Training and Learning to Avoid Steroids (ATLAS) Program | 1506 students in grades 9–12; high school football players from 31 schools in Portland, Oregon | 3 |
| *Goldberg et al., 1996* | | |
| Alternative Schools: Alpha, Beta, and ACE | 240 students in high school; mostly disruptive and delinquent youths who would otherwise be excluded from school | 4 |
| *Gold and Mann, 1984* | | |
| Values Clarification | 72 students in grade 9; nondelinquent, average intelligence, orphaned or single-parent family boys in a residential school | 5 |
| *Thompson and Hudson, 1982* | | |
| Values Clarification Program | 217 students in high school | 3 |
| *Goodstadt and Sheppard, 1983* | | |
| **Middle/junior high school grades** | | |
| Affective and Cognitive Drug Education | 266 students in grades 6–7; a rural midwestern area | 3 |
| *Sarvela and McClendon, 1987* | | |
| Delinquency Vulnerability Prevention | 1094 students in grade 7; boys nominated by teachers and principals as headed for trouble with the law | 4 |
| *Reckless and Dinitz, 1972; Dinitz, 1982* | | |
| Drug Education | 935 students in grades 7–9; 2 suburban junior high schools | 4 |
| *Stuart, 1974* | | |
| Here's Looking at You, 2000 (curriculum only) | 895 students in grades 5–7; children from rural farm or rural non-farm towns in New Hampshire from 4 school districts | 3 |
| *Stevens et al., 1996* | | |
| HLAY 2000 (Here's Looking At You 2000) | 463 students in grades 7–8; Yadkin City, NC | 3 |
| *Kim et al., 1993* | | |
| **Elementary school grades** | | |
| Orientation Program (peer-led discussion group and/or slide presentation) | 87 students in grades 1–8; students from lower- to middle-income area on north side of Chicago | 5 |
| *Sloan et al., 1984* | | |

Notes
a  Frequency distribution represents the number of outcomes for which the program group out-performed the comparison group (positive effects) or the comparison group out-performed the program group (negative effects). Statistically significant positive and negative outcomes are reflected in the columns "+*" and "−*" respectively. Statistically nonsignificant effects or outcomes for which only the direction of effect was known are in the "+" and "−" columns.

study showed that the intervention *increased* drug use among the treatment students. Sarvela and McClendon (1987; methods rating = 3) compared an information-only curriculum to an experimental one that included drug information as well as "affective" education. The affective lessons included lectures and discussions about different lifestyles, values, alternatives to drug use and decision-making. The main emphasis was on values clarification. The youths exposed to this experimental curriculum (which was delivered primarily lecture-style with discussions) also *used alcohol more* at the end of the program than the control group. These negative effects were counterbalanced by positive effects or trends on the use of other drugs. These studies have

| Follow-up (months) | Outcome | Frequency distribution[a] | | | | | Effect size[b] | |
|---|---|---|---|---|---|---|---|---|
| | | −* | − | 0 | + | s+* | | |
| 8.75 | AOD | 0 | 1 | 0 | 1 | 0 | −.03 | (2) |
| 6 | Crime | 0 | 2 | 0 | 0 | 0 | | |
| | Anti-Soc./Aggr. | 0 | 0 | 0 | 2 | 1 | | |
| 3.75 | Anti-Soc./Aggr. | 0 | 0 | 0 | 0 | 1 | | |
| 6 | AOD | 1 | 0 | 0 | 0 | 0 | | |
| 0 | AOD | 2 | 0 | 0 | 2 | 1 | .05 | (5) |
| 39 | Crime | 0 | 2 | 0 | 0 | 0 | −.02 | (2) |
| | Drop-out/Truancy | 0 | 2 | 1 | 2 | 0 | .07 | (2) |
| 3 | Crime | 3 | 1 | 0 | 0 | 0 | −.23 | (4) |
| | AOD | 6 | 0 | 0 | 0 | 0 | −.26* | (6) |
| 27 | AOD | 0 | 0 | 0 | 2 | 0 | | |
| 0 | AOD | 0 | 1 | 0 | 1 | 0 | .11 | (2) |
| .25 | Drop-out/Truancy | 0 | 0 | 0 | 2 | 0 | | |
| | Anti-Soc./Aggr. | 0 | 0 | 0 | 1 | 0 | | |

b  The mean effect size is based only on those outcomes for which an effect size could be calculated. This may be fewer than the number of effects represented in the frequency distribution. Significance is based on the observed effect size data and may disagree with the frequency distribution if the authors performed a different test or used a different criterion, such as a one-tail test.

helped to guide the field away from instructional programs focusing on information and affective education and more towards social competency promotion. It is interesting, however, that the average effect size for measures of substance use for these programs is +0.08 (not significant). This effect size is small, but actually larger than the average effect size for the instructional programs that are generally thought of as more promising (see Table 4.17). The average effect size for these residual programs is elevated by one weak study (McAlister *et al.*, 1980; methods rating = 1) which reported significant positive findings, with an effect size of +0.54.

In summary, the evidence from these "residual" instructional programs suggest that they *do not work* to reduce crime (Gold and Mann, 1984; Stuart, 1974; Reckless and Dinitz, 1972; Dinitz, 1982) or drop-out/truancy (Reckless and Dinitz, 1972; Dinitz, 1982; Sloan, Jason and Bogat, 1984). Evidence is mixed regarding the effect of these programs on substance use, and evidence suggests that the programs are successful for reducing other conduct problems (Gold and Mann, 1984; Thompson and Hudson, 1982), but the supporting studies are both conducted in alternative or residential school settings.

A NOTE ON VIOLENCE-PREVENTION INSTRUCTION

Included in the instructional programs described in the forgoing section are programs that are often called "violence prevention programs." These are programs involving instruction focused on reducing violent behavior. These instructional programs are usually designed to improve students' social, problem-solving and anger management skills, promote beliefs favorable to nonviolence, and increase knowledge about conflict and violence. As noted above, relatively few evaluations of instructional programs have assessed program effects on actual violent behavior. The absence of rigorous evaluation of these programs has been noted in other reviews. For example, Brewer *et al.* (1995) summarize evaluations of eight violence prevention curricula and note that the quality of the evaluations of these programs is uniformly poor. No study used random assignment of subjects to treatment and comparison conditions. Only four of the studies assessed program effects on aggressive or violent behavior, and two of these studies suffered from serious methodological flaws. The other two studies reported positive results on measures of aggressive behavior, but no corresponding positive changes on attitudes towards violence. More recently, Drug Strategies (1998) summarized information about 84 currently available classroom-based educational programs aimed at preventing aggression and violence for the general student population. They searched for rigorous evaluations[14] of these programs and found none. They did find published evaluations that used pretest/post-test comparison group designs for eleven different programs, but only seven of these included measures of any problem behavior. These programs (and others which are not currently available to schools) are summarized in various sections of this report, depending on the content of the program. Table 4.12 provides a brief summary of selected violence prevention programs. This table excludes several elementary level programs designed to reduce problem behavior (e.g. Fast Track) but not usually considered violence prevention programs. The main summary tables include all school-based programs whose evaluations included an assessment of effects on violence or aggressive behavior. Table 4.12 includes only those programs that specifically target aggressive behavior or anger or are normally considered to be "violence prevention programs."

These programs are considered to "work," using the Maryland Report criteria because at least two positive significant findings have been reported and the preponderance of the evidence is positive. Also, recall that among all instructional programs (including those not currently available to schools), the evidence suggests a small but consistent positive effect on measures of crime for instructional programs that focus on teaching social competency skills and use cognitive-behavioral methods (Table 4.9), and for programs that establish norms against violence (Table 4.6). These more general findings accord with the specific findings for violence prevention curricula in

*Table 4.12* Summary of effects on violence and aggression of selected violence prevention curricula

| Program name | Table | Effects on aggression or violence |
| --- | --- | --- |
| Anger Control Training | 9 | Positive effects on four measures of aggression: 3 (S), 1 (NS) |
| BrainPower Program | 9 | Positive effects on aggression (S) |
| Bullying Prevention | 6 | Positive effects on antisocial behavior and bullying behavior (no significance tests reported) |
| Gang Resistance Education and Training (GREAT)[a] | 10 | Positive effects on six measures of crime: 2 (S), 4 (NS) |
| PACT[a] | 9 | Positive effect on suspensions (NS) |
| Peacebuilders | 6 | Positive effect on fighting-related injuries (S) |
| Peacemakers Program | 9 | Positive effects on suspensions for violent behavior, and four measures of aggression (S) |
| Reconnecting Youth | 9 | Eggert *et al.* (1995): two positive findings (1 S, 1 NS); one negative (NS) finding on anger |
| Responding in Peaceful and Positive Ways | 9 | Positive effects on violent and problem behavior (NS) |
| Safe Dates | 6 | Positive effects on sexual violence, dating violence (NS); positive effect on use of physical force (S) |
| Second Step | 9 | Grossman *et al.* (1997): five of seven measures of physical aggression/delinquency favor treatment group (NS) Orpinas *et al.* (1995): one positive and one negative effect on aggression (NS) |
| Social Competence Promotion | 9 | Positive effects on delinquent behavior (S) |
| Sociomoral Reasoning Development Reasoning Development | 9 | Positive effects on behavioral referrals at 6 and 18 months (S); positive effects on court/police contacts at 6 months (S), but not at 18 months |
| Think First[a] | 9 | Positive effects (NS) on aggression; positive effects (S) on incident referrals |
| Violence Prevention Curriculum for Adolescents | 9 | Positive effect on risk of suspension (NS) |

Notes
S = statistically significant; NS = statistically nonsignificant.
a Suppressed from main tables due to low methods rating.

Table 4.12. All of the significant effects from reasonably rigorous studies are for programs with a focus on normative change and that make use of cognitive-behavioral methods.

Instructional programs are the most common approach used by schools to reduce problem behavior. Our review of the more rigorous studies of this approach suggests that a certain class of these programs are effective for reducing crime, substance use, drop-out/truancy and other forms of anti-social behavior. Instructional interventions that teach social competency skills *and* make use of high levels of modeling and practice, provide specific and frequent feedback about new behaviors, provide cues to prompt the behavior, and use techniques to generalize the new behavior to different settings work.[15] The effects of other instructional programs, even those teaching important social competency skills, are less consistently positive and the effects are smaller. The evidence in favor of these other instructional programs is not sufficient to move them in to the "works" category.

Instructional programs using cognitive-behavioral methods do not have large effects on measures of problem behavior. Table 4.17 shows that the magnitude of the effects of such programs on crime and substance use is generally small (i.e. *ES*s less than 0.10). Several interventions aimed at changing the classroom or school environment, as opposed to individual behaviors, beliefs and attitudes discussed earlier, show larger effects on these outcomes. Also, considerable variability in the magnitude of effects is observed within the most effective instructional category. For example, the average effect on substance use for Botvin's Life Skills Training is +0.19, while for Alert it is +0.04. Alert's effects are only slightly greater than the average effect for DARE (+0.02), which is generally considered ineffective for reducing substance use. This small effect for instructional programs suggests that *no* instructional program is likely to have a dramatic effect on substance use. Replacing DARE in our nation's schools with Alert or even Life Skills Training is not likely to make a major difference. The small effects for instructional programs in general suggests that such programs should not form the centerpiece of the nation's drug prevention strategy. Rather, such programs should be embedded within more comprehensive programs using the additional strategies identified elsewhere in this chapter.

*Modifying behavior and teaching thinking skills*

The methods used in the most effective instructional programs are often used to reduce problem behaviors in the absence of a major curricular component. These activities involve either behavior modification or coaching and rehearsal in specific "thinking skills." Behavior modification interventions focus directly on changing behaviors by rewarding desired behavior and punishing undesired behavior. Several well-known programs for delinquent youths (e.g. Achievement Place) rely on these methods, as do many educational programs – especially those serving special education populations. Many programs for delinquent and "at-risk" populations also attempt to alter thinking skills. These "cognitive-behavioral training" interventions are based on a substantial body of research indicating that delinquents are deficient in a number of thinking skills necessary for social adaptation. Delinquents often do not think before they act, believe that what happens to them is due to fate or chance rather than to their own actions, misinterpret social cues, fail to consider alternative solutions to problems, and lack interpersonal skills necessary for effective communication. Programs often combine behavioral and cognitive methods in an attempt to alter immediate behavior and promote the generalization of behavior change to other settings.

As indicated above, instructional programs that rely on cognitive-behavioral methods, such as feedback, reinforcement and behavioral rehearsal, are the most effective for reducing substance use in the general population. Meta-analyses (Garrett, 1985; Izzo and Ross, 1990; Lipsey, 1992) have also concluded that the most effective delinquency prevention and treatment programs incorporate strategies aimed at developing social skills and using cognitive-behavioral strategies.

The programs reviewed below incorporate many of the same principles found in the more effective instructional programs. These programs differ in that they are often targeted at students identified as at especially high-risk for engaging in delinquent activities, are delivered in small groups or individually, and provide more intensive intervention than is possible with classroom-based instructional programs. A small number of these studies have applied behavioral methods to entire classrooms with favorable outcomes. These studies will be reviewed first, followed by summaries of a few of the many high-quality studies of interventions using behavioral and cognitive-behavioral methods at the individual level. All of the studies are shown in Table 4.13.

CLASSROOM-BASED STRATEGIES IN ELEMENTARY SCHOOLS

In a 3-year discipline management study implemented in nine schools, Mayer et al. (1983; methods rating = 4) demonstrated positive effects for a program that trained teams of school personnel to use behavioral strategies for reducing student vandalism and disruption. Each team also met regularly to plan and implement programs on a school-wide basis that would teach students alternative behavior to vandalism and disruption. These included lunch-room and playground management programs and classroom management programs that stressed the use of specific positive reinforcement. The school and classroom-management strategies incorporated into the program were behavioral, e.g. they involved behavioral analysis to identify and eliminate antecedent conditions that preceded disorderly events, identification and use of positive reinforcers, and so on. Graduate student consultants worked with each teacher about twice per week and conducted about two team meetings per month during the school year. The study showed that rates of student off-task behavior decreased significantly and vandalism costs plummeted in the project schools. These results replicated results from an earlier pilot study (Mayer and Butterworth, 1979; methods rating = 4). Note that in addition to relying on behavioral methods, the school team approach used in these studies resembles that used in the PDE method described

*Table 4.13* Cognitive-behavioral, behavioral modeling or behavior modification interventions

| Program name and citation | Students | Method rating |
|---|---|---|
| **High school grades** | | |
| Behavioral Group Counseling<br>*Thompson and Hudson, 1982* | 72 students in grade 9;<br>nondelinquent, average intelligence,<br>orphaned or single-parent family<br>boys in a residential school | 5 |
| Contingency Management<br>*Brooks, 1975* | 40 students in grades 9–12; students<br>with 9 or more days of truancy in<br>the first 8 weeks of school | 5 |
| **Middle/junior high and high school grades** | | |
| ACE (Academy for Community<br>Education)<br>*Gottfredson, 1990* | 135 students in grades 7–12; youths<br>at high-risk for delinquent behavior,<br>drawn from the Miami public<br>schools | 4 |
| **Middle/junior high school grades** | | |
| Behaviorally Based Preventive<br>Intervention (2 years of program plus<br>booster)<br>*Bry, 1982; Bry and George, 1979, 1980* | 80 students in grades 7–8; students<br>with low academic motivation,<br>family problems or discipline<br>referrals | 5 |
| Preparation through Responsive<br>Educational Programs (PREP)<br>*Wodarski and Filipczak, 1982; Filipczak<br>and Wodarski, 1982* | 60 students in grades 7–8; students<br>in a suburban school with academic<br>or social problems | 4 |
| Rational Behavior Therapy (RBT)<br>*Zelie et al., 1980* | 60 students in grades 7–9; a large<br>midwestern city, referred to the vice<br>principal for disciplinary action | 4 |
| **Elementary school grades** | | |
| Anger Coping<br>*Lochman, 1985, 1992; Lochman et al.,<br>1984; Lochman and Curry, 1986* | 83 students in grades 4–6; boys<br>identified by teachers as aggressive<br>and disruptive | 4 |
| Anger Coping and Goal Setting<br>*Lochman et al., 1984; Lochman et al.,<br>1985* | 76 students in grades 4–6; boys with<br>high teacher ratings of aggression | 4 |
| Anger Coping and Teacher Consultation<br>*Lochman et al., 1989* | 32 students in grades 4–6; boys with<br>high teacher ratings of aggression | 3 |
| Assertiveness/Social Skills Training<br>*Rotheram et al., 1982; Rotheram, 1982;<br>Rotheram, 1980* | 274 students in grades 4–6;<br>southern California | 4 |
| Behavioral Intervention Program for<br>Conduct Problem Children<br>*Kent and O'Leary, 1976* | 32 students in grades 2–4; students<br>(from 6 schools) with conduct<br>problems and academic difficulties | 4 |
| Behavioral Program to Modify Attendance<br>*Barber and Kagey, 1977* | 2120 students in grades 1–3; a<br>school ranked below the country's<br>other schools with regards to attendance | 3 |
| DUSO – Developing Understanding of Self<br>and Others Program<br>*Gerler, 1980* | 26 students in grade 0; a rural<br>central PA school district, virtually<br>none had attended day care or<br>nursery school | 4 |
| External and Self Regulation at Wave 5<br>*Bolstad and Johnson, 1972* | 45 students in grades 1–2;<br>disruptive students in 1st and<br>2nd grades in Eugene, OR from 9<br>classrooms | 4 |
| Good Behavior Game (GBG)<br>*Dolan et al., 1993; Kellam et al., 1994* | 289 students in grade 1 | 4 |
| HDP – Human Development Program<br>*Gerler, 1980* | 26 students in grade 0; a rural<br>central PA school district, virtually<br>none had attended day care or<br>nursery school | 4 |

| Follow-up (months) | Outcome | Frequency distribution[a] | | | | | Effect size[b] | |
|---|---|---|---|---|---|---|---|---|
| | | −* | − | 0 | + | +* | | |
| 3.75 | Anti-Soc./Aggr. | 0 | 0 | 0 | 0 | 1 | | |
| 0 | Drop-out/Truancy | 0 | 0 | 0 | 0 | 1 | 3.09* | (1) |
| 0 | Crime | 1 | 1 | 0 | 0 | 0 | −.18 | (2) |
| | AOD | 0 | 1 | 0 | 0 | 0 | −.21 | (1) |
| | Drop-out/Truancy | 0 | 0 | 0 | 2 | 0 | .35 | (2) |
| | Anti-Soc./Aggr. | 0 | 1 | 0 | 1 | 0 | −.18 | (2) |
| 60 | Crime | 0 | 0 | 1 | 0 | 2 | .57 | (2) |
| | AOD | 0 | 0 | 1 | 1 | 0 | .44 | (2) |
| | Drop-out/Truancy | 0 | 0 | 0 | 0 | 1 | | |
| 48 | Drop-out/Truancy | 0 | 0 | 0 | 1 | 0 | | |
| | Anti-Soc./Aggr. | 0 | 0 | 0 | 2 | 1 | | |
| 1.5 | Anti-Soc./Aggr. | 0 | 0 | 0 | 0 | 3 | 1.14* | (3) |
| 36 | AOD | 0 | 0 | 0 | 2 | 1 | .35 | (3) |
| | Crime | 0 | 0 | 0 | 1 | 0 | .12 | (1) |
| | Anti-Soc./Aggr. | 0 | 1 | 0 | 0 | 0 | −.22 | (1) |
| 1 | Anti-Soc./Aggr. | 0 | 0 | 0 | 0 | 2 | | |
| .75 | Anti-Soc./Aggr. | 0 | 0 | 0 | 1 | 1 | .64 | (2) |
| 12 | Anti-Soc./Aggr. | 0 | 0 | 0 | 0 | 2 | | |
| 9 | Anti-Soc./Aggr. | 0 | 1 | 0 | 0 | 2 | | |
| 1 | Drop-out/Truancy | 0 | 1 | 0 | 1 | 0 | | |
| 36 | Drop-out/Truancy | 0 | 0 | 0 | 1 | 2 | .94 | (3) |
| 0 | Anti-Soc./Aggr. | 0 | 0 | 0 | 0 | 1 | | |
| 0 | Anti-Soc./Aggr. | 0 | 0 | 0 | 1 | 1 | .26* | (2) |
| 36 | Drop-out/Truancy | 0 | 0 | 0 | 1 | 2 | .80 | (3) |

Table 4.13 Continued

| Program name and citation | Students | Method rating |
|---|---|---|
| Instructions<br>*Bierman et al., 1987* | 16 students in grades 1–3; peer rejected boys; rural predominantly white middle- to working-class schools | 5 |
| Prohibitions<br>*Bierman et al., 1987* | 16 students in grades 1–3; peer rejected boys; rural predominantly white middle- to working-class schools | 5 |
| Project Aware<br>*Elardo and Caldwell, 1979* | 68 students in grades 4–5; integrated inner-city schools | 3 |
| Response Cost<br>*Forman, 1980* | 13 students in grades 3–5; referred to school psychologist for aggressive behavior (inner-city school) | 4 |
| Response Cost<br>*Olexa and Forman, 1984* | 32 students in grades 4–5; enrolled in Title 1 programs, 3 southeast schools | 3 |
| Social Skills and Academic Training<br>*Coie and Krehbiel, 1984* | 20 students in grade 4; children identified as having both serious academic and social problems | 5 |
| Social Skills Training<br>*Coie and Krehbiel, 1984* | 20 students in grade 4; children identified as having both serious academic and social problems | 5 |
| Teacher-Only Intervention<br>*Bloomquist et al., 1991* | 52 students in grades 1–4; students with mild to moderately severe ADHD from 3 suburban schools | 4 |
| Vandalism and Violence Prevention<br>*Mayer and Butterworth, 1979* | 228 students in grades 4–6; mostly lower SES and minority areas | 4 |
| Vandalism and Violence Prevention<br>*Mayer et al., 1983* | 216 students in grades 4–8; Los Angeles County | 4 |
| First Step to Success<br>*Walker et al., 1998* | 46 students in grade 0; kindergarteners identified as at-risk for developing serious antisocial behavior patterns | 5 |

Notes

a  Frequency distribution represents the number of outcomes for which the program group out-performed the comparison group (positive effects) or the comparison group out-performed the program group (negative effects). Statistically significant positive and negative outcomes are reflected in the columns "+*" and "–*" respectively. Statistically nonsignificant effects or outcomes for which only the direction of effect was known are in the "+" and "–" columns.

above in the school management section. It is not possible to disentangle the separate contributions of these two effective strategies.

Dolan et al. (1993; methods rating = 4) and Kellam et al. (1994; methods rating = 4) reported on the Good Behavior Game (GBG):[16] a group-based behavior management program based on sound behavioral principles. Small student teams are formed within each classroom, and the teams are rewarded for achieving behavioral standards. Because the team reward depends upon the behavior of each member of the team, peer pressure is used constructively in this program to achieve positive behavior.

These strategies were tested separately in randomized trials in which nineteen schools were randomly assigned to receive ML, GBG or no program. Within each treatment school, first grade classrooms were randomly assigned to receive or not receive the program. Also, the incoming

| Follow-up (months) | Outcome | Frequency distribution[a] | | | | | Effect size[b] | |
|---|---|---|---|---|---|---|---|---|
| | | −* | − | 0 | + | +* | | |
| 12 | Anti-Soc./Aggr. | 1 | 0 | 0 | 1 | 1 | .59 | (2) |
| 12 | Anti-Soc./Aggr. | 1 | 0 | 0 | 0 | 2 | .65 | (2) |
| 0 | Anti-Soc./Aggr. | 0 | 0 | 0 | 0 | 1 | | |
| 0 | Anti-Soc./Aggr. | 0 | 1 | 0 | 2 | 2 | | |
| 1.25 | Anti-Soc./Aggr. | 5 | 1 | 1 | 1 | 0 | −.59 | (8) |
| 1 | Anti-Soc./Aggr. | 0 | 1 | 1 | 1 | 0 | .00 | (1) |
| 1 | Anti-Soc./Aggr. | 0 | 2 | 0 | 1 | 0 | | |
| 1.5 | Anti-Soc./Aggr. | 0 | 3 | 0 | 1 | 0 | −.17 | (2) |
| 0 | Anti-Soc./Aggr. | 0 | 0 | 0 | 0 | 1 | | |
| 0 | Anti-Soc./Aggr. | 0 | 0 | 0 | 0 | 1 | | |
| 0 | Anti-Soc./Aggr. | 0 | 0 | 0 | 0 | 2 | 1.09* | (2) |

b  The mean effect size is based only on those outcomes for which an effect size could be calculated. This may be fewer than the number of effects represented in the frequency distribution. Significance is based on the observed effect size data and may disagree with the frequency distribution if the authors performed a different test or used a different criterion, such as a one-tail test.

first graders were randomly assigned to these conditions. Hence, two comparison groups, one internal and one external, were available. This design feature allowed a control against the possibility of spill-over effects to control classrooms in the same schools. The program lasted for 2 years. Only students who stayed in their schools for an entire year ($n = 864$) were included in the analysis of first-year outcomes. Academic achievement and aggressive behavior (rated by both teachers and peers) were measured.

At the end of the first year of the program, the results were somewhat inconsistent, both across genders and depending upon which measure of aggressiveness and control group was used. Comparing with control classrooms in the same school, GBG males were rated by their peers but not by their teachers as significantly less aggressive at the end of the first grade. The opposite pattern was found for females: teacher ratings but not peer ratings of aggression were significantly lower for GBG students. Compared to control classrooms in different schools, GBG males were rated by their teachers but not by their peers as less aggressive at the end of the first grade, and none of the comparisons of GBG females with the external controls showed significant differences. Kellam and Rebok (1992) recommended caution in interpreting the teacher ratings, as the teachers were responsible for delivering the intervention. Our analysis pooled data for males and females, teacher and peer raters and found an overall significant effect of the intervention on aggressive behavior.

Kellam *et al.* (1994) reported the results of a follow-up at sixth grade. Only students who had experienced 2 full years of the intervention (in grades 1 and 2) and took part in the 6-year follow-up assessment ($n = 590$) were retained in the analysis. The early positive effects of GBG on aggression were no longer evident for the total population of females or males (not shown on Table 4.13 because the direction of the effect could not be ascertained). When subgroups of subjects who differed on their levels of teacher-observed first grade aggression were examined, a significant reduction in teacher-rated aggression at grade 6 was observed, but only for males at or above the median on first grade aggressive behavior. These post-hoc subgroup findings are based on a post-hoc design of lower scientific rigor.

INDIVIDUALLY TARGETED BEHAVIORAL AND COGNITIVE-BEHAVIORAL
STRATEGIES

Three of the highest quality studies in this category contrasted different forms of cognitive and behavioral training applied to high-risk populations. Coie and Krehbiel (1984; methods rating = 5) compared an intensive academic skills program with a social skills training program which involved coaching and practice in skills necessary for positive interaction with peers. In their work, the academic skills training (discussed later and shown in Table 4.15) improved academic achievement, peer acceptance, and classroom behavior. The groups receiving social skills training also improved on some measures of reading achievement (although these effects were not sustained 1 year later) and on peer ratings of social status. Neither group improved significantly in terms of their disruptive behavior, although the academic skills training group tended in the positive direction. The authors noted that very little aversive behavior was observed either before or after the intervention, and suggested that their classroom observations of aversive behavior may not have been sufficiently sensitive. Peer ratings, which did evidence positive effects, may be more sensitive to changes in behavior.

Bierman, Miller and Stabb (1987; methods rating = 5) extended this work by testing the effectiveness of a behavior modification component which directly rewarded compliance with rules. They randomly assigned peer-rejected boys to receive social skills instruction and coaching (the "instructions" condition), a set of rules and the application of a response cost procedure that removed rewards when rules were violated (the "prohibitions" condition), or a combination of the strategies. The "prohibitions" condition led to immediate and sustained reductions (after 6 weeks) in observed negative behavior. The "instructions" condition was not immediately effective, but resulted in longer-term improvement of observed negative behaviors. Interestingly, neither condition was effective for reducing teacher or peer ratings of aggression, suggesting that it is more difficult to change the reputation of aggressive boys than it is to change their actual behavior. Forman (1980; methods rating = 4) showed that brief cognitive training and behavioral interventions decrease aggressive behavior relative to a brief tutoring condition, although the behavioral intervention decreased disruptive behavior to a somewhat greater extent than the cognitive intervention. Taken together, these studies suggest that aggressive and antisocial behavior responds both to direct behavioral intervention and to coaching in cognitive-behavioral skills.

Lochman's work with highly aggressive boys is reported in a series of research articles beginning in the mid 1980s. Lochman's anger-coping intervention is based on research showing that aggressive children tend to attribute hostility to other people's intentions and to misperceive their own aggressiveness and responsibility for conflict. In addition to targeting specific cognitive skills (shown in Box 4.7), the intervention uses behavioral techniques (operant conditioning) to reward compliance with group rules. The program is targeted at boys in grades 4 through 6 who are identified as aggressive and disruptive by their teachers. A school counselor and a mental health professional from a Community Guidance Clinic co-led groups of aggressive boys for twelve to eighteen group sessions, each 45 minutes to an hour. Importantly, this cognitive training is augmented with teacher consultation in which the mental health professional running the children's group assists the children's regular teachers in classroom management in general and in helping the targeted youths generalize new skills to the regular classroom.

---

**Box 4.7**

- Establishing group rules and contingent reinforcements
- Using self-statements to inhibit impulsive behavior
- Identifying problems and social perspective-taking
- Generating alternative solutions and considering the consequences to social problems
- Modeling videotapes of children becoming aware of physiological arousal when angry, using self-statements, and using a set of problem-solving skills to solve social problems
- Having the boys plan and make their own videotape of inhibitory self-statements and social problem solving
- Dialoging, discussion and role-playing to implement social problem solving skills with children's current anger arousal problems

---

The effectiveness of this "anger coping" intervention was investigated in a series of studies which systematically varied features of the program to learn more about its essential elements. In one study (Lochman *et al.*, 1984; methods rating = 4), 76 boys from eight elementary schools ranging in age from 9 to 12 were studied. They were not randomly assigned to experimental conditions, but pre-treatment measures showed the groups to be similar on the outcome measures of interest. In comparison to aggressive boys receiving no treatment or minimal treatment, aggressive treatment group boys reduced their disruptive-aggressive off-task behavior in school and their aggressive behavior as rated by their parents directly after the intervention. A 3-year follow-up study was conducted when these and some boys from other earlier studies were 15-years old (Lochman, 1992; methods rating = 4). The study found that the intervention had a significant effect on self-reported alcohol and substance use, but no significant effect on self-reported criminal behavior. It can be argued that a reduction in delinquency of this magnitude ($ES = 0.12$, approximately equivalent to a 5-percentage point difference in crime rate between the treatment and control group) in a highly delinquent population is practically meaningful even if it is not statistically significant. Also, the treatment group in this follow-up study was significantly younger than the comparison group, which worked against finding program effects as younger age was associated with higher rates of delinquency.

Other studies that stand out as exceptionally rigorous demonstrations of the efficacy of this type of intervention strategy are Walker *et al.*'s (1998; methods rating = 5) "First Step to Success" and Thompson and Hudson's (1982; methods rating = 5) Behavioral Group Counseling. Walker *et al.* (1998) randomly assigned at-risk kindergarteners to receive the program or to a wait-list control group. Students in the intervention group were exposed to 3 months of school and parent intervention. The school-based intervention is a behavior modification program delivered first by a trained consultant during the classroom period, and then taken over by the regular classroom teacher (who is trained and supported by the consultant). The parent intervention consists of six parent training lessons designed to assist parents in helping their children adjust to school and perform well. Teacher reports of aggressive and maladaptive behavior declined substantially following the treatment.

Thompson and Hudson (1982) contrasted the effects of behavioral group counseling with a values clarification intervention delivered to orphaned ninth grade boys in a residential home. Behavioral counseling consisted of 15 weeks of weekly meetings during which a counselor trained in behavioral counseling procedures led activities aimed at understanding problems in behavioral terms and helping students to modify their behaviors. Behavioral techniques included role playing, rational behavior therapy, environmental manipulation and contracting. During the 15-week post-treatment phase, the behavioral counseling group had significantly fewer acts of maladaptive behavior than did the control group or placebo groups.

Interventions relying solely on behavior modification strategies have also been successful. Brooks (1975; methods rating = 5) studied a contingency management approach to reducing truancy among high school students. Students carried daily attendance cards, had all of their teachers sign them, and were rewarded with tickets at the end of each day according to the number of teacher signatures and positive comments they received. Tickets were periodically exchanged for chances to win prizes. The intervention period lasted 8 weeks. Truancy dropped dramatically for the treatment students and increased for a randomly assigned control group.

Bry's work also used behavioral monitoring and reinforcement with high-risk youths and measured each of the four outcomes included in this analysis. In this intervention, junior high school students' tardiness, class preparedness, class performance, classroom behavior, school attendance and disciplinary referrals were monitored weekly for 2 years. Students met with program staff weekly and earned points contingent on their behavior which could be used for a class trip of the students' choosing. Frequent parent notification was used. Bry conducted two studies, both involving random assignment of high-risk youths to receive behavioral monitoring and reinforcement or not. A third study reported on the long-term follow-up of the subjects from the earlier studies. In the first study of students in two suburban schools (Bry and George, 1979; methods rating = 5), experimental students in one of the two schools had significantly better grades and attendance at the end of the program than did controls. In the replication study involving urban schools, experimental students received significantly better grades and had better attendance (Bry and George, 1980; methods rating = 5). Bry (1982; methods rating = 5) reports that in the year after the intervention ended, experimental students displayed significantly fewer problem behaviors at school than did controls and experimental students reported significantly less substance use and criminal behavior. These differences were marginally significant ($p < .10$) in this underpowered study. Five years after the program ended, experimental youth were 66 percent less likely to have a juvenile record than were controls.

SUMMARY

The studies included in this category are among the most rigorous studies of school-based prevention, with an average methods rating of 3.9 (see Table 4.3). These rigorous studies of targeted behavior modification and cognitive skill-training demonstrate clear positive effects on school attendance and persistence (Brooks, 1975; Bry and George, 1979, 1980; Bry, 1982; Gerler, 1980) and aggressive, antisocial behavior (studies finding significant positive effects are too numerous to list). Only one study in this category found an overall significant negative effect, and it was for a brief (8-week) response cost intervention for which the teachers were not well trained, according to the authors (Olexa and Forman, 1984). The effect sizes for studies in this category are among the highest observed for any school-based strategy, and they are observed at all levels of schooling and for group contingency behavior management strategies (e.g. Dolan *et al.*, 1993) as well as for individually-targeted programs. Only a handful of studies reported results on crime or substance use. Bry showed a statistically significant reduction for criminal behavior and a marginally significant reduction in substance use, and these results are from two different studies. Lochman (1992) also reported a significant reduction in substance use. One study (Gottfredson, 1990) reported a significant negative effect on self-reported delinquent behavior. This was for a study of a token reinforcement system implemented in an alternative school for delinquents.

Using cognitive behavioral methods, behavioral modeling and behavior modification methods works to increase school attendance and persistence ($\overline{ES} = 1.10$, $p < .05$), and aggressive and antisocial behavior ($\overline{ES} = 0.34$, $p < .05$). The limited evidence on substance use and criminal behavior suggests positive effects, but must be considered mixed due to the negative results from one study conducted in an alternative school setting.

## Counseling, social work, and other therapeutic interventions

Many studies have examined the effect of counseling interventions on delinquency. Lipsey's (1992) meta-analysis of juvenile delinquency treatment effects shows that, for juvenile justice and non-juvenile justice interventions alike, counseling interventions are among the least effective for reducing delinquency. Twenty-four studies of individual counseling in non-juvenile justice settings yielded an effect size of −0.01 on measures of recidivism. These programs are not necessarily school-based.

A popular form of school-based counseling is the Student Assistance Program (SAP). These programs are among the most common programs found in schools, accounting for approximately half of the expenditures of Drug-Free Schools and Communities funds (Hansen and O'Malley, 1996, citing General Accounting Office, 1993) administered through the US Department of Education. These programs involve group counseling for students with alcoholic parents, counseling for students who are using drugs or alcohol or whose poor academic performance places them at risk for substance use, and work with parent and community groups to develop ways of dealing with substance abuse problems. Often the peers of student clients are involved as crisis managers, group facilitators and referral agents. SAP counselors are school-based but employed by mental health departments or other outside agencies. After surveying the scant literature on the effectiveness of SAP programs, Hansen and O'Malley (1996) concluded that evaluations are "universally absent."

*Table 4.14* Counseling, social work and other therapeutic interventions

| Program name and citation | Students | Method rating |
|---|---|---|
| **High school grades** | | |
| Peer Culture Development (PCD) | 180 students in high school; | 2 |
| *Gottfredson, G.D. 1987* | Chicago public schools | |
| **Middle/junior high school grades** | | |
| Explicit Bibliotherapy | 33 students in grades 7–9; schools | 4 |
| *Sheridan et al., 1984* | in State College, PA | |
| Group Counseling (structured aural, | 96 students in grade 6; an | 5 |
| structured visual, and unstructured) | upper/middle-class elementary | |
| *Crow, 1971* | school in Texas | |
| Structured Group Counseling | 32 students in grades 7–9; schools | 4 |
| *Sheridan et al., 1984* | in State College, PA | |
| **Elementary school grades** | | |
| Peer Culture Development (PCD) | 180 students in upper elementary; | 4 |
| *Gottfredson, G.D. 1987* | Chicago public schools | |

Notes
a  Frequency distribution represents the number of outcomes for which the program group out-performed the comparison group (positive effects) or the comparison group out-performed the program group (negative effects). Statistically significant positive and negative outcomes are reflected in the columns "+*" and "−*" respectively. Statistically nonsignificant effects or outcomes for which only the direction of effect was known are in the "+" and "−" columns.

Low rigor is a general problem in evaluations of school-based counseling and similar interventions. We located five studies of school-based counseling interventions containing eight treatment-control comparisons. Only five of these comparisons from three studies are of sufficiently high rigor to be included on Table 4.14. The average rigor of the studies in this category (2.9; see Table 4.3) is the lowest of all categories.

No conclusive statement about the effectiveness of school-based counseling programs on crime or substance use can be derived from the studies shown on Table 4.14. One studied peer group counseling, a popular method used both in schools and in treatment programs for at-risk youths and adjudicated delinquents. This type of counseling usually involves an adult leader guiding group discussions in which participants are encouraged to recognize problems with their own behavior, attitudes and values. Peer pressure to adopt pro-social attitudes is expected to occur. G.D. Gottfredson (1987; methods rating = 2 and 4 for the high school and elementary school comparisons) reviewed evidence pertaining to peer group counseling programs in general and evaluated the strategy in a large-scale school-based program. As many negative as positive effects were found in the elementary version of the program, and the one significant positive effect (on self-reported attendance) was not supported by official attendance records. In the high school program, treatment youths reported significantly more delinquent behavior, more drug use and more tardiness to school. Presumably, these interventions backfire when students are brought into closer association with negative

| Follow-up (months) | Outcome | Frequency distribution[a] | | | | | Effect size[b] | |
|---|---|---|---|---|---|---|---|---|
| | | −* | − | 0 | + | +* | | |
| 0 | Crime | 1 | 1 | 0 | 0 | 0 | −.21 | (2) |
| | AOD | 1 | 0 | 0 | 0 | 0 | −.39* | (1) |
| | Drop-out/Truancy | 1 | 2 | 0 | 0 | 0 | −.12 | (1) |
| | Anti-Soc./Aggr. | 0 | 1 | 0 | 2 | 0 | .03 | (3) |
| 0 | Drop-out/Truancy | 0 | 0 | 0 | 1 | 0 | .03 | (1) |
| | Anti-Soc./Aggr. | 0 | 0 | 0 | 1 | 0 | .10 | (1) |
| 0 | Anti-Soc./Aggr. | 0 | 0 | 0 | 1 | 0 | | |
| 0 | Drop-out/Truancy | 0 | 1 | 0 | 0 | 0 | −.15 | (1) |
| | Anti-Soc./Aggr. | 0 | 0 | 0 | 1 | 0 | .36 | (1) |
| 0 | Crime | 0 | 1 | 0 | 1 | 0 | −.18 | (1) |
| | AOD | 0 | 0 | 1 | 0 | 0 | .00 | (1) |
| | Drop-out/Truancy | 0 | 2 | 0 | 0 | 1 | .08 | (3) |
| | Anti-Soc./Aggr. | 0 | 1 | 0 | 2 | 0 | .05 | (3) |

b The mean effect size is based only on those outcomes for which an effect size could be calculated. This may be fewer than the number of effects represented in the frequency distribution. Significance is based on the observed effect size data and may disagree with the frequency distribution if the authors performed a different test or used a different criterion, such as a one-tail test.

peers during the peer counseling sessions. Gottfredson also notes that frequent discussions of parent/home issues in the groups may have led to a weakening of parental bonding (which was measured and found to be lower among treatment students) and a subsequent increase in delinquency. No other studies measured effects on drug use or delinquency. Replication is needed.

Effects on other outcomes in the counseling studies (truancy, drop-out and antisocial or aggressive behavior) failed to find any positive effects. Two different studies of reasonable rigor failed to find significant effects on truancy or drop-out (G.D. Gottfredson, 1987; Sheridan, Baker and Lissovoy, 1984) and three failed to find positive effects on antisocial behavior (Crow, 1971; G.D. Gottfredson, 1987; Sheridan, Baker and Lissovoy, 1984).

SUMMARY

School-based counseling approaches to crime reduction show no promise for reducing substance use or crime. G.D. Gottfredson (1987) found null or negative effects on crime and substance use in two comparisons involving separate populations, and the mean effect sizes across all studies are $-0.37$ ($p < .05$) for crime and $-0.19$ ($p > .05$) for substance use. However, only one study of sufficient methodological rigor has been conducted, so it is premature to conclude that such programs do not work to reduce these outcomes. Two or more studies are available to assess the effects on other outcomes, however. These studies suggest that school-based counseling *does not work* to reduce truancy or drop-out (G.D. Gottfredson, 1987; Sheridan, Baker and Lissovoy, 1984) or antisocial behavior (Crow, 1971; G.D. Gottfredson, 1987; Sheridan, Baker and Lissovoy, 1984). The average effect sizes across all studies in this category (shown in Table 4.17) suggest a negative effect on crime, substance use and truancy/drop-out ($\overline{ES} = -0.13$, $p > .05$), and a small, nonsignificant positive effect on antisocial behavior ($\overline{ES} = 0.06$, $p > .05$).

*Mentoring, tutoring, and work study*

Several studies have examined the effect of providing youths (usually at elevated risk for problem behavior) with special attention in the form of tutoring, mentoring or apprenticeship. These strategies usually involve one-on-one interaction with an older, more experienced person to provide advice or assistance. They are differentiated from counseling in that the older adult is generally not a professional counselor, and the interaction is generally not focused on the individuals' problem behavior. Such strategies – especially mentoring – have become popular as delinquency prevention strategies. OJJDP's allocation for juvenile mentoring programs for fiscal year 2000 is $13.5 million.

Studies of these individual-attention strategies are shown on Table 4.15. The most rigorous study is of the Quantum Opportunities program by Hahn, Leavitt and Aaron (1994; methods rating = 4). This program provides both in- and out-of-school services to disadvantaged high school students. This program stands out from all others of its type (that have been evaluated) by providing intensive, long-term services, as well as cash and scholarship incentives for participants. The program spans the four high school years (including summers) and includes 250 hours *each year* of each of the following services: academic assistance (e.g. computer-assisted instruction, peer tutoring, homework assistance), service activities (e.g. community service activities, jobs) and a curriculum focusing on life/family skills and planning for college and jobs. Services are provided in the community during the after-school hours and in some sites the school provided space for the program. Participating students receive hourly stipends and bonuses for their participation.

A randomized experiment was used to evaluate the program. After 1 year of services, no differences were observed between the treatment and control students. After 2 years, differences favoring the treatment subjects appeared on measures of academic and functional skills as well as on educational expectations. A survey conducted in the fall following scheduled high school graduation showed that experimental students graduated at higher rates, dropped out of school at lower rates, and continued on to post-secondary education at higher rates than did control students. Experimental subjects were more likely to report that their lives had been a success and that they were hopeful about the future. Significant effects on self-reports of "trouble with the police" and having children were also observed. A separate report (Taggart, 1995; cited in Greenwood, Model, Rydell and Chiesa, 1996) reports a 70 percent reduction in arrests for the treatment subjects relative to the control subjects by the time of expected high school graduation.

Although the Quantum Opportunities program was clearly successful, the results for the remaining studies in this category do not support a positive effect on crime. Gottfredson (1986; methods rating = 5) examined effects on delinquent behavior of a program of services provided to high-risk secondary school students. Students' behavioral and academic problems were diagnosed, and individual plans were developed by school specialists (either teachers or counselors assigned to work individually with the high-risk students for this project). Counseling and tutoring services were provided consistent with the individual plans, and the specialists also acted as advocates for the students, worked with the students' parents and tried to involve the students in extracurricular activities to increase bonding to the school. On average, school specialists met twice per month directly with the target students and the students also participated in peer counseling and "rap" sessions with other students. Random assignment of 869 eligible high-risk youths to treatment and control conditions yielded equivalent groups. After 2 years of treatment, the targeted youths were significantly better off than the control students on several measures of academic achievement. Students were promoted to the next grade at a higher rate after the first year in the program, graduation rates were higher, and the percentage of students scoring in the bottom quartile of a standardized achievement tests was lower. Also, target students had significantly fewer disciplinary referrals than control students. However, the services did not result in a reduction in delinquency, substance use, absences from school, drop-out, or several other measures of antisocial behavior for the treated versus the untreated students. In fact, treatment students reported significantly *more* drug use. The study suggests that even relatively small doses of tutoring lead to improvements in academic outcomes. But these positive results were probably off-set by the

*Table 4.15* Mentoring, tutoring and work study

| Program name and citation | Students | Method rating |
|---|---|---|
| **High school grades** | | |
| Kansas City Work/Study Experiment (3 years of intervention) *Ahlstrom and Havighurst, 1982; Ahlstrom and Havighurst, 1971* | 230 students in grades 8–10; inner-city boys screened as socially maladjusted | 3 |
| Kansas City Work/Study Experiment (5 years of intervention) *Ahlstrom and Havighurst, 1982; Ahlstrom and Havighurst, 1971* | 230 students in grades 8–12; inner-city boys screened as socially maladjusted | 3 |
| Kansas City Work/Study Experiment (6 years of intervention) *Ahlstrom and Havighurst, 1982; Ahlstrom and Havighurst, 1971* | 230 students in grades 8–12; inner-city boys screened as socially maladjusted | 3 |
| Quantum Opportunities Program (QOP) *Hahn et al., 1994* | 250 students in grades 9–12; disadvantaged students from families receiving public assistance | 4 |
| Resource Program *Trice et al., 1982* | 48 students in grade 10; disruptive students | 3 |
| The Minnesota Youth Advocate Program *Higgins, 1978* | 74 students in high school; youths released from state or county correctional institution | 3 |
| Work-Study Program *Longstreth et al., 1964* | 146 students in grades 10–12; boys identified as potential drop-outs | 4 |
| **Middle/junior high and high school grades** | | |
| Project Pathe (schoolwide intervention plus additional services) *Gottfredson, 1986; Gottfredson, 1990* | 869 students in grades 6–12; high-risk students, Charleston County, SC | 5 |
| **Middle/junior high school grades** | | |
| Across Ages: With Mentoring *LoSciuto et al., 1996* | 483 students in grade 6; schools in Philadelphia's most stressed neighborhoods | 3 |
| Project RAISE *McPartland and Nettles, 1991* | 1634 students in grades 6–7; at-risk students attending middle school in impoverished neighborhoods in Baltimore | 3 |
| **Elementary school grades** | | |
| Academic Skills Training *Coie and Krehbiel, 1984* | 20 students in grade 4; children identified as having both serious academic and social problems | 5 |
| Companionship Program *Alden et al., 1975* | 32 students in grades K-1; poverty-level children from 4 public elementary schools in Danville, IL, racially mixed neighborhoods | 5 |
| Primary Mental Health Project *Elkin et al., 1988* | 108 students in grades 2–5; urban and suburban Rochester, NY schools with no long-standing severe problems | 4 |
| Structured Academic Program *Alden et al., 1975* | 32 students in grades K-1; poverty-level children from 4 public elementary schools in Danville, IL, racially mixed neighborhoods | 5 |

Notes

a  Frequency distribution represents the number of outcomes for which the program group out-performed the comparison group (positive effects) or the comparison group out-performed the program group (negative effects). Statistically significant positive and negative outcomes are reflected in the columns "+*" and "−*" respectively. Statistically nonsignificant effects or outcomes for which only the direction of effect was known are in the "+" and "−" columns.

| Follow-up (months) | Outcome | Frequency distribution[a] | | | | | Effect size[b] | |
|---|---|---|---|---|---|---|---|---|
| | | −* | − | 0 | + | +* | | |
| 0 | Crime | 0 | 3 | 0 | 0 | 0 | −.21 | (3) |
| 0 | Drop-out/Truancy | 0 | 1 | 0 | 0 | 0 | −.07 | (1) |
| 0 | Crime | 0 | 0 | 0 | 3 | 0 | .24 | (3) |
| 3 | Crime | 0 | 0 | 0 | 0 | 1 | .32* | (1) |
| | Drop-out/Truancy | 0 | 0 | 0 | 0 | 1 | .74* | (1) |
| 24 | Drop-out/Truancy | 0 | 0 | 0 | 3 | 1 | .75* | (3) |
| 0 | Crime | 0 | 2 | 0 | 0 | 0 | −.09 | (2) |
| | Drop-out/Truancy | 0 | 0 | 0 | 1 | 0 | .40 | (1) |
| 5 | Crime | 0 | 1 | 0 | 0 | 0 | −.23 | (1) |
| | Drop-out/Truancy | 0 | 0 | 0 | 1 | 0 | .08 | (1) |
| 0 | Crime | 0 | 0 | 2 | 0 | 0 | .00 | (2) |
| | AOD | 1 | 0 | 0 | 0 | 0 | −.21* | (1) |
| | Drop-out/Truancy | 0 | 1 | 1 | 1 | 0 | −.03 | (3) |
| | Anti-Soc./Aggr. | 0 | 2 | 0 | 1 | 1 | .05 | (4) |
| 0 | AOD | 0 | 0 | 1 | 0 | 0 | .00 | (1) |
| | Drop-out/Truancy | 0 | 0 | 0 | 0 | 1 | | |
| 0 | Drop-out/Truancy | 0 | 0 | 0 | 0 | 1 | .18* | (1) |
| 1 | Anti-Soc./Aggr. | 0 | 0 | 0 | 3 | 0 | | |
| .25 | Anti-Soc./Aggr. | 0 | 0 | 0 | 2 | 0 | | |
| .5 | Anti-Soc./Aggr. | 0 | 0 | 0 | 0 | 1 | .39* | (1) |
| .25 | Anti-Soc./Aggr. | 0 | 0 | 0 | 2 | 0 | | |

b  The mean effect size is based only on those outcomes for which an effect size could be calculated. This may be fewer than the number of effects represented in the frequency distribution. Significance is based on the observed effect size data and may disagree with the frequency distribution if the authors performed a different test or used a different criterion, such as a one-tail test.

counseling intervention which brought high-risk youths together to discuss (and therefore make more salient to others) their poor behavior.

The remaining studies in this category also found no significant effects on crime (Ahlstrom and Havighurst, 1971, 1982; methods rating = 3; Higgins, 1978; methods rating = 3; Longstreth, Shanley and Rice, 1964; methods rating = 4). These were primarily work-study or mentoring programs for older delinquent boys. Aside from Gottfredson (1986), only one study measured effects on substance use. This study of mentoring by elderly community members (LoSciuto *et al.*, 1996; methods rating = 3) showed no significant effect on substance use.

Studies of tutoring for younger children are more positive, but with one exception do not reduce problem behaviors significantly. A rigorous study already described above in the cognitive-behavioral training section also involved intensive tutoring for rejected fourth grade children. Coie and Krehbiel (1984; methods rating = 5) compared an academic skills program with a social skills training program which involved coaching and practice in skills necessary for positive interaction with peers to a control condition. Academic skills training improved academic achievement and peer acceptance, and improved positive classroom behaviors. Significant effects on disruptive behavior were not found, although the academic skills training group tended in the positive direction. The authors found that the academic skills training helped the students attend better to their classroom work. Because they spent more time on-task, they tended to be less disruptive. The teacher began to give them more positive attention, and peers began to like them better. Similarly, Rappaport, Alden, and Seidman (1975; methods rating = 5) found that first and second graders who were either tutored or the benefi- ciary of an adult "companion" who attempted to develop a "committed human relationship" with the child tended to be rated by their teacher as being less disruptive after treatment, but the differences were not statistically significant. Finally, the Primary Mental Health Project (Elkin, Weissberg and Cohen, 1988; methods rating = 4) reported a positive significant effect on a measure of acting out for a program that offered elementary school students the opportunity to develop a trusting relationship with an adult in a play-room context. These programs targeting elementary school children all show positive results. The small sample sizes employed in most of the studies work against finding a "significant" effect.

## SUMMARY

The studies in this section primarily target students at elevated risk for engag- ing in delinquency and provide special services intended to help them perform better in school, adjust better to school, attend school more regu- larly or give them an alternative to school (such as work). All of these services might plausibly curb misbehavior in the present and reduce future criminal activity. One study (Hahn, Leavitt and Aaron, 1994) found a positive effect on crime, but four other studies failed to replicate the finding and the mean effect size across all studies is close to zero ($\overline{ES} = 0.03$). The strategy cannot be regarded as promising. Two studies (LoSciuto *et al.*, 1996; Gottfredson, 1986) found no positive effect on substance use. Four studies (Hahn, Leavitt and Aaron, 1994; LoSciuto *et al.*, 1996; McPartland and Nettles, 1991; Trice, Parker and Safer, 1982) found positive effects on drop-out or school persistence and the preponderance of evidence supported this positive effect ($\underline{ES}=0.18$, $p>.05$). Effects of these programs on measures of antisocial behavior and aggression are generally positive and reach statistical significance in two studies, therefore placing them in the "works" category (Elkin, Weissberg and Cohen, 1988; Gottfredson, 1986). The Quantum Opportunities program should be replicated, and additional, larger studies should be conducted to get a better read on the effect of these programs on antisocial behavior and conduct problems.

*Recreational, community service, enrichment, and leisure activities*

Some programs offer recreational, enrichment, or leisure activities as a delinquency prevention strategy. These programs historically have been based on one of the following assumptions: (1) "idle hands are the devil's workshop;" (2) children, especially those who do not fit the academic mold, will suffer from low self-esteem if they are not able to display their other competencies; or (3) students need to vent their energy. With the rise in violent crime, the typical rationale for alternative activities programs is that occupying youths' time will keep them out of harm's way – the "safe haven" theory. Drop-in recreation centers, after-school and week-end programs, dances, community service activities and other events are offered as alternatives to the more dangerous activities. After-school programs have enjoyed a recent boost in popularity in light of evidence that 22 percent of violent juvenile crime occurs between 2 p.m. and 6 p.m. on school days (Snyder, Sickmund and Poe-Yamagata, 1996). This is more than would be expected if juvenile crime were uniformly distributed across the waking hours.

Relevant research on alternative activities is found both in basic research on the causes and correlates of delinquency and in evaluations of prevention programs involving these activities. Basic research has examined the plausibility of the "idle hands are the devil's workshop" rationale for explaining delinquency and found it lacking. Several studies have found that time spent in leisure activities is unrelated to the commission of delinquent acts (Gottfredson, 1984b; Hirschi, 1969). Time spent on activities which reflect an underlying commitment to conventional pursuits (e.g. hours spent on homework) is related to the commission of fewer delinquent acts, while time spent on activities which reflect a (premature) orientation to adult activities (e.g. time spent riding around in cars) is related to the commission of more delinquent acts. But the myriad activities of adolescents that have no apparent connection to these roles (e.g. clubs, volunteer and service activities, youth organizations, sports, hobbies, television, etc.) are unrelated to the commission of delinquent acts. Simply spending time in these activities is unlikely to reduce delinquency unless they provide direct supervision when it would otherwise *be lacking.*

Alternative activities programs have been found to *not* prevent or reduce alcohol, tobacco and other drug use in several reviews of the effectiveness of drug prevention (Botvin, 1990; Hansen, 1992; Schaps *et al.*, 1981; Schinke, Botvin and Orlandi, 1991). More recent evidence of the impotence of alternative activities programs comes from the National Structured Evaluation (NSE; Stoil, Hill and Brounstein, 1994), a major study of the effectiveness of prevention activities initiated in 1991 by the Center for Substance Abuse Prevention (CSAP), which examined hundreds of different program models in operation during or after 1986. The NSE found that alternative activities *alone* do not reduce alcohol and other drug use, alcohol and other drug-related knowledge and attitudes, or other risk and protective factors related to alcohol and other drug use. However, when these drug-free activities appeared as secondary components in programs primarily aimed at psycho-social skill development, they were effective for reducing alcohol and other drug use and related risk and protective factors. Note that the reviews and the NSE summarize evidence related to broadly defined alternative activities programs operating in both school and community contexts. They do not tell us whether the null findings apply equally to programs in these different settings.

Few evaluations of the effect of school-based recreation, community service, leisure and enrichment activities on delinquency other than substance use are available. They are summarized in Table 4.16. These studies all combine an emphasis on alternative activities with other components such as instruction in skills related to the alternative activity. One program (Ross *et al.*, 1992; methods rating = 4) involved instruction and supervised homework and self-esteem building exercises in a school-based after-school program for elementary school children. The study did not assess program effects on actual delinquent behavior due to the young age of the children, but it did measure antisocial behavior and low self-control, a potent risk

*Table 4.16* Recreation, community service, enrichment and leisure activities

| Program name and citation | Students | Method rating |
| --- | --- | --- |
| **Middle/junior high and high school grades** | | |
| Teen Outreach<br>  *Allen et al., 1994* | 2086 students in grades 7–12; 66 sites around the country | 4 |
| **Middle/junior high school grades** | | |
| Across Ages: Without Mentoring<br>  *LoSciuto et al., 1996* | 490 students in grade 6; schools in Philadelphia's most stressed neighborhoods | 3 |
| Magic Me<br>  *Cronin, 1996* | 508 students in grades 6–8; at-risk middle school students in Maryland and California | 4 |
| **Elementary school grades** | | |
| ADEPT Drug and Alcohol Community Prevention Project (ADACPP)<br>  *Ross et al., 1992* | 888 students in grades K–6; primarily African-American students identified as latchkey children | 4 |

Notes
a  Frequency distribution represents the number of outcomes for which the program group out-performed the comparison group (positive effects) or the comparison group out-performed the program group (negative effects). Statistically significant positive and negative outcomes are reflected in the columns "+*" and "−*" respectively. Statistically nonsignificant effects or outcomes for which only the direction of effect was known are in the "+" and "−" columns.

factor for later delinquency. The study found no significant effect on a teacher rating of acting out behavior, but it *increased* risk-taking and impulsiveness, an important negative side effect most likely due to grouping high-risk youths with lower-risk youths in the absence of a strong intervention.

Cronin (1996; methods rating = 4) reported on a community service program which also involved reflection/discussion sessions for "processing" the service experience. Cronin reported a significant negative effect on substance use, a nonsignificant trend favoring the comparison group on a measure of rebellious behavior, and a significant positive effect on self-reports of class-cutting.

The two remaining programs on Table 4.16 (LoSciuto *et al.*, 1996; methods rating = 3; Allen *et al.*, 1994; methods rating = 4) both report on community service activities for teens. The Teen Outreach program for students in grades 7–12 showed a significant positive effect on school suspensions. The component of the Across Ages program that involved a community service activity with no mentoring had no significant effects on drug use or attendance.

SUMMARY

Research clearly supports the crime-prevention potential of providing direct adult supervision of high-risk juveniles when they would otherwise be unsupervised, but designing such interventions so that they will reach the intended population and counteract potential negative effects of grouping high-risk youths remains a challenge. The evidence summarized above does

| Follow-up (months) | Outcome | Frequency distribution[a] | | | | | Effect size[b] | |
|---|---|---|---|---|---|---|---|---|
| | | −* | − | 0 | + | +* | | |
| 0 | Anti-Soc./Aggr. | 0 | 0 | 0 | 0 | 1 | .15* | (1) |
| 0 | AOD | 0 | 1 | 0 | 0 | 0 | −.12 | (1) |
| | Drop-out/Truancy | 0 | 0 | 0 | 1 | 0 | | |
| 0 | AOD | 1 | 1 | 0 | 0 | 0 | −.16 | (2) |
| | Drop-out/Truancy | 0 | 0 | 0 | 1 | 1 | .21 | (2) |
| | Anti-Soc./Aggr. | 0 | 1 | 0 | 0 | 0 | −.13 | (1) |
| 0 | Anti-Soc./Aggr. | 0 | 0 | 0 | 1 | 0 | | |

b The mean effect size is based only on those outcomes for which an effect size could be calculated. This may be fewer than the number of effects represented in the frequency distribution. Significance is based on the observed effect size data and may disagree with the frequency distribution if the authors performed a different test or used a different criterion, such as a one-tail test.

not allow a conclusion about the effects of recreational, community service, or enrichment programs on crime because no studies have directly assessed such effects. The evidence accords with previous meta-analyses of the effects of such programs on substance use: they do not work (Cronin, 1996; LoSciuto et al., 1996, $\overline{ES} = -0.14$, $p > .05$). One study (Allen et al., 1994) found a significant effect on suspensions, but positive results for measures of antisocial behavior and aggression are not replicated in other studies and the overall effect size for these results is very small (0.03, $p > .05$). Effects on school attendance and persistence appear promising; however: Cronin's (1996) "Magic Me" students self-reported fewer days cut than comparison students, and LoSciuto et al.'s (1996) "across ages" students had fewer days of nonattendance ($p < .01$). Perhaps these recreational and enrichment strategies could be coupled with more potent intervention strategies to increase student participation in the other activity.

These conclusions pertain only to *school-based* recreation and leisure activities. It is possible (although not yet tested) that *community-based* recreation programs are more effective than the more broadly defined alternative activities programs summarized here (see Chapter 5). It is also possible that features of the implementing organization and the community context within which the programs operate moderate the programs' effectiveness. Better research is clearly needed to isolate these characteristics of programs and contexts. At this point in time, expectations for these programs far exceed their empirical record. Because some studies have found backfire effects, it is particularly important to proceed with due caution.

**Scientific conclusions: what works, what is promising, and what does not work?**

Table 4.17 provides the basis for Table 4.18, which summarizes the evidence across the relevant categories of school-based prevention discussed in this chapter. Programs that "work" (indicated by a "●") are those for which at least two different reasonably rigorous studies have found significant positive effects on measures of problem behavior and for which the preponderance of evidence is positive. Promising strategies (indicated by a "−") are those for which only one reasonably rigorous study has found significant positive effects on measures of problem behavior. If the preponderance of evidence for these strategies is positive, they are regarded as "promising" until replication confirms the effect. Strategies that do not work (indicated by a "○") are those for which at least two reasonably rigorous studies have found no significant positive effects on measures of problem behavior and for which the preponderance of evidence is not positive. Question marks on the table ("?") indicate outcomes for which no rigorous studies existed, or whose results varied substantially from study to study. These indicate areas requiring additional research. The specific studies supporting each conclusion are cited in the relevant summary sections above.

The results in Table 4.18, using the Scientific Methods Scale (SMS) criteria for judging effectiveness, correspond for the most part with conclusions based on the meta-analytic approach, the results of which are shown in Table 4.17. Sometimes the counts (which form the basis of the results in Table

4.18) are based on more information because all studies are eligible for summary using this method as long as the direction of the effect is known. Effects for interventions to change norms and expectations are shown in Table 4.18 to "work" for reducing crime and antisocial behavior, for example, while in the meta-analytic results these effects cannot be computed. Also, the meta-analytic summary includes all studies for which an effect size could be computed regardless of the methodological rigor of the study. This accounts for some of the discrepancies between the two sources. For example, the average effect size for studies involving classroom or instructional management on crime measures is 0.18 ($p < .05$), based on five different contrasts. But only one of these contrasts comes from a study whose methodological rigor was a level 3 on the SMS, so this strategy is regarded as "promising." Similarly, the average size of the effect of counseling interventions on crime is $-0.37$ ($p < .05$), but because these negative results are based on only one reasonably rigorous study, we cannot conclude that this strategy is ineffective. Both summary methods agree on the following:

1  Several school-based prevention strategies are effective for reducing one or more of the problem behavior outcomes examined in this report.
2  Except for effects on truancy and drop-out, strategies that focus on changing the environment are somewhat more effective than those focusing only on changing individuals' attitudes, behaviors or beliefs.
3  The most effective strategies (across all four outcomes) are: school and discipline management interventions; interventions to establish norms and expectations for behavior; and instructional programs that teach social competency skills using cognitive-behavioral methods.
4  The least effective strategies (across all four outcomes) are: instructional programs that do not use cognitive-behavioral methods; counseling, social work and other therapeutic interventions; and recreation and leisure programs.

Additional research is needed to better understand the potential of certain intervention strategies. For the classroom instruction and management category, positive effects on school attendance and substance use are fairly consistent across studies, but effects on antisocial behavior and crime are mixed. Effects on substance use for instructional programs that do not use cognitive-behavioral strategies are also mixed. The results of studies in these categories are heterogeneous. Research is needed to better understand the essential elements of these programs. Similarly, the effects of studies involving regrouping of students are somewhat inconsistent. Replications of this promising strategy are sorely needed because methodological shortcomings in the existing studies reduce confidence in their results. A final area requiring replication is the mentoring, tutoring and work study category. Only one of the several studies showed positive effects on crime, but its effects were consistent across several different outcomes of interest. These results require replication, and we need a better understanding of the critical elements that differentiate this effective program from the others. The mentoring studies are also interesting because they seem to produce consistent positive effects on school attendance which do not translate into positive effects on substance use. Finally, the studies of

Table 4.17 Mean effect size by program category and outcome type

| Program category | Outcome type | Effect size | | | |
|---|---|---|---|---|---|
| | | Mean† | Minimum | Maximum | N‡ |
| **Environmentally focused interventions** | | | | | |
| School and discipline management interventions | Crime | 0.27* | 0.12 | 0.65 | 5 |
| | AOD | 0.24* | 0.15 | 0.33 | 2 |
| | Truancy/Dropouts | -0.05 | -0.10 | 0.00 | 2 |
| | Anti-Soc./Aggr. | 0.13 | -0.10 | 0.37 | 6 |
| Interventions to establish norms or expectations for behavior | AOD | 0.09 | -0.23 | 0.31 | 12 |
| Classroom or instructional management | Crime | 0.18* | -0.16 | 0.27 | 5 |
| | AOD | 0.17* | 0.03 | 0.25 | 5 |
| | Truancy/Dropouts | 0.15 | 0.05 | 0.32 | 4 |
| | Anti-Soc./Aggr. | 0.05 | -0.86 | 0.45 | 11 |
| Reorganization of grades or classes | Crime | 0.24* | 0.23 | 0.36 | 2 |
| | Truancy/Dropouts | 0.16 | -0.07 | 0.38 | 4 |
| | Anti-Soc./Aggr. | 0.23* | 0.23 | 0.23 | 2 |
| **Individually focused interventions** | | | | | |
| Self-control or social competency instruction using cognitive-behavioral or behavioral instructional methods | Crime | 0.08 | -0.10 | 0.41 | 8 |
| | AOD | 0.05* | -0.44 | 0.37 | 30 |
| | Truancy/Dropouts | 0.23 | 0.17 | 0.36 | 2 |
| | Anti-Soc./Aggr. | 0.30* | -0.37 | 1.62 | 24 |
| Self-control or social competency instruction without cognitive-behavioral or behavioral instructional methods | Crime | 0.02 | -0.30 | 0.16 | 12 |
| | AOD | 0.03 | -0.22 | 0.29 | 25 |
| | Truancy/Dropouts | 0.02 | -0.25 | 0.25 | 9 |
| | Anti-Soc./Aggr. | 0.07 | -0.24 | 0.39 | 14 |
| Other instructional programs | Crime | -0.05 | -0.23 | -0.02 | 2 |
| | AOD | 0.07 | -0.26 | 0.54 | 5 |
| Cognitive behavioral, behavioral modeling or behavior modification interventions | Crime | -0.01 | -0.18 | 0.11 | 2 |
| | AOD | 0.23 | -0.21 | 0.44 | 3 |
| | Truancy/Dropouts | 1.10* | 0.35 | 3.09 | 5 |
| | Anti-Soc./Aggr. | 0.34* | -0.59 | 1.14 | 12 |

| Intervention | Outcome | | | | |
|---|---|---|---|---|---|
| Counseling, social work and other therapeutic interventions | Crime | −0.37* | −0.67 | −0.18 | 3 |
| | AOD | −0.19 | −0.39 | 0.00 | 2 |
| | Truancy/Dropouts | −0.13 | −0.77 | 0.29 | 6 |
| | Anti-Soc./Aggr. | 0.06 | 0.03 | 0.36 | 4 |
| Mentoring, tutoring and work study | Crime | 0.03 | −0.23 | 0.32 | 6 |
| | AOD | −0.11 | −0.21 | 0.00 | 2 |
| | Truancy/Dropouts | 0.18 | −0.32 | 0.75 | 8 |
| | Anti-Soc./Aggr. | 0.18 | 0.05 | 0.39 | 2 |
| Recreation, community service, enrichment and leisure activities | AOD | −0.14 | −0.16 | −0.12 | 2 |
| | Anti-Soc./Aggr. | 0.03 | −0.13 | 0.15 | 2 |
| All environmentally focused interventions | Crime | 0.24* | −0.16 | 0.65 | 12 |
| | AOD | 0.13* | −0.23 | 0.40 | 20 |
| | Truancy/Dropouts | 0.09 | −0.10 | 0.38 | 10 |
| | Anti-Soc./Aggr. | 0.14* | −0.86 | 0.57 | 21 |
| All individually focused interventions | Crime | −0.02 | −0.67 | 0.41 | 33 |
| | AOD | 0.03* | −0.44 | 0.54 | 68 |
| | Truancy/Dropouts | 0.13* | −0.77 | 3.09 | 32 |
| | Anti-Soc./Aggr. | 0.20* | −0.59 | 1.62 | 58 |

Note

Effect sizes for all studies (regardless of methods rating) are included in the analyses for this table.

*  $p < .05$

†  Inverse variance weighted mean effect size (random effects model).

‡  Number of effect sizes contributing to the analysis.

*Table 4.18* Summary of what works in school-based crime prevention

| Strategy | Crime | AOD | Anti-Soc./ Aggr. | Drop-out/ Truancy |
|---|---|---|---|---|
| **Environmentally focused interventions** | | | | |
| School and discipline management interventions | ● | ● | ● | ? |
| Interventions to establish norms or expectations for behavior | ● | ● | ● | ? |
| Classroom or instructional management methods | – | ● | ? | ● |
| Reorganization of grades or classes | – | – | ● | ● |
| **Individually focused interventions** | | | | |
| Self-control or social competency instruction using cognitive-behavioral or behavioral instructional methods | ● | ● | ● | ● |
| Self-control or social competency instruction without cognitive-behavioral or behavioral instructional methods | ? | ? | ○ | ○ |
| Other instructional programs | ○ | ? | ?[a] | ○ |
| Cognitive behavioral, behavioral modeling or behavior modification interventions | ? | ? | ● | ● |
| Counseling, social work and other therapeutic interventions | ? | ? | ○ | ○ |
| Mentoring, tutoring, and work study | ? | ○ | ● | ● |
| Recreation, community service, enrichment and leisure activities | ? | ○ | ? | – |

Notes
● = Works          – = Promising
○ = Doesn't work   ? = Unknown or mixed
a  Evidence is positive but limited to alternative or residential settings.

younger children in this category produce consistently positive effects which are usually not statistically significant because the studies are underpowered. Clearly larger replication studies are needed in this area.

## Future directions

Gottfredson (1997) discussed the relatively small size of the effects of school-based preventive interventions. The small size of the effects is even more evident in this report because effect sizes have been computed. The average effect size across all outcome measures and all studies included in this report is 0.11 ($p < .05$). By any reckoning, this is a "small" effect. Future work in this area must find ways to increase the yield of the typical school-based program. As discussed in Gottfredson (1997), these efforts should focus on specifying theories underlying school-based prevention so that intervention can be more closely aligned with the critical causal variables, and improving the level of implementation of prevention programs. A recent National Study of Delinquency Prevention in Schools (Gottfredson and Gottfredson, 1996) found that the quality of implementation of school-based prevention programs varies a great deal from activity to activity, and that the typical program is implemented with only mediocre quality. This suggests that within any of the categories found to be effective for reducing problem behavior, a wide range of effects is possible depending on the strength and fidelity of program implementation. It is likely that the effectiveness of prevention activities can be boosted considerably if we can find ways to simply improve the quality of implementation of existing programs and practices.

## Notes

1 The editorial assistance of Roger Weissberg and the research assistance of Todd Armstrong, Jennifer Castro, Elaine Eggleston, Paul Hirschfield, Veronica Puryear, John Ridgely and Shannon Womer are gratefully acknowledged. An earlier version of this chapter appeared in Gottfredson, D.C. (1997). Some sections are abstracted from Gottfredson, D.C. (2001). Partial support was provided by a grant from the National Institute of Justice and a gift from Jerry Lee.

2 Of course, more money is spent on maintaining basic educational services. The largest proportion of spending for children and youth in all states is tied to schools (Holmes, Gottfredson and Miller, 1992) – mostly to maintain basic education processes. An argument can be made for counting these large basic education expenditures as prevention expenditures because they are directed at improving the social capital of the citizenry (e.g. education and proper conduct) which protects youths from later involvement in a variety of problem behaviors. Because the evidence for a connection between basic education programs and practices and crime is largely indirect, such basic education functions will be given short shrift in this chapter. Researchers and policy-makers should devote more attention, however, to understanding the crime prevention potential of large federal entitlement programs such as Chapter I of Title I of the Elementary and Secondary Education Act, which distributes approximately $8 billion in federal funds to local school districts to enhance basic educational processes.

3 The Office of Justice Programs (OJP) spends over $1 billion on law enforcement assistance and approximately $323 million on the construction of new federal prisons per year.

4 This category of conduct problems is labeled "antisocial/aggressive" on the tables in this chapter. It includes a variety of different measures of misbehavior, about half of which are specifically labeled as aggressive behavior or another antisocial behavior, such as "disrespect/defiance," "minor delinquent behavior" or "rebellious behavior." Approximately half are non-specific measures of what can be assumed to be conduct problems, including "acting out," conduct ratings, referrals for behavior problems, and school responses to such referrals (e.g. suspensions and expulsions).

5 In most tables and summaries the instruction category is disaggregated into theoretically relevant types of instruction.

6 Recall that most school-based interventions include several components. Occasionally, the study was designed to provide information about the effectiveness of each component separately. In these cases, each separate component was classified into one of the program types and placed on the relevant table. Most often, an effect estimate was provided only for the entire program. In these cases, a judgment was made about which component best described the program or practice and the study was placed on that table.

7 If at least one treatment-control contrast from a study has a methods rating of 3 or above, all contrasts for the study are included in the tables.

8 Because school and discipline management interventions often involve changes to the way office referrals are handled, official school records were not considered as outcome measures for this category. One study was eliminated because it reported only office referrals.

9 Several reports have been published from these studies. Included on the table are only those treatment-control contrasts which involve a measure of problem

behavior (many of the studies reported on a combined measure of problem behavior and intentions to engage in problem behavior) and for which the direction of the effect could be ascertained. In most reports, the direction of non-significant effects was not reported.

10  This effect is considered statistically significant if a one-tailed test is used and not statistically significant if a two-tailed test is used.

11  Felner *et al.* (1993; methods rating = 2) report on the long-term follow-up of this study and on a downward extension of the project to students entering junior high and middle school. This replication studied 1,965 students in eight geographically and demographically diverse schools. Unfortunately, most important potential pre-existing differences between the STEP and non-STEP students are not measured or adequately controlled in this study.

12  A more extensive summary of DARE evaluations can be found in an earlier version of this report (Gottfredson, 1997).

13  Although the curriculum is labeled "affective," our coding of the content placed it in the social competency skills category.

14  The criteria for rigorous evaluation used were: (a) published, peer reviewed report using (b) pre-test/post-test, control group designs, with (c) adequate sample size and appropriate statistical tests that included (d) outcome data for at least 2 years that measured violent or aggressive behavior.

15  Also see the discussion of interventions to establish school norms. These interventions often involve instruction and are generally more effective than the instructional programs included in this section.

16  An instructional intervention – Mastery Learning (ML) – was also tested in the same study. Results are not reported here because we could not ascertain the direction of the effects of ML on measures of problem behavior from the published reports.

# References

Ahlstrom, W.M. and Havighurst, R.J. (1971) *400 losers: Delinquent boys in high school.* San Francisco, CA: Jossey-Bass.

Ahlstrom, W. and Havighurst, R.J. (1982) The Kansas City work/study experiment. In D.J. Safer (ed.), *School programs for disruptive adolescents.* Baltimore, MD: University Park Press, 259–75.

Alden, L., Rappaport, J. and Seidman, E. (1975) College students as interventionists for primary-grade children. *American Journal of Community Psychology,* 3(3), 261–71.

Allen, J.P., Kuperminc, G., Philliber, S. and Herre, K. (1994) Programmatic prevention of adolescent problem behaviors: The role of autonomy, relatedness, and volunteer service in the Teen Outreach Program. *American Journal of Community Psychology,* 22(5), 617–38.

Amerikaner, M. and Summerlin, M.L. (1982) Group counseling with learning disabled children: Effects of social skills and relaxation training on self-concept and classroom behavior. *Journal of Learning Disabilities,* 15(6), 340–3.

Arbuthnot, J. (1992) Sociomoral reasoning in behavior-disordered adolescents: Cognitive and behavioral change. In J. McCord and R.E. Tremblay (eds), *Preventing antisocial behavior: Interventions from birth through adolescence.* New York, NY: Guilford Press, 283–310.

Arbuthnot, J. and Gordon, D.A. (1986) Behavioral and cognitive effects of a moral reasoning development intervention for high-risk behavior-disordered adolescents. *Journal of Consulting and Clinical Psychology,* 54(2), 208–16.

Barber, R.M. and Kagey, J.R. (1977) Modification of school attendance for an elementary population. *Journal of Applied Behavior Analysis,* 10(1), 41–8.

Battistich, V., Schaps, E., Watson, M. and Solomon, D. (1996) Prevention effects of the Child Development Project: Early findings from an ongoing multisite demonstration trial. *Journal of Adolescent Research*, 11(1), 12–35.

Battistich, V., Solomon, D., Watson, M., Solomon, J. and Schaps, E. (1989) Effects of an elementary school program to enhance prosocial behavior on children's cognitive-social problem-solving skills and strategies. *Journal of Applied Developmental Psychology*, 10, 147–69.

Becker, H.K., Agopian, M.W. and Yeh, S. (1992) Impact evaluation of Drug Abuse Resistance Education (DARE). *Journal of Drug Education*, 22(4), 283–91.

Bell, R.M., Ellickson, P.L. and Harrison, E.R. (1993) Do drug prevention effects persist into high school? How Project ALERT did with ninth graders. *Preventive Medicine*, 22, 463–83.

Bierman, K.L., Miller, C.L. and Stabb, S.D. (1987) Improving the social behavior and peer acceptance of rejected boys: Effects of social skill training with instructions and prohibitions. *Journal of Consulting and Clinical Psychology*, 55(2), 194–200.

Bloomquist, M.L., August, G.J. and Ostrander, R. (1991) Effects of a school-based cognitive-behavioral intervention for ADHD children. *Journal of Abnormal Child Psychology*, 19(5), 591–605.

Bolstad, O.D. and Johnson, S.M. (1972) Self-regulation in the modification of disruptive classroom behavior. *Journal of Applied Behavior Analysis*, 5(4), 443–54.

Botvin, G.J. (1990) Substance abuse prevention: Theory, practice, and effectiveness. In M. Tonry and J.Q. Wilson (eds), *Drugs and crime*. Chicago, IL: University of Chicago Press, 461–519.

Botvin, G.J., Baker, E., Botvin, E.M., Filazzola, A.D. and Millman, R.B. (1984) Prevention of alcohol misuse through the development of personal and social competence: A pilot study. *Journal of Studies on Alcohol*, 45, 550–2.

Botvin, G.J., Baker, E., Dusenbury, L., Botvin, E.M. and Diaz, T. (1995) Long-term follow-up results of a randomized drug abuse prevention trial in a white middle-class population. *Journal of the American Medical Association*, 273(14), 1106–12.

Botvin, G.J., Baker, E., Filazzola, A.D. and Botvin, E.M. (1990) A cognitive-behavioral approach to substance abuse prevention: One-year follow-up. *Addictive Behaviors*, 15, 47–63.

Botvin, G.J., Baker, E., Renick, N.L., Filazzola, A.D. and Botvin, E.M. (1984) A cognitive-behavioral approach to substance abuse prevention. *Addictive Behaviors*, 9, 137–47.

Botvin, G.J., Batson, H.W., Witss-Vitale, S., Bess, V., Baker, E. and Dusenbury, L. (1989) A psychosocial approach to smoking prevention for urban black youth. *Public Health Reports*, 104(6), 573–82.

Botvin, G.J., Dusenbury, L., Baker, E., James-Ortiz, S. and Kerner, J. (1989) A skills training approach to smoking prevention among Hispanic youth. *Journal of Behavioral Medicine*, 12(3), 279–96.

Botvin, G.J., Schinke, S.P., Epstein, J.A., Diaz, T. and Botvin, E.M. (1995) Effectiveness of culturally focused and generic skills training approaches to alcohol and drug abuse prevention among minority adolescents: Two-year follow-up results. *Psychology of Addictive Behaviors*, 9(3), 183–94.

Botvin, G.J., Schinke, S.P. and Orlandi, M.A. (1995) School-based health promotion: Substance abuse and sexual behavior. *Applied and Preventive Psychology*, 4, 167–84.

Brewer, D.D., Hawkins, J.D., Catalano, R.F. and Neckerman, H.J. (1995) Preventing serious, violent, and chronic juvenile offending: A review of evaluations of selected strategies in childhood, adolescence, and the community. In J.C. Howell, B. Krisberg, J.D. Hawkins and J.J. Wilson (eds), *A sourcebook: Serious, violent, and chronic juvenile offenders*. Thousand Oaks, CA: Sage, 61–141.

Brooks, B.D. (1975) Contingency management as a means of reducing school truancy. *Education*, 95(3), 206–11.

Bry, B.H. (1982) Reducing the incidence of adolescent problems through preventive intervention: One- and five-year follow-up. *American Journal of Community Psychology*, 10(3), 265–76.

Bry, B.H. and George, F.E. (1979) Evaluating and improving prevention programs: A strategy for drug abuse. *Evaluation and Program Planning*, 2, 127–36.

Bry, B.H. and George, F.E. (1980) The preventive effects of early intervention on the attendance and grades of urban adolescents. *Professional Psychology*, 11, 252–60.

Bryk, A.S. and Driscoll, M.E. (1988) *The high school as community: Contextual influences and consequences for students and teachers*. Madison, WI: University of Wisconsin, National Center on Effective Secondary Schools.

Campanelli, P.C., Dielman, T.E., Shope, J.T., Butchart, A.T. and Renner, D.S. (1989) Pretest and treatment effects in an elementary school-based alcohol misuse prevention program. *Health Education Quarterly*, 16(1), 113–30.

Caplan, M., Weissberg, R.P., Grober, J.S., Sivo, P.J., Grady, K. and Jacoby, C. (1992) Social competence promotion with inner-city and suburban young adolescents: Effects on social adjustment and alcohol use. *Journal of Consulting and Clinical Psychology*, 60(1), 56–63.

Clayton, R.R., Cattarello, A., Day, L.E. and Walden, K.P. (1991) Persuasive communication and drug prevention: An evaluation of the DARE program. In L. Donohew, H.E. Sypher and W.J. Bukoski (eds), *Persuasive communication and drug abuse prevention*. Hillsdale, NJ: Lawrence Erlbaum, 295–313.

Clayton, R.R., Cattarello, A.M. and Johnstone, B.M. (1996) The effectiveness of Drug Abuse Resistance Education (Project DARE): Five-year follow-up results. *Preventive Medicine*, 25, 307–18.

Clayton, R.R., Cattarello, A. and Walden, K.P. (1991) Sensation seeking as a potential mediating variable for school-based prevention intervention: A two-year follow-up of DARE. *Health Communication*, 3(4), 229–39.

Cohen, J. (1962) The statistical power of abnormal-social psychological research: A review. *Journal of Abnormal and Social Psychology*, 65, 145–53.

Coie, J.D. (1997) *Testing developmental theory of antisocial behavior with outcomes from the Fast Track Prevention Project*. Paper presented at the meeting of the American Psychological Association, Chicago, IL.

Coie, J.D. and Krehbiel, G. (1984) Effects of academic tutoring on the social status of low-achieving, socially rejected children. *Child Development*, 55, 1465–78.

Coie, J.D., Underwood, M. and Lochman, J.E. (1991) Programmatic intervention with aggressive children in the school setting. In D.J. Pepler and K.H. Rubin (eds), *The development and treatment of childhood aggression*. Hillsdale, NJ: Lawrence Erlbaum, 389–410.

Comer, J.P. (1985) The Yale-New Haven Primary Prevention Project: A follow-up study. *Journal of the American Academy of Child Psychiatry*, 24(2), 54–160.

Comer, J.P., Haynes, N.M. and Hamilton-Lee, M. (1989) School power: A model for improving black student achievement. In W.D. Smith and E.W. Chunn (eds), *Black education: A quest for equity and excellence*. New Brunswick, NJ: Transaction Publishers, 187–200.

Conduct Problems Prevention Research Group (1992) A developmental and clinical model for the prevention of conduct disorder: The FAST Track Program. *Development and Psychopathology*, 4, 509–27.

Conduct Problems Prevention Research Group (1997) *Prevention of antisocial behavior: Initial findings from the Fast Track Project*. Paper presented at the meeting of the

Society for Research in Child Development, Washington, DC.

Cook, R., Lawrence, H., Morse, C. and Roehl, J. (1984) An evaluation of the alternatives approach to drug abuse prevention. *The International Journal of the Addictions,* 19(7), 767–87.

Cook, T.D., Hunt, H.D. and Murphy, R.F. (1998) *Comer's School Development Program in Chicago: A theory-based evaluation.* Chicago, IL: Institute for Policy Research, Northwestern University.

Cronin, J. (1996) *An evaluation of a school-based community service program: The effects of Magic Me.* Ellicott City, MD: Gottfredson Associates, Inc.

Crow, M.L. (1971) A comparison of three group counseling techniques with sixth graders. *Elementary School Guidance and Counseling,* 6(1), 37–42.

Dielman, T.E., Shope, J.T., Butchart, A.T. and Campanelli, P.C. (1986) Prevention of adolescent alcohol misuse: An elementary school program. *Journal of Pediatric Psychology,* 11(2), 259–282.

Dielman, T.E., Shope, J.T., Butchart, A.T., Campanelli, P.C. and Caspar, R.A. (1989) A covariance structure model test of antecedents of adolescent alcohol misuse and a prevention effort. *Journal of Drug Education,* 19(4), 337–61.

Dielman, T.E., Shope, J.T., Leech, S.L. and Butchart, A.T. (1989) Different effectiveness of an elementary school-based alcohol misuse prevention program. *Journal of Social Health,* 59(6), 255–63.

Dinitz, S. (1982) A school-based prevention program to reduce delinquency vulnerability. In D.J. Safer (ed.), *School programs for disruptive adolescents.* Baltimore, MD: University Park Press, 279–96.

Dodge, K.A. and Conduct Problems Prevention Research Group (1993) *Effects of intervention on children at high risk for conduct problems.* Paper presented at the meeting of the Society for Research in Child Development, New Orleans, LA.

Dolan, L.J., Kellam, S.G., Brown, C.H., Werthamer-Larsson, L., Rebok, G.W., Mayer, L.S., Laudolff, J., Turkkan, J.S., Ford, C. and Wheeler, L. (1993) The short-term impact of two classroom-based preventive interventions on aggressive and shy behaviors and poor achievement. *Journal of Applied Developmental Psychology,* 14, 317–45.

Drug Strategies (1998) *Keeping score: Women and drugs: Looking at the federal drug control budget.* Washington, DC: Drug Strategies.

Dryfoos, J.G. (1990) *Adolescents at risk: Prevalence and prevention.* New York: Oxford University Press.

Duke, D.L. (1989) School organization, leadership, and student behavior. In O.C. Moles (ed.), *Strategies to reduce student misbehavior.* Washington, DC: US Department of Education, 19–46.

Durlak, J.A. (1995) *School-based prevention programs for children and adolescents.* Thousand Oaks, CA: Sage.

Eggert, L.L., Seyl, C.D. and Nicholas, L.J. (1990) Effects of a school-based prevention program for potential high school drop-outs and drug abusers. *The International Journal of the Addictions,* 25(7), 773–801.

Eggert, L.L., Thompson, E.A., Herting, J.R. and Nicholas, L.J. (1995) Reducing suicide potential among high-risk youth: Tests of a school-based prevention program. *Suicide and Life-Threatening Behavior,* 25(2), 276–96.

Eggert, L.L., Thompson, E.A., Herting, J.R., Nicholas, L.J. and Dicker, B.G. (1994) Preventing adolescent drug abuse and high school drop-out through an intensive school-based social network development program. *American Journal of Health Promotion,* 8(3), 202–15.

Elardo, P.T. and Caldwell, B.M. (1979) The effects of an experimental social development program on children in the middle childhood period. *Psychology in the Schools*, 16(1), 93–100.

Elias, M.J., Weissberg, R.P., Hawkins, J.D., Perry, C.L., Zins, J.E., Dodge, K.A., Kendall, P.C., Gottfredson, D.C., Rotheram-Borus, M.J., Jason, L.A. and Wilson-Brewer, R. (1994) The school-based promotion of social competence: Theory, research, practice, and policy. In R.J. Haggerty, L.R. Sherrod, N. Garmezy and M. Rutter (eds), *Stress, risk, and resilience in children and adolescents: Processes, mechanisms, and interventions*. Cambridge: Cambridge University Press, 268–316.

Elkin, J.I.W., Weissberg, R.P. and Cowen, E.L. (1988) Evaluation of a planned short-term intervention for schoolchildren with focal adjustment problems. *Journal of Clinical Child Psychology*, 17(2), 106–15.

Ellickson, P.L. and Bell, R.M. (1990) Drug prevention in junior high: A multi-site longitudinal test. *Science*, 247, 1299–305.

Ellickson, P.L., Bell, R.M. and McGuigan, K. (1993) Preventing adolescent drug use: Long-term results of a junior high program. *American Journal of Public Health*, 83(6), 856–61.

Ennett, S.T., Rosenbaum, D.P., Flewelling, R.L., Bieler, G.S., Ringwalt, C.L. and Bailey, S.L. (1994) Long-term evaluation of Drug Abuse Resistance Education. *Addictive Behaviors*, 19(2), 113–25.

Farrell, A.D. and Meyer, A.L. (1997) The effectiveness of a school-based curriculum for reducing violence among urban sixth-grade students. *American Journal of Public Health*, 87(6), 979–84.

Feindler, E.L., Marriott, S.A. and Iwata, M. (1984) Group anger control training for junior high school delinquents. *Cognitive Therapy and Research*, 8(3), 299–311.

Felner, R.D. and Adan, A.M. (1988) The School Transitional Environmental Project: An ecological intervention and evaluation. In R.H. Price, E.L. Cowen, R.P. Lorion and J. Ramos-McKay (eds), *14 ounces of prevention: A casebook for practitioners*. Washington, DC: American Psychological Association, 111–22.

Felner, R.D., Brand, S., Adan, A.M., Mulhall, P.F., Flowers, N., Sartain, B. and DuBois, D.L. (1993) Restructuring the ecology of the school as an approach to prevention during school transitions: Longitudinal follow-ups and extensions of the School Transitional Environment Project (STEP). *Prevention in Human Services*, 10(2), 103–36.

Felner, R.D., Ginter, M. and Primavera, J. (1982) Primary prevention during school transitions: Social support and environmental structure. *American Journal of Community Psychology*, 10(3), 277–90.

Filipczak, J. and Wodarski, J.S. (1982) Behavioral intervention in public schools: Short-term results. In D.J. Safer (ed.), *School programs for disruptive adolescents*. Baltimore, MD: University Park Press, 195–9.

Forman, S.G. (1980) A comparison of cognitive training and response cost procedures in modifying aggressive behavior of elementary school children. *Behavior Therapy*, 11, 594–600.

Foshee, V.A., Bauman, K.E., Arriaga, X.B., Helms, R.W., Koch, G.G. and Linder, G.F. (1998) An evaluation of Safe Dates, an adolescent dating violence prevention program. *American Journal of Public Health*, 88(1), 45–50.

Foshee, V.A., Linder, G.F., Bauman, K.E., Langwick, S.A., Arriaga, X.B., Heath, J.L., McMahon, P.M. and Bangdiwala, S. (1996) The Safe Dates Project: Theoretical basis, evaluation design, and selected baseline findings. *American Journal of Preventive Medicine*, 12(5), 39–47.

Garrett, C.J. (1985) Effects of residential treatment on adjudicated delinquents: A meta-analysis. *Journal of Research in Crime and Delinquency*, 22(4), 287–308.

General Accounting Office (1993) *Drug Education: Limited Progress in Program Evaluation.*

*Statement of Eleanor Chemlinshy before the Subcommittee on Select Education and Civil Rights, Committee on Education and Labor, House of Representatives, GAO/T-PEMD-93-2.*

Gerler, E.R., Jr. (1980) A longitudinal study of multimodal approaches to small group psychological education. *The School Counselor*, 27, 184–91.

Gersick, K.E., Grady, K. and Snow, D.L. (1988) Social-cognitive skill development with sixth graders and its initial impact on substance use. *Journal of Drug Education*, 18(1), 55–70.

Gesten, E.L., Flores de Apodaca, R., Rains, M., Weissberg, R.P. and Cowen, E.L. (1979) Promoting peer-related social competence in schools. In M.W. Kent and J.E. Rolf (eds), *The primary prevention of psychopathology: Social competence in children*. Hanover, NH: University Press of New England, 220–47.

Gesten, E.L., Rains, M.H., Rapkin, B.D., Weissberg, R.P., Flores de Apocada, R., Cowen, E.L. and Bowen, R. (1982) Training children in social problem-solving competencies: A first and second look. *American Journal of Community Psychology*, 10(1), 95–115.

Gold, M. and Mann, D.W. (1984) *Expelled to a friendlier place: A study of effective alternative schools*. Ann Arbor, MI: The University of Michigan Press.

Goldberg, L., Elliot, D., Clarke, G.N., MacKinnon, D.P., Moe, E., Zoref, L., Green, C., Wolf, S.L., Greffrath, E., Miller, D.J. and Lapin, A. (1996) Effects of a multidimensional anabolic steroid prevention intervention. *Journal of American Medical Association*, 276(19), 1555–62.

Goodstadt, M.S. and Sheppard, M.A. (1983) Three approaches to alcohol education. *Journal of Studies on Alcohol*, 44(2), 362–80.

Gottfredson, D.C. (1986) An empirical test of school-based environmental and individual interventions to reduce the risk of delinquent behavior. *Criminology*, 24(4), 705–31.

Gottfredson, D.C. (1987) An evaluation of an organization development approach to reducing school disorder. *Evaluation Review*, 11(6), 739–63.

Gottfredson, D.C. (1990) Changing school structures to benefit high-risk youths. In P.E. Leone (ed.), *Understanding troubled and troubling youth*. Newbury Park, CA: Sage, 246–71.

Gottfredson, D.C. (1997) School-based crime prevention. In L.W. Sherman, D.C. Gottfredson, D. MacKenzie, J. Eck, P. Reuter and S. Bushway, *Preventing crime: What works, what doesn't, what's promising: A report to the United States Congress*. Washington, DC: US Department of Justice, Office of Justice Programs.

Gottfredson, D.C. (2001) *Schools and Delinquency*. New York: Cambridge University Press.

Gottfredson, D.C., Fink, C.M., Skroban, S. and Gottfredson, G.D. (1997) Making prevention work. In R.P. Weissberg, T.P. Gullotta, R.L. Hampton, B.A. Ryan and G.R. Adams (eds), *Issues in children's and families' lives (Volume 9): Healthy children 2010: Establishing preventive services*. Thousand Oaks, CA: Sage, 219–52.

Gottfredson, D.C., Gottfredson, G.D. and Hybl, L.G. (1993) Managing adolescent behavior: A multiyear, multischool study. *American Educational Research Journal*, 30(1), 179–215.

Gottfredson, D.C., Gottfredson, G.D. and Skroban, S. (1996) A multimodel school-based prevention demonstration. *Journal of Adolescent Research*, 11(1), 97–115.

Gottfredson, D.C., Sealock, M.D. and Koper, C.S. (1996) Delinquency. In R.J. DiClemente, W.B. Hansen and L.E. Ponton (eds), *Handbook of adolescent health risk behavior*. New York: Plenum Press, 259–88.

Gottfredson, G.D. (1984a) A theory-ridden approach to program evaluation: A method for stimulating researcher-implementer collaboration. *American Psychologist*, 39(10), 1101–12.

Gottfredson, G.D. (1984b) *The Effective School Battery: User's Manual.* Odessa, FL: Psychological Assessment Resources, Inc.

Gottfredson, G.D. (1987) Peer group interventions to reduce the risk of delinquent behavior: A selective review and a new evaluation. *Criminology,* 25(3), 671–714.

Gottfredson, G.D. and Gottfredson, D.C. (1985) *Victimization in schools.* New York: Plenum Press.

Gottfredson, G.D. and Gottfredson, D.C. (1996) *A national study of delinquency prevention in schools: Rationale for a study to describe the extensiveness and implementation of programs to prevent adolescent problem behavior in schools.* Unpublished manuscript, Gottfredson Associates, Inc., Ellicott City, MD.

Gottfredson, G.D., Rickert, D.E., Gottfredson, D.C. and Advani, N. (1984) Standards for program development evaluation plans. *Psychological Documents,* 14(2), 32 (ms. No. 2668).

Graham, J.W., Johnson, C.A., Hansen, W.B., Flay, B.R. and Gee, M. (1990) Drug use prevention programs, gender, and ethnicity: Evaluation of three seventh-grade Project SMART cohorts. *Preventive Medicine,* 19, 305–13.

Greenberg, M.T. (1996) *The PATHS Project: Preventive Intervention for Children, Final Report to NIMH (Grant Number R01MH42131).* Rockville, MD: National Institute on Mental Health.

Greenberg, M.T., Kusche, C.A., Cook, E.T. and Quamma, J.P. (1995) Promoting emotional competence in school-aged children: The effects of the PATHS curriculum. *Development and Psychopathology,* 7, 117–36.

Greenwood, C.R., Delquadri, J.C. and Hall, R.V. (1989) Longitudinal effects of Class-wide Peer Tutoring. *Journal of Educational Psychology,* 81(3), 371–83.

Greenwood, C.R., Terry, B., Utley, C.A., Montagna, D. and Walker, D. (1993) Achievement, placement, and services: Middle school benefits of ClassWide Peer Tutoring used at the elementary school. *School Psychology Review,* 22(3), 497–516.

Greenwood, P.W., Model, K.E., Rydell, C.P. and Chiesa, J. (1996) *Diverting children from a life of crime: Measuring costs and benefits.* Santa Monica, CA: RAND.

Grossman, D.C., Neckerman, H.J., Koepsell, T.D., Liu, P., Asher, K.N., Beland, K., Frey, K. and Rivara, F.P. (1997) Effectiveness of a violence prevention curriculum among children in elementary school: A randomized controlled trial. *Journal of the American Medical Association,* 277(20), 1605–11.

Hahn, A., Leavitt, T. and Aaron, P. (1994) *Evaluation of the Quantum Opportunities Program (QOP): Did the program work?: A report on the post secondary outcomes and cost-effectiveness of the QOP Program.* Unpublished manuscript, Brandeis University, Waltham, MA.

Hansen, W.B. (1992) School-based substance abuse prevention: A review of the state of the art in curriculum: 1980–1990. *Health Education Research,* 7, 403–30.

Hansen, W.B. and Graham, J.W. (1991) Preventing alcohol, marijuana, and cigarette use among adolescents: Peer pressure resistance training versus establishing conservative norms. *Preventive Medicine,* 20, 414–30.

Hansen, W.B., Johnson, C.A., Flay, B.R., Graham, J.W. and Sobel, J. (1988) Affective and social influences approaches to the prevention of multiple substance abuse among seventh grade students: Results from Project SMART. *Preventive Medicine,* 17, 135–54.

Hansen, W.B. and O'Malley, P.M. (1996) Drug use. In R.J. DiClemente, W.B. Hansen and L.E. Ponton (eds), *Handbook of adolescent health risk behavior.* New York: Plenum Press, 161–92.

Harmon, M.A. (1993) Reducing the risk of drug involvement among early adolescents: An evaluation of Drug Abuse Resistance Education (DARE). *Evaluation Review,* 17(2), 221–39.

Hausman, A., Pierce, G. and Briggs, L. (1996) Evaluation of comprehensive violence prevention education: Effects on student behavior. *Journal of Adolescent Health*, 19, 104–10.

Hawkins, J.D., Arthur, M.W. and Catalano, R.F. (1995) Preventing substance abuse. In M. Tonry and D. Farrington (eds), *Building a safer society: Strategic approaches to crime prevention*. Chicago, IL: University of Chicago Press, 343–427.

Hawkins, J.D., Catalano, R.F., Kosterman, R., Abbott, R. and Hill, K.G. (1999) Preventing adolescent health-risk behaviors by strengthening protection during childhood. *Archives of Pediatrics and Adolescent Medicine*, 153(3), 226–34.

Hawkins, J.D., Catalano, R.F. and Miller, J.Y. (1992) Risk and protective factors for alcohol and other drug problems in adolescence and early adulthood: Implications for substance abuse prevention. *Psychological Bulletin*, 112(1), 64–105.

Hawkins, J.D., Catalano, R.F., Morrison, D.M., O'Donnell, J., Abbott, R.D. and Day, L.E. (1992) The Seattle Social Developmental Project: Effects of the first four years on protective factors and problem behaviors. In J. McCord and R.E. Tremblay (eds), *Preventing antisocial behavior: Interventions from birth through adolescence*. New York, NY: Guilford Press, 139–61.

Hawkins, J.D., Doueck, H.J. and Lishner, D.M. (1988) Changing teaching practices in mainstream classrooms to improve bonding and behavior of low achievers. *American Educational Research Journal*, 25(1), 31–50.

Hawkins, J.D., Von Cleve, E. and Catalano, R.F. (1991) Reducing early childhood aggression: Results of a primary prevention program. *Journal of the American Academy of Child and Adolescent Psychiatry*, 30(2), 208–17.

Haynes, N.M. (1994) School development effect: Two follow-up studies. In N.M. Haynes (ed.), *School Development Program research monograph*. New Haven, CT: Yale Child Study Center.

Hecht, M.L., Corman, S.R. and Miller-Rassulo, M. (1993) An evaluation of the Drug Resistance Project: A comparison of film versus live performance media. *Health Communication*, 5(2), 75–88.

Higgins, P.S. (1978) Evaluation and case study of a school-based delinquency prevention program: The Minnesota Youth Advocate Program. *Evaluation Quarterly*, 2(2), 215–34.

Hirschi, T. (1969) *Causes of delinquency*. Berkeley, CA: University of California Press.

Holmes, A.B., Gottfredson, G.D. and Miller, J. (1992) Resources and strategies for findings. In J.D. Hawkins and R.F. Catalano (eds), *Communities that care*. San Francisco, CA: Jossey Bass.

Howell, J.C., Krisberg, B., Hawkins, J.D. and Wilson, J.J. (eds) (1995) *A sourcebook: Serious, violent, and chronic juvenile offenders*. Thousand Oaks, CA: Sage, 191–210.

Hudley, C.A. (1994) The reduction of childhood aggression using the BrainPower Program. In M. Furlong and D. Smith (eds), *Anger, hostility, and aggression: Assessment, prevention, and intervention strategies for youth*. Brandon, VT: Clinical Psychology Publishing Co., Inc., 313–44.

Hunter, J.E. and Schmidt, F.L. (1990) *Methods of meta-analysis: Correcting error and bias in research findings*. Newbury Park, CA: Sage.

Institute of Medicine (1994) *Reducing risks for mental disorders: Frontiers for preventive intervention research*. Washington, DC: National Academy Press.

Izzo, R.L. and Ross, R.R. (1990) Meta-analysis of rehabilitation programs for juvenile delinquents: A brief report. *Criminal Justice and Behavior*, 17(1), 134–42.

Johnson, C.A., Pentz, M.A., Weber, M.D., Dwyer, J.H., Baer, N., MacKinnon, D.P., Hansen, W.B. and Flay, B.R. (1990) Relative effectiveness of comprehensive community programming for drug abuse prevention with high-risk and low-risk adolescents. *Journal of Consulting and Clinical Psychology*, 58(4), 447–56.

Johnson, G. and Hunter, R. (1985) *Law-related education as a delinquency prevention strategy: A three-year evaluation of the impact of LRE on students.* Unpublished manuscript, Center for Action Research, Boulder, CO.

Jones, E.M., Gottfredson, G.D. and Gottfredson, D.C. (1997) Success for some: An evaluation of a Success for All Program. *Evaluation Review,* 21(6), 643–70.

Kaufman, J.S., Jason, L.A., Sawlski, L.M. and Halpert, J.A. (1994) A comprehensive multi-media program to prevent smoking among black students. *Journal of Drug Education,* 24(2), 95–108.

Kellam, S.G. and Rebok, G.W. (1992) Building developmental and etiological theory through epidemiologically based preventive intervention trials. In J. McCord and R.E. Tremblay (eds), *Preventing antisocial behavior: Interventions from birth through adolescence.* New York, NY: Guilford Press, 162–95.

Kellam, S.G., Rebok, G.W., Ialongo, N. and Mayer, L.S. (1994) The course and malleability of aggressive behavior from early first grade into middle school: Results of a developmental epidemiologically-based preventive trial. *Journal of Child Psychology and Psychiatry,* 35(2), 259–81.

Kenney, D.J. and Watson, T.S. (1996) Reducing fear in the schools: Managing conflict through student problem solving. *Education and Urban Society,* 28(4), 436–55.

Kent, R.N. and O'Leary, K.D. (1976) A controlled evaluation of behavior modification with conduct problem children. *Journal of Consulting and Clinical Psychology,* 44(4), 586–96.

Kim, S., McLeod, J.H. and Shantzis, C. (1993) An outcome evaluation of Here's Looking At You 2000. *Journal of Drug Education,* 23(1), 67–81.

Krug, E.G., Brener, N.D., Dahlberg, L.L., Ryan, G.W. and Powell, K.E. (1997) The impact of an elementary school-based violence prevention program on visits to the school nurse. *American Journal of Preventive Medicine,* 13(6), 459–63.

Law Enforcement News (1996) Truth and DARE: Washington cities shelve anti-drug curriculum. New York: John Jay College of Criminal Justice.

Lindstrom, P. (1996) *Partnership in crime prevention: Police-school cooperation.* Paper presented at the meeting of the American Society of Criminology, Chicago, IL.

Lipsey, M.W. (1992) Juvenile delinquency treatment: A meta-analytic inquiry into the variability of effects. In T.D. Cook, H. Cooper, D.S. Cordray, H. Hartmann, L.V. Hedges, R.J. Light, T.A. Louis and F. Mosteller (eds), *Meta-analysis for explanation.* New York: Russell Sage Foundation, 83–127.

Lipsey, M.W. and Derzon, J.H. (1998) Predictors of violent or serious delinquency in adolescence and early adulthood: A synthesis of longitudinal research. In R. Loeber and D.P. Farrington (eds), *Serious and violent juvenile offenders: Risk factors and successful interventions.* Thousand Oaks, CA: Sage, 86–105.

Lipsey, M.W. and Wilson, D.B. (1993) The efficacy of psychological, educational, and behavioral treatment: Confirmation from meta-analysis. *American Psychologist,* 48(2), 1181–209.

Lipsey, M.W. and Wilson, D.B. (2001) Practical meta-analysis. In L. Bickman and D. Rog (eds), *Applied social research methods series.* Thousand Oaks, CA: Sage.

Lochman, J.E. (1985) Effects of different treatment lengths in cognitive behavioral interventions with aggressive boys. *Child Psychiatry and Human Development,* 16(1), 45–56.

Lochman, J.E. (1992) Cognitive-behavioral intervention with aggressive boys: Three-year follow-up and preventive effects. *Journal of Consulting and Clinical Psychology,* 60(3), 426–32.

Lochman, J.E., Burch, P.R., Curry, J.F. and Lampron, L.B. (1984) Treatment and generalization effects of cognitive-behavioral and goal-setting interventions with aggressive boys. *Journal of Consulting and Clinical Psychology*, 52(5), 915–16.

Lochman, J.E. and Curry, J.F. (1986) Effects of social problem-solving training and self-instruction training with aggressive boys. *Journal of Clinical Child Psychology*, 15(2), 159–64.

Lochman, J.E., Lampron, L.B., Burch, P.R. and Curry, J.F. (1985) Client characteristics associated with behavior change for treated and untreated aggressive boys. *Journal of Abnormal Child Psychology*, 13(4), 527–38.

Lochman, J.E., Lampron, L.B., Gemmer, T.C., Harris, S.R. and Wyckoff, G.M. (1989) Teacher consultation and cognitive-behavioral interventions with aggressive boys. *Psychology in the Schools*, 26, 179–88.

Longstreth, L.E., Shanley, F.J. and Rice, R.E. (1964) Experimental evaluation of a high-school program for potential drop-outs. *Journal of Educational Psychology*, 55(4), 228–36.

LoSciuto, L. and Ausetts, M.A. (1988) Evaluation of a drug abuse prevention program: A field experiment. *Addictive Behaviors*, 13, 337–51.

LoSciuto, L., Rajala, A.K., Townsend, T.N. and Taylor, A.S. (1996) An outcome evaluation of Across Ages: An intergenerational mentoring approach to drug prevention. *Journal of Adolescent Research*, 11(1), 116–29.

MacKinnon, D.P., Johnson, C.A., Pentz, M.A., Dwyer, J.H., Hansen, W.B., Flay, B.R. and Wang, E.Y. (1991) Mediating mechanisms in a school-based drug prevention program: First-year effects of the Midwestern Prevention Project. *Health Psychology*, 10(3), 164–72.

Malvin, J.H., Moskowitz, J.M., Schaeffer, G.A. and Schaps, E. (1984) Teacher training in affective education for the primary prevention of adolescent drug abuse. *American Journal of Drug and Alcohol Abuse*, 10(2), 223–35.

Mayer, G.R. and Butterworth, T.W. (1979) A preventive approach to school violence and vandalism: An experimental study. *Personnel and Guidance Journal*, 57, 436–41.

Mayer, G.R., Butterworth, T., Nafpaktitis, M. and Sulzer-Azaroff, B. (1983) Preventing school vandalism and improving discipline: A three-year study. *Journal of Applied Behavior Analysis*, 16(4), 355–69.

McAlister, A., Perry, C., Killen, J., Slinkard, L.A. and Maccoby, N. (1980) Pilot study of smoking, alcohol, and drug abuse prevention. *American Journal of Public Health*, 70(7), 719–21.

McCord, J., Tremblay, R.E., Vitaro, F. and Desmarais-Gervais, L. (1994) Boys' disruptive behaviour, school adjustment, and delinquency: The Montreal Prevention Experiment. *International Journal of Behavioral Development*, 17(4), 739–52.

McPartland, J.M. and Nettles, S.M. (1991) Using community adults as advocates or mentors for at-risk middle school students: A two-year evaluation of Project RAISE. *American Journal of Education*, 99, 568–86.

Moberg, D.P. and Piper, D.L. (1990) An outcome evaluation of Project Model Health: A middle school health promotion program. *Health Education Quarterly*, 17(1), 37–51.

Moskowitz, J.M., Malvin, J., Schaeffer, G.A. and Schaps, E. (1983) Evaluation of a junior high school primary prevention program. *Addictive Behaviors*, 8, 393–401.

Moskowitz, J.M., Schaps, E. and Malvin, J.H. (1982) Process and outcome evaluation in primary prevention: The Magic Circle Program. *Evaluation Review*, 6(6), 775–88.

Moskowitz, J.M., Schaps, E., Schaeffer, G.A. and Malvin, J.H. (1984) Evaluation of a substance abuse prevention program for junior high school students. *The International Journal of the Addictions*, 19(4), 419–30.

Nelson, G. and Carson, P. (1988) Evaluation of a social problem-solving skills program for third- and fourth-grade students. *American Journal of Community Psychology*, 16(1), 79–99.

Newman, I.M., Anderson, C.S. and Farrell, K.A. (1992) Role rehearsal and efficacy: Two 15-month evaluations of a ninth-grade alcohol education program. *Journal of Drug Education*, 22(1), 55–67.

O'Donnell, J., Hawkins, J.D., Catalano, R.F., Abbott, R.D. and Day, L.E. (1995) Preventing school failure, drug use, and delinquency among low-income children: Long-term intervention in elementary schools. *American Journal of Orthopsychiatry*, 65(1), 87–100.

Olexa, D.F. and Forman, S.G. (1984) Effects of social problem-solving training on classroom behavior of urban disadvantaged students. *Journal of School Psychology*, 22, 165–75.

Olweus, D. (1991) Bully/victim problems among schoolchildren: Basic facts and effects of a school based intervention program. In D.J. Pepler and K.H. Rubin (eds), *The development and treatment of childhood aggression*. Hillsdale, NJ: Lawrence Erlbaum, 411–18.

Olweus, D. (1992) Bullying among schoolchildren: Intervention and prevention. In R. DeV. Peters, R.J. McMahon and V.L. Quinsey (eds), *Aggression and violence throughout the life span*. Newbury Park, CA: Sage, 100–25.

Olweus, D. and Alsaker, F.D. (1991) Assessing change in a cohort-longitudinal study with hierarchical data. In D. Magnusson, L.R. Bergman, G. Rudinger and B. Torestad (eds), *Problems and methods in longitudinal research: Stability and change*. Cambridge: Cambridge University Press, 107–32.

Orpinas, P., Parcel, G.S., McAlister, A. and Frankowski, R. (1995) Violence prevention in middle schools: A pilot evaluation. *Journal of Adolescent Health*, 17(6), 360–71.

Patterson, G.R. (1982) *Coercive family process*. Eugene, OR: Castalia Publishing.

Pedro-Carroll, J.L. and Alpert-Gillis, L.J. (1997) Preventive interventions for children of divorce: A developmental model for 5 and 6 year old children. *Journal of Primary Prevention*, 18(1), 5–23.

Pedro-Carroll, J.L. and Cowen, E.L. (1985) The Children of Divorce Intervention Program: An investigation of the efficacy of a school-based prevention program. *Journal of Consulting and Clinical Psychology*, 53(5), 603–11.

Pedro-Carroll, J.L., Cowen, E.L., Hightower, A.D. and Guare, J.C. (1986) Preventive intervention with latency-aged children of divorce: A replication study. *American Journal of Community Psychology*, 14(3), 277–90.

Pentz, M.A., Dwyer, J.H., MacKinnon, D.P., Flay, B.R., Hansen, W.B., Wang, E.Y.I. and Johnson, C.A. (1989) A multicommunity trial for primary prevention of adolescent drug abuse: Effects on drug use prevalence. *Journal of the American Medical Association*, 261(22), 3259–66.

Pentz, M.A., MacKinnon, D.P., Flay, B.R., Hansen, W.B., Johnson, C.A. and Dwyer, J.H. (1989) Primary prevention of chronic diseases in adolescence: Effects of the Midwestern Prevention Project on tobacco use. *American Journal of Epidemiology*, 130(4), 713–24.

Pentz, M.A., Trebow, E.A., Hansen, W.B., MacKinnon, D.P., Dwyer, J.H., Johnson, C.A., Flay, B.R., Daniels, S. and Cormack, C. (1990) Effects of program implementation on adolescent drug use behavior: The Midwestern Prevention Project (MPP). *Evaluation Review*, 14(3), 264–89.

Pepler, D.J., King, G. and Byrd, W. (1991) A social-cognitively based social skills training program for aggressive children. In D.J. Pepler and K.H. Rubin (eds), *The development and treatment of childhood aggression*. Hillsdale, NJ: Lawrence Erlbaum, 361–79.

Perry, C.L., Grant, M., Ernberg, G., Florenzano, R.U., Langdon, M.C., Myeni, A.D., Waahlberg, R., Berg, S., Andersson, K., Fisher, K.J., Blaze-Temple, D., Cross, D.,

Saunders, B., Jacobs, D.R., Jr. and Schmid, T. (1989) WHO collaborative study on alcohol education and young people: Outcomes of a four-country pilot study. *The International Journal of the Addictions*, 24(12), 1145–71.

Perry, C.L., Williams, C.L., Veblen-Mortenson, S., Toomey, T.L., Komro, K.A., Anstine, P.S., McGovern, P.G., Finnegan, J.R., Forster, J.L., Wagenaar, A.C. and Wolfson, M. (1996) Project Northland: Outcomes of a communitywide alcohol use prevention program during early adolescence. *American Journal of Public Health*, 86(7), 956–65.

Reckless, W.C. and Dinitz, S. (1972) *The prevention of juvenile delinquency: An experiment.* Columbus, OH: Ohio State University Press.

Reyes, O. and Jason, L.A. (1991) An evaluation of a high school drop-out prevention program. *Journal of Community Psychology*, 19, 221–30.

Ringwalt, C., Ennett, S.T. and Holt, K.D. (1991) An outcome evaluation of Project DARE (Drug Abuse Resistance Education). *Health Education Research*, 6(3), 327–37.

Ringwalt, C., Greene, J., Ennett, S., Iachan, R., Clayton, R.R. and Leukefeld, C.G. (1994) *Past and Future Directions of the DARE Program: An Evaluation Review: Draft Final Report (Grant Number 91-DD-CX-K053).* Washington, DC: National Institute of Justice.

Rosenbaum, D.P., Flewelling, R.L., Bailey, S.L., Ringwalt, C.L. and Wilkinson, D.L. (1994) Cops in the classroom: A longitudinal evaluation of Drug Abuse Resistance Education (DARE). *Journal of Research in Crime and Delinquency*, 31(1), 3–31.

Rosenthal, R. and Rubin, D.B. (1982) A simple, general purpose display of magnitude of experimental effect. *Journal of Educational Psychology*, 74(2), 166–9.

Ross, J.G., Saavedra, P.J., Shur, G.H., Winters, F. and Felner, R.D. (1992) The effectiveness of an after-school program for primary grade latchkey students on precursors of substance abuse. *Journal of Community Psychology, OSAP Special Issue*, 22–38.

Rotheram, M.J. (1980) Social skills training programs in elementary and high school classrooms. In D.P. Rathjen and J.P. Foreyt (eds), *Social competence: Interventions for children and adults.* New York: Pergamon, 69–112.

Rotheram, M.J. (1982) Social skills training with underachievers, disruptive and exceptional children. *Psychology in the Schools*, 19, 532–9.

Rotheram, M.J., Armstrong, M. and Booraem, C. (1982) Assertiveness training in fourth- and fifth-grade children. *American Journal of Community Psychology*, 10(5), 567–82.

Sarason, I.G. and Sarason, B.R. (1981) Teaching cognitive and social skills to high school students. *Journal of Consulting and Clinical Psychology*, 49(6), 908–18.

Sarvela, P.D. and McClendon, E.J. (1987) An impact evaluation of a rural youth drug education program. *Journal of Drug Education*, 17(3), 213–31.

Schaps, E., DiBartolo, R., Moskowitz, J., Palley, C.S. and Churgin, S. (1981) A review of 127 drug abuse prevention program evaluations. *Journal of Drug Issues*, 11(1), 17–43.

Schaps, E., Moskowitz, J.M., Condon, J.W. and Malvin, J. (1984) A process and outcome evaluation of an affective teacher training primary prevention program. *Journal of Alcohol and Drug Education*, 29, 35–64.

Schinke, S.P., Botvin, G.J. and Orliandi, M.A. (1991) *Substance abuse in children and adolescents: Evaluation and intervention.* Newbury Park, CA: Sage.

Severson, H.H., Glasgow, R., Wirt, R., Brozovsky, P., Zoref, L., Black, C., Biglan, A., Ary, D. and Weissman, W. (1991) Preventing the use of smokeless tobacco and cigarettes by teens: Results of a classroom intervention. *Health Education Research*, 6(1), 109–20.

Shapiro, J.P. and Paulson, R.A. (1998) *The Peacemakers Program, year II: Final report.* Unpublished manuscript, Center for Research, Quality Improvement and Training, Applewoods Centers, Inc., Cleveland, OH.

Sheehan, M., Schonfeld, C., Ballard, R., Schofield, F., Najman, J. and Siskind, V. (1996) A three-year outcome evaluation of a theory-based drink driving education program. *Journal of Drug Education*, 26(3), 295–312.

Sheridan, J.T., Baker, S.B. and de Lissovoy, V. (1984) Structured group counseling and explicit bibliotherapy as in-school strategies for preventing problems in youth of changing families. *The School Counselor*, 32, 134–41.

Sherman, L.W., Gottfredson, D.C., MacKenzie, D., Eck, J., Reuter, P. and Bushway, S. (1997) *Preventing crime: What works, what doesn't, what's promising: A report to the United States Congress.* Washington, DC: US Department of Justice, Office of Justice Programs.

Shope, J.T., Copeland, L.A., Maharg, R. and Dielman, T.E. (1996) Effectiveness of a high school alcohol misuse prevention program. *Alcoholism: Clinical and Experimental Research*, 20(5), 791–8.

Shope, J.T., Copeland, L.A., Marcoux, B.C. and Kamp, M.E. (1996) Effectiveness of a school-based substance abuse prevention program. *Journal of Drug Education*, 26(4), 323–37.

Shope, J.T., Dielman, T.E., Butchart, A.T., Campanelli, P.C. and Kloska, D.D. (1992) An elementary school-based alcohol misuse prevention program: A follow-up evaluation. *Journal of Studies on Alcohol*, 53(2), 106–21.

Shope, J.T., Kloska, D.D., Dielman, T.E. and Maharg, R. (1994) Longitudinal evaluation of an enhanced Alcohol Misuse Prevention Study (AMPS) curriculum for grades six–eight. *Journal of School Health*, 64(4), 160–6.

Shure, M.B. and Spivak, G. (1979) Interpersonal cognitive problem solving and primary prevention: Programming for preschool and kindergarten children. *Journal of Clinical Child Psychology*, 8, 89–94.

Shure, M.B. and Spivak, G. (1980) Interpersonal problem solving as a mediator of behavioral adjustment in preschool and kindergarten children. *Journal of Applied Developmental Psychology*, 1, 29–44.

Shure, M.B. and Spivak, G. (1982) Interpersonal problem-solving in young children: A cognitive approach to prevention. *American Journal of Community Psychology*, 10(3), 341–56.

Skroban, S.B., Gottfredson, D.C. and Gottfredson, G.D. (1999) A school-based social competency promotion demonstration. *Evaluation Review*, 23(1), 3–27.

Sloan, V.J., Jason, L.A. and Bogat, G.A. (1984) A comparison of orientation methods for elementary school transfer students. *Child Study Journal*, 14(1), 47–60.

Snow, D.L., Tebes, J.K., Arthur, M.W. and Tapasak, R.C. (1992) Two-year follow-up of a social-cognitive intervention to prevent substance use. *Journal of Drug Education*, 22(2), 101–14.

Snyder, H.N., Sickmund, M. and Poe-Yamagata, E. (1996) *Juvenile offenders and victims: 1996 update on violence.* Washington, DC: Office of Juvenile Justice and Delinquency Prevention.

Solomon, D., Watson, M.S., Delucchi, K.L., Schaps, E. and Battistich, V. (1988) Enhancing children's prosocial behavior in the classroom. *American Educational Research Journal*, 25(4), 527–54.

Sorsdahl, S.N. and Sanche, R.P. (1985) The effects of classroom meetings on self-concept and behavior. *Elementary School Guidance and Counseling*, 20, 49–56.

Spoth, R.L., Redmond, C. and Shin, C. (1999) *Randomized trial of brief family interventions for general populations: Adolescent substance use outcomes four years following baseline.* Ames, IA: Iowa State University, Institute for Social and Behavioral Research.

Stevens, M.M., Freeman, D.H., Jr., Mott, L. and Youells, F. (1996) Three-year results of prevention programs on marijuana use: The New Hampshire Study. *Journal of Drug Education*, 26(3), 257–73.

Stoil, M., Hill, G. and Brounstein, P.J. (1994) *The seven core strategies for ATOD prevention: Findings of the National Structured Evaluation of What is Working Well Where.* Paper presented at the meeting of the American Public Health Association, Washington, DC.

Stuart, R.B. (1974) Teaching facts about drugs: Pushing or preventing? *Journal of Educational Psychology,* 66(2), 189–201.

Taggart, R. (1995) *Quantum Opportunity Program.* Philadelphia, PA: Opportunities Industrialization Centers of America.

Thompson, D.G. and Hudson, G.R. (1982) Values clarification and behavioral group counseling with ninth-grade boys in a residential school. *Journal of Counseling Psychology,* 29(4), 394–9.

Tobler, N.S. (1986) Meta-analysis of 143 adolescent drug prevention programs: Quantitative outcome results of program participants compared to a control or comparison group. *Journal of Drug Issues,* 16(4), 537–67.

Tobler, N.S. (1992) Drug prevention programs can work: Research findings. *Journal of Addictive Diseases,* 11(3), 1–28.

Tobler, N.S. and Stratton, H.H. (1997) Effectiveness of school-based drug prevention programs: A meta-analysis of the research. *Journal of Primary Prevention,* 18(1), 71–128.

Tremblay, R.E. and Craig, W.M. (1995) Developmental crime prevention. In M. Tonry and D.P. Farrington (eds), *Building a safer society: Strategic approaches to crime prevention.* Chicago, IL: University of Chicago Press, 151–236.

Tremblay, R.E., Kurtz, L., Mâsse, L.C., Vitaro, F. and Pihl, R.O. (1994) *A bimodal preventive intervention for disruptive kindergarten boys: Its impact through mid-adolescence.* Montreal, Canada: University of Montreal, Research Unit on Children's Psycho-Social Maladjustment.

Tremblay, R.E., McCord, J., Boileau, H., Charlebois, P., Gagnon, C., LeBlanc, M. and Larivée, S. (1991) Can disruptive boys be helped to become competent? *Psychiatry,* 54, 148–61.

Tremblay, R.E., Pagani-Kurtz, L., Vitaro, F., Mâsse, L.C. and Pihl, R.O. (1995) A bimodal preventive intervention for disruptive kindergarten boys: Its impact through mid-adolescence. *Journal of Consulting and Clinical Psychology,* 63(4), 560–8.

Tremblay, R.E., Vitaro, F., Bertrand, L., LeBlanc, M., Beauchesne, H., Boileau, H. and David, L. (1992) Parent and child training to prevent early onset of delinquency: The Montreal Longitudinal-Experiment Study. In J. McCord and R.E. Tremblay (eds), *Preventing antisocial behavior: Interventions from birth through adolescence.* New York, NY: Guilford Press, 117–38.

Trice, A.D., Parker, F.C. and Safer, D.J. (1982) A comparison of senior high school interventions for disruptive students. In D.J. Safer (ed.), *School programs for disruptive adolescents.* Baltimore, MD: University Park Press, 333–40.

Walker, H.M., Kavanagh, K., Stiller, B., Golly, A., Severson, H.H. and Feil, E. (1998) First step to success: An early intervention approach for preventing school antisocial behavior. *Journal of Emotional and Behavioral Disorders,* 6(2), 66–80.

Weinstein, R.S., Soule, C.R., Collins, F., Cone, J., Mehlhorn, M. and Simontacchi, K. (1991) Expectations and high school change: Teacher-researcher collaboration to prevent school failure. *American Journal of Community Psychology,* 19(3), 333–63.

Weissberg, R.P. and Caplan, M. (1994) *Promoting social competence and preventing antisocial behavior in young urban adolescents.* London: Thomas Coram Research Unit, University of London.

Weissberg, R.P., Gesten, E.L., Carnrike, C.L., Toro, P.A., Rapkin, B.D., Davidson, E. and Cowen, E.L. (1981) Social problem-solving skills training: A competence-building intervention with second- to fourth-grade children. *American Journal of Community Psychology*, 9(4), 411–23.

Weissberg, R.P., Gesten, E.L., Rapkin, B.D., Cowen, E.L., Davidson, E., Flores de Apodaca, R. and McKim, B.J. (1981) Evaluation of a social-problem-solving training program for suburban and inner-city third-grade children. *Journal of Consulting and Clinical Psychology*, 49(2), 251–61.

Weissberg, R.P. and Greenberg, M.T. (1998) School and community competence-enhancement and prevention programs. In W. Damon (Series Ed.), I.E. Sigel and K.A. Renninger (Vol. Eds), *Handbook of child psychology: Vol. 4. Child psychology in practice* (5th edn). New York: John Wiley and Sons, 877–954.

Werch, C.E., Anzalone, D.M., Brokiewicz, L.M., Felker, J., Carlson, J.M. and Castellon-Vogel, E.A. (1996) An intervention for preventing alcohol use among inner-city middle school students. *Archives of Family Medicine*, 5(3), 146–52.

Wilhelmsen, B.U., Laberg, J.C. and Klepp, K. (1994) Evaluation of two student and teacher involved alcohol prevention programmes. *Addiction*, 89, 1157–65.

Wodarski, J.S. (1987a) Evaluating a social learning approach to teaching adolescents about alcohol and driving: A multiple variable evaluation. In B.A. Thyer and W.W. Hudson (eds), *Progress in behavioral social work*. New York: The Haworth Press, 121–44.

Wodarski, J.S. (1987b) Teaching adolescents about alcohol and driving: A two year follow-up. *Journal of Drug Education*, 17(4), 327–44.

Wodarski, J.S. and Filipczak, J. (1982) Behavioral intervention in public schools: Long-term follow-up. In D.J. Safer (ed.), *School programs for disruptive adolescents*. Baltimore, MD: University Park Press, 201–14.

Zelie, K., Stone, C.I. and Lehr, E. (1980) Cognitive-behavioral intervention in school discipline: A preliminary study. *The Personnel and Guidance Journal*, 59, 80–3.

# 5 Communities and crime prevention

*Brandon C. Welsh and Akemi Hoshi*

This chapter aims to review the existing scientific evidence on the effectiveness of community-based programs to prevent crime. More often than not, community-based crime prevention is thought to be some combination of developmental (Tremblay and Craig, 1995) and situational (Clarke, 1995) crime prevention. Unlike these two crime prevention strategies, there is little agreement in the academic literature on the definition of community prevention and the types of programs that fall within it (Bennett, 1996). Hope (1995, p. 21) defines community crime prevention as "actions intended to change the social conditions that are believed to sustain crime in residential communities." Local social institutions (e.g. families, associations, churches, youth clubs) are usually the medium by which these programs are delivered to tackle delinquency and crime problems (Hope, 1995, p. 21). This chapter instead focuses on the community as the setting for programs to prevent crime. Community mobilization, gang membership prevention, gang member intervention, mentoring, afterschool recreation, and gun buy-back programs are the different types of community-based programs covered here.

This chapter updates Sherman's (1997) review of community-based crime prevention. We used the same program categories as Sherman, as well as the same criteria for deciding what programs to include: (1) the community was the focus of the intervention; (2) an outcome or impact evaluation was conducted; and (3) there was an outcome measure of delinquency or crime. As with the other chapters in this volume, programs are evaluated on the Scientific Methods Scale, which ranks scientific studies from 1 (weakest) to 5 (strongest) on overall internal validity (see Chapter 2).

To identify new evaluations of community-based crime prevention programs, we studied review papers and other relevant sources on community crime prevention that have been published since Sherman's chapter (Catalano *et al.*, 1998; Hope, 1998; Howell, 1998; Rosenbaum, Lurigio and Davis, 1998; Herrenkohl *et al.*, 2001) and searched selected criminology journals. We also contacted a number of leading researchers in the field.[1]

This chapter is divided into nine sections. The first section overviews the main theories that have been advanced to explain the community-level influence on crime and offending and that have been used to inform community crime prevention programs. The next five sections review community-based crime prevention programs meeting the criteria for inclusion in five distinct programmatic areas: community mobilization, gang prevention and intervention (divided into gang membership prevention and gang member intervention), mentoring, afterschool recreation, and the removal of criminogenic commodities (specifically, gun buy-back programs), respectively. The seventh section presents conclusions on the effectiveness of the different types of programs reviewed. Here we identify what works, what does not work, what is promising and what is unknown. The eighth section discusses key methodological issues and priorities for research in evaluating community crime prevention programs, and the final section provides some concluding remarks.

## Community crime prevention theory

Numerous theories have been advanced over the years to explain the community-level influence on crime and offending and have come to form the basis of community crime prevention programs (for excellent reviews, see Byrne and Sampson, 1986; Reiss and Tonry, 1986; Farrington, 1993; Sampson and Lauritsen, 1994; Wikström, 1998). Bennett (1998) identifies four main theories that have informed community-based crime prevention programs: community disorganization, community disorder, community empowerment and community regeneration. These four theories are the focus of this section.

### Community disorganization theory

More commonly referred to as social disorganization theory, the theory of community disorganization largely developed out of the research by Shaw and McKay (1942, 1969) on the relationship between delinquency and urban areas in Chicago neighborhoods from the 1900s to 1950s. According to community disorganization theory, offending or, more specifically, male juvenile delinquency, as was the focus of Shaw and McKay's work, was seen as a result of the disruption of community social order or organization, which is maintained by such social institutions as the family, church, and school, as well as community centers and organized clubs for young people (e.g. YM/YWCA). Giving rise to this breakdown in social organization and, hence, the variation in delinquency rates across communities, were three key structural factors: low economic status, ethnic heterogeneity and residential mobility (Sampson and Lauritsen, 1994, p. 44).

This has been named the "classic" view of social disorganization theory (Wikström, 1998). More "contemporary" views of social disorganization and its relationship to offending have noted the importance of other structural influences on offending, such as family disruption and weak social cohesion, which can involve, for example, an absence of neighborhood or collective efficacy (Sampson, Raudenbush and Earls, 1997).

Under the general framework of community disorganization theory, the scope for the prevention of offending and crime, at least during the first half of the twentieth century, was seen to rest "in a program of the physical rehabilitation of slum areas and the development of community organization" (Burgess, 1942, p. xi). In more recent decades, community disorganization theory has given rise to programs emphasizing the empowerment or mobilization of community residents to take preventive action to reduce crime in their neighborhoods (Rosenbaum, Lurigio and Davis, 1998, p.212).

## Community disorder theory

Community disorder theory has its roots in the "Broken Windows" hypo-thesis of Wilson and Kelling (1982), which postulates that disorderly behav-ior is the precursor to more serious street crime and decay, by engendering fear amongst community members and producing a spiral of decline and weakened social controls. Kelling and Coles (1996), in a recent follow-up to the Broken Windows perspective, describe the general thrust of community disorder theory:

...disorderly behavior unregulated and unchecked signals to citizens that the area is unsafe. Responding prudently, and fearful, citizens will stay off the streets, avoid certain areas, and curtail their normal activities and associations. As citizens withdraw physically, they also withdraw from roles of mutual support with fellow citizens on the streets, thereby relin-quishing the social controls they formerly helped to maintain within the community, as social atomization sets in. Ultimately the result for such a neighborhood ... is increasing vulnerability to an influx of more dis-orderly behavior and serious crime.

(Kelling and Coles, 1996, p. 20)

Largely an urban phenomenon, disorder is, in its widest sense, "incivility, boorish behavior that disturbs life" (Kelling and Coles, 1996, p. 14). Skogan (1990, p. 4) distinguishes between social and physical disorder: the former is related to behavior (e.g. public drinking, begging, loitering), while the latter involves "visual signs of negligence and unchecked decay" (e.g. abandoned buildings and vehicles, litter, graffiti). The scope for crime prevention, as guided by this theory, rests largely with efforts to tackle the disorderly behav-ior when it is minor and/or conditions prior to them taking root in the community and resulting in more serious criminal offending and social decline. Preventive action is to take place largely through a partnership between police and local community residents.

## Community empowerment theory

The theory of community empowerment is concerned with the sharing of power with residents, often of public housing estates, in decision-making processes and management activities that impact on, either directly or indi-rectly, those social conditions believed to sustain crime in residential settings. Community empowerment, as noted by Bennett (1998, p.376), is believed to make residents "more satisfied, which, in turn, will encourage them to stay and take greater interest in, and responsibility for, their area of residence." Programs that attempt to empower communities can take many different forms, including providing services for the community such as afterschool recreation programs.

## *Community regeneration theory*

Drawing largely upon the work of Taub, Taylor and Dunham (1984), Bennett (1998) assembles the influences of local economic conditions or, at least, the perceptions held by residents about such matters on community crime prevention, under a theory called community regeneration. The theory of community regeneration is not confined to the interests of community safety alone; the overall well-being or "wellness" of the community is of central concern. At the level of which safety from crime is one element, is of central concern. At the level of safety for one's person or property, community regeneration theory is largely concerned with the effect (or the perceived effect on the part of community residents) of the community's economic base or the resources at its disposal to ward off the onset of factors conducive to less than desirable levels of delinquency and crime, such as the "flight" of middle- and upper-class residents, the loss of public and private services, and an increase in rental properties. Bennett states that "Several important factors in shaping this perception are the level of investment in the community, commercial interest in the area, and the level of maintenance of the housing stock" (1998, p.376). According to Taub, Taylor and Dunham (1984, p.187), corporate investment and its relationship to individual investment is also an important protective factor against neighborhood decline and crime:

When corporate investment is at a high enough level, then the market for individual investment becomes secure enough that individuals choose to spend on rehabilitation, to withstand the fears of crime or impending racial change, and to take part in other actions that collec-tively determine the quality of neighborhood life.

The community regeneration theory encapsulates Hope's "resource mobilization" paradigm, which holds that "it may not be sufficient merely to promote social cohesion in communities if they are starved of resources to address the social and economic conditions that are undermining that cohe-sion" (Hope, 1995, pp.34–5). As a consequence, Hope (1995) argues that any efforts at the development of a community-based crime prevention scheme should first be concerned with the transfer of both economic and political resources to local institutions and residents. (This latter view pre-sents an overlap between community empowerment and regeneration theo-ries.) This transfer of resources, it is argued, will contribute to the empowerment of communities, help integrate marginalized youth into the wider community, and enable the community to tackle key community-level risk factors for delinquency (Hope, 1995, p.35).

## Community mobilization

Comprehensive crime prevention strategies frequently involve the mobil-ization of community members to participate actively in planning and imple-menting prevention activities. According to Sherman (1997, Chapter 3, p.9), the definition of community mobilization has varied greatly, "from the cre-ation of formal community development organizations to the mobilization of resources from outside the community to help solve local problems like crime and unemployment." Hope (1995) refers to community mobilization as resource mobilization and claims that while the promotion of social cohesion in communities is important to preventing crime, resource mobilization is concerned with "the transfer of economic and political resources to empower local communities, to give youth a stake in conformity, and to relieve the frustration of blocked aspirations and relieve deprivation that induce delinquency" (p. 35).

Table 5.1 provides an overview of key elements of four community mobilization programs meeting the criteria for inclusion in this review. All of the programs were carried out in the United States. The age of participating subjects is not identified for the four programs. With the exception of the program by Fagan (1987), this is because the programs did not target one age group specifically, but were area-based or city-wide events. All of the programs took place in high-crime areas.

Treatment duration in three of the four programs was four years; information for the duration of the fourth program (Bibb, 1967) was not available. Only the program by Fowler and Mangione (1986) evaluated program effects during the post-intervention phase; all of the other studies measured immediate outcomes only. The methodological ratings of the four programs was low. Two programs (Fowler and Mangione, 1986; Fagan, 1987) did not use comparison groups and each received a scientific methods score of 2. The program by Bennett and Lavrakas (1989) used a nonequivalent control group, defined as the area around the target areas. The fourth program (Bibb, 1967), although often deemed as "the best-known single experiment in community organization" (Klein, 1995, p. 140), was not assigned a scientific methods score, because no information on the evaluation design was reported. It is unfortunate that the efforts of this comprehensive community-based intervention program shifted away from community empowerment and was taken over by the politics of the day, which led to a displacement of immediate objectives to a more "general challenge to local sources of political power, in which the mundane aims of crime prevention became subsumed in the broader political struggle" (Hope, 1995, p. 37).

The results of the three other programs were mixed. While Fowler and Mangione (1986) initially reported lower crime rates and less fear of crime, only fear of crime remained a desirable effect at the later follow-up. The Neighborhood Anti-Crime Self-Help program (Bennett and Lavrakas, 1989) had no desirable effects on crime rates in nine out of ten cities. It was, however, successful in reducing fear of crime in most areas. Fagan (1987) claims that serious juvenile violent crime was reduced in three of the six high-crime cities he evaluated. It is not clear, however, if an evaluation was done for the other three cities.

The Neighborhood Anti-Crime Self-Help program (Bennett and Lavrakas, 1989) was a comprehensive crime prevention scheme sponsored by the Eisenhower Foundation and started in 1983. Ten community-based organizations in ten high-crime cities defined the target areas; the comparison areas were defined as the ring around the target areas. The study's primary data source was panel surveys of heads of households; monthly police recorded crime statistics were also used. Interventions ranged from individual-level social service

*Table 5.1* Community mobilization programs

| Study author, name, and location | Age at intervention | Context of intervention | Duration and type of intervention | Sample size | Follow-up[a] and results[b] | Scientific methods score |
|---|---|---|---|---|---|---|
| Bibb (1967), Mobilization for Youth, New York, NY | n.a. | Nonresidential centers, street, school | n.a.; community mobilization, detached workers, individual and family services, job training, education | n.a. | Immediate outcome: (no measure of delinquency) | (no information on evaluation design) |
| Fowler and Mangone (1986), Hartford Experiment, Hartford, CT | n/a | Community | 4 years; community organization, recreation, localized policing, environmental modification | 5,000 residents (North Asylum Hill area) | 1 year: informal social control +, burglary rate +, robbery rate +, fear of crime + 3 years: informal social control +, burglary rate −, robbery rate 0, fear of crime + | 2 (before-after) |
| Fagan (1987), Violent Juvenile Offender Research and Development Program, USA | n.a. | Neighborhood-based organizations | 4 years; violent crisis-intervention, mediation, family support, youth skill development | 6 high-crime cities | Immediate outcome: serious juvenile crime + (for 3 cities)[c] | 2 (before-after) |
| Bennett and Lavrakas (1989), Neighborhood Anti-Crime Self-Help Program, USA | n/a | Community-based organizations | 3–4 years; neighborhood watch, crime prevention education, youth employment, recreation | 10 high-crime inner cities | Immediate outcome: crime rate + (for 1 city), crime rate − (for 2 cities), crime rate 0 (for 7 cities); quality of life + (for 3 cities), quality of life 0 (for 7 cities); fear of crime + (for 6 cities), fear of crime − (for 1 city), fear of crime 0 (for 3 cities) | 3 (experimental-control, before-after) |

Notes

T = treatment group; C = control group; n/a = not applicable; n.a. = not available.
a  The period of time in which program effects were evaluated after the intervention had ended.
b  "0" = no intervention effects; "+" = desirable intervention effects; "−" = undesirable intervention effects.
c  It is not clear if an evaluation was done for the other three cities.

provisions to community-wide changes of social structure. Most cities sponsored a variety of activities, which can be broadly grouped into two main categories: (1) opportunity reduction (e.g. neighborhood watch) with public education, and (2) individual- or community-based developmental prevention (e.g. youth employment, recreation). Three sites had both components implemented and the other sites concentrated on one approach or the other. In two sites, program activity was generally very low.

In the ten high-crime inner city areas in which prevention activities took place, crime went down in one area, crime increased in two areas, and crime remained the same in seven areas (all compared to control areas). The program had the strongest impact on residents' fear of crime: six communities showed a desirable change. This strong effect on fear of crime was also shown in the preliminary evaluation findings of the program (Curtis, 1987). Generally, programs with an opportunity reduction focus had the most desirable outcomes. In sum, the program "did not seem to achieve the 'ultimate' goals of crime reduction and improved quality of life" (Bennett and Lavrakas, 1989, p. 361).

Fowler and Mangione (1986) evaluated the National Institute of Justice-sponsored Hartford Experiment. This program used a three-pronged approach to reduce criminal opportunities: physical environment modification, police service reorganization and community organization. The idea was that crime prevention efforts must be multifaceted. The focus of the analysis was the interaction between human behavior and physical environment. It was hypothesized that "the proper design and effective use of the built environment can lead to a reduction in crime and fear" (Fowler and Mangione, 1986, p. 89).

Interventions for the community organization component included block watch and recreational programs. The police service component stressed police centralization in the form of a unit assigned permanently to the area. The physical design component focused on narrowing entrances to streets to restrict traffic flow and visually defining the boundaries of the neighborhood.

The Hartford program expected improvements in three areas: informal social control, burglary and robbery rates, and fear of crime. As mentioned above, fear of crime decreased significantly. Informal social control improved more slowly, but showed a significant positive outcome. The initial reductions in burglary and robbery rates, however, were followed by increases in the third and fourth years of the program. It should be noted that the level of police involvement was significantly reduced in the latter part of the program. The authors contend that a continued reduction in crime rates would have been expected had the police component remained strong. Also, the authors concluded that informal social control by itself is not enough to reduce crime in a community.

From the four community mobilization programs reviewed here, we are left to conclude that this strategy of preventing crime in communities is of unknown effect. The scientific rigor of the evaluations of these programs as a group is very poor, with only one program (Bennett and Lavrakas, 1989) having an evaluation design that meets our threshold for making an assessment of effectiveness (i.e. a scientific methods score of 3 or higher; see

Chapter 2). Furthermore, Bennett and Lavrakas (1989) report mixed results for the program's effect on crime. Of the ten high crime inner-city areas that received the program (compared to control areas), crime rates went down in one area, crime rates increased in two areas, and crime rates remained unchanged in seven areas. Similar mixed results were reported for program effects on fear of crime and quality of life.

Had the methodological rigor of the two other programs that measured crime (Fowler and Mangione, 1986; Fagan, 1987) met the scientific methods score threshold, this would not have resulted in any clear change to our conclusion. This is because the program by Fowler and Mangione (1986), at the most recent assessment of 3 years post-intervention, showed mixed results for its effect on crime. On the basis of the aggregate findings of these programs, it would seem plausible to recommend further testing. However, with no new evaluations of community mobilization programs in more than 10 years, it is questionable whether further testing is merited.

## Gang prevention and intervention

The presence of youth gang violence in the United States is a source of great public concern. According to the 1997 National Youth Gang Survey (Office of Juvenile Justice and Delinquency Prevention, 1999), about 30,500 youth gangs and 816,000 gang members were active. Although the prevalence of youth gangs and gang membership declined overall from 1996 to 1997, small cities and rural counties report increasingly more gang activity. Youth gang members were estimated to be involved in 3,340 homicides in 1997, almost two-thirds of which took place in large cities. Despite a slight decrease from 1996 to 1997, youth gang involvement in other types of criminal activity remained high.

The history of response to youth gang problems has produced two primary strategies: gang membership prevention and gang member intervention. The early youth gang work emphasized prevention, which was followed by intervention (Howell, 1998). We review programs for both types of strategies.

Gang membership prevention programs focus on discouraging children and young people from joining gangs. The target is usually high-risk youth. Gang member intervention programs, on the other hand, target active gangs and gang members. The primary component of these programs is the "detached worker," whose role is "to redirect gang energy toward legitimate activity, including school work, as well as to discourage crime" (Sherman, 1997, Chapter 3, p. 14). The role of these workers varies across programs and in the extent to which they focus on gangs as groups or on gang members as individuals. Crisis intervention is another component of gang member intervention programs. The idea is to mediate and intervene in conflict situations between opposing gangs.

### Gang membership prevention

The key features of three gang membership prevention programs are summarized in Table 5.2. We located two evaluations of Gang Resistance

Table 5.2 Gang membership prevention programs

| Study author, name, and location | Age at intervention | Context of intervention | Duration and type of intervention | Sample size | Follow-up[a] and results[b] | Scientific methods score |
|---|---|---|---|---|---|---|
| Thrasher (1936), Boys Club, New York, NY | 7–13 years (juniors), 13–18 years (intermediates), 18+ years (seniors) | Non-residential center | 4 years (1927–31); recreational and athletic activities, health service, vocational placement | 2,520 members (approximately)[c] | Immediate outcome: delinquency/truancy rate 0 | 2 (before-after) |
| Woodson (1981), House of Umoja, Philadelphia, PA | 13–19 years | Residential center (house) | 3 years; crisis intervention, self-discipline, problem solving, job training, leadership | 30 members (maximum) | Immediate outcome: gang homicides + | 2 (before-after) |
| Thompson and Jason (1988), BUILD, Chicago, IL | 8th graders (14 years) | Public school, community | 12 months; T1 = 12 gang prevention classes, T2 = 12 gang prevention classes and afterschool recreational program, C = no treatment | 117 children in 6 schools (3T and 3C); T1 = 36, T2 = 38, C = 43 | Immediate outcome: (T1 and T2 vs. C): gang membership 0 (Small N joined gangs; 1 of 74 experimentals, 4 of 43 comparison) | 3 (experimental-control, before-after) |

Notes

T = treatment group; C = control group.

a The period of time in which program effects were evaluated after the intervention had ended.

b "0" = no intervention effects; "+" = desirable intervention effects; "–" = undesirable intervention effects.

c 63% of the 4,000 membership capacity of the Boys Club.

Education and Training (GREAT; Palumbo and Ferguson, 1995; Esbensen and Osgood, 1999), but because the programs were delivered in a school setting they have not been included in this review (see Chapter 4). All of the programs were carried out in the United States. At the start of treatment, the age of the subjects ranged from 7 to around 19 years. Thrasher (1936) evaluated an all-round intervention in a Boys Club. The program analyzed by Woodson (1981) took place in a residential setting, and the program evaluated by Thompson and Jason (1988) involved classroom education and after-school activities.

The sample size varied considerably across the three programs, ranging from a high of approximately 2,500 members in Thrasher (1936) to a low of 30 in Woodson (1981). Treatment duration varied from 1 year in the program by Thompson and Jason (1988) to 4 years in Thrasher (1936). The methodological rating of the three programs was very low. Only the program by Thompson and Jason (1988) employed a comparison group.

Only the program by Woodson (1981) produced a desirable result for outcomes of interest to this review. While Thompson and Jason's (1988) program seems to be promising, the results were not statistically significant (only 1 in 74 experimental youth joined gangs, compared to 4 of 43 comparison youth). The New York Boys Club evaluated by Thrasher (1936) found no immediate beneficial effects.

The New York Boys Club, started in 1927, was one of the first attempts to prevent gang membership in a population of potential gang members. This 4-year study tested the hypothesis that recreational, health and vocational services could prevent delinquency among under-privileged boys. Boys were classified according to their age into junior members (7–13 years), intermediates (13–18 years), and seniors (18 years and over). While the club was unable to reach its estimated 4,000 member capacity (63 percent of members were enrolled according to monthly membership statistics), an exact measurement of membership was problematic because of bookkeeping and accounting difficulties.

Analyses at the end of the 4 years showed that the Boys Club had no effect on juvenile delinquency or truancy. Also, the number of offenses committed by club members increased after membership; however, this finding seemed to be the result of increasing age rather than the effect of club participation. Overall, the accumulation of risk factors of family disorganization, poverty, school problems and social disturbance created dynamics that were "beyond the power of the Boys Club to neutralize" (Thrasher, 1936, p. 78).

Another community-based gang prevention program is the House of Umoja (Woodson, 1981), which started in the early 1970s in Philadelphia. This unique grassroots program was initiated by two community residents, David and Falaka Fattah, and is based on the African extended family concept. The House of Umoja consisted of a residential and nonresidential program for youths involved in gangs, offering a sanctuary from street life. "Umoja," a Swahili word meaning "unity within the family," is the underlying philosophy of the program. The residential population was limited to 30 young people, between the ages of 13 and 19. The intervention for target youths (also a maximum of 30 members at one time) included educational development, job training, employment assistance, individual and group counseling, and self-discipline and leadership training. The program also organized a gang summit, which resulted in a gang warfare truce.

Woodson's (1981) conclusion after 3 years (1975 through 1977) of observation, interviews, and in-depth study was that the House of Umoja was effective in reducing the number of gang deaths in Philadelphia. According to him, gang homicides "declined from an average of thirty-nine deaths per year to six in 1976 and to just one death in 1977" (Woodson, 1981, p. 46). These desirable results, however, might not be due to the House of Umoja alone, as other programs operating in Philadelphia at the time claimed credit for part of this reduction in gang homicides (Howell, 1998, p. 287).

Similar to community mobilization, our assessment of the effectiveness of gang membership prevention was hindered by weak evaluation designs of the programs in this category. On the scale of scientific methods, two of the three programs received a score of 2 and the other program (Thompson and Jason, 1988) received a score of 3. For the latter program, fewer subjects in the treatment compared to the control group joined gangs, but the difference was not statistically significant. We are left to conclude that this type of community crime prevention is of unknown effectiveness.

### Gang member intervention

Table 5.3 summarizes key characteristics of nine intervention programs targeted at active gangs and gang members. All of the programs were carried out in the United States; three programs were implemented in Los Angeles (Klein, 1968, 1971; Torres, 1981) and three in Chicago (Gold and Mattick, 1974; Spergel, 1986; Spergel and Grossman, 1997). All of the studies except two, Goldstein and Glick (1994) and Torres (1981), used detached workers in some form, and while most programs intervened in multiple settings (e.g. street, home, school), the emphasis was clearly on the street work of the detached worker. The workers varied in the extent to which they focused on gangs or on individual gang members. Two of the nine programs (Gold and Mattick, 1974; Kennedy, Piehl and Braga, 1996b) were implemented citywide. In the remaining seven programs, sample size varied considerably from a high of 576 gang members (Klein, 1968) to a low of 58 members (Spergel, 1986). Although we know that Torres (1981) analyzed seven gangs, the precise number of members was not provided. Treatment duration varied from 10 months (Spergel, 1986) to 6 years (Gold and Mattick, 1974). The Latino Hills Project (Klein, 1968) followed subjects for 2 years postintervention, while almost all of the other programs had no follow-up once the program ended. At the start of treatment, the age of subjects ranged from 10 to about 24 years, and for two of the nine programs, the age of subjects was not available (Torres, 1981; Goldstein and Glick, 1994).

All nine programs received a scientific methods score between 2 and 3. Six of the nine studies employed control groups and each was given a score of 3. Six of the nine programs showed desirable effects for outcomes of interest to this review. Reduced gang cohesion, delinquency and homicides were some of the desirable results achieved by the gang member intervention programs. The 6-year effort of the Chicago Youth Development Project (Gold and Mattick, 1974) resulted in no desirable effects for outcomes of education,

Table 5.3 Gang member intervention programs

| Study author, name, and location | Age at intervention | Context of intervention | Duration and type of intervention | Sample size | Follow-up[b] and results | Scientific methods score |
|---|---|---|---|---|---|---|
| Miller (1962), The Midcity Project, Boston, MA | 12–21 years | Street, home, community | 3 years; detached workers, community organization, family service, gang work, recreation, job referral | 377 members (T = 205 members in 7 gangs, C = 172 members in 11 gangs) | Immediate outcome: disapproved behavior 0 (school oriented behavior +), illegal acts 0 (girls +, minor offenses +), court appearances 0 | 3 (experimental-control, before-after) |
| Klein (1968), Group Guidance Project, Los Angeles, CA | 12–20 years | Street, community, home | 4 years; detached workers, individual and family counseling, de-isolation, group guidance, community organization, recreational activities | 576 members in 4 gangs | Immediate outcome: delinquency – (especially ages 12–15) | 2 (before-after) |
| Klein (1968, 1971), Latino Hills Project, Los Angeles, CA | 12–20 years | Street | 18 months; detached workers, recreational activities, employment, education, individual therapy | 100 gang members | Immediate outcome: gang cohesion +, delinquency +, 6 months: gang cohesion +, delinquency +, 2 years: gang cohesion 0, delinquency 0 | 2 (before-after) |
| Gold and Mattick (1974), Chicago Youth Development Project, Chicago, IL | 10–19 years | Street, non-residential community center | 6 years; detached workers, community organization, parent education, recreational activities, counseling | 4 city boroughs: T = 2, C = 2 | Immediate outcome: cohesion 0, delinquency 0. Immediate outcome: education 0, arrest rate 0, employment 0 | 3 (experimental-control, before-after) |
| Torres (1981), Gang Violence Reduction Project, Los Angeles, CA | n.a. | Street | 4 years; crisis intervention, truce meetings, feud mediation, job referral, recreation | 7 gangs | Immediate outcome: homicide rate (among target gangs) +, intergang violence (among target gangs) + | 2 (before-after) |
| Spergel (1986), Crisis Intervention Services Project, Chicago, IL | 14–29 years | Street, community | 10 months; detached workers, crisis intervention, conflict mediation, communication. | 2 Chicago areas: T = 1, C = 1 | Immediate outcome: serious gang crimes (for juveniles) +, less serious gang crimes 0, serious gang crimes (adults) – | 3 (experimental-control, before-after) |

| Goldstein and Glick (1994), Aggression Replacement Training (ART), New York, NY | n.a. | Community-based organizations (e.g. graffiti-expunging projects) counseling, referral for service, community organization, developmental activities | 4 months; 32 ART sessions (skill acquisition, anger control, moral education) | 65 members of 10 gangs (T = 38, C = 27) | 4 months: interpersonal skills +, anger control 0, work adjustment +, recidivism + | 3 (experimental-control, before-after) |
|---|---|---|---|---|---|---|
| Spergel and Grossman (1997), Gang Violence Reduction Project, Chicago, IL | 17–24 years | Street, community | 4 years: detached workers, community mobilization, job referral, crisis counseling, educational programs, recreational activities, interagency coordination | 252 members of 4 gangs (T = 125 in 2 gangs, C = 127 in 2 gangs) | Immediate outcome: gang crime + | 3 (experimental-control, before-after) |
| Kennedy et al. (1996), Braga et al. (1999), Boston Gun Project, Boston, MA | 24 years and under | Street, school | 2 years; communication of ceasefire strategy to gangs, deterrence through multi-agency intervention, detached workers, social services, drug treatment | 1 city (Boston) | Immediate outcome: youth homicide victims per month (mean) +; within-Boston analysis (before-after): youth homicide victims per month (mean) +, gun assaults per month (mean) +, gang violence + | 3 (experimental-control, before-after – comparison of trends in youth homicide victims in 39 major US cities over same time period) |

Notes

T = treatment group; C = control group; n.a. = not available.

a   The period of time in which program effects were evaluated after the intervention had ended.

b   "0" = no intervention effects; "+" = desirable intervention effects; "–" = undesirable intervention effects.

employment or crime. Similarly, the detached worker study in Boston (Miller, 1962) proved to be ineffective on all measures of delinquency.

For the Group Guidance Project (Klein, 1968), officially recorded arrests of gang members were found to have increased during the study period. The program, implemented in 1961 in Los Angeles, attempted to de-isolate gang members from their community. Detached workers intervened in street, community and home settings to offer "group guidance." The 4-year experiment used a before-after design in which the 4 years before the intervention constituted the baseline period. The author explains the undesirable outcome as the group guidance efforts leading to increased gang cohesiveness, which in turn resulted in more favorable conditions for delinquency.

To test the group cohesion hypothesis, Klein (1968, 1971) implemented another study, the Latino Hills Project, which operated for 18 months in the same Los Angeles neighborhood. In contrast to the previous program, project staff concentrated on working with gang members individually, and with a much smaller number (N = 100). Interventions included assisting gang members get jobs, tutoring, recreation and individual counseling. The program reduced gang cohesiveness and gang member arrests. While these desirable outcomes held for 6 months after completion of the program, 2 years later gang cohesion and delinquency rates had returned to baseline level.

Spergel evaluated two Chicago gang member intervention programs, which incorporated the component of "crisis intervention." Unlike programs that try to transform gangs into clubs, the focus here is to intervene in crisis situations that could lead to inter-gang violence. Spergel (1986) evaluated the Crisis Intervention Services Project (CRISP), which operated for a 10-month period in a well-known gang area in Chicago. Crisis intervention and mediation, both well implemented, were the primary components, while counseling and community organization constituted secondary interventions. Spergel described the program as a "mixed social intervention or crisis intervention approach, with strong deterrent and community involvement characteristics" (1995, p. 255). The study analyzed the number and type of gang incidents and arrived at mixed results. While crime and gang crime in target and control areas increased overall, serious gang crimes for juveniles in the target area increased but at a lower rate than for juveniles in the comparison areas. However, the program showed no effect on less serious gang crimes. Undesirable results were also found, with young adults in the program area showing higher rates of serious crime than their counterparts in the control area. CRISP seemed to be more effective for juvenile than for young adult gang members.

According to Howell (1995), Spergel and Grossman (1997) conducted one of the most promising gang violence prevention and intervention programs. Taking place in the Little Village area of Chicago, the Gang Violence Reduction Project represented a 4-year inter-organizational and community-wide approach to youth gang problems and incorporated elements such as community mobilization, job referral, crisis counseling, educational programs and recreational activities. The study targeted more than 200 youths of two of the city's most violent gangs and made a comparison to other youth gangs not receiving the intervention.

At the end of the program, desirable effects were found at the individual and community level. The level of serious gang violence for the target gang members was lower than that for the comparison gangs. At the area level of analysis, Little Village had a smaller increase in gang violence compared to the comparison area. In sum, the Little Village Gang Violence Reduction Project appeared to be a successful, innovative approach in the control of serious gang violence problems. The close cooperation of police, community youth workers and probation officers was likely a key ingredient of its success.

Unlike traditional gang member intervention approaches, the Boston Gun Project or Operation Ceasefire (Kennedy, Piehl and Braga, 1996b), implemented in 1996, used a gang suppression strategy focusing on firearms. According to Kennedy, Piehl and Braga (1996b), the goal of this multi-agency suppression approach "will not be to eliminate gangs as such, or to prevent all gang-related crime; it will be explicitly focused on violence and violence prevention" (p. 165). The two main elements of the intervention were: (1) a direct law-enforcement attack on illicit firearms traffickers illegally supplying youth with guns, and (2) a strong deterrent to gang violence (Braga, Kennedy and Piehl, 1999). The response to violence was pulling every "lever" available, including shutting down drug markets, serving warrants, enforcing probation restrictions and making disorder arrests (Kennedy, 1997). The Ceasefire Working Group delivered its message clearly: "we're ready, we're watching, we're waiting: who wants to be next?" (Kennedy, 1998). The Ceasefire strategy was aimed at all gang areas of the city and did not establish any comparison areas; therefore, analysis of impacts within Boston followed a basic before-after design. Additionally, a comparison was made with the trends in youth homicide in Boston and 39 major US cities over the same time period.

The before-after evaluation showed a 69 percent reduction in the mean monthly number of youth homicide victims across Boston. The intervention was also associated with statistically significant decreases in the mean monthly number of city-wide gun assault incidents (Braga, Kennedy and Piehl, 1999) and overall gang violence (Kennedy, Piehl and Braga, 1996b). The comparison of youth homicide trends in Boston relative to those in major US cities revealed that "Only Boston experienced a significant reduction in the monthly count of youth homicides coinciding with the implementation of the Operation Ceasefire program" (Braga, Kennedy and Piehl, 1999, p. 42).

The scientific quality of the nine gang member intervention programs is moderately strong. We rated six programs as having level 3 evaluation designs and three (Klein, 1968, 1971; Torres, 1981) as having level 2 designs. The six programs with the most rigorous evaluation designs show mixed results for outcomes of delinquency, crime, and violent crime. Miller (1962) and Gold and Mattick (1974) report no intervention effects, and Spergel (1986) reports an undesirable effect on serious gang crimes for adults and a desirable effect on serious gang crimes for juveniles. The other three high-quality programs (Goldstein and Glick, 1994; Kennedy, Piehl and Braga, 1996b; Spergel and Grossman, 1997) report desirable intervention effects on outcomes of interest.

Also, important to arriving at an overall assessment of the effectiveness of intervening with already active gangs and gang members to reduce crime is the work of Malcolm Klein (1968, 1971). Klein (1968) found that the Los Angeles Group Guidance Project led to increased gang crime, which he believed was a result of detached workers enhancing, not decreasing, gang cohesion. As noted above, Klein's (1971) follow-up study to apply the gang cohesion theory in an explicit attempt to minimize gang cohesion showed desirable results at a 6-month post-intervention follow-up. Program effects were found to have worn-off at a 2-year follow-up.

On the basis of the six high quality programs and the weight of the evidence (all nine programs), it is our conclusion that gang intervention programs focused on reducing cohesion among juvenile gangs and individual juvenile gang members, but not increasing gang cohesion, is a promising community crime prevention modality. Replications of some of the early, successful gang intervention programs and the highly successful Boston Gun Project (Kennedy, Piehl and Braga, 1996b) seem to be warranted.

## Community-based mentoring

Community-based mentoring programs typically involve nonprofessional volunteers spending time with young individuals in a "supportive, nonjudgmental manner while acting as role models" (Howell, 1995, p. 90). Compared to the interventions of detached workers with gang members, these interventions take a much broader focus on crime risk factors and intervene at a much earlier age (10–14 years), which, according to developmental theorists, "provides a more promising focus for intervention and prevention" (Sherman, 1997, Chapter 3, p. 20).

Table 5.4 gives an overview of key elements of seven mentoring programs meeting the criteria for inclusion in this review. Again, all of the programs took place in the United States. Unlike gang programs, these studies focus on a much broader population. Intervention settings included home, school and community. Most of the programs measured a variety of outcomes, including behavior problems, truancy, academic failure, drug and alcohol use, and delinquency.

Sample size varied considerably across the seven studies, ranging from a high of 959 children in Tierney and Grossman (1995) to a low of 42 children in Fo and O'Donnell (1974). With the exception of the study by Goodman (1972), there was a modestly high sample retention rate across the programs. Treatment lasted from 12 weeks to 4 years, and the length of follow-up was from immediate outcome to 6 months. The scientific methods score among the programs ranged from 2 to 5. Four programs (Fo and O'Donnell, 1974, 1975; Tierney and Grossman, 1995; Hahn, 1999) used randomized controlled experimental designs to evaluate program effects and three received a rating of 5 on the scientific methods scale.

Two (Fo and O'Donnell, 1975; Hahn, 1999) of the seven programs measured crime outcomes (police arrests and court records).[2] The other programs have been included in this review because they provided measures of disruptive and aggressive behavior and antisocial acts and there is considerable continuity between these behaviors and offending (see e.g. Farrington,

1998). Goodman (1972) is the one exception – it measured self-esteem, peer relations, and schoolwork – but has been included here because it is one of the earliest community-based mentoring programs.

Fo and O'Donnell (1974, 1975) evaluated two experimental mentoring programs called "Buddy System," which took place in Hawaii in the early 1970s. The age range of the at-risk youth in both programs was 11–17 years and the mentors were between 17 and 65 years. The first Buddy System program (Fo and O'Donnell, 1974) lasted 12 weeks and consisted of two 6-week interventions. Forty-two children with behavior management problems were randomly assigned to three treatment groups and one control group. In all three experimental groups, mentors received $10 to spend on each mentee per month. While the "relationship" and "social approval" treatment groups spent the money in a non-contingent way on the mentee, the "social and material reinforcement" treatment group provided social approval and money contingent on appropriate behaviors of the youngsters.

Fo and O'Donnell's (1974) assessment of program effectiveness focused on truancy rate, academic achievement and behavior problems (e.g. fighting) of the children. Results after the first 6 weeks showed a substantial reduction in truancy for those mentees who received the social approval and social and material reinforcement treatment, but not for those in the relationship treatment group or no-treatment control group. After "stabilization" of the target behavior, all mentees were switched to the social and material reinforcement condition for the second intervention period. Results from the second 6 weeks of intervention showed lower truancy rates for all treatment groups compared to the control group. Academic achievement was assessed in the same fashion but no effect was found across treatment or time periods. Child problem behaviors were also reduced through social and material reinforcement treatment. These findings indicate that the use of contingency procedures may be highly effective. However, the small sample size and short intervention periods limit the strength of these findings.

Fo and O'Donnell (1975) evaluated a second, much larger and longer Buddy System program. This program lasted 1 year and included a sample of 442 children and youth, ages 10–17 years. Much less complex than the first program, comparisons were made only between those who received mentoring and those who did not. The results of this program were rather interesting: while the Buddy System seemed to be effective for youngsters with prior offenses, it was not for those without any criminal history. One explanation for this outcome could be that mentees with no prior offenses formed relationships with delinquent youngsters. This possibility could not be assessed. Importantly, the authors note that "The results raise the spectre of possible iatrogenic treatment effects of the Buddy System approach with youngsters with no record of prior major offenses" (Fo and O'Donnell, 1975, p. 524). Harmful effects caused by interventions designed to "do good" is a particularly important issue facing social interventions of all kinds, and has recently been the subject of important empirical work (Dishion, McCord and Poulin, 1999).

The scientific quality of the seven community-based mentoring programs is very strong, with five programs having a scientific methods score of 4 or higher. As noted above, only two (Fo and O'Donnell, 1975; Hahn, 1999) of

Table 5.4 Community-based mentoring programs

| Study author, name, and location | Age at intervention | Context of intervention | Duration and type of intervention | Sample size | Follow-up[a] and results[b] | Scientific methods score |
|---|---|---|---|---|---|---|
| Goodman (1972), Companionship Therapy, Berkeley, CA | 10–11 years | Community, home | 2 years; tutoring and mentoring, conversation, weekly meetings and activities | 162 children (T = 88, C = 74) Note: high attrition of C | Immediate outcome: self-esteem 0, peer relations 0, school work 0 (no measure of delinquency) | 2 (before-after) |
| Fo and O'Donnell (1974), The Buddy System, Hawaii | 11–17 years | Community, school | 12 weeks: 1st intervention (6 weeks): T1 = relationship, T2 = social approval, T3 = social and material reinforcement, C = no participation; 2nd intervention (6 weeks): T1 = T2 = T3 = social and material reinforcement, C = no participation | 42 children (T = 11, T2 = 9, T3 = 15, C = 7) | Immediate outcome (after 1st intervention): truancy rate +, academic achievement 0, (T3 vs. C): problem behaviors (e.g. fighting) +; Immediate outcome (after 2nd intervention): (T1, T2 and T3 vs. C): truancy +, academic achievement 0; (T3 vs. C): problem behaviors (e.g. fighting) + | 5 (randomized experiment) |
| Fo and O'Donnell (1975), The Buddy System, Hawaii | 10–17 years | Community, school | 12 months: mentoring, recreation | 442 children (T = 264, C = 178) | Immediate outcome: criminal activity (for youths with priors) +, criminal activity (for youths with no priors) – | 5 (randomized experiment) |

| Reference / program | Age | Setting | Intervention | Sample | Outcomes | Design |
|---|---|---|---|---|---|---|
| Dicken et al. (1977), Companionship Therapy, San Diego, CA | 6–13 years | Community, home | 1 semester of school; mentoring, companionship, social and recreational activities | 66 children (T = 43, C = 23) | Immediate outcome: teacher-rated behavior (e.g. temper tantrums, self-esteem, aggression) 0, parent-rated behavior (e.g. temper tantrums, self-esteem, aggression) + | 3 (experimental-control, before-after) |
| Green (1980), Big Brothers/Big Sisters Organization, Nassau County, NY | 7–16 years | Non-residential center | 6 months; T1 = Big Brothers/Big Sisters program, T2 = Big Brothers/Big Sisters program waiting list, C = no participation | 120 children (T1 = 60, T2 = 30, C = 30) | Immediate outcome: self-esteem, aggression + | 4 (experimental-control, before-after and statistical analyses) |
| Tierney and Grossman (1995), Big Brothers/Big Sisters Program, USA | 10–16 years (90% between 10–14 years) | Non-residential agencies | 12 months; mentoring; recreational activities, communication | 959 children in 8 centers (T = 487, C = 472) | Immediate outcome: disruptive classroom behavior 0, self-esteem 0, maladaptive behavior 0; 6 months; drug use onset +, alcohol use onset +, antisocial activities +, academic performance + | 5 (randomized experiment) |
| Hahn (1999), Opportunity Institute (no date), Quantum Opportunities Program (QOP), USA | 15 years | Community-based agency, home | 4 years; education, service activities, skill development, community service | 250 youths at 5 sites (T = 125, C = 125) | 3 months; police arrests +, school achievement +, high school drop-out rates + | 4 (randomized experiment) |

Notes

T = treatment group; C = control group.

a  The period of time in which program effects were evaluated after the intervention had ended.

b  "0" = no intervention effects; "+" = desirable intervention effects; "–" = undesirable intervention effects.

the seven programs provided direct measures of crime. These two programs had methods scores of 5 and 4, respectively. Their effects on crime are mixed. Fo and O'Donnell (1975) found desirable effects on criminal activity for youths with prior offenses and undesirable effects on criminal activity for youths with no prior offenses. Hahn (1999) found desirable effects on criminal activity.

On the basis of these two programs alone, no clear assessment can be made of the crime prevention effectiveness of community-based mentoring. In also considering the evidence provided by the four programs that measured outcomes related to offending (e.g. disruptive and aggressive behavior), we find that community-based mentoring is a promising approach to preventing crime.

## Afterschool recreation

Community-based recreation programs are premised on the belief that providing pro-social opportunities for young people in the afterschool hours can reduce their involvement in delinquent behavior in the community. Afterschool programs seek to target a range of risk factors for delinquency and later criminal behavior, including alienation and association with delinquent and violent peers. Afterschool recreation programs, however, generate some controversy since they could also create opportunities for victims and offenders to intersect, producing conflicts and violence.

Table 5.5 summarizes key elements of three afterschool recreation programs. Two (Brown and Dodson, 1959; Schinke, Orlandi and Cole, 1992) of the three programs were carried out in the United States, and the third (Jones and Offord, 1989) was conducted in Ottawa, Canada. Two programs took place in the context of public housing projects and one was based in a Boys Club (Brown and Dodson, 1959). Sample size varied considerably but only Jones and Offord (1989) provided information on the number of study participants (N = 905). The other two programs were implemented at numerous sites. Brown and Dodson (1959) evaluated the impact of a neighborhood Boys Club on delinquency in an area compared to two no-treatment control areas. Schinke, Orlandi and Cole (1992) assessed program effects using fifteen different sites.

Treatment duration ranged from 32 months in Jones and Offord (1989) to 9 years in Brown and Dodson (1959). Information on the length of intervention for Schinke, Orlandi and Cole (1992) was not available. Only Jones and Offord (1989) assessed program effects in the period after the program ended. The methodological rigor of the evaluation designs was moderate, with an average scientific methods score of 3.3. All programs showed desirable effects. Lower rates of delinquency, police arrests and drug activity were some of the desirable results achieved by the afterschool recreation programs.

The 32-month Ottawa program (Jones and Offord, 1989), implemented in 1980 in a public housing complex, recruited low-income children (ages 5 to 15) to participate in afterschool activities aimed at improving skills in sports, music, dance, scouting and other nonsport areas. The Participate and Learn Skills (PALS) program sought to advance children toward higher skill

Table 5.5 Afterschool recreation programs

| Study author, name, and location | Age at intervention | Context of intervention | Duration and type of intervention | Sample size | Follow-up[a] and results[b] | Scientific methods score |
|---|---|---|---|---|---|---|
| Brown and Dodson (1959), Boys Club, Louisville, KT | 5–17 years | Non-residential centers | 9 years; recreational activities, sports, small-group work, constructive activities | 3 sites: T = 1, C = 2 | Immediate outcome: delinquency rate +[c] | 3 (experimental-control, before-after) |
| Jones and Offord (1989), Participate and Learn Skills, Ottawa, Canada | 5–15 years | Public housing | 32 months; non-school, skill development | 905 children (T = 417, C = 488) | Immediate outcome: police arrests + 16 months: police arrests +, self-concept +, prosocial skills +, community integration + | 3 (experimental-control, before-after) |
| Schinke et al. (1992), Boys and Girls Clubs (BGC), USA | Preteens-adolescents | Public housing | n.a.; T1 = BGC (recreation, education, leadership, guidance and counseling), T2 = BGC + drug prevention, C = no BCG | 15 sites: T1 = 5, T2 = 5, C = 5 | Immediate outcome (T1 and T2 vs. C): drug activity +, parental involvement in youth activities +, vandalized housing units +; (T1 vs. C in 2 sites): police arrests + | 4 (experimental-control, before-after and matching) |

Notes

T = treatment group; C = control group; n.a. = not available.

a   The period of time in which program effects were evaluated after the intervention had ended.

b   "0" = no intervention effects; "+" = desirable intervention effects; "−" = undesirable intervention effects.

c   Significance tests were not reported.

levels and to integrate children from the housing complex into activities in the wider community. It was also assumed that this skill-development program could affect other areas of a child's life (e.g. pro-social attitudes and behaviors). The housing project was matched with another public housing complex, which did not provide this specialized treatment. Children in the program housing site fared better than their control counterparts on a range of measures. The strongest program effect was found for juvenile delinquency. During the 32 months of the program, the monthly average of juveniles (in the age-eligible program range) charged by the police was 80 percent less (0.2 vs. 1.0) at the experimental site compared to the control site. This statistically significant effect was diminished somewhat in the 16 months post-intervention: 0.5 juveniles were charged per month at the experimental site compared to 1.1 at the control site. Possibly, the effects of the program were wearing off. Substantial gains were observed in skill acquisition, as measured by the number of levels advanced in an activity, and in integration in the wider community among experimental site children compared with the controls. Spill-over effects on participating children included an increase in self-esteem, but no change in behavior at school or home was observed.

Schinke, Orlandi and Cole (1992) analyzed the impact of the Boys and Girls Clubs in public housing sites across the United States. The study's goal was to compare "substance abuse and other problem behavior rates between youth who lived in public housing developments and youth who do and do not have access to Boys and Girls Clubs" (Schinke, Orlandi and Cole, 1992, p. 120). The evaluation design used three groups of five housing project sites: ten treatment sites and five control sites. Five sites had a traditional Boys and Girls Club (BGC) program, five sites received the BGC program in combination with a substance abuse prevention program called Self-Management and Resistance Training (SMART Moves), and five sites had no intervention, which served as the control groups. Evaluation results showed that housing projects with BGC, with and without SMART Moves, had fewer damaged units and less criminal activity than housing projects without clubs. There was also an overall reduction in substance abuse, drug trafficking and other drug-related criminal activity.

All three of the afterschool recreation programs had a scientific methods score of 3 or higher. Each program produced desirable effects on delinquency or crime, and the program by Schinke, Orlandi and Cole (1992) also reported lower rates of drug activity for program participants compared to controls. The desirable, aggregate crime effect of these programs is weakened somewhat by Brown and Dodson (1959) not reporting significance tests and Jones and Offord (1989) finding evidence of program effects on crime wearing off in the post-intervention follow-up. Overall, we agree with Sherman *et al.*'s (1998) assessment that, based on the same three evaluation studies, community-based afterschool recreation programs represent a promising approach to preventing juvenile crime, but restricted to "areas immediately around the recreation center" (p. 10).

# Gun buy-backs

In the US, criminal gun violence is a leading social and public health problem (Mercy, 1993). Gun violence accounts for about 70 percent of all homicides in the US, a proportion higher than any Western democracy (Zimring and Hawkins, 1997) and higher than many developing countries and countries in transition (Walker, 1999). Gun-related deaths and injuries also exact enormous monetary costs on government and victims (Miller and Cohen, 1996; Cook *et al.*, 1999). Various strategies have been employed in the US and elsewhere to reduce gun violence, including improving gun safety (e.g. trigger locks), reducing the availability of guns (e.g. bans on ownership, confiscating or buying-back guns), restricting ownership, sales, and transfers of guns, and enforcing laws against carrying concealed guns (Sherman, 2000).

Gun buy-back programs represent a community-based approach to reducing gun violence and have been the subject of evaluation research. In the US, this approach has emerged as a popular anti-violence initiative. The popularity of gun buy-back programs is reflected "both in their volume and in the variety of their themes and inducements, which range from the sacred to the profane" (Rosenfeld and Perkins, 1995, p. 1).

We identified three gun buy-back programs (Callahan, Rivara and Koepsell, 1996; Rosenfeld, 1996) that have been the subject of scientific evaluations, and these programs are summarized in Table 5.6. One other published report on a gun buy-back program was identified (Kennedy, Piehl and Braga, 1996a), but has not been included here because it did not assess effects on criminal gun-related injuries or deaths.

All three programs were carried out in the US. There was a wide range of participating subjects. This is because all three programs did not focus on one group of people specifically but were city-wide events. Two programs operated in St. Louis (Rosenfeld, 1996) and were the same intervention carried out at different times (1991 and 1994), and the third program took place in Seattle (Callahan, Rivara and Koepsell, 1996). The programs targeted the availability of firearms in communities as a risk factor for gun homicides. Treatment duration varied from 6 days (Callahan, Rivara and Koepsell, 1996) to 2 months (Rosenfeld, 1996). For the 1991 and 1994 St. Louis programs, the follow-up period to assess treatment effects went beyond immediate outcome: 1 year and 5 months, respectively. For the Seattle program, results were measured at the completion of the program.

The 1991 St. Louis program was deemed one of the most successful in terms of number of firearms collected (7,500). The basic idea of this 2-month intervention was that taking firearms off the street would lead to a reduction in firearm-related injuries and deaths. Handguns, rifles, shotguns and other firearms were exchanged for $25 and $50 certificates.

The 1994 St. Louis program received far less publicity and attracted fewer guns (1,200) than its 1991 predecessor. Targeting the same area and age group, this second program lasted 1 month. Results of both programs were disappointing. There was no reduction in gun homicides or gun assaults at any time. One obvious explanation is that these programs do not affect the flow of new guns into private hands (Kennedy, Piehl and Braga, 1996a).

Table 5.6 Gun buy-back programs

| Study author, name, and location | Age at intervention | Context of intervention | Duration and type of intervention | Sample size | Follow-up[a] and results[b] | Scientific methods score |
|---|---|---|---|---|---|---|
| Rosenfeld (1996), St. Louis, 1991 Gun Buy-Back Program, St. Louis, MO | 18–54+ years | Community | 2 months; buy-back of 7,500 firearms | 1 city (St. Louis in 1991) | Immediate outcome: gun homicides 0, gun assaults 0 1 year: gun homicides 0, gun assaults 0 | 3 (before-after, some control – comparison of trends in the same type of crimes committed without guns) |
| Rosenfeld (1996), St. Louis, 1994 Gun Buy-Back Program, St. Louis, MO | 18–54+ years | Community | 1 month; buy-back of 1,200 firearms | 1 city (St. Louis in 1994) | Immediate outcome: gun homicides 0, gun assaults 0 5 months: gun homicides 0, gun assaults 0 | 3 (before-after, some control – comparison of trends in the same type of crimes committed without guns) |
| Callahan et al. (1996), Seattle Gun Buy-Back Program, Seattle, WA | 44.3 years (mean) | Community | 6 days; buy-back of 1,772 firearms | 1 city (Seatle in 1992) | Immediate outcome: gun crimes 0, homicide 0, gun injuries (from medical records) 0 | 3 (before-after, some control – comparison of trends in the same type of crimes committed without guns) |

Notes
a The period of time in which program effects were evaluated after the intervention had ended.
b "0" = no intervention effects; "+" = desirable intervention effects; "−" = undesirable intervention effects.

Rosenfeld estimated that in St. Louis many participants would eventually replace their turned-in guns. Further, many participants possessed more than one gun, which they did not turn in.

The Seattle gun buy-back program operated for only 6 days in September of 1992. Seattle residents of all ages turned in 1,772 firearms in exchange for $50 vouchers. The program was evaluated using three sets of data: participant survey, police and medical records, and community awareness/support interviews. The program showed no effect on gun crimes, homicides or gun injuries. Callahan, Rivara and Koepsell (1996) estimated that the program removed less than 1 percent of local stockpiles. In addition, participation was high among women and the elderly, two low-risk gun-crime offending groups.

Each of the three gun buy-back programs had a scientific methods score of 3, and each found no effect on criminal gun violence (homicide, assault) relative to a comparison of trends in the same types of crimes committed without guns in the same geographical area. Sherman (1997, Chapter 3, p. 29) notes the following reasons for the failure of gun buy-back programs to reduce criminal violence:

1   They often attract guns from areas far from the program city.
2   They may attract guns that are kept locked up at home, rather than being carried on the street.
3   Potential gun offenders may use the cash from the buy-back program to buy a new and potentially more lethal firearm; the buy-back cash value for their old gun may exceed market value substantially.

As we did not locate any new evaluation study of gun buy-back programs since Sherman's (1997) review, his previous assessment of the effectiveness of this type of community-based violence prevention scheme is equally applicable today, which is: gun buy-back programs do not work in reducing criminal gun violence or, more specifically, "Gun buyback programs operated without geographic limitations on the eligibility of people providing guns for money fails to reduce gun violence in cities" (Sherman *et al.*, 1998, p.8).

## Scientific conclusions

Sherman (1997), in his review of the effectiveness of community crime prevention, which used the same criteria employed in this chapter and throughout this book, concluded that "there are no community-based programs of 'proven effectiveness' by scientific standards to show with reasonable certainty that they 'work' in certain kinds of settings" (Chapter 3, p. 30). We also reached the conclusion that community-based crime prevention does not, at the present time, demonstrate evidence of proven effectiveness in reducing crime. Although this is disappointing news from a policy perspective, it is nevertheless important from a scientific perspective, because it directs our attention towards other crime prevention programs that show evidence presently of proven effectiveness. Importantly, it is not a claim that nothing works and that community-based crime prevention should be abandoned, as the following attests.

Three community crime prevention approaches were deemed to be promising enough to merit further replication and evaluation. The first is gang intervention programs focused on reducing cohesion among juvenile gangs and individual gang members. An important part of this finding is that gang intervention programs should not be focused on increasing gang cohesion. Increasing gang cohesion was found to produce harmful or iatrogenic treatment effects for participating members in one early gang intervention program.

The second promising approach of community crime prevention is community-based mentoring. The scientific quality of the seven programs we reviewed in this area was very strong. The third promising approach is afterschool recreation. All three of the afterschool recreation programs had a scientific methods score of 3 or higher, and each program produced desirable effects on delinquency or crime. Our rating of this class of programs as "promising" instead of "effective" is based on one program not reporting significance tests and another reporting evidence of program effects wearing off. The promising nature of afterschool recreation programs is limited to the prevention of juvenile crime and in areas immediately around the recreation center.

Gun buy-back campaigns, a popular community-based anti-violence initiative, was found to not work in reducing its targeted outcomes of criminal gun-related deaths and injuries. Our conclusion that this type of program is not effective is based on three programs with level 3 evaluation designs, which, according to Sherman (1997, Chapter 3, p. 29), provides "moderate evidence of no effect." Although this level of scientific evidence is not sufficient for a recommendation that there be no further replication and evaluation of gun buy-back programs, if its failure to address proximate causes of gun violence (see section on gun buy-backs) and its potentially prohibitive expense are also considered, then there seem to be sufficient grounds to support such a recommendation.

Lastly, we found that the two strategies of community mobilization and gang membership prevention are of unknown effect in preventing crime. The community mobilization programs reviewed were very weak methodologically and reported mixed results for effects on crime. With an unknown level of scientific evidence and no new evaluations of this type of community-based crime prevention program in more than 10 years, it is questionable whether further replication and evaluation of community mobilization is merited. Weak evaluation designs also limited our assessment of the effectiveness of gang prevention programs.

## Evaluating community crime prevention

Scientific knowledge of the effectiveness of community-based crime prevention programs is hampered by a number of methodological issues (see Lurigio and Rosenbaum, 1986; Rosenbaum, 1988; Hope, 1995, 1998; Farrington, 1997; Sherman, 1997; Catalano et al., 1998). As shown above, in a number of the program areas reviewed in this chapter, methodologically weak evaluation designs and hence low scores on the Scientific Methods Scale, prevented us from being able to say more about the effectiveness of community crime prevention. Disappointingly, the words of Dennis Rosenbaum, more than a decade ago, still seem applicable today: "The primary reason why we do not know 'what works' in community crime prevention is the quality of the evaluation research" (1988, p. 381).

Catalano *et al.* (1998, pp. 278–80) identify three key methodological issues that need to be addressed as part of impact evaluations of community crime prevention programs: (1) mixed units of analysis, (2) heterogeneity of effect across different populations, and (3) systematic attrition, accretion and ecological validity. Arguably, issues (2) and (3) are not encountered only in evaluations of community-based programs; they also face evaluations of programs in other institutional settings or contexts in which crime prevention takes place (e.g. schools). Issue (1), on the other hand, is more often applicable to community-based programs. Mixed units of analysis occur when the unit of analysis differs from the unit of assignment. For example, if the community is the unit that is assigned to experimental or control conditions, it follows that the community should be the unit of analysis in assessing the impact of the intervention. All too often, however, communities are assigned but individuals are the unit of analysis in evaluating the impact of the intervention. As noted by Biglan and Ary (1985, cited in Catalano *et al.*, 1998, p. 279), "Community, school, or classroom differences are thus confounded with program effects on individuals."

Random assignment is problematic in the design of community-based crime prevention programs (Farrington, 1983, 1997). The difficulty stems primarily from the need to randomize a large enough number of communities to "gain the benefits of randomization in equating experimental and control communities on all possible extraneous variables" (Farrington, 1997, p. 160). As a rule of thumb, at least 50 units in each category are needed (Farrington, 1997). This number is relatively easy to achieve with individuals but very difficult to achieve with larger units such as communities. For larger units such as communities, the best and most feasible design usually involves before-and-after measures in experimental and control communities, together with statistical control of extraneous variables. Another important limiting factor for carrying out randomized controlled experiments with communities is the financial cost associated with this type of evaluation design.

One proposal for advancing knowledge about community crime prevention without unduly compromising methodological rigor and, hence, the confidence that can be placed in observed outcomes, is to define communities at the level of census tract, which could, for a large city, produce hundreds of units for assignment and analysis (Sherman, 1997, Chapter 3, p. 38). However, randomly assigning census tracts to conditions could lead to problems of contamination, since the areas are not clearly distinct. Catalano *et al.* (1998, p. 279) report on a number of alternatives that can be adopted when resources do not allow for the minimum number of units to be randomly assigned, some of which include: "matching communities prior to randomization on variables related to the outcomes of interest," "randomized block and factorial designs to stratify communities by factors known to affect key outcomes," and "generalized estimating equations to estimate both the individual- and group-level components of variation."

## Conclusion

This chapter reviewed the scientific evidence on the effectiveness of community-based crime prevention programs. We located 29 community-based programs meeting the criteria for inclusion, and organized them by six different approaches: community mobilization, gang membership prevention, gang member intervention, mentoring, afterschool recreation, and gun buy-backs.

The results of the present review of community-based crime prevention programs are very similar to those of Sherman's (1997) review. We did not find one type of community-based program to be of proven effectiveness in preventing crime. However, there is empirical evidence to conclude that some community-based interventions are promising and thus are deserving of further replication and evaluation. The promising programs are: gang member intervention, community-based mentoring and afterschool recreation.

This chapter has several main limitations. First, only 29 community-based crime prevention programs could be identified. Moreover, since Sherman's (1997) review, only two new programs (Kennedy, Piehl and Braga, 1996b; Hahn, 1999) could be added to our updated review. Second, the methodological rigor of the 29 programs is of weak to moderate strength, with the mean scientific methods score being just over 3 (the program by Bibb, 1967, could not be assigned a score). Only four programs used randomized-experimental designs to assess the effectiveness of the interventions. Sixteen programs used experimental-control designs with before and after measures (mostly quasi-experimental designs), and the remaining programs used simple one-group (no control group) before-after designs.

A third limitation of this chapter is that we did not review the increasingly popular version of community-based crime prevention programs that have come to be known as comprehensive community partnerships or initiatives (Hope, 1998; Rosenbaum, Lurigio and Davis, 1998), examples of which include Communities That Care (Hawkins and Catalano, 1992), the Comprehensive Communities Program (see Rosenbaum, Lurigio and Davis, 1998, pp. 218–19), and the Texas City Action Plan to Prevent Crime (National Crime Prevention Council, 1994). In their review of comprehensive community programs, Rosenbaum, Lurigio and Davis report on the findings of process but not outcome evaluations of these programs. We did not locate any published evaluations that measured program effects on crime.

Advancing knowledge about the effectiveness of community-based crime prevention requires attention to many important methodological issues – these programs are among the most difficult to evaluate. But there is also the need for more experimentation with this form of crime prevention; more specifically, with the three program types that we rated as promising: gang member intervention, community-based mentoring, and afterschool recreation. A higher quality and an increased but targeted quantity of evaluation research offers to be of great benefit to community crime prevention science and policy.

## Notes

1   For helpful responses, we are very grateful to John Eck, Andrew Hahn, Tim Hope, David Kennedy, Richard Rosenfeld and Lawrence Sherman.

2   We did not review the Quantum Opportunities Program (Hahn, 1999) here, because it is reviewed in Chapter 4.

## References

Bennett, T.H. (1996) Community crime prevention in Britain. In T. Trenczek and H. Pfeiffer (eds), *Kommunale Kriminalprävention: Paradigmenwechsel und Wiederentdeck-ung alter Weisheiten*. Bonn, Germany: Forum Verlag Godesberg, 169–83.

Bennett, T.H. (1998) Crime prevention. In M. Tonry (ed.), *The handbook of crime and punishment*. New York: Oxford University Press, 369–402.

Bennett, S.F. and Lavrakas, P.J. (1989) Community-based crime prevention: An assessment of the Eisenhower Foundation's neighborhood program. *Crime and Delin-quency*, 35, 345–64.

Bibb, M. (1967) Gang-related services for mobilization for youth. In M. Klein and B.G. Myerhoff (eds), *Juvenile gangs in context*. Englewood Cliffs, NJ: Prentice-Hall, 175–82.

Biglan, A. and Ary, D. (1985) Methodological issues in research on smoking preven-tion. In C. Bell and R.J. Batjes (eds), *Prevention research: Deterring drug abuse among children and adolescents*. National Institute on Drug Abuse research monograph no. 63. Washington, DC: US Government Printing Office, 170–95.

Braga, A.A., Kennedy, D.M. and Piehl, A.M. (1999) *Problem-oriented policing and youth violence: An evaluation of the Boston Gun Project*. Final report submitted to the National Institute of Justice. Cambridge, MA: John F. Kennedy School of Govern-ment, Harvard University.

Brown, R.J. and Dodson, D.W. (1959) The effectiveness of a boy's club in reducing delinquency. *Annals of the American Academy of Political and Social Science*, 322, 47–52.

Burgess, E.W. (1942) Introduction. In C.R. Shaw and H.D. McKay, *Juvenile delin-quency and urban areas: A study of rates of delinquents in relation to differential character-istics of local communities in American cities*. Chicago, IL: University of Chicago Press, ix–xiii.

Byrne, J.M. and Sampson, R.J. (eds) (1986) *The social ecology of crime*. New York: Springer-Verlag.

Callahan, C., Rivara, F. and Koepsell, T. (1996) Money for guns: Evaluation of the Seattle gun buy-back program. In M.R. Plotkin (ed.), *Under fire: Gun buy-backs, exchanges, and amnesty programs*. Washington, DC: Police Executive Research Forum, 81–95.

Catalano, R.F., Arthur, M.W., Hawkins, J.D., Berglund, L. and Olson, J.J. (1998) Com-prehensive community- and school-based interventions to prevent antisocial behav-ior. In R. Loeber and D.P. Farrington (eds), *Serious and violent juvenile offenders: Risk factors and successful interventions*. Thousand Oaks, CA: Sage, 248–83.

Clarke, R.V. (1995) Situational crime prevention. In M. Tonry and D.P. Farrington (eds), *Building a safer society: Strategic approaches to crime prevention: Vol. 19. Crime and justice: A review of research*. Chicago, IL: University of Chicago Press, 91–150.

Cook, P.J., Lawrence, B.A., Ludwig, J. and Miller, T.R. (1999) The medical costs of gunshot injuries in the United States. *Journal of the American Medical Association*, 282, 447–54.

Curtis, L.A. (1987) The retreat of folly: Some modest replications of inner-city success. *Annals of the American Academy of Political and Social Science*, 494, 71–89.

Dicken, C., Bryson, R. and Kass, N. (1977) Companionship therapy: A replication in experimental community psychology. *Journal of Consulting and Clinical Psychology*, 45, 637–46.

Dishion, T.J., McCord, J. and Poulin, F. (1999) When intervention harms: Peer groups and problem behavior. *American Psychologist*, 54, 755–64.

Esbensen, F.-A. and Osgood, D.W. (1999) Gang Resistance Education and Training (GREAT): Results from the national evaluation. *Journal of Research in Crime and Delinquency*, 36, 194–225.

Fagan, J. (1987) Neighborhood education, mobilization, and organization for juvenile crime prevention. *Annals of the American Academy of Political and Social Science*, 494, 54–70.

Farrington, D.P. (1983) Randomized experiments on crime and justice. In M. Tonry and N. Morris (eds), *Crime and justice: A review of research: Vol. 4*. Chicago, IL: University of Chicago Press, 257–308.

Farrington, D.P. (1993) Have any individual, family or neighbourhood influences on offending been demonstrated conclusively? In D.P. Farrington, R.J. Sampson and P.-O.H. Wikström (eds), *Integrating individual and ecological aspects of crime*. Stockholm, Sweden: National Council for Crime Prevention, 7–37.

Farrington, D.P. (1997) Evaluating a community crime prevention program. *Evaluation*, 3, 157–73.

Farrington, D.P. (1998) Predictors, causes, and correlates of male youth violence. In M. Tonry and M.H. Moore (eds), *Youth violence: Vol. 24. Crime and Justice: A review of research*. Chicago, IL: University of Chicago Press, 421–75.

Fo, W.S.O. and O'Donnell, C.R. (1974) The buddy system: Relationship and contingency conditioning in a community intervention program for youth with nonprofessionals as behavior change agents. *Journal of Consulting and Clinical Psychology*, 42, 163–9.

Fo, W.S.O. and O'Donnell, C.R. (1975) The buddy system: Effect of community intervention on delinquent offenses. *Behavior Therapy*, 6, 522–4.

Fowler, F.J. and Mangione, T.W. (1986) A three-pronged effort to reduce crime and fear of crime: The Hartford experiment. In D.P. Rosenbaum (ed.), *Community crime prevention: Does it work?* Beverly Hills, CA: Sage, 87–108.

Gold, M. and Mattick, H.W. (1974) *Experiments on the streets: The Chicago youth development project*. Ann Arbor, MI: Institute for Social Research.

Goldstein, A.P. and Glick, B. (1994) *The prosocial gang: Implementing aggression replacement training*. Thousand Oaks, CA: Sage.

Goodman, G. (1972) *Companionship therapy: Studies in structured intimacy*. San Francisco, CA: Jossey-Bass.

Green, B.C. (1980) *An evaluation of a big brothers' program for father-absent boys: An eco-behavioral analysis*. Unpublished Ph.D. dissertation. New York: New York University.

Hahn, A. (1999) Extending the time of learning. In D.J. Besharov (ed.), *America's disconnected youth: Toward a preventive strategy*. Washington, DC: Child Welfare League of America Press, 233–65.

Hawkins, J.D. and Catalano, R.F. (1992). *Communities that care: Action for drug abuse prevention*. San Francisco, CA: Jossey-Bass.

Herrenkohl, T.I., Hawkins, J.D., Chung, I.-J., Hill, K.G. and Battin-Pearson, S. (2001) School and community risk factors and interventions. In R. Loeber and D.P. Farrington (eds), *Child delinquents: Development, intervention, and service needs*. Thousand Oaks, CA: Sage, 211–46.

Hope, T. (1995) Community crime prevention. In M. Tonry and D.P. Farrington (eds), *Building a safer society: Strategic approaches to crime prevention: Vol. 19. Crime and justice: A review of research.* Chicago, IL: University of Chicago Press, 21–89.

Hope, T. (1998) Community crime prevention. In C. Nuttall, P. Goldblatt and C. Lewis (eds), *Reducing offending: An assessment of research evidence on ways of dealing with offending behaviour.* London, UK: Research and Statistics Directorate, Home Office, 51–62.

Howell, J.C. (ed.) (1995) *Guide for implementing the comprehensive strategy for serious, violent, and chronic juvenile offenders.* Washington, DC: Office of Juvenile Justice and Delinquency Prevention, US Department of Justice.

Howell, J.C. (1998) Promising programs for youth gang violence prevention and intervention. In R. Loeber and D.P. Farrington (eds), *Serious and violent juvenile offenders: Risk factors and successful interventions.* Thousand Oaks, CA: Sage, 284–312.

Jones, M.B. and Offord, D.R. (1989) Reduction of anti-social behaviour in poor children by nonschool skill development. *Journal of Child Psychology and Psychiatry,* 30, 737–50.

Kelling, G.L. and Coles, C.M. (1996) *Fixing broken windows: Restoring order and reducing crime in our communities.* New York: Free Press.

Kennedy, D.M. (1997) Pulling levers: Chronic offenders, high-crime settings, and a theory of prevention. *Valparaiso University Law Review,* 31, 449–84.

Kennedy, D.M. (1998) Pulling levers: Getting deterrence right. *National Institute of Justice Journal,* July, 2–8.

Kennedy, D.M., Piehl, A.M. and Braga, A.A. (1996a) Gun buy-backs: Where do we stand and where do we go? In M.R. Plotkin (ed.), *Under fire: Gun buy-backs, exchanges and amnesty programs.* Washington, DC: Police Executive Research Forum, 141–74.

Kennedy, D.M., Piehl, A.M. and Braga, A.A. (1996b) Youth violence in Boston: Gun markets, serious youth offenders, and a use-reduction strategy. *Law and Contemporary Problems,* 59, 147–96.

Klein, M. (1968) *From association to guilt: The group guidance project in juvenile gang intervention.* Los Angeles, CA: University of Southern California.

Klein, M. (1971) *Street gangs and street workers.* Englewood Cliffs, NJ: Prentice-Hall.

Klein, M. (1995) *The American street gang: Its nature, prevalence and control.* New York: Oxford University Press.

Lurigio, A.J. and Rosenbaum, D.P. (1986) Evaluation research in community crime prevention: A critical look at the field. In D.P. Rosenbaum (ed.), *Community crime prevention: Does it work?* Beverly Hills, CA: Sage, 19–44.

Mercy, J.A. (1993). The public health impact of firearm injuries. *American Journal of Preventive Medicine,* 9 (supplement), 8–11.

Miller, T.R. and Cohen, M.A. (1996) Costs. In R.R. Ivatury and C.G. Cayten (eds), *The textbook of penetrating trauma.* Baltimore, MD: Williams and Wilkins, 49–58.

Miller, W.B. (1962) The impact of a "total-community" delinquency control project. *Social Problems,* 10, 168–91.

National Crime Prevention Council (1994) *Taking the offensive to prevent crime: How seven cities did it.* Washington, DC: NCPC.

Office of Juvenile Justice and Delinquency Prevention (1999) *1997 National Youth Gang Survey: Summary.* Washington, DC: OJJDP, US Department of Justice.

Opportunity Institute (no date) *Quantum Opportunities Program.* Unpublished report. Alexandria, VA: Opportunity Institute.

Palumbo, D.J. and Ferguson, J.L. (1995) Evaluating Gang Resistance Education and Training (GREAT): Is the impact the same as that of Drug Abuse Resistance Education (DARE)? *Evaluation Review,* 19, 597–619.

Reiss, A.J., Jr. and Tonry, M. (eds) (1986) *Communities and crime: Vol. 8. Crime and justice: A review of research.* Chicago, IL: University of Chicago Press.

Rosenbaum, D.P. (1988) Community crime prevention: A review and synthesis of the literature. *Justice Quarterly*, 5, 323–95.

Rosenbaum, D.P., Lurigio, A.J. and Davis, R.C. (1998) *The prevention of crime: Social and situational strategies.* Belmont, CA: Wadsworth.

Rosenfeld, R. (1996) Gun buy-backs: Crime control or community mobilization? In M.R. Plotkin (ed.), *Under fire: Gun buy-backs, exchanges and amnesty programs.* Washington, DC: Police Executive Research Forum, 1–28.

Rosenfeld, R. and Perkins, M. (1995) Crime prevention or community mobilization? Reflections on gun buy-back programs. Paper presented at the meeting of the American Association for the Advancement of Science, Atlanta, GA.

Sampson, R.J. and Lauritsen, J. (1994) Violent victimization and offending: Individual-, situational-, and community-level risk factors. In A.J. Reiss, Jr. and J.A. Roth (eds), *Understanding and preventing violence: Vol. 3. Social influences.* Washington, DC: National Academy Press, 1–114.

Sampson, R.J., Raudenbush, S.W. and Earls, F. (1997) Neighborhoods and violent crime: A multilevel study of collective efficacy. *Science*, 277, 918–24.

Schinke, S.P., Orlandi, M.A. and Cole, K.C. (1992) Boys and Girls Clubs in public housing developments: Prevention services for youth at risk. *Journal of Community Psychology*, OSAP Special Issue, 118–28.

Shaw, C.R. and McKay, H.D. (1942) *Juvenile delinquency and urban areas: A study of rates of delinquents in relation to differential characteristics of local communities in American cities.* Chicago, IL: University of Chicago Press.

Shaw, C.R. and McKay, H.D. (1969) *Juvenile delinquency and urban areas: A study of rates of delinquency in relation to differential characteristics of local communities in American cities.* Revised edition. Chicago, IL: University of Chicago Press.

Sherman, L.W. (1997) Communities and crime prevention. In L.W. Sherman, D.C. Gottfredson, D.L. MacKenzie, J.E. Eck, P. Reuter and S.D. Bushway. *Preventing crime: What works, what doesn't, what's promising.* Washington, DC: National Institute of Justice, US Department of Justice, 3–1, 3–49.

Sherman, L.W. (2000) Gun carrying and homicide prevention. *Journal of the American Medical Association*, 283, 1193–5.

Sherman, L.W., Gottfredson, D.C., MacKenzie, D.L., Eck, J.E., Reuter, P. and Bushway, S.D. (1998) Preventing crime: What works, what doesn't, what's promising. *Research in Brief*, July. Washington, DC: National Institute of Justice, US Department of Justice.

Skogan, W.G. (1990) *Disorder and decline: Crime and the spiral of decay in American neighborhoods.* New York: Free Press.

Spergel, I.A. (1986) The violent gang problem in Chicago: A local community approach. *Social Services Review*, 60, 94–129.

Spergel, I.A. (1995) *The youth gang problem: A community approach.* New York: Oxford University Press.

Spergel, I.A. and Grossman, S.F. (1997) The Little Village Project: A community approach to the gang problem. *Social Work*, 42, 456–70.

Taub, R.P., Taylor, D.G. and Dunham, J.D. (1984) *Paths of neighborhood change: Race and crime in urban America.* Chicago, IL: University of Chicago Press.

Thompson, D.W. and Jason, L.A. (1988) Street gangs and preventive interventions. *Criminal Justice and Behavior*, 15, 323–33.

Thrasher, F.M. (1936) The Boys' Club and juvenile delinquency. *American Journal of Sociology*, 41, 66–80.

Tierney, J.P. and Grossman, J.B. (1995) *Making a difference: An impact study of Big Brothers/Big Sisters.* Philadelphia, PA: Public/Private Ventures.

Torres, D. (1981) *Gang violence reduction project: Fourth evaluation report*. Sacramento, CA: California Youth Authority.

Tremblay, R.E. and Craig, W.M. (1995) Developmental crime prevention. In M. Tonry and D.P. Farrington (eds), *Building a safer society: Strategic approaches to crime prevention: Vol. 19. Crime and justice: A review of research*. Chicago, IL: University of Chicago Press, 151–236.

Walker, J. (1999) Firearm abuse and regulation. In G. Newman (ed.), *Global report on crime and justice*. New York: Oxford University Press, 151–70.

Wikström, P.-O., H. (1998) Communities and crime. In M. Tonry (ed.), *The handbook of crime and punishment*. New York: Oxford University Press, 269–301.

Wilson, J.Q. and Kelling, G.L. (1982) Broken windows: The police and neighborhood safety. *Atlantic Monthly*, March, 29–38.

Woodson, R. (1981) *A summons to life: Mediating structures and the prevention of youth crime*. Cambridge, MA: Ballinger.

Zimring, F.E. and Hawkins, G. (1997) *Crime is not the problem: Lethal violence in America*. New York: Oxford University Press.

# 6 Labor markets and crime risk factors

*Shawn D. Bushway and Peter Reuter*[1]

## Introduction

Employment and crime have a complex relationship. For an individual, they can be substitutes or complementary activities. For example, some people choose crime rather than legitimate work because of an expectation that they can make more money from crime and/or because they find it more rewarding in other ways (Katz, 1989; Bourgois, 1995). On the other hand, the workplace can offer opportunities for certain kinds of crimes that are more difficult to commit elsewhere, such as theft of inventory or selling of gambling services.

The relationship between employment and crime at the community level is equally ambiguous. Crime in a community is the outcome of the inter-action between propensity and opportunity to commit crime. For example, in a given community over time, high employment may be associated with reduced presence of residents (i.e. lessened guardianship) and greater wealth, thus increasing criminal opportunities. On the other hand, low unemployment also provides better legitimate work opportunities for potential offenders, thus reducing their propensity to commit crime. Looking across communities, one can see the same potentially countervailing influences; poor communities offer weak job prospects but also (except for drug markets) financially unrewarding criminal opportunities. At this level, crime rates may depend not on the level of employment but on a much more fundamental set of social and individual characteristics.

Pure theory is not likely then to provide guidance about the strength or direction of the relationship between employment and crime. However, it is at least plausible that a strong negative relationship exists. At the descriptive level, those who commit crimes tend to be out of the labor force, unemployed or in low paying jobs. The communities in which crime, particularly violent crime, is so heavily concentrated show persistently high jobless rates. Increasing employment and the potential for employment for individuals and communities that are currently at high risk of persistent joblessness may have a substantial preventive effect on crime. Thus a comprehensive assessment of crime prevention programs should include those aimed at increasing employment.

Our review, which covers only research done in the United States, includes any evaluated program that aims to increase the employment of individuals or populations at risk of serious criminal involvement. We exclude general macro-economic policies (e.g. looser monetary policy aimed at lowering interest rates) though these may in theory reduce crime; such policies are driven by other factors and in any case the evidence on the aggregate relationship between employment and crime is very ambiguous. We include, however, a range of community and individual programs which do not specifically target crime, as indicated by the frequent omission of crime, or even risk-factors for crime, as an outcome measure. Thus, much of this review assesses just how effective such job training and job creation programs are at increasing employment for the targeted community or individual, even if they do not target criminal justice-involved offenders. The crime consequences are inferred from our review of the relationship between employment and crime at various levels.

For policy purposes the reciprocal relationship of crime and employment presents a major challenge. Areas of high crime are unattractive for investment. Both property and personnel are at risk; goods are stolen, premises damaged, employees assaulted and customers intimidated. Attracting capital requires a reduction in crime so as to allay the legitimate concerns of investors, employers and customers. On the other hand, crime reduction on a large scale may require the creation of employment opportunities for the large numbers of young adults that are the source of so much of the crime in the area. Unfortunately, many offenders lack the skills needed to obtain and retain attractive jobs; that is, positions that pay enough to avoid poverty (well above the minimum wage for a two-parent, two-child household with only one wage earner) and which offer potential progress and a sense of accomplishment. Thus, improving their work force skills may be essential even when capital, a prerequisite for new jobs, can be attracted into the community.

Existing programs aimed at reducing crime through employment and/or increasing employment in high crime areas fall into the following two main categories:

- Supply-side programs aim to improve the attractiveness of individuals to employers. Mostly these programs increase the potential productivity of the worker through education or job training. However, the category includes programs that take account of the fact that many high-risk individuals are handicapped by their location. These programs move people to jobs, either by transportation subsidies or by actually providing access to housing in lower crime communities nearer areas of high employment potential. The latter also may have crime prevention effects by allowing high-risk children to grow up in communities with more employed adult role models.
- Demand-side programs aim to reduce the costs of employment borne by the employer. One way to do this is through wage supplements or subsidized bonds (insuring the employer against theft by the employee) for ex-offenders. Another alternative is community development programs which lower costs for businesses locating in particularly needy communities. The influx of capital into communities characterized by low employment and high crime should generate jobs and thus, by a variety of mechanisms, reduce crime in the community.

The next section briefly surveys the theoretical and empirical literature on the relationship between crime and employment at various levels. The third and fourth sections survey supply and demand side programs, respectively. Each examines the evaluation evidence on program outcomes: Only a very few evaluations include explicit findings on the crime consequences of the intervention; the rest providing only employment measures. The final section then offers conclusions and recommendations for future research.

## The relationship between employment and crime

The relationship between crime and employment has been a long standing issue in research, involving a range of paradigms.[2] Fagan and Freeman (1999) and Freeman (1995) provide recent reviews, particularly focused on understanding how the returns from crime and legitimate work jointly affect the decision to engage in crime. We propose here to give more attention to the multiplicity of relationships between the criminal participation and work opportunities that operate at different levels (individual and community) and at different points in an individual's life-span (school, young adult, adult). Our goal is not to make theoretical contributions but to give a better grounding to an analysis of programmatic and policy options.

### Theoretical perspective

Fagan and Freeman (1999) and Uggen (1994) have identified four major theoretical explanations for the link between employment and crime: economic choice; social control; strain; and labeling theory.

*Economic choice theory* (Ehrlich, 1973) posits that an individual makes choices between legal and illegal work based partly on the relative economic attractiveness of the two options. Moral values still influence actions but are assumed not to change with economic opportunities. It is, like economic theory generally, about response to changes or differences. If legal work becomes less rewarding or if illegal work becomes more rewarding, individuals may shift to crime and away from legal work. Education plays a role in framing choices; low educational attainment, which now puts young males at risk of frequent periods of unemployment and of achieving only low paying and unsatisfactory jobs, will be associated with high crime participation. This is exactly what Freeman claims happened in the late 1980s:

> Given the well-documented growth of [legitimate] earnings inequality and fall in the job opportunities for less-skilled young men in this period, and the increased criminal opportunities due to the growth of demand for drugs, the economist finds appealing the notion that the increased propensity for crime is a rational response to increased job market incentives to commit crime.
>
> (Freeman, 1995, pp. 177–8)

Notice that within this theory, the crimes in question are income-generating crimes which are used to replace income gained from legitimate means. The theory offers no account of non-income generating crime. Much violent crime is expressive (e.g. an enactment of drunken anger) rather than instrumental (e.g. aimed at ensuring success of a robbery). However, economic theory is not entirely silent on violent crime. Employment should raise the opportunity cost of incarceration (i.e. what the individual loses with his freedom), both through loss of earnings and the loss of work experience; this might deter acts that endanger the individual's freedom.

The economic choice framework allows individuals to engage in both legitimate work and crime simultaneously. This is appropriate as most offenders also maintain some relationship to the workplace over their criminal careers (e.g. Reuter, MacCoun and Murphy, 1990). What may be affected by changes in the relative attractiveness of crime and legitimate work is the allocation of time between the two types of income-generating activities; better employment opportunities reduce the fraction of time spent in crime. Importantly, this theory has further implications beyond a simple contemporaneous choice of legal versus illegal work. The individual, particularly in adolescent years, also has to decide how much to invest in human capital (education and other workforce relevant skills). If the legal labor market opportunities appear weak, a youth is less likely to make adequate investment in acquiring the human capital necessary for success in the legal labor market. As a result, this theory can explain both participation in income-generating crime and under-investment in human capital that reduces legitimate income later.

*Control theory* claims that employment exerts social control over an individual (Gottfredson and Hirschi, 1990). The absence of employment for an individual leads to a breakdown of positive social bonds for that individual. That in turn is hypothesized to induce the individual to increase his criminal activity, both violent and income-related. This theory, expanded naturally to cover not just individuals but areas, is a key part of William Julius Wilson's analysis of inner-city problems. Using a series of carefully constructed studies of poverty areas in Chicago, he concludes that "many of today's problems in the inner-city ghetto neighborhoods – crime, family dissolution, welfare, low levels of social organization and so on – are fundamentally a consequence of a disappearance of work" (Wilson, 1996, p.xiii). Employment is seen as the main builder of pro-social bonds and institutions in a community and its absence results in large-scale disorder.

*Anomie* is another more aggregate level theory (for a concise summary targeted to this issue, see Uggen, 1994). This theory suggests that frustration caused by income inequality and other aggregate level problems will cause individuals to resort to crime out of frustration. High unemployment rates may contribute, in that unemployment also generates frustration.

One small area of theory that explicitly includes the idea that crime itself could be criminogenic is *labeling theory* (Lemert, 1951). Individuals who participate in crime acquire stigmatic labels (both to others and to themselves) and are then denied opportunities because of these labels. What is intriguing about this theory is that it suggests the very real possibility of feedback between employment and crime. This feedback suggests that cessation from crime will be difficult once criminal activity has been initiated, particularly if the offender acquires an official record (see Schwartz and Skolnick, 1964; Nagin and Waldfogel, 1994, 1995; Bushway, 1996).

Labeling theory points also to a community level connection between crime and employment; that is, joblessness in an area may be caused by past criminal activity of the residents, as well as the converse. In a sense, the community or area is "labeled," which makes it difficult for the community to attract investment. This is a point first made forcefully by former NIJ Director James K. Stewart (1986).

These theories, potentially complementary, point to important potential feedback between crime and unemployment. Programs aimed solely at improving an individual's employability (motivated by economic choice) or solely at increasing the number of jobs in an area (motivated by all four theories) are vulnerable, the first to the failure of program graduates to find jobs and the second simply to the difficulty of providing jobs in high-risk neighborhoods. In the extreme case, a community including many individuals with low human capital, limited ties to positive social structures and institutions and negative labels is likely to be characterized by both high crime and low employment, with complex interaction between the two problems. Theory suggests that areas characterized by both high crime and low employment require attention to all three factors: weak social institutions, low human capital and negative labels.

### Research on crime and employment

We now review empirical research aimed at assessing the relationship between crime and employment,[3] a necessary bridge between the theories and the program evaluations. This research has been conducted at many different levels of aggregation, including national time-series data, state and local cross-sectional data and individual-level data.

### National level

A review by Chiricos (1986) finds that most national level analyses have yielded weak results on the crime–employment relationship. Freeman (1995) claims that this is primarily because of problems with the time-series statistical model with national data. One exception is a paper by Cook and Zarkin (1985). They report mixed results from an analysis of business cycles from 1933 to 1982. In general, crime increased over this period. However, homicide rates did not vary systematically with the business cycle. On the other hand, the burglary and robbery rates were higher during the economic downturns than during the upturns. This is consistent with the hypothesis that low employment generates an increased propensity to commit property crime while violent crime is driven by other factors. At the same time, they found that auto-theft was actually pro-cyclical – auto-theft increased faster when the economy improved and more slowly when the economy declined. This is consistent with the hypothesis that the opportunity for auto-theft increases when employment (and hence disposable income and the stock of new cars) increases. We shall present no other findings at this level of aggregation because it seems to provide least insight into those policy issues with which we are particularly concerned.

*Community level*

Chiricos does find, however, that at lower levels of aggregation (states, counties and cities), roughly half of all reported studies show a positive and statistically significant relationship between employment and crime, using post-1970 data.[4] The fraction of positive results increases to almost 75 percent of all studies when property crimes are analyzed separately from violent crimes.

*Individual level*

Analyses of individual level data have attracted more attention as these data have become available. Studies of the 1945 Philadelphia birth cohort have shown that unemployment is associated with crime (e.g. Wolfgang, Figlio and Sellin, 1972), a finding that is reported in numerous other studies. However, the causality is uncertain. Sampson and Laub (1993) argue that employment per se or by itself does not reduce crime or increase social control; it is only stability, commitment and responsibility that may be associated with getting a job that has crime reducing consequences. Gottfredson and Hirschi (1990) argue that the relationship is essentially spurious, a reflection of a common third factor which they call the level of individual social control.

Economic choice theory is supported by evidence showing that human capital influences earnings, and earnings influence recidivism by ex-offenders (Needels, 1996). Social control theory seems to have relevance, too, within the context of economic choice. Farrington *et al.* (1986) tie crime more directly to employment by examining the timing of crime and employment over almost 3 years for a sample of teenage males in England. They show that property crimes are committed more frequently during periods of joblessness. However, this relationship held only for those who were predisposed to crime (as reflected by self-reports on earlier criminal activity and moral values); otherwise spells of joblessness did not induce more criminal offending.

This brief review establishes that researchers have found a relationship between crime and employment, and that a number of mechanisms, operating both at the individual and community level, may explain the relationship. The key remaining question is whether or not programs aimed at increasing employment for at-risk populations can attain that goal and reduce crime.

## Supply side programs

### *Job training and education*

The earliest labor market-oriented crime prevention programs followed just this logic – providing legitimate employment or employment skills to at-risk individuals in order to reduce their criminal activity. Numerous programs were developed to provide basic education, vocational training and work experience for youth in high crime and high unemployment communities.

The Training and Employment Services division of the Employment and Training Administration of the Department of Labor spends large sums ($5.5 billion in FY 2000[5]) on skills-developing programs aimed at increasing the employment prospects of individuals who are at high risk of being persistently unemployed. Most of these interventions target youth, particularly adolescents, on the reasonable (but not unassailable) assumption that early interventions have higher pay-off if successful. The other large set of interventions targets those already involved with the criminal justice system, since they are also known to have little education or training.

We will consider these two groups of interventions separately, since the division corresponds to differences in institutions and outcome measures. The programs for youth generally are provided by social service agencies, while those for offenders frequently occur in correctional settings. Moreover, criminal justice program evaluations almost always include recidivism as an outcome measure, and sometimes do not include employment, while the general population programs always include employment, but rarely crime, as an outcome measure.

## Job training programs connected to the criminal justice system

### Introduction

Targeting human capital development programs at offenders while in, or just leaving, the criminal justice system has the merit of focusing resources on the highest risk group. It is a human services equivalent of Willie Sutton's famous line about the banks; in this case, we are going where the crime is. Like Sutton's strategy, it also has an obvious weakness; just as banks are well guarded, so offenders in the criminal justice system have already developed behavior patterns that are difficult to reverse with educational programs.

We divide programs by age of the target population: juvenile and adult. That reflects the fact that juveniles seem most suitable for programs that focus on the development of human capital, as is true of education generally; adult programs give more emphasis on reintegration into the workforce. We will also distinguish programs by whether they are in prison or post-release.

### Juvenile offenders[6]

Juvenile correctional institutions generally give more emphasis to rehabilitation than do adult correctional facilities. Education and training programs frequently fit into a broad array of habilitation and rehabilitation services generally. Indeed, it is difficult to identify the main effects of these programs alone, precisely because they are imbedded into a larger set (e.g. cognitive therapy, substance abuse treatment) which may interact with education and training. Moreover, there are only two studies that concentrate on the juvenile justice system (see Table 6.1). Both evaluations point to a problem in getting participants to complete the program once started; high drop-out rates indicate either that the program was poorly implemented or it was unattractive to many of the participants. Both programs also involved a relatively low level of services for the clients; even if they were well done it would seem implausible that they could have large behavioral consequences.

For example, Leiber and Mawhorr (1995) used a variety of matched control groups to assess the impact of the Second Chance program on youth who were in court but not yet sentenced to an institution. Second Chance involves sixteen weekly group meetings aimed at developing certain social skills, along with a pre-employment training program (including how to conduct an independent job search, interview for a job and demonstrate good work habits). With 85 program entrants (only 57 of whom completed it), the test does not have much statistical power. The findings were of no significant differences in official arrests; the control group actually showed lower recidivism than the experimental group (completers or drop-outs).

The evaluation pointed to the lack of treatment integrity.

An OJJDP review of correctional educational programs noted the lack of rigorous evaluation of juvenile vocational education programs within the criminal justice system (OJJDP, 1994).[7] The one "rigorous" evaluation cited by OJJDP is the New Pride program in Denver. New Pride is a community-based program that provides a year of intensive non-residential treatment and training, including participation in an on-site business run by the program. The evaluation consisted of tracking the success of the program participants without any comparison group. This is a poor evaluation design that does not meet minimal standards (less than a "1" on our scale). Widespread replication of this program, while encouraged by its evaluators (James and Granville, 1984), is not justified by the quality of the evaluation.

*Adult offenders*

Though both theory and political rhetoric emphasize juveniles as the most suitable targets for training and education, a large fraction of adult offenders in the criminal justice system have poor education and employment records. That fact was the original source of interest in the early 1960s in assessing whether recidivism might be reduced by providing these adults with additional educational and job skills. Moreover, the life course model of crime suggests that many adult offenders may be more receptive to work than adolescents.

Secondary reviews from the early 1970s, after these programs had been around for roughly 10 years, were uniformly negative. The Department of Labor's Manpower Administration sponsored research on these programs, and provided a comprehensive review of the research in 1973 (Rovner-Piecznik, 1973). Despite strong commitment and great enthusiasm by program operators, the study reluctantly reported that very few programs led to a substantial decline in recidivism. By way of explanation, the report highlighted problems in persuading correctional institutions to focus on education and post-release objectives. The report also highlighted the great educational deficits of the offenders, generally high school drop-outs reading several years below grade level with no discernible job skills. The author concluded "that we entertain no fantasies about the degree of change which manpower projects for the offender can help to bring about. Some offenders will remain unemployed and unemployable no matter what programs are available" (Rovner-Piecznik, 1973, p.77).

*Table 6.1* Criminal justice system programs

| Studies | Scientific methods score (number of cases treatment/control) | Description of intervention and findings |
|---|---|---|
| **Youth** | | |
| Greenwood and Turner, 1993, Paint Creek Youth Center | 3 (73/75) | PCYC offers a comprehensive array of intervention services and activities including counseling, peer support and skills training. One year follow-up data showed no significant differences in arrests or self-reported delinquency between experimental and control groups. |
| Leiber and Mawhor, 1995, Second Chance program | 3 (57/56) | Rehabilitative strategy that uses social skills training, pre-employment training and job placement opportunities (4 months). Youths who received the treatment intervention are as likely to be involved in official offending as are the equivalent matched comparison (37% compared to 29%). |
| **Adults** | | |
| Adams et al., 1994, PERP | 3 (5,608/8,001) | Participation in academic and vocational programs bore no relation to reincarceration; percentage of inmates who were returned to prison did not vary significantly across groups of program and non-program inmates. |
| Berk et al., 1980, TARP | 5 (775/200) | Intervention included the eligibility for unemployment benefits at several levels of the alternative of job counseling. Membership in any of the three experimental groups eligible for payments of job counseling had no statistically significant impact on either property or non-property arrests. |
| Mallar and Thornton, 1978, Baltimore LIFE | 5 (216/216) | Treatment groups received either income maintenance (3 months), job placement or both. Financial aid treatment groups were re-arrested for property crimes 8.3% less (statistically significant) than control and job assistance groups; they were re-arrested 7% less for other crimes (not statistically significant). |
| Finn and Willoughby, 1996, JTPA | 3 (521/734) | Findings suggest that ex-offender status had no effect on employment at termination or follow-up; only the barrier of being long-term unemployed negatively influenced prospect of employment. |
| Hartmann et al., 1994, KPEP | 2 (156) | Treatment included employment skills classes, job club peer support, life skills and GED training. Offenders who successfully completed the program were significantly less likely to recidivate than those who did not (felony arrest $p < .004$; any arrest $p < .005$). |
| Henry, 1988, CADD | 3 (34/56) | Provided inmates with job training and skills along with substance abuse counseling. No difference found between inmates working with substance abuse counseling. No the proportion of disciplinary reports per month in prison. |
| Home Builders Institute, 1996, TRADE | 1 (219) | Involves an 8 week pre-apprenticeship carpentry training program for incarcerated adult offenders. Well over half of program graduates were placed in related jobs in 4 out of the 5 sites; 3 month recidivism rate (7.3%) is consistent or better than those of other vocational programs. |

| Study | No. | (N treatment/control) | Description |
|---|---|---|---|
| Lattimore et al., 1990, Vocational Delivery System | 4 | (154/130) | VDS involved the use of vocational skills training, job readiness and employment skills training. Thirty-six percent of the experimental group compared to 46% of the control group were re-arrested following release (statistically significant $p<.10$). |
| Maguire et al., 1988, PIRP | 4 | (399/497) | Intervention involved participation in prison industry for at least 6 continuous months. After controlling for differences between the two groups, the recidivism rates for industry and non-industry participants were virtually identical. |
| Menon et al. 1992, Project RIO | 3 | (Evaluation not clear) | RIO provides services such as educational and vocational training pre-release and job search and placement assistance post-release. It also uses vouchers from the Targeted Jobs Tax Credit program and federal bonding as special incentives for prospective employers. Positive and significant impact on employment and negative and significant impact on recidivism, particularly for the high risk offenders. |
| Piliavin and Masters, 1981, Supported Work | 5 | (2,200 ex-offenders, 1,400 ex-addicts; 1,200 youth) | Low-skilled and low-wage rate jobs provided for participants for no longer than 12-18 months. Found little effect on delinquents' post-program employment or on their criminal activity after program participation; for adult offenders and drug addicts, especially those over 35, increased employment and reduced crime effects were found. |
| Saylor and Gaes, 1996, PREP | 3 | (over 7,000) | Treatment group had either worked in prison industry, or had received in-prison vocational instruction. Long-term findings (8 years) show that male prison industry subgroup had 20% longer survival times (time before committing new offense) than comparison group; training program subgroup had 28% longer survival times; both results are statistically significant. |
| Spencer, 1980, Ex-Offender Clearinghouse | 4 | (478/478) | Ex-offenders enrolled in the Clearinghouse program were significantly more likely to obtain employment and/or constructive activity than those not enrolled. Treatment involved career counseling, job placement and special counseling services. |
| Van Stelle et al., 1995, STEP | 3 | (89/42) | Provides in-prison training, as well as post-release transition services such as job placement assistance. There were no significant differences between graduates and controls with regard to arrest after release. |
| Vera Institute of Justice, 1972, Manhattan Court Employment Project | 4 | (214/91) | Offers counseling and vocational opportunities such as job training or academic placement for a period of 90 days in lieu of traditional court disposition. During the initial 23 months of operation, the re-arrest rate for the successfully dismissed group was about 50% less than that of the terminated or control groups ($p<.01$). No reported results for entire treatment group vs. control group. |
| Baker and Sadd, 1981, Court Employment Project | 5 | (410/256) | Offers counseling and vocational opportunities such as job training or academic placement for a period of 120 days in lieu of traditional court disposition. There was no difference in recidivism between the treatment and control groups initially, after 12 months or after 23 months. |

Notes

PERP = Prison Education Research Project; TARP = Transitional Aide Research Project; LIFE = Living Insurance for Ex-Offenders; JTPA = Job Training Partnership Act; KPEP = Kalamazoo Probation Enhancement Program; CADD = Computer Aided Design and Drafting; TRADE = Training, Restitution, Apprenticeship, Development and Education; PIRP = Prison Industry Research Project; RIO = Re-Integration of Offenders; PREP = Post Release Employment Project; STEP = Specialized Training and Employment Project.

These disappointing conclusions were communicated to a much broader audience with Martinson's (1974) widely read review of 231 rehabilitative (including employment-based) programs. Martinson concluded that "with few and isolated exceptions the rehabilitative efforts that have been reported so far have had no appreciable effect on recidivism" (p.25). This report has often been held responsible for the decline of the rehabilitative model in corrections and has limited the research done on these programs.

The sheer numbers of offenders, however, have led correctional officials to continue their efforts to curtail recidivism by reintegrating ex-offenders into the workforce. Evaluators have also continued their efforts to identify the causal impact of these programs on recidivism. In this section, we rely on a recent comprehensive review/meta-analysis of 53 experimental or quasi-experimental treatment-control comparisons based on 33 evaluations of prison education, vocation and work programs by Wilson, Gallagher and MacKenzie (2000). This list includes 19 studies conducted during the 1990s and includes all of the evaluations included in our 1997 chapter (Bushway and Reuter, 1997) and listed in Table 6.1.

Wilson and his colleagues report that most of the evaluations find that participants in the treatment programs are less likely to recidivate than those who do not participate in a treatment program. The average effect is substantial. If we assume that the non-participants have a recidivism rate of 50 percent, the program participants have a recidivism rate of 39 percent, a reduction of more than 20 percent. Moreover, the studies that include a measure of employment (roughly one third also measure employment outcomes) found that program participants were substantially more likely to be employed than non-participants. Finally, the studies with the largest employment effect tended also to have the largest reduction in recidivism, validating in some sense the mechanism by which these types of programs are thought to reduce recidivism.

Wilson and his colleagues, however, include a strong caveat to these findings that is consistent with our earlier report. These results are based on studies that are extremely weak methodologically. Eighty-nine percent of the comparisons rate a 1 or 2 on the Scientific Methods Scale. What this means in practice is that there are very poor controls for pre-existing differences between program participants and non-participants. Unobserved differences in motivation (or other factors) could account for much of the resulting change in behavior attributed to the training programs. Only three studies used an experimental design and only one of the non-experimental studies, Saylor and Gaes (1996), used what Wilson, Gallagher and MacKenzie (2000) considered to be the strong statistical controls for selection bias between the participants and non-participants.

A closer examination of the Saylor and Gaes (1996) study of 7,000 individuals in the US Bureau of Prisons system makes the importance of controls for individual differences clear. Inmates were considered to have participated in the program if they had participated in industrial work within the prison, or had received in-prison vocational training or apprenticeship training. One year after release from prison, 6.6 percent of the program participants had either had their parole revoked or been re-arrested, compared with 20 percent of the non program participants, a dramatic 67 percent decline in recidivism. However, because prisoners self-select into these employment programs, it is unreasonable to assume that participants are identical to non-participants. The authors found that participants differed from non-participants in terms of age, prior records, length of incarceration, race, rate of prior violence and security level. When controls for these differences were included in the model, the program participants had a 6.6 percent recidivism rate versus a 10.1 percent recidivism rate for the non-participants, a greatly reduced difference of 35 percent. Other differences not observed by the authors are clearly possible, so even this estimate should be viewed as a liberal estimate of the program impact.

We include two of the experimental studies in Table 6.1. This experimental design explicitly controls for pre-program differences. A close look at these two programs is illustrative of the types of problems faced by rigorous evaluations in this area.

Specialized Training and Employment Project (STEP) was run by the Wisconsin Department of Corrections and was evaluated by the University of Wisconsin Medical School (Van Stelle, Lidbury and Moburg, 1995). This program randomly assigned a well-defined group of offenders to a 6-month program prior to release that included participation incentives, classroom and job training in the institution, and post-release employment assistance. This project showed no decline in recidivism after the first year of the program, but the process evaluation stressed the extraordinary difficulty in implementing a program of this intensity within the prison system. Among other problems, attrition among staff and prisoners alike was a significant impediment both to program implementation and to adequate evaluation.

Lattimore, Witte and Baker (1990) report a randomized control trial for 18–22-year-old offenders in two North Carolina prisons. Two hundred ninety-five inmates were enrolled in a Vocational Delivery System (VDS) aimed at identifying vocational interests and aptitudes, providing appropriate training for the individual and then helping with post-release employment. Subjects were picked from all inmates in the two institutions who were aged 18–22, committed for property offenses, had IQ no less than 70, were in good health and within 8 to 36 months of an in-state release. Data were available for 154 of the experimental and 130 of the controls at approximately the two-year mark.[8] "(T)hose participating in the program were more likely than control group members to complete vocational training and other programs ... VDS participants were less likely to be arrested following release from prison" (Latti-more, Witte and Baker, 1990, p. 117). At 24 months the control group showed a 50 percent recidivism rate (based on arrest records) compared to 40 percent for the experimental group. The difference was only weakly significant (10 percent level) and barely that for tests on other outcome measures. This relatively large effect exists even though only 18 percent of the people assigned to the VDS program actually completed the program. This level of attrition is worrisome, despite the overall positive result, if for no other reason than because it highlights the apparent difficulty in implementing this type of program. Clearly, even the best of these evaluations has limited scope and serious methodological limitations. As noted by Wilson, Gallagher and MacKenzie 2000, it would be foolhardy to conclude on this type of limited evidence that vocational programs for incarcerated offenders work. The only reasonable conclusion is a two-fold statement that (a) it is possible that vocational programs aimed at inmates can reduce recidivism and (b) rigorous evaluations of existing programs need to be implemented to verify that these programs increase employment and reduce recidivism.

Another approach for individuals involved in the criminal justice system was the pre-trial intervention, a major movement during the 1970s. The concept of pre-trial diversions was attached to the labor market in the Court Employment Project. This was evaluated twice by the Vera Institute, first in the late 1960s (Vera Institute of Justice, 1972), and then again during 1977–9 (Baker and Sadd, 1981). In the first less rigorous study, non-serious offenders were offered the opportunity to participate in a 90-day job training and placement program. Successful completion of the program resulted in the dismissal of all charges. Less than half of the participants successfully completed the program. Twelve months after the completion of the program, only 15.8 percent of the successful completers had recidivated, compared to 31 percent of the non-completers and the control group. Again, the problem of selection bias precludes concluding that the program worked – the difference between all the program participants (23.6 percent recidivism rate) and the control group was not statistically significant. Low dosage, problems with implementation and data collection are cited as reasons for the weak results.

By the time the more rigorous study was undertaken almost 8 years later, the program had been taken over by the New York City government and had grown significantly. Four hundred and ten arrestees were assigned to the program, while 256 controls went through the normal court process. The evaluators found no statistically significant difference between recidivism for the two groups, during the diversion period, 12 months after the diversion or 23 months after the diversion. Partial explanations for the failure of the program include the large disturbance in the program immediately before the evaluation due to New York City's budget crisis. However, the evaluators concluded that there were systematic problems with the structure of the pre-trial diversions. For example, counselors did not believe that it was realistic to change the attitude of offenders towards work in 4 months, especially since participants typically lived in criminogenic environments removed from the world of work. Therefore, the training program was not seen as a route to real employment (and hence non-recidivism) but rather as a route away from jail time. In addition, the evaluators felt that the prosecutors had started using the program to control offenders who would otherwise have their cases dismissed, instead of diverting cases which would not be dismissed away from the courts (Hillsman, 1982).

Another approach concentrates on transitional assistance after an individual leaves prison. Job Training Partnership Act (JTPA) programs have attempted to help ex-prisoners by giving them (a) job search assistance, (b) remedial education, (c) occupational skills, (d) work experience, (e) on-the-job training, or (f) customized training for a particular employer. One evaluation of these programs (Finn and Willoughby, 1996) looked at all 521 ex-prisoners who enrolled in JTPA training programs in the state of Georgia for 1 year starting in July 1989. These enrollees were compared to 734 non-offender JTPA participants. The researchers found no sign of any difference in employment outcomes for the two groups, either at program termination or 14 weeks after termination. This result is hard to interpret. Other studies have shown a consistent difference between ex-offenders and other workers. Perhaps the finding of no difference indicates that JTPA programs have helped eliminate some of the stigma of offending. However, since JTPA programs are generally regarded as only minimally effective at improving employment outcomes, that conclusion is hypothetical at best.

Another large federally-funded program tried in the late 1970s involved the use of income supplements during post-release in order to lessen the need to commit crime for money at a time when it may be particularly difficult to find a job. These randomized experiments known collectively as the Transitional Aid Research Project (TARP; Berk, Lenihan and Rossi, 1980) showed that no combination of job training and transitional income support could reduce arrest rates. TARP built on a smaller Baltimore LIFE (Living Insurance for Ex-Offenders) experiment, carefully designed and evaluated (Mallar and Thornton, 1978; Berk, Lenihan and Rossi, 1980; Myers, 1982): The LIFE evaluations found that even combinations of job assistance and counseling for 1 year had no impact on recidivism but that the transitional payments did make a statistically significant difference. Perhaps TARP could not maintain the program integrity of LIFE once the program was expanded.

Despite the failure of TARP, long-term follow-up of the Georgia TARP subjects by Needels (1996) demonstrated that the intuition of these programs is still valid: Needels found that the ex-offenders with jobs commit fewer crimes than the ex-offenders without jobs, and those with higher earnings commit fewer crimes than those with lower earnings. Even after 30 years of trying, however, no program – in-prison training, transitional assistance (both in kind and monetary assistance) or pre-trial diversion – has consistently shown itself capable (through a rigorous random assignment evaluation) of decreasing recidivism through labor-market orientated programs, inside or outside of prison. Perhaps offenders are too deeply entrenched in crime, or the criminal justice system is not an effective delivery system for these types of programs.

Offender-based programs come late in criminal careers, simply because incarceration or even conviction tends to come late. There are strong arguments for intervening early. The next subsection reviews programs that are aimed at high-risk youth before they become involved with the criminal justice system.

### Job training and education programs for at-risk youth

A large number of relatively well-funded governmental programs have tried to boost the labor market performance of at-risk youths (high school dropouts, kids from poor households or poor communities). Although we cannot estimate total expenditures for all such job training programs, the largest single program, Job Corps, enrolled 60,000 youth at a total cost of $1.3 billion in 1999, while youth activities under Title II-C of the JTPA (Job Training and Partnership Act)[9] had a total cost of $130 million in 1999. These programs have undoubtedly attracted more federal funding than any other program category in this review. Encouragingly, there are also many rigorous evaluations, with most studies using some form of randomized experiment (methods score 4 or higher; see Table 6.2). In reviewing the findings of these

*Table 6.2* Non-criminal justice system: at-risk youth

| Studies | Scientific methods score (number of cases treatment/control) | Description of intervention and findings |
|---|---|---|
| **Summer jobs/subsidized work** | | |
| Ahlstrom and Havighurst, 1982, Kansas City Work/Study | 3 (~100/~100) | Combines work experience program with a modified academic program. There appeared to be a negative effect on arrest, as the experimental group was more likely to be arrested by the age of 16 than was the comparison group (51% versus 36%). |
| Cave and Quint, 1990, Career Beginnings | 5 (621/612) | Services of Career Beginnings include summer jobs, workshops and classes, counseling and the use of mentors lasting from junior year of high school through graduation. Experimentals were 9.7% more likely to attend college than controls (statistically significant); they therefore worked less and earned less. |
| Farkas et al., 1982, YIEPP | 4 (2,778/1,255) | Guaranteed full-time summer jobs and part-time school-year jobs to disadvantaged youth who stayed in school. School-year employment doubled from 20% to 40%, while summer employment increased from about 35% to 45%; however, YIEPP was unable to attain its goals of increased school enrollment and success despite the school enrollment requirement. |
| Grossman and Sipe, 1992, STEP | 5 (1,613/1,613) | Program, lasting 15 months, involves remediation, life skills, summer jobs over 2 years and school-year support. STEP had little or no impact on youth's educational experience and had not altered employment patterns for either in-school or out-of-school youth. |
| Maynard, 1980, Supported Work | 5 (570/682) | Structured transitional employment program which offers limited term employment at relatively low wage rates for up to 12 or 18 months, combined with peer group support and close supervision. Up to 18 months post-program, there was a significantly larger percentage of treatment group youth employed; there was no significant impact on arrest rate of youths. |
| Summer Youth Employment and Training Program (SYETP) | N/A | Provides summer jobs for youth. Program appears to greatly increase summer employment rates among disadvantaged youth in sites where jobs are provided; have not investigated whether SYETP creates positive long-term impacts on employment after participants leave their summer jobs. |
| **Short-term training programs** | | |
| Kemple and Snipes (2000), Career Academy (CA) | 4 (959/805) | Academic and career-related high school (HS) courses provided students with work-based learning experiences. CAs produced little change in outcomes for students at low or medium risk of HS drop-out. For students at high risk of HS drop-out, CA was associated with 33.9% lower rate of school drop-out, 36.6% lower rate of arrest and higher rates of school performance and attendance. |
| Fogg and Sum (1999), Youth Opportunity Areas (YOAs) | 2 (990, No comparison) | Targeted out-of-school youths in high-poverty neighborhoods for education, employment and training programs. Pre/post comparison found a 6.3% increase in labor force participation, 6.9% decrease in unemployment, and similar increases in weekly hours of employment and wages. There was also a 9.2–21.0% decrease in high school drop-out. 7.0–63.1% increase in high school graduation, and similar increase in |

| Study | | Description |
|---|---|---|
| Needels et al. (1998), Youth Fair Chance (YFC) | 3 (1,365/1,225) | post-secondary education. No significance testing reported. One-stop employment and education services to persons living in high-poverty areas. Youths in YFC areas relative to youths in non-YFC areas had an increase in employment (12.5% vs. –1.8%, NS) but a decrease in school enrollment. No differences for rates of public assistance, substance abuse, criminal or gang involvement, or single parenthood. |
| Bloom et al., 1994, JTPA | 5 (total of 4,777) | Federal government's major training program for disadvantaged youth which provides average of 5 months of services including on-the-job training, classroom training, and job search assistance (average of 420 hours of service). After 30 months no increase in earnings was found, and there was no decrease in crime rates. |
| Hahn et al. (1994), Quantum Opportunities Program (QOP) | 4 (125/125) | Offered disadvantaged high school students mentoring combined with financial incentives. QOP youths, relative to control youths, were 53.8% less likely to be in trouble with police, less likely to need help with a substance abuse problem, and 54% less likely to be a HS drop-out. QOP youths were also more highly involved in school and volunteer activities, and were more optimistic about the future. |
| Cave et al., 1993, JOBSTART | 5 (988/953) | Provides instruction in basic academic skills, occupational skills training, training related support services and job placement assistance. JOBSTART led to a significant increase in the rate of GED attainment, or completion of high school. In the final 2 years of the follow-up, experimentals' earnings appeared to overtake those of controls, but the magnitude of this impact was not significant. |
| Wolf et al., 1982, 70001 Ltd. | 4 (535/440) | Provides job search assistance, educational services and job preparation classes to high school drop-outs (average of 80–90 hours of services are given). On long-term follow-up (24–40 months), there were no significant earnings impact reported; however, significant positive impact on GED attainment. |

**Intensive residential programs**

| Study | | Description |
|---|---|---|
| Mallar et al., 1982, Job Corps | 3 (4,334/1,457) | Residential program provides intensive skills training, basic education, support services and job placement for 1 year. Average over first 4 years after program exit of 15% earnings increase and 15% reduction in serious (felony) crime. Also, a large and significant increase in GED attainment and college enrollment. |
| Schochet et al. (2000), Job Corps | 5 (9,409/5,977) | Experimental evaluation on average 22 months after enrollment. JC youths, relative to non-JC youths, had a 16% lower rate of arrest or being charged with a criminal complaint and a 21% lower rate of conviction. JC youths were more likely to receive a GED or high school diploma and to be employed at 30 months post-assignment, but were no more likely to attend college. There was an 8% increase in earnings by the end of the follow-up period. |
| Wolf et al., 1987, California Conservation Corps (CCC) | 3 (943/1,083) | Combines work sponsored by various public resource agencies with youth development activities for up to 1 year. CCC is not an effective way of raising the earnings of all participants when they first enter the labor market; however, it did improve earnings of disadvantaged residential corps members and significantly increased their hours worked, post-program. |

Notes

CA = Career Academy; JC = Job Corps; JTPA = Job Training Partnership Act; QOP = Quantum Opportunities Program; STEP = Specialized Training and Employment Project; YFC = Youth Fair Chance; YIEPP = Youth Incentive Entitlement Pilot Project; YOA = Youth Opportunity Area; N/A = not available.

evaluations, we rely primarily on three reviews of the literature: Donohue and Siegelman (1996), Heckman (1994) and US Department of Labor (1995).

Programs aimed at youth tend to take three forms, arrayed below in order of increasing expense and program intensity.

1  *The provision of summer work or other forms of subsidized employment in either public or private sector organizations.*[10] These programs typically cost about $1,000 (in terms of 1995 US dollars) per participant and lasted about 3 months. The Summer Youth Employment and Training Program (SYETP) is the Department of Labor's current summer jobs program, providing minimum wage summer jobs and some education to hundreds of thousands of disadvantaged youth, aged 14–21. Less typical is the more intense Supported Work program from the late 1970s, which provided about 1 year of full-time public sector employment to minority high school drop-outs aged 17–20, with job search assistance at the end of the work period.

2  *Short-term training with job placement for out-of-school youth.* These programs typically last about 6 months and cost $2,500 to $5,000 per participant. For example, the federal government's principal program for disadvantaged youth, JTPA, enrolled 125,000 out-of-school youth aged 16 to 21 for 5 months, during which they received on-the-job training, classroom training and job search assistance. JOBSTART was a large scale demonstration program, designed as a more intensive version of JTPA, lasting 7 months and including more classroom training, at a cost of $5,000 per participant.

3  *Long-term, intensive residential programs providing vocational and life skills training, general education and job placement after graduation.* The most prominent of these programs is Job Corps, a residential program aimed at extremely disadvantaged populations. In 1999, Job Corps received $1.3 billion and enrolled 60,000 new youth in tailored 1-year programs that included classroom training in basic education, vocational skills and a wide range of supportive services (including health care), at a cost of roughly $15,000 per student.

Very few evaluations of these programs measure change in criminal behavior, simply because crime prevention is not generally a primary objective and its measurement requires substantial and complex additional data collection.[11] Crime control is a secondary effect which may result from increased employment, the primary objective. The remainder of this section will briefly review the principal evaluations of these programs, starting with the subsidized work programs.

Subsidized work programs are the cheapest and least intensive of any of the training programs aimed at at-risk youth. Although all subsidized work programs show a marked increase in employment for the targeted population over the time period of the subsidy, no evaluation has shown any long-term effect on employment. For example, Piliavin and Masters (1981) used a randomized assignment of 861 youth (average age 18) in five sites to evaluate Supported Work. The program lasted 12–18 months and provided work experience along with a stipend in a sheltered work environment. Two-thirds of the youth had an arrest before entry into the program and 28 percent had been incarcerated, for an average of 20 weeks; they were predominantly Black (78 percent) and Hispanic (16 percent).

The labor market outcome differences were non-significant and small; e.g. at 36 months the experimental group worked 83.3 hours per month, compared to 75.8 for the control group. The crime differences were weakly significant (10 percent level). At 27 months, 30 percent of the experimental group had been arrested, compared to 39 percent of the control group; the difference was larger and had greater statistical significance for those without prior arrest. Although this effect size is relatively large (a 30 percent difference between controls and experimentals more than 2 years after the program ended), the evaluators concluded that there was no evidence of an effect for youth. As in the VDS case, the evaluators point to failure of most participants to complete the program as one of the sources of error in the study. Overall, the conclusions from this literature seem robust – subsidized work does not increase productivity in any appreciable way and these types of jobs do not appear to be supportive of non-criminal behavior.[12]

The picture is only slightly less gloomy for short-term skill training programs. None of the rigorous evaluations in this category have shown any lasting impact on employment outcomes, although some of the programs show a short-term gain in earnings. It is again not surprising then that the one evaluation that looked at crime showed no lasting impact (JOBSTART). A slightly more detailed look at the data shows that while there are no employment gains, there are some educational gains from these programs. JOB-START and other programs effectively doubled the fraction of GED recipients. Although GED completion is in fact correlated with higher earnings, it apparently serves as a credentialing device rather than a training device (i.e. the fact of earning a GED indicates an ability to sustain consistent effort but working toward the diploma does not actually develop skills). This helps explain why the earnings gains showed in these programs are not long lasting. Eventually, those without GEDs are also able to acquire similar jobs; it just takes them longer without the GED credentials. These programs are generally unable to increase productivity in any meaningful way within the constraints of a short-term non-intensive program.

*Job Corps*

The most rigorously evaluated program, and one of the longest lasting programs in this area, is Job Corps, a long-term, primarily residential training program with emphasis on academic and vocational credentials. The residential component is seen as a key feature of the program because it provides people who are drawn from largely debilitating environments with the experience of living in a structured community committed to learning. The idea is that this environment is what makes the vocational and educational components actually work. The non-residential programs are seen as a way to reach individuals – primarily women with children – who would otherwise not be able to take advantage of Job Corps. Job Corps is by far the most intensive and expensive non-military training sponsored by the federal government. The high cost is a consequence of the residential element of the program and its severely disadvantaged population (over 80 percent are high school drop-outs).

There have been two major evaluations of Job Corps, one in 1982 and one in 2000. The 1982 Job Corps evaluation was not a randomized experiment. It had to use a comparison group drawn from persons eligible but not likely to participate in Job Corps because of geographic location. Despite these limitations, the study was carefully done and generally regarded as credible, although Donohue and Siegelman (1996) raise serious questions about the magnitude of the decline in the homicide rate for enrollees.[13]

The evaluation found that 4 years after graduating from Job Corps, enrollees earned on average $1,300 more per year than the control group, a difference of 15 percent. These achievements corresponded with real increases in educational achievement. Enrollees were five times as likely to get a GED or finish high school, and twice as likely to go to college. Also, there was a significant decline in arrests for serious crimes, especially theft. However, there was also an unexplained increase in minor arrests, especially traffic incidents.

The 2000 evaluation (Schochet, Burghardt and Glazerman, 2000) was a large experiment involving random assignment based on all 80,883 applicants who applied to Job Corps between November 1994 and February 1996. Almost 6,000 subjects (N = 5,997) were assigned to a control group and not allowed to sign up for Job Corps for 3 years. They were allowed to participate in other training programs, and during the follow-up period 64 percent participated in some type of education program, receiving on average a half year of education, including vocational training. It deserves noting that the control group in this more recent study, unlike the first study, is composed of motivated youth, since they applied to participate in Job Corps. The fact that they can and do make use of other educational opportunities should be kept in mind in considering the results of this study.

The treatment group included 9,409 applicants. Of these, 27 percent did not enroll, and another 28 percent participated for less than 3 months. The average participant enrolled for 8 months and received roughly one additional school year of education, including vocational training. The study participants were interviewed at 12 and 30 months after random assignment with reasonable response rates. The results are based on the 11,787 control and treatment members who completed the 30-month interviews. Due to the large sample, even small differences are statistically significant. Outcomes studied include education, work, welfare receipt, crime, health and living arrangements. At the 30-month interview the average youth had been out of the Job Corps for 20 months. As a result, the outcomes must be considered short-term, especially when compared with the earlier study. A 48-month follow-up is currently underway.

In the 2000 study, the participants were 70 percent more likely to receive a GED or high school degree, and more than twice as likely to have vocational certification than non-participants. Unlike the earlier evaluation, Job Corps participants were no more likely to attend college. Employment is rather more difficult to evaluate, since participants were less likely than non-participants to work during their participation in Job Corps. As a result, it takes the Job Corps workers some time to "catch up," to peers who have been working the entire time period. It appears that this finally occurs in the last 4 months of the study. Job Corps participants were only 3 percent more likely to be working than non-participants but the weekly wages of Job Corps participants were 8 percent higher than the control group. This is comparable to the academic estimates of 5–8 percent increase in wages for every additional year of schooling. It remains to be seen if these gains are stable over a longer period of time.

In the 30-month follow-up period 23.3 percent of the treatment group were arrested compared to 27.7 percent of the control group, a difference of 15.9 percent. The treatment group was also 17 percent less likely to be convicted. As in the 1982 study, the biggest difference occurs during the first year of follow-up, when the treatment group is enrolled in Job Corps. Because Job Corps is a highly structured program that is usually residential, this finding is not surprising. It is tempting to dismiss this finding as the result of "incapacitation" and not real behavioral change.[14] However, if, as suggested in the introduction, involvement in the criminal justice system leads to future problems through labeling, this small difference could be meaningful for later outcomes. Furthermore, unlike in the 1982 study, it is also true that there is a 17 percent difference in arrests during the last 6 months of the 30-month follow-up when virtually all applicants have graduated from Job Corps. This result at least suggests a true impact of work on criminality. The 2000 study also replicates the finding from the 1982 study that Job Corps participants who do commit crimes tend to be involved in less serious events than the non-participants who commit crimes.

Although the effects are basically uniform across most of the examined subgroups, young men (16–17 year olds) and older men (22–4) without high school credentials saw the largest employment gains and crime drops among male participants. The link between employment gains and crime drops is an encouraging sign that real progress is being measured. However, there was little evidence that Job Corps had any impact on drug use. In fact, there was little meaningful difference between participants and non-participants in lifestyle issues like family formation and place of residence. This finding raises some doubt about the lasting impact of this program since movement out of disadvantaged neighborhoods and better family relationships are thought to be highly correlated with long-term declines in criminality. The 48-month follow-up should provide a better overall picture of long-term employment gains and drops in criminal activity.

### School-based programs

The failure of all but the most intensive job training programs for at-risk youth to have any effect on either employment or crime is troubling. There are several possible explanations for this finding:

1  The first, and simplest, explanation is that low dosage programs over a 6-month period (or less) lack statistical power to make a measurable impact.

2  More substantively, these lower dosage programs simply might not be

enough to counterbalance a failed academic career that often finds 15- and 16-year-olds reading at the fifth grade level. Extensive training is required to raise reading levels four grade levels or more.

3   A structured positive environment is an important component of any successful program, especially for young males.

The second and third points, taken together, suggest that the vast majority of at-risk youth will not benefit from after-the-fact job training without a highly structured environment that affects more than their job skills. In some ways, this conclusion suggests that someone's orientation towards learning is just as important as their access to learning.

This finding is consistent with the Clinton Administration's effort to make schooling more relevant by connecting training to real jobs to a school environment through the enacted School to Work Opportunities Act. The emphasis on the school-to-work transition is supposed to make students and schools more motivated to learn, and decrease drop-outs (Rosenbaum, 1996). This belief is based in part on the success of Job Corps in connecting education to success in the labor market. A recent evaluation of the School to Work (STW) implementation (Hershey *et al.*, 1999) attempts to assess the implications of this philosophy on education in the United States. Although 4 years is too short a time to expect dramatic changes in orientation in the decentralized educational system found in the United States, the main findings are no doubt discouraging to proponents of this approach. In general, the report finds that any change in focus is small, and incremental. Overall participation in STW programs remains low, with most participation focused on short-term activities, such as job shadowing, rather than career skills development. On the more positive side, student surveys demonstrated a doubling in the number of African-American students who participated in career-related academics. In general, the authors report that the energy behind the STW initiatives is fading, the victim in large part of the perception that these programs are primarily vocational in an age where college non-vocational education is growing in importance. This perception persists despite an effort to emphasize a broader career orientation aimed at all students. It is unlikely that this type of perceptual hurdle can be overcome, especially in the absence of concrete evidence that more career focused academic orientations lead to better life outcomes for any large, defined group of students.

Some school-based programs are not based on the school-to-work model. Evaluations of these programs are neither as numerous nor as rigorous as those for job training programs. The evidence also suggests that anti-drop-out programs, because they involve working within the complex environments of schools (see Chapter 4), are extremely difficult to implement.

The strongest positive evaluation is for the Quantum Opportunities Program (QOP), a demonstration program offering extensive academic assistance, adult mentoring, career and college guidance, a small stipend and money set aside for a college fund. Services totaling 1,286 hours over 4 years (equivalent to about 6 hours per week) were provided to children from AFDC (Aid for Families with Dependent Children) families throughout high school, at a total cost per participant of $10,600. The rigorous evaluation of

100 students in four sites (random assignment, scientific methods score = 4) found that 42 percent of the QOP students were in post-secondary education versus only 16 percent of the controls; a total of 63 percent of the QOP students graduated from high schools, versus only 42 percent of the control group (US Department of Labor, 1995). This evaluation has no long-term follow-up of employment outcomes. However, the increase in enrollment in college is likely to be a good predictor of improved labor market performance.

In this evaluation, adult mentors were assessed to be the most important element. Apparently, the mentors provide the necessary focus and motivation for students to change their behavior and perform better in school. Yet notice that in QOP, the key elements of the school-to-work philosophy – direct connections to the labor market, and contextual learning – were not used. As in Job Corps, QOP students were in routine contact with adults who projected a positive attitude about meaningful employment.

It is impossible within the context of the current literature to determine if mentoring or a school-to-work program (or some combination) is better able to change the motivation of the at-risk youth. However, it is clear that individuals need to become focused on obtaining meaningful and productive employment as an important goal before they will/can take advantage of job training or schooling. We will discuss ways to change the orientation of youth later in this section.

### *Job training for adults in the general population*

Mother Nature has her own way of changing motivation, called aging. It is possible that the same individuals who are not reachable as at-risk youth may be reachable by similar programs when they have reached adulthood. Programs aimed at adults in the general population within the context of a crime prevention discussion, however, are not as interesting as programs aimed at youth, since adults who have not offended by age 25 are at low risk of offending. And, if they have offended by age 25, chances are they will be already involved with the criminal justice system. But some people out of the criminal justice system may benefit from training in order to find meaningful employment. These older adults may have a reduced propensity to commit crime due to maturation. As a result, the number of crimes prevented by such a training program might be less than for younger participants, but at the same time, these individuals may be finally ready to take advantage of training programs that are offered. In reviewing the extensive literature on job training for the general population, Heckman concludes the following:

> Employment and training programs increase the earnings of female AFDC recipients. Earnings gains are (a) modest, (b) persistent over several years, (c) arise from several different treatments, (d) are sometimes quite cost-effective ... For adult males the evidence is consistent with that for adult women.
>
> (Heckman, 1994, p. 112)

Consistent with these findings, older ex-offenders in the Supported Work program appear more responsive to the program than younger ex-offenders. In addition, older subjects in the Baltimore Life experiment also recidivated less often relative to their controls than did younger subjects. The authors of the Supported Work program conclude "the evidence in this experiment and elsewhere suggests older disadvantaged workers, including those who are known offenders, may be much more responsive (than younger workers) to the opportunity to participate in employment programs" (Piliavin and Masters, 1981, p.45).

## Housing dispersal and mobility programs

Much of the above discussion has been focused on at-risk individuals, rather than places. But depressed urban areas deserve special attention in this chapter, given the simultaneous existence of high crime and low employment in these areas. A decade ago, William Julius Wilson (1987) identified the movement of jobs from the inner city to the suburbs as the key factor in the growing concentration of African-American poverty and the social problems related to that hyper-segregation. More recently he has argued that only an employment oriented policy can reduce the social problems of these communities (Wilson, 1996). Yet, as we will see in the following section, stimulating true economic development in the inner city through tax incentives or direct capital subsidies has proven very difficult. Substantial economic forces[15] have led to the movement of businesses to the suburbs, and these forces are extremely difficult to counteract (Hughes, 1993).

As a result, policy makers have recently begun to develop ways to change the supply of labor by bringing inner-city residents to suburban jobs, instead of bringing jobs to inner-city residents. One way to do this is to physically relocate inner-city residents to the suburbs (housing dispersal programs).

The only published outcome evaluation of the housing dispersal concept is based on what is known as the Gautreaux housing mobility program in Chicago. Starting in 1979, the Gautreaux program has given 6,000 inner-city families (primarily single mothers) vouchers that allow them to relocate to low poverty neighborhoods throughout a six county area in and around Chicago. The program, started as the result of a federal court ruling in a housing discrimination case, also allowed families to move within the city of Chicago. Families were assigned to the suburbs or the city based on the location of apartment openings when they became eligible for the program. Because the waiting list was long, and because families were placed at the back of the list when they rejected an opening, very few families rejected an apartment when it was offered, regardless of the location.

Rosenbaum (1992) took advantage of this natural experiment to compare the employment and educational outcomes of the city movers with the suburban movers (scientific methods score = 4). He found that women who moved to the suburbs were 28 percent more likely to be employed than the women who moved inside the city, on average 5.5 years after moving. This was true even though the wage gains attributed to the move were the same for all women who worked, regardless of their location. In addition, he found that 9 years (on average) after the move, the children of the suburban movers were doing significantly better than the children of the city movers (scientific methods score = 3[16]). Although criminal activity was not measured, the children of the suburban movers dropped out of high school only 25 percent as often as the city movers, were in college track courses 1.6 times as often as the city movers, were 2.5 times as likely to attend college, were more than 4 times as likely to earn $6.50 an hour if working, and only 38 percent as likely to be unemployed. These results suggest that for children in these environments, relocation can be an effective tool to change their focus towards posit-ive outcomes like meaningful employment.

These large positive results led to significant optimism on the part of policymakers about the benefits associated with simply relocating poor famil-ies to non-poverty areas. Several programs modeled on the Gautreaux pro-grams were spawned and now operate in Cincinnati, Memphis, Dallas, Milwaukee and Hartford. In 1992, the US Department of Housing and Urban Development (HUD) provided $168 million to fund Moving to Opportunity as a demonstration program for the housing mobility concept. Moving to Opportunity has five sites in large cities – Baltimore, Boston, Chicago, New York and Los Angeles – and is funded for at least 10 years. The project has been set up with a rigorous evaluation component (scientific methods score = 4) – households were randomly assigned to either place-ment in a suburban location with less than 10 percent poverty, placement in the central city, or no treatment. About 1,300 families were given vouchers to allow them to relocate in low poverty suburbs, along with extensive counsel-ing about relocation and assistance in finding a new apartment.

Several evaluations of these programs are now available and are listed in Table 6.3. Perhaps not surprisingly, in each case, households assigned to the experimental treatment were less likely to move than the households assigned to the comparison group, suggesting that moving to low poverty neighborhoods is a non-trivial exercise for impoverished single-parent house-holds. Katz, Kling and Liebman's (1999) study of the Boston experiment found that the families who were assigned to move to low poverty neighbor-hoods had better life outcomes than the control groups and the unrestricted movers, despite the fact that less than half of the assigned households actu-ally moved. In general, the mothers had significant improvements in their mental health, feelings of safety, and victimization relative to the control group. The boys in the sample had 10 to 15 percent reductions in their problem behavior relative to the boys in the control group.

Ludwig, Duncan and Hirschfield (1999) and Ludwig, Duncan and Pinkston (2000) evaluate the MTO experiment in Baltimore. Once again only half of the experimental households actually took advantage of the vouchers to move. They find that the mothers in the experimental settings were 9.2 percent less likely to be on welfare 3 years after moving than the control groups. Children in the treatment and comparison groups were both less likely to be arrested for violent crimes than the children in the control groups. Contrary to predictions, members of the treatment group had higher arrest rates than the comparison group. In addition, children in both groups had more arrests for property offenses than the control group, perhaps because of the increased opportunity.

Both sets of authors warn against making too much of these early results,

*Table 6.3* Moving to opportunity

| Studies | Scientific methods score (number of cases treatment/control) | Description of intervention and findings |
|---|---|---|
| Ludwig *et al.* (2000), Moving To Opportunity – Baltimore (MTO) | 5 (Exp./Comp./Con. 252/188/198) | Eligible families with children who resided in public housing were randomly assigned to a control group or one of two treatment groups: experimental group received housing subsidies valid only in low poverty areas; comparison group received unrestricted housing subsidies. Experimental treatment relative to controls had 6.7% decrease in welfare receipt first year post-program (9.2% decrease 3 years post-program) and with 5.6% increase in welfare-to-work exits. Smaller decreases were evident for comparisons relative to controls. |
| Katz *et al.* (1999), Moving To Opportunity – Boston (MTO) | 5 (Exp./Comp./Con. 240/120/180) | Experimental treatment relative to controls had 10.6–15.0% reduction in problem behavior in boys, 6.5% reduction in criminal victimization, and similar improvements in feelings of safety, child's physical health and adult mental health. Smaller changes were evident for comparisons. |
| Ludwig *et al.* (1999), Moving To Opportunity – Baltimore (MTO) | 5 (Exp./Comp./Con. 252/188/198) | Treatment families that relocated had children at higher risk for criminal involvement. Experimental treatment relative to controls had 7% decrease in violent crime arrests (10% decrease for comparisons relative to controls), in first year post-program, but property crime arrests increased 8% for experimental youths. No change was evident among comparisons. |

Notes

MTO = Moving To Opportunity
Exp. = experimental group
Comp. = comparison group
Con. = control group.

but it would appear safe to conclude that moving to lower poverty areas does have the potential at least to marginally help poor urban women and their children isolated in inner-city public housing communities. It bears repeating that housing dispersal programs have met significant opposition from suburban residents afraid of the impact of poor minority families on their communities. For example, the expansion of Moving to Opportunity to include more than 1,300 families was defeated after it became a political issue in the 1994 election. The Mount Laurel decision in New Jersey, a two-decade-old, court-enforced dispersal strategy, is now being undermined by legislators. In addition, minorities sometimes voice a concern that the dispersal of minorities to the suburbs will weaken minority political power (Hughes, 1993). Given these problems, it seems politically unlikely that housing mobility programs will ever include a large fraction of the residents of poor inner-city neighborhoods.[17]

This reality, however frustrating, suggests that perhaps a strategy aimed at integrating workplaces instead of neighborhoods might be easier to implement. Using this logic, a useful approach to the problem of inner-city poverty is mobility programs which provide transportation for inner-city residents to the suburbs (Hughes, 1993). Such a program recognizes (and takes advantage of) the power of the suburban labor markets to increase residents' incomes while avoiding the political problems associated with housing dispersal. This idea is relatively new, and as a result only a small number of programs are in operation in the United States.[18]

HUD has funded an $18 million demonstration program in five sites starting in 1996 and running for 4 years. The strategy has three main components: a metropolitan-wide job placement service to connect inner-city residents with suburban jobs, a targeted commute mechanism to provide transportation to the jobs, and a support services mechanism which will try to ameliorate some of the problems that may result from a long-distance commute into a primarily white suburban location. Rigorous evaluation with random assignment is currently being undertaken by Public/Private Ventures. Mid-stream process evaluations (all that is available now) suggest that implementation and operation of this type of program is difficult, particularly in tight labor markets. Tight labor markets mean that motivated workers can find decent jobs on their own close to where they live. The remaining workers often need serious training and skill development. As a result, these reverse commuting programs are spending time and resources on both worker training and job development.

The mobility programs are rooted in theoretically very different approaches to reducing central-city crime. Housing dispersal programs attempt to break up the poverty community. Reverse commuting preserves the community but at a cost: the long commuting causes reduced guardianship and parenting that have potentially negative effects in the home communities. Children also do not benefit in the same way because they continue to live in depressed environments. These reverse commuting programs might serve to increase employment and decrease the criminal activity of a particular person, but the programs will probably not have the indirect anti-criminogenic effects of housing dispersal programs.

## Demand-side programs

### Bonding and wage supplements

All the programs described in the previous section focused on changing individual behavior. Yet employers may feel that certain individuals, particularly ex-offenders, represent a potential risk. A criminal history record appears to be a predictor of low job attachment (in part because of the risk of future arrest and incarceration), poor performance, theft and malingering. To overcome these barriers, a number of programs offer to compensate employers for the risk associated with hiring workers with a criminal record, thus increasing the demand for this kind of labor.

One class of programs directly lowers the employer's wage payments, either with a subsidy or through a targeted job tax credit (i.e. the employer of a particular class of worker is able to deduct the payments or some portion of them, from taxable income). This reduces the employer's labor cost since the government pays part of the wage. The programs are transitional and are intended to last just long enough for the offender to acquire a work history that of itself will increase future prospects. The second class of program is more indirect and takes the form of subsidized bonding of offenders, thus reducing the cost for the employer of insuring himself against specific crimes, such as inventory theft; such bonding is normally provided by private corporations.

The federal government, however, has provided little funding for these programs. In 1995, the Department of Labor discontinued the Targeted Jobs Tax Credit, for which the annual budget never exceeded $10 million, with most of that targeted to other disadvantaged groups. Some state Departments of Corrections (e.g. Texas) do offer wage subsidies. However, no evaluation identifies the impact of these on either employment or crime. In addition, some researchers (US Department of Labor, 1995) feel that these programs actually hurt ex-offenders by clearly identifying their ex-offender status. The one independent review of the Targeted Jobs Tax Credit was not optimistic that these programs improved employment among ex-prisoners (Jacobs, McGahey and Minion, 1984).

### Enterprise zones

Community development programs use demand-side policies to help particular neighborhoods. Although these programs are focused on depressed areas, community development programs, like housing dispersal programs, can be used in a wider array of settings. They are of particular interest for crime prevention because they propose to help both individuals and neighborhoods. New jobs present more opportunities for legitimate work to compete with illegitimate opportunities often present in these communities. Jobs visibly available in an area may also provide motivation for young people to continue their education and to enroll in training programs. The economic activity that new or expanded businesses represent can also lead to increased social interactions among residents and strengthen social institutions (churches, business organizations, schools), which can exert a positive influence on individuals who might otherwise revert to crime.

Enterprise zones are one relatively new policy tool focusing tax incentives at generally small, economically depressed geographic areas (Papke, 1993; Erickson and Friedman, 1991). These programs typically use investment incentives, labor incentives and financial incentives to encourage job development (Erickson and Friedman, 1991). The investment incentives include credits for property taxes, franchise taxes, sales taxes, investment taxes and other possibly state-idiosyncratic employer taxes (e.g. inventory tax credits). The labor incentives include a tax credit for job creation, for hiring a zone resident or some other disadvantaged person, and for training expenditures. Finally, the finance incentives sometimes include an investment fund associated with the program and preferential treatment for federal bond programs. These programs are based on the assumption that employers are sensitive to state and local tax incentives in their location decisions. The academic literature shows mixed results about the validity of this claim, although recent evidence suggests that investment is more responsive to state and local taxes than previously thought (Bartik, 1991).

As of 1995, 34 states had a total of 3,091 active enterprise zone programs (median = 16), and the Federal Empowerment Zone and Enterprise Community Program has introduced 106 more zones (Wilder and Rubin, 1996). The state zones are limited in the value of the incentives they can offer, precisely because federal taxes (e.g. corporate profits tax) are so large and cannot be waived by the state. According to Erickson and Friedman (1991), the median zone population for the state programs is about 4,500 persons and the median zone size is about 1.8 square miles. Zone designation is usually based on unemployment rates, population decline, poverty rates, median incomes, the number of welfare recipients or the amount of property abandonment. The federal government provided direct funding of about $40 million in 1999. Beginning in 2000, the government will provide $1.5 million each year for the next 10 years. The federal evaluation will be completed by Abt Associates in December 2000.

All evaluations consider only the immediate economic outcomes of these programs, and do not examine the larger social implications, such as crime reductions (see Table 6.4). Only Bartik and Bingham (1997) show an awareness of this shortcoming. The evaluations also do not attempt to determine the impacts of individual incentives. The incentives are typically used in concert, so that the economic growth in any given zone cannot be attributed to any one incentive; nor is it possible to separate out component effects using econometric techniques.

The main theoretical concern about enterprise zones is that they will simply relocate existing jobs rather than create new jobs. In fact, the British government, which pioneered these zones, abandoned its enterprise zone program after researchers found that nearly all jobs in enterprise zones (86 percent) represented relocation from neighboring communities. The US experience is somewhat more optimistic: the literature seems to agree that, of all the new jobs found in enterprise zones, roughly 25 percent are due to relocation, 25 percent are due to new business and 50 percent are due to expansion of existing businesses (Wilder and Rubin, 1996). Of course, not all the jobs that appear in the enterprise zone should be attributed directly to the zone incentives. However, the primary modes of evaluation in this field,

*Table 6.4* Enterprise zones

| Studies | Scientific methods score (number of cases treatment/control) | Description of intervention and findings |
|---|---|---|
| Bondonio and Engberg (2000), Enterprise Zone (EZ) | 3 (Ns unclear) | Targeted tax breaks and other incentives to depressed economic areas to encourage growth. The impact of EZs at zip code level in five states found no effect of the presence of EZ, level of monetary value of incentives, or other program characteristics on local employment growth. |
| Greenbaum and Engberg (2000), Enterprise Zone (EZ) | 3 (341/3,241) | The impact of EZs at zip code level in six states found that areas that were worse off economically were most likely to be designated as EZs. Comparison of EZs with a matched sample of non-EZs found no impact on housing values, rent, ownership, occupancy, income or employment. |
| Greenbaum and Engberg (1999), Enterprise Zone (EZ) | 3 (303/1,102) | The impact of EZs at place level in 22 states found that EZs raised housing values in areas with low housing vacancy rates, but had a negative impact in areas with high vacancy rates. |
| Greenbaum and Engberg (1999), Enterprise Zone (EZ) | 3 (345/2,897) | Comparison of EZs with a matched sample of non-EZs found no overall employment growth, but a positive impact on employment growth among new establishments which was offset by losses among existing establishments. |
| Boarnet and Bogart, 1996, Enterprise Zone (EZ) | 3 (7/21) | New Jersey EZs have no impact on employment and business growth. |
| Papke, 1994 | 3 (15/24) | Indiana EZs decrease zone unemployment by 19%. |
| Bostic, 1996 | 3 (5/27) | California EZs in small cities increase business construction. |
| Office of the Auditor General, California, 1988 | 1 (13) | Survey of firms indicates small net increase in economic activity with wide variability across zones. |
| Dowall et al., 1994 | 2 (13) | Although employment growth and increased business activity increased in all CA zones, researchers concluded that zone incentives could not be linked to growth. |
| Erickson and Friedman, 1991 | 1 (35) | EZs in 17 states appear to create jobs in areas with development potential. EZs are ineffective in highly distressed areas. |
| GAO, 1988 | 2 (3) | Three rural Maryland EZ zones showed significant increases in employment and investment after zone designation. |
| HUD, 1996 | 1 (10) | Interviews with zone managers in ten zones in nine states show zones lead to significant new investment and job growth. |
| Jones, 1985 | 2 (1/1) | Connecticut EZ has no impact on building activity. |
| Jones, 1987 | 2 (1/1) | Illinois EZ has an impact on building activity. |
| Wilder and Rubin, 1996 | 1 (1) | Firm-level survey data show increase in jobs due to Indiana EZ in Evanston. |

correlation and before-and-after without comparison group (scientific methods score 1 and 2), do not allow researchers to isolate the contribution of the zone incentives.

In addition, most of these studies use data from surveys of zone firms or zone managers; these lack credibility as measures since both groups have an incentive to place a positive bias on the outcomes.[19] These studies generally conclude that the zones increase jobs and investment, although results vary by zone.[20]

Three studies (Papke, 1994; Boarnet and Bogart, 1996; Bostic, 1996) attain a level 3 scientific methods score by performing before-and-after studies of a particular state's enterprise zone (EZ) program (Indiana, New Jersey and California, respectively) with comparison groups from other eligible areas in the state. Each study also uses data collected by independent agencies, so the data is unlikely to be biased by EZ participants. The first two studies used econometric methods to control for selection bias; the study by Bostic did not.

The results of the first two studies contrast strongly – the New Jersey study found that the zones had no impact on total employment or property values in municipalities with zones,[21] while the Indiana study found that the zones led to a long-term 19 percent decline in unemployment rates in municipalities with enterprise zones. The Indiana researcher was somewhat surprised by the magnitude of this effect, given that the employment incentives were limited in the Indiana zones. But the study also found that firms responded to reductions in inventory taxes by increasing inventory by 8 percent and reducing capital machinery by 13 percent. These changes in inventory and machinery may represent the conversion of firms from manufacturing to more emphasis on distribution, generating a positive impact on employment. Bostic's study used investment growth rather than employment as the principal outcome measure. He found that the EZs had a significant but small impact on commercial construction permits and an insignificant impact on the number of businesses in an area.

More recently, there have been four studies by a group of researchers which attempt to go beyond these single state studies to look at variation across states for state enterprise zones (Bondonio and Engberg, 2000; Engberg and Greenbaum, 1999; Greenbaum and Engberg, 1999, 2000). These studies include the most rigorous econometric controls yet employed for pre-existing differences between places with enterprise zones and places without enterprise zones. These studies also made use of impartial Census Bureau data from 1980 and 1990 on housing values, housing vacancy, employment and area income. The broadest study (Engberg and Greenbaum, 1999) looks at 303 enterprise zones located in places with between 5,000 and 50,000 people in 22 states. The study finds that the enterprise zone has no overall impact on housing markets. They do find that zones with low vacancy rates see an increase in housing values after the start of enterprise zones, while zones actually reduce the housing value growth rate for places with high vacancy rates. This suggests that enterprise zones are actually harmful in the most depressed locations.

A similar analysis was conducted for zones located in larger metropolitan urban areas based on zip code data for six states (Greenbaum and Engberg,

2000). Once again they find that zones have no impact on the overall housing values, and in fact lead to declines in the average growth in housing values in California and Virginia, rents in California and Florida, and occupancy rates in Florida and Pennsylvania. Zone impacts on income and employment outcomes are either negative or insignificant. Unlike the previous report by Engberg and Greenbaum (1999) the results did not appear to depend on the initial values of the zones in 1980.

Bondonio and Engberg (2000) did a similar study with advanced controls for selection bias on enterprise zones in five states and found no effect of the zones on employment outcomes. Bondonio and Engberg also looked at separate components for each of the enterprise zones and found that the monetary value of the incentives did not increase the probability of success. This result contrasts with the suggestions of reviewers like Bartik (1991).

Finally, in attempt to peel back the layers of the onion on what may be going on in these enterprise zones, Greenbaum and Engberg (1999) look at establishment level employment statistics for enterprise zones in metropolitan areas in six states using a matched sample difference-in-difference approach. They found that enterprise zones increased employment and business activity in new establishments while decreasing employment and business activity in old establishments. The net effect was a small decrease in employment. Essentially, this study finds that, as in the UK, zones lead to increased churning of business activity without any net gains in employment. They suggest that perhaps the political nature of the zones tends to over-emphasize new businesses without paying much attention to existing businesses. It is also possible that depressed areas that did not get zones (the matched comparison places) received other types of public investment tailored to existing businesses.

This new body of rigorous research on many zones over a number of states certainly raises serious questions about the ability of enterprise zones to significantly change the business environments in depressed urban areas. The upcoming evaluation of the Federal Empowerment Zones, due to be released in December of 2000, should either validate this negative conclusion or suggest that federal zones, as opposed to state zones, have the ability to make an impact.

### Community Development Block Grants

The 1974 Community Development Block Grant (CDBG) Program represents the other major federally funded program aimed directly at revitalizing distressed neighborhoods. Instead of relying on tax credits as incentives, this program provides direct funding to local governments. In 1992, CDBGs provided local jurisdictions with $4.8 billion to be spent on activities that support any one of three objectives: benefiting low- and moderate-income persons, preventing or eliminating slums or blight, or addressing other urgent community needs. The program funding breaks down broadly into five main areas: housing (38 percent), public facilities (22 percent), economic development (12 percent), public services (9 percent), and acquisition and clearance (6 percent). The remaining 13 percent is for administration of the program. Although there are no outcome evaluations of this program,[22] the sheer size of the economic development component of this program ($251 million in 1992) demands inclusion in this section.

Most of what follows is based on a 1995 funding process evaluation sponsored by the Department of Housing and Urban Development (Urban Institute, 1995). The evaluation, like those for Enterprise Zones, considers only economic outcomes. A full 78 percent of the $251 million economic development grant money was spent on loans and grants to private businesses. Most of the recipient businesses were small, and 37 percent of these businesses were minority owned. These loans seemed to perform better than the non-geographically targeted Small Business Administration loans. According to the HUD report, these loans were more important to the business activities of the recipients than the EZ tax incentives,[23] but neighborhood residents held a comparable number of the newly created jobs under both programs (approximately 30 percent).

An effort was made to provide a before-and-after study of 250 census tracts in the CDBG program (scientific methods score = 2), using a survey on all CDBG funding and census data from 1980 and 1990. This study found a clear relationship between the level of funding and tract income: tracts that saw an increase in income received $1,247 per capita, tracts that were stable between the two time periods received $844 per capita and tracts that declined received $737 per capita. Improvement in low-income tracts usually only occurred through gentrification or out-migration of low income people, but in several instances the arrival of major industrial facilities resulted in an increase in income for the tract residents.[24]

In more general terms, the researchers concluded that the existence of an income-mix among neighborhood residents and a healthy commercial district appeared to help development. Within the context of this review, these factors could signal the existence of a certain level of social control that would allow community programs to be effective. Neighborhoods without these factors may not have enough social capital to take advantage of any community-based program.

### Weed and Seed

The demand-side programs (Community Development Block Grants and Enterprise Zones) involve such a broad array of incentives and funds that it will be hard to determine what might explain any positive findings and thus what is worth replicating. Furthermore, neither represents a focused effort to solve the crime problems present in the inner city. Policymakers focused on this problem within the Department of Justice have observed that these areas are characterized by weak attachment of individuals and communities to the legal labor market (Wilson, 1987). This means that resources are not being directed towards success in that market. For example, low employment rates provide little incentive for individuals to make the necessary investments in human capital, limit the adverse consequences of arrest and incarceration, and limit the number of pro-social role models who may support an individual in the common struggles of working life. Neighborhoods where many males support themselves through some drug selling will not have many of the social institutions that support legitimate work, making it more difficult for individuals to make the transition to legitimate work. Wilson (1996) argues that youth who grow up in communities where people do not regularly work do not learn necessary job skills, such as how to dress or how to arrive on time. Rosenbaum (1996) also argues that youth have difficulty finding employment when they live in impoverished neighborhoods because their friends and family are not likely to provide many job connections. The perceived returns from continuing in school or from acquiring human capital in other ways is therefore low. This leads to low rates of high school graduation rates and high attrition in training programs, maintaining the under-investment in human capital of the previous generation in high poverty neighborhoods.

In this environment, criminal activity is both a reason for the poor attachment and an obstacle to creating a stronger bond with the legal labor market. For example, high neighborhood crime rates provide individuals with an alternative economy in which to earn a living while deterring employers from seriously considering locating in these areas. Criminal activity is a major obstacle for any positive programs aimed at creating legal employment. A large fraction of adult criminal offenders are substance users; their involvement with expensive illicit drugs, such as cocaine and heroin, is distinctive. This represents a major employment handicap, which has to be addressed before realistic employment can occur. The same forces are at work in the community at large. Evidence from Bostic (1996) shows that places with high crime rates have a hard time attracting employers. Crime has to be addressed before businesses will invest in an area.

Policymakers have concluded that if they want to "reattach" communities or individuals to the legal labor market, then they must simultaneously "detach" these communities or individuals from crime, and provide opportunities for legal activity. This line of reasoning represents the basic premise of Operation Weed and Seed.

Operation Weed and Seed represents an ambitious federal, state, and local effort to improve the quality of life in targeted high crime areas in urban settings, launched in 1991 by the Department of Justice. Weed and Seed programs can be found in over 200 sites nationwide with an average funding level of about $225,000. There are some key components of this strategy, including a) enhanced coordination among local actors to solve local problems, b) weeding out criminals from target areas through concentrated efforts of local law enforcement, c) proactive community policing intended to maintain a stable low crime equilibrium and d) seeding efforts, consisting of human service provision and neighborhood revitalization effort to prevent and deter further crime.

A major national evaluation of Weed and Seed was released in 1999 (Dunworth *et al.*, 1999; see Table 6.5). From our perspective, this evaluation is unfortunately weak, consisting of a before-and-after (scientific methods score = 2) study of only eight Weed and Seed sites. This poor design is the result of the political process which moved forward on the attractive notion of Weed and Seed without an evaluation strategy.

Weeding activity tended to predominate, with increased special operations for targeted law enforcement. In general, local prosecutors' offices were not brought into the program, resulting in a fair amount of churning: arrests

*Table 6.5* Weed and Seed

| Studies | Scientific methods score (number of cases treatment/control) | Description of intervention and findings |
|---|---|---|
| Dunworth *et al.* (1999), Weed and Seed | 2 (No comparison) | Interagency effort to remove offenders from target areas and to deter further crime through community revitalization. Pre/post comparison after 2 years found a 6.1–45.9% decrease in index crime rates in 6 of 10 target areas relative to surrounding city (in 3 target areas an increase of 1.9–13.8%). Significant decreases in the percentage of respondents reporting crime as a big problem (4 of 8 sites) and victimization (3 of 8 sites). Significant increases in the percentage of respondents indicating greater police effectiveness (5 of 8 sites) and improved quality of life (6 of 8 sites). |

without incarceration. The Boston Gun Project has clearly demonstrated the value of including the prosecutor's office in any local law enforcement crackdown. Youth programs in a wide array of categories including job training tended to dominate the seeding activity, followed by a neighborhood beautification program. Adult employment and economic advancement programs only played a minor role in most sites. Seeding activity tended to be less well implemented relative to weeding, and usually followed the weeding program sequentially, instead of occurring simultaneously. Weeding activities without seeding tended to alienate community residents. In terms of the desired outcomes, five of the eight sites had decreases in Type 1 offenses[25] reported to the police 4 years after the implementation of Weed and Seed. These decreases exceeded the rates of decline in the cities as a whole. This comparison is not wholly satisfying, as the authors recognized, because of the differences between a small inner-city neighborhood (the target area) and a large metropolitan area. It is noteworthy that the pattern of crime in the Weed and Seed site was consistently in the same direction as the observed pattern for the city as a whole, making it possible that the observed pattern is simply the result of city-wide changes in crime rates.

Results of a neighborhood survey conducted at 2-year intervals showed that four sites had substantial reductions in perceptions of neighborhood declines, but only one site showed a decline in the victimization experiences of the respondents. In general, although there were no negative findings, the survey results showed little impact. This could reflect the difficulties associated with this part of the evaluation, which had substantial non-response rates. The problems led to the use of in-person interviews in the first wave and phone interviews in the second wave, which may not be comparable.

A fair review of Weed and Seed based on this evaluation must conclude that there has been little sustained impact. This could be the result of many factors, including the relative paucity of the funding initiative, the lack of coordination of the Weed and Seed components, and the relative failure of the seeding initiatives. Funding at $225,000 per area is simply not enough money to make a difference with such a large and structurally complex problem.

## Conclusions

We feel confident in stating that programs that aim to shift more poor people out of crime and into employment must accomplish at least these three steps:

Step 1. Reduce the attraction of crime.
Step 2. Treat substance abuse problems.
Step 3. Provide social and educational supports to help high-risk individuals obtain employment.

At the individual level, Job Corps is the "poster child" for this approach. Step 1 is accomplished by removing youth from their neighborhoods and placing them in an intensive, pro-social, residential environment. Step 2 is accomplished through the provision of substance abuse treatment at most of the centers as part of the program. Step 3 is accomplished through the development of bonds with the program leaders, the use of the extensive job networks developed by Job Corps, and the actual education and training that takes place at the Job Corps centers. Gautreaux and Moving to Opportunity accomplish Step 1 and Step 3 simultaneously (women with obvious substance abuse problems are not eligible for the program) by moving families out of the inner city and into the suburbs; crime is less attractive because the networks of offenders are less dense. Mentoring was found to be the most important part of the Quantum Opportunities Program – perhaps because it provided students with an older role model who could help them redirect their attention towards school and away from less "productive" alternatives (Step 3).

The preponderance of individual-level programs in the above examples is not a coincidence. Implementation of programs at the community level is almost by definition difficult (see Chapter 5). The community-level program that is closest to this logic, Weed and Seed, has had difficulty implementing the Seed (which includes job training) part of the program systematically. Detaching a community from crime without providing alternatives is unlikely to be effective, and will probably antagonize local residents.

One reason that implementing programs at the community level is more difficult than implementing programs for individuals is simply scale. It is always easier to affect change with one person rather than 1,000 people. But we do not believe that the problem is just one of scale. It is also possible that at the community level the process is not linear. In other words, one cannot expect to reconnect people to legal work one at a time until the majority of people in the community are focused on work rather than crime or other enterprises. Perhaps, instead, it is necessary to create large-scale change before people are willing to tackle the types of changes these different programs will inevitably inspire. This problem is a natural result of the type of neighborhood effects discussed above. Since what your neighbors do matters, policymakers might need to get substantial numbers of people moving together, in order to allow them to support one another. This conclusion is the basis for the US Department of Labor (1995) recommendation that poor neighborhoods should be saturated with a range of interventions intended to alleviate poverty so that "the employment outcomes of some person within a community can lead to 'spillover effects' as other people in the neighborhood are influenced by the positive actions of their peers" (p.63).

The Youth Opportunity Act is the Department of Labor's response to that charge. The goal is to saturate low-income, high crime communities with educational, employment and training programs aimed at 16–24 year old out-of-school youth. The level of funding is impressive ($250 million a year targeted at 42 sites). For the first time ever, community-level outcomes will be studied along with individual-level outcomes, formally recognizing the link between individual-level and community-level outcomes. Results from a three-site pilot study started in 1996 are cautiously optimistic (see Table 6.2). An audit of the process at the three pilot sites, however, showed that implementing intensive programs in highly disadvantaged areas can be a very difficult process, a lesson learned earlier in the Community Block Grant Program and Weed and Seed (Office of Inspector General, 2000).

One final caveat about community-level programs seems worthwhile. The very programs that are the most successful at the individual level may be harmful at the community level. Programs like Gautreaux and Job Corps which take people out of the community at least temporarily also paradoxically may worsen the situation of those who remain, since the movers are likely to be among the more forward looking adults in these fragile inner-city communities. Similarly, programs like reverse commuting, though they may bring important benefits for individuals, may exacerbate problems if the long commutes reduce still further the extent of adult supervision of children that is such an important component of effective community. This of course suggests the attractions of the converse, bringing some middle-class households back into the neighborhoods that are so devastated. But this type of strategy places the burden on Step 1 far more than in any individual-based programs. It is relatively easy to "detach" an individual, particularly a motivated individual, from crime. But it is still unclear whether police have developed effective strategies that can reduce crime dramatically over a long enough time to encourage capital investment by new residents and businesses. These are the types of questions that need to be addressed in future research.

## Notes

1 The authors would like to recognize the excellent research assistance of Jennifer Borus and Robert Apel.

2 Employment, like crime, has many dimensions. Jobs vary in wage rates, work satisfaction and duration. Measured correlation between employment rates and crime may be confounded by failure to measure variation in job quality adequately.

3 We focus here on employment measures rather than unemployment because in many areas the problem is less a matter of formally defined unemployment than low labor force participation rate. In the face of persistent unemployment, discouragement may lead many to drop out even from job search.

4  This may reflect the higher quality of post-1970 data, itself a consequence of the activities of the Law Enforcement Assistance Administration (as well as its successor federal agencies) and the criminal justice system investment in computers, among other factors.

5  It is difficult to classify all job training programs in terms of our programmatic interest. For example, Job Training and Partnership Act (JTPA) Title-IIA ($955 million in FY, 1999) is aimed at economically disadvantaged adults; some of those adults may be involved with the criminal justice system and others may still be young enough to be reasonably classified as "youth," but many may be at slight risk of serious criminal involvement. Given the large number of other JTPA Titles that were more directly targeted at disadvantaged youth, we did not include any of Title-IIA.

6  We identify the targets as offenders rather than ex-offenders because in fact what is known is that they have committed a crime. The ex-offender status is a goal rather than a description.

7  Note once again that the Vocational Delivery System and Supported Work programs cited above are not technically part of the juvenile criminal justice system.

8  Differences in release date meant that a uniform follow-up period would have excluded significant periods of post-release exposure for some participants.

9  JTPA is the main federal funding source for job training programs in the US. JTPA funds a number of discrete program types including a) job search assistance, b) remedial education, c) occupational training, d) work experience, e) on-the-job training and f) customized training for a particular employer.

10  Strictly speaking, the provision of a job is not a job training or education program. However, many employment skills are learned on the job; employment increases future employability.

11  Self-report from program participants about crime involves inquiring about sensitive behaviors. Official record checks of criminal histories requires information from a different set of agencies, with different sensitivities, from those providing the other outcome data.

12  This result is consistent with the conclusion of Sampson and Laub (1990) who find that the critical variable is not the job but the social bonds of the workplace, bonds that probably are absent in a short-term subsidized work environment.

13  The reported reduction in homicide rates suggests that the control group had extraordinarily high homicide rates compared to their peers, thus making suspect the claimed reduction in homicides for the experimental subjects. Homicide reductions accounted for a large share of the dollar benefits estimated in the evaluation. On the other hand, the figure used for estimating the value of a life for homicides was much lower than reported elsewhere in the literature; it is possible that the errors roughly cancel out.

14  In fact, the males who are in the non-residential programs are no less likely to be arrested than the control group.

15  Massey and Denton (1993) argue that the strong desire for racial segregation has also been an impetus for the exit of jobs.

16  The sample is different for the children and the mothers. The children come from a sample originally composed in 1982. They were re-interviewed in 1989. Only 59 percent of the original sample could be relocated, and most of those relocated had moved from another location, not the location where the first interview was done. The potential for bias exists because the harder to locate families might vary by suburban or urban location.

17  Of course, many of the same objectives met by housing dispersal programs could be met by encouraging gentrification of older depressed neighborhoods, though gentrification often involves the exit of current residents.

18  Within this area, we noted the absence of any discussion of the role of crime in driving business to the suburbs, or the potential crime prevention effects of new job connections in the suburbs.

19  In an attempt to determine what would have happened if the zones had not existed, these surveys ask zone firms and zone managers how many of the jobs were due directly to the incentives. It is in the self-interest of both sets of agents to provide positive answers.

20  The surveys did provide useful insight into the elements of programs which seemed to work best. Bostic (1996) concludes that the incentives provide only marginal incentive for firms to locate in zoning areas. Program success in California depends on supplementing the tax incentives with an active local government or community effort, mainly with marketing. Wilder and Rubin (1996) conclude that places with severe economic blight need additional assistance beyond enterprise zones, and autonomous management of the zone is effective. Finally, Erickson and Friedman (1991) conclude that the most successful state programs restrict the number of zones, use a competitive award process (which pulls together local resources), and provide significant incentives to these limited, targeted areas.

21  This result is especially interesting given that a before-and-after study by Rubin (1990) found substantial effects in New Jersey.

22  The lack of outcome evaluations is attributed to the flexibility of the programs, the lack of credible evidence about what would have occurred in the absence of the program and the inability to conceptualize and measure clear outcomes at a neighborhood level.

23  A full 80 percent of recipients said that the loan was crucial to their activity, while EZ incentives are typically important for 30 to 40 percent of all EZ businesses (Wilder and Rubin, 1996).

24  Although these numbers appear to suggest that higher CDGB funding generates improvements, this conclusion is not possible without some other comparison. For example, there may be selection bias; better organized communities, which are more likely to be improving economically anyway, may do better in the grant application process.

25  Under the Uniform Crime Report, there are eight Type 1 offenses: homicide/non-negligent manslaughter, forcible rape, robbery, assault, burglary, larceny, motor vehicle theft, and arson.

# References

Adams, K., Bennet, K.J., Flanagan, T.J., Marquart, J.W., Cuvelier, S.J., Fritsch, E., Gerber, J., Longmire, D.R. and Burton, V.S., Jr. (1994) A large scale multidimensional test of the effect of prison education programs on offenders' behavior. *The Prison Journal*, 74, 433–49.

Ahlstrom, Winton and Robert J. Havighurst (1982) The Kansas City work/study experiment. In Daniel J. Safer (ed.), *School programs for disruptive adolescents*. Baltimore, MD: University Park Press, 259–75.

Baker, Sally and S. Sadd (1981) *Diversion of felony arrests: An experiment in pretrial intervention: An evaluation of the Court Employment Project, summary report*. Washington, DC: US Department of Justice, National Institute of Justice.

Bartik, Timothy J. (1991) *Who benefits from state and local economic development policies?*. Kalamazoo, MI: W.E. Upjohn Institute for Employment Research.

Bartik, Timothy J. and Richard D. Bingham (1997) Can economic development programs be evaluated? In Richard Bingham and Robert Mier (eds), *Significant issues in urban economic development*. Newbury Park, CA: Sage.

Berk, R.A., K.J. Lenihan and P.H. Rossi (1980) Crime and poverty: Some experimental evidence from ex-offenders. *American Sociological Review*. 45, 766–86.

Bloom, Howard, Orr, L.L., Cave, G., Bell, S.H., Doolittle, F. and Lin, W. (1994) *The National JTPA Study: Overview of impacts, benefits, and costs of Title IIA*. Bethesda, MD: Abt Associates.

Boarnet, Marlon G. and William T. Bogart (1996) Enterprise zones and employment: Evidence from New Jersey. *Journal of Urban Economics*, 40, 198–215.

Bondonio, Daniele and John Engberg (2000) States' enterprise zone policies and local employment: What lessons can be learned? *Regional Science and Urban Economics*, 30, 519–49.

Bostic, Raphael W. (1996) *Enterprise zones and the attraction of businesses and investment: The importance of implementation strategies and program incentives.* Washington, DC: Division of Research and Statistics, Board of Governors of the Federal Reserve System.

Bourgois, Phillipe (1995) *In search of respect: Selling crack in El Barrio.* New York: Cambridge University Press.

Bushway, S.D. (1996) *The impact of a criminal history record on access to legitimate employment.* Unpublished Ph.D. dissertation, Pittsburgh, PA: Carnegie Mellon University.

Bushway, S. and Reuter, P. (1997) Labor markets and crime risk factors. In L.W. Sherman, D.C. Gottfredson, D.L. MacKenzie, J. Eck, P. Reuter and S. Bushway, *Preventing crime: What works, what doesn't, what's promising* (pp. 1–59, Chapter 6). Washington, DC: National Institute of Justice, US Department of Justice.

Cave, G., Doolittle, F., Bos, H. and Toussaint, C. (1993) *JOBSTART: Final report on a program for high school dropouts.* New York: Manpower Demonstration Research Corp.

Cave, George and Janet Quint (1990) *Career beginnings impact evaluation: Findings from a program for disadvantaged high school students.* New York: Manpower Demonstration Research Corp.

Chiricos, Ted (1986) Rates of crime and unemployment: An analysis of aggregate research evidence. *Social Problems*, 34, 187–212.

Cook, Philip and Gary Zarkin (1985) Crime and the business cycle. *Journal of Legal Studies*, 14, 115–28.

Donohue, J.J. and Peter Siegelman (1996) *Is the United States at the optimal rate of crime? Allocating resources among prisons, police, and social programs.* Working paper for the American Bar Foundation.

Dowall, D.E., Beyeler, M. and Wong, C.-C.S. (1994) *Evaluation of California's enterprise zone and employment and economic incentive programs.* Berkeley, CA: University of California-Berkeley.

Dunworth, Terence, Gregory Mills, Gary Cordner and Jack Greene (1999) *National evaluation of weed and seed cross-site analysis, research report.* Washington, DC: US Department of Justice, National Institute of Justice.

Ehrlich, I. (1973) Participation in illegitimate activities: A theoretical and empirical investigation. *Journal of Political Economy*, 81, 521–65.

Engberg, John and Robert Greenbaum (1999) State enterprise zones and local housing markets. *Journal of Housing Research*, 10, 163–87.

Erickson, Rodney A. and Susan W. Friedman (1991) Comparative dimensions of state enterprise zone policies. In R.E. Green, (ed.), *Enterprise zones: New dimensions in economic development.* Newbury Park, CA: Sage Focus Edition, pp. 155–76.

Fagan, J. and Freeman, R.B. (1999) Crime and work. In M. Tonry (ed.), *Crime and justice: A review of research.* Chicago, IL: University of Chicago Press, pp. 113–78.

Farkas, G., Smith, D.A., Stromsdorfer, E.W., Trask, G. and Jerrett, R. (1982) *Impacts from the Youth Incentive Entitlement Pilot Projects: Participation, work and schooling over the full program period.* New York: Manpower Demonstration Research Corp.

Farrington, D.P., Gallagher, B., Morley, L., St. Ledger, R.J. and West, D.J. (1986) Unemployment, school leaving and crime. *British Journal of Criminology*, 26, 335–56.

Finn, Mary A. and Katherine G. Willoughby (1996) Employment outcomes of ex-offender Job Training Partnership Act (JTPA) Trainees. *Evaluation Review,* 20, 67–83.

Fogg, Neeta and Andrew Sum (1999) *The employment status and job characteristics of out-of-school youth in the three initial YOA demonstration sites: Key findings of wave two follow-up surveys.* Boston, MA: Northeastern University, Center for Labor Market Studies.

Freeman, Richard B. (1995) The labor market. In J.Q. Wilson and Joan Petersilia (eds.), *Crime.* San Francisco, CA: Institute for Contemporary Studies, pp. 171–91.

GAO (US General Accounting Office) (1988) *Enterprise zones: Lessons from the Maryland experience.* Washington, DC: GAO.

Gottfredson, Michael and Travis Hirschi (1990) *A general theory of crime.* Stanford, CA: Stanford University Press.

Greenbaum, Robert and John Engberg (1999) The impact of state enterprise zones on urban business outcomes. Under review.

Greenbaum, Robert and John Engberg (2000) An evaluation of state enterprise zone policies: Measuring the impact on urban housing market outcomes. *Policy Studies Review,* 17, 29–46.

Greenwood, Peter and Susan Turner (1993) Evaluation of the Paint Creek Youth Center: A residential program for serious delinquents. *Criminology,* 31, 263–80.

Grossman, J.B. and Sipe, C.L. (1992) *Summer Training and Education Program (STEP): Report on long-term impacts.* Philadelphia, PA: Public/Private Ventures.

Hahn, Andrew, Tom Leavitt and Paul Aaron (1994) *Evaluation of the Quantum Opportunities Program (QOP): Did the program work?* Waltham, MA: Brandeis University, Center for Human Resources.

Hartmann, David, P. Friday and Kevin Minor (1994) Residential probation: A seven year follow-up study. *Journal of Criminal Justice,* 22, 503–15.

Heckman, James J. (1994) Is job training oversold? *The Public Interest,* Spring, 91–115.

Henry, Patrick (1988) *Effects of private industry participation on inmates adjustment experiences before and after release.* St. Petersburg, FL: Department of Sociology, Eckerd College.

Hershey, Alan M., Marsha K. Silverberg, Joshua Haimson, Paula Hudis and Russell Jackson (1999) *Expanding options for students: Report to congress on the national evaluation of school-to-work implementation.* Princeton, NJ: Mathematica Policy Research.

Hillsman, Sally (1982) Pretrial diversion of youthful adults: A decade of reform and research. *The Justice System Journal,* 7, 361–87.

Home Builders Institute (1996) *Project TRADE (Training, Restitution, Apprenticeship, Development and Education) report.* Washington, DC: Home Builders Institute.

HUD (US Department of Housing and Urban Development) (1996) *Expanding housing choices for HUD-assisted families.* Washington, DC: US Department of Housing and Urban Development, Office of Policy Development and Research.

Hughes, Mark Alan (1993) *Over the horizon: Jobs in the suburbs of major metropolitan areas.* Philadelphia, PA: Public/Private Ventures.

Jacobs, James B., Richard McGahey and Robert Minion (1984) Ex-offender employment, recidivism and manpower policy: CETA, TJTC, and future initiatives. *Crime and Delinquency,* 30, 486–506.

James, Thomas S. and Jeanne M. Granville (1984) Practical issues in vocational education for serious juvenile offenders. In R. Mathias, P. DeMuro and R. Allinson (eds), *Violent juvenile offenders: An anthology.* San Francisco, CA: National Council on Crime and Delinquency, pp. 337–45.

Jones, E.R. (1985) *Enterprise zone programs and neighborhood revitalization: The first two years.* Working Paper. Urbana, IL: Department of Urban and Regional Planning, University Illinois.

Jones, E.R. (1987) Enterprise zones for the black community – promise or product: A case study. *The Western Journal of Black Studies*, 11, 1–10.

Katz, Jack (1989) *The seductions of crime.* New York: Basic Books.

Katz, Lawrence F., Jeffrey R. Kling and Jeffrey B. Liebman (1999) Moving to opportunity in Boston: Early impacts of a housing mobility program. Unpublished manuscript, Washington, DC: National Bureau of Economic Research.

Kemple, James J. and Jason C. Snipes (2000) *Career academies: Impacts on students' engagement and performance in high school.* New York: Manpower Demonstration Research Corp.

Lattimore, Pamela K., Ann Dryden Witte and Joanna R. Baker (1990) Experimental assessment of the effect of vocational training on youthful property offenders. *Evaluation Review*, 14, 115–33.

Leiber, Michael J. and Tina L. Mawhorr (1995) Evaluating the use of social skills training and employment with delinquent youth. *Journal of Criminal Justice*, 23, 127–41.

Lemert. Edwin (1951) *Social pathology.* New York: McGraw-Hill.

Ludwig, Jens, Greg J. Duncan and Paul Hirschfield (1999) Urban poverty and juvenile crime: Evidence from a randomized housing-mobility experiment. Unpublished manuscript, Washington, DC: Georgetown Public Policy Institute.

Ludwig, Jens, Greg J. Duncan and Joshua C. Pinkston (2000) Neighborhood effects on economic self-sufficiency: Evidence from a randomized housing-mobility experiment. Unpublished manuscript, Washington, DC: Georgetown Public Policy Institute.

Maguire, Kathleen E., Timothy J. Flanagan and Terence P. Thornberry (1988) Prison labor and recidivism. *Journal of Quantitative Criminology*, 4, 3–18.

Mallar, Charles and Craig V.D. Thornton (1978) Traditional aid for released prisoners: Evidence from the LIFE experiment. *Human Resources*, 13, 208–36.

Mallar, C., Kerachsy, S., Thornton, C. and Long, D. (1982) *Third follow-up report of the evaluation of the economic impact of the job corps.* Princeton, NJ: Mathematica Policy Research, Inc.

Martinson, Robert (1974) What works? Questions and answers about prison reform. *Public Interest*, 35, 22–54.

Massey, D.S. and Denton, N.A. (1993) *American Apartheid: Segregation and the making of the underclass.* Cambridge, MA: Harvard University Press.

Maynard, R. (1980) *The impact of supported work on young school dropouts.* New York: Manpower Demonstration Research Corporation.

Menon, Ramdas, Craig Blakely, Dottie Carmichael and Laurie Silver (1992) *An evaluation of Project RIO outcomes: An evaluative report.* College Station, TX: Public Policy Resources Laboratory.

Myers, Samuel (1982) Racial differences in postprison employment. *Social Science Quarterly*, 63, 655–69.

Nagin, Daniel and Joel Waldfogel (1994) The effect of conviction on income over the life course. Working paper, New Haven, CT: Yale University.

Nagin, Daniel and Joel Waldfogel (1995) The effects of criminality and conviction on the labor market status of young British offenders. *International Review of Law and Economics*, 15, 109–26.

Needels, Karen (1996) Go directly to jail and do not collect? A long-term study of recidivism, employment and earnings patterns among prison releasees. *Journal of Research on Crime and Delinquency*, 33, 471–96.

Needels, Karen, Mark Dynarski and Walter Corson (1998) *Helping young people in high-poverty communities: Lessons from Youth Fair Chance.* Princeton, N.J.: Mathematica Policy Research.

Office of the Auditor General, California (1988) *A review of the economic activity in the state's enterprise zones and employment and economic incentive areas.* Sacramento, CA: CAO.

Office of Inspector General (2000) Audit findings from the first 18 months of the three Kulick Youth Opportunity Pilot Sites suggest additional innovation is needed for youth training undertaken with JTPA demonstration grant funds. Office of Audit, Report No. 06-00-0002-03-340.

Office of Juvenile Justice and Delinquency Prevention (1994) *Effective practices in juvenile correctional education: A study of the literature and research 1980–1992.* Washington, DC, US Department of Justice.

Papke, Leslie E. (1993) What do we know about enterprise zones? In James M. Poterba (ed.), *Tax policy and the economy.* Cambridge, MA: MIT Press.

Papke, Leslie E. (1994) Tax policy and urban development: Evidence from the Indiana Enterprise Zone Program. *Journal of Public Economics,* 54, 37–49.

Piliavin, Irving and Stanley Masters (1981) *The impact of employment programs on offenders, addicts, and problem youth: Implications from supported work.* Madison, WI: University of Wisconsin, Institute for Research and Poverty Discussion.

Reuter, Peter, Robert J. MacCoun and Patrick J. Murphy (1990) *Money from crime: The economics of drug selling in Washington, DC.* Santa Monica, CA: RAND.

Rosenbaum, James E. (1992) Black pioneers: Do their moves to the suburbs increase economic opportunity for mothers and children? *Housing Policy Debate,* 2, 1179–213.

Rosenbaum, J.E. (1996) *Institutional networks and informal strategies for improving work-entry for disadvantaged youth: New directions for research and policy.* Evanston, IL: Northwestern University.

Rovner-Pieczenik, Roberta (1973) *A review of manpower R&D projects in the correctional field (1963–1973).* Manpower Research Monograph, no. 28. Washington, DC: US Department of Labor.

Rubin, M. (1990) Urban enterprise zones: do they work? Evidence from New Jersey. *Public Budgeting and Finance,* 10, 3–17.

Sampson, R.J. and Laub, J.H. (1990) Crime and deviance over the life course: The salience of adult social bonds. *American Sociological Review,* 55, 609–27.

Sampson, R.J. and Laub, J.H. (1993) *Crime in the making: Pathways and turning points through life.* Cambridge, MA: Harvard University Press.

Saylor, William G. and Gerald G. Gaes (1996) *PREP: Training inmates through industrial work participation, and vocational and apprenticeship instruction.* Washington, DC: US Federal Bureau of Prisons.

Schochet, Peter Z., John Burghardt and Steven Glazerman (2000) *National Job Corps study: The short-term impacts of job corps on participants' employment and related outcomes.* Princeton, NJ: Mathematica Policy Research.

Schwartz, Richard D. and Jerome H. Skolnick (1964) Two studies of legal stigma. In Howard S. Becker (ed.), *The other side: Perspectives of deviance.* New York: Free Press, 103–17.

Spencer, F. (1980) The effects of an experimental vocational intervention model upon hard-core unemployed ex-offenders. *Journal of Offender Counseling, Services and Rehabilitation,* 4, 343–56.

Stewart, James K. (1986) The urban strangler. *Policy Review,* Summer: 6–10.

Uggen, Christopher (1994) Innovators, retreatists, and the conformist alternative: A job quality model of work and crime. Unpublished paper. Madison, WI: University of Wisconsin-Madison.

Urban Institute (1995) *Federal funds, local choices: An evaluation of the community develop- ment block grant program.* Washington, DC: Urban Institute, Center for Public Finance and Housing.

US Department of Labor (1995) *What's working (and what's not).* Washington, DC: Office of the Chief Economist, US Department of Labor.

Van Stelle, Kit, Julie R. Lidbury and D. Paul Moberg (1995) *Final evaluation report: Spe- cialized Training and Employment Project (STEP).* Madison, WI: University of Wisconsin Medical School, Center for Health Policy and Program Evaluation.

Vera Institute of Justice (1972) *Pre-trial intervention: The Manhattan court employment project.* New York: Vera Institute of Justice.

Wilder, Margaret G. and Barry M. Rubin (1996) Rhetoric vs. reality: A review of studies on state enterprise zone programs. *Journal of the American Planning Associ- ation,* Fall, 472–91.

Wilson, David B., Catherine A. Gallagher and Doris L. MacKenzie (2000) A meta- analysis of corrections-based education, vocation, and work programs for adult offenders. *Journal of Research in Crime and Delinquency,* 37, 346–68.

Wilson, William Julius (1987) *The truly disadvantaged: The inner city, the underclass and public policy.* Chicago, IL: University of Chicago Press.

Wilson, William Julius (1996) *When work disappears: The world of the new urban poor.* New York: Alfred A. Knopf.

Wolf, Wendy, Sally Leiderman and Richard Voith (1987) *The California Conservation Corps: An analysis of short-term impacts on participants.* Philadelphia, PA: Public/Private Ventures.

Wolf, Wendy, John M. Kelley, Jerene Good and Richard Silkman (1982) *The impact of pre-employment services on the employment and earnings of disadvantaged youth.* Philadel- phia, PA: Public/Private Ventures.

Wolfgang, Marvin, Robert Figlio and Thorstin Sellin (1972) *Delinquency in a birth cohort.* Chicago, IL: University of Chicago Press.

# 7    Preventing crime at places

*John E. Eck*[1]

## The importance of places for prevention

> Individual behavior is a product of an interaction between the person and the setting. Most criminological theory pays attention only to the first, asking why certain people might be more criminally inclined or less so. This neglects the second, the important features of each setting that help to translate criminal inclinations into action.
>
> (Felson and Clarke, 1998, p. 1)

Some locations are crime hot spots. Offenders and targets repeatedly meet there at the same time and with little supervision. These places are the sites for a very large proportion of crime. If we can prevent crime at these high crime places, we then may have a substantial impact on crime. Because place strategies are applied close to situations in which crime is likely to occur, potential victims are more likely to use them, and offenders are more likely to be influenced by them. In this chapter, we will see that there are a large number of place-focused prevention tactics with evidence of effectiveness.

Place-focused strategies work in ways similar to those of hot spot police patrols (see Chapter 8, this volume). Police hot spot patrolling and place strategies are employed when and where they are most likely to be needed. In fact, police hot spot patrolling is a place-focused strategy. The principle differences between place strategies considered here and hot spot patrols are that they are far more varied than hot spot police patrols, they can be applied by a greater variety of people and organizations, and they usually require little use of enforcement.

A place is a small area reserved for a narrow range of functions, often controlled by a single owner, and separated from the surrounding area. By "small" we mean that a location is smaller than a neighborhood. Often, a person standing anywhere within a place can see or hear activities in any other part of the place. Technology can extend these senses. Because they are usually small and have a single owner, it is easier to control activities within places. Places include stores, homes, apartment buildings, street corners, subway stations and airports. There are mobile places as well, for example buses, subways, ships and planes.

The concentration of crime at places is predicted by routine activity theory (Cohen and Felson, 1979; Felson, 1994) and offender search theory (Brantingham and Brantingham, 1981). Some of the original evidence for clustering of crime at places was found in Boston (Pierce, Spaar and Briggs, 1986) and Minneapolis (Sherman, Gartin and Buerger, 1989). Additional evidence for crime concentration at places has been found for specific types of crime. Over 20 years ago, it was found that most convenience stores had no or few robberies, but a few had many robberies (Crow and Bull, 1975). A growing body of research has revealed that in high burglary neighborhoods most residences have no burglaries, but a few residences suffer repeated burglaries (Farrell, 1995; Forrester, Chatterton and Pease, 1988; Forrester *et al.*, 1990; Polvi *et al.*, 1990). Among drinking establishments, a few bars have most tavern-related violence (Sherman, Schmidt and Velke, 1992). Ten percent of the fast food restaurants in San Antonio, Texas, account for one-third of the property crimes at such restaurants (Spelman, 1995b). In Kansas City and Indianapolis, gun crimes were found to be highly concentrated at a few places (Sherman and Rogan, 1995b). Drug dealing is highly concentrated in a few locations, even in areas with a high volume of drug dealing (Eck, 1994; Sherman and Rogan, 1995a; Weisburd, Green and Ross, 1994). This clustering is most apparent when compared to repeat offending and repeat victimizations. Combining the results from several studies, Spelman estimated that 10 percent of the victims in the United States are involved in about 40 percent of the victimizations, 10 percent of the offenders are involved in over 50 percent of the crimes, and 10 percent of the places are sites for about 60 percent of the crimes (Spelman and Eck, 1989). Further, the concentration of crimes at a few places is relatively stable over time (Spelman, 1995a, 1995b). These findings suggest that something about a few places facilitates crime and something about most places prevents crime. The most important something is criminal opportunity – something worth taking or someone worth attacking, and no one who will stop it.

### Blocking criminal opportunities

The oldest forms of crime prevention were undertaken with the knowledge that making changes to places might prevent criminal events. These changes involve making crime more difficult, more risky, less rewarding or less excusable. This approach is known as opportunity blocking (Clarke, 1992, 1995; Clarke and Homel, 1997). Opportunity blocking does not have to be done at places. It can also be built into targets, for example, designing anti-theft devices into automobiles (Clarke, 1995) or printing holograms and photos on credit cards to curtail forgery and fraud. Designing methods for blocking crime opportunities is the domain of situational crime prevention (Clarke, 1992, 1995).

Place-focused prevention has a much longer history than efforts to prevent people from becoming offenders. More importantly, opportunity blocking at places is used much more widely and in more settings than any other form of crime prevention. The vast majority of efforts to block crime opportunities at places are carried out and paid for by businesses, individuals and local governments. Nevertheless, our knowledge of which place-based prevention strategies work is severely limited because places themselves have only recently become a subject of study (Eck and Weisburd, 1995).

Opportunity blocking at places may have a greater direct effect on offenders than other crime prevention strategies. This is because place-focused tactics might influence offenders when they are deciding to commit a specific crime. Most offender-based strategies try to sway offenders' minds weeks, months or years before they confront a tempting criminal opportunity. If offenders pay closer attention to the situation immediately before them than to the uncertain long-term risks of their behavior, then it is quite possible that prevention at places may have a greater impact on offending than increases in penalties or less tangible increases in risks (e.g. decreases in police response time, increased police presence or greater numbers of arrests and convictions). Because hot spots of crime are themselves clustered, if crime at these few places can be substantially reduced, communities can be made safer.

Although opportunity blocking takes a different approach than programs designed to change the life-course of potential and existing offenders, these two approaches can work together. Keeping cookies out of sight of toddlers is not only different from instructing them not to take the cookies, and sanctioning them when they yield to temptation, it reinforces instructions by eliminating the temptation. For people with low self-control and low ability to see long-term consequences of behavior (Gottfredson and Hirschi, 1990), addressing the immediate circumstances surrounding crime opportunities may amplify the effectiveness of other strategies designed to address the prevalence of such offenders.

There are other possible advantages to place-based prevention. Most place-based prevention does not rely on the imposition of criminal sanctions. This reduces the economic costs associated with catching and punishing offenders. Further, this reduces the social costs from the disproportionate application of criminal sanctions to some groups relative to others (but see Norris and Armstrong, 1999). Another advantage of place-based prevention is that it can distribute the costs of prevention more equitably. The risk of crime at places is often under partial control of people who own these places. To the extent that owners' decisions give rise to situations that create crime, owners should be the ones who bear the burden of prevention costs. Most other prevention strategies shift the cost burden of prevention to the public through the police or other government agencies or government-funded programs.

The evaluations selected for review were required to meet three criteria. First, they had to involve opportunity blocking at places. An exception is made for public areas because area opportunity blocking is not covered elsewhere in this book, and increasingly opportunity blocking is used to address crime hot spots within larger areas. Second, they had to examine intentional changes in places and show that the changes preceded changes in crime. Third, each evaluation had to report outcome data, typically a measure of crime. Studies of implementation and management that did not measure an impact on crime were not examined.

This chapter does not review police efforts at places that relied solely on patrolling, investigations or other enforcement. These are reviewed in Chapter 8 of this volume. This chapter does review evaluations of interventions involving police agencies when other agencies or institutions could also have implemented the intervention. Nuisance abatement, for example, has

*Table 7.1* Summary of evaluations

| | | % of interventions |
|---|---|---|
| **Reports examined** | 89 | – |
| **Interventions examined** | 109 | 100 |
| **Country of setting** | | |
| Great Britain | 54 | 50 |
| United States | 41 | 38 |
| Australia | 7 | 6 |
| Continental Europe | 4 | 4 |
| Canada | 3 | 3 |
| **Crimes addressed** | | |
| Violent | 38 | 35 |
| Serious property and violent | 61 | 56 |
| Drug dealing | 7 | 6 |
| Minor crimes and disorders | 20 | 18 |
| **Methods scores** | | |
| 1 – correlation/cross section | 4 | 4 |
| 2 – before/after (no control group) | 39 | 36 |
| 3 – before/after with control and time series | 57 | 52 |
| 4 – large sample quasi-experiments | 6 | 6 |
| 5 – randomized experiments | 3 | 3 |
| **Crime change** | | |
| Down | 98 | 90 |
| No change | 9 | 8 |
| Up | 3 | 3 |

been implemented by police agencies, but prosecutors' offices, city attorneys and citizen groups have also used it. In short, who implemented the tactic was of less importance than the fact that the tactic was applied at places.

Table 7.1 summarizes the evaluations examined. When a report described several separate quasi-experiments, they were treated as distinct interventions. Almost half of the evaluations were conducted in the United Kingdom. Over a third of the studies were from the United States, but only seven studies were funded by agencies of the US Justice Department, whose function is to conduct research into crime prevention. The programs addressed a wide variety of offenses, ranging from murder to vandalizing parking meters.

Evaluations were graded using the scientific methods score (see Chapter 2, this volume). The modal score was 3, but a substantial number of evaluations only scored 2. Though few studies scored 1, only seven percent had scores of 4 or 5. The vast majority of these evaluations reported some crime reduction attributable to the intervention being examined.

## General findings

How much can we conclude about specific types of intervention, at specific places, against specific crimes? The answer is that if we rely solely on the empirical evidence, as we do in this chapter, we usually cannot be very confident about what works where. A limitation of a strictly empirical approach, particularly one that assumes that the randomized experiment is the penultimate research design, is that it overlooks or discounts other scientifically valid bodies of evidence and theory. To help address this weakness, a brief summary of the theory and non-experimental research is included in each of the sections that follow. For this reason, the results reported in this chapter should be treated as conservative.

Four categories and nine subcategories of places were examined: residential places; money spending places (retail stores, banks and money handling businesses, and bars and drinking establishments); transportation places (public transportation facilities, parking lots, and airports); and other public places (open urban spaces and public coin machines). The nine types of places examined were selected because these were the places for which evaluations existed. Clearly, our knowledge about place-focused tactics is limited to relatively few place types. Within each category, we examine a variety of crime prevention tactics.

## Apartments and residences

This section examines six types of interventions at residential properties, many in public housing in Great Britain and the United States. Public housing complexes have become notorious for high crime rates in the United States. Public housing complexes often have higher rates of violent crimes and drug arrests than nearby neighborhoods or surrounding cities, but there is a great deal of variation among housing projects within each of the cities (Dunworth and Saiger, 1994). In Britain, public (council) housing estates can also be a problem. First, we review efforts to reduce crime by restricting movement through apartment complexes. Next, we look at improving security by improving locks and barriers on windows and doors. Third, we examine property marking. Improving watching of residences is the subject of the fourth subsection. In the fifth subsection, we look at the effectiveness of multiple tactic interventions to prevent burglaries at dwellings with a history of burglary. Finally, we will turn to methods to compel place managers to reduce drug dealing on their rental property. Table 7.2 summarizes the evaluations of crime prevention in residential settings.

### *Restricting pedestrian access and movement*

Oscar Newman's works (1972, 1980) stimulated interest in the link between the built environment and crime in residential areas. Newman compared two public housing complexes and asserted that the differences in design were the principal reasons for the differences in crime. The limited number of places observed and the failure to take into account other differences (most notably the age distribution of tenants) suggests that his conclusions may have been overstated (Mawby, 1977; Mayhew, 1979; Merry, 1981; Taylor, Gottfredson and Brower, 1980). Other studies of the influence of design have compared more sites (Coleman, 1985; Poyner, 1983; Poyner and Webb, 1991). All pointed to the association of design features and crime, particularly features that allow unfettered movement through residential complexes. Two of these evaluations examined changes to residential sites that broke up large residential complexes into smaller components.

*Table 7.2* Residences

| Study | Methods score | Tactic | Setting | Results |
|---|---|---|---|---|
| Allatt, 1984 | 3 | target hardening | British public housing | 52% reduction relative to controls in burglary |
| Anderson *et al.*, 1995a, b; Chenery *et al.*, 1997 | 3 | graded response depending on number of prior burglaries or thefts from vehicles | British public housing (Huddersfield) | 30% reduction in burglary relative to controls and 20% reduction in theft from vehicles relative to controls |
| Chatterton and Frenz, 1994 | 2 | CCTV including dummy cameras | elderly housing complexes, Manchester, Great Britain | 79% decline in burglary and attempted burglary |
| Gabor, 1981 | 3 | property marking | residential dwellings, Canada | 75% increase in burglary |
| Laycock, 1985, 1991 | 3 | property marking that was highly publicized | public housing, Great Britain | 62% reduction in burglary |
| Tilley and Webb, 1994 | 3 | improving security of doors and windows | Birmingham public housing, Great Britain | 59% reduction in burglary |
|  | 3 | improved door locks and removal of prepayment meters | Bradford public housing, Great Britain | 91% reduction in burglary |
| Forrester *et al.*, 1988, 1990; Pease, 1991; Tilley, 1993a | 3 | removal of pay gas meters; cocoon neighborhood watch; security survey and hardware installation | public housing, Great Britain | 40% reduction in burglary in 1 year; continued drop over next 3 years |
| Bennett and Durie, 1999 | 2 | cocoon neighborhood watch; security advice, hardware installation, and other actions as needed | residential neighborhood in Great Britain | very small reduction in target area but substantial reduction in surrounding areas |
| Meredith and Paquette, 1992 | 2 | crime watch (and target hardening) | apartment building | 82% drop in burglary, little drop in other crimes |
| Popkin *et al.*, 1995a, b | 1 | guards, design changes, enforcement, identification cards, and other changes | two high-rise public housing buildings, Chicago | 40% to 64% drop in drug dealing; 74% to 88% drop in shootings and fighting |
| Newman, 1996 | 2 | restricting pedestrian movement and other design changes | Bronx public housing | 54% drop in reported crime; 62% drop in burglary, robbery and assault |

| Study | Methods score | Tactic | Setting | Results |
|---|---|---|---|---|
| Poyner, 1994 | 3 | closing walkways connecting buildings and installation of entry phone | London public housing | reported reduction in purse snatches |
| Eck and Wartell, 1998 | 5 | threat of nuisance abatement | private residential rental property, San Diego, CA | 59% drop relative to controls in reported crime for most stringent intervention, 51% drop for less stringent intervention; not significant |
| Green, 1993, 1995, 1996 | 4 | nuisance abatement | private residential properties with drug dealing in Oakland, CA | 15% decline in arrests, 38% decline in field contacts, 14% decline in calls |
| Hope, 1994 | 3 | closing or selling of property | 3 addresses used for drug dealing in St. Louis, MO | 54%, 67% and 95% reduction in calls for service |
| Lurigio *et al.*, 1993 | 2 | nuisance abatement | residential properties in Cook County, IL | no difference between treated and untreated blocks relative to drug dealing |
| Mazerolle *et al.*, 1998 | 5 | nuisance abatement and other civil remedies | private properties in Oakland, CA | substantial reduction in drug selling behavior and physical disorder, as well as improvements in orderly behavior. Precise estimates difficult to estimate with data provided |

The Clawson Point public housing complex was changed by reducing the number of foot routes through the project, creating separate areas within the complex, improving lighting and enhancing the surface appearance of buildings. Newman (1980, 1996) claimed a 54 percent decline in the crime rate and a 62 percent decline in the rate of serious crime (burglary, robbery and assault) though he did not employ a control group.

In another evaluation, Poyner (1994) looked at the effects of removing elevated walkways connecting buildings in a British public housing complex. The walkways were thought to facilitate robberies of residents. Poyner's before-after (without a control) design found a reduction in purse snatching, but found no reduction in burglary. An entry phone was installed at one entrance and this, too, may have contributed to the decline in purse snatches. Although auto thefts around the buildings declined, it was unclear if this was due to the removal of the walkways or the presence of the workers removing the walkways.

Restricting the movements of pedestrians was part of a 1991 effort to reduce crime in several of Chicago's worst public housing buildings (Popkin et al., 1995a). The approach included door-to-door police inspections of all units within the buildings. Ground-floor entrances were enclosed in new lobbies, and guard stations were installed along with metal detectors. Residents were issued identification cards to present when entering the buildings. In addition to housing authority and private security, the Chicago Public Housing Authority organized tenant patrols. Finally, a set of drug prevention services was provided to tenants.

Samples of residents in two complexes were interviewed to find out if conditions had improved. The surveys found that 74 percent and 88 percent of respondents (depending on the complex) said shootings and fighting in their building had declined, and 40 percent and 64 percent of the residents said drug dealing in their building had declined (Popkin et al., 1995a). Retrospective assessments by residents substituted for pre-treatment measures of crime and drug problems. The lack of control groups and true pre-treatment measures of crime, along with the implementation of multiple simultaneous interventions, means that we do not know if restricted foot access made an improvement.

Collectively, these evaluations suggest possible beneficial effects of reducing pedestrian movement through large public housing complexes. The weak designs used to evaluate these programs temper our confidence in these types of interventions.

## *Target hardening*

Providing locks and improved security to access points is a commonly used burglary prevention tactic. Two evaluations of improved locks and doors in English public housing complexes provide some insight into the effectiveness of this tactic. Both studies used a pre-post design compared to a control area. In one complex, burglary declined 59 percent. In the other, burglary declined over 90 percent relative to the control area (Tilley and Webb, 1994).

The displacement of burglars to less protected locations is commonly raised as a threat to the effectiveness of place-focused interventions. Patricia Allatt (1984) was one of the first evaluators to explicitly test for displacement effects. In addition to identifying the target residences that received improved ground-floor entrance security, she examined the residences in the area immediately adjacent to the target area. She also used a control area that was far enough from the treatment area that it would not be contaminated by displacement. Allatt found that burglaries in the target area increased by 9 percent 1 year after implementation, but burglaries in the control area had increased 77 percent. This suggests the program may have reduced burglaries. Burglaries increased 86 percent in the displacement area but, relative to the control area, this was only a 9 percent increase over what could have been expected without the program (Allatt, 1984). Thus, she concluded that displacement may have occurred, but it was small relative to the overall program effect on the target area.

Target hardening appears to reduce burglaries without major displacement effects. However, with only two studies, more rigorous evaluations would make valuable contributions to our knowledge of what works in place-focused crime prevention.

*Property marking*

A third approach to controlling burglaries is to make burglary targets unattractive to offenders. Laycock (1985, 1991) reports on the evaluation of a property marking campaign in three isolated Welsh communities. A 62 percent decline in burglaries was reported for residents who participated in the program (as measured by the presence of property marking decals on their windows or doors), compared to a control group of non-participating residents (Laycock, 1985, 1991). There is strong circumstantial evidence that the publicity of the property marking scheme contributed a great deal to these results (Laycock, 1991). Though results might be due to property marking and publicity, the results could also occur if less vulnerable residents participated in the program and more vulnerable residents did not participate. Contradictory results were found in a Canadian neighborhood where property marking was applied. Seasonally adjusted burglaries per dwelling unit went up 75 percent in the 18 months after the program began compared to the 24 months before the program (Gabor, 1981). In the absence of a relevant control group, it is impossible to determine if burglaries were already going up, but would have risen faster without the program. Nevertheless, with two contradictory studies, we cannot be confident that property marking is an effective method for reducing burglaries to residences.

*Closed-circuit television (CCTV)*

CCTV was used in fifteen housing complexes for elderly residents in Manchester, England (Chatterton and Frenz, 1994). The evaluators reported a decline in burglary and burglary attempts of 79 percent across all complexes. Again, natural trends in burglary were not reported. This single weak study is insufficient as a basis for crime prevention policy. As we will see, however, these findings are consistent with evaluations of CCTV in other settings.

*Multi-tactic interventions and repeat victimizations*

Crime prevention in residential settings often involves the use of a variety of measures. Evaluations usually cannot estimate the relative effectiveness of the component parts, but they can show whether crime prevention possibly occurred. A Canadian apartment building program included apartment watch (like neighborhood watch but for apartment dwellers), target hardening, property marking, lighting improvements and an assortment of other interventions. Reported burglaries dropped 82 percent from the year before to the year after the prevention measures were put in place. No control group was used, so this drop may have been due to a trend toward fewer burglaries in the surrounding area (Meredith and Paquette, 1992).

Evidence, particularly from Great Britain, suggests that a few victims are repeatedly victimized (Farrell, 1995). There have been evaluations of three repeat residential burglary programs. In each program, a comprehensive analysis phase was used to determine the level of repeat victimization and the form of the response.

The Kirkholt public housing complex has received considerable attention because it showed that focusing on residences with previous burglaries prevents more burglaries (Forrester, Chatterton and Pease, 1988; Forrester *et al.*, 1990; Pease, 1991; Tilley, 1993a). A number of interventions were used at each targeted residence, including target hardening and organizing residents in surrounding homes to watch the burgled house. However, two tactics deserve special mention. The residences in Kirkholt had coin-operated gas meters with which residents used to buy gas for heating and cooking. Meters were periodically emptied, but for weeks the meters could contain a great deal of cash. These meters were a target in many of the Kirkholt burglaries and removing them was a tactic in the project. Another part of the Kirkholt project was organizing the residents surrounding burgled dwellings to watch the victimized home – "cocoon neighborhood watch" – instead of organizing the entire neighborhood. Burglaries declined by 40 percent in the first year after the start of the program, and continued to decline over the next 3 years (controlling for seasonality and surrounding area trends) (Forrester, Chatterton and Pease, 1988; Forrester *et al.*, 1990).

The Huddersfield program used a graded response to repeat victimization (Anderson, Chenery and Pease, 1995a, b). Residents reporting their first burglary received a "bronze" response: crime prevention advice, cocoon neighborhood watch and improvement in dwelling security. If a resident was burgled a second time within a year, the police stepped up patrolling of the location and put warning stickers on the dwelling. This was the "silver" response. If a third burglary was reported within a year, then the "gold" response was put into place: the use of video surveillance of the location and even more intense police patrols. A similar graded response was used for vehicle crime. Evaluators reported a reduction in repeat burglary victimization (compared to the surrounding area). Though burglary and thefts from motor vehicles remained relatively stable for the rest of the police area, there was a 30 percent decline in burglary from before implementation to March 1996 in the target area. Thefts from motor vehicles declined by 20 percent, but these effects took longer to become visible. There was no evidence of displacement and some evidence suggesting a diffusion of benefits (Chenery, Holt and Pease, 1997). Significance tests were only reported for the displacement analysis.

The Cambridge repeat burglary program was not as effective as the Kirkholt or Huddersfield programs. In two wards (Castle and Arbury) of this English town, when a burglary was reported, the police applied a variety of interventions, depending on the situation. The actions included cocoon neighborhood watch, loan alarms, security advice to victims, security upgrades, and advice to nearby residents. In addition, several neighborhood-level interventions were layered on top of these, including having postal delivery people watch for suspicious activity, enhancing neighborhood watch if one already existed, holding crime prevention seminars, increasing directed police patrols, and providing local residents with crime information. Some efforts were made to engage high-risk youth in activities designed to keep them out of trouble. Residential burglaries for 12 months prior to the program were compared to 12 months during the program for both areas, and the rest of Cambridge. Burglary declined in Castle by three percent and declined in Arbury by six percent. The rest of the city had a decline in burglary of 19 percent. When smaller areas within these wards were examined as treatment areas and comparable controls were introduced, the treatment areas still fared worse than the controls. The authors suggest that even though the police delivered the program as intended, the take-up rate by citizens was low (Bennett and Durie, 1999).

Crime prevention programs based on repeat victimizations are interesting. But the mixed results and the possibility that British housing and construction patterns may differ substantially from those found elsewhere make it imperative that further research and testing be applied before such programs are widely adopted (Stedman and Weisel, 1999).

### Reducing drug dealing and crime in private rental places

Despite the fact that the management of private rental housing has only recently been examined as a crime risk factor, we have strong evidence that improving management of rental properties can reduce drug related crime. A study of retail drug dealing locations in San Diego found that smaller apartment buildings were more likely to be selected by drug dealers than the larger buildings, primarily because owners of the smaller buildings had fewer resources to control the behaviors of place users (Eck, 1994, 1995, 1999). Spelman (1993) found that houses that had been abandoned by their owners were magnets for crime. A number of evaluations have probed the effectiveness of compelling place managers to control the behaviors of people who use their properties.

The civil law has been the primary tool used to make owners of private rental property evict drug dealers or make physical changes to their property. In three case studies from St. Louis, where police officers helped change the ownership of drug houses, calls for service from the blocks with the houses declined 54 percent to 94 percent relative to nearby blocks, suggesting a decline in drug selling (Hope, 1994).

Most efforts to influence landlords threaten civil action, but do not typically result in the transfer of property ownership or the seizure of property. Nuisance abatement programs threaten court action to seize property if owners take no action to curtail drug dealing.

An evaluation of an abatement program run by the State's Attorney Office in Cook County, Illinois, compared the perceptions of people living near 30 abated properties to the perceptions of residents of nearby untreated blocks. Evaluators found no difference in perceptions (Lurigio *et al.*, 1993). If the abatement program did reduce drug dealing or related crime, nearby residents did not notice it. This design did not have a true pre-treatment measure of crime, but only perceptions of change, measured after the program was underway.

More rigorous evaluations have found substantial support for the threat of civil abatement. In Oakland, California, evaluators examined 275 abated drug-dealing sites. Green found a 15 percent decline in arrests, a 38 percent decline in field contacts, and a 14 percent decrease in citizen calls, relative to citywide changes in these measures (1993, 1995, 1996).

An experiment with threatened abatement in San Diego, California, also

found evidence of effectiveness. Following police drug enforcement, properties were randomly assigned to three groups. Owners of properties in one
group received a letter from the police ("letter" group). Owners of properties in another group met with a narcotics detective and a city codes inspector ("meeting" group). Owners of properties in a third (control) group
received no follow-up contact from the police or the city. No landlord was
taken to court and no property was seized. But in the 30 months following
treatment, the properties in the meeting group had significantly fewer
reported crimes than the control places. The letter group also had a decline
in crimes, but this was not statistically significant (Eck and Wartell, 1998).

In a randomized experiment of 100 drug locations from Oakland, California, half were treated with a civil remedy program, including nuisance abatement, health and safety code inspections and pressure on property owners to
clean up the site. The control sites received typical police interventions:
arrests, surveillance and field interrogations. Relative to the 50 control locations, the 50 civil remedy locations showed a significant reduction in drug
dealing activity and improved physical conditions (Mazerolle, Roehl and
Kadleck, 1998).

Four of the five studies report some reduction in crime or calls for service
at treated drug properties or the block around the properties. Since the four
studies with positive effects are more rigorous than the single study showing
no effect, we can be confident that holding owners responsible for drug
dealing on their property may reduce drug related crime.

### Conclusions about residences

As a group, these evaluations – from the weakest to the strongest – suggest
that improvements in crime reduction can be achieved; nevertheless, it is
hard to be precise about what works at which types of residential sites and
against which crimes. One set of tactics, however, does have several rigorous
evaluations: nuisance abatement. We have sufficient evidence to claim that it
works. Holding private landlords accountable for drug dealing on their property by threatening civil action reduces drug dealing, related crime and disorder. A weaker body of evidence suggests that reducing the ability of people
to move freely about large public housing complexes can reduce crime.

Addressing repeat victimization deserves more attention in the United
States, but there is insufficient evidence to recommend that this tactic be
applied wholesale at this time. Still, repeat victimization prevention research
in housing and other settings should be undertaken. Finally, by standards
used in this book, the evidence for target hardening is so weak it is of
unknown effectiveness. Of particular concern is the lack of significance tests
in target hardening evaluations that could show observed crime reductions
were not due to chance.

### Retail stores

Places that sell goods to the public are frequent crime sites. The theft of
goods represents a large proportion of these crimes. Both patrons and
employees commit these thefts. In addition to thefts, robberies of store clerks

and burglaries after store hours are troublesome. In this section we examine all of these crime types. First, we look at convenience store robberies. Much has been written on this topic, but most of it describes correlational studies with very small samples, comparing stores with and without robberies. Second, we consider burglaries and robberies in other retail settings. Third, we examine credit card fraud. The fourth subsection looks at shoplifting prevention. Finally, we look at thefts by employees. Table 7.3 summarizes the evaluations of crime prevention in retail stores.

### Convenience store robberies

Although convenience stores have received considerable attention in the crime prevention literature, robberies of these retail establishments peaked around 1980–1, declined through 1983 and remained stable for the next 10 years at around 16,000 per year. Over the same period, the number of such stores has increased and gas station robberies have trended upward (Bellamy, 1996). Comparisons of convenience stores with and without robberies have been carried out for over two decades. These studies attempted to find store features that were associated with few or no robberies. The studies generally suffer from three major scientific problems. They usually examine a variety of store features using a small sample of stores. Since these features are often correlated with each other, it is difficult to determine which features are related to robberies. Next, since the store features and robberies are measured at about the same time, it is unclear if the features preceded the robberies (and could possibly have influenced the chances of the crime) or whether the robberies cause store managers to change the store's features. Finally, most convenience stores have no robberies, but a few have many robberies. Prevention measures may work in the few stores with repeated robberies but have no influence on the other stores (Crow and Bull, 1975). It is not surprising, therefore, that these studies arrived at contradictory findings.

One of the most debated questions is whether two clerks reduce the risk of robberies. Hunter and Jeffery (1992) cite a number of studies showing that stores with fewer robberies are associated with two clerks being on duty. LaVigne (1991) provides evidence that the number of clerks is unrelated to robberies. Another study, conducted by Robert Figlio, compared 230 convenience stores with two or more clerks on duty at night, to 346 stores with only one clerk on duty, and examined a subsample of one-clerk stores before and after they shifted to two clerks. The evaluation found no impact on robberies by the switch to two clerks, compared to similar stores that did not increase the number of clerks from one to two. However, for stores with robberies prior to the switch, two clerks did reduce the chances of a robbery (National Association of Convenience Stores, 1991).

The Gainesville (Florida) Police Department evaluated a city ordinance requiring two clerks to be on duty. The police department found that convenience store robberies declined immediately after the ordinance took place (Clifton, 1987). Although the short-term reduction may have been due to the arrest of several active convenience store robbers just before the ordinance took place (Wilson, 1990), robberies of these stores in Gainesville

*Table 7.3* Retail stores

| Study | Methods score | Tactic | Setting | Results |
|---|---|---|---|---|
| Crow and Bull, 1975 | 5 | variety | convenience stores | stores with 2 prior robberies had 30% fewer robberies relative to controls |
| Crow and Erickson, 1984 | 4 | surveillance cameras | convenience stores | no significant change in robberies |
| National Association of Convenience Stores, 1991 | 4 | two clerks | convenience stores | 15% reduction in robberies over 2-year period in high robbery stores |
|  | 2 | CCTV | convenience stores | 15% reduction in robberies over 2-year period |
|  | 2 | video monitors for patrons and staff | convenience stores | 53% reduction in robberies |
| Poyner and Webb, 1992 | 2 | widening aisles in open market | public market in Birmingham, Great Britain | 44% reduction in thefts from purses |
| Burrows and Speed, 1996 | 3 | electronic monitoring of phone lines | electronic retail stores | noticeable decline in wire cut burglaries but amount difficult to determine from chart provided |
| Jacques, 1994 | 2 | metal shutters | electronic retail stores | 53% drop in losses due to ram-raiding burglaries |
| Taylor *et al.*, 1980; Tilley and Hopkins, 1998 | 3 | variety of offender risk enhancing tactic tailored to each business | businesses in Belgrave area of Leicester | 25% reduction compared to surrounding area or city |
|  | 3 |  | businesses in West End area of Leicester | no change compared to surrounding area and a 23% reduction compared to the city |
| Masuda, 1993 | 2 | profiling offenders, training, liaison with law enforcement | retail store chain | 82% decline in credit card fraud losses |
| Masuda, 1996 | 3 | computer-aided positive identification at point of sales | retail stores | 90% reduction in credit card fraud losses |
| Webb, 1996 | 2 | lowering limits for use of credit cards, improved information exchange, and other tactics | point of sales in retail establish-ment in Great Britain | 25% to 41% decrease in credit card fraud losses nationwide |
| Challinger, 1996 | 3 | requiring proof of purchase for refund, and related procedures to prevent refund fraud | retail stores | decline in losses and reports |

| Study | Methods score | Tactic | Setting | Results |
|---|---|---|---|---|
| Bamfield, 1994 | 3 | EAS to prevent shoplifting | retail stores | 32% reduction in shrinkage |
| DiLonardo, 1996 | 3 | EAS to prevent shoplifting | retail stores | 47% decline in shrinkage over 5 years |
| | 3 | EAS to prevent shoplifting | retail stores | 80% decrease when installed. When reinstalled over 80% decline repeated |
| | 3 | EAS to prevent shoplifting | retail stores | 52% decrease in shrinkage |
| DiLonardo and Clarke, 1996 | 3 | ink tags to prevent shoplifting | retail stores | 14% reduction in inventory shrinkage |
| | 3 | ink tags replace EAS to prevent shoplifting | retail stores | 47% decline in inventory shrinkage |
| Farrington *et al.*, 1993 | 3 | uniformed guards | retail stores in Great Britain | no measurable impact on shoplifting |
| | 3 | store redesign | retail stores in Great Britain | 58% drop in shoplifting at one store and 80% decline in another in target items stolen |
| | 3 | tagging | retail stores in Great Britain | 76% reduction in shoplifting at one store and 93% reduction in another in target items stolen |
| Beck and Willis, 1999 | 3 | 3 levels of CCTV: high, medium and low, differing in part on the basis of consistent monitoring | 15 stores of British fashion retail chain: 3-high, 6-medium, and 6-low | changes in items missing based on repeated inventory counts: high-level down 35% and medium-level up 23%, relative to low-level stores serving as a control group |
| McNees *et al.*, 1980 | 3 | awards for compliance to prevent shoplifting by elementary school children | single convenience store | 58% decline in shoplifting of targeted items. Estimated increase in profits of 42% during program |
| Masuda, 1992 | 2 | increased frequency of inventory counts to prevent employee theft | retail stores | elimination of shrinkage for targeted products; 85% decline in shrinkage of non-targeted products |

continued to decline for 7 years after the ordinance (Bellamy, 1996). Other changes in stores' operations, or the controversy surrounding Florida-wide efforts to increase the number of clerks, may have sensitized the convenience store industry and the police to this problem. Thus, many other changes could have created the long-term reduction, so we cannot be certain the decline was due to the two-clerk rule.

One of the first randomized experiments in crime prevention was undertaken over 20 years ago to determine if convenience stores robberies could be reduced. Crow and Bull (1975) matched 120 stores according to previous robberies and other characteristics. These stores were randomly assigned to either a control group or a prevention group. The type of prevention was selected based on site visits, so it was not possible to determine what tactics had what effects. The treated stores with two or more prior robberies had 30 percent fewer robberies after treatment than the untreated stores with two or more previous robberies.

In a later convenience store study, cameras and silent alarms did not appear to prevent robberies when 55 convenience stores in Columbus, Ohio, and New Orleans, Louisiana, receiving these devices were compared to 53 stores in Dayton, Ohio, and Baton Rouge, Louisiana, not receiving them (Crow and Erickson, 1984). In the treated stores signs announcing the equipment were posted. These changes were accompanied by publicity in the treatment areas. No significant changes in robberies were found.

The National Association of Convenience Stores (1991) reported on two other interventions evaluated by Robert Figlio. The use of interactive CCTV (allowing communication between the clerk and the personnel in a remote location) reduced robberies in 189 stores by a statistically significant 31 percent in the first year following the installations. By the second year, the reduction had shrunk to 15 percent, which was not statistically significant. No control stores were used in the analysis. One chain of 81 stores installed color video monitors that were visible to patrons and staff. Robbery rates were reported to have declined by 53 percent a year after installation. Again, no control stores were used.

These studies by the convenience store industry suggest that there are two types of stores: those with few or no robberies where crime prevention efforts are unlikely to influence future robberies, and a fewer number of stores with several robberies where prevention efforts may be productive.

### Burglary and purse snatching in other retail places

Burrows and Speed (1996) report on an effort to curb "wire-cut" burglaries of electronics stores. Since alarm systems in these stores are connected to a remote monitoring station, burglars cut the telephone lines before entering. Electronically monitoring the integrity of the phone lines appears to have reduced losses from these types of burglaries. Unfortunately, the authors only show a graph of the data without reporting the figures for burglaries or losses. Trends in wire-cut burglaries were compared to other types of burglaries and indicated that the decline was unlikely to be due to a general decline in burglaries, independent of the preventive tactic studied.

"Ram-raiding" involves crashing a vehicle (often stolen) into the front of a retail establishment and then removing valuable products. The costs of the damage to the store are considerable and often exceed the costs of the stolen merchandise (Jacques, 1994). This is a problem in Great Britain, but its extent in the United States is unknown. Jacques (1994) reports that the installation of metal shutters in six large retail establishments cut burglary costs 53 percent (from an average of £20,892 sterling to £9,613 sterling). In one store, burglars shifted to roof entry, thus providing evidence of limited displacement in burglary tactics. No control stores were examined.

Addressing repeat burglaries of commercial establishments may be an effective method of preventing commercial break-ins. Police in Leicester, England, contacted businesses with multiple burglaries and applied a variety of tactics to increase the risk to offenders. The tactics applied (silent alarms, covert CCTV, devices to collect forensic evidence and proximity alarms) depended on the nature of the situation, so it is impossible to establish which tactics were effective and under what circumstances. Taylor (1999) compared the number of burglaries per month for the 12 months prior and the 11 months after the intervention in the West End area. In the Belgrave area of Leicester, he compared the average monthly burglary figures for the preceding 4 years to the number of burglaries in the month following the intervention. In both areas, he reports substantial declines in commercial burglary. Though Taylor does not provide actual counts in his article, the graph he shows for the West End gives only equivocal evidence for the program's success. In another report on this project, Tilley and Hopkins (1998) use before-after victimization survey data for the two sites to demonstrate that there was a reduction. They also showed how the changes in commercial burglary for the two sites compared to Leicester as a whole (minus the target areas). In the two target areas combined, commercial burglary went down 41 percent (40 percent in the West End and 43 percent in Belgrave), but declined only 17 percent for the city. Finally, the area surrounding the West End had as much of a reduction in commercial burglary as the target area, though the area surrounding Belgrave had only an 18 percent reduction. It is difficult to know if the results for the West End are due to weak program effects, or to a diffusion of crime prevention benefits. Overall, however, this study provides mixed evidence for the application of repeat victimization targeting in commercial settings.

Thefts from shoppers can also be a problem. In shopping markets in one British city, women's purses were being taken from their shopping bags. The aisles of the markets were widened to reduce the bumping of patrons that facilitated the thefts. Poyner and Webb (1992) report a 44 percent decline in thefts from the 3 years prior to the changes to the 2 years after the changes. Changes in nearby markets make them unsuitable as control places, so we have no evidence about background trends.

### Credit card fraud

Three evaluations examined attempts to prevent credit card fraud at the point of sales. All three involved staff training and increased attention to customers. Two studies describe providing clerks with more information about potential offenders, either through liaison with police authorities (Masuda,

1993) or by providing computer-aided identification of shoppers wishing to use credit cards (Masuda, 1996). A before-after comparison of losses showed an 82 to 90 percent reduction. No control stores were examined.

Lowering the limit for credit card purchases may also reduce thefts. A British experiment coupling lowered limits with improved information exchange about possible offenders may have reduced fraud losses by 25 to 41 percent nationwide, depending on the length of the pre-treatment period used (Webb, 1996).

Although these studies used weak evaluation designs, they consistently showed that tightening restrictions on credit card use and use of information about people with a history of credit card fraud reduced this crime. Such findings indicate that many losses sustained by retailers are due to their choices about how to conduct business. Challinger's (1996) evaluation of refund fraud reduction reinforces this point. Refund fraud involves the return of stolen goods for a refund. The store ends up paying for the merchandise twice, the first time at the wholesale price and the second time at the retail price. Challinger (1996) reports that requiring proof of purchase may reduce the losses from this form of theft. For confidentiality reasons, he does not report the amount of losses for stores involved in his evaluation.

### Shoplifting

Shoplifting is an extremely common crime. Two anti-shoplifting interventions, electronic article surveillance and ink tags, have received multiple evaluations. A third method, use of CCTV, has received less attention. Electronic article surveillance (EAS) involves placing tags on merchandise that only clerks can remove at time of payment. If a clerk does not remove the tag, an alarm sounds when the shopper takes it out of the store. EAS technology improves employee surveillance of goods. Ink tags deface the merchandise, if it is taken from the store without paying. This destroys the value of the goods to thieves.

Five evaluations of EAS were reviewed and each reported reductions in shoplifting. All compared crime or shrinkage (unaccounted-for declines in inventory) before the installation of EAS to the same measures after, and all used a control store to measure background trends. The reduction in shrinkage varied from 32 percent (Bamfield, 1994) to 80 percent (DiLonardo, 1996). Farrington and his colleagues (1993) report even greater reductions in shoplifting in the two stores they examined (76 and 93 percent). Furthermore, EAS was found to be more effective than security guards (no improvement) but not store redesign (50 to 80 percent improvement) (Farrington *et al.*, 1993). Unfortunately, with one exception (Farrington *et al.*, 1993), significance tests were not reported, so we cannot determine the probability that the reported reductions were due to chance.

Ink tags may also reduce shoplifting, but we have fewer studies and they used weaker evaluation designs. DiLonardo and Clarke (1996) report on two quasi-experiments involving ink tags. Both used repeated inventory counts to measure inventory reduction before and after the installation of the tags. In the first study, fourteen new stores were compared to the chain-wide average. Shrinkage was reduced 14 percent in the new stores. In the second study, ink tags were installed in four stores, but no control stores were used. Shrinkage declined by 47 percent. As we will see below, repeated inventory counts have been linked to reduced employee theft, so we cannot be certain that the changes reported in these two ink tag studies are due to the ink tags or the method of measuring shrinkage.

A British fashion retail chain studied three levels of CCTV to curb shoplifting (Beck and Willis, 1999). In three stores, high-level CCTV was used – multiple cameras, full-time watching by staff, monitors at all public entrances and recording capability. Six stores received a medium-level system – similar number of cameras watched by the store manager as time permitted, monitors at public entrances and recording capability. Six other stores received a low-level system – up to twelve of the cameras were dummies, monitors at all public entrances, but no capability to record. We can treat the low-level stores as controls and the other two types of stores as forms of treatment. Theft reduction was measured by inventory counts before installation and at 3- and 6-month intervals following installation. After 3 months, the number of items lost per week had declined by 40 percent, 17 percent, and 20 percent for the high-, medium- and low-level stores, respectively. After 6 months, the number of items lost per week had declined by 26 percent for the high-level store, but increased by 32 percent and 9 percent for the medium- and low-level stores, respectively (Beck and Willis, 1999). These results suggest that CCTV may curb retail theft, but staff monitoring may be critical to its success.

The final shoplifting evaluation is a case study of a single store where the problem was minor thefts by elementary school children. Combinations of individual and collective rewards were offered to the children for refraining from stealing small items. The period before the program, program period and a period after the program ended were compared. Shoplifting of targeted items declined by 58 percent and profits increased 42 percent during the program period compared to the periods before and after the program.

Shoplifting appears to be controllable by the use of EAS technology, and possibly ink tags, and CCTV as well. If more evaluations had used significance tests, we might have classified EAS as "works." In the absence of this information, EAS must be placed in the "do not know" category. Store redesign in the prevention of shoplifting is, however, the only promising intervention, and further evaluation and replication appear warranted.

### Employee theft

Masuda (1992) examined the effectiveness of increasing the frequency with which articles at great risk of theft are counted. Since the increased inventory counts were unknown to shoppers but were known to store employees, it is reasonable to assume that the 100 percent reduction in shrinkage he found was due to the deterrence of employees. The 85 percent reduction in non-target item shrinkage may be attributable to diffusion of benefits. The absence of an uncontaminated control makes it hard to determine if this change was an unexpected program effect or evidence of declining shrinkage independent of the intervention.

## Banks and money-handling places

The robbery of banks and other places that provide money-handling services is a serious problem in many countries. In this section we will examine evaluations of security measures in US and Swiss banks, British post offices and Australian betting shops. Table 7.4 summarizes evaluations of crime prevention at banks and money-handling places.

Guards may prevent bank robberies. A study of 236 banks in the Philadelphia area found one less robbery per year at banks with guards compared to banks without them, controlling for the surrounding area, police response time, proximity to major streets and other prevention measures used. Screens protecting tellers and cameras were not associated with fewer robberies (Hannan, 1982). Since these tactics are often found together, the evidence about the effectiveness of any specific measure is weak. Though this is a correlational study, the evaluator made special efforts to control for temporal order. Information about security measures came from surveys and only crimes reported after the survey were used in the analysis. Because we can be sure that the interventions were installed prior to the crimes, this evaluation was given a scientific methods score of 2.

Two other studies provide better evidence that screens protect clerks from robberies. A study of over 300 Swiss banks found that banks with screens had a 52 percent lower robbery rate than banks without them (Grandjean, 1990). Ekblom (1987, 1988) examined the installation of bulletproof barriers to protect post office clerks. He estimated that the barriers reduced robberies from 55 percent to 65 percent, net of changes in control group robberies. Both studies found evidence for displacement, but even accounting for displacement, robberies declined substantially.

Clarke and McGrath (1990) examined the effects of time-lock cash boxes and safes on Australian betting shop robberies. Relative to control places, robberies may have been reduced by 52 to 139 percent. The results may be

*Table 7.4* Banks and money-handling places

| Study | Methods score | Tactic | Setting | Results |
| --- | --- | --- | --- | --- |
| Clarke and McGrath, 1990 | 3 | time-lock cash boxes and safes | Betting shops in Australia | robberies declined |
| Clarke et al., 1991 | 1 | security screens, and other measures | Banks in Victoria, Australia | 52% to 139% drop in bank robberies |
| Ekblom, 1987, 1988 | 3 | counter screen barriers in front of clerks | Post offices in London | 55% to 65% reduction in robberies |
| Grandjean, 1990 | 2 | bulletproof screens for tellers | Banks in Switzerland | 52% reduction in robberies |
| Hannan, 1982 | 2 | security guards, screens and cameras | Banks in Philadelphia, PA area | reduction of one robbery per year for most robbery-prone banks due to guards |

highly unstable given that there were three interventions throughout a 10-year period.

An examination of a drop in the number of bank robberies in Victoria, Australia, asserts that this was due to the installation of screens protecting clerks, guards, cameras and other security devices (Clarke, Field and McGrath, 1991). After increasing from 1979 through 1987, the number of bank robberies dropped to levels similar to those found in earlier years. Similar patterns of growth and rapid decline were found in bank robberies in an adjacent state and in robberies of other businesses. It is unclear whether the protective measures were installed only in Victoria's banks and when they were installed.

We do not know what works to prevent crimes at banks and other money-handling places because the scientific methods scores for the interventions are either below 3 or significance tests were not reported. These evaluations suggest the possibility that guards, bulletproof screens and secure cash containers might reduce crimes, but more rigorous evaluations are needed to draw firm conclusions.

## Bars, taverns and drinking establishments

The research literature consistently points to a relationship between the presence of bars and crime in the surrounding area (Block and Block, 1995; Roncek and Meier, 1991; Roncek and Bell, 1981; Roncek and Pravatiner, 1989). Despite this reputation, most bars may be relatively crime free while a few may be hot spots of crime (Engstad, 1975; Homel and Clark, 1994; Sherman, Schmidt and Velke, 1992). The behavior of bartenders and bouncers may have contributed to violence in these places (Homel and Clark, 1994) and changes in bar management practices (from server training and changes in legal liability of bartenders) may reduce assaults (Putnam, Rockett and Campbell, 1993), drunk driving (Saltz, 1987), and traffic accidents (Wagenaar and Holder, 1991).

Two Australian programs to reduce violence created agreements among pub managers to improve the training of bouncers, reduce crowds of youths, and improve relationships with police, along with other tactics (Homel *et al.*, 1997). In one evaluation, observers reported a 53 percent reduction in assaults per 100 hours of observation in the first year of the program. The prevention effects decayed over time. Three years after implementation, the reduction had declined to 15 percent. No control pubs were observed (Homel *et al.*, 1997). The other evaluation examined serious assaults at downtown pubs for the year before and 4 years after the management accord, and compared these changes to the same period for six other cities in the same state. Serious assaults declined 40.5 percent in the target city, but increased 14.3 percent in the control cities (Felson *et al.*, 1997).

The consistent results from Australia and the United States, summarized in Table 7.5, suggest that changing the management of drinking places is a promising method for prevention of drinking-related offenses.

*Table 7.5* Bars and taverns

| Study | Methods score | Tactic | Setting | Results |
|---|---|---|---|---|
| Felson *et al.*, 1997 | 3 | code of practice for pubs | bars and drinking establishments in Geelong, Australia | 60% decline in serious assaults, net controls |
| Homel *et al.*, 1997 | 2 | training for bouncers, code of practice | bars and drinking establishments in Australian town | 53% decline in assaults/100 hours of observation first year after implemented, but only 15% decline compared to 3 years after |
| Putnam *et al.*, 1993 | 3 | training of alcohol servers and police enforcement | alcohol sales outlets in one Rhode Island community | decline in alcohol-related assaults and vehicle crash injuries, relative to control communities |
| Saltz, 1987 | 3 | changing serving policies and training | Navy enlisted club in California | over 50% reduction in driving when drunk |

## Public transportation

Two types of public transportation have been subjects of evaluations: buses and subways. Evaluations investigated prevention measures directed at four types of crime: crimes against riders, attacks on staff, fare evasion, and vandalism. The types of interventions have been quite varied, ranging from complete system design to volunteer citizen patrols. Table 7.6 summarizes evaluations of crime prevention in public transportation.

### Incivilities and crimes against the public

The Washington, DC, Metro System has been singled out in crime prevention literature as having been designed to prevent crime (LaVigne, 1997). "Designing in" crime prevention may be effective, but it is difficult to determine if a design is effective. LaVigne (1997) compared the Washington, DC, Metro to three other urban rail transit systems and found that it had less crime than the other systems. She also compared subway station crime to crime in the areas above ground. If the system had no influence on crime then the above-ground crime and station crime should be correlated. If the system design prevented crime, then there should be no relationship between station and above-ground crime. LaVigne (1997) found that, except for assaults, ground level and station crime were not correlated. Although this is not a strong research design, it is the best evidence available that system design influences crime patterns.

To improve passenger confidence in the safety of the New York subway system, an intensive clean-up program was undertaken to remove graffiti from all train cars and stations. Rapid clean-up would deprive vandals of the benefit of seeing their graffiti (Sloan-Howitt and Kelling, 1990). By treating

*Table 7.6* Public transportation facilities

| Study | Methods score | Tactic | Setting | Results |
|---|---|---|---|---|
| LaVigne, 1997 | 1 | subway system design | Washington, DC, metro subway | system design may prevent crime |
| Carr and Spring, 1993 | 2 | improved cleaning and vandalism repair; patrolling | public transportation system, Victoria, Australia | 45% improvement in train availability; 42% reduction in crimes against persons |
| Felson *et al.*, 1996 | 3 | 63 different tactics implemented about the same time | Port Authority Bus Terminal, New York City | reduction in robberies and assaults but not compared to surrounding area; reductions in incivilities |
| Kenney, 1986 | 3 | Guardian Angels | subways | no detectable impact on crime |
| Poyner, 1988 | 1 | CCTV | buses | steady decline in vandalism |
| Webb and Laycock, 1992 | 3 | CCTV (and other tactics) | stations on London Underground | 11% to 28% reduction in robberies |
| Chaiken *et al.*, 1974 | 2 | exact fare requirement | buses in New York City | 90% decline in robberies of bus drivers |
| Poyner and Warne, 1986 | 2 | protective screens for drivers | buses in Cleveland, Great Britain | 90% reduction in assaults on drivers |
| Clarke, 1993 | 3 | automatic gates to prevent fare evasion | London Underground | 10% increase in ticket sales |
| Clarke *et al.*, 1994 | 2 | modification of ticket vending machines | London Underground | elimination of problem of slug use within 4 months of modification |
| DesChamps *et al.*, 1992 | 2 | increase in rush hour attendants to check tickets, training in fraud detection | ferry terminal | 20% reduction in fare evasion rate |
| van Andel, 1989 | 2 | recruiting over 1,100 young unemployed people as public transit monitors | buses, metro trains and trams in 3 large cities in the Netherlands | 18% to 72% decrease in fare dodging depending on city and mode of transport, 60% decline in attack or harassment victimizations |
| Weidner, 1997 | 3 | installation of new fare gates | stations on New York City subway | fare evasions declined in target station |

the physical appearance of the system, it was hoped that this would make the public feel safe and bring more people into the system. More riders would increase the number of people watching out for each other, and this could drive down crime. This chain of events is expected, according to the "Broken Windows" hypothesis (Wilson and Kelling, 1982). Sloan-Howitt and Kelling

(1990) show that graffiti was virtually eliminated and, despite increased police attention to graffiti, arrests for this offense also declined.

A similar effort was used by the Victoria (Australia) transit system that includes trains, trams and buses. The Victoria program involved rapid repair and cleaning of vandalized equipment, along with stepped up police enforcement. Carr and Spring (1993) show that train availability increased 45 percent and reported crimes against persons dropped 42 percent.

Another comprehensive program to clean up a problematic transit facility has been described by Felson and colleagues (1996). The title of their paper, "Redesigning Hell," suggests the state of disrepair into which the New York Port Authority Bus Terminal had fallen. Sixty-three interventions were made at the terminal, at about the same time. These included closing off spaces, improving shopping, cleaning, increased enforcement, and other measures to remove situations that facilitated offending or increased the number of patrons and their ability to watch each other. Although robberies and assaults declined in the station, they also declined in the surrounding area. Outside crime control efforts or diffusion of crime control benefits to the surrounding area may account for these parallel trends. Annual surveys of patrons that began with the clean-up in 1991 show declines in incivilities and disorder.

Vandalism against buses is another problem in transit systems. Poyner (1988) describes how the installation of CCTV on a portion of a bus fleet was followed by reduced vandalism throughout the fleet. There was also a public information campaign directed at the group of people most likely to be responsible for the damage, school children. Poyner attributes the diffusion of benefits from the targeted buses to the entire set of buses to offenders' confusion over which buses had the CCTV. Unfortunately, this evaluation only describes trends in vandalism after CCTV was installed.

All three of these transit system clean-up campaigns were accompanied by increases in police enforcement (as well as other changes), and it is impossible to disentangle the enforcement effects from clean-up effects with the evidence presented in these evaluations.

Kenney (1986) evaluated the effectiveness of Guardian Angel patrols at stations by comparing crime changes to control stations without these patrols. He found that these patrols had no discernible impact on crime in the patrolled stations. This may be because the base rates of crime in the stations were too low to detect an effect (Kenney, 1986).

Webb and Laycock (1992) also found no evidence that the Guardian Angels reduced crime in the London Underground. They did find that the installation of CCTV in London Underground stations reduced robberies 11 to 28 percent, relative to control stations without CCTV. Twenty-two months of data before CCTV installation and 26 months after installation at selected stations were compared.

On the whole, we have limited information about how to prevent incivilities and crime against transit. In part, this is due to the difficulty in assessing system-wide designs and comprehensive changes. Selecting a control system and disentangling the effects of multiple interventions is very difficult. Rapid clean-up and repair to deprive offenders of the pleasure of seeing their graffiti appears to be effective, but the evidence to date is weak.

## Attacks on bus drivers

The two evaluations of attacks on bus drivers provide evidence that these crimes can be reduced. The rise in robberies of bus drivers in the late 1960s and early 1970s prompted New York City officials, along with transportation officials in other US cities, to remove accessible cash that was the target of the robbers. They required passengers to give exact fares and prohibited bus drivers from giving change. Fares were put in secure boxes. Chaiken, Lawless and Stevenson (1974) reported a 90 percent reduction in bus driver robberies following these changes. The Stanford Research Institute (1970) reported similar results in its review of the effect of exact fare systems in eighteen other cities (Clarke, 1992, p. 216).

If the target of the attack cannot be removed, then perhaps it can be protected. A bus company in northern England used two approaches to protect its drivers from assaults by riders (Poyner and Warne, 1986). They first simplified the fare system so it would be less aggravating. They also installed protective screens around bus drivers. Assaults on drivers declined 90 percent following the installation of screens. Assaults on all employees fell during this period, but not as much as it fell for drivers (37 percent).

## Fare evasion

Transit systems suffer from people who try to enter without paying the correct fare. Fare evasion can simply mean jumping gates or moving through entries without paying, or it can involve the use of slugs in gates or ticket machines. Three evaluations examined the redesign of gates or ticket machines to curtail fare evasion. All three reported evidence of declines in this form of theft. Clarke (1993) reports an increase in ticket sales of 10 percent, relative to control stations where new automatic gates were not installed. Clarke, Cody and Natarajan (1994) show that one form of slug use was totally eliminated by modifying ticket machines so they would not accept a type of coin for which a slug could be substituted. This was a system-wide change so no control stations were available. Finally, Weidner (1997) gives results of the effect on fare evaders of the installation of new gates in the New York City subway. While arrests declined in the target station, they increased in adjacent control stations. Whether this was due to changes in police enforcement, displacement or background trends cannot be determined from the evidence provided.

Two evaluations without control groups examined personnel changes to reduce fare evasion. Increases in the number of ticket takers at a Canadian ferry terminal may have reduced fare evasion by 20 percent, although there were no control sites to assess background trends (DesChamps, Brantingham and Brantingham, 1992). A Dutch effort to reduce fare evasion in three cities decreased fare dodging by 18 to 78 percent. Authorities recruited over 1,100 unemployed young people to monitor ticket use on the buses, trains and trams in the three cities. This report (van Andel, 1989) also claims that there was a 60 percent drop in assaults on harassment of patrons.

## Conclusions about transportation system prevention

Although there are several evaluations of crime prevention in transportation settings, we know relatively little about the effectiveness of these interventions. This is in part due to the variety of crime types that are applicable to transportation systems. It is also due to the number of settings (buses, trains and stations) within the system, as well as the variety of victims (patrons, staff and facilities). Thus, a large number of studies are needed to learn what works to prevent crime in transit systems. However, there are methodological complications that make learning about crime prevention effectiveness quite difficult. Many of the systems are large, and there are few, if any, plausible control settings available to measure background trends. Places within systems are linked, so internal changes to part of a system can influence crime in other parts of the system. If untreated parts of the system are used as controls, diffusion of benefits or displacement effects can confound the findings. We cannot, therefore, identify with reasonable certainty a specific tactic against a specific crime that works across similar settings in other cities.

## Parking lots and garages

Evaluations of crime prevention in parking lots and garages examined changes in people who watch cars. These people were often security guards, although one evaluation looked at placing a taxi business near the entrance to a parking garage to increase informal guardianship (Poyner, 1991). Another set of interventions used closed-circuit television to centralize watching. Table 7.7 summarizes evaluations of crime prevention in parking lots and garages.

### Guards and security attendants

Five evaluations are available reporting on the effectiveness of adding security guards to parking lots. Four showed reductions in car-related crimes (Barclay *et al.*, 1996; Laycock and Austin, 1992; Poyner, 1991, 1994) and one found no improvement (Hesseling, 1995a). Although these studies suggest auto thefts and thefts from automobiles might be prevented by increasing people who watch lots, there are two important caveats. Poyner (1991) notes that parking lot strategies that control access may curb thefts *of* vehicles, but may be ineffective at controlling thefts *from* vehicles. The failure of Hesseling (1995a) to find a reduction in thefts from vehicles may be due to the way the guards were deployed. Thus, what the guards do may be as important as their deployment. Second, none of these studies examined personal violence against people using parking facilities. In conclusion, because of the mixed results of the evaluations, we do not know if guards or security attendants prevent crimes in parking lots.

### Closed-circuit television

There are seven evaluations from Great Britain of the effects of CCTV on vehicle crimes (thefts of vehicles, thefts from vehicles and damage to vehicles), but no evaluations of its effect on other crimes in parking facilities (Poyner, 1991; Tilley, 1993b). The weakest of the evaluations found no effect (Coven-

*Table 7.7* Parking facilities

| Study | Methods score | Tactic | Setting | Results |
|---|---|---|---|---|
| Barclay *et al.*, 1996 | 3 | security guards on bikes | commuter parking lot | 53% reduction in car thefts/month |
| Hesseling, 1995a | 3 | guards | parking area in Rotterdam | 2% increase in thefts from automobiles relative to control |
| Laycock and Austin, 1992 | 3 | security attendant | parking area | 52% to 60% in auto theft reduction |
| Poyner, 1994 | 2 | guard | parking area | reduction in auto thefts. Amount cannot be estimated |
| Poyner, 1991 | 3 | restricting foot access, improved lighting, increased guardianship | parking garage | 29% increase in thefts from vehicles, 35% reduction in thefts of vehicles |
| | 3 | CCTV | parking lots | 71% and 94% reduction in thefts from cars |
| Tilley, 1993b | 3 | CCTV | parking lots, Hartlepool, Great Britain | 75% reduction in theft of autos, 60% reduction in theft from autos |
| | 2 | CCTV | one parking lot, Hull, Great Britain | 45% reduction in damage to autos, 89% reduction in theft of autos, and 76% reduction in theft from autos |
| | 2 | CCTV | one parking lot, Lewisham, Great Britain | 75% reduction in auto crimes |
| | 3 | CCTV | one parking lot, Bradford, Great Britain | 73% to 78% reduction in theft from autos, 49% to 75% reduction in thefts of autos |
| | 2 | CCTV | one parking lot, Wolverhampton, Great Britain | 18% reduction in thefts of autos, 46% reduction in thefts from autos |
| | 2 | CCTV | 5 parking lots, Coventry, Great Britain | no discernible pattern in auto crimes |

try lots, in Tilley, 1993b). The other six evaluations found varying levels of decline in vehicle crimes. In the CCTV parking lots evaluated, thefts *from* vehicles declined 46 to 94 percent, and thefts *of* vehicles dropped 18 to 89 percent, depending on the evaluation. We do not know if these results can be replicated in the United States. There is no empirical basis for recommending CCTV to prevent parking lot violence. The results suggest that CCTV should be tested in high vehicle crime parking lots within the United States. Because of the lack of significance tests we must classify CCTV in parking facilities as having "unknown" prevention effectiveness.

## Conclusions about parking facilities

Evaluations in parking lots and garages outside the United States consistently support the hypotheses that guards and CCTV reduce vehicle-related property crime. Though several CCTV studies had scientific methods scores of 3, they lacked significance tests. Therefore, CCTV's effectiveness in parking lots is "unknown." These studies do not report on violent crimes in parking lots, including robberies and car jacking. The highly crime-specific nature of intervention effectiveness suggests that we must be careful in drawing inferences about the effectiveness of interventions to places and settings.

# Airports

Aircraft hijacking by armed passengers has been a problem since World War I. Wilkinson (1977) has documented the worldwide trends in this problem. From 1948 (when records were first kept) through 1957 there were 15 attempts worldwide, and none involved aircraft originating in the United States. In the next decade, there were 48 hijackings worldwide (23 of them North American originating flights). In 1968, the number of worldwide aircraft hijackings increased rapidly from 38 that year to 82 the next. In response, policymakers implemented a number of strategies, including treaties to ensure the return of hijackers and aircraft. By 1973, hijacking attempts had dropped to 22 worldwide and 2 in the United States (Wilkinson, 1977).

Since several interventions were put into place over a short time period during the early 1970s, it is difficult to determine which tactics made the greatest contribution to the decline. Sky marshals (armed plainclothes security guards) were assigned to selected flights beginning in 1970. To thwart parachuting from aircraft, modifications were made to the rear doors of Boeing 727s and DC 9s to prevent them from being opened in flight (Landes, 1978). In early 1973, the US and Cuba signed a treaty that required each country to extradite or punish hijackers (Landes, 1978). Table 7.8 summarizes evaluations of schemes to prevent crime in airports.

Landes (1978) attempted to determine the effectiveness of sky marshals and passenger screening. He used a time series analysis of 64-quarter years and 143 incidents. He also controlled for hijacking of aircraft originating from foreign airports to remove worldwide trends in skyjacking and attempted to remove the effects of the Cuba treaty. He provides evidence for an 82 percent decline in US hijacking due to the combined effects of the Cuba treaty, sky marshals and passenger screening. He then estimated the contribution of the three policies: screening was the cause of a decline of 45 percent, sky marshals created a 28 percent decline, and the remainder (9 percent) was probably attributed to the Cuba treaty.

Two other studies, using annual data for different time periods and weaker evaluation designs, also found large declines in aircraft hijacking in the United States following passenger baggage screening (Easteal and Wilson, 1991; Wilkinson, 1977). These studies did not attempt to estimate the effects of different hijacking programs.

The variation in aircraft hijacking from year to year and the virtually simultaneous implementation of multiple prevention methods at airports

*Table 7.8* Airports

| Study | Methods score | Tactic | Setting | Results |
|---|---|---|---|---|
| Easteal and Wilson, 1991 | 2 | passenger screening with metal detectors | US airports and originating flights | 64% reduction in hijacking of passenger aircraft |
| Landes, 1978 | 3 | passenger screening with metal detectors | US airports and originating flights | 45% reduction in hijacking of passenger aircraft |
| | 3 | sky marshals | US airports and originating flights airports | 28% reduction in hijacking of passenger aircraft |
| Wilkinson, 1977 | 3 | passenger screening with metal detectors | | 41% reduction in hijacking of passenger aircraft in US, 3% drop world-wide |

around the world make it difficult to come to definitive conclusions regarding any particular intervention. Nevertheless, the weight of the evidence supports the effectiveness of passenger screening.[2]

These findings are important. They demonstrate the potential utility of opportunity blocking against highly determined offenders. They also illustrate some of the difficulties of evaluating place-focused prevention (multiple simultaneous interventions, detecting reductions in rare events, and the difficulty of finding control places). Further, they may have implications for other places.

Given these findings about the use of metal detectors to screen for weapons at airports, are they effective at other places? We do not know. Evaluations are scant and weak. A New York City study of the use of metal detectors found that weapon carrying in schools with metal detectors ($n = 19$) was lower than in schools without the devices ($n = 96$), but there were no differences in assaults within or outside these schools (Centers for Disease Control and Prevention, 1993). This evaluation has a scientific methods score of 4; although there was a decline in risk factors for violence, there was no significant decline in violence. In the residential places section, we noted an evaluation of a multi-tactic intervention in a particularly troubled set of public housing buildings (Popkin *et al.*, 1995a). Metal detectors were a part of this program, but it is impossible to determine what, if any, influence they had because so many other things were implemented at the same time. We cannot, therefore, be confident about the transferability of this tactic to very different settings.

## Open public spaces

The places considered in this section are open spaces in cities, including street corners and segments. Four types of interventions will be examined. The first is the control of problem offenders. The second is improved lighting. The third is the use of closed-circuit television (CCTV). Fourth, we examine street closures and rerouting. Table 7.9 summarizes evaluations of crime prevention at open public spaces.

*Table 7.9* Open public places

| Study | Methods score | Tactic | Setting | Results |
|-------|---------------|--------|---------|---------|
| Bjor *et al.*, 1992 | 2 | ban on public drinking and high risk offenders and closing of a parking site | open spaces of downtown area, Sweden | 8% reduction in drunkenness arrests; 64% reduction in disorderly conduct arrests |
| Ramsay, 1990, 1991 | 2 | ban on public drinking | open spaces of a British downtown area | No change on assaults; 33% reduction in insults from strangers |
| Atkins *et al.*, 1991 | 2 | lighting | 39 sections of London | no systematic effect of lighting |
| Ditton and Nair, 1994 | 2 | lighting | Glasgow neighborhood | 32% to 68% reduction in victimizations; 14% reduction in reported crime |
| Painter, 1994 | 2 | lighting | London | 86% reduction in street robberies, auto crimes and threats |
| | 2 | lighting | London | 78% reduction in street robberies, auto crimes and threats |
| | 2 | lighting | London | 100% reduction in street robberies, auto crimes and threats (base rates too small to be meaningful) |
| Painter and Farrington, 1997, 1999a, 2000 | 4 | lighting | Dudley, Great Britain, housing estate | 26% reduction in property and violent crime in treatment area, net change in control area. Significance tests used |
| Painter and Farrington, 1999b | 4 | lighting | Stoke-on Trent, Great Britain, housing estate | Significant decline in property and violent crime in treatment area net of control area. Evidence of diffusion of benefits beyond target area |
| Brown, 1995 | 3 | CCTV | town center, Newcastle-upon-Tyne, Great Britain | decline in burglary (18%), criminal damage (9%), auto theft (7%), theft from auto (11%), other theft up (7%) |
| | 3 | CCTV | town center, Birmingham, Great Britain | charts suggest reductions in robbery, burglary and theft but do not allow calculation of reductions |
| | 3 | CCTV | town center, King's Lynn, Great Britain | charts suggest reductions in burglary, assaults, thefts from autos and |

| Study | Methods score | Tactic | Setting | Results |
|---|---|---|---|---|
| | | | | thefts of autos but do not allow calculation of reductions |
| Ditton and Short, 1999 | 3 | CCTV | Airdrie town center, Scotland | reported crime dropped 79% and property crimes dropped about 52% |
| Ditton and Short, 1999 | 3 | CCTV | Glasgow town center, Scotland | crime increased 109% and property crime increased 123%. Probably was not implemented to prevent crime |
| Armitage *et al.*, 1999 | 3 | CCTV | Burnley town center, Great Britain | Substantial declines in total reported crime, including violent crime, drug crimes, motor vehicle theft, criminal damage, burglary, fraud and handling stolen goods. Some displacement of criminal damage, but large diffusion of benefits for most other crimes |
| Mazerolle *et al.*, 1999 | 3 | CCTV | 3 separate sites in Cincinnati, OH | 50% reduction in calls for service in one site, 17% reduction in another, and no reduction in the third. Surrounding areas had increases in calls for service |
| Wagner, 1997 | 2 | street closures | St. Louis, MO | 3% crime rise, but reported crime rose over twice as fast in control neighborhood and surrounding area |
| Atlas and LeBlanc, 1994 | 3 | street closures | Florida town | 8% decline in burglary, drops in larceny and auto theft. No change in robbery or aggravated assault |
| Lasley, 1996, 1998 | 3 | street barricades | Los Angeles, CA | 65% reduction in homicides |
| Matthews, 1992 | 2 | street closures and rerouting | Finsbury Park, London | reduction in prostitution activity |
| Matthews, 1993 | 2 | street closures and rerouting | Streatham, London | reduction in prostitution activity |
| Newman, 1996 | 3 | street closures | Dayton, OH | 26% reduction in reported crime and 50% reduction in violent crime |

## Controlling problem offenders

Two efforts to control public drinking to reduce assaults and incivilities in downtown areas provide evidence that controlling problem offenders may be effective. Ramsay (1990, 1991) reports on the banning of public drinking in one English town. Comparing the year before and the year after the ban (with no control group), he found no changes in assaults, but surveys of people using the area suggest that there may have been a reduction in incivilities. A Swedish effort to reduce disorder at an annual festival reported a decline in drunkenness and disorderly conduct arrests following the prohibition of public drinking, banning high-risk offenders, and the closing of a popular camping site (Bjor, Knutsson and Kuhlhorn, 1992). This study compared arrests at the previous year's festival to arrests at the festival with the pared arrests at the previous year's festival to arrests at the festival with the restrictions, without control area comparisons.

### Lighting

Lighting campaigns seek to enhance the ability of people to provide protection for each other. In 1979, a study reviewed 60 lighting evaluations and found that they were too weak to draw useful conclusions (Tien et al., 1979). Over 20 years later, we are beginning to know more about the effectiveness of lighting, primarily because of work in Great Britain, particularly by Kate Painter.

In the 1980s, a borough in London upgraded all of its street lighting. Atkins, Husain and Storey (1991) compared reported crimes the year before the relighting to the year following for 39 sections of the borough. No control areas were used, so background trends in crime cannot be assessed, but daytime crime was used as a control. There was a decline in crime during the night and day, leading the authors to conclude the lighting was ineffective. Surveys of residents of one area found no changes in perceptions of security. Pease (1999) has criticized these conclusions on two grounds. First, daytime hours are inappropriate controls because they are susceptible to treatment contamination (i.e. diffusion of benefits to daylight hours). Second, illuminating areas that are not crime hot spots says nothing about the effectiveness of lighting areas where crime is concentrated. Most of the areas relit in this London borough were low crime areas so the relighting would have had a minimal impact on crime.

A Scottish study of relighting in a Glasgow neighborhood and a small town near Glasgow found that there was a short-term reduction in victimizations that varied from 32 percent to 68 percent, depending on how victimization was measured (respondent victimizations, victimization of respondents' children, victimization of other family members, victimization of friends or car victimization). Reported crime dropped 14 percent. The evaluators compared a 3-month period prior to relighting to a 3-month period following (Ditton and Nair, 1994). No control group was used and the results for the two neighborhoods were combined.

Painter (1994) conducted three separate evaluations, with similar designs, in "crime prone" areas within London. She examined lighting improvements on two separate street segments and a footpath. Pedestrians were interviewed before and after the lighting improvement. All interviews were conducted after dark and were completed within 6 weeks of the relighting. No interviews were conducted in control areas. Substantial reductions in robberies, auto crimes and threats were reported in two sites (86 percent, 79 percent). These crimes were eliminated in the third site, but the number of crimes before relighting was small so this could have been the result of other factors.

The final two lighting studies we will examine are the most rigorous yet conducted and provide the greatest evidence that lighting may prevent crime in public areas. One housing estate in England had the lighting of its roadways (not paths) improved, while a nearby very similar housing estate received no upgrade in its lighting. Before-and-after victimization surveys of residents of the treatment and control neighborhoods showed a 41 percent decline in victimizations per 100 households in the estate with the improvements, compared to a 15 percent decline in victimizations per 100 households in the estate without the lighting upgrades. These results were statistically significant and no evidence of spatial, temporal or target displacements were found (Painter and Farrington, 1997). Similar results were found for the same lighting project when a youth self-report survey for antisocial acts was used to measure crime reduction (Painter and Farrington, 2000).

In an evaluation of lighting improvements in Stoke-on-Trent, England, Painter and Farrington found statistically significant crime reduction effects in the treated area (households with a crime victimization went down 25.8 percent) compared to the control area (households with a crime victimization went up 12.3 percent). Additionally, the area surrounding the treatment area had a 21.2 percent drop in victimized households (Painter and Farrington, 1999a, 1999b; Welsh and Farrington, 1999). This indicates a possible, and substantial, diffusion of prevention benefits beyond the target area (Clarke and Weisburd, 1994).

The recent lighting studies from Great Britain appear to remove the lingering doubts about lighting's efficacy. Lighting appears to work in public areas, especially residential communities. Generalizing beyond these types of settings is highly speculative, given the rudimentary nature of current lighting theory (Painter and Farrington, 1997). Lighting may be effective in some places, ineffective in others and counter-productive in still other circumstances. The problematic relationship between lighting and crime increases when one considers that offenders need light to detect potential targets in low-risk situations (Fleming and Burrows, 1986). As Pease (1999) correctly points out, we should address the specific conditions where lighting is effective, rather than assume it is always effective.

## Closed-circuit television

Closed-circuit television (CCTV) enhances the ability of a designated guardian to watch people in an area and to call for police intervention if potential trouble is detected. This is supposed to increase the risks of offending, but only if the CCTV surveillance is well known to the people who use the area. This project was unable to locate any published scientific evaluations of the use of CCTV in urban areas of the United States.

A number of CCTV evaluations have been conducted in Great Britain (Brown, 1995). As deployed, a set of video cameras are posted in city center areas and monitored at a central station. The cameras cover many, but not all, locations in the target area. Finding locations with clear unobstructed views, year round, can be difficult. CCTV cameras were installed around the town center of Newcastle-upon-Tyne in late 1992 and early 1993. The evaluation used a time series of 23 months prior to the installation of cameras, 4 months during and 14 months after, and compared CCTV-covered areas to uncovered areas in the same periods. It found that burglaries declined by 18 percent, auto thefts dropped 9 percent, thefts from autos went down 11 percent and other thefts declined 7 percent. No effect was found for robberies (Brown, 1995).

Brown (1995) used a similar design to assess the impact of CCTV in Birmingham. He compared reported crime 12 months before, 2 months during and 30 months after installation to control areas. Unfortunately, no figures were provided with the reported charts, but visual inspection of the time-series charts provided suggests reductions in robbery, burglary and thefts. Similar results were reported for another town center in Great Britain, King's Lynn. Four quarters of reported crime before installation were compared to seven quarters after. A control area was used. Again, the data was not given, but visual inspection of the charts suggests reductions in burglary, assaults, thefts from vehicles and thefts of vehicles. Significance tests were not reported in any of these case studies.

Ditton and Short (1999) examined CCTV in two Scottish cities: Airdrie and Glasgow. Twelve cameras were placed in the center of Airdrie. Controlling for crime trends in the surrounding area and seasonal fluctuations, reported crime declined 79 percent from the 12 months prior to the 12 months after implementation. Property crimes dropped 52 percent in the same period. There was no evidence of displacement. No significance tests were reported.

Thirty-two cameras were placed in the center of Glasgow. Controlling for seasonality and crime trends in the surrounding area, reported crime increased 109 percent and property crime increased 123 percent from the 24 months prior to the 12 months after implementation. Some of this may have been due to increased reporting from CCTV and natural variation in crime. But two other explanations are also plausible. First, CCTV may not have been fully implemented. Glasgow had two untrained CCTV operators (the same as Airdrie with a third the cameras) and the evaluators found that for some periods no one was monitoring the cameras. Second, Ditton and Short reported that at one troublesome crime hot spot, the police caused a reduction in formal and informal surveillance after implementation of CCTV. This could have sparked a surge in crime (Ditton and Short, 1999, fn. 14). Unlike the Airdrie program, the Glasgow program appears to have been started as an image building exercise and used by the police to increase investigative arrests, rather than prevent crime. Given this, the Glasgow results cannot be reliably used to evaluate CCTV as a prevention method.

In the English city of Burnley, cameras were deployed in three city center beats. Total crime for 1997 went down by 24 percent in the area, but increased in the control area by 3 percent, compared to 1994 (the year prior to installation). A zone around the treatment beats was used to measure displacement. None was found. Violent crime showed a 27 percent reduction in the treatment beats while it went up by 46 percent in the control area. The 9 percent reduction in the buffer suggests a diffusion of benefits effect. Drug crimes, motor vehicle thefts, burglaries and criminal damage all declined. Evidence for diffusion of benefits was found for drug crimes and motor vehicle theft. Some burglaries may have displaced, but that is unclear. There is clearer evidence for the displacing of criminal damage. The evaluators also report data that can be interpreted as evidence of strong diffusion of benefits with regard to crime type. One would not expect fraud and handling stolen goods to be affected by CCTV, yet they declined in the treatment area and the buffer area (53 percent and 12 percent respectively), while increasing by 586 percent in the control areas (Armitage, Smyth and Pease, 1999).

Only one study of the effectiveness of CCTV in open public places was found for the United States. In Cincinnati, evaluators studied the effectiveness of three different installations of CCTV on troublesome corners. At each location a single camera was mounted on a pole. It scanned the area and was monitored by the desk sergeant at the district station. So, unlike the British installations, these CCTV cameras were not deployed in clusters, but alone, and instead of being monitored in a communications center, they were monitored in police stations by people with many other tasks. Further, no signs were used in the area to demarcate the CCTV surveillance area (though there was much publicity about each installation). In a before-after comparison of 200-feet radii around the cameras, using the surrounding police districts as controls, one site had a 50 percent reduction in the weekly average calls for service (from 4 to 2 calls per week), another site had no change (3 per week), and a third site had a 17 percent decline in the weekly average calls for service (from 12 to 10 per week). The site with the largest reduction may have had a diffusion of benefits out as far as 500 feet, but the site with the 17 percent reduction may have displaced crimes to a radius of 500 feet. The surrounding police districts in each case experienced a modest increase in weekly calls for service over the same period (Mazerolle, Hurley and Chamlin, 1999). No significance tests were described.

The effectiveness of CCTV in open spaces appears promising but the lack of significance tests forces a rating of unknown, given the criteria used. This probably understates the evidence for its effectiveness.

### Street closures

Research suggests that areas with easy access have more crime than areas with street layouts that restrict access (Beavon, Brantingham and Brantingham, 1994; Greenberg and Rohe, 1984; Newman, 1980; Wagner, 1997; White, 1990). In this section, we will examine five evaluations that support the hypothesis that closing and rerouting automobile traffic can reduce crime.

Wagner (1997) evaluated the effectiveness of reducing access to a St. Louis neighborhood in 1984. He compared reported crime trends for the 5 years following the street modifications in the treated neighborhood to crime trends in a similar untreated adjacent neighborhood, the surrounding police district and the city. Wagner found that crime rose 3 percent from

1985 through 1989 in the treated neighborhood, but it rose over twice as fast in the control neighborhood (7.7 percent), the police district (6.6 percent), and the city (6.1 percent). The absence of pre-treatment measures of crime and the lack of significance tests make this a particularly weak evaluation.

In 1986, the citizens of Miami Shores, Florida (near Miami, in Dade County), voted to close off 67 streets (Atlas and LeBlanc, 1994). The closings took place between July 1988 and March 1991. The evaluation compared changes in reported crime within the town to the changes in the same crimes in the surrounding county and Miami. Mean 1986 and 1987 crimes (before installation) were compared to the mean number of reported crimes in 1991 and 1992 (Atlas and LeBlanc, 1994). There were no significant changes in reported robberies and aggravated assaults within Miami Shores compared to the two control jurisdictions. Relative to changes in Dade County, reported burglaries declined significantly – at least 8 percent. Larcenies and auto theft in Miami Shores also declined significantly, relative to changes in Miami and Dade County.

Street closures were also used in Dayton, Ohio. The Five Oaks neighborhood is a half-mile square area containing 2,000 homes on a grid street layout. Closing streets subdivided the neighborhood into small areas and made it so people could no longer drive directly through Five Oaks. Newman (1996) summarized the City of Dayton evaluation results (Office of Management and Budget, 1994). Police-reported crime statistics showed that crime in the city rose 1 percent, but that total crime in the target neighborhood declined 26 percent, and violent crime declined 50 percent. Significance tests were not reported. Citizen surveys reported that over half of the residents felt crime had declined. Newman also reports that housing values increased after having declined prior to the street closures.

Two efforts to curb prostitution activity in London neighborhoods used road closures and rerouting coupled with increased police enforcement. In Finsbury Park, police had steadily increased enforcement for 2 years prior to changes in the street closures. However, with the changes in the streets, "Soliciting and curb-crawling virtually disappeared and the area was transformed from a noisy and hazardous 'red-light' district into a relatively tranquil residential area" (Matthews, 1992, p. 94). Reported crime declined 50 percent for the 12-month period after the street closures compared to the previous 12 months. Observations of the area suggest that most of the prostitutes left the area, but did not displace to adjacent neighborhoods (Matthews, 1992).

In the Streatham neighborhood of London, street closures were also used in conjunction with increased police enforcement. Matthews (1993) reports a decline in traffic flow along key streets. Although police enforcement was maintained, arrests of "curb-crawlers" seeking sexual services declined by two-thirds (comparing the first quarter of 1990, after the program, to the first quarter of 1988, before the program began). Interviews of residents suggest a decline in noticeable prostitution activity, although some of this activity may have shifted to the periphery of that area.

The final evaluation of street closures was a retrospective analysis of the Los Angeles Police Department's Operation Cul-De-Sac. In 1990, the Los Angeles Police Department installed traffic barriers on fourteen streets in a South Central Los Angeles neighborhood with a high level of drug activity, shootings and homicides. Much of the violence was created by disputes over drug sales locations by local gang members. The barriers were designed to make the drive-up purchase of drugs more difficult and prevent drive-by shootings. This effort was part of a larger law enforcement effort to suppress these crimes. Two years following the installation of the barriers, the barriers were abandoned, and then removed, as the police became embroiled in the controversy surrounding the Rodney King beating.

The evaluation of the Los Angeles Police Department project compared reported crimes in the neighborhood for four quarters before the barriers were installed, the eight quarters while they were being maintained, and sixteen quarters after the program was abandoned (Lasley, 1996). Reported crime for the four adjacent areas was also examined. If one uses the surrounding beats as control areas, the net effect of the installation of the barriers (before compared to during) was that homicides decreased 65 percent. In fact, during the 2 years when the barriers were installed there was just one killing in the target area. Once the barriers were no longer maintained and were removed (comparing the installed period, to the after period), homicides rose 800 percent, relative to the surrounding area killings. Total violent crimes (homicide, rape, street robbery, aggravated assault and purse snatching) declined from the pre-program period to the 2 years during the program (8 percent for the first year and 37 percent for the second year), and then rose again after the program fell into disuse. At the same time, the surrounding areas remained relatively stable. Lasley attributes most of the decline in violent crime to changes in aggravated assaults. Significance tests were not reported for any of these comparisons.

Closing streets makes escaping more difficult. In the case of prostitution cruising and drive-by shootings, the offenders are likely to follow a circular driving pattern in their search for targets. By making circular driving patterns harder and increasing the chances that offenders will find themselves at the end of a dead-end street, criminal behavior may be thwarted.

The street closure evaluations used moderately strong designs and their conclusions are consistent with theory and prior research. This gives us confidence that street closings are promising. In at least three of the programs, the street closures were undertaken along with police crackdowns. Matthews (1992) hypothesizes that street closures and enforcement may be more effective when used together than when used separately and enforcement should be used prior to street changes. This opportunity-blocking tactic for controlling crime in open urban areas deserves more attention.

### Conclusions for open urban places

Four types of tactics were considered in this section. There is some evidence that controlling offenders, particularly public drinking, may be useful. However, the evaluations are small in number and weak in design, leaving its effectiveness unknown.

Lighting has received considerable attention but, until recently, the results were uncertain because of weak evaluation designs. Evaluation designs have improved to the point where we can rate this prevention technique as "works." Nevertheless, the conditions under which lighting is effective are largely unknown, and we do not know if offenders use lighting to their advantage in some situations. Rigorous testing of lighting in a variety of situations needs to be undertaken, particularly in the United States.

The installation of CCTV in urban areas might be a fruitful area for research, but its effectiveness is unknown. Though several evaluations had scientific methods scores of 3, the absence of significance tests limits what we can claim for the effectiveness of this tactic. We cannot recommend the adoption of this tactic, except for purposes of testing.

Finally, most street closure evaluations have been conducted with greater rigor than the other tactics. We also have evidence that is consistent with theory and research. This tactic appears to be "promising" and deserves more attention, particularly in high crime areas.

## Public coin machines

Parking meters and public telephones are the principal subject of this section. These devices occupy small, but important, places in cities and are subject to fraud and vandalism. The six studies we will examine here show reductions in property offenses due to changes in the physical structure (target hardening) or operations of these devices, and these evaluations are summarized in Table 7.10.

*Table 7.10* Public coin machines

| Study | Methods score | Tactic | Setting | Results |
|---|---|---|---|---|
| Barker and Bridgeman 1994 | 2 | publicity, target hardening, electronic monitoring | public telephones in Great Britain | 49% reduction in vandalism/theft |
| Challinger, 1991; Wilson, 1988 | 2 | hardened coin boxes, and other changes, and rapid repair | Australian public telephones | 48% reduction in vandalism |
| Bichler and Clarke, 1996 | 3 | removing international dialing capacity and disabling telephone keypads to prevent pay phone toll fraud | Port Authority Bus Terminal, Manhattan | 37% reduction in calls and 72% reduction in minutes of phone use. No displacement found |
| LaVigne, 1994 | 3 | restrictions on inmate phone use and phone system | Rikers Island, New York | 46% reduction in telephone related fights. 49% reduction in phone costs |
| Decker, 1972 | 4 | installation of slug rejecting parking meters and warning signs on parking meters | parking meters in New York | reduction in slug use due to changes in meters. Short-term reduction with two labels, but no long-term effect of any labels |

Two evaluations examined the effectiveness of strengthening the material used in public telephone cash boxes. Target hardening was supplemented by other prevention measures in both instances. In Britain, electronic monitoring of phone booths helped identify attacks quickly and act as a deterrent (Barker and Bridgeman, 1994). The evaluators reported a 49 percent reduction in attacks on cash compartments as a result of these changes. Australian evaluators claimed a comparable reduction in vandalism incidents following a combined target hardening and rapid repair program (Challinger, 1991). Both studies have weak designs due to their absence of control places.

Fraudulent use of public telephones has been addressed in two studies. [In both, new systems were installed that prohibited calls which prior analysis suggested were likely to be fraudulent.] At the New York Port Authority Bus Terminal, international calls were blocked, keypads were disabled to prevent routing calls through outside automated systems, and the number of available phones were reduced and relocated (Bichler and Clarke, 1996). Calls and number of minutes of phone use declined from the pre-intervention period to the post-intervention period. This is indirect evidence of a drop in fraudulent phone use because one cannot distinguish between reduced legitimate phone use due to increased inconvenience to users and reduced illegitimate phone use.

LaVigne (1994) evaluated the effects of restricting inmate access to phones at Rikers Island, a New York City jail facility. The Department of Corrections restricted inmate phone use to control the costs of fraudulent calls. Not only did phone costs go down, but also phone-related fights among inmates declined, controlling for overall trends in fights and changes in inmate population.

Finally, Decker (1972) examined the effectiveness of a target hardening method to prevent slug use in parking meters (i.e. installation of meters that reject certain types of slugs and display the last coin inserted). Rates of slug use were measured in ten areas of New York City. Slug use declined in all areas. In another study, Decker (1972) looked at the effectiveness of warning labels on parking meters. He found short-term reductions in slug use for some labels but, overall, the labels were less effective than meters that reject slugs.

These evaluations imply that target hardening is a promising method for reducing theft and vandalism. When evaluators looked for displacement effects, they were not found. LaVigne's (1994) evaluation suggests that illegal use of some facilities might stimulate other more serious criminal behavior and blocking minor offenses might reduce other more serious crimes. The Rikers Island evaluation is an illustration of the possible diffusion of crime prevention benefits (Clarke and Weisburd, 1994).

## The effectiveness of place-focused prevention

Table 7.11 summarizes the findings described in this chapter. Tactics that "work" have two or more positive studies with a scientific methods score of 3 or more and reported the statistical significance of findings. By this standard, nuisance abatement works to control drug dealing and related crime at private rental places. It had four evaluations rated 3 or more, including two

*Table 7.11* Summary of place-specific findings

| | Works | Does not work | Promising | Unknown |
|---|---|---|---|---|
| **Residential** | nuisance abatement | | | target hardening restricting movement guards CCTV cocoon watch property marking |
| **Commercial** stores | | | multiple clerks store design | EAS CCTV target hardening frequent inventory counts prohibiting offenders electronic monitoring ink tags guards cameras restricting movement |
| banking and money handling | | | | cameras target hardening guards |
| bars and taverns | | | server training | |
| **Transport** public transportation | | | | removing targets rapid cleanup design informal watching |
| parking lots | | | | CCTV guards restricting movement |
| airports | | | metal detectors guards | |
| **Public setting** open spaces | lighting | | street closures | CCTV prohibiting offenders controlling drinking |
| public facilities | | | target hardening | removing targets signs |

randomized experiments. Lighting high crime public areas also appears to work. It had two level 3 evaluations showing positive effects. Though there are some evaluations that indicate lighting is ineffective at preventing crime, these negative findings appear to be the consequence of weak research designs. They also indicate that the effectiveness of lighting is variable, depending on the circumstances under which it is used (Pease, 1999).

To be classified as "does not work," an intervention had to meet the same qualifications as "works," but the findings reported no relationship between the intervention and crime. There are no tactics in this category. This may be because many evaluations were insufficiently powerful to detect ineffective programs. Partially offsetting this conclusion is the fact that when rigorous and weak evaluations of the same tactic were available, the weak designs were more likely to reject the tactic than the strong designs. An alternative explanation is that most opportunity blocking at places works well. The question is at which places and in what circumstances does a tactic work well. If a large proportion of the studies examined circumstances where some effort was made to find a suitable intervention for a place crime problem then the vacuum in the "does not work" category is not surprising. This vacuum will be filled when attempts are made to expand the use of place tactics to unsuitable locations.

"Promising" tactics had to have at least one evaluation with a scientific methods score of 3, use significance tests and show that crime declined. If significance tests had been used in all studies, it is possible that some tactics of unknown effectiveness might have been classified as promising, and some promising tactics might have been found to work. Seven interventions had sufficient scientific evidence to be classified as promising. Putting metal detectors in this category reveals the limits of the application of standard social science research methods. Few would question the efficacy of metal detectors and passenger screening to prevent aircraft hijacking, but because this tactic has not been widely studied and many of the studies use weak research methods, we cannot put this tactic in the works category. We know little about its effectiveness in other settings. Street closures may be another tactic that is underrated because of weak evaluations and the lack of significance tests.

The "unknown" category contains most of the interventions. Many of these tactics had several studies showing positive effects, but the evaluations had methods scores less than 3, or did not report significance test results. Examples of these tactics include CCTV in stores and parking lots, and EAS in retail stores. Consistent findings that CCTV reduces crime in a variety of settings suggest that their effectiveness in stores and parking areas may be underrated by the criteria used here. Other tactics had several weak studies with conflicting results. Finally, some tactics may not prevent crime. Cameras were ineffective at preventing robberies of convenience stores in two studies, one of which was a rigorous test.

In conclusion, blocking crime opportunities at places reduces crime in many circumstances. Over 90 percent of the interventions reported evidence of crime reduction following the installation of an opportunity-blocking tactic. This evidence is encouraging but it must be tempered by four considerations. First, we know little about the place- and crime-specific effects of these tactics. That there is a great deal of uncertainty about what works, at which places, against which crimes, should not distract us from the broader finding that opportunity blocking tactics at places can be productive. Second, 94 percent of these evaluations are case studies, typically with a single site. We cannot treat these interventions as a random sample of all interventions of this type. Programs described in reports may have a higher proportion of successes than unreported programs. Nevertheless, authors of many of the evaluations asserted that their places were hot spots of crime and had resisted other interventions, such as police enforcement. Thus, the interventions may have tackled tougher problems than would be found at the average place. Third, many of the evaluations studied the effect of multiple interventions implemented at about the same time. Even when the effects of a single tactic were identified, other changes were reported that could have confounded the evaluation results. Thus, we might learn that crime was prevented, but we do not know what caused the prevention.

Fourth, the scientific rigor supporting the conclusions is usually moderate at best, and is frequently weak. About a third of the evaluations did not have control groups and evaluators often did not report significance levels for crime reductions. This means that many tactics were not put to a test sufficiently hard to uncover their weaknesses. Interestingly, however, we saw with both lighting and nuisance abatement that the weaker tests were more likely to find no effect than the hard tests. This gives us some hope that increasingly rigorous tests will find even more place-focused tactics that work.

### Displacement is limited

Do place specific interventions merely cause criminals to go to other places? If 100 percent of the crime were shifted somewhere else, place-focused prevention would be worthless. In the last 10 years, there have been a number of reviews of the empirical evidence and theoretical underpinnings for displacement. Theoretical explorations based on a rational choice perspective find no basis for believing offenders always completely displace if they cannot attack their favorite targets (Barnes, 1995; Barr and Pease, 1990; Bouloukos and Farrell, 1997; Cornish and Clarke, 1987; Eck, 1993). Reviews of empirical studies find no evidence to suggest that these interventions increase crime by displacing, that there is often no displacement, but when displacement does occur it does not overwhelm other gains from blocking crime opportunities (Cornish and Clarke, 1987; Eck, 1993; Hesseling, 1995b).

Perhaps more displacement would be found if evaluators were more diligent in searching for it. Many older prevention evaluations did not test for it. However, recent studies designed explicitly to detect displacement find little of it. In short, if the evidence for limited displacement is weak, the evidence for large amounts of displacement is even weaker. At this time our best conclusion, based on the evidence, is that, at worst, displacement may suppress effectiveness, but it does not drive effectiveness to zero.

### Prevention benefits can spread

Overlooked in the concern about displacement is the possibility of just the opposite effect, diffusion of crime prevention benefits (Clarke and Weisburd, 1994). This occurs when places or targets that did not receive the intervention nevertheless had their risk of crime reduced because of the intervention. In the evaluations examined in this chapter, there are a number of examples of possible diffusion of benefits effects (Felson *et al.*, 1997; LaVigne, 1994; Masuda, 1992; Poyner, 1988; Scherdin, 1992; see also Welsh and Farrington, 1999). There are good theoretical reasons to believe diffusion of benefits might be common. Under some circumstances offenders may be uncertain about the scope of prevention efforts and avoid both the blocked opportunities and similar unblocked opportunities. When this occurs, prevention may spread. Further, evaluations using controls contaminated by diffusion effects underestimate the effectiveness of the tested interventions. If diffusion of benefits is common, the place-focused approaches may be far more effective than the evidence suggests.

### *Situational crime prevention and problem solving are promising*

The assessment of what we know about the effectiveness of place-focused crime prevention tactics is based on the assumption that, if a tactic has been shown to be effective against a type of crime at a type of place, it will reduce these crimes at most such places. But if crime problems are highly situational, such an approach has major limitations.

There is another valid approach to addressing crime problems. Instead of testing generic solutions to crimes, one can conduct a thorough examination of a problem and then craft a unique intervention to address it. Situational crime prevention (Clarke, 1992) and problem-oriented policing (Goldstein, 1990) advocate this approach. Many of the evaluations reviewed here studied multiple simultaneous interventions selected following some form of problem analysis. One of the three randomized experiments was a study of problem solving (Crow and Bull, 1975). Repeat victimization interventions (Anderson, Chenery and Pease, 1995a; Bennett and Durie, 1999; Forrester, Chatterton and Pease, 1988; Tilley and Hopkins, 1998) are also forms of problem solving because the complex interventions are based on site-specific analysis. It is difficult to determine how many of the tactics reviewed in this chapter were selected because of site-specific analysis of the crime problem, but more than half provide some evidence of this. In these cases the evaluation results reflect the joint effectiveness of the analysis and the response. This implies that we have good evidence for the effectiveness of problem-solving and situational crime prevention. And, as mentioned earlier, this would help explain the high success rate of the interventions tested.

## Improving effectiveness through research and evaluation

What can be done to improve our knowledge of place-focused prevention effectiveness? First, more criminologists, prevention practitioners, the police and public officials must take opportunity blocking seriously. Most debates over preventing crime are conflicts between people who believe harsher punishment is effective and those who believe social programs and rehabilitation prevent more crime. Both camps miss two fundamental facts about crime. It cannot be committed if there is no opportunity (Felson and Clarke, 1998). Further, for most people, such a debate is practically irrelevant because they do not punish or rehabilitate offenders. If one takes into account the spending of individuals, businesses, public agencies and other groups, it is safe to say that far more is spent on opportunity blocking than any other form of crime prevention. Yet we know little about how much of this money is spent well and its impact on society (see Welsh and Farrington, 1999). Providing citizens with scientifically based prevention information they can put to use should be a priority.

Second, researchers studying opportunity blocking should improve their evaluation methods. As we have seen, more rigorous evaluations are more likely to reveal crime reduction effects than weak designs. Weak designs undermine confidence in potentially effective programs and fail to distinguish them from truly ineffective interventions. Control groups and significance tests serve important functions, and should be applied whenever feasible. The most advanced evaluations now include buffer areas for detecting displacement and diffusion of benefits effects.

Third, we need valid alternatives to the "randomized experiment paradigm." Many places are imbedded in large, complex and unique systems – subway systems, chains of stores, apartment buildings, malls, subdivisions and others. When a system exerts an influence on places, valid controls are difficult, if not impossible, to find. System influences make it hard to isolate treatment places from control places and, if they can be isolated, the results have little generalizability. Further, with low base rates for many crimes, statistical power is impossible to achieve within reasonable time periods. The case of metal detectors in airports to thwart hijacking is a case in point: air transportation is a strong system and there never were many hijackings, so the evaluations are weak. No sensible person would claim that these metal detectors are ineffective and demand their removal. Yet, when we use the classic experimental design as the benchmark, this is exactly what we are implying.

Randomized experiments are not the gold standard of all sciences. There are many sciences that do not use them, yet have made far greater contributions to humanity than criminology. One alternative is to examine the causal mechanism by which a place-focused tactic should influence crime and the context within which the tactic was implemented (Beck and Willis, 1999; Pawson and Tilley, 1994). Another approach is to develop valid models of complex situations, and then simulate the implementation of prevention methods prior to field experiments.

Fourth, we need to expand on existing theories to develop a detailed theory of crime patterns and hot spots. We have learned that crime is concentrated at places, and we have begun to realize that crime prevention at places works best at places that are crime hot spots. Routine activity theory (Felson, 1994) and crime pattern theory (Brantingham and Brantingham, 1993) offer solid foundations for such a theory. We have elementary theories for displacement (Bouloukos and Farrell, 1997; Eck, 1993) and diffusion of benefits (Clarke and Weisburd, 1994). Situational crime prevention provides a useful road map for action. Nevertheless, there is a great deal of work to be done before we can accurately predict crime concentrations in a wide variety of places and offer clear and detailed prescriptions for their prevention.

Because the number of possible places is so large, and the situations found at these places so diverse, the fifth thing we need to do is to make better use of information from evaluations with weak designs. Evaluation designs that are weak by social science standards may be acceptable to decision makers who fund such efforts and even weak evaluations can contain valuable information. Local governments and businesses produce untold numbers of weak evaluations. Those who want to build knowledge in this area must discover ways of learning from the many attempts to address very specific crime problems, even when level 1 and 2 designs are used. This requires ways of finding, cataloging and synthesizing weak evaluations. It may require the development of interval level methods weights so that the collective contribution of these studies can be ascertained. Or there may be ways of using meta-analysis to mine information from these studies.

Finally, we should abandon the search for generic solutions, ones that work under all circumstances for all times (Pease, 1999). Though many opportunity blocking tactics appear to work in many places, there is no guarantee they will hold up as they are tried in different types of places. These tactics are being applied where they are most plausible, so success is most likely. As people try them in other less plausible places, there is greater likelihood of failure. And, over time, circumstances will change and some of these changes will undercut the effectiveness of even the most successful tactic. Offenders may adapt. Facilitating features of the environment may disappear. At the same time, new opportunity blocking mechanisms will be discovered. If we look for general principles of prevention, rather than general tactics, we may have greater success for longer periods. Such knowledge will come quicker, if theory development and testing are coupled more closely to solution development and evaluation.

## Notes

1  I owe thanks to the members of the University of Maryland team who gave me valuable advice throughout the preparation of the original review: Lawrence Sherman, Denise Gottfredson, Doris MacKenzie, Peter Reuter and Shawn Bushway. Special thanks are due to Larry Sherman for spearheading this effort and seeing the value of a chapter reviewing place-based prevention. David Farrington and Brandon Welsh were very helpful in the preparation of the revisions and updating of this chapter. Ronald Clarke was enormously generous with his time, library, and copies of documents. He suggested numerous ways of improving the chapter. Michael Hough and Gloria Laycock provided insightful criticism. Lisa Growette undertook the tedious job of editing the chapter and her suggestions have improved it a great deal. Finally, I have benefited greatly from the comments of students and police officials who have read the initial report. Nevertheless, I retain exclusive claim to all errors and omissions that this chapter contains.

2  This chapter was written a year before the events of 11 September 2001. The lessons from these events regarding the effectiveness of passenger screening have yet to be fully grasped. One lesson may be that passenger screening displaced the method of attack from the use of guns to the use of knives (Malcolm Gladwell, 2001). It is undeniable that the hijackers of 11 September selected weapons that screeners either allowed on planes or had difficulty detecting. Gladwell, however, makes the point that screening and other airport security has made hijacking less frequent, but more fatal. His first point is probably true and his second point is probably false. In the absence of passenger screening, it is likely that the hijackers would have used firearms to carry out the same ends. The increased lethality of hijacking, reported by Gladwell, probably has more to do with changes in the motivation of hijackers – a shift from monetary gain or transportation to a foreign country, both of which involve the survival of the hijacker, to the use of planes as human guided munitions to create havoc. It is highly unlikely that such a shift in motivation is due to airport security.

So a second possible lesson might be that prevention measures are only effective against the threat they were designed to address. Though we call any seizing of an aircraft "hijacking," there are many types of hijacking and no single precaution can address them all. If new forms of hijacking develop, we cannot expect old forms of prevention to be effective against them.

Finally, a third possible lesson is that security deteriorates over time as the threat abates. Security is expensive, and efforts to process the maximum number of people at the least cost may have resulted in a diminution of the effectiveness of passenger screening.

## References

Allatt, P. (1984) Residential security: Containment and displacement of burglary. *Howard Journal of Criminal Justice*, 23, 99–116.

Anderson, D., Chenery, S. and Pease, K. (1995a) *Biting back: Tackling repeat burglary and car crime* (Vol. 58). London: Home Office.

Anderson, D., Chenery, S. and Pease, K. (1995b) *Preventing repeat victimizations: A report on progress in Huddersfield* (Briefing Note 4/95). London: Home Office.

Armitage, R., Smyth, G. and Pease, K. (1999) Burnley CCTV evaluation. In K. Painter and N. Tilley (eds), *Surveillance of public space: CCTV, street lighting and crime prevention* (Vol. 10). Monsey, NY: Criminal Justice Press, 225–50.

Atkins, S., Husain, S. and Storey, A. (1991) *The influence of street lighting on crime and fear of crime* (Vol. 28). London: Home Office.

Atlas, R. and LeBlanc, W.G. (1994) The impact on crime of street closures and barricades: A Florida case study. *Security Journal*, 5, 140–5.

Bamfield, J. (1994) Electronic article surveillance: Management learning in curbing theft. In M. Gill (ed.), *Crime at work: Studies in security and crime Prevention*. Leicester: Perpetuity Press, 155–73.

Barclay, P., Buchley, J., Brantingham, P.J., Brantingham, P. and Whinn-Yates, T. (1996) Preventing auto theft in suburban Vancouver commuter lots: Effects of a bike patrol. In R.V. Clarke (ed.), *Preventing mass transit crime* (Vol. 6). Monsey, NY: Criminal Justice Press, 133–62.

Barker, M. and Bridgeman, C. (1994) *Preventing vandalism: What works?* (Vol. 56). London: Home Office.

Barnes, G.C. (1995) Defining and optimizing displacement. In J.E. Eck and D. Weisburd (eds), *Crime and place* (Vol. 4). Monsey, NY: Criminal Justice Press, 95–114.

Barr, R. and Pease, K. (1990) Crime placement, displacement, and deflection. In M. Tonry and N. Morris (eds), *Crime and justice: A review of research* (Vol. 12). Chicago, IL: University of Chicago Press, 227–318.

Beavon, D.J.K., Brantingham, P.L. and Brantingham, P.J. (1994) The influence of street networks on the patterning of property offenses. In R.V. Clarke (ed.), *Crime prevention studies* (Vol. 2). Monsey, NY: Criminal Justice Press, 115–48.

Beck, A. and Willis, A. (1999) Context-specific measures of CCTV effectiveness in the retail sector. In K. Painter and N. Tilley (eds), *Surveillance of public space: CCTV, street lighting and crime prevention* (Vol. 10). Monsey, NY: Criminal Justice Press.

Bellamy, L.C. (1996) Situational crime prevention and convenience store robbery. *Security Journal*, 7, 41–52, 251–69.

Bennett, T. and Durie, L. (1999) *Preventing residential burglary in Cambridge: From crime audits to targeted strategies* (Vol. 108). London: Home Office.

Bichler, G. and Clarke, R.V. (1996) Eliminating pay phone toll fraud at the Port Authority Bus Terminal in Manhattan. In R.V. Clarke (ed.), *Preventing mass transit crime* (Vol. 6). Monsey, NY: Criminal Justice Press, 93–116.

Bjor, J., Knutsson, J. and Kuhlhorn, E. (1992) The celebration of Midsummer Eve in Sweden: A study in the art of preventing collective disorder. *Security Journal*, 3, 169–74.

Block, R. and Block, C. (1995) Space, place and crime: Hot spot areas and hot place of liquor-related crime. In J.E. Eck and D. Weisburd (eds), *Crime and place* (Vol. 4). Monsey, NY: Criminal Justice Press, 145–84.

Bouloukos, A.C. and Farrell, G. (1997) On the displacement of repeat victimization. In G. Newman, R.V. Clarke and S.G. Shoham (eds), *Rational choice and situational crime prevention: Theoretical foundations.* Dartmouth, NH: Dartmouth University Press, 219–32.

Brantingham, P.L. and Brantingham, P.J. (1981) Notes on the geometry of crime. In P.J. Brantingham and P.L. Brantingham (eds), *Environmental criminology.* Beverly Hills, CA: Sage, 27–54.

Brantingham, P.L. and Brantingham, P.J. (1993) Environment, routine, and situation: Toward a pattern theory of crime. In R.V. Clarke and M. Felson (eds), *Routine activity and rational choice* (Vol. 5). New Brunswick, NJ: Transaction, 259–94.

Brown, B. (1995) *CCTV in town centres: Three case studies* (Vol. 68). London: Home Office.

Burrows, J. and Speed, M. (1996) Crime analysis: Lessons from the retail sector. *Security Journal,* 7, 53–60.

Carr, K. and Spring, G. (1993) Public transport safety: A community right and a communal responsibility. In R.V. Clarke (ed.), *Crime prevention studies* (Vol. 1). Monsey, NY: Criminal Justice Press, 147–56.

Centers for Disease Control and Prevention (1993) Violence-related attitudes and behaviors of high school students: New York City, 1992. *Morbidity and Mortality Weekly Report,* 42, 773–7.

Chaiken, J.M., Lawless, M.W. and Stevenson, K.A. (1974) *Impact of police on crime: Robberies on the New York City subway system* (R-1424-NYC). New York: The New York City Rand Institute.

Challinger, D. (1991) Less telephone vandalism: How did it happen? *Security Journal,* 2, 111–19.

Challinger, D. (1996) Refund fraud in retail stores. *Security Journal,* 7, 27–35.

Chatterton, M.R. and Frenz, S.J. (1994) Closed-circuit television: Its role in reducing burglaries and the fear of crime in sheltered accommodation for the elderly. *Security Journal,* 5, 133–9.

Chenery, S., Holt, J. and Pease, K. (1997) *Biting back II: Reducing repeat victimization in Huddersfield* (Vol. 82). London: Home Office.

Clarke, R.V. (ed.) (1992) *Situational crime prevention: Successful case studies.* Albany, NY: Harrow and Heston.

Clarke, R.V. (1993) Fare evasion and automatic ticket collection in the London Underground. In R.V. Clarke (ed.), *Crime prevention studies* (Vol. 1). Monsey, NY: Criminal Justice Press.

Clarke, R.V. (1995) Situational crime prevention. In M. Tonry and D.P. Farrington (eds), *Building a safer society: Strategic approaches to crime prevention* (Vol. 19). Chicago, IL: University of Chicago Press, 91–150.

Clarke, R.V., Cody, R. and Natarajan, M. (1994) Subway slugs: Tracking displacement on the London Underground. *British Journal of Criminology,* 34, 122–38.

Clarke, R.V., Field, S. and McGrath, G. (1991) Target hardening of banks in Australia and displacement of robberies. *Security Journal,* 2, 84–90.

Clarke, R.V. and Homel, R. (1997) A revised classification of situational crime prevention techniques. In S.P. Lab (ed.), *Crime prevention at the crossroads.* Cincinnati, OH: Anderson, 17–30.

Clarke, R.V. and McGrath, G. (1990) Cash reduction and robbery prevention in Australian betting shops. *Security Journal,* 1, 160–3.

Clarke, R.V. and Weisburd, D. (1994) Diffusion of crime control benefits:

Observations on the reverse of displacement. In R.V. Clarke (ed.), *Crime prevention studies* (Vol. 2). Monsey, NY: Criminal Justice Press, 165–84.

Clifton, W., Jr. (1987) *Convenience store robberies in Gainesville, Florida: An intervention strategy by the Gainesville Police Department.* Gainesville, FL: Gainesville Police Department.

Cohen, L.E. and Felson, M. (1979) Social change and crime rate trends: A routine activity approach. *American Sociological Review*, 44, 588–608.

Coleman, A. (1985) *Utopia on trial.* London: Hilary Shipman.

Cornish, D. and Clarke, R.V. (1987) Understanding crime displacement: An application of rational choice theory. *Criminology*, 25, 933–47.

Crow, W.J. and Bull, J.L. (1975) *Robbery deterrence: An applied behavioral science demonstration – final report.* La Jolla, CA: Western Behavior Sciences Institute.

Crow, W.J. and Erickson, R.J. (1984) *Cameras and silent alarms: A study of their effectiveness as a robbery deterrent.* Jackson Hole, WY: Athena Research Corporation.

Decker, J.F. (1972) Curbside deterrence: An analysis of the effect of a slug rejection device, coin view window and warning labels on slug usage in New York City parking meters. *Criminology*, 10, 127–42.

DesChamps, S., Brantingham, P. and Brantingham, P. (1992) The British Columbia transit fare evasion audit. In R.V. Clarke (ed.), *Situational crime prevention: Successful case studies* (1st edn). Albany, NY: Harrow and Heston, 139–50.

DiLonardo, R.L. (1996) Defining and measuring the economic benefit of electronic article surveillance. *Security Journal*, 7, 3–9.

DiLonardo, R.L. and R.V. Clarke (1996) Reducing the rewards of shoplifting: An evaluation of ink tags. *Security Journal*, 7, 11–14.

Ditton, J. and Nair, G. (1994) Throwing light on crime: A case study of the relationship between street lighting and crime prevention. *Security Journal*, 5, 125–32.

Ditton, J. and Short, E. (1999) Yes, it works, no, it doesn't: Comparing the effects of open-street CCTV in two adjacent Scottish town centres. In K. Painter and N. Tilley (eds), *Surveillance of public space: CCTV, street lighting and crime prevention* (Vol. 10). Monsey, NY: Criminal Justice Press, 201–24.

Dunworth, T. and Saiger, A.J. (1994) *Drugs and crime in public housing: A three city analysis.* Washington, DC: National Institute of Justice.

Easteal, P.W. and Wilson, P.R. (1991) *Preventing crime on transport.* Canberra: Australian Institute of Criminology.

Eck, J.E. (1993) The threat of crime displacement. *Criminal Justice Abstracts*, 25, 527–46.

Eck, J.E. (1994) *Drug markets and drug places: A case-control study of the spatial structure of illicit drug dealing.* Unpublished Ph.D. dissertation, College Park, MD: University of Maryland.

Eck, J.E. (1995) A general model of the geography of illicit retail marketplaces. In J.E. Eck and D. Weisburd (eds), *Crime and place* (Vol. 4). Monsey, NY: Criminal Justice Press, 67–94.

Eck, J.E. (1999) Drug market places: How they form and how they can be prevented. In C.S. Brito and T. Allen (eds), *Problem-oriented policing: Crime-specific problems, critical issues and making POP work* (Vol. 2). Washington, DC: Police Executive Research Forum, 91–112.

Eck, J.E. and Wartell, J. (1998) Improving the management of rental properties with drug problems: A randomized experiment. In L. Mazerolle and J. Roehl (eds), *Civil remedies and crime prevention* (Vol. 9). Monsey, NY: Criminal Justice Press, 161–86.

Eck, J.E. and Weisburd, D. (eds) (1995) *Crime and place* (Vol. 4). Monsey, NY: Criminal Justice Press.

Ekblom, P. (1987) *Preventing robberies at sub-post offices: An evaluation of a security initiative* (Vol. 9). London: Home Office.

Ekblom, P. (1988) Preventing post office robberies in London: Effects and side effects. *Journal of Security Administration*, 11, 36–43.

Engstad, P.A. (1975) Environmental opportunities and the ecology of crime. In R.A. Silverman and J.J. Teevan (eds), *Crime in Canadian society*. Toronto: Butterworth, 193–211.

Farrell, G. (1995) Preventing repeat victimization. In M. Tonry and D.P. Farrington (eds), *Building a safer society: Strategic approaches to crime prevention* (Vol. 19). Chicago, IL: University of Chicago Press, 469–534.

Farrington, D.P., Bowen, S., Buckle, A., Burns-Howell, T., Burrows, J. and Speed, M. (1993) An experiment on the prevention of shoplifting. In R.V. Clarke (ed.), *Crime prevention studies* (Vol. 1). Monsey, NY: Criminal Justice Press, 93–120.

Felson, M. (1994) *Crime and everyday life: Insight and implications for society*. Thousand Oaks, CA: Pine Forge Press.

Felson, M., Belanger, M.E., Bichler, G.M., Bruzinski, C.D., Campbell, G.S., Fried, C.L., Grofik, K.C., Mazur, I.S., O'Regan, A.B., Sweeney, P.J., Ullman, A.L. and Williams, L.M. (1996) Redesigning Hell: Preventing crime and disorder at the Port Authority Bus Terminal. In R.V. Clarke (ed.), *Preventing mass transit crime* (Vol. 6). Monsey, NY: Criminal Justice Press, 5–92.

Felson, M., Berends, R., Richardson, B. and Veno, A. (1997) Reducing pub hopping and related crime. In R. Homel (ed.), *Policing for prevention: Reducing crime, public intoxication and injury* (Vol. 7). Monsey, NY: Criminal Justice Press, 115–32.

Felson, M. and Clarke, R.V. (1998) *Opportunity makes the thief: Practical theory for crime prevention* (Vol. 98). London: Home Office.

Fleming, R. and Burrows, J. (1986) The case for lighting as a means of preventing crime. *Research Bulletin, Research and Planning Unit*, 22, 14–17.

Forrester, D.H., Chatterton, M.R. and Pease, K. (1988) *The Kirkholt Burglary Prevention Demonstration Project, Rochdale* (Vol. 13). London: Home Office.

Forrester, D.H., Frenz, S., O'Connell, M. and Pease, K. (1990) *The Kirkholt Burglary Prevention Project: Phase II* (Vol. 23). London: Home Office.

Gabor, T. (1981) The crime displacement hypothesis: An empirical examination. *Crime and Delinquency*, 26, 390–404.

Gladwell, M. (2000) Annals of aviation: Safety in the skies – airline security and its limits. *The New Yorker*, 1 October, 50–3.

Goldstein, H. (1990) *Problem-oriented policing*. New York: McGraw-Hill.

Gottfredson, M.R. and Hirschi, T. (1990) *A general theory of crime*. Stanford, CA: Stanford University Press.

Grandjean, C. (1990) Bank robberies and physical security in Switzerland: A case study of the escalation and displacement phenomena. *Security Journal*, 1, 155–9.

Green, L. (1993) *Treating deviant places: A case study examination of the Beat Health Program in Oakland, California*. Unpublished Ph.D. dissertation, Newark, NJ: Rutgers, The State University of New Jersey.

Green, L. (1995) Cleaning up drug hotspots in Oakland, California: The displacement and diffusion effects. *Justice Quarterly*, 12, 737–54.

Green, L. (1996) *Policing places with drug problems*. Thousand Oaks, CA: Sage.

Greenberg, S.W. and Rohe, W.M. (1984) Neighborhood design and crime: A test of two perspectives. *Journal of the American Planning Association*, 49, 48–61.

Hannan, T.H. (1982) Bank robberies and bank security precautions. *Journal of Legal Studies*, 11, 83–92.

Hesseling, R. (1995a) Theft from cars: Reduced or displaced? *European Journal of Criminal Policy and Research*, 3, 79–92.

Hesseling, R.B.P. (1995b) Displacement: A review of the empirical literature. In R.V. Clarke (ed.), *Crime prevention studies* (Vol. 3). Monsey, NY: Criminal Justice Press 197–230.

Homel, R. and Clark, J. (1994) The prediction and prevention of violence in pubs and clubs. In R.V. Clarke (ed.), *Crime prevention studies* (Vol. 3). Monsey, NY: Criminal Justice Press, 1–46.

Homel, R., Hauritz, M., Wortley, R., McIlwain, G. and Carvolth, R. (1997) Preventing alcohol-related crime through community action: The Surfers' Paradise Safety Action Project. In R. Homel (ed.), *Policing for prevention: Reducing crime, public intoxication and injury* (Vol. 7). Monsey, NY: Criminal Justice Press, 35–90.

Hope, T. (1994) Problem-oriented policing and drug market locations: Three case studies. In R.V. Clarke (ed.), *Crime prevention studies* (Vol. 2). Monsey, NY: Criminal Justice Press, 5–32.

Hunter, R.D. and Jeffrey, C.R. (1992) Preventing convenience store robbery through environmental design. In R.V. Clarke (ed.), *Situational crime prevention: Successful case studies* (1st edn). Albany, NY: Harrow and Heston, 194–204.

Jacques, C. (1994) Ram raiding: The history, incidence and scope for prevention. In M. Gill (ed.), *Crime at work: Studies in security and crime prevention*. Leicester: Perpetuity Press, 42–55.

Kenney, D.J. (1986) Crime on the subways: Measuring the effectiveness of the Guardian Angels. *Justice Quarterly*, 3, 481–96.

Landes, W.M. (1978) An economic study of US aircraft hijacking, 1961–1976. *Journal of Law and Economics*, 21, 1–32.

Lasley, J.R. (1996) *Using traffic barriers to "design out" crime: A program evaluation of LAPD's Operation Cul-De-Sac. Report to the national institute of justice.* Fullerton, CA: California State University.

Lasley, J.R. (1998) *"Designing out" gang homicides and street assaults.* Washington, DC: National Institute of Justice.

LaVigne, N.G. (1991) *Crimes of convenience: An analysis of criminal decision-making and convenience store crime in Austin, Texas.* Unpublished M.A. thesis, Austin, TX: University of Texas at Austin.

LaVigne, N.G. (1994) Rational choice and inmate disputes over phone use on Rikers Island. In R.V. Clarke (ed.), *Crime prevention studies* (Vol. 3). Monsey, NY: Criminal Justice Press, 109–26.

LaVigne, N.G. (1997) Safe transport: Security by design on the Washington Metro. In R.V. Clarke (ed.), *Preventing mass transit crime* (Vol. 6). Monsey, NY: Criminal Justice Press, 163–98.

Laycock, G. (1985) *Property marking: A deterrent to domestic burglary?* (Vol. 3). London: Home Office.

Laycock, G. (1991) Operation identification, or the power of publicity? *Security Journal*, 2, 67–72.

Laycock, G. and Austin, C. (1992) Crime prevention in parking facilities. *Security Journal*, 3, 154–60.

Lurigio, A.J., Davis, R.C., Regulus, T.A., Gwiasda, V.E., Popkin, S.J., Dantzker, M.L., Smith, B. and Ouellet, L. (1993) *An evaluation of the Cook County State's Attorney's Office Narcotics Nuisance Abatement Unit.* Chicago, IL: Illinois Criminal Justice Information Authority.

Masuda, B. (1992) Displacement vs. diffusion of benefits and the reduction of inventory losses in a retail environment. *Security Journal*, 3, 131–6.

Masuda, B. (1993) Credit card fraud prevention: A successful retail strategy. In R.V. Clarke (ed.), *Crime prevention studies* (Vol. 1). Monsey, NY: Criminal Justice Press, 121–34.

Masuda, B. (1996) An alternative approach to the credit card fraud problem. *Security Journal*, 7, 15–21.

Matthews, R. (1992) Developing more effective strategies for curbing prostitution. In R.V. Clarke (ed.), *Situational crime prevention: Successful case studies* (1st edn). Albany, NY: Harrow and Heston, 89–98.

Matthews, R. (1993) *Kerb-crawling, prostitution and multi-agency policing* (Vol. 43). London: Home Office.

Mawby, R.I. (1977) Defensible space: A theoretical and empirical appraisal. *Urban Studies*, 14, 169–79.

Mayhew, P. (1979) Defensible space: The current status of a crime prevention theory. *Howard Journal of Penology and Crime Prevention*, 18, 150–9.

Mazerolle, L., Roehl, J. and Kadleck, C. (1998) Controlling social disorder using civil remedies: Results for a randomized field experiment in Oakland, California. In L. Mazerolle and J. Roehl (eds), *Civil remedies and crime prevention* (Vol. 9). Monsey, NY: Criminal Justice Press, 141–6.

Mazerolle, L.G., Hurley, D.C. and Chamlin, M. (1999) *Surveillance cameras in Cincinnati: An analysis of the impacts across three study sites.* Cincinnati, OH: Division of Criminal Justice, University of Cincinnati.

McNees, M.P., Schnelle, J.F., Kirchner, R.E. and Thomas, M.M. (1980) An experimental analysis of a program to reduce retail theft. *American Journal of Community Psychology*, 8, 379–85.

Meredith, C. and Paquette, C. (1992) Crime prevention in high-rise rental apartments: Findings of a demonstration project. *Security Journal*, 3, 161–9.

Merry, S.F. (1981) Defensible space undefended: Social factors in crime prevention through environmental design. *Urban Affairs Quarterly*, 16, 397–422.

National Association of Convenience Stores (1991) *Convenience store security report and recommendations.* Alexandria, VA: National Association of Convenience Stores.

Newman, O. (1972) *Defensible space.* New York: Macmillan.

Newman, O. (1980) *Community of interest.* Garden City, NY: Anchor Press.

Newman, O. (1996) *Creating defensible space.* Washington, DC: US Department of Housing and Urban Development.

Norris, C. and Armstrong, G. (1999) CCTV and the social structuring of surveillance. In K. Painter and N. Tilley (eds), *Surveillance of public space: CCTV, street lighting and crime prevention* (Vol. 10). Monsey, NY: Criminal Justice Press, 157–78.

Office of Management and Budget (1994) *Evaluation of the Five Oaks Neighborhood Stabilization Plan.* Dayton, OH: Office of Management and Budget.

Painter, K. (1994) The impact of street lighting on crime, fear and pedestrian use. *Security Journal*, 5, 116–24.

Painter, K. and Farrington, D.P. (1997) The crime reducing effect of improved street lighting: The Dudley project. In R.V. Clarke (ed.), *Situational crime prevention: Successful case studies* (2nd edn). Guilderland, NY: Harrow and Heston, 209–26.

Painter, K. and Farrington, D.P. (1999a) Improved street lighting: Crime reducing effects and cost–benefit analysis. *Security Journal*, 12(4), 17–32.

Painter, K. and Farrington, D.P. (1999b) Street lighting and crime: Diffusion of benefits in the Stoke-on-Trent project. In K. Painter and N. Tilley (eds), *Surveillance of public space: CCTV, street lighting and crime prevention* (Vol. 10). Monsey, NY: Criminal Justice Press, 77–122.

Painter, K. and Farrington, D.P. (2001) Evaluating situational crime prevention using a young people's survey. *British Journal of Criminology*, 40, 266–84.

Pawson, R. and Tilley, N. (1994) What works in evaluation research? *British Journal of Criminology*, 34(3), 291–306.

Pease, K. (1991) The Kirkholt project: Preventing burglary on a British public housing estate. *Security Journal*, 2, 73–7.

Pease, K. (1999) A review of street lighting evaluations: Crime reduction effects. In K. Painter and N. Tilley (eds), *Surveillance of public space: CCTV, street lighting and crime prevention* (Vol. 10). Monsey, NY: Criminal Justice Press, 47–76.

Pierce, G.L., Spaar, S. and Briggs, L.R. (1986) *The character of police work: Strategic and tactical implications.* Boston: Center for Applied Social Research. Northeastern University.

Polvi, N., Looman, T., Humphries, C. and Pease, K. (1990) Repeat break-and-enter victimizations: Time-course and crime prevention opportunity. *Journal of Police Science and Administration*, 17, 8–11.

Popkin, S.J., Gwiasda, V.E., Rosenbaum, D.P., Anderson, A.A., Olson, L.M., Lurigio, A.J. and Taluc, N. (1995a) *An evaluation of the Chicago Housing Authority's anti-drug initiative: A model of comprehensive crime prevention in public housing.* Cambridge, MA: Abt Associates Inc.

Popkin, S.J., Olson, L.M., Lurigio, A.J., Gwiasda, V.E. and Carter, R.G. (1995b) Sweeping out drugs and crime: Residents' views of the Chicago Housing Authority's Public Housing Drug Elimination Program. *Crime and Delinquency*, 41, 73–99.

Poyner, B. (1983) *Design against crime: Beyond defensible space.* London: Butterworths.

Poyner, B. (1988) Video cameras and bus vandalism. *Journal of Security Administration*, 11, 44–51.

Poyner, B. (1991) Situational crime prevention in two parking facilities. *Security Journal*, 2, 96–101.

Poyner, B. (1994) Lessons from Lisson Green: An evaluation of walkway demolition on a British housing estate. In R.V. Clarke (ed.), *Crime prevention studies* (Vol. 3). Monsey, NY: Criminal Justice Press, 127–50.

Poyner, B. and Warne, C. (1986) *Violence to staff: A basis for assessment and prevention.* London: Tavistock.

Poyner, B. and Webb, B. (1991) *Crime free housing.* London: Butterworths-Architecture.

Poyner, B. and Webb, B. (1992) Reducing theft from shopping bags in city center markets. In R.V. Clarke (ed.), *Situational crime prevention: Successful case studies* (1st edn). Albany, NY: Harrow and Heston.

Putnam, S.L., Rockett, I.R. and Campbell, M.K. (1993) Methodological issues in community-based alcohol-related injury prevention projects: Attribution of program effects. In T.K. Greenfield and R. Zimmerman (eds), *Experience with community action projects: New research in the prevention of alcohol and other drug problems* (Vol. 14). Rockville, MD: Center for Substance Abuse Prevention, 31–9.

Ramsay, M. (1990) *Lagerland lost: An experiment in keeping drinkers off the streets in central Coventry and elsewhere* (Vol. 22). London: Home Office.

Ramsay, M. (1991) A British experiment in curbing incivilities and fear of crime. *Security Journal*, 2, 120–5.

Roncek, D.W. and Bell, R. (1981) Bars, blocks and crime. *Journal of Environmental Systems*, 11, 35–47.

Roncek, D. and Meier, P.A. (1991) Bars, blocks and crimes revisited: Linking the theory of routine activities to the empiricism of "hot spots." *Criminology*, 29, 725–55.

Roncek, D.W. and Pravatiner, M.A. (1989) Additional evidence that taverns enhance nearby crime. *Sociology and Social Research*, 73, 185–8.

Saltz, R.F. (1987) The role of bars and restaurants in preventing alcohol-impaired driving: An evaluation of server education. *Evaluation in Health Professions*, 10, 5–27.

Scherdin, M.J. (1992) The halo effect: Psychological deterrence of electronic security systems. In R.V. Clarke (ed.), *Situational crime prevention: Successful case studies* (1st edn). Albany, NY: Harrow and Heston, 133–8.

Sherman, L.W., Gartin, P.R. and Buerger, M.E. (1989) Hot spots of predatory crime: Routine activities and the criminology of place. *Criminology*, 27, 27–55.

Sherman, L.W. and Rogan, D.P. (1995a) Deterrent effects of police raids on crack houses: A randomized, controlled experiment. *Justice Quarterly*, 12, 755–81.

Sherman, L.W. and Rogan, D.P. (1995b) Effects of gun seizure on gun violence: "Hot spots" patrol in Kansas City. *Justice Quarterly*, 12, 673–94.

Sherman, L.W., Schmidt, J.D. and Velke, R.J. (1992) *High crime taverns: A RECAP project in problem-oriented policing. Final report to the National Institute of Justice.* Washington, DC: Crime Control Institute.

Sloan-Howitt, M. and Kelling, G.L. (1990) Subway graffiti in New York City: "Getting up" vs. "Meaning it and cleaning it." *Security Journal*, 1, 131–6.

Spelman, W. (1993) Abandoned buildings: Magnets for crime? *Journal of Criminal Justice*, 21, 481–95.

Spelman, W. (1995a) Criminal careers of public places. In J.E. Eck and D. Weisburd (eds), *Crime and place* (Vol. 4). Monsey, NY: Criminal Justice Press, 115–44.

Spelman, W. (1995b) Once bitten, then what? Cross-sectional and time-course explanations of repeat victimization. *British Journal of Criminology*, 35, 366–83.

Spelman, W. and Eck, J.E. (1989) Sitting ducks, ravenous wolves, and helping hands: New approaches to urban policing. *Public Affairs Comment*, 35(2), 1–9.

Stanford Research Institute (1970) *Reduction of robbery and assault of bus drivers. Vol. 3. Technological and operational methods.* Stanford, CA: Stanford Research Institute.

Stedman, J. and Weisel, D.L. (1999) Finding and addressing repeat burglaries. In C.S. Brito and T. Allen (eds), *Problem-oriented policing: Crime-specific problems, critical issues and making POP work* (Vol. 2). Washington DC: Police Executive Research Forum, 3–28.

Taylor, G. (1999) Using repeat victimization to counter commercial burglary: The Leicester experience. *Security Journal*, 12(1), 41–52.

Taylor, R.B., Gottfredson, S.D. and Brower, S. (1980) The defensibility of defensible space. In T. Hirschi and M. Gottfredson (eds), *Understanding crime*. Beverly Hills, CA: Sage, 53–71.

Tien, J.M., O'Donnell, V.F., Barnett, A. and Mirchandani, P.B. (1979) *Phase I report: Street lighting projects.* Washington, DC: US Government Printing Office.

Tilley, N. (1993a) *After Kirkholt: Theory, method and results of replication evaluations* (Vol. 47). London: Home Office.

Tilley, N. (1993b) *Understanding car parks, crime and CCTV: Evaluation lessons from safer cities* (Vol. 42). London: Home Office.

Tilley, N. and Hopkins, M. (1998) *Business as usual: An evaluation of the small business and crime initiative* (Vol. 95). London: Home Office.

Tilley, N. and Webb, J. (1994) *Burglary reduction: Findings from safer cities schemes.* (Vol. 51). London: Home Office.

van Andel, H. (1989) Crime prevention that works: The case of public transport in the Netherlands. *British Journal of Criminology*, 29, 47–56.

Wagenaar, A.C. and Holder, H.D. (1991) Effects of alcoholic beverage server liability on traffic crash injuries. *Alcoholism: Clinical and Experimental Research*, 15, 942–7.

Wagner, A.E. (1997) A study of traffic pattern modification in an urban crime prevention program. *Journal of Criminal Justice*, 25(1), 19–30.

Webb, B. (1996) Preventing plastic credit card fraud in the UK. *Security Journal*, 7, 23–5.

Webb, B. and Laycock, G. (1992) *Reducing crime on the London Underground: An evaluation of three pilot projects* (Vol. 30). London: Home Office.

Weidner, R.R. (1997) Target hardening at a New York City subway station: Decreased fare evasion – at what price? In R.V. Clarke (ed.), *Preventing mass transit crime* (Vol. 6). Monsey, NY: Criminal Justice Press, 117–32.

Weisburd, D., Green, L. and Ross, D. (1994) Crime in street level drug markets: A spatial analysis. *Criminologie*, 27, 49–67.

Welsh, B.C. and Farrington, D.P. (1999) Value for money? A review of the costs and benefits of situational crime prevention. *British Journal of Criminology*, 39(3), 345–68.

White, G.F. (1990) Neighborhood permeability and burglary rates. *Justice Quarterly*, 7, 57–67.

Wilkinson, P. (1977) *Terrorism and the liberal state.* New York: John Wiley and Sons.

Wilson, J.Q. and Kelling, G.L. (1982) Broken windows. *Atlantic Monthly*, March, 29–38.

Wilson, J.V. (1990) *Gainesville convenience store ordinance: Findings of fact. Conclusions and recommendations.* Washington, DC: Crime Control Research Corporation.

Wilson, P. (1988) Reduction of telephone vandalism: An Australian case study. *Security Journal*, 1, 149–54.

# 8 Policing for crime prevention

*Lawrence W. Sherman and John E. Eck*[1]

The more police we have, the less crime there will be. While citizens and public officials often espouse that view, others claim that police make only minimal contributions to crime prevention in the context of far more powerful social institutions, like the family and labor markets. The truth appears to lie in between. Whether additional police prevent crime may depend on how well they are focused on specific objectives, tasks, places, times and people. Most of all, it may depend upon putting police where serious crime is concentrated, at the times it is most likely to occur: policing focused on risk factors.

The value of policing focused on risk factors is the most powerful conclusion reached from three decades of research. Simply hiring more police does not prevent serious crime. Community policing without a clear focus on crime risk factors generally shows no effect on crime. But directed patrols, proactive arrests and problem solving at high-crime "hot spots" have shown substantial evidence of crime prevention. Police can prevent robbery, disorder, gun violence, drunk driving and domestic violence, but only by using certain methods under certain conditions.

One of the most striking recent findings is the extent to which the police themselves create a risk factor for crime simply by using bad manners. Modest but consistent scientific evidence supports the hypothesis that the less respectful police are towards suspects and citizens generally, the less people will comply with the law. Changing police "style" may thus be as important as focusing police "substance." Making both the style and substance of police practices more "legitimate" in the eyes of the public, particularly high-risk juveniles, may be one of the most effective long-term police strategies for crime prevention.

This chapter begins with a review of the eight major hypotheses about how the police can prevent crime (Box 8.1). It then describes the varying strength of the scientific evidence on those hypotheses, in relation to the "rigor" of the scientific methods used to test them. The available studies are summarized for both their conclusions and their scientific rigor. The chapter then attempts to simplify these results by answering the questions about what works, what does not, and what's promising. Major gaps in our knowledge are also examined. The chapter concludes with recommendations derived from these findings for both evaluation research and police practices to be developed for evaluation.

**Box 8.1 – Eight major hypotheses about policing and crime**

Other things being equal:

**Numbers of police** The more police a city employs, the less crime it will have.

**Rapid response to emergency calls** The shorter the police travel time from assignment to arrival at a crime scene, the less crime there will be.

**Random patrols** The more random patrol a city receives, the more a perceived "omnipresence" of the police will deter crime in public places.

**Directed patrols** The more precisely patrol presence is concentrated at the "hot spots" and "hot times" of criminal activity, the less crime there will be in those places and times.

**Reactive arrests** The more arrests police make in response to reported or observed offenses of any kind, the less crime there will be.

**Proactive arrests** The higher the police-initiated arrest rate for high-risk offenders and offenses, the lower the rates of serious violent crime.

**Community policing** The more quantity and better quality of contacts between police and citizens, the less crime.

**Problem-oriented policing** The more police can identify and minimize proximate causes of specific patterns of crime, the less crime there will be.

## Varieties of police crime prevention

### Numbers of police

The claim that hiring more police results in less crime is not a "theory" in a truly scientific sense. The idea was developed not as a mathematical equation but as a general "doctrine" of public policy in the heat of democratic debate. The doctrine was based not just on speculation, but also on the apparent results of several "demonstration projects" with some empirical results. These included the court supervised "Bow Street Runners" (Lee, 1901 [1971]; Pringle, 1955) and the privately operated but publicly chartered Thames River "Marine Police" (Stead, 1977). As the level of violence throughout the nineteenth century declined while the number of police increased (Gurr *et al.*, 1977, pp. 93–6, 140), many observers concluded that the more police, the less crime.

### Rapid response to emergency calls

The general form of this claim is that the shorter the police travel time from assignment to arrival at a crime scene, the more likely it is that police can arrest offenders before they flee. This claim is then extended to rapid response producing three crime prevention effects. One is a reduction in harm from crimes interrupted in progress by police intervention. Another, more general, benefit of rapid response time is a greater deterrent effect from the threat of punishment reinforced by response-related arrests. The third hypothesized prevention effect comes from the incapacitation through imprisonment of offenders prosecuted more effectively with evidence from response-related arrests. All of these claims presume, of course, that police are notified during or immediately after the occurrence of a crime. This premise, like the hypotheses themselves, is empirically testable, and its falsification could logically falsify the hypotheses built upon the assumption of its validity.

### Random patrols

Early beat officers were directed to check in at specific places at specific times, with rigid supervision of the prescribed patrol patterns (Reiss, 1992). The increasing emphasis on rapid response to emergency calls in automobiles gradually put an end to directed patrols, allowing officers to patrol at random far beyond their assigned beats. This policy was justified by the theory that unpredictability in patrol patterns would create a perceived "omnipresence" of the police that deters crime in public places. Chicago Police Chief and Berkeley Criminology Dean Orlando W. Wilson (1963, p. 232) was a widely cited proponent of this view. Although he favored the use of police workload analysis to determine how many officers should be assigned to different beats and shifts, modern police practice shows little variation in patrol presence by time and place. Nonetheless, many police chiefs and mayors claim that hiring more officers to patrol in this fashion would reduce crime.

### Directed patrols

Since the advent of computerized crime analysis, however, a far greater precision in the identification of crime patterns has become possible. Police have used that precision to focus patrol resources on the times and places with the highest risks of serious crime. The hypothesis is that the more patrol presence is concentrated at the "hot spots" and "hot times" of criminal activity, the less crime there will be in those places and times. The epidemiological underpinning for this claim is NIJ-funded research showing that the risk of crime is extremely localized, even within high crime neighborhoods, varying widely from one address to another (Pierce, Spaar and Briggs, 1988; Sherman, Gartin and Buerger, 1989).

### Reactive arrests

Like police patrol, arrest practices can be either unfocused or focused on crime-risk factors. Reactive arrests (in response to specific citizen complaints) are like random patrol in that they cast a wide net, warning all citizens that they can be arrested for all law violations at all times. This net is necessarily quite thin. Observations of thousands of police encounters with criminal suspects show that police choose *not* to arrest suspects in the majority of the cases in which there was legal basis to do so (Black, 1980, p. 90; Smith and Visher, 1981, p. 170). The frequent decision not to arrest has been noticed by crime victims' advocacy groups, who argue that more arrests will produce less crime. This hypothesis, like deterrence generally, is expressed at two levels of analysis: the "general" or community-wide, and the "specific" or individual-level. The individual-level hypothesis has been questioned for decades by social scientists, and even some police, who suggest exactly the opposite: that arrest, especially for minor offenses (which are by far the most common), provokes a response from offenders making them more likely to commit future crime than if they had not been arrested.

### Proactive arrests

Like directed patrol, proactive (police-initiated) arrests concentrate police resources on a narrow set of high-risk targets. The hypothesis is that a high certainty of arrest for a narrowly defined set of offenses or offenders will accomplish more than low arrest certainty for a broad range of targets. In recent years the theory has been tested with investigations of four primary high risk targets: chronic serious offenders, potential robbery suspects, drug market places and areas and high-risk places and times for drunk driving. All but the first can be tested by examining the crime rate. The hypothesis about chronic serious offenders is tested by examining the rate at which such offenders are incapacitated by imprisonment from further offending.

Another version of the proactive arrest hypothesis is called "zero tolerance," based on the "broken windows" theory (Wilson and Kelling, 1982). The theory is that areas appearing disorderly and out-of-control provide an attractive climate for violent crime – just as a window with one broken pane attracts more stones than a completely unbroken window. The crime prevention hypothesis is that the more arrests police make (for even petty disorder), the less serious crime there will be (Skogan, 1990).

### Community vs. problem-oriented policing

The hypotheses about community- and problem-oriented policing are less focused than the others, so much so that some observers have even advised against trying to test them (Moore, 1992, p. 128). They both involve far more variations and possible combinations of police activities than the narrow deterrence hypotheses. As in the school- and community-based programs reviewed in Chapters 4 and 5, community and problem-oriented policing are put into practice more like a "stew" of different elements than a single type of "food." Yet it is just this flexibility that proponents hypothesize give them their power. Crime problems vary so widely in nature and cause that effective policing for prevention must vary accordingly, and arguably require many elements to succeed.

While community- and problem-oriented policing are often said to be overlapping strategies (Skogan, 1990; Moore, 1992), they actually have very different historical and theoretical roots. Community policing arises from the crisis of legitimacy after the urban race riots of the 1960s, the proximate causes of which several blue-ribbon reports blamed on police (President's Commission on Law Enforcement and Administration of Justice, 1967; National Advisory Commission on Civil Disorders, 1968). The reports claimed police had lost contact with minority group residents, both by changing from foot patrols to radio cars and by taking a more legalistic approach to law enforcement. In various ways, most notably "team policing" (Task Force Report, 1967; Sherman, Milton and Kelly, 1973), the police were urged to increase their contact with citizens in more positive settings than just responding to emergencies. Thus for almost three decades the Community Policing hypothesis has been that increasing the quantity and quality of police–citizen contact (Kelling, 1988) reduces crime.

Problem-oriented policing, in contrast, arose from the crisis of police effectiveness at crime prevention provoked in the 1970s by some of the very studies reviewed in this chapter. As one of its early sponsors, Gary Hayes (1979), put it, the studies told police chiefs that nothing they were doing – putting more police on the street into random patrols, rapid responses – was working to fight crime. The strategy of problem-oriented policing conceived by Professor Goldstein (1979) provided a new paradigm in which to focus innovation, regardless of any contact with the citizenry. Where the core concept of community policing was community involvement for its own sake, the core concept for problem-oriented policing was *results*: the effect of police activity on public safety, including (but not limited to) crime prevention. Nonetheless, community policing has also been justified by its hypothesized effects on crime, not the least of which has been the rationale for the 100,000 federally funded police officers.

### Community policing

The crime prevention effects of community policing are hypothesized to occur in four major ways.

### Neighborhood watch

This hypothesis justifies one of the most widespread community policing programs, "block watch": increasing volunteer surveillance of residential neighborhoods by residents, which should deter crime because offenders know the neighbors are watching.

### Community-based intelligence

This hypothesis justifies the many community meetings (Sherman *et al.*, 1973) and informal contacts police sought through storefront offices, foot patrol (Trojanowicz, 1986) and other methods: increasing the flow of intelligence from citizens to police about offenses and offenders, which then increases the probability of arrest for crime and the deterrent incapacitative effects of arrest. The increased flow of citizen intelligence can also increase police effectiveness at crime prevention through problem-solving strategies.

### Public information about crime

This hypothesis is just the reverse of the last one: increased flow of police intelligence about crime back to citizens improves citizen ability to protect themselves, especially in light of recent changes in crime patterns and risks.

The latest version of this idea is "reverse 911" (reverse emergency calls) under which police fax out warnings of criminal activity to a list of residential and business fax numbers requesting the service.

### Police legitimacy

Given the historical roots of community policing, perhaps the most theoretically compelling version of its crime prevention hypothesis addresses police legitimacy, or public confidence in the police as fair and equitable (Eck and Rosenbaum, 1994). Recent theoretical and basic research work in "procedural justice" (Tyler, 1990) provides a more scientifically elaborate version of this hypothesis than its proponents in the 1960s intended. The claim is not just that police must be viewed as legitimate in order to win public cooperation with law enforcement. The claim is that a legitimate police institution fosters more widespread obedience of the law itself. Gorer (1955, p. 296) even attributes the low levels of violent crime in England to the example of law-abiding masculinity set by nineteenth-century police, a role model that became incorporated into the "English character." There is even evidence that the police themselves become less likely to obey the law after they have become disillusioned with its apparent lack of procedural justice (Sherman, 1974).

### Problem-oriented policing

Problem-oriented policing offers infinite specific hypotheses about crime prevention, all under this umbrella claim: the more accurately police can identify and minimize proximate causes of specific patterns of crime, the less crime there will be. In recent years this claim has taken two major forms.

### Criminogenic commodities

The more police can remove criminogenic substances from the micro-environments of criminal events, the fewer crimes there will be. This claim arises from the growing emphasis on the causation of criminal events as partly independent of the causation of individual criminality (Hirschi, 1986). Like the theories about preventing crime in places (Chapter 7), the premise is that many crimes require certain preconditions, such as guns or cash or moveable property (Cohen and Felson, 1979).

### Converging offenders and victims

Another precondition of violent criminal events is that victims and offenders must intersect in time and space. A major problem-solving theory of crime prevention is to keep the more basic elements of criminal events from combining: the more police can reduce the intersection of motivated offenders in time and space with suitable targets of crime, the less crime there will be.

## Testing the hypotheses

All of these hypotheses pose formidable challenges to scientific testing. The measurement of crime is difficult under any circumstances, let alone in relation to experiments or natural variation in police practices. Control over police practices is difficult for police administrators under normal conditions, let alone under experimental protocols. Measuring the many dimensions of police activity, from effort to manners, is expensive and often inaccurate. Only a handful of studies have managed to produce strong scientific evidence about any of these hypotheses. But the accumulated evidence of the more numerous weaker studies can also provide some insights on policing for crime prevention.

Police research varies little by *methods* of measurement. In the police evaluation literature, crime is almost always measured either by official crime reports (with all their flaws) or by victimization surveys of the public (with all their costs). Police practices are measured either not at all, through citizen perceptions of those practices, through police records, or (rarely) through direct observation of police patrol activity. It is not clear that any of these methods except the last is superior to any others in drawing valid inferences about the actual practices of the police. Thus the greatest difference across police evaluations lies not in their methods of measurement, but in their basic research designs: the logical structure for drawing conclusions about cause and effect.

Evaluations of police crime prevention generally follow five basic research designs, which can be ranked for overall strength of the inferences they can suggest about cause and effect. These designs are:

1 correlations at the same point in time (e.g. in 1995 the cities with the most police had the most crime);
2 before-and-after differences in crime without a comparison group (e.g. doubling drunk driving arrests was followed by a 50 percent reduction in fatal accidents);
3 before-and-after differences with comparison (e.g. the 50 percent reduction in fatal crashes compared to a 10 percent increase in fatal crashes in three cities of comparable size that did not increase arrests);
4 before-and-after large sample comparisons of treated and untreated groups (e.g. 30 neighborhoods organized for neighborhood watch compared to 30 that were not); and
5 randomized controlled experiments (300 offenders selected by a computerized equal probability program to be arrested had higher repeat offending rates than 300 offenders selected to be given warnings only).

No matter how strong the evaluation research design, the measurement of police activity remains the Achilles heel of police research. Most of the evidence reviewed in this chapter leaves police actions largely unmeasured. This measurement gap leaves all the research open to varying interpretations. The most serious threat of that gap is the confusion of two different kinds of conclusions when programs have no impact on crime: (1) the police activity did not affect crime, and (2) the police did not perform all or sufficient levels of the activity in the first place. Such activity as foot patrol, for example, might show much greater effects on crime than we report here if foot patrols were actually performed. Whether, or how much, foot patrol was actually delivered in the studies we cite remains largely unknown. The only solution to this problem is increased investment in police research, with substantial resources for measuring exactly what police do – and where and when they do it. Only then can we tell the difference between programs that "do not work," and programs that simply "did not happen."

## Scientific evaluations

This section reviews and interprets the reported tests of each of the hypotheses. The discussion attempts to integrate both the scientific score of the various studies and the number of studies converging on the same conclusion. More detailed discussion is offered for some of the major findings, in order to connect the evidence more clearly to the hypotheses. The main concern throughout this section is the cumulative success or failure of the studies in ruling out competing theories in the attempt to provide a conclusive test of each hypothesis.

### Numbers of police

There are two questions one needs to answer when addressing the effect of the numbers of police on crime. The first involves the *absolute effectiveness* of police; would we have more crime if we had no police? The second question involves the *marginal effect* of adding more police to an existing police force; does adding more police have an additional crime prevention effect, over and above what we have already achieved from having a police agency in place?

In principle, we can answer the first question by comparing cities before the addition or subtraction of police forces. Since there are no examples of fully developed metropolitan cities without a police agency suddenly creating a police agency, the answer to this question must be sought using other comparisons. There are several examples of police strikes.[2] Analysis of crime levels before, during and after strikes can show the influence of police agencies on crime. The upper part of Table 8.1 shows that the police strike evidence, while weak in both measurement and design, is fairly consistent in showing the effect of this natural experiment: crime rates skyrocket instantly.

The strongest design is the Makinen and Takala (1980) study of crime in Helsinki before and during a police strike. The Helsinki measures included systematic observation counts of fights in public places, as well as emergency room admissions for assault-related injuries. Both measures rose substantially during the strike despite severe winter weather. The only purportedly negative evidence on this conclusion is the Pfuhl (1983) study of police-recorded crime in eleven American police strikes, in which 89 percent of the "strike" period in the analysis consisted of non-strike days. Both the measure and the definition of the strike period hopelessly confound cause and effect, rendering the study irrelevant to the conclusion reached from the stronger evidence.

*Table 8.1* Numbers of police

| Studies | Scientific methods score | Findings |
|---|---|---|
| **Effects of no police at all** | | |
| Andenaes, 1974 | 2 | 1944: no Danish Police, large robbery and larceny increase |
| Clark, 1969 | 2 | Police strike, major increase in violent and property crime |
| Russell, 1975 | 2 | Same as preceding (Boston) |
| Sellwood, 1978 | 2 | Same as preceding (Liverpool) |
| Makinen and Takala, 1980 | 2 | Same as preceding (Helsinki) |
| Pfuhl, 1983 | 1 | No crime increase during quarters with police strike |
| **Marginal effectiveness of additional police officers** | | |
| Marvell and Moody, 1996 | 1 | Higher police numbers in cities reduce most types of crime |
| Marvell and Moody, 1996 (review of 36 studies of police effect on crime) | 2 | Little evidence that more police reduce crime; weak methods |
| Eck and Maguire, 2000 (review 27 studies of police effect on *violent* crime) | 2 | Little evidence that more police reduce crime; weak methods |

The more police a city employs, the less crime it will have.

None of the strike findings have comparison groups, so in theory it is possible that crimes would have risen dramatically during the strike period even without the strike. The substantial magnitudes of some of the increases, however, greatly exceed typical daily variations in crime in big cities. In the Montreal police strike of 1969, for example, there were 50 times more bank robberies and 14 times more commercial burglaries than average (Clark, 1969). Thus despite the weak research design, the large effect size suggests that abolishing a police force can cause crime to increase.

Whether adding more officers to an already large police force causes crime to decrease, however, is somewhat less clear (bottom half of Table 8.1). Studies of the marginal effect of police and crime suffer from a number of difficulties. First, not only might additional police cause a decline in crime, one might expect additional crime to result in the hiring of more police. This simultaneity effect makes it very hard to sort out what causes what. The second problem is temporal order. When comparing cities with higher and lower levels of policing, we do not know whether the addition of the police in cities with more police preceded or followed their current crime levels. Finally, there is a great deal of measurement error in the counts of police officers and in the crime rates (Eck and McGuire, 2000). Criminologists have tried to address this question for over a quarter of a century, with no consistent result.

A review of 36 correlational studies, most of them weak in research design, found little evidence that more police reduce crime (Marvell and Moody, 1996). A recent review of 27 studies of the effect of police numbers on violent crime (including nine studies not reviewed by Marvell and Moody) came to similar conclusions (Eck and Maguire, 2000). Recent published findings by

Marvell and Moody (1996), Levitt (1997) and Lundman (1997) try to address the simultaneity problem by using longitudinal data and through the use of various time series modeling. At best, they show mixed results for the marginal effect of police numbers on crime.

There are two reasons to be agnostic about these recent findings. First, the history of research on this issue has shown an oscillation between findings of a marginal crime reduction effect and of no effect, as researchers use ever more sophisticated statistical modeling. These models have proven to be highly sensitive to the way the statistical analysis is conducted and which variables are used in the analysis. Until a body of research consistently shows the same result, even when different modeling techniques and variables are used, there is no reason to believe such oscillations will not continue. Second, without a coherent and detailed causal mechanism showing how numbers of police translate into reduced crime, controlling for the way these officers are used, there is no satisfactory way of interpreting a statistical association between police numbers and crime numbers.

The Marvell and Moody (1996, p. 632) analysis gives a tantalizing hint as to how numbers might translate into crime prevention. Their study allows a test of the hypothesis that the prevention benefits of hiring more police officers are greater in higher crime cities than across the country in general. The analysis estimates that for each additional officer added to a police force in a big city, 24 Part 1 (see Chapter 6, note 25) crimes are prevented annually. For each officer hired anywhere in a state, only four Part 1 crimes are prevented. States, on average, have much lower crime rates than the big cities (over 250,000 population); in 1995 the rate of Part I crimes was 8,563 per 100,000 in the big cities, compared to 5,624 per 100,000 across all police agencies. The Marvell and Moody estimate shows that six times as much crime is prevented for each officer added in cities than is added in all places on average. This result is consistent with other studies finding that putting more police in areas and places with high frequencies of crime is far more effective than additional police in low crime areas and places. If larger cities are putting their officers in high crime areas because they have more high crime areas to patrol than do smaller jurisdictions, this would explain Marvell and Moody's findings. It would also suggest that the question of marginal effectiveness cannot be disentangled from the effectiveness of the police deployment strategies. In short, if numbers of police on the payroll matter, they matter only if more police are used where there is more crime.

The evidence for the absolute effectiveness of police is thus weak but consistent: police agencies have a crime prevention effect. The evidence for the marginal effectiveness of adding police officers willy-nilly to police agencies is weak and inconsistent, in the absence of clear indicators of what they do and where they do it.

### Rapid response to emergency calls

One major theory about the crime prevention benefits of hiring more officers is that it reduces police response time. The research on this theory is an excellent example of how different conclusions can result from research results with very different levels of scientific strength. The initial studies of the response time hypothesis produced strong support, suggesting that shaving minutes off response time could lead to the arrest of many more offenders. The extension of this hypothesis into a strategy of policing included the development of emergency call (911) systems to speed victim contact with police radio dispatchers, and the hiring of more police nation-wide in the early 1970s in order to reduce average response times and deter crime through greater certainty of arrest. Only the 1977 NIJ response time analysis in the Kansas City and the NIJ replications in four other cities, were able to call that strategy into question, and open the door to more focused alternatives (Goldstein, 1979).

The original test of the hypothesis was based on a scientifically weak research design, a non-random sample of 265 police responses to citizen calls by the Los Angeles Police Department (Isaacs, 1967) (see Table 8.2). Its results were confirmed by a later study in Seattle (Clawson and Chang, 1977): the probability of arrest per police response increased as police time in travel to the scene decreased. Two other studies (Brown, 1974; Holliday, 1974, as cited in Chaiken, 1978) failed to find that pattern, perhaps because, as Chaiken (1978, p. 130) observes, "the curves are essentially flat for response times larger than three minutes, and therefore a substantial amount of data for responses under three minutes is needed to observe any effect."

The Kansas City (1977) response time analysis took a far more systematic approach to the issue. Its first step was to divide crimes into victim–offender "involvement" (e.g. robbery, assault, rape) and after-the-crime "discovery" categories (e.g. burglary, car theft). It then focused response time analysis on involvement crimes, since the offender would not be present at the discovery crimes. The analysis then divided the involvement crime "response time" into three time periods: crime initiation to calling the police ("reporting time"), police receipt of call to dispatch ("dispatch time"), and "travel time" of police from receipt of dispatch to arrival at the scene. Using systematic observation methods and interviews of victims, the Kansas City study (1977, Vol. 2, p. 39) found that there was no correlation between response-related arrest probability and reporting time once the time exceeded 9 minutes. The average reporting time for involvement crimes is 41 minutes (KCPD 1977, Vol. 2, p. 23). Cutting police travel time for such crime from 5 to 2.5 minutes could require a doubling of the police force, but it would have almost no impact on the odds of making an arrest.

*Table 8.2* Rapid response

The shorter the police travel time from assignment to arrival at a crime scene, the less crime there will be.

| *Studies* | *Scientific methods score* | *Findings* |
|---|---|---|
| Isaacs, 1967 | 1 | Shorter police travel time, more arrests |
| Clawson and Chang, 1977 | 1 | Same as preceding |
| Pate *et al.*, 1976 | 1 | Police travel time unrelated to arrest |
| Kansas City (MO) Police, 1977 | 2 | Same as preceding, most crimes |
| Spelman and Brown, 1981 | 2 | Same as preceding |

Police chiefs in the Police Executive Research Forum (PERF) told NIJ that they did not think citizens in their own communities would take so long to call the police. NIJ responded by commissioning PERF to replicate the citizen-reporting component of the response time analysis in four other cities. Over 4,000 interviews about 3,300 "involvement" crimes produced unequivocal support for the findings of the Kansas City response time analysis (Spelman and Brown, 1981). The probability of arrest in those serious crimes was only 29 per 1,000 reports, with 75 percent of serious crimes being discovered by victims long after the crimes occurred. Of the 25 percent that directly involved the victims, almost half were reported 5 minutes or more after the crime was completed. The findings were consistent across cities, including one that had a 911 system and three that did not.

The conclusion that reduced response time will not reduce crime is based on strong but indirect evidence. The evidence is strong because it is based on sound logical argument, large samples, careful measurement and a replicated research design in five diverse cities showing little variation in arrest rates by police *travel* time, the main factor that tax dollars can affect. It is indirect because an experimental test of the effects of reduced police travel time on city-wide arrest and crime rates has never been conducted. Yet there is neither empirical nor theoretical justification for such an expensive test. Given the strong evidence of citizen delays in reporting involvement crimes, and the small proportion of serious crimes that feature direct victim–offender involvement, further tests of this theory seem to be a waste of tax dollars. Those dollars might be better spent on communicating the findings to the general public, which still puts great priority on police travel time for public safety (Sherman, 1995).

### Random patrols

Another major theory about the benefits of more police is that they can conduct more random patrols. Table 8.3 summarizes the evidence for the police numbers hypothesis tested at the level of uniformed patrols within cities, in non-directed or random patrol patterns. The table shows weak evidence of no effect of moderate variations in numbers or method of patrols. The most famous test of the *random* preventive patrol hypothesis, the Kansas City Preventive Patrol Experiment (Kelling *et al.*, 1974), reveals some of the difficulty in testing this claim. This experiment claimed to have varied the dosage of patrol presence for 1 year across three groups of five randomly assigned beats each, preceded and followed by extensive measures of crime from both household surveys and official records. The results of the experiment showed no statistically significant differences in crime across the three groups.

Many criminologists conclude from this experiment that there is no crime prevention effect of adding patrol presence in a big city, where low density of crime makes the extra patrol a mere drop in the bucket (Felson, 1994). Yet the experiment has been criticized for its failure to measure the actual differences in patrol dosage and the possible lack of them (Larson, 1975), its inadequate statistical power to detect large percentage differences in crime as not due to chance (Fienberg, Larntz and Reiss, 1976), and its failure to assign

*Table 8.3* Random patrol

The more random patrol a city receives, the more a perceived "omnipresence" of the police deters crime in public places.

| Studies | Scientific methods score | Findings |
|---|---|---|
| Kelling *et al.*, 1974 | 3 | No difference in crime by number of police cars assigned |
| Police Foundation, 1981 | 3 | No difference in crime by number of foot patrol assigned |
| Trojanowicz, 1986 | 3 | Foot patrol areas had fewer crimes than controls, but no significance tests reported |

patrol dosage at random (Farrington, 1983). Similar limitations are found in the Newark Foot Patrol Experiment (Police Foundation, 1981), where despite large victimization surveys no crime prevention effects were detected in association with adding or eliminating daytime and early evening foot patrols from selected patrol beats.

The weakness of the evidence is even greater for the one study claiming to find a crime prevention effect from random patrols not focused on crime risks (Trojanowicz, 1986). The design of this study was limited to recorded crime and calls for service, with no victimization surveys. After daytime foot patrols were added to fourteen beats in Flint, Michigan for 3 years, the official crime counts in those beats were down by 9 percent in the foot patrol beats and up 10 percent in the other beats city-wide. Large increases in burglary and robbery in the foot patrol areas were matched by reportedly greater increases in the rest of the city. No significance tests were reported, nor were there any controls for the demographic characteristics of the areas selected for foot patrol compared to the rest of the city. Since the foot patrol areas were not selected at random, it is possible that those areas might have experienced different crime trends even without the foot patrols.

None of the studies are able to distinguish failures of implementation from failures of impact. No systematic observations were made to measure the number of hours of patrol actually delivered. No indirect indicators of patrol time on the street, such as officers' logs, were analyzed to estimate the dosage of patrol presence. Foot patrol in particular is known for difficulty in keeping police out of doors, since there are so many invitations for police to go inside where they can stay warm and dry. Until there is more investment in measuring the amount of visible police patrol, our knowledge of its effects must remain provisional. It must also continue to combine possible failures of implementation with possible failures of impact from well implemented programs.

Nonetheless, there is little evidence that changing the number of officers patrolling beats has a consistent and measurable impact on crime. These results are consistent with the non-experimental studies of the marginal value of adding more police officers to established police forces. As we will see below, where officers are deployed and what they do there is far more important than simply how many are assigned to each beat.

## Directed patrols

The evidence from the *directed* preventive patrol hypothesis is more volumi-
nous, scientifically stronger (in two tests), and consistently in the opposite
direction from the weight of the (weak) evidence on the random patrol
hypothesis. In order to be assigned to this category, the studies had to indicate that they were somehow focused on high-crime places, times or areas. In
the New York City study (Press, 1971, p. 94) (see Table 8.4), for example, the
test precinct was known as a high robbery area, and had over three times as
many robberies per week as each group of five areas in the Kansas City experiment. All eight of the reported tests of the directed patrol hypothesis show
crime reductions in response to increased patrol presence.

The crime prevention effects of extra uniformed patrol in marked police
cars at high crime "peaks" are especially evident in two very different
research designs imposed on one large NIJ study designed to improve upon
the Kansas City Preventive Patrol Experiment. Based on the NIJ-funded
research showing extreme concentrations in spatial and temporal distribu-
tions of crime, the Minneapolis Police Department (MPD) reorganized its
entire patrol force in 1988–9 to test a pattern of directed patrols at hot spots
during hot times. With the unanimous consent of the City Council, the MPD
substantially reduced patrols in low crime areas in order to provide 2 to 3
hours of extra patrol each day during high crime hours at 55 street corner
hot spots. The corners were randomly selected for extra patrols from a carefully compiled list of 110 high crime locations that were visually separate
from each other (Buerger, Petrosino and Cohn, 1995). Both the patrolled
and unpatrolled hot spots were subjected to over 7,000 randomly selected
hours of observations by independent researchers over the course of a year.
The observers recorded every minute of 24,813 instances of police presence

*Table 8.4* Directed patrol

The more precisely patrol presence is concentrated at the "hot spots" and "hot times" of
criminal activity, the less crime there will be in those places and times.

| Studies | Scientific methods score | Findings |
| --- | --- | --- |
| Press, 1971 | 3 | 40% more police, reductions of outdoors crime |
| Chaiken *et al.*, 1975 Chaiken, 1978 | 3 | Police on subways at night, reduced crime |
| Dahman, 1975 | 2 | More police, reductions of outdoors crime |
| Schnelle *et al.*, 1977 | 2 | 400% more patrol, less Part 1 crime |
| Sherman and Weisburd, 1995 | 5 | 100% more patrol, less observed hot spot crime |
| Koper, 1995 | 4 | Longer patrol visits, longer post-visit crime-free time |
| Reiss, 1995 Review: Barker *et al.*, 1993 | 2 | Squad focused on hot spots, where street crime dropped |
| Burney, 1990 | 2 | Saturation patrols, reduced street crime |
| Fritsch, Caeti and Taylor, 1999 | 3 | Undirected saturation patrolling was less effective than truancy and curfew patrolling in curbing gang violence |

in the hot spots, and 4,014 observed acts of crime and disorder (Koper, 1995, p. 656).

Koper's (1995) analysis of the Minneapolis Hot Spots Patrol data found a very strong relationship between the length of each police patrol presence (which averaged 14 minutes) and the amount of time the hot spot was free of crime *after* the police left the scene. The longer the police stayed before they left, the longer the time until the first crime (or disorderly act) after they left. This relationship held for each additional minute of police presence from 1 to 15 minutes, after which the relationship began to reverse. Thus the "Koper curve" in the Minneapolis data suggests the optimum length of a police patrol visit to a hot spot for the purpose of deterring crime is about 15 minutes.

Koper's correlational analysis of all police presences observed in both the extra-patrol and no-extra-patrol hot spots combined is consistent with the results of Sherman and Weisburd's (1995) comparisons of the two groups. The experimental analysis found that there was an average of twice as much patrol presence and up to half as much crime in the extra-patrol hot spots as in the no-extra-patrol group. The observational data showed crime or disorder in 4 percent of all observed minutes in the control group compared to 2 percent in the experimental group (Sherman and Weisburd, 1995, p. 64). Most of the difference in the observed crime was found when police were *not* present in the hot spots. Crime-related calls for service increased for both groups of hot spots over the 1-year experiment as well as city-wide, but the average growth per hot spot was up to three times as great in the no-extra-patrol group (17 percent) as in the extra-patrol group (5 percent) (Sherman and Weisburd, 1995, p. 644).

The retort to these findings is that crime simply moved elsewhere (but see the discussion of displacement in Chapter 7). So, too, can a reduction of crime in one city be questioned on the grounds that offenders may have focused on other jurisdictions. Neither empirical evidence nor theory supports such universal pessimism (Eck, 1993). Routine activity theory (Cohen and Felson, 1979; Felson, 1994) suggests that crime is likely to happen in certain places and times, and not in others, so there are only a limited number of alternatives for offenders. It suggests that if crime is displaced at all, it will be displaced to other hot spots. That argument is still consistent with the experimental–comparison group analysis, given the rising numbers of calls in the experimental year relative to the baseline year. But it does not explain away Koper's cross-sectional analysis of the effects of longer patrol presence on post-patrol crime rates.

Fritsch, Caeti and Taylor (1999) push further the idea of focusing police attention. They examined the effectiveness of saturation patrolling to suppress gang violence. They compared before-and-after results for five high gang violence areas that received the patrols to five comparison areas that received no additional patrols. The target areas had 20 percent greater reductions in crime than the control areas. Most interestingly, in the three target areas with the greatest reductions in crime the saturation patrols were used to enforce truancy and curfew violations. The two target areas with the lowest declines (neither statistically significant) deployed undirected saturation patrols. The authors found only slight spatial displacement. These results suggest that focusing directed patrol on high crime areas is productive, but that it can be made even more productive by having officers use tactics that are problem specific (see problem-oriented policing, below).

In summary, while there is very little empirical support for the effectiveness of adding more police across the board, there is a consistent body of strong scientific support for concentrating police patrols at places and times where crime is the most likely to occur. Patrolling low crime areas is unlikely to improve safety, but more patrolling in high crime places can be effective.

### Reactive arrests

The evidence in support of the reactive arrest hypothesis is remarkably unencouraging at both the community and individual levels of analysis. As a matter of general deterrence, the tests are all fairly weak and generally negative. As a matter of individual deterrence, the results are consistently negative for juveniles, and contradictory for two different groups of domestic assailants, employed and unemployed. The scientific evidence for the latter is among the strongest available in the police literature, while the evidence about juveniles is much weaker. Taken as a whole, these results make a vivid demonstration of the complexity of police effects on crime (see Table 8.5).

The evidence on the *general deterrent* effects of reactive (Reiss, 1971) arrests is based on correlational analyses, with and without temporal order. There is some weak evidence that there is a threshold beyond which the effect of increased arrest rates becomes evident, while no such effect is apparent below the "tipping point" of minimum dosage level (Tittle and Rowe, 1974). This evidence is complicated by the suggestion that the arrest effects are only evident among cities of less than 10,000 people, even with the "tipping point." The finding by Greenberg, Kessler and Logan (1979) and Greenberg and Kessler (1982) of no deterrent effects in big cities throws great doubt on a simple claim of general deterrence. Here again, without focusing arrests on high-risk persons or places, the effects of higher arrest levels may get lost in the many factors causing crime.

The consistent *individual level* evidence of the criminogenic effects of arrests for juveniles is all longitudinal, but only one of the studies is a randomized experiment (Klein, 1986). The other studies are natural observations of the difference in self-reported offending before and after juvenile offenders were arrested. These studies cannot adequately control for the rival hypothesis that the same factors that led to the youth being arrested also caused a higher level of repeat offending. A pattern of "defiance" (Sherman, 1993), for example, would account for both variables and their correlation. The Klein (1986) experiment reported some difficulties in maintaining random assignment, but still managed to make the formal charging of juveniles in police custody a matter of equal likelihood across cases. Holding juvenile characteristics relatively constant, then, Klein found that the more legalistic the processing of a juvenile suspect, the higher the official recidivism rate.[3] In interpreting these results, it is necessary to recall that most juvenile arrests are for fairly minor offenses, and that most juveniles with one police contact never have another (Wolfgang, Figlio and Sellin, 1972). Thus to a certain degree, arresting some juveniles and not others for such offenses may be perceived as arbitrary or procedurally unfair.

*Table 8.5* Reactive arrests

The more arrests police make in response to reported or observed offenses of any kind, the less crime there will be.

| Studies | Scientific methods score | Findings |
|---|---|---|

### General deterrence
The higher the arrest rate per crime for each type of crime in a city, the lower the city's rate of that type of crime

| Studies | Scientific methods score | Findings |
|---|---|---|
| Tittle and Rowe, 1974 | 2 | Cities with higher arrest rates beyond a "tipping point" have less crime, but under tipping point no arrest effects |
| Logan, 1975 | 2 | No correlation of arrest rates and crime across cities |
| Brown, 1978 | 2 | Deterrent effect limited to cities under 10,000 people |
| Greenberg et al., 1979 | 2 | No effect of arrest rates on crime across cities |
| Greenberg and Kessler, 1982 | 3 | No arrest rate effect even when other factors controlled |
| Chamlin, 1988 | 3 | More arrests reduce robberies, not 4 types of property crimes |
| Chamlin, 1991 | 3 | No arrest rate effect for cities over 10,000 |

### Specific deterrence
Individual offenders arrested for an offense are less likely to repeat that offense in the future than offenders who are not arrested.

#### Juvenile offenses

| Studies | Scientific methods score | Findings |
|---|---|---|
| Gold and Williams, 1970 | 2 | Arrested juveniles offend more post-arrest than those not arrested |
| Klein, 1986 | 4 | More formal arrest processing increased recidivism |
| Esbensen, Huizinga 1991 | 2 | Same as preceding |
| and Smith and Gartin, 1989 | 2 | Arrested juveniles offend less post-crime than those not arrested, if they are first offenders; others offend more if arrested |
| Farrington, 1977 | 2 | Arrested juveniles offend more post-arrest than those not arrested |

#### Domestic violence

| Studies | Scientific methods score | Findings |
|---|---|---|
| Sherman and Berk, 1984 | 4 | Arrest reduced recidivism 50% |
| Dunford et al., 1990 | 5 | Arrest had no effect on recidivism at 6 months |
| Dunford, 1992 | 5 | Arrest increased offense frequency at 12 months |
| Dunford, 1990 | 5 | Arrest warrant reduced absent offender recidivism 50% |
| Sherman et al., 1991 | 5 | Arrest had no effect on recidivism at 6 months; short arrest increased recidivism after 12 months |
| Sherman et al., 1992 (Milwaukee) | 4 | Arrest deters employed, criminogenic for unemployed |
| (Omaha) | 4 | Same as preceding |
| Berk et al., 1992a | 5 | Arrest reduced recidivism |
| Berk et al., 1992b | 4 | Arrest deters employed, not unemployed |
| Pate et al., 1991 | 5 | Arrest reduced recidivism |
| Pate and Hamilton, 1992 | 4 | Arrest deters employed, criminogenic for unemployed |
| Hirschel et al., 1990 | 5 | Arrest increases official recidivism |
| Marciniak, 1994 | 4 | Arrest deters in areas of high employment and marriage; increases recidivism in areas of low employment and marriage |

The evidence on the effects of arrest for misdemeanor domestic violence is contradictory across cities but consistent within arrestee characteristics. While three experiments have found some evidence of deterrent effects of arrest (Sherman and Berk, 1984; Pate, Hamilton and Annan, 1991; Berk1992a), three other experiments have found some evidence that arrest increases the frequency of officially detected offending (Sherman *et al.*, 1991; Hirschel *et al.*, 1990; Dunford, 1992). All four of these six experiments for which the data have been analyzed separately by employment status of the offender show consistent results. Arrest increases repeat offending among unemployed suspects while reducing it among employed suspects. Marciniak (1994) has shown that this difference operates even more powerfully at the census tract level than at the individual level, with arrest backfiring irrespective of individual employment status in neighborhoods of concentrated unemployment and single parent households. There is a literature raising concerns about measurement issues in these data (Garner *et al.*, 1995; Fagan, 1996) that are not generally raised about other studies in the police literature. Yet there is no other example in the police literature of six similar randomized experiments all testing similar hypotheses with similar (though not identical) designs. These studies feature a scientific methods score that is twice the mean of all studies classified for this chapter. The consistency of the effects of arrest on crime for employed and unemployed offenders even extends to similarity in effect sizes.

### Proactive arrests

Like the evidence on focused patrol, the evidence on the focused proactive arrest hypothesis is generally supportive across a wide range of studies and research designs. While most of the studies are relatively modest in scientific strength, there are some randomized controlled experiments. With the exception of arrests targeted on drug problems, there appear to be substantial results from focusing scarce arrest resources on high-risk people, places, offenses and times (see Table 8.6).

The evidence on high-risk people comes from two strong (level 4) evaluations of police units aimed at repeat offenders. The Washington, DC unit employed pre-arrest investigations, designed to catch offenders in the act of crime to enhance the strength of evidence. The Phoenix police unit employed post-arrest investigations, designed to enhance the evidence in the offenders' latest case based upon the length and nature of the offender's prior record. Both projects aimed at increasing the incarceration rate of the targeted offenders, and both succeeded. Just how serious or active the offenders were is an important issue in these studies, one that could illuminate future analyses of money invested per crime prevented.

Two weaker studies use national samples of cities to test the effects of police arrest rates for minor offenses on robbery (Wilson and Boland, 1978; Sampson and Cohen, 1988). Both employ multivariate models to control for the effects of some of the other factors that could influence the city's robbery rate. Both find that the higher the per capita rates of traffic arrest, the lower the rates of robbery. One uncontrolled factor in these analyses is the number of pedestrian robbery opportunities. This may be much higher in cities

*Table 8.6* Proactive arrests

The higher the arrest rates for high-risk offenders and offenses, the lower the rates of serious violent crime.[1]

| Studies | Scientific methods score | Findings |
|---|---|---|
| **Repeat offenders** | | |
| Martin and Sherman, 1986 | 4 | Targeted offenders more likely to be arrested and incarcerated (Washington) |
| Abrahamse *et al.*, 1991 | 4 | Post-arrest case enhancement increases odds of arrestees being incarcerated (Phoenix) |
| **Traffic and disorderly conduct arrests** | | |
| Wilson and Boland, 1978 | 2 | Cities with higher arrest rates have less crime |
| Sampson and Cohen, 1988 | 2 | Same as preceding |
| Weiss and McGarrell, 1996 | 3 | Increased traffic tickets, reduced robbery |
| **Drug market areas** | | |
| Kleiman, 1988 (Lynn) | 2 | Crackdown on heroin market, violence down |
| Kleiman, 1988 (Lawrence) | 2 | Crackdown on heroin market, violence up |
| Zimmer, 1990 | 2 | Crackdown on heroin market, violence down |
| Kleiman, 1988 (NYC) | | |
| Sviridoff *et al.*, 1992 | 3 | Crackdown on crack market, violence flat |
| Uchida *et al.*, 1992 (Birmingham) | 3 | Inconsistent changes in violence after arrests up |
| Uchida *et al.*, 1992 (Oakland) | 3 | Buy and bust plus door-to-door, robbery down Each strategy alone, no effect |
| Sherman and Rogan, 1995 | 5 | Raids of crack houses reduced crime for 12 days |
| Weisburd and Green, 1995 | 4 | Crackdowns on hot spots reduced disorder; no effects on violence or property crime |
| Annan and Skogan, 1993 | 3 | Drug crackdown in public housing, no effect on crime |
| **Drunk driving** | | |
| Ross, 1973 (UK) | 2 | Arrests up sharply, drop in crashes decays over time |
| Ross, 1975 (Scandinavia) | 2 | Same as preceding |
| Ross, 1977 (Cheshire 1) | 2 | Same as preceding |
| Ross, 1977 (Cheshire 2) | 2 | Same as preceding |
| Hurst and Wright, 1980 (NZ1) | 2 | Same as preceding |
| Hurst and Wright, 1980 (NZ2) | 2 | Same as preceding |
| Ross *et al.*, 1982 (France) | 2 | Same as preceding |
| Homel, 1993 | 3 | Increased state arrest rate reduced deaths over 10 years, but not in comparable states |
| **Zero tolerance arrests** | | |
| Boydstun, 1975; Sherman, 1990 | 3 | More field interrogations, fewer outdoor crimes |
| Reiss, 1985 | 3 | More police regulation of conduct, fewer "soft" crimes |
| Pate and Skogan 1985; Skogan, 1990 | 3 | Same as preceding |
| Sherman, 1990 | 2 | Disorder crackdown, no robbery reduction |
| Kelling and Coles, 1996 | 2 | Fare-beating, crackdown, robbery reduction in subways |
| Novak *et al.*, 1999 | 3 | No decline in burglary or robbery following proactive disorder enforcement |

where there is less use of automobiles, such as New York City, in which under 3 percent of the US population recently suffered 12 percent of the reported robberies. Since that is the only crime type for which New York is so disproportionate, and since other dense, pedestrian cities like Baltimore and Boston also have high robbery rates, there may be a spurious relationship between traffic enforcement and robbery. That is, the more cars per capita, the fewer robbery opportunities and the more traffic enforcement opportunities.

That is just the kind of limitation in causal inference that experiments can address. Quasi-experimental evidence on this hypothesis was reported by the Hudson Institute study of the Indianapolis Police Department, in which substantial increases in traffic enforcement in a high robbery area were followed by a sharp reduction in robbery (Weiss and McGarrell, 1996).

The evidence on drug crackdowns shows no consistent reductions in violent crime during or after the crackdown is in effect. The strongest evidence is the randomized experiment in raids of crack houses (Sherman and Rogan, 1995), in which crime on the block dropped sharply after a raid. The rapid decay of the deterrent effect in only 7 days, however, greatly reduces the cost-effectiveness of the labor-intensive raid strategy. Only the high yield of guns seized per officer-hour invested (Shaw, 1994) and its possible connection to community gun violence over a longer time period (Sherman, Shaw and Rogan, 1995) showed great cost-effectiveness. Other drug enforcement strategies in open-air markets have even less encouraging results, with the exception of the Jersey City experiment in which the principal outcome measure was disorder, not violence.

The evidence on drunk driving, in contrast, is one of the great success stories of world policing. Despite relatively low scientific method scores, the sheer numbers of consistent results from quasi-experimental evaluations of proactive drunk driving arrest crackdowns suggest a likely cause and effect. The ability of the police to control drunk driving appears to be a direct and linear function of the amount of effort they put into it (Homel, 1990). Since more deaths are caused annually by drunk driving than by homicide, the cost effectiveness of saving lives through enforcement of "driving under the influence" laws may well be far greater than for homicide prevention. The evidence on drunk driving prevention sees far clearer than anyway we know how to have police prevent murders.

The evidence for the *broken windows/zero tolerance arrests* hypothesis (Wilson and Kelling, 1982) is inconsistent and the research designs are only moderately strong. The specific tactics by which this is accomplished can be controversial, and some methods used in the 1982 Newark test have been described in the literature as "unconstitutional" (Skolnick and Bayley, 1985, p.199), including the ordering of loitering teenage males off street corners on the grounds of obstructing traffic. Field interrogations have often been a flash point of poor police-community relations, yet they have also been a favorite crime prevention tactic for police in both the US and Europe. The evidence from both the San Diego field interrogation experiment (Boydstun, 1975) and the Oakland city center study (Reiss, 1985) suggest that it is possible to regulate public behavior in a polite manner that fosters rather than hinders police legitimacy. That possibility, however, is by no means guaranteed. Novak *et al.* (1999) provide evidence that proactive drinking enforce-ment arrests had no discernible impact on crime in the area studied.

The larger concern about zero tolerance is its long-term effect on people arrested for minor offenses. Even while massive arrest increases, such as those in New York City in the mid-1990s, may reduce violence in the short run -- especially gun violence -- they may also increase serious crime in the long run. The negative effects of an arrest record on labor market participa-tion are substantial (Schwartz and Skolnick, 1964; Bushway, 1996). The effects of an arrest experience over a minor offense may permanently lower police legitimacy, both for the arrested person and their social network of family and friends. The criminogenic effect of arrest may make arrestees more defiant (Sherman, 1993) and more prone to anger in domestic viol-ence and child abuse. The data suggest that zero tolerance programs should be evaluated in relation to long-term effects on those arrested, as well as short-term effects on community crime rates. Program development to foster greater legitimacy in the course of making the arrests is also advisable, based on findings from procedural justice research (see hypothesis on police legiti-macy below). This could include, for example, a program to give arrested minor offenders an opportunity to meet with a police supervisor who would explain the program to them, answer questions about why they are being arrested, and give them a chance to express their views about the program while listening respectfully to them. Such innovations would not be expen-sive, but would also pose many testable hypotheses.

Overall, proactive arrests may be effective at preventing crime when they are directed at repeat offenders and when used to reduce drunk driving injuries and fatalities. There is weak evidence that they can reduce violent crime, and conflicting (but generally negative) evidence that they can reduce drug sales. The evidence for zero tolerance of disorder arrests is equivocal.

### Community policing

The results of available tests of the community policing hypotheses are mixed (see Table 8.7). The evidence against the effectiveness of police organizing communities into neighborhood watches is consistent and relat-ively strong. The evidence about the crime prevention benefits of more information flowing from citizens to police is at best only promising. The two tests of police sending more information to citizens are both very strong, but clearly falsify the hypothesis. The tests of increasing police legitimacy are the most promising, especially since they draw on a powerful theoretical perspective that is gaining growing empirical support.

One of the most consistent findings in the literature is also the least well-known to policymakers and the public. The oldest and best known commun-ity policing program, *Neighborhood Watch*, is ineffective at preventing crime. That conclusion is supported by moderately strong evidence, including a randomized experiment in Minneapolis that tried to organize block watch programs with and without police participation in areas that had not requested assistance (Pate, McPherson and Silloway, 1987). The primary problem found by the evaluations is that the areas with highest crime rates

*Table 8.7* Community policing

Increasing the quantity and quality of police–citizen contact reduces crime. Tests of this basic hypothesis omitting measurement of an intervening causal mechanism have been done.

| Studies | Scientific methods score | Findings |
|---|---|---|
| **Neighborhood Watch** | | |
| Lindsay and McGillis, 1986 | 3 | Burglary reduced for 18 months |
| Pate *et al.*, 1987; | 4 | No effect of block watch on crime |
| Skogan, 1990 | | Poorer areas had less surveillance |
| Rosenbaum, Lewis and Grant, 1986 | 3 | Same as preceding |
| Bennett, 1990 | 3 | Same as preceding |
| **Intelligence from citizens to police** | | |
| *Community meetings* | | |
| Wycoff and Skogan, 1993 | 3 | No drop in victimization after increase in police–community meetings in target district |
| Skogan *et al.*, 1995 | 3 | After 18 monthly police–community meetings in each beat in 5 districts, reductions in some crimes and victimization measures but not others |
| *Door-to-door contacts* | | |
| Wycoff *et al.*, 1985; Skogan, 1990 | 3 | Door-to-door police visits; victimization dropped |
| Pate and Skogan, 1985; Skogan, 1990 | 3 | Door-to-door visits and storefront, crime dropped |
| Laycock, 1991 | 3 | Door-to-door visits, burglary down by 62% |
| Sherman *et al.*, 1995 | 3 | Door-to-door visits, no drop in crime |
| Uchida *et al.*, 1992 | 3 | Visits plus Buy and Bust, crime down |
| Uchida *et al.*, 1992 | 3 | Visits alone, no crime reduction |
| Davis and Taylor, 1997 | 5 | Home visits after domestic violence failed to reduce repeat violence |
| *Storefronts* | | |
| Wycoff and Skogan, 1986 | 3 | Storefront open, no drop in victimization |
| Uchida *et al.*, 1992 | 3 | Storefront open, no difference in crime |
| Pate and Skogan 1985; Skogan, 1990 | 3 | (See above under "door-to-door") |
| **Increasing the flow of information from police to citizens** | | |
| Pate *et al.*, 1986 (Newark) | 5 | Monthly newsletter with crime data failed to reduce victimizations of recipients |
| Pate *et al.*, 1986 (Houston) | 5 | Same as preceding |
| Davis and Taylor, 1997 | 5 | Public education about domestic violence failed to reduce violence |
| **Legitimacy** | | |
| Skogan, 1990 (Houston) | 3 | Door knock visits reduced fear of police, reduced crime |
| Tyler, 1990 | 1 | Definition of past police treatment as fair increases expected obedience to law in the future |
| Paternoster *et al.*, 1997 | 2 | Definition of treatment at arrest as fair, lower recidivism in domestic violence |
| Skogan *et al.*, 1995 | 3 | Perceived increased responsiveness of police to community in 4 districts, perceived reduction in serious crime in 3 of those 4 |

are the most reluctant to organize (Hope, 1995). Many people refuse to host or attend community meetings, in part because they distrust their neighbors. Middle-class areas, in which trust is higher, generally have little crime to begin with, making measurable effects on crime almost impossible to achieve. The program cannot even be justified on the basis of reducing middle-class fear of crime and flight from the city, since no such effects have been found. Rather, Skogan (1990) finds evidence that Neighborhood Watch increases fear of crime.

Another popular program for increasing contact between police and public is *community meetings*. The careful NIJ evaluation of the Madison, Wisconsin community policing project in which meetings played a central role found no reduction in crime (Wycoff and Skogan, 1993). A different approach to the meetings in Chicago shows more promise, with the meetings focused much more precisely on specific crime patterns in the area and ideas for what the police should do to attack those problems. While the crime reduction evidence for "community policing, Chicago style" is mixed, it is striking that Chicago has mobilized high crime communities to participate in these meetings (Skogan, 1996). Unlike Neighborhood Watch meetings, the Chicago meetings are held in public places rather than local residences. The best attendance at these meetings for almost 2 years has been found in the police districts with the highest crime rates.

A less popular but often effective community policing practice is *door-to-door visits* by police to residences during the daytime. These visits may be used to seek information, such as who is carrying guns on the street (Sherman, Shaw and Rogan, 1995). The visits may be used to give out information, such as burglary reduction tips (Laycock, 1991) or advice on how to deal with domestic violence (Davis and Taylor, 1997). The visits may be used simply to introduce local police officers to local residents, to make policing more personal (Wycoff *et al.*, 1985). Four out of seven available tests of the door-to-door visits show modestly strong (level 3) evidence of substantial crime prevention. In the NIJ-funded Houston test, for example, the overall prevalence of household victimization dropped in the target area substantially, with no reduction in the comparison area (Wycoff *et al.*, 1985). The prevention effects were primarily for car-break-ins and other minor property crime.

Here again, however, there was a substantial "Matthew effect": the benefits of the program were highly concentrated among white middle-class home-owners, with virtually no benefit for the Asian, Hispanic and African-American minorities living in rental housing in the target area (Skogan, 1990). It may be that door-to-door visits work in very specific circumstances, or for certain kinds of people or areas, but are ineffective as a generic prevention strategy. A major investment in additional research would be needed to say what these specific circumstances might be.

A far more popular program is far less effective. *Police storefronts* are often requested by communities, often staffed during business hours by a mix of sworn police, paid civilians and unpaid volunteers. The evidence from tests of substations in Houston, Newark and Birmingham (Alabama) consistently shows no impact on crime. While there are some positive citizen evaluations associated with storefronts, the problems of staffing the offices once they are open may counterbalance any non-crime benefits.

Increasing the *flow of information* from police to public has been tested in the form of police newsletters. In two randomized experiments, the Newark and Houston police departments found no effect of newsletters on the victimization rates of the households receiving them. The finding was true for both newsletters with and without specific data on recent crimes in the community.

The most promising approach to community policing is also the most theoretically coherent. Based on two decades of laboratory and field studies on the social psychology of "procedural justice," a growing body of research suggests that *police legitimacy* prevents crime. Tyler (1990) finds a strong correlation across a large sample of Chicago citizens between perceived legitimacy of police and willingness to obey the law. The legitimacy was measured by citizen evaluations of how police treated them in previous encounters. This finding is consistent with the Houston door-to-door experiment, in which citizen fear of police after a major scandal over police beating to death a Mexican immigrant was reduced by the door-to-door visits (Wycoff *et al.*, 1985). Community policing Chicago style (Skogan, 1996) also finds the greatest perceived reduction in serious crime in the districts where surveys showed police were "most responsive" to citizen concerns. The most powerful test of this hypothesis is the Paternoster *et al.* (1997) reanalysis of the Milwaukee Domestic Violence Experiment, which found that repeat domestic violence was lowest among arrestees who thought police had treated them respectfully; a powerful effect on recidivism was associated with police simply taking the time to listen to the offender's side of the story. The capacity of police legitimacy to prevent crime is something community policing may well be effective at creating; Skogan's (1994, p.176) review of six community policing evaluations (scientific methods scores = 2 or 3) found every one showed positive or improved perceptions of police in the treated areas.

Still in progress, but with encouraging preliminary results, is the Australian test of *community accountability conferences*. The Australian Federal Police in the Australian capital, Canberra, use this procedure as an alternative to prosecuting juveniles. Only cases in which the offender(s) admit(s) guilt and the victim(s) are willing to attend the conference are eligible. The conference of offenders and victims with their respective families and friends is led by a trained police officer, who focuses the discussion on what happened, what harm it caused and how the harm can be repaired. The officer tries to insure that everyone, especially victims, is allowed to have their say. Sometimes offenders apologize, but always an agreement for repaying the cost of the crime to the victim is reached; failure to do so results in the case being prosecuted. Preliminary findings from subsequent interviews with victims and offenders in a randomized experiment show that the procedure greatly increases respect for police and a perception of justice, regardless of the outcomes (Strang, 1996). This method may turn out to have long-term effects on police legitimacy in the eyes of both juvenile offenders and their families, which could in turn reduce crime, as it did among youthful offenders charged with violent – but not property – crimes in Canberra, and among very young offenders charged with property crimes in Indianapolis (McGarrell *et al.*, 2001).

The interesting point about the Australian model of community policing is that it builds on actual community ties rather than anonymous geographic areas. Moreover, the attendees form a community of concern about the criminal act bringing them together, holding the offender accountable for over an hour to a "village-like" community rather than for a few minutes to a distant and anonymous judge. Of all the approaches to community policing yet tried, this one may have the most focused empowerment of "community" to prevent future crimes.

### Problem-oriented policing

The tests of this hypothesis are generally more positive than the tests of community policing. As Moore (1992) suggests, however, this may be due to a process of selective reporting, in which failures are not included. The most basic problem with testing this very rich and complex hypothesis is that it is essentially about insight, imagination and creativity. The essence of problem-oriented policing as Goldstein (1979) defined it is science itself (Sherman and Strang, 1996): classification, prediction and causation. Evaluations of the scientific method, paradoxically, are not readily susceptible to the scientific method – except in gross comparison to *un*scientific methods. From this perspective, problem-oriented policing embraces all of the other strategies described in this chapter, with the problem to be solved that of crime prevention.

This section reviews some evidence on police efforts to prevent crime that do not fall into the preceding seven hypotheses, and that self-consciously adopted a scientific process that involved police officers in analyzing crime patterns, imagining and creating an intervention, and testing it in the field (see Table 8.8). We divide the problem-oriented policing evaluations into two groups. The first group of studies focuses on problem places (see Chapter 7 for a more extensive review of place-based prevention and its relationship to problem-oriented policing). The second group focuses on removing guns – a crime facilitator – from offenders.

These two categories simply reflect a convergence of police and criminological thinking about the proximate causes of criminal events. There is nothing in the basic problem-oriented policing (POP) strategy (Goldstein, 1979) that requires the use of these two approaches. Many others are possible. If problem-oriented policing succeeds at making scientific research and development the core technology of police work (Reiss, 1992), we may expect that its approaches to crime prevention will evolve with the evolution of knowledge about crime causation.

Much of police work is geographically oriented, so it is not surprising that police problem-solving projects often focus on *hot places*. Five evaluations have been conducted of problem solving at places. With one notable exception they all found substantial and significant reductions in target offenses at the places receiving the treatment, compared to control places.

The exception is the Minneapolis RECAP (REpeat Call Address Policing) experiment. Here, four police officers were unable to implement a broad mix of efforts to separate potential victims and offenders across a sample of 250 target addresses. The YMCA refused to limit access to its lobby during evening hours, the Public Library refused to bar intoxicated persons, public

*Table 8.8* Problem-oriented policing

The more accurately police can identify and minimize proximate causes of specific patterns of crime, the less crime there will be.

| Studies | Scientific methods score | Findings |
|---|---|---|
| **Problem places** | | |
| The more precisely police can focus attention on the characteristics of places that facilitate crime, the fewer crimes there will be. | | |
| Hope, 1994 | 3 | Forced closure or sale of property reduced drug dealing |
| Sherman, 1990; Buerger, 1994 | 5 | Unable to get landlords to restrict offender access |
| Krimmel and Mele, 1998 | 3 | Reduced auto theft following targeting vehicle dump sites |
| Braga et al., 1999 | 5 | Reductions in violent and property crime, disorder and drug selling |
| Mazerolle et al., 2000 | 3 | Reductions in violence and property crime |
| **Reducing gun carrying in public** | | |
| The more police can remove guns from public places or deter people from carrying them in the micro-environments of criminal events, the fewer crimes there will be. | | |
| Sherman et al., 1995 | 3 | Increased gun seizures, reduced gun crimes |
| Kennedy et al., 1996 | 2 | Reduced gun carrying, fewer gun crimes |

housing officials were unable to segregate young "disabled" but predatory alcoholics from elderly co-residents, and private landlords resisted efforts to evict drug dealers (Sherman, 1990; Buerger, 1994). The large volume of the police workload may have made the intervention too weak to have an effect (Buerger, 1994). Case studies of place-focused problem solving generally shows that interventions with landlords can be effective, if the police employ threats of civil remedies (see Chapter 7). Here again, without better measurement of the hours and nature of police problem-solving activity, it is difficult to distinguish failures to implement problem-solving from failures of problem-solving efforts to prevent crime.

The evidence on *gun carrying* is also strong. In the NIJ Kansas City Gun Experiment, police focused traffic enforcement and field interrogations on gun crime hot spots during hot times (Sherman, Shaw and Rogan, 1995). With special training in the detection of carrying concealed weapons, police focused on seizing illegally carried weapons. Gun seizures in the target area rose by 60 percent, and gun crimes dropped by 49 percent. A similar area in a different part of town showed no change in either guns seized or gun crimes. In Boston, police have used a mix of strategies to discourage gun carrying in public places among juveniles, especially gang members and probationers. Qualitative evidence from an NIJ project suggests gun carrying by the high-risk groups has been substantially reduced, while early quantitative evidence shows an elimination of juvenile gun homicide (Kennedy, Piehl and Braga, 1996). In Indianapolis, increased efforts to get guns off the streets reduced gun crime as well (McGarrell et al., 2001).

The evidence on problem-solving efforts focused on *alcohol* and *prostitution* is also encouraging, and was presented in Chapter 7 in the discussions of taverns, bars, traffic barriers and street closures.

In summary, we can state that there is considerable evidence based on strong evaluations that problem-oriented policing is an effective way to reduce crime. The evidence available addresses problem solving focusing on places or firearms, and we lack similar evaluations of problem-solving projects using other approaches. But the principle is sound conceptually.

## Conclusions

For all of its scientific limitations, the evidence shows substantial consistency on a number of the hypotheses, and some tentative conclusions on others. All science, of course, is provisional, with better research designs or theories revealing previously undiscovered patterns. It is no small achievement that police crime prevention research has developed to the point of having reached some conclusions to discard.

The available evidence supports two major conclusions about policing for crime prevention. One is that the effects of police on crime are complex, and often surprising. The other is that the more focused the police strategy, the more likely it is to prevent crime. The first conclusion follows from the findings that arrests can sometimes increase crime, that traffic enforcement may reduce robbery and gun crime, that the optimal deterrent effect of a police patrol may be produced by 15 minutes of presence in a hot spot, and that prevention effects generally fade over time without modification and renewal of police practices. The second conclusion follows from the likely failure to achieve crime prevention merely by adding more police or shortening response time across the board.

The substantial array of police strategies and tactics for crime prevention (Reiss, 1995) has a small but growing evaluation literature. Using the standard of at least two consistent findings from level 3 scientific methods score (well-measured, before-after studies with a comparison group) *and* a preponderance of the other evidence in support of the same conclusion, the research shows several practices to be supported by strong evidence of effectiveness, and several with strong evidence of ineffectiveness.

### What works

- increased directed patrols in street-corner hot spots of crime
- proactive arrests of serious repeat offenders
- proactive drunk driving arrests
- arrests of employed suspects for domestic assault
- problem-oriented policing

### What does not work

- neighborhood block watch
- arrests of some juveniles for minor offenses
- arrests of unemployed suspects for domestic assault

- drug market arrests
- community policing with no clear crime-risk factor focus
- adding extra police to cities, regardless of assignment or activity

Several other strategies fail to meet the test of strong evidence for generalizable effectiveness, but merit much more research and development because of encouraging findings in the initial research.

*What is promising*

- police traffic enforcement patrols against illegally carried handguns
- community policing with community participation in priority setting
- community policing focused on improving police legitimacy
- warrants for arrest of suspect absent when police respond to domestic violence

Notably absent from these findings, however, are many topics of great concern to police. Police recreation activities with juveniles, such as Police Athletic Leagues, also remain unevaluated. Automated identification systems, in-car computer terminals, and a host of other new technologies costing billions of dollars remain unevaluated for their impact on crime prevention. There is clearly a great deal of room for further testing of hypotheses not listed here due to the absence of available scientific evidence.

## Notes

1   We want to give special thanks to Lisa Growette for her assistance in this effort. Another special debt of gratitude is owed our fellow editors and chapter writers for their extreme patience, and particularly Brandon Welsh for his persistence against great odds. Needless to say, all errors in this chapter are ours.
2   And, in one case, the arrest of the entire Copenhagen police force by the Nazis in 1944, which was equivalent to a strike because the occupying German army did nothing to enforce civilian criminal laws before or after arresting the police (Andenaes, 1974).
3   There was no difference in the self-reported offending data, but only 60 percent of the offenders gave follow-up interviews.
4   Given the potential for vehicular homicide attached to drunk driving, that offense is included here in the definition of violent crime. It would not, however, be classified that way for most other purposes.

## References

Abrahamse, Allan F., Patricia A. Ebener, Peter W. Greenwood, Nora Fitzgerald and Thomas E. Kosin (1991) An experimental evaluation of the phoenix repeat offender program. *Justice Quarterly*, 8, 141–68.

Andenaes, Johannes (1974) *Punishment and deterrence*. Ann Arbor, MI: University of Michigan Press.

Annan, Sampson and Skogan, Wesley (1993) *Drug enforcement in public housing: Signs of success in Denver*. Washington, DC: Police Foundation.

Barker, M., Geraghty, J., Webb, B. and Key, T. (1993) The prevention of street robbery. Police Research Group Crime Prevention Series Paper No. 44. London: Police Department, Home Office.

Bennett, Trevor (1990) *Evaluating Neighborhood Watch.* Basingstoke: Gower.

Berk, Richard A., Alec Campbell, Ruth Klap and Bruce Western (1992a) A Bayesian analysis of the Colorado spouse abuse experiment. *Journal of Criminal Law and Criminology*, 83, 170–200.

Berk, Richard A., Alec Campbell, Ruth Klap and Bruce Western (1992b) The deterrent effect of arrest in incidents of domestic violence: A Bayesian analysis of four field experiments. *American Sociological Review*, 57, 698–708.

Black Donald (1980) *The manners and customs of the police.* NY: Academic Press.

Boydstun, John (1975) *The San Diego Field Interrogation Experiment.* Washington, DC: Police Foundation.

Braga, Anthony A., David L. Weisburd, Elin J. Waring, Lorraine Green Mazerolle, William Spelman and Francis Gajewski (1999) Problem-oriented policing in violent crime places: A randomized controlled experiment. *Criminology*, 37(3), 541–80.

Brown, Don W. (1974) Evaluation of police patrol operations. Unpublished M.A. Thesis, University of Ottawa.

Brown, Don W. (1978) Arrests and crime rates: When does a tipping effect occur? *Social Forces*, 57, 671–82.

Buerger, Michael E. (ed.) (1994) *The crime prevention casebook: Securing high crime locations.* Washington, DC: Crime Control Institute.

Buerger, Michael E., Anthony Petrosino and Ellen G. Cohn (1995) Hot spots of crime: Operationalizing theoretical concepts for field research. In John Eck and David Weisburd (eds), *Crime and place.* Monsey, N.Y.: Criminal Justice Press, 237–58.

Burney, E. (1990) *Putting street crime in its place: A report to the Community/Police Consultative Group for Lambeth.* London: Goldsmith's College.

Bushway, Shawn (1996) The impact of a criminal history record on access to legitimate employment. PhD Dissertation, H. John Heinz School of Public Policy and Management, Carnegie Mellon University.

Chaiken, Jan M. (1978) What is known about deterrent effects of police activities. In James A. Cramer (ed.), *Preventing crime.* Beverly Hills, CA: Sage Publications.

Chaiken, Jan M., M. Lawless and K. Stevenson (1975) The impact of police activity on crime: Robberies on the New York City Subway System. *Urban Analysis*, 3, 173–205.

Chamlin, Mitchell (1988) Crimes and arrest: An autoregressive integrated moving average (ARIMA) approach. *Journal of Quantitative Criminology*, 4, 247–58.

Chamlin, Mitchell (1991) A longitudinal analysis of the arrest–crime relationship: A further examination of the tipping effect. *Justice Quarterly*, 8, 187–99.

Clark, Gerald (1969) What happens when the police go on strike. *New York Times Magazine*, Nov. 16, sec. 6, pp. 45, 176–85, 187, 194–5.

Clawson, C. and S.K. Chang (1977) The relationship of response delays and arrest rates. *Journal of Police Science and Administration*, 5, 53–68.

Cohen, Lawrence and Marcus Felson (1979) Social change and crime rate trends: A routine activities approach. *American Sociological Review*, 44, 588–607.

Dahman, J.S. (1975) *Examination of police patrol effectiveness.* McLean, Va.: Mitre Corporation.

Davis, Robert C. and Bruce G. Taylor (1997) A proactive response to family violence: The results of a randomized experiment. *Criminology*, 35(2), 307–33.

Dunford, Franklyn W. (1990) System-initiated warrants for suspects of misdemeanor domestic assault: A pilot study. *Justice Quarterly*, 7, 631–53.

Dunford, Franklyn W. (1992) The measurement of recidivism in cases of spouse assault. *Journal of Criminal Law and Criminology*, 83, 120–36.

Dunford, Franklyn W., David Huizinga and Delbert S. Elliott (1990) The role of arrest in domestic assault: The Omaha Police Experiment. *Criminology*, 28, 183–206.

Eck, John E. (1993) The threat of crime displacement. *Criminal Justice Abstracts*, 25, 527–46.

Eck, John and Edward Maguire (2000) Have changes in policing reduced violent crime? An assessment of the evidence. In Alfred Blumstein and Joel Wallmann (eds), *The crime drop in America*. New York: Cambridge University Press, 207–65.

Eck, John E. and Dennis Rosenbaum (1994) The new police order: Effectiveness, equity and efficiency in community policing. In Dennis Rosenbaum (ed.), *The challenge of community policing: Testing the promises*. Thousand Oaks: Sage.

Esbensen, F.A. and Huizinga, D. (1991) Juvenile victimization and delinquency. *Youth and Society*, 23, 202–28.

Fagan, Jeffrey (1996) *The criminalization of domestic violence: Promises and limits*. Research Report. Washington, DC: National Institute of Justice.

Farrington, David P. (1977) The effects of public labeling. *British Journal of Criminology*, 17, 112–25.

Farrington, David P. (1983) Randomized experiments on crime and justice. In Michael Tonry and Norval Morris (eds), *Crime and justice: An annual review of research*. Chicago: University of Chicago Press.

Felson, Marcus (1994) *Crime and everyday life*. Thousand Oaks, CA: Pine Forge Press.

Fienberg, Stephen E., Kinley Larntz and Albert J. Reiss, Jr. (1976) Redesigning the Kansas City Preventive Patrol Experiment. *Evaluation*, 3, 124–31.

Fritsch, Eric J., Tory J. Caeti and Robert W. Taylor (1999) Gang suppression through saturation patrol, aggressive curfew, and truancy enforcement: A quasi-experimental test of the Dallas anti-gang initiative. *Crime and Delinquency*, 45(1), 122–39.

Garner, Joel, Jeffrey Fagan and Christopher D. Maxwell (1995) Published findings from the NIJ spouse assault replication program: A critical review. *Journal of Quantitative Criminology*, 8, 1–29.

Gold, Martin and Jay Williams (1970) National study of the aftermath of apprehension. *Prospectus*, 3, 3–12.

Goldstein, Herman (1979) Improving policing: A problem-oriented approach. *Crime and Delinquency*, 25, 236–58.

Gorer, Geoffrey (1955) *Exploring English character*. London: Cresset.

Greenberg, David and Ronald C. Kessler (1982) The effects of arrests on crime: A multivariate panel analysis. *Social Forces*, 60, 771–90.

Greenberg, David F., Ronald C. Kessler and Charles H. Logan (1979) A panel model of crime rates and arrest rates. *American Sociological Review*, 44, 843–50.

Gurr, Ted Robert, Peter N. Grabosky and Richard C. Hula (1977) *The politics of crime and conflict: A comparative history of four cities*. Beverly Hills, CA: Sage.

Hayes, Gary (1979) Personal communication with the first author.

Hirschel, David, Ira W. Hutchison III, Charles W. Dean, Joseph J. Kelley and Carolyn E. Pesackis (1990) *Charlotte Spouse Assault Replication Project: Final report*. Charlotte, NC: University of North Carolina at Charlotte.

Hirschi, Travis (1986) On the compatibility of rational choice and social control theories of crime. In Derek B. Cornish and Ronald V. Clarke (eds), *The reasoning criminal*. NY: Springer-Verlag, 105–18.

Holliday, L.P. (1974) A methodology for radio car planning. Unpublished Ms., New York City RAND Institute.

Homel, Ross (1990) Random breath testing and random stopping programs in Australia. In R.J. Wilson and R. Mann (eds), *Drinking and driving: Advances in research and prevention*. NY: Guilford Press.

Homel, Ross (1993) Reference supplied upon request.

Hope, T. (1994) Problem-oriented policing and drug-market locations: Three case studies. In R.V. Clarke (ed.), *Crime prevention studies: Volume 2.* Monsey, New York: Criminal Justice Press, 5–32.

Hope, Tim (1995) Community crime prevention. In Michael Tonry and David P. Farrington (eds), *Building a safer society. Crime and justice*, Vol. 19. Chicago: University of Chicago Press.

Hurst, P. and P. Wright (1980) Deterrence at last: The Ministry of Transport's alcohol blitzes. Paper Presented to the Eighth International Conference on Alcohol, Drugs and Traffic Safety, Stockholm.

Isaacs, H. (1967) A study of communications, crimes and arrests in a metropolitan police department. Task force report: Science and technology, a report to the president's commission on law enforcement and administration of justice. Washington, DC: USGPO.

Kansas City, Missouri Police Department (1977) *Response time analysis.* Kansas City, MO: MPD.

Kelling, George L. (1988) Community policing. Presentation to the Executive Sessions on the Police, Kennedy School of Government, Harvard University.

Kelling, George L. and Catherine M. Coles (1996) *Fixing broken windows: Restoring order and reducing crime in our communities.* NY: Free Press.

Kelling, George L., Antony M. Pate, Duane Dieckman and Charles Brown (1974) *The Kansas City Preventive Patrol Experiment: Technical report.* Washington, DC: Police Foundation.

Kennedy, David M., Anne M. Piehl and Anthony A. Braga (1996) Youth violence in Boston: Gun markets, serious youth offenders, and a use-reduction strategy. *Law and Contemporary Problems*, 59, 147–96.

Kleiman, Mark (1988) Crackdowns: The effects of intensive enforcement on retail heroin dealing. In Marcia Chaiken (ed.), *Street-level drug enforcement: Examining the issues.* Washington, DC: National Institute of Justice.

Klein, Malcolm (1986) Labeling theory and delinquency policy: An empirical test. *Criminal Justice and Behavior*, 13, 47–79.

Koper, Christopher (1995) Just enough police presence: Reducing crime and disorderly behavior by optimizing patrol time in crime hot spots. *Justice Quarterly*, 12, 649–72.

Krimmel, John T. and Marie Mele (1998) Investigating stolen vehicle dump sites: An interrupted time series quasi-experiment. *Policing: An International Journal of Police Strategies and Management*, 21(3), 479–89.

Larson, Richard (1975) What happened to patrol operations in Kansas City. *Journal of Criminal Justice*, 3, 299–330.

Laycock, Gloria (1991) Operation identification, or the power of publicity? *Security Journal*, 2, 67–72.

Lee, W.L. Melville (1901) [1971] *A history of police in England.* Montclair, NJ: Patterson-Smith.

Levitt, Steven D. (1997) Using electoral cycles in police hiring to estimate the effect of police on crime. *American Economic Review*, 87(3), 270–91.

Lindsay, Betsy and Daniel McGillis (1986) Citywide community crime prevention: An assessment of the Seattle program. In Dennis Rosenbaum (ed.), *Community crime prevention: Does it work?* Beverly Hills, CA: Sage.

Logan, Charles H. (1975) Arrest rates and deterrence. *Social Science Quarterly*, 56, 376–89.

Lundman, Richard (1997) Police levels and crime: Additional evidence. Paper presented at the annual meeting of the American Society of Criminology, November 22, San Diego.

McGarrell, E., S. Chermak, A. Weiss and J. Wilson (2001) Reducing firearms violence through directed police patrol. *Criminology and Public Policy*, 1(1), 119–48.

Makinen, Tuija and Hannu Takala (1980) The 1976 police strike in Finland. *Scandinavian Studies in Criminology*, 7, 87–106.

Marciniak, Elizabeth (1994) Community policing of domestic violence: Neighborhood differences in the effect of arrest. PhD Dissertation, University of Maryland.

Martin, Susan and Lawrence Sherman (1986) Selective apprehension: A police strategy for repeat offenders. *Criminology*, 24, 55–72.

Marvell, Thomas B. and Carlisle E. Moody (1996) Specification problems, police levels and crime rates. *Criminology*, 34, 609–46.

Mazerolle, Lorraine Green, Justin Ready, William Terrill and Elin Waring (2000) Problem-oriented policing in public housing: The Jersey City evaluation. *Justice Quarterly*, 17(1), 129–58.

Moore, Mark (1992) Problem-solving and community policing. In Michael Tonry and Norval Morris (eds), *Modern policing. Crime and justice*, Vol. 15. Chicago: University of Chicago Press.

National Advisory Commission on Civil Disorders (1968) *Report*. NY: Bantam Books.

Novak, Kenneth, Jennifer L. Hartman, Alexander M. Holsinger and Michael G. Turner (1999) The effects of aggressive policing of disorder on serious crime. *Policing: An International Journal of Police Strategies and Management*, 22(2), 171–90.

Pate, Antony M. and Edwin E. Hamilton (1992) Formal and informal deterrents to domestic violence: The Dade County Spouse Assault Experiment. *American Sociological Review*, 57, 691–8.

Pate, Antony, Edwin E. Hamilton and Sampson Annan (1991) *Metro-Dade Spouse Abuse Replication Project: Draft final report*. Washington, D.C.: Police Foundation.

Pate, Antony, Amy Ferrara, Robert A. Bowers and Jon Lorence (1976) *Police response time: Its determinants and effects*. Washington, DC: Police Foundation.

Pate, Antony M., Marlys McPherson and Glenn Silloway (1987) *The Minneapolis Community Crime Prevention Experiment: Draft evaluation report*. Washington, DC: Police Foundation.

Pate, Antony M. and Wesley Skogan (1985) *Coordinated community policing: The Newark experience. Technical report*. Washington, DC: Police Foundation.

Pate, Antony M., M.A. Wycoff, W.G. Skogan and L.W. Sherman (1986) *Reducing fear of crime in Houston and Newark: A summary report*. Washington, DC: Police Foundation.

Paternoster, Raymond, Bobby Brame, Ronet Bachman and Lawrence W. Sherman (1997) Do fair procedures matter? The effect of procedural justice on spouse assault. *Law and Society Review*, 31, 163–204.

Pfuhl, Erdwin H., Jr. (1983) Police strikes and conventional crime: A look at the data. *Criminology*, 21, 489–503.

Pierce, Glenn, Susan A. Spaar and LeBaron Briggs, IV. (1988) The character of police work: Strategic and tactical implications. Unpublished Ms., Northeastern University, Center for Applied Social Research.

Police Foundation (1981) *The Newark Foot Patrol Experiment*. Washington, DC: Police Foundation.

President's Commission on Law Enforcement and Administration of Justice (1967) *The challenge of crime in a free society*. Washington, DC: USGPO.

Press, S.J. (1971) *Some effects of an increase in police manpower in the 20th Precinct of New York City*. NY: New York City RAND Institute.

Pringle, Patrick (1955) *Hue and cry: The birth of the British police*. London: Museum Press.

Reiss, Albert J. Jr. (1971) *The police and the public.* New Haven: Yale University Press.

Reiss, Albert J. Jr. (1985) *Policing a city's central district: The Oakland story.* Washington, DC: National Institute of Justice.

Reiss, Albert J. Jr. (1992) Police organization in the twentieth century. In Michael Tonry and Norval Morris (eds), *Modern policing. Crime and justice,* Vol. 15. Chicago: University of Chicago Press.

Reiss, Albert J. Jr. (1995) The role of the police in crime prevention. In P.-O. Wikstrom, R.V. Clarke and J. McCord (eds), *Integrating crime prevention strategies: Propensity and opportunity.* Stockholm: National Council for Crime Prevention.

Rosenbaum, Dennis, Dan A. Lewis and Jane A. Grant (1986) Neighborhood-based crime prevention: Assessing the efficacy of community organizing in Chicago. In Dennis Rosenbaum (ed.), *Community crime prevention: Does it work?* Beverly Hills, CA: Sage.

Ross, H. Laurence (1973) Law, science and accidents: The British Road Safety Act of 1967. *Journal of Legal Studies,* 2, 1–78.

Ross, H. Laurence (1975) The Scandinavian myth: The effectiveness of drinking-and-driving legislation in Sweden and Norway. *Journal of Legal Studies,* 4, 285–310.

Ross, H. Laurence (1977) Deterrence regained: The Cheshire Constabulary's "Breathalyser Blitz." *Journal of Legal Studies,* 6, 241–9.

Ross, H. Laurence (1992) *Confronting drunk driving: Social policy for saving lives.* New Haven: Yale University Press.

Ross, H. Laurence, R. McCleary and T. Epperlein (1982) Deterrence of drinking and driving in France: An evaluation of the law of July 12, 1978. *Law and Society Review,* 17, 241–9.

Russell, Francis (1975) *A city in terror: 1919 – the Boston police strike.* New York: Viking.

Sampson, Robert and Jacqueline Cohen (1988) Deterrent effects of police on crime: A replication and theoretical extension. *Law and Society Review,* 22, 163–89.

Schnelle, J.F., R.E. Kirchner, Jr., J.D. Casey, P.H. Uselton Jr. and M.P. McNees (1977) Patrol evaluation research: A multiple-baseline analysis of saturation police patrolling during day and night hours. *Journal of Applied Behavioral Analysis,* 10, 33–40.

Schwartz, D. and J. Skolnick (1964) Two studies of legal stigma. In H. Becker (ed.), *The other side: Perspectives of deviance.* New York: Free Press.

Sellwood, A.V. (1978) *Police strike – 1919.* London: W.H. Allen.

Shaw, James W. (1994) Community policing against crime: Violence and firearms. PhD dissertation, University of Maryland at College Park.

Sherman, Lawrence W. (1974) Becoming bent. In Lawrence W. Sherman (ed.), *Police corruption: A sociological perspective.* NY: Anchor-Doubleday.

Sherman, Lawrence W. (1990) Police crackdowns: Initial and residual deterrence. In Michael Tonry and Norval Morris (eds), *Crime and justice: A review of research,* Vol. 12. Chicago: University of Chicago Press.

Sherman, Lawrence W. (1993) Defiance, deterrence, and irrelevance: A theory of the criminal sanction. *Journal of Research in Crime and Delinquency,* 30, 445–73.

Sherman, Lawrence W. (1995) The police. In James Q. Wilson and Joan Petersilia (eds), *Crime.* San Francisco: ICS Press.

Sherman, Lawrence W. and Richard A. Berk (1984) The specific deterrent effects of arrest for domestic assault. *American Sociological Review,* 49, 261–72.

Sherman, Lawrence W., Patrick R. Gartin and Michael E. Buerger (1989) Hot spots of predatory crime: Routine activities and the criminology of place. *Criminology,* 27, 27–55.

Sherman, Lawrence W., Catherine H. Milton and Thomas Kelly (1973) *Team policing: Seven case studies.* Washington, DC: Police Foundation.

Sherman, Lawrence and Dennis P. Rogan (1995) Deterrent effects of police raids on crack houses: A randomized, controlled experiment. *Justice Quarterly*, 12, 755–81.

Sherman, Lawrence W., Janell D. Schmidt, Dennis P. Rogan, Patrick R. Gartin, Ellen G. Cohn, Dean J. Collins and Anthony R. Bacich (1991) From initial deterrence to long-term escalation: Short-custody arrest for poverty ghetto domestic violence. *Criminology*, 29, 821–50.

Sherman, Lawrence W., Janell D. Schmidt, Dennis P. Rogan, Patrick R. Gartin, Ellen G. Cohn, Dean J. Collins and Anthony R. Bacich (1992) The variable effects of arrest on criminal careers: The Milwaukee Domestic Violence Experiment. *Journal of Criminal Law and Criminology*, 83, 137–69.

Sherman, Lawrence W., James W. Shaw and Dennis P. Rogan (1995) *The Kansas City Gun Experiment: Research in brief.* Washington, DC: National Institute of Justice.

Sherman, Lawrence W. and Heather Strang (1996) Policing domestic violence: The problem-solving paradigm. Paper presented to the Conference on Problem-Oriented Policing as Crime Prevention, Stockholm, Swedish National Police College.

Sherman, Lawrence and David A. Weisburd (1995) General deterrent effects of police patrol in crime "hot spots": A randomized, controlled trial. *Justice Quarterly*, 12, 625–48.

Skogan, Wesley (1990) *Disorder and decline.* New York: Free Press.

Skogan, Wesley (1994) The impact of community policing on neighborhood residents: A cross-site analysis. In Dennis Rosenbaum (ed.), *The challenge of community policing: Testing the promises.* Thousand Oaks: Sage.

Skogan, Wesley *et al.* (1995) *Community policing in Chicago, year two.* Chicago: Illinois Criminal Justice Information Authority.

Skogan, Wesley (1996) *Community policing in Chicago, year three.* Chicago: Illinois Criminal Justice Information Authority.

Skolnick, Jerome and David Bayley (1985) *The new blue line.* NY: Free Press.

Smith, Douglas and Visher, Christy (1981) Street-level justice: Situational determinants of police arrest decisions. *Social Problems*, 29, 167–78.

Smith, Douglas and Patrick R. Gartin (1989) Specifying specific deterrence: The influence of arrest on future criminal activity. *America Sociology Review*, 54, 94–106.

Spelman, William and Brown, Dale K. (1981) *Calling the police: A replication of the citizen reporting component of the Kansas City response time analysis.* Washington, DC: Police Executive Research Forum.

Stead, Philip John (1977) Patrick Colquhoun. In Philip John Stead (ed.), *Pioneers in policing.* Montclair, NJ: Patterson-Smith.

Strang, Heather (1996) Shaming conferences: Community policing and the victim's perspective. Paper presented at the 48th Annual Meeting of the American Society of Criminology, November 20–23, 1996, Chicago.

Sviridoff, Michelle, S. Sadd, R. Curtis and R. Grinc (1992) *The neighborhood effects of street-level drug enforcement: Tactical narcotics teams in New York.* NY: Vera Institute of Justice.

Task Force Report (1967) *The police. A report to the President's Commission on Law Enforcement and Administration of Justice.* Washington, DC: USGPO.

Tittle, Charles R. and Alan R. Rowe (1974) Certainty of arrest and crime rates: A further test of the deterrence hypothesis. *Social Forces*, 52, 455–62.

Trojanowicz, Robert (1986) Evaluating a neighborhood foot patrol program: The Flint, Michigan Project. In Dennis Rosenbaum (ed.), *Community crime prevention: Does it work?* Beverly Hills, CA: Sage.

Tyler, Tom (1990) *Why people obey the law.* New Haven: Yale University Press.

Uchida, Craig D., Brian Forst and Sampson O. Annan (1992) *Modern policing and the control of illegal drugs: Testing new strategies in two American cities. Research report.* Washington, DC: National Institute of Justice.

Weisburd, D. and Green, L. (1995) Policing drug hot spots: The Jersey City Drug Market Analysis Experiment. *Justice Quarterly*, 12, 711–36.

Weiss, Alex and Edmund McGarrell (1996) Paper presented to the American Society of Criminology, Chicago, November.

Wilson, James Q. and Barbara Boland (1978) The effect of the police on crime. *Law and Society Review*, 12, 367–90.

Wilson, James Q. and George L. Kelling (1982) Broken windows: The police and neighborhood safety. *Atlantic Monthly*, 249, 29–38.

Wilson, O.W. (1963) *Police administration.* NY: McGraw-Hill.

Wolfgang, Marvin, Robert Figlio and Thorsten Sellin (1972) *Delinquency in a birth cohort.* Chicago: University of Chicago Press.

Wycoff, Mary Ann, Antony M. Pate, Wesley Skogan and Lawrence W. Sherman (1985) *Citizen contact patrol in Houston: Executive summary.* Washington, DC: Police Foundation.

Wycoff, Mary Ann and Wesley Skogan (1993) *Community policing in Madison: Quality from the inside out. An evaluation of implementation and impact. Research report.* Washington, DC: National Institute of Justice.

Zimmer, Lynn (1990) Proactive policing against street-level drug trafficking. *American Journal of Police*, 11, 43–74.

# 9 Reducing the criminal activities of known offenders and delinquents

## Crime prevention in the courts and corrections

*Doris Layton MacKenzie*[1]

## Introduction

Past behavior is the best predictor of future behavior. From this perspective, it is reasonable to attempt to prevent crime by preventing known offenders from continuing their criminal behavior. This chapter focuses on the options for dealing with actual perpetrators once they are identified so that crime in the community can be reduced. While traditional crime prevention efforts are directed toward those who are not yet involved in crime, a broader definition includes any setting that reduces crime in the community. By definition, therefore, included as crime prevention are programs in the courts and corrections that focus on reducing the criminal activities of known offenders.

For policy purposes, recent interventions for reducing crime through the courts and corrections can be classified into six categories:

- *Incapacitation* or depriving the offender of the capacity to commit crimes, usually through detention in prison or capital punishment;
- *Deterrence* or punishment that is so repugnant that neither the punished offender (specific deterrence) nor others (general deterrence) will commit the crime in the future;
- *Community restraints* or the surveillance and supervision of offenders in the community in order to reduce their capacity and/or opportunity for criminal activities;
- *Structure, discipline and challenge* programs that use physically and/or mentally stressful experiences to change the offenders in a positive way (rehabilitation) or deter them from later crime (specific deterrence);
- *Rehabilitation* or treatment directed toward changing the offender and thereby preventing future criminal behavior of the treated individual;
- *Combining rehabilitation and restraint* in order to insure that offenders make changes that are associated with a reduction in future criminal behavior.

As shown in Table 9.1, these are not mutually exclusive categories. The categorization is a heuristic device to classify a wide range of programs, policies and interventions currently existing in criminal justice systems throughout the United States. They represent different strategies for controlling

*Table 9.1* Different strategies for preventing known offenders from committing crimes in the community

**Crime prevention in the courts and corrections**

| | *Incapacitation* | *Deterrence* | *Community restraints* | *Structure, discipline and challenge* | *Rehabilitation* | *Combining restraints and rehabilitation* |
|---|---|---|---|---|---|---|
| **Mechanism for impact** | Imprisonment removes offenders' capacity to commit crimes in community (General) | Punitive punishment will keep those in the community from committing crimes (General) | Increased surveillance and change offenders control in the community will decrease offenders' capacity to commit crimes | Experience will change offenders in a positive way so they will not continue to commit criminal behavior | Change aspects of offenders that are changeable and associated with criminal behavior | Offenders can be coerced into rehabilitation (forced to take steps to positively change) |
| | Small number of high-rate offenders can be identified and imprisoned during their active criminal career (Specific) | Punitive punishment programs (with will keep punished individuals from committing more crimes (Specific) | Increased surveillance and control in the community will decrease offenders' opportunity to commit crimes | General and specific deterrence | Intensive, adequately implemented treatment (with integrity) of sufficient duration (dosage) | Offenders can be coerced to remain in treatment longer |
| | General and specific deterrence | | Specific deterrence | | Target higher risk cases | Coercion will not diminish the effectiveness of treatment |
| | | | | | Cognitive, skill oriented and behavioral treatment methods | |

crime in the community. Most have some theoretical rationale for expecting a reduction in crime; they differ enormously in the mechanism anticipated to produce the reduction in crime.

Support for these different strategies of crime prevention in the courts and corrections have changed enormously in the past 30 years. In the 1970s, the strong emphasis on rehabilitation that had existed since the turn of the century gave way first to a focus on equality and fairness in sentencing, and then to an increased focus on incapacitation, deterrence and restraint strategies of crime prevention. Today, incapacitation is the primary justification for imprisonment in the US criminal justice system (Zimring and Hawkins, 1995).

A dramatic increase in offender populations accompanied this change in philosophy. The increase was unprecedented. It followed a period of relative stability in incarceration rates that had existed throughout most of the twentieth century. For example, from 1945 to 1974 the average incarceration rate was 106 inmates per every 100,000 individuals in the population. Incarceration rates fluctuated only slightly, from a low of 93 inmates per 100,000 to a maximum rate 119 (Blumstein and Cohen, 1973). Since that time, however, incarceration rates have grown enormously. By 1985, the number of inmates per 100,000 US residents was 313; this grew to 600 by 1995 (Bureau of Justice Statistics, BJS, 1996).

This increase impacted the total correctional populations and not just prisons. Since 1980, the total estimated correctional population rose 179 percent from 1.8 million in 1980 to 5.1 million in 1994 (BJS, 1995). For parole populations the increase was 213 percent, for probation populations the increase was 1,565 percent (BJS, 1995).

While this analysis of crime prevention focuses on how effective these different strategies are in reducing crime, it is important to remember that each strategy has impacts other than crime reduction. For example, analysis of the costs and benefits is critically important in any examination of policy relevant issues. This has been the focus of much of the discussion on incapacitation because of the large impact associated with policies that increase the need for building, operating and maintaining the prisons necessary for incapacitation. On the other hand, with the exception of some drug treatment studies, there are fewer discussions and less research examining the costs and benefits of rehabilitation. Yet, such analysis is important. A high quality, intensive treatment program for offenders can be relatively costly. The advantages of the program must be weighed against the costs. Such issues, among others, are important in policy decisions.

However, the focus of this chapter is on strategies that reduce crime in the community. From this perspective, issues such as costs, prison crowding, reducing risk factors, public opinion, and the politicalization of decision making are considered important only if they have a direct impact on criminal activities and crime prevention. In the following sections of this chapter, these topics are discussed only when they are such an important part of the interpretation of the impact of some programs that they cannot be easily dismissed. In general, the focus of this review is on activities in the courts and corrections that have a direct bearing on preventing crime by reducing the criminal activities of known offenders and delinquents.

Given the scope of programs and evaluations, examining crime prevention techniques in the criminal justice system is a very large assignment and decisions had to be made about what was important to emphasize in this review. Limitations on time and space meant that some important topics had to be omitted from this chapter. Some obvious examples are capital punishment, deterrence research not directly related to court or correctional programs and the impact of transferring juveniles to adult courts. Nor are the relatively new programs on restorative justice and mediation examined. These are important and current topics, and the interested reader should refer to the recent summaries of the work.

### Examining the scientific evidence

In evaluating the research and assessing the effectiveness of the six identified strategies of crime reduction, this chapter uses three different methods: (1) reviews of the research literature; (2) reviews of meta-analyses used to examine groups of studies; and (3) the scientific methods score combined with significance tests. There were several reasons for the decision to use the different methodologies to review the research and draw conclusions about effectiveness in crime prevention. First, some strategies of crime prevention do not lend themselves to program evaluation that can be easily categorized using the scientific methods score designed to assess the quality of the science. For example, incapacitation research uses complex statistical models to estimate the crimes prevented by various policy decisions. Such studies do not easily lend themselves to the scoring methodology used for evaluating specific programs. For this reason, the literature on incapacitation is reviewed and, on the basis of the simulation research, conclusions are drawn about the effectiveness of incapacitation strategies.

Reviews of the literature were also used to judge the effectiveness of several other programs. Most often this was because current reviews of the literature were available, and there was little research that had been completed in the past 5 or 6 years that would change the conclusions of the previous reviews. For example, the discussion of shock probation and the Scared Straight programs were based on past literature reviews.

Broad assessments of treatment effects have greatly benefited from the rise of a new statistical technique, meta-analysis, that enables researchers to aggregate the continuously growing research literature in order to examine and compare the effect sizes for treatment versus control group comparisons. In some areas, such as the rehabilitation literature, there is a body of research using meta-analyses to examine the effectiveness of programs. Wherever possible, these meta-analyses are used to draw conclusions about programs. The rationale for this decision is that meta-analysis techniques are respected statistical techniques that offer a different picture of effectiveness from that of the scientific methods scale. The meta-analysis technique permits the aggregation of a large body of research literature in order to examine and compare the effect sizes for treatment versus control group comparisons. The meta-analyses reported herein summarize a large number of studies and control for important methodological issues.

There is an enormous body of literature on crime prevention efforts in criminal justice. Much of this literature is not research examining the impact of crime prevention strategies. Few of the research studies are of sufficient quality to permit conclusions regarding the effectiveness of the program studied. In order to evaluate the quality of the research, as described in Chapter 2, this chapter uses the Scientific Methods Scale. Topics were chosen and the previously described categories were identified by examining current research publications. Most of the studies reviewed examine the recidivism of offenders who receive some treatment, service or regime. The focus was on research that had been completed since 1987. In most other cases, the discussion of a topic is based on published reviews of the literature or meta-analyses.

Two problems that continually arose in the research were the small number of subjects and attrition. Even if a strong experimental design is used, a study will not have sufficient power to detect a possible difference if the number of subjects is small. This was particularly a problem with studies using juvenile subjects. Attrition is another problem. Some studies used as comparison groups those who had dropped out of the program being studied. At times this is referred to as a comparison between the "motivated" individuals and others. The problem is that these groups can be assumed to differ prior to receiving any treatment and, therefore, no conclusion can be drawn about the effect of the program being studied. This is a serious problem with some of the drug treatment studies.

Frequently, random assignment studies did not fulfill the requirements for a score of 5, the highest score on the scale, because the assignment process was not successful, there were too few subjects, or subjects were lost during the study. If the effect of these problems could be assumed to be minimal from a research perspective, such studies were given a score of 4. Other studies that scored 4 were quasi-experimental designs with careful statistical controls for differences among subjects. These studies were also required to have limited attrition during the study and sufficient numbers of subjects.

The next sections of this chapter review the proposed strategies for preventing crimes through the use of the criminal justice system. Studies for juveniles and for drug-involved offenders are evaluated in separate sections because of the particular focus of these studies. Conclusions about what works, what does not and what is promising are based on a careful examination of the literature reviews, meta-analyses, statistical significance and the Scientific Methods Scale.

## Incapacitation

The concept of incapacitation is simple – for as long as offenders are incarcerated they clearly cannot commit crimes outside of prison. Crime is reduced because the incarcerated offenders are prevented from committing crimes in the community. At least while they are in prison, they cannot continue to commit crimes. A secondary benefit of incarceration is thought to be the indirect effect of deterring (or inhibiting) others from committing crimes because of the threat of incarceration (general deterrence effect). Furthermore, individuals who spend time in prison may be deterred from continuing their criminal activities when they are released (a specific deterrent effect).

Most people accept the notion that crime prevention through incapacitation is a primary justification of imprisonment (Zimring and Hawkins, 1995). Generally accepted, also, is the fact that some individuals should be incapacitated for long periods of time because of the seriousness of their offenses and the threat they pose if released. Questions arise over how broadly the incapacitation strategy should be used and whether it is a cost efficient and effective crime prevention strategy. Some ask that prison space be reserved for only a small select group of dangerous, repeat offenders. Others advocate a general incapacitation strategy that would incarcerate a substantial number of felons. The success of incapacitation in reducing crime in the community remains a controversial subject.

During the mid-1970s, interest in incapacitation as a crime prevention strategy grew, in part, due to concerns about the efficacy of rehabilitation, rising crime rates and public fear of crime. Originally, incapacitation strategies were supported because of what seemed to be the logical utility of keeping offenders in prison so they could not commit crimes. In some jurisdictions increases in incarceration rates were accompanied by decreases in crime rates. This correlation was used to justify incapacitation policies. However, careful scientific examination requires more than an association between two variables because both could easily be caused by some third factor. Furthermore, correlational studies examining the association between incarceration rates and arrest rates within jurisdictions have not found any consistent relationship between the two (Zimring and Hawkins, 1995).

More rigorous research examining the effectiveness of incapacitation in reducing crime has focused on developing models to estimate the impact of incarceration on individual level offending (Zimring and Hawkins, 1995; Spelman, 1994). Estimating the crime prevention benefits that can be obtained through incarceration is a complicated process. The researcher must estimate how frequently offenders commit crimes and the duration of active criminal careers. The majority of studies examining incapacitation effects demonstrate a small but positive effect in reducing crime. Frequently, however, this crime prevention effect is associated with significant increases in prison populations. Issues of concern relate to whether this reduction is worth the additional costs for building and maintaining prisons and jails, and whether there are other more cost-effective methods of crime reduction.

Early research on incapacitation used official records to estimate individual-level offense rates (Clarke, 1974; Greenberg, 1975; Van Dine, Conrad and Dinitz, 1977; Petersilia and Greenwood, 1978; Blumstein and Cohen, 1979). These incapacitation studies offered widely divergent estimates of the incapacitative effect of imprisonment because there were no generally accepted estimates of these rates nor did researchers know how long criminals continued to commit crimes (e.g. the length of the "career" of crime).

Surveys of prisoners conducted during the late 1970s and early 1980s were designed to answer the questions about the individual crime rates and criminal careers of offenders (Peterson, Greenwood and Lavin, 1977; Peterson and Braiker, 1980; Peterson and Braiker with Polich, 1981; Marques and Ebener, 1981; Peterson *et al.*, 1982; Chaiken and Chaiken, 1982; Greenwood with Abrahamse, 1982). Using these estimates, researchers examined the number of crimes prevented by actual and hypothetical criminal justice practices and sanctioning policies. In general, reviews of these "collective" incapacitation strategies demonstrated a modest reduction in crime combined with substantial increases in prison populations (Visher, 1987).

Increases in prison populations and the research findings of large differences in crime rates of individual offenders moved attention towards a more selective strategy of incapacitating a small group of offenders. Encouragement for this selective incapacitation as a crime control strategy also came from research that revealed a small number of very active offenders (6 percent of the cohort) accounted for a disproportionately large number of the arrests (52 percent) in a Philadelphia birth cohort (Wolfgang, Figlio and Sellin, 1972). Incapacitation advocates argued that crime could be reduced if these "career criminals" were identified and incapacitated. This "selective incapacitation" strategy would identify the offenders who were predicted to commit serious crimes at high rates so that they could be incarcerated for long periods of time. Further support for the benefits of incapacitation as a correctional strategy came from the proposal that, although there were enormous costs to incarcerating large numbers of felons, there were also substantial costs if they were released and continued to commit crimes (in terms of such factors as criminal processing, loss to victims, etc.) (Zedlewski, 1987). Some of the practices that can be attributed to these incapacitation strategies are habitual offender laws, mandatory sentences and the more recent three-strikes laws.

Greenwood with Abrahamse (1982) examined whether selective incapacitation policies could reduce the robbery rate in California using simulations. They found evidence that through the use of a selective incapacitation strategy the robbery rate could be reduced by about 15 percent, and the number of incarcerated robbers would be reduced by about 5 percent. However, they cautioned that their analysis had several limitations and they suggested that the work should be replicated in other jurisdictions. Other researchers reviewed Greenwood and Abrahamse's results and concluded that the original analysis greatly overstated the effects of the proposed selective incapacitation (Cohen, 1983, 1984; Spelman, 1994; Von Hirsch and Gottfredson, 1984; Visher, 1987). Estimates resulting from these studies indicated substantially smaller incapacitative effects than those found by Greenwood and Abrahamse. Furthermore, substantial increases in the prison population were predicted (Blumstein et al., 1986). Research also suggests that identifying future offenders in order to selectively incarcerate them will prove difficult (Greenwood and Turner, 1987; Gottfredson and Gottfredson, 1994).

Surprisingly there was little research on the magnitude of incapacitation effects during the decade of the 1980s when the incapacitation philosophy drove the largest increase in incarceration in American history (Zimring and Hawkins, 1995). A few more recent studies were completed in the early 1990s (Miranne and Geerken, 1991; Horney and Marshall, 1991; English and Mande, 1992). In one recent study, Cohen and Canela-Cacho (1994) studied the relationship between incarceration and levels of violent crime using both national data and corrections data from six states. According to them, chang-

_Courts and corrections_ 337

ing prison policies, such as guidelines, mandatory minimum prison terms, and restrictions on parole release, have played a major part in the rising prison populations over the last decade. In comparison to the past, a higher proportion of those who are arrested in the US are sentenced to prison and those who are committed to prison stay there for longer periods of time.

In their research, Cohen and Canela-Cacho (1994) used sophisticated estimating techniques taking into consideration the fact that high-rate offenders are over-represented among inmates while low-rate offenders are disproportionately found among the offenders who remain free, and the fact that termination of criminal careers reduces the crime prevention effects derived from increased incarceration. They estimate that the incapacitation effects during periods of low incarceration rates are probably much greater than previously estimated but the increasing numbers of offenders being incarcerated today bring only marginal returns for incapacitation effects. This occurs because the expanding prison populations are likely to include an increasing number of offenders who would be low-rate.

The focus on tougher sentencing laws has led to increasingly rigid sentencing statutes and these have particularly impacted repeat offenders. By 1994, 30 states had introduced "three-strikes" legislation and ten had passed tougher sentencing for repeat offenders (Benekos and Merlo, 1996). The "three-strikes and you're out" baseball metaphor is used throughout the country in reference to criminal sanctions that become increasingly severe for each conviction an offender receives until they are considered to be "out" or in prison for life. Greenwood *et al.* (1994) estimated the crime prevention impact of the California three-strikes law, one of the most sweeping of the laws. Although the first two "strikes" accrue for serious felonies, the third strike that triggers the life sentence can be any felony. According to their estimates the new law would reduce serious felonies committed by adults in California between 22 and 34 percent below what would have occurred had the previous law remained in effect. The researchers caution that, while these results appear encouraging for crime prevention, it will come at great financial cost due to the large estimated increase in prison population. For example, the California three-strikes law, if applied in all eligible cases, would reduce the number of serious felonies in a year by about 28 percent or 329,000 crimes. However, this would cost an additional $5.5 billion a year in criminal justice funding for the costs of the construction and operation of prisons. This can be translated as a cost of $16,000 per serious felony prevented.[2]

In summary, there is now a body of research examining the crime prevention effect of incapacitation:

- Incapacitation policies prevent crime because offenders who are imprisoned do not have the opportunity to commit crimes.
- There are a small number of offenders who commit a large number of crimes. If they could be incapacitated a large number of crimes would be prevented.

However, there are many unresolved questions that make the effectiveness of this strategy questionable. Most important are the following issues:

- It is not yet possible to predict who will be the high frequency offenders in the future; therefore targeting them for increased prison sentences is impossible.
- Increased use of incapacitation as a crime prevention strategy must address the expected increases in imprisonment rates and the associated financial costs that accompany such strategies.
- Large increases in the use of incapacitation may have limited returns because the additional offenders not now incarcerated are lower-frequency offenders who would not be committing many crimes in the community, thus reducing the return on investment for every new dollar expended.
- Large increases in the use of incapacitation may also have limited returns because offenders who are incarcerated for lengthy periods of time may be at the end of their criminal career and therefore would not be committing crimes in the community.
- True estimates of the crimes prevented are difficult to obtain because both the frequency of criminal participation and the duration of careers must be estimated.

Furthermore, recent studies of the impact of the increases in imprisonment rates that have occurred in the past 25 years have revealed that the impact has had a major impact on minority populations in urban environments (Tonry, 1995). Other disadvantages of increased use of imprisonment strategies are the unintended consequences of imprisonment on the families and communities of those who are imprisoned (Clear, 1996).

## Deterrence

Deterrence strategies are based on early criminological theory proposing that sufficiently repugnant punishments will inhibit individuals from committing crime. Deterrence could be an expected impact of incapacitation, community restraints and challenge programs. However, this is secondary to the primary mechanism that is expected to have an impact on crime prevention for these strategies. Here, the programs classified as deterrence are those with a primary purpose of deterring either the individual offender or others through the repugnant nature of the sanction. At the individual level, specific deterrence is explained by the fact that the pain generated by the punishment will serve to discourage future criminality. It assumes a rational choice model of decision-making where the offender perceives that the costs and benefits of punishment are not outweighed by the crime. General deterrence refers to the impact the threatened punishment has on other potential offenders, thus reducing the chance that they will commit crimes.

Deterrence is the rationale given for programs such as Scared Straight, chain gangs and shock probation. These are distinguished from other strategies because the major emphasis is on the punitive nature of the punishment and not on reducing crime through restraint, discipline or challenge. Another deterrence strategy is that of fines, particularly day fines. These fines are designed to be fair, given the difference in the economic circumstances of the individual offenders, thereby making this sanction more punitive than traditional fines.

Research examining two types of deterrence programs is reviewed in this section. It is important to note that other programs, such as incapacitation policies that threaten offenders with longer prison sentences as well as programs requiring offenders to participate in emotionally and physically strenuous programs (e.g. structure, discipline and challenge), are also expected to deter offenders. However, they are viewed as potentially having other impacts and, therefore, they have been examined in separate sections.

### Monetary penalties

Fines are frequently used as criminal penalties for a wide variety of cases in American courts (Hillsman, 1990; Hillsman *et al.*, 1984; Casale, Silvia and Hillsman, 1986; Cole *et al.*, 1987). However, many of the fine sentences are composites of fines and other non-custodial sanctions and not stand-alone sanctions. Judges have wide discretion in setting fines. They are not uniformly imposed, and jail sentences are sometimes used as alternatives to fines, particularly for the poor. Rarely are fines in the US used as the sole sanction for more serious cases or for repeat offenders. In contrast, in Western Europe fines are the most often imposed sentence for most crimes and are a major alternative to imprisonment (Hillsman, 1990). One of the differences between the use of fines in the United States and other countries is the fact that American judges are not able to set fines that are proportionate to the severity of the offense, but are also equitable and fair given the difference in the economic circumstances of the individual offenders. "Day" or "unit" fines as they are called in Western Europe are linked to both the offender's daily income and to the gravity of the crime.

In terms of crime prevention, fines may act as a deterrent to criminal activities. Most studies of fines, however, have focused on setting just and proportionate levels for the amount of the fine, or on compliance, cost savings, or prison population impact issues. Until recently little was known about the use of fines as criminal penalties in the United States (see Hillsman *et al.*, 1984; Casale, Silvia and Hillsman, 1986; Cole *et al.*, 1987; Glaser and Gordon, 1988; Hillsman and Green, 1987, 1988). However, the three studies assessed here examine the impact of fines on criminal activities (Table 9.2).

Gordon and Glaser (1991) did examine the impact of traditional fines on recidivism in a quasi-experimental study comparing financial penalties with similar sentences (probation or probation plus jail). Offenders who received a fine with probation have lower recidivism rates (25 percent) than offenders who received only probation (36 percent). Similarly, those who received a fine with probation and jail (37 percent) had lower recidivism than offenders who received only probation and jail without the fines (50 percent). However, these differences were not significant.

As yet, there are few jurisdictions in the United States that use the day fine concept (Hillsman, 1990). Two studies have examined the impact of day fines on the recidivism of offenders. One study assessed the recidivism of offenders sentenced in Milwaukee's Municipal Court Day-Fine Pilot Project

*Table 9.2* Fines and day fines and recidivism

| Study | Scientific methods score | Findings |
|-------|--------------------------|----------|
| Gordon and Glaser (1991) Fines | 3 | Probation + fine had fewer arrests (25%) than probation only (36%); Probation + jail + fine had fewer arrests (37%) than probation + jail only (50%) |
| Worzella (1992) Fines | 3 | No differences between day fine group in new ordinance violations (33%) and conventional fine group (34%) |
| Turner and Petersilia (1996) Day fines | 5 | Day fine group had fewer technical violations (9%) than conventional sentenced group (22%); Day fine group had fewer re-arrests (11%) than conventional sentenced group (17%) |

and compared the recidivism rates to a comparison group who received traditional fines (Worzella, 1992). There was no difference in the percentage of the groups who committed further violations of municipal ordinances but the day-fined group had fewer arrest warrants (neither measure was significantly different). In another study, Turner and Petersilia (1996) evaluated a multi-site structured fines demonstration project. While most of the research focused on the implementation and development of the day fine programs, there was some outcome data from one of the jurisdictions. Day fines were associated with reductions in both technical violations (9 percent compared to 22 percent) and re-arrests (11 percent to 17 percent) but only the technical violation difference was significant.

Overall, there is a limited amount of research examining the effectiveness of fines in reducing the recidivism of offenders. The Gordon and Glaser (1991) study suggests that fines as additions to other sanctions may be effective in reducing recidivism. Since fines could potentially reduce the cost of courts and corrections, and day fines address the problems of inequality, this strategy appears to be a promising avenue for future research.

### Shock probation, shock parole and split sentences

The programs in this section have been grouped together because their major emphasis has been on specific deterrence of the offender participants. Shock probation or parole programs are a form of split sentence in which offenders are incarcerated for unspecified short periods of time in prisons or jails followed by a period of community supervision. The idea is that a short period of incarceration would "shock" offenders into abandoning criminal activity and into more conventional and law-abiding behavior. During their incarceration there are no special programs for them and they are mixed with other offenders in the jail or prison. Reviews of the research examining shock programs have provided little evidence of a deterrent effect. Studies examining the recidivism of shock probationers with similar probation groups have found no differences and in some cases the shock probationers have done demonstrably worse (Vito, 1984; Vito and Allen, 1981; Boudouris and Turnbull, 1985; Finckenauer, 1982).

"Scared Straight" is another program designed to deter young offenders or at-risk juveniles from continuing criminal activities. They are taken to maximum security institutions where inmates tell them the horrors and difficulties of life in prison. Studies of these programs have not indicated any differences between those who participated in the programs and comparison groups and in some cases the re-arrest rates were higher for those who participated in the program (Buckner and Chesney-Lind, 1983; Lewis, 1983). Overall, there is no evidence that deterrence programs such as these effectively reduce the future criminal activities of the offender participants (see also section on rehabilitation below).

## Community restraints

Many of the sanctions and correctional options categorized as community restraints are referred to as intermediate sanctions or alternative punishments. However, here the term community restraint refers to the fact that a group of these alternative punishments increase the amount of surveillance and control over offenders while they are in the community. In a sense, they might be referred to as "semi-incapacitation" because they are expected to reduce offenders' ability to commit crimes. Examples of restraint programs are intensive supervision, house arrest, electronic monitoring and halfway houses. Theoretically, increasing the surveillance and control over offenders in the community will prevent criminal activities by reducing both their capacity and their opportunity to commit crimes. Additionally, it is expected that the punitive nature of the sanctions will act as a specific deterrence to reduce the offenders' future criminal activity.

In response to the record numbers of convicted offenders and widespread prison crowding, correctional officials in recent years have expanded the range of intermediate sanctions that fall between traditional probation and complete incarceration (Cullen, Wright and Applegate, 1996; Tonry and Lynch, 1996; Byrne, Lurigio and Petersilia, 1992; Harland, 1996; Smykla and Selke, 1995). House arrest, intensive supervision, curfew, day reporting and other intermediate sanctions fulfill many purposes. They provide graduated punishments that may be more appropriate than either probation or prison for some offenses, and they maintain a higher level of offender restraint and accountability than does standard probation or parole supervision. In addition, intermediate sanctions may provide enhanced levels of treatment or services for problems that are common among criminal offenders, such as drug abuse, low education levels and unemployment. Finally, when used in lieu of confinement, intermediate sanctions may reduce prison or jail populations and associated costs.

This section examines sanctions that increase the restraints on offenders in the community and studies assessing the effectiveness of these restraints in reducing criminal activity. The term restraints is used to refer to activities such as contacts with agents, urine testing (see section on drug-involved offenders below) and employment verification that represent control over offenders and increased accountability. It is these restraints and not the rehabilitation that is the primary focus of the research. Thus, this section examines whether the sanctions are effective in preventing the future criminal activities of these offenders.

## Intensive Community Supervision

Compared to regular probation and parole services, Intensive Community Supervision, usually called Intensive Supervised Probation (or Parole) or ISP, was designed to provide increased restraints on offenders in the community (Lurigio and Petersilia, 1992; Petersilia and Turner, 1993a; Cullen, Wright and Applegate, 1996; Tonry and Lynch, 1996). Studies of ISP do indeed reveal that there are increased direct contacts between the offenders and the supervising probation or parole agent. Many programs combine other options such as electronic monitoring and/or home confinement with increased agent-offender contacts. Furthermore, indirect methods of observation are also frequently combined with the ISP programs. In many cases offenders are required to report for more frequent urine testing or agents may conduct regular employment verification. In all, these direct and indirect observations provide substantially increased levels of control within probation and parole programs. However, the type and level of demands placed on offenders differs enormously by jurisdiction. Offenders are often required to pay fines, keep a mandatory curfew, or provide community service, and these additional requirements also differ by jurisdiction.

ISP programs grew dramatically in the 1980s, and by 1990 virtually every state in the nation had developed some type of ISP program. In part, this was the result of the initial research examining the programs in New Jersey and Georgia where the findings suggested that ISP led to a significant decrease in reincarceration (in Georgia, see Erwin, 1986) and re-arrests (in New Jersey, see Pearson, 1987). However, critical reviews of the research demonstrated that the data did not support the initial unqualified conclusions about the ability of the ISP programs to reduce crime. Recognizing the limitations of the prior research, Petersilia and Turner (1993b) used an experimental design to evaluate fourteen ISP programs in nine states. This experimental design with random assignment of offenders to ISP and control groups eliminated many of the past methodological problems of the earlier studies. Recidivism was measured using both arrests and technical violations. When ISP participants were compared to the control group, there were no significant differences in arrests. At the end of the 1-year study period, about 37 percent of the ISP participants and 33 percent of the control offenders had been arrested. In comparison, the researchers found a significant difference when the technical violation rates were examined. The average ISP violation rate was found to be 65 percent for ISP participants compared with 38 percent for the controls. In summary, while there was no evidence that the increased surveillance in the community deterred offenders from committing crimes, it did appear that this additional control increased the probability that technical violations would be detected. As shown in Table 9.3, there is a fairly substantial body of research now available on ISP. Few of the studies found statistically significant differences between ISP participants and comparisons, and the direction of the differences between the ISP groups and the comparison groups varied, sometimes favoring ISP, sometimes favoring the alternative. Thus, there is no evidence that recidivism is reduced by increasing the surveillance and other restraints over offenders on ISP. In fact, the increased surveillance may be associated with increases in technical violations.

*Table 9.3* Intensive Supervised Probation/Parole (ISP) and home confinement/electronic monitoring

| Study | Scientific methods score | Findings |
|---|---|---|
| Austin and Hardyman (1991) EM | 5 | Electronic monitoring arrested (14%) more than controls (11%) |
| Baumer and Mendelsohn (1991) EM | 5 | Electronic monitoring more revocations (21%) than manual supervision (18%) |
| Petersilia and Turner (1993b) ISP | 5 | ISP sample in 10 states had higher recidivism than comparison. ISP samples in 4 states had lower recidivism than comparison |
| Jolin and Stipack (1991) ISP | 4 | Recidivism rates higher for ISP than electronic monitoring and work release groups |
| Fallen *et al.* (1981) ISP | 3 | Recidivism lower for ISP |
| Erwin (1986) ISP | 3 | Recidivism rates lower for ISP than probationers and lower for prison releasees |
| Mitchell and Butter (1986) ISP | 3 | Recidivism higher for ISP than parolees and CCC |
| Pearson (1987) ISP | 3 | ISP recidivism rates lower |
| Byrne and Kelly (1989) ISP | 3 | ISP lower recidivism |
| Latessa (1991) ISP | 3 | Recidivism rates higher for ISP offenders than three comparison samples |
| Austin and Hardyman (1991) ISP | 3 | ISP-electronic monitoring offenders arrested more than parolees |
| National Council on Crime and Delinquency (1991) ISP | 3 | Recidivism rates for ISP-jail probationers and ISP-parolees higher than comparisons but rates lower for ISP parolees than comparison |
| Latessa (1992) ISP | 3 | Recidivism rates higher for ISP |
| Moon and Latessa (1993) ISP | 3 | ISP drug program participants had lower recidivism rates |
| Latessa (1993a) ISP | 3 | ISP groups had higher recidivism than probationers |
| Molof (1991) ISP | 2 | ISP group had lower recidivism than probationers |

Although research has not revealed a significant relationship between levels of surveillance and recidivism, there is some evidence that increased treatment of offenders in ISP programs may be related to significant reductions in re-arrests. Follow-up analyses by the RAND researchers (Petersilia and Turner, 1993b) and also researchers evaluating ISP programs in Massachusetts (Byrne and Kelly, 1989), Oregon (Jolin and Stipack, 1991) and Ohio (Latessa, 1993a) have found evidence that re-arrests are reduced when offenders receive treatment services in addition to the increased surveillance and control of the ISP programs. For example, Petersilia and Turner (1993b) reported a 10 to 20 percent reduction in recidivism for those who were most active in programs while they were in the community. However, the research designs used in these evaluations do not reach the experimental rigor of the random assignment study by RAND that examined the effect of increasing the surveillance and control of ISP participants.

### Home confinement

Home confinement is designed to regulate and restrict the freedom of the offender within the community (Renzema, 1992; Baumer and Mendelsohn, 1992). The terms "house arrests," "home confinement" and "electronic monitoring" are often used interchangeably. However, it is important to note that house arrest, home confinement and more recently "community control" are terms describing the programs, while electronic monitoring is a tool used to monitor the compliance with the requirements of the sentence. During the 1980s, technological advances made it possible to monitor offenders electronically to insure that the offender was complying with the requirements of the program. Unlike ISP, house arrest is usually a sentence given by the court that is much more restrictive than ISP.

In general, home confinement programs had targeted low-risk offenders, such as those convicted of Driving While Intoxicated (DWI). However, more recently, home confinement has been used for parolees (Beck and Klein-Saffran, 1989) or other more serious offenders (Baumer, Maxfield and Mendelsohn, 1993; Baumer and Mendelsohn, 1991; Austin and Hardyman, 1991). Early research examining the effectiveness of the home confinement programs suffered from poor research designs, lack of program integrity, and the low-risk offenders placed in the programs. Recidivism rates of the low-risk offenders placed in home confinement programs are usually very low. Therefore, many studies do not have the power to detect small differences that might be expected between the program and control groups. Two studies (see Table 9.3) using experimental designs found no significant difference in recidivism when the behavior of offenders who are electronically monitored on home confinement is compared with those being manually supervised (Austin and Hardyman, 1991; Baumer and Mendelsohn, 1991).

### Community facilities: residential and day reporting

Halfway houses, also called community residential centers, pre-release centers or restitution centers, are nonconfining residential facilities for adjudicated adults or juveniles, or those subject to criminal or juvenile proceedings (pre-trial period). They are intended as an alternative to confinement for persons not suited for probation or who need a period of readjustment to the community after imprisonment. The facilities are included as community restraints because most of the research reviews have focused on their use as additional restraint and not on the details of the services provided.

The results from studies of halfway houses are mixed. In an early review of studies of correctional halfway houses, Allen *et al.* (1976) examined 35 studies. The majority of the studies used quasi-experimental designs or non-experimental designs; only two used true experimental designs. The evidence was about equally divided between lower recidivism for the halfway house residents and no differences in recidivism in comparison to control groups in the quasi-experimental and experimental designs. In a later study focusing on parolees in halfway houses, Latessa and Allen (1982) examined 44 studies with sufficiently rigorous methodology to enable the researchers to draw reasonable assessments of post-release outcomes. As Allen *et al.* (1976) had found earlier, the results were mixed – at times showing halfway house residents having lower recidivism rates and at times showing no differences or that halfway house residents did worse on recidivism rates.

Day reporting centers are a more recent correctional option that require offenders who are on pre-trial release, probation or parole to appear at specific locations on a frequent and regular basis. Unlike the halfway houses, the day reporting centers are non-residential: offenders are required to report to the centers but they return to their homes at night. While at the centers they are required to participate in services (treatment, employment search, etc.) or activities (urine test, meetings with agents) provided by the agency or other community agencies. These programs are currently being widely implemented in the United States. The programs are rapidly increasing. In 1990, there were only thirteen centers in the United States, by 1995 at least 114 centers were operating in 22 states (Parent *et al.*, 1995). The centers emphasize both strict surveillance and high levels of treatment and other services to offenders. As with the other intermediate sanctions, there is a tension between providing increased surveillance and increased treatment in the day reporting centers, and centers vary greatly in the emphasis placed on one or the other. While there have been some descriptive studies of day reporting programs, to date there have been no impact evaluations examining the effectiveness of the programs in preventing crime.

### Summary of community restraints

A large body of research, including random assignment studies, consistently shows the failure of community restraint programs to lower recidivism. Restraining offenders in the community by increasing surveillance and control over their activities does not reduce their criminal activities. In general, they are arrested as often as their counterparts who receive less surveillance. The increased surveillance may actually increase the probability of detection and, thus, result in more technical violations. Most research has focused on the restraining aspects of these community programs and not the treatment services delivered to the offenders. That is, the research fails to clearly identify and rigorously examine (from a research perspective) the impact of the therapeutic aspects of the community programs. When the researchers have mentioned the therapeutic integrity of the programs, it is often to note that the anticipated services or staffing did not occur (see, for example, Sontheimer and Goodstein's (1993) or Greenwood, Deschenes and Adam's (1993) study of the Skillman aftercare program discussed in the juvenile programs section below). Questions remain about the impact of additional treatment within a program that increases restraints.

## Structure, discipline and challenge

Correctional boot camps for adults and for juveniles focus on structure, discipline and physical and/or mental challenge (see Table 9.4). The experiences of

*Table 9.4* Juvenile and adult correctional boot camps (BC)

| Study | Scientific methods score | Findings |
|---|---|---|
| Peters (1996a) Juvenile | 5 | More BC juveniles (38.8%) recidivated than control group (35.5%) |
| Peters (1996b) Juvenile | 5 | Fewer BC juveniles (28.1%) recidivated than control group (31%) |
| Peters (1996c) Juvenile | 5 | More BC juveniles (71.8%) recidivated than control group (50%) |
| Bottcher *et al.* (1996) Juvenile | 5 | More BC juveniles (77.7%) re-arrested than control group (77.1%) |
| MacKenzie *et al.* (1995) Adult | 4 | Compared to probationers BC releasees had fewer re-arrests in one state and more in two states; fewer revocations in three states. Compared to parolees BC releases had fewer re-arrests in four states; fewer revocations in five states and more revocations in one state |
| Flowers, Carr and Ruback (1991) Adult | 3 | Compared with those sentenced to various alternatives, male BC graduates were reincarcerated less often. But when graduates were compared with groups most similar to BC graduates the reincarceration rates were higher for BC graduates |
| MacKenzie and Parent (1991) Adult | 3 | BC graduates had fewer arrests and reconvictions for new crimes when compared to samples of parolees and probationers but more arrests for technical violations. Those dismissed from the program had fewer arrests than graduates but were the same in reconviction rates |
| Texas Department of Criminal Justice (1991) Adult | 2 | BC releasees were reincarcerated more than parolees, ISP and restitution center releasees |
| Florida Department of Corrections (1990) Adult | 2 | There were no differences between BC graduates and prison releasees in new felonies. BC graduates had more new misdemeanors but fewer technical violations |
| NYDCS and NYDP (1992, 1993) Adult | 2 | Male BC graduates reincarcerated less for new crimes and parole violations compared to: (1) parolees sentenced before the program began; (2) those who refused to enter; (3) dismissals from the program |
| NYDCS and NYDP (1993) Adult | 2 | Female BC graduates reincarcerated less for new crimes and parole violations compared to: (1) parolees sentenced before the program began; (2) those who refused to enter; (3) dismissals from the program |

the offenders in the programs are anticipated to change them in a positive way so that their future criminal activities will be reduced. The mechanism for this change is attributed to various factors such as self-esteem or increased bonds with staff and peers. Some also expect that these punitive programs will discourage others from committing crimes or that the individuals who spend time in the programs will be deterred from future criminal activities. At times programs combine therapeutic programming with structure, discipline and challenge aspects. The studies of the programs focus on the recidivism rates of those who are released from the programs and compare these rates to comparison groups who served different sentences. Thus, the studies examine the specific deterrence or positive change impacts of the programs.

### Boot camps for adults

Boot camp prisons, alternatively called shock incarceration, regimented discipline or intensive incarceration, are correctional programs designed to be similar to military basic training. These relatively new programs began in 1983 in Georgia and Oklahoma but rapidly spread throughout the nation (MacKenzie, 1990; MacKenzie and Parent, 1991). The early programs emphasized the military aspects of discipline, comportment and drill and ceremony. More recently the programs have changed to include more programming and treatment and many have de-emphasized the military focus of the programs. As has occurred with other correctional options, the boot camp programs vary tremendously when cross-program comparisons are made in type of population served, treatment components, aftercare or follow-up supervision, and emphasis on military drill and ceremony. The majority of the state department of corrections have opened boot camp programs and increasing numbers of programs are being opened for juveniles and for jail inmates.

To date, there have been no random assignment studies examining the effectiveness of boot camp prisons for adult offenders. Most of the existing research had limited scientific rigor (scientific methods scores of 3). Some of the research has made use of statistical controls to adjust for original differences between the boot camp releasees and comparison groups to examine their performance in the community (e.g. MacKenzie *et al.*, 1995). In general, the results show no significant differences in recidivism between offenders who are sent to boot camps when compared to others, including those who either served a longer period of time in prison or those who served their sentence on probation (MacKenzie, Shaw and Gowdy, 1993; MacKenzie and Shaw, 1993; Flowers, Carr and Ruback, 1991; Florida Department of Corrections, 1990). However, in programs where a substantial number of offenders were dismissed from the boot camp prior to completion, the recidivism rates for those who completed the program were significantly lower than the rates for those who were dismissed (MacKenzie *et al.*, 1995; NYDCS and NYDP, 1993). Thus, while there is no evidence that the boot camps actually change offenders, there is some indication that the programs can be used to "signal" which offenders will have difficulty completing probation or parole. That is, offenders who remain in the program and complete it are at less risk for recidivism than those who are dismissed (either voluntarily dropping out or for misbehavior).

In a further exploratory analysis examining program differences and recidivism rates, MacKenzie *et al.* (1995) found some commonality among programs where the boot camp releasees had lower recidivism rates than comparison groups on some but not all measures of recidivism. In particular, these programs: (1) devoted more than 3 hours per day to therapeutic activities such as therapy, counseling, drug treatment and education; (2) there was some type of follow-up for the offenders in the community after they left the boot camp; and (3) participants had to volunteer for the program.

## Boot camps for juveniles

Four random assignment studies have been completed examining the recidivism of juveniles released from boot camps (see Table 9.4). With cooperative funding from the National Institute of Justice (NIJ) and the Office of Juvenile Justice and Delinquency Prevention (OJJDP) of the US Department of Justice, a carefully designed experimental study examining boot camps in three sites was completed. Funding was provided for sites to develop innovative demonstration programs, if they were willing to permit researchers to randomly assign juveniles to the boot camps or some alternative. Three sites were selected to participate. The fourth study of juvenile boot camps was conducted by the California Youth Authority (CYA; Boutcher *et al.*, 1996). This study used random assignment to evaluate the effectiveness of the CYA juvenile boot camp. The California legislature provided funding to the CYA to develop a pilot program and complete a random assignment study to evaluate its effect. All of the four studies of the juvenile boot camps were judged to score 5 on the methods assessment. The results from the three demonstration camps revealed no significant differences in recidivism between the boot camp youth and the control groups. In the fourth site, the CYA, more of the boot camp youth were reincarcerated than the control youth. These results led the CYA to abolish their boot camp. Obviously, these results present little support for the boot camps as crime prevention techniques.

## Summary

The boot camps reviewed in this section do not, as a whole, appear to be good candidates for crime prevention. In general, findings indicate no difference between the offenders who participated and those who did not. There was some suggestion in the research examining adult boot camps that enhanced therapeutic programming within the boot camps may have had an impact on reducing recidivism, but the research is exploratory and did not use a strong methodology. The juvenile programs appeared less hopeful. Several issues deserve attention. First, more information is needed about the therapeutic integrity of the programs and how the programs compare to the alternatives where the control groups spent time. Possibly, the failure to find differences in recidivism may be because the control groups were receiving enhanced treatment while the juveniles in the boot camps were spending time on physical activities. Such physical activities may have health benefits but they may not address the criminogenic needs of these offenders. Questions remain about how rehabilitation can be combined with these programs and whether this would enhance or conversely reduce the effectiveness of the rehabilitation.

## Rehabilitation and treatment

In contrast to incapacitation, rehabilitation strategies focus on changing individual offenders so they will not continue their criminal activities upon return to the community. The research goal is to identify and understand the individual differences that explain criminal behavior and how interventions can be used to change individuals so they will not continue to commit crimes. The work is based on psychological theories of learning, cognition and the general principles of human development applied to the analysis of illegal behavior (Andrews and Bonta, 1994). Research has focused on examining the components of programs that are effective in reducing recidivism.

Since the mid-1970s there have been major changes in how the courts and corrections manage offenders in the United States. One of the most visible influences on this change was the report by Martinson (1974) that was widely interpreted as showing that "nothing works" in rehabilitation. Critics (Gendreau, 1981; Gendreau and Ross, 1979, 1981, 1987; Goutfredson, 1979; Cullen and Gilbert, 1982; Greenwood and Zimring, 1985; Halleck and Witte, 1977; Palmer, 1975; Van Voorhis, 1987) argued against this conclusion, saying it was not that treatment programs could not potentially reduce recidivism, but instead that it was impossible to draw any conclusions from the research because:

- the research methodology was so inadequate that few studies warranted any unequivocal interpretations about what works; and,
- the programs studied were so poorly implemented and delivered in such a weakened form that they would not reasonably be expected to have an impact.

Reviews of evaluations published after Martinson's essay indicated that substantial research exists showing the effectiveness of correctional treatment (Gendreau, 1981; Gendreau and Ross, 1979, 1981, 1987; Goutfredson, 1979; Cullen and Gilbert, 1982; Greenwood and Zimring, 1985; Halleck and Witte, 1977; Van Voorhis, 1987). Today, while there is still some debate about the effectiveness of rehabilitation (e.g. Lab and Whitehead, 1988; Whitehead and Lab, 1989) recent literature reviews and meta-analyses demonstrate that rehabilitation programs can effectively change offenders (Andrews and Bonta, 1994; Andrews, Bonta and Hoge, 1990; Andrews et al., 1990; Palmer, 1975; Gendreau and Ross, 1979, 1987). For example, in a series of literature reviews, the proportion of studies reporting positive evidence of treatment effectiveness varied from near 50 percent to 86 percent: 75 percent (Kirby, 1954), 59 percent (Bailey, 1966), 50 percent (Logan, 1972), 48 percent (Palmer's 1975 re-tabulation of studies reviewed by Martinson), 86 percent (Gendreau and Ross, 1979) and 47 percent (Lab and Whitehead, 1988).[3] The important issue is not whether something works but what works for whom (Andrews et al., 1990).

What is clear is that some approaches to treatment are better than others. Psychological researchers emphasize that effective treatment programs must follow some basic principles (Gendreau and Ross, 1979, 1987; Cullen and Gendreau, 1989). First, treatment must directly address characteristics that can be changed (dynamic) and that are directly associated with an individual's criminal behavior (criminogenic factors). There are numerous risk factors associated with criminal activity. Age, gender and early criminal involvement are some examples. In comparison to others, young males who began criminal activities at a young age are higher risks for future criminal activities. But these "static" characteristics such as age, gender and past history, while predictive of recidivism, cannot be changed in treatment. Instead, the "dynamic" or changeable factors should be the target of treatment programs.

Equally important is the distinction between factors that are criminogenic and those that are not. Criminogenic factors are those that are directly associated with criminal behavior. Research has revealed some dynamic factors that are also criminogenic: attitudes, cognitions, behaviors regarding employment, education, peers, authority, substance abuse and interpersonal relationships that are directly related to an individual's criminal behavior. Less promising targets for reducing future criminal behavior include increasing self-esteem without touching antisocial propensity or increasing the cohesiveness of antisocial peer groups. While factors such as self-esteem may be correlated with criminal behavior, changing them will not necessarily reduce future criminal activities. That is, criminals may have relatively strong self-concepts but they may continue to commit crimes. Treatment programs that target such non-criminogenic factors will not be particularly successful in reducing recidivism.

Also important in determining whether a treatment program will be effective is the therapeutic integrity of the program, or the need for effective programs to be delivered as planned and designed. Poorly implemented programs, delivered by untrained personnel, where offenders spend only a minimal amount of time in the program, can hardly be expected to successfully reduce recidivism. Furthermore, programs must target offenders who are at sufficient risk for recidivism so that this reduction is measurable. Many offenders are low-risk for future recidivism. Treatment programs that provide intensive services for such offenders will show little reduction in future criminal activities because few of these offenders will recidivate anyway.

The final principle of effective treatment is the need to deliver treatment in a style and mode that addresses the learning styles and abilities of offenders. For example, more effective programs follow a cognitive behavioral and social leaning approach rather than nondirective relationship-oriented counseling or psycho-dynamic, insight-oriented counseling.

Using these principles as the basis to classify studies of treatment as appropriate or inappropriate, Andrews et al. (1990) undertook a meta-analysis of 154 treatment comparisons.[4] Most often studies were classified as appropriate because the treatment was behavioral in nature. Few studies could be classified on the basis of risk or treatment integrity because the information was not available. Inappropriate treatments were those that employed deterrence (e.g. "Scared Straight"), nondirective approaches, non-behavioral milieu approaches and group interactions. They found appropriate treatment was significantly more effective than inappropriate services and criminal justice sanctions (warnings, probation, intensive probation, custody).

Lipton and Pearson (1996) found some, but limited, evidence corroborating the finding that treatment programs could be classified by the appropriateness of the treatment provided. Preliminary findings from a meta-analysis of the first 500 coded evaluation studies (they anticipate over 1,500 studies) replicated the findings of the Andrews *et al.* (1990) study on the significance of the appropriateness of treatment. However, they reported having some difficulty in identifying exactly what characteristics are associated with effective treatment.

In summary, there is evidence that:

- rehabilitation is effective in reducing the criminal behavior of at least some offenders.

The evidence from the meta-analyses suggests that effective correctional treatment programs appear to follow some basic principles. In order to effectively reduce recidivism, treatment programs appear to need to:

- be carefully designed to target the specific characteristics and problems of offenders that can be changed in treatment (dynamic characteristics) and those that are predictive of the individual's future criminal activities (criminogenic), such as antisocial attitudes and behavior, drug use, and anger responses;
- be implemented in a way that is appropriate for the participating offenders and utilizes therapeutic techniques that are known to work (e.g. designed by knowledgeable individuals, programming provided by appropriately educated and experienced staff, use of adequately evaluated programs) and require offenders to spend a reasonable length of time in the program considering the changes desired (deliver sufficient dosage);
- give the most intensive programs to offenders who are at the highest risk of recidivism;
- use cognitive and behavioral treatment methods based on theoretical models, such as behaviorism, social learning or cognitive behavioral theories of change, that emphasize positive reinforcement contingencies for pro-social behavior and is individualized as much as possible.

More information is needed regarding:

1  how to ensure that treatment programs have adequate integrity;
2  what should be targeted in the treatment (antisocial attitudes, values, employment behavior, education, etc.); and
3  what method should be used to deliver the treatment (required staff training, outpatient, in-prison programs).

## Juvenile offenders

### Treatment programs for juveniles

Rehabilitation has particular appeal for use with juveniles. Juvenile crime is often serious and it may represent a large proportion of the total criminal activity in a community. However, it is usually assumed that adolescents deserve and require special handling because at this stage of life they are in a formative period and criminal behavior at this stage will not necessarily be continued into adulthood. Theoretically, rehabilitation has been the focus of correctional programs for juveniles. However, in practice, as occurs with adult programs, juvenile programs may be poorly implemented. Juveniles have a potentially long adulthood in front of them, therefore strategies that reduce the future criminal activities of juveniles are also particularly import-ant. An effective preventive intervention at an early age, that results in reduced criminality over a lifetime, can have a substantial payoff.

The most extensive meta-analysis examining the effectiveness of delin-quency outcome studies was conducted by Lipsey (1992). In a meta-analysis of juvenile delinquency programs, Lipsey examined the effectiveness of 443 different research studies.[5] This meta-analysis improved on previous reviews of delinquency treatment research by (1) broadening the coverage of the literature through an exhaustive search for relevant studies and (2) coding sufficient detail from each eligible study. Among other criteria, the studies included in Lipsey's analysis were those that provided some intervention or treatment that had as its aim the reduction, prevention, treatment or remedi-ation of delinquency or antisocial behavior problems similar to delinquency. Delinquency was defined as behavior chargeable under applicable laws. Studies were included in the analysis only if the majority of the subjects were between the ages of 12 and 21.

Findings from the Lipsey (1992) study revealed that overall in 64.3 percent of the studies the treatment group did better (in most cases this refers to a reduction in recidivism) than the control group. The mean effect size for the studies was .172, which was comparable to previous meta-analyses of more highly selected sets of studies. One way to understand this effect size is to translate it into a comparison to a baseline of 50 percent. This effect size is equivalent to an average reduction in recidivism from 50 to 45 percent. That is, considering all treatment program studies combined, 45 percent of those who received treatment would be expected to recidivate in comparison to 50 percent of the non-treated control group.

In more detailed analyses, Lipsey identified those characteristics most important in determining differences among treatment and control groups. In comparison to 50 percent recidivism rate for the control group, only 32 to 38 percent of the juveniles who were given employment, multi-modal and behavior programs were estimated to recidivate.

Overall, the results of the meta-analysis indicate that more effective pro-grams:

- were judged to provide larger amounts of meaningful contact (treatment integrity) and were longer in duration (more dosage);
- were provided by the researcher or in situations where the researcher was influential in the treatment setting;
- provided behavioral, skills-oriented and multi-modal treatment.

There was also some evidence that more effective programs targeted higher-risk juveniles, but this effect was small and nonsignificant. On the other hand, treatment in public facilities, custodial institutions and in the juvenile justice system were less effective than alternatives. This suggests that treatment provided in community settings may be more effective. However,

Lipsey cautions that this conclusion is confounded with dosage (intensity) and needs a more refined breakdown before definite conclusions can be drawn.

It is interesting that effective programs were those that were either provided by the researcher or where the researcher was influential in the treatment setting. This may indicate that treatment delivered or administered by the researcher was better implemented than typical programs.

The best treatment types show delinquency effects of meaningful practical magnitude, in the range of 10 to 20 percent reduction in recidivism. On the other hand, there is no evidence that programs emphasizing deterrence treatments are effective and, in fact, such programs were estimated to increase recidivism (e.g. 62 percent of those who received a deterrence program were estimated to recidivate in comparison to 50 percent of the controls).

In comparing his results to the earlier findings by Andrews, Zinger *et al.* (1990), Lipsey asserts that with few exceptions the largest effect sizes occurred for treatment that would be classified by Andrews, Zinger *et al.* as clinically relevant. Similarly, as found by Andrews, Zinger *et al.*, deterrence treatments were associated with negative effects (e.g. an increase in recidivism). Few studies of interventions deal exclusively with the most serious or most violent juvenile offenders so, at this point, little can be said about the effectiveness of programs for these offenders.

## *Juvenile residential programs*

One type of program particularly popular during the late 1970s and early 1980s was the wilderness or outward bound-type programs. These programs emphasize physical challenge and demand that individuals excel beyond what they feel they can do. Outcome evaluations have been extremely rare (Gendreau and Ross, 1987). Recently, however, several other wilderness-type programs have been studied. Perhaps the most frequently cited study of this type of program is the VisionQuest study by Greenwood and Turner (1987). They examined the behavior of the juveniles during the 6 to 18 months after release from the program (controlling for prior arrests). Youth from Vision-Quest had fewer re-arrests (39 percent) than youth who had served time in a probation camp or who had refused to accept the VisionQuest placement and were placed in other programs (71 percent). While the results appear positive, as shown in Table 9.5 the research methodology (methods scores of 2) makes it impossible to draw conclusions regarding the program's effectiveness.

In a more recent study, Deschenes, Greenwood and Marshall (1996) examined the Nokomis Challenge Program in the Michigan Department of Social Services. Nokomis was designed as an intensive treatment program for low- to medium-risk juveniles. The focus of the program was on relapse prevention. Male youth were expected to spend less time in the residential facility but a longer time in community treatment when compared with youth in the training schools. Findings indicated that the Nokomis youth had significantly more felony arrests after release (48 percent) than did the comparison (23 percent). It is important to note that examination of the implementation

*Table 9.5* Juvenile residential programs (residential) and community supervision and aftercare (community)

| Study | Scientific methods score | Findings |
|---|---|---|
| Deschenes, Greenwood *et al.* (1996) Residential | 3 | Nokomis group (48%) had more arrests than control (23%) |
| Greenwood and Turner (1993) Residential | 3 | Paint Creek youth had fewer official arrests (51%) than control youth (61%); Paint Creek youth self-reported more serious offenses (75%) than control (62%) |
| Castellano and Soderstrom (1992) Residential | 2 | Spectrum youth did not differ from control youth in recidivism |
| Greenwood and Turner (1987) Residential | 2 | VisionQuest (39%) had fewer arrests than YCC Control (71%) |
| Barton and Butts (1990) Community | 5 | ISP juveniles had more charges but control group had more serious charges |
| Greenwood *et al.* (1993) Community | 5 | Detroit: aftercare group (22%) had more arrests than controls (18%); Pittsburgh: aftercare group had fewer arrests (49%) compared to controls (48%) |
| Land *et al.* (1990) Community | 5 | ISP youth (mostly status offenders) with no prior delinquent offenses had fewer delinquent offenses (12%) than control group (28%); ISP youth with prior delinquent offenses had more delinquent offenses (57%) than control group (33%) |
| Sontheimer and Goodstein (1993) Community | 5 | ISP juveniles had fewer re-arrests (50%) than parolees (74%) |
| Gottfredson and Barton (1993) Community | 4 | Institutionalized juveniles had fewer arrests than non-institutionalized |
| Weibush (1993) Community | 3 | ISP youth had more felony complaints (51%) than probationers (38%) but fewer than parolees (57%); ISP youth had more adjudications (77%) than probationers (62%) but fewer than parolees (78%) |
| Minor and Elrod (1990) Community | 2 | ISP group had more self-reported criminal and status offenses |
| Elrod and Minor (1992) Community | 2 | ISP group had fewer status offenses but more criminal offenses (68%) than control group (67%) |

of the program revealed that the aftercare phase of the program failed to provide many of the expected treatment programs. There was limited substance abuse treatment and control group youth had more family counseling than the treatment group.

Castellano and Soderstrom (1992) completed a study of the Spectrum program in Illinois. This wilderness program was modeled after outward bound. The 30-day course focuses on teaching wilderness survival and group living skills to pre-delinquent and delinquent juveniles. A comparison of recidivism rates indicated that 75 percent of the Spectrum participants were re-arrested in the follow-up period compared with 62.6 percent of the matched comparison group (nonsignificant).

In a random assignment study, RAND researchers examined the effectiveness of the Paint Creek Youth Center (PCYC) in southern Ohio (Greenwood and Turner, 1993). The program targeted youth convicted of serious felonies who were required to spend an average of almost a year in residential treatment. While the program was located in a rural setting, it would not be classified as a wilderness or challenge program because these activities were not a major component of the program. The distinguishing features of the PCYC were: small size, problem-oriented focus, cognitive/behavioral methods, family group therapy and intensive community reintegration and aftercare. Youth were randomly assigned to either the PCYC or regular training schools. Their behavior in the community after release was compared. The design was weakened because a relatively large number of the youth (25 percent) were removed from the PCYC and sent to the training schools to serve the remainder of their term. Furthermore, 27 percent of the remaining youth did not complete all three phases of the residential program. Official records of recidivism indicated that 50.7 percent of the PCYC youth (including those who were removed) and 61.3 percent of the control group had been arrested during a 1-year follow-up. The difference was nonsignificant. The small numbers of offenders in the study limits the power to detect differences between groups. This along with the loss of 25 percent of the PCYC youth makes it difficult to draw any definitive conclusions from the research.

Overall, these studies of juvenile residential programs had very mixed results. Although several of the studies were well designed, problems with the small number of subjects, attrition and program implementation limit the conclusions that can be drawn about the effectiveness of the programs in preventing crime. The one program that included both a strong research design and a reduction in recidivism, although this difference was not significant, was Paint Creek. Interestingly, this program followed many of the principles proposed by Andrews, Zinger *et al.* (1990). High-risk youth were targeted for participation in the intensive program that used a cognitive/behavioral mode of treatment. However, problems with the research design severely limited the potential for detecting differences even if the program had indeed been effective. Most notably, the focus of the program was not on wilderness or challenge activities.

The other programs reviewed in this section either targeted individuals who were lower risks for recidivism (Nokomos, Spectrum), were of short duration (Spectrum), were less behavioral in treatment philosophy, or focused on non-criminogenic factors, such as physical challenge (Spectrum). Thus, from the perspective of the research on rehabilitation (see section on rehabilitation and the Andrews, Zinger *et al.*, 1990 study), we would not expect them to be effective in reducing future criminal behavior.

### Community supervision and aftercare for juveniles

Approximately 55 percent of adjudicated juveniles are given probation (Butts, Snyder and Finnegan, 1994). Furthermore, those knowledgeable about juvenile corrections increasingly argue for aftercare and transitional services for juveniles following a period of incarceration. Both of the recent meta-analyses (e.g. Andrews, Zinger *et al.*, 1990; Lipsey, 1992) suggest there will be greater reductions in recidivism if treatment is provided in community settings instead of in institutions. However, national surveys of intensive supervision and aftercare programs for juveniles completed during the 1980s revealed that few programs had been evaluated (Armstrong, 1988; Krisberg *et al.*, 1989). Additionally, the evaluations that had been completed were severely limited in scientific rigor.

Most recent studies of community programs have focused on the increased surveillance and restraint aspects of the programs and not the enhanced services (see Table 9.5). While some of the programs enhance services, the research is designed to compare the increased surveillance and restraint with or without increased services. The treatment and restraint components cannot be untangled, and since the research designs focus on surveillance the outcomes are more indicative of the effectiveness of restraints than rehabilitation. Additionally, when the treatment integrity is examined, few differences are found between the experimental program and the control in either the services delivered or the impact on risk factors.

Using a random assignment design, Land, McCall and Williams (1990) examined the North Carolina Court Counselors' Intensive Protective Supervision Project (ISP). The majority of the subjects were status offenders who entered the program as runaways or truants. The program was designed to enhance both the surveillance and services provided to the juveniles. The results indicated that youth with no prior delinquent offenses had fewer delinquent offenses compared to the control group (11.9 percent compared to 27.5 percent) but the ISP youth with prior delinquent offenses had more delinquent offenses (57.1 percent compared to 33.3 percent). However, there were only a small number of youth with prior delinquencies. Whether the results were the effect of surveillance or services could not be distinguished in the research design.

In another study of youth in the community, Weibush (1993) compared the performance of youth on intensive supervision (ISP) with comparison groups of youth on probation and parole. During the 18-month follow-up, a larger percent of the ISP youth received felony complaints (50.6 percent) than the probationers (37.9), but fewer felonies than the parolees (56.6 percent). Similarly, a larger percent of the ISP group were adjudicated (76.5) when compared to the probationers (61.6 percent), but fewer than the parolees (77.6). The results were not significant. Furthermore, it is difficult to draw conclusions because the groups were not randomly assigned and the groups differed prior to the treatment.

Sontheimer and Goodstein (1993) examined whether a juvenile intensive supervision program (ISP) in Pennsylvania had an impact on juveniles' propensity to reoffend (a rehabilitative or deterrent effect) or whether the restraints provided by the officers limited the opportunity juveniles had to reoffend. The program was an intensive aftercare program for serious juvenile offenders. Probation officers supervising juveniles in the aftercare program were required to have frequent contacts with the juveniles and significant others; however, other than these additional contacts, there was no statement of the mission or philosophy of the program. Significantly fewer of the experimental group were re-arrested (50 percent) than the controls (74 percent) and their mean number of re-arrests were fewer (1.02 compared to 2.07 for the controls).

Minor and Elrod (1990,1994) examined the impact of an enhanced treatment program for juveniles on intensive and moderate levels of supervision. While there were no significant differences between the groups, juveniles in the enhanced treatment ISP program had more criminal offense complaints than the juveniles on ISP but without the enhanced treatment. Follow-up analyses also indicated that the intervention did have an effect on those who had more lengthy criminal backgrounds (e.g. the higher-risk group). The major problem with this research was that the number of subjects was so small there was no power to detect any difference that might have existed.

Greenwood, Deschenes and Adams (1993) studied the Skillman aftercare program in Michigan and Pennsylvania. The programs were designed to provide treatment components, hence the term "aftercare," along with intensive supervision. Subjects were randomly assigned to either the aftercare ISP or the control. Results indicated no significant difference between the experimental and control groups in the proportion of the youth who were re-arrested, or who self-reported either offending or drug use in a 1-year follow-up period. However, an examination of what the programs provided for the youth indicated that in comparison to the control group the aftercare group did not participate more in education or work activities, had little family support, and did not associate less with delinquent peers. Thus, despite the fact that the program was designed to promote changes in these risk factors there was little evidence of such change. Consistent with the previous meta-analyses of rehabilitation, it appears that the program did not have the required "treatment integrity" to bring about the changes in the risk (criminogenic) factors associated with criminal behavior.

The above studies compared the ISP programs in the community to other community alternatives. Studies by Barton and Butts (1990) and Gottfredson and Barton (1993) were designed to compare the recidivism of those who spent time on community supervision with others who had spent time in training schools. Barton and Butts (1990) evaluated an in-home ISP program compared to commitment to traditional training schools in a random assignment study. They found that the ISP groups had a higher mean number of charges but the mean seriousness of the charges was greater for the control group. These differences were not significant when time in the community was controlled in the statistical analysis. Gottfredson and Barton (1993) used a nonequivalent comparison group design to compare the effect of the closing of a juvenile training facility to the performance of juveniles who were then managed in the community. They found that the juveniles who had spent time in the institution had significantly lower recidivism rates than the comparison group. It is important to note that the comparison group was not intensively supervised in the community and there is little information about what services they may have received in the community.

In summary, most of the results reveal no significant difference between the experimental condition and the controls. In part, this reflects the small number of subjects in the studies which means there is little power to detect any differences that might exist between the groups. Two studies by Land, McCall and Williams (1990) and Sontheimer and Goodstein (1993) did find lower recidivism rates for the experimental groups. In both cases it appears that the experimental group received more services than the comparison. Again, this suggests the importance of meeting the rehabilitative needs of such offenders. This may also be why the institutionalized juveniles in the Gottfredson and Barton (1993) study had lower recidivism rates – because of the services and rehabilitation they received when they were in the institution. Whether or not the juvenile is in a facility or on ISP may not be as important as whether appropriate rehabilitation programs are a part of the correctional option.

## Education and work programs for adult offenders

### Adult Basic Education

We identified thirteen recent studies that examined whether Adult Basic Education (ABE) and/or GED training are associated with reductions in recidivism (see Table 9.6). Many of these evaluations were assessed as low in scientific merit (scientific methods scores of level 1 or 2) because the studies compared only participants or completers with others. No attempt was made to identify a reasonable comparison group or to compare the characteristics (such as sex, race, age, prior criminal activity, etc.) of the participants to the comparisons. As a result, we do not know what types of individuals entered and/or completed the educational programs. There is a good chance that volunteers for program participation are already at a lower risk for recidivism than others who were not willing or interested in obtaining education. Thus, in these situations, we cannot conclude that the educational program changed the offenders. Of the thirteen available evaluations, five studies (Harer, 1995a, 1995b; Ohio Department of Rehabilitation and Corrections, 1995; Texas Youth Commission, 1993; Walsh, 1985) were rated at level 3 or 4 on the Scientific Methods Scale. However, many of these did not use statistical significance tests, and those that did failed to produce significant findings. Furthermore, generally speaking, the effect sizes were moderate or low. Only the study by Walsh (1985) found that GED completers had a significantly lower re-arrest rate (16 percent) than the comparison group (44 percent). Therefore, we conclude that ABE and/or GED education appears to be a promising strategy for reducing recidivism.

### Vocational education programs

Since lack of education and unemployment tend to be correlated with crime, reduction of these two risk factors has been proposed by many as a means to reduce crime. Many criminal justice system-based programs have been developed in an attempt to increase educational achievement and employability for offenders. Though they share a number of similarities, the primary focus of these programs vary. Some programs, such as the Manhattan Court Employment Project, have attempted to divert offenders from the criminal justice system and into stable employment (Baker and Sadd, 1979). Others,

*Table 9.6* Adult Basic Education (ABE), correctional industries, vocational education (Voc Ed) and work programs for adult offenders

| Study | Methods score | Findings |
| --- | --- | --- |
| Harer (1995a) ABE | 4 | ABE participants whom entered prison with an 8th grade education level or less had a lower rate of re-arrest or parole revocation (46.7%) than non-participants (52.2%); ABE participants with some high school education were re-arrested or had their parole revoked at a higher rate (57.8%) than non-participants (54.5%); ABE participants who had already obtained a high school diploma prior to admission were re-arrested or had their parole revoked at a lower rate (31.2%) than non-participants (38.9%); ABE participants with some college education at admission were re-arrested or had their parole revoked at a higher rate (31.6%) than non-participants (29.3%) |
| Harer (1995b) ABE | 4 | Inmates with an educational level of 8th grade or less who participated in correctional education programming (GED, ABE, ACE) had a lower rate of reincarceration (45%) than equivalent non-participants (52.9%); inmates with some high school education upon entry who participated in correctional education programs (ABE, GED, ACE) had a lower rate of reincarceration (47.1%) than equivalent non-participants (62.7%); inmates with a high school diploma who participated in academic education (ACE) had a lower reincarceration rate (24.5%) than equivalent non-participants (39.2%) |
| Ohio Department of Rehabilitation and Corrections (1995) ABE | 3 | ABE participants had more reincarcerations (32.3%) than non-participants (30.6%); GED completers had a lower reincarceration rate (27.9%) than non-participants (32.3%); GED participants had a lower reincarceration rate (24.1%) than non-participants (32.3%) |
| Texas Youth Commission (1993) ABE | 3 | GED completers were re-arrested at a lower rate (41.3%) than the control group (53.5%); reincarceration rates for GED completers was lower (10.1%) than non-completers (19.1%) |
| Walsh (1985) ABE | 3 | In a 42-month follow-up, GED completers had a lower re-arrest rate (16%) than the comparison group (44%); GED non-completers had a higher re-arrest rate (32%) than non-participants (44%) |
| Siegal and Basta (1997) ABE | 2 | PALS participants were re-arrested at a lower rate (35%) than non-participants (46%) and reconvicted at a lower rate (20%) than non-participants (22%); GED participants had a lower rate of re-arrest (24%) than non-participants (46%) but were not different from non-participants in reconviction rates |
| Piehl (1995) ABE | 2 | Educational program completers had fewer reincarcerations (33.5%) than those who were eligible but did not complete a program (40.2%) |
| Adams *et al.* (1994) ABE | 2 | After an average of 25 months, Windham participants returned to prison at a lower rate (23.0%) than non-participants (23.7%); Windham non-mandatory participants were returned to prison at a lower rate (22.2%) than non-mandatory non-participants (22.3%); Windham mandatory participants had a lower return rate (23.1%) than |

*Table 9.6* Continued

| Study | Methods score | Findings |
|---|---|---|
| | | mandatory non-participants (25.3%); Windham participants who enrolled in 100 or fewer hours of academic training had a higher rate of return to prison (25%) than non-participants (23.6%); inmates who were schooled for 101–200 hours had a lower reincarceration rate (20.7%) than non-participants (23.6%); academic participants who received 201–300 hours of class time had a lower return rate (21.8%) than non-participants (23.6%); inmates who received 301+ hours of educational training had a lower reincarceration rate (16.6%) than non-participants (23.6%) |
| Fabelo (1992) ABE | 2 | Fewer GED participants and completers were returned to prison (0%) than controls (9%); drop-outs were reincarcerated at a higher rate (19%) than the control group (9%) |
| NYDCS (1992) ABE | 2 | Inmates who satisfactorily participated in a GED program were returned to prison at a lower rate (34.0%) than unsatisfactory program participants (39.1%) |
| Porporino and Robinson (1995) ABE | 2 | ABE program graduates had a lower reincarceration rate (30.1%) than those that withdrew from the program (41.6%); ABE participants had a lower reincarceration rate (30.1%) than non-completers (35.7%) |
| Schumacker *et al.* (1990) ABE | 2 | Vocational participants experienced a lower reconviction or reincarceration rate (21%) than the control group (28%); vocational/academic participants had lower reconviction/reincarceration rates (19%) compared to control group (28%); academic participants had lower reconviction/reincarceration rates (22%) than the comparison group (28%) |
| Ramsey (1988) ABE | 2 | GED completers were reincarcerated at a lower rate (16%) than non-participants (36%); GED completers had a lower re-arrest rate (32%) than the comparison group (38%); GED participants were reincarcerated at a lower rate (33%) than the comparison group (36%); GED participants were re-arrested at a lower rate (32%) than non-participants (38%) |
| Maguire *et al.* (1988) C. Industries | 4 | Industry participants have fewer felony re-arrests (29%) than controls (34%) |
| Saylor and Gaes (1996) C. Industries | 3 | Industry participants had a 24% lower risk of a new offense recommitment than matched controls; vocational/training/apprenticeship participants had a 33% lower risk of new offense recommitment than matched controls; industry/training/apprenticeship participants had a 23% lower risk of new offense recommitment than matched controls |
| Saylor and Gaes (1996) C. Industries | 3 | After 6 months, industry participants had fewer parole revocations (4.9%) than controls (6.6%); after 12 months, industry participants had fewer parole revocations (6.6%) than controls (10.1%) |
| Anderson (1995a) C. Industries | 2 | After 2 years, correctional industry program completers had a lower rate of |

| Study | Methods score | Findings |
|---|---|---|
| | | return to prison (28.7%) than those who participated but did not complete (30.1%) and those who did not participate (31.3%) |
| Boudouris (1985) C. Industries | 2 | In-prison vocational, industry or farm work experience had fewer returns to prison (9%) than those with education alone (24%) and fewer re-arrests and revocations (30%) than those with education alone (38%) |
| Bloom *et al.* (1994) Voc Ed | 5 | Male youth JTPA completers with prior arrests had a higher rate of recommitment (59.2%) than controls with prior arrests (55.7%); male youth JTPA completers with no prior arrests had higher arrest rates (25.8%) than controls with no prior arrests (18.7%); female youth JTPA completers had higher arrest rates (7%) than controls (5.3%) |
| Harer (1995a) Voc Ed | 4 | Educational (including vocational) participation reduced the probability of arrest or parole revocation within 3 years of release; one course for each 6 months of prison term reduced recidivism 4.2% or, on average, 28.6% (one course) to 32.8% (no courses); any education (including vocational) course completers (at least half of a course per 6 months) had fewer re-arrests or parole revocations (30.1%) than those who completed less than half a course per 6 months (39%) and those who completed no courses (44.5%) |
| Lattimore *et al.* (1990) Voc Ed | 4 | Vocational education participants had lower new crime reconviction rates (36%) than controls (46%) |
| Saylor and Gaes (1996) Voc Ed | 3 | Vocational/training/apprenticeship participants had a lower risk of new offense recommitment than matched controls; industry/training/ apprenticeship participants had a lower risk of new offense recommitment than matched controls |
| Van Stelle *et al.* (1995) Voc Ed | 3 | STEP program graduates had higher average number of parole violations (M = 6) than controls (M = 1); STEP program graduates had more re-arrests (24%) than controls (19%); STEP program graduates had fewer reincarcerations (22%) than controls (28%) |
| Adams *et al.* (1994) Voc Ed | 3 | Vocational education (only) participants had fewer returns to prison (20.9%) than controls (25.1%) |
| Downes *et al.* (1995) Voc Ed | 3 | Vocational education participants had more unsuccessful parole outcomes (24%) than controls (20%) |
| McGee (1997) Voc Ed | 2 | After an average follow-up period of 3 years, male vocational education program completers had fewer returns to prison (13.4%) than matched non-completers (38%); female vocational education program completers had fewer returns to prison (5%) than matched comparison non-completers (25%); vocational education program completers who were employed had fewer returns to prison (8.7%) than matched comparison non-completers (38%) |
| Ryan (1997) Voc Ed | 2 | Job training program participants had fewer positive parole outcomes (25%) than non-participants (41%) |

*Table 9.6* Continued

| Study | Methods score | Findings |
|-------|---------------|----------|
| Piehl (1995)<br>Voc Ed | 2 | Vocational and education program completers had lower recidivism (35%) than eligible controls (40.2%) |
| Anderson (1995b)<br>Voc Ed | 2 | Vocational education completers (28.7%) had fewer returns to prison than controls (31.3%) |
| Schumacker *et al.* (1990)<br>Voc Ed | 2 | Vocational education participants had fewer parole violations (21%) than controls (28%) |
| Uggen (1997)<br>Work | 5 | Employment program participants (43%) had same re-arrest rates as controls (43%); young ex-offender participants had fewer re-arrests (46%) than young ex-offender non-participants (51%); older ex-offender participants had fewer re-arrests (26%) than older non-participants (36%) |
| Clark *et al.* (1992)<br>Work | 5 | Enhanced employment search program participants had lower rates of misconduct violations (56.7%) than matched controls (66.7%); enhanced employment search program participants had fewer average number of misconduct violations (M = 1.03) than matched controls (M = 1.23); enhanced employment search program participants had longer average time to first misconduct violation (M = 125.2) than matched controls (M = 81.8); enhanced employment search program participants had lower rates of return to prison (13.3%) than matched controls (33%) |
| Turner and Petersilia (1996)<br>Work | 4 | Work release participants had lower re-arrest rates (22.3%) than controls (30.2%), lower reconviction rates (7.1%) than controls (7.6%), higher return to jail rates (3.4%) than controls (0%), higher rates of return to prison for new crimes (4.7%) than controls (3.6%) and higher rates of return to prison for violations (25.9%) than controls (1.0%) |
| Menon *et al.* (1992)<br>Work | 3 | High-risk employment program participants had fewer re-arrests (48%) and reconvictions (23%) than high-risk non-participants (57% re-arrests, 38% reconvictions); low-risk participants had fewer re-arrests (16%) and reconvictions (0.6%) than comparisons (18% re-arrests, 1% reconvictions) |
| Latessa and Travis (1991)<br>Work | 3 | Halfway house participants (with more services and employment assistance) had fewer new crime convictions (29.5%) than probation comparison non-participant subjects (30.7%) |
| Milkman (1985)<br>Work | 3 | *Average/re-arrests by city*<br>Those who received program services and were placed in jobs had higher average number of re-arrests (Boston, M = .0145, NS; Chicago, M = .0133, NS) than comparisons (Boston, M = .0125; Chicago, M = .0125) in two sites and had a lower average number of re-arrests (San Diego, M = .0098, NS) than comparisons (M = .0107) in one site; those who received program services and were placed in jobs had higher average number of AFBI Part I crime re-arrests (Boston, M = .0076, NS; Chicago, M = .0083, NS) than comparisons (Boston, M = .0072; Chicago, M = .0080) in two sites and had a lower average number of AFBI Part I crime re-arrests (San Diego, M = .0036, NS) than comparisons (M = .0054) in one site; those who received program services and were placed in jobs had higher average number of "income producing |

| Study | Methods score | Findings |
|---|---|---|
| | | crime re-arrests" in all cities (Boston, M = .0098, NS; Chicago, M = .0090, NS; San Diego, M = .0064, NS) than comparisons (Boston, M = .0083; Chicago, M = .0082; San Diego, M = .0061). Those who were placed in jobs (experimental and comparison groups) had lower average number of re-arrests in all cities (Boston, M = .067, NS; Chicago, M = .058, S; San Diego, M = .053, NS) than non-placed (Boston, M = .078; Chicago, M = .088; San Diego) |
| Washington State Department of Corrections (1995) Work | 2 | Work ethic camp (WEC) participants had a lower average number of "community custody inmate" violations per offender (M = 2.2) than controls (M = 2.9); WEC participants had a higher rate of return to prison (25%) than controls (24%); WEC participants and controls were re-arrested at the same rate (35%) |
| Hartmann *et al.* (1994) Work | 2 | Halfway house employment program completers had lower re-arrest rates (52%) than non-completers (75%); halfway house employment program completers had lower felony re-arrest rates (44%) than non-completers (69%) |

Notes
M = mean average; NS = non-significant.

such as the POWER program, project TRADE, and the Wisconsin STEP program, have attempted to provide general education and vocational education to offenders during or following incarceration. Still other programs have attempted to provide inmates with hands-on industrial experience, such as the Canadian CORCAN program and the US Federal Bureau of Prisons' UNICOR program. (See section on Correctional Industries.) Pre- and post-release financial and job search assistance have been provided through work release programs, day reporting centers, and halfway houses. Some programs combine elements of several separate approaches, sometimes integrating vocational education, trade apprenticeship, prison industrial work experience and pre-release job search assistance.

According to our assessment of the research, vocational education programs provided to offenders in prison or residential settings are effective in reducing recidivism. Vocational education participants had significantly lower recidivism than controls in two relatively strong studies (Lattimore, Witte and Baker, 1990; Saylor and Gaes, 1996). Harer (1995a, 1995b), in two different studies, also found that education participants had significantly lower recidivism rates. However, this study combined all education programs with the vocational education, so the effect of the vocational education cannot be separated. Results from the other studies of reasonable scientific rigor were mixed. Several studies (Van Stelle, Lidbury and Moberg, 1995; Downes, Monaco and Schreiber, 1995) found higher rates of recidivism for the vocational education participants on some measures of recidivism but only one of the comparisons was significant. Vocational education participants in one study (Adams *et al.*, 1994) had a lower recidivism rate but the difference was not statistically significant. Thus, while there are some inconsistencies in the findings, the preponderance of the evidence suggests that vocational education programs are effective.

We do not know if community vocational training programs such as those established under the Job Training Partnership Act can be effective. The only available, yet very well designed, evaluation found that the program completers had higher recidivism rates than the comparisons (Bloom *et al.*, 1994).

### Correctional industries

Correctional industry is a term used to describe various offender employment-related activities that occur almost exclusively during an offender's term of incarceration. While some industrial facilities are located outside of prison walls, correctional industry workers are typically serving time in some type of residential facility (Correctional Industries Association, 1998). Offenders who participate in correctional industry programs tended to be older, serving longer sentences, had better pre-incarceration employment records and were less likely to be drug users than a sample of non-industry participants (Flanagan *et al.*, 1988).

Correctional industries produce a wide range of products and services for both government and private sector consumers, including furniture, health technology, automobile parts, institutional and jail products, signs, printing products, textiles and apparel, traffic paint and food products. As well as providing valuable skills and work experience that inmates can use outside of prison, correctional industry experience can provide opportunities for inmates to develop better time management skills, self-discipline and work ethics (Maguire, Flanagan and Thornberry, 1988). However, correctional industries often use outmoded production techniques and equipment, train inmates in areas that already have an excess of laborers or that require professional licenses that are difficult for ex-offenders to acquire. These and other problems associated with correctional industries make it more challenging for offenders to secure gainful employment outside of the supported work environment of prison.

Many correctional industry programs contain other intervention components, such as job search or vocational education/apprenticeship training. This makes evaluations of correctional-industry-only programs relatively rare. Therefore, evaluations of multi-component programs, including vocational education, correctional industries, and job search assistance or work release services are reviewed in this section. Unfortunately, evaluations of combined approaches make it extremely difficult to assess the effectiveness of correctional industry participation alone. Another problem with correctional industry evaluations is their relatively weak scientific rigor. Nearly all the evaluations reviewed here include some substantial methodological shortcomings. Typically, there is a failure to use random assignment. A related methodological problem in these evaluations is the failure to deal adequately with the issue of subject selection bias. A selection bias most commonly occurs when offenders who are less likely to recidivate (even without the program) are compared to a group of offenders who were initially more likely to engage in future criminal behavior. Since those who work in correctional industries are different from those who do not the groups differ prior to the work experience.

Our assessment of the research on correctional industries indicates that multi-component correctional industry programs are effective in reducing recidivism. Significant differences between industry participants and others have been found in at least two studies (Saylor and Gaes, 1996), showing that industry participants have lower recidivism rates. However, the differences between the recidivism rates of the groups are small. Most likely, the differences are significant because the sample sizes have been large. From a statistical perspective, small differences can be detected with large samples more readily than with smaller samples. An important consideration is whether the size of this difference is of practical significance. The difference in recidivism rates, in most cases, was less than 5 percentage points. Most evaluations focused on multi-component programs and, therefore, the effectiveness of correctional industry programs alone could not be assessed.

### Other work programs

Work programs for offenders in prison may be designed to give them work experience, help with the transition to the community or provide housing or other assistance for offenders in the community. In prisons, inmates frequently perform work such as cleaning, maintenance, painting or grounds keeping. In most cases, this work is not designed to have an impact on recidivism. However, one in-prison work activity program is the Washington State McNeil Island Work Ethic Camp, designed to provide an intensive employment experience within the prison environment that gives offenders the "opportunity to develop a positive work ethic and crime-free lifestyle through a regimented program" (Campbell, 1996).

Other work programs provide employment opportunities and/or services for offenders in community settings. For example, a work release program may allow participants to leave the facility during their last few months in prison either to seek employment or, more commonly, to participate in some type of work program (Turner and Petersilia, 1996). The goal of this type of program is to ease the participants' transition from institution to community and promote productive, stable employment following release. According to Turner and Petersilia (1996), work release has been a part of many correctional systems for nearly 80 years and, while 43 states have statutes allowing work release programs, only about one-third of these states actually operate such programs.

Other types of community employment programs attempt to ease the transition from prison to the community by assisting participants to obtain information and assistance in employment while they are in prison or upon release. We assessed the research examining programs that attempt to provide work experiences, work ethics or employment services to offenders (see Table 9.6). We found some types of community employment programs are effective in reducing the recidivism of offenders (Uggen, 1997; Clark, Hartter and Ford, 1992). For example, Clark, Hartter and Ford (1992) found that an enhanced employment search program reduced the number of violations and returns to prison. Similarly, when Uggen (1997) compared the recidivism of different aged participants in an employment program he found the participants had lower re-arrest rates. However, the mixed results found by Milkman (1985), Uggen (1997) and Turner and Petersilia (1996) led us to have some concern about the effectiveness of different implementations of community employment programs.

Transitional programs that begin individualized employment preparation and job search assistance in prison and continue upon release hold promise for reducing recidivism. Menon and colleagues (1992) found significantly lower recidivism for the high-risk participants suggesting that, for some individuals, transitional employment is effective.

There is insufficient research to draw conclusions about the effectiveness of work ethics programs or in-prison work programs (Washington State Department of Corrections, 1995). Nor is there sufficient research to determine whether halfway houses with enhanced employment services are effective (Latessa and Travis, 1991). Furthermore, no conclusion can be drawn about the type of offenders (different risk levels or ages) who may benefit from community work programs (Uggen, 1997; Menon *et al.*, 1992). Finally, there is no evidence that work release programs that focus on increased supervision requirements and surveillance are effective; and such programs may lead to increased technical violations (Turner and Petersilia, 1996).

## Cognitive skills programs

Cognitive-behavioral therapies comprise a number of different approaches which attempt to change behavior by changing the dysfunctional ways an individual thinks – their attitudes, beliefs and thinking patterns (Porporino, Fabiano and Robinson, 1991). Thus, cognitive-behavioral rehabilitation programs in a correctional setting focus on changing the problematic thought processes of offenders which are contributing to criminal behavior. There are over twenty different types of cognitive-behavioral therapies which generally fall into two different areas: (1) moral reasoning and development and (2) information processing (Mahoney and Lyddon, 1988). This review will examine rehabilitation programs which provide examples of these two approaches; Moral Reconation Therapy focuses on moral reasoning and development, and Reasoning and Rehabilitation focuses on information processing.

### Moral Reconation Therapy

The moral development approach suggests that individuals with higher levels of moral reasoning are better able to choose to engage in behavior which is "right" rather than behavior which is considered to be "wrong" (Arbuthnot and Gordon, 1988). Moral Reconation Therapy (MRT) was developed in the tradition of the moral development approach as a way of reducing recidivism by increasing the moral reasoning abilities of offenders (Little and Robinson, 1988). Specifically, the program incorporates seven elements of treatment: confrontation and assessment of self, assessment of current relationships, reinforcement of positive behavior, identity-formation, enhancement of self-concept, decreasing hedonistic orientation and increasing delay of gratification, and development of higher stages of moral reasoning (Little and Robinson, 1988).

Our assessment of the research on Moral Reconation Therapy determined that it is effective in reducing the recidivism of offenders (see Table 9.7 for

*Table 9.7* Cognitive skills programs, Moral Reconation Therapy (MRT) and Reasoning and Rehabilitation (R&R)

| Study | Scientific methods score | Findings |
|---|---|---|
| Little *et al.* (1996) MRT | 3 | MRT participants had a lower reincarceration rate (41.2%) than control group (56.2%), fewer mean re-arrests (M = 2.70) than control group (M = 3.37), and fewer mean additional days of sentence (M = 793.1) than control group (M = 990.4) |
| Little *et al.* (1995a) MRT | 3 | MRT participants had a lower reincarceration rate (44.3%) than control group (59.8%) |
| Little *et al.* (1995b) MRT Study 1 | 3 | MRT participants had a lower rate of reincarceration (48.9%) than the control group (58.5%) and had fewer re-arrests (74.0%) than the control group (79%) |
| Study 2 | | MRT participants had lower reincarceration rate (40.0%) than control group (52.3%), fewer re-arrests for any offense (61.0%) than control group (73.8%) and more re-arrests for DWI offenses (31.3%) than control group (29.2%) |
| Little *et al.* (1993a) MRT | 3 | MRT participants had a lower rate of reincarceration (31.3%) than the control group (40%) |
| Little *et al.* (1993b) MRT | 3 | MRT participants had a lower rate of reincarceration (37.1%) than the control group (54.9%), received fewer additional days of sentence (M = 511) than control group (M = 550), had fewer re-arrests (M = 2.6) than control group (M = 2.8), and had been re-arrested (73%) less than control group (77%) |
| Little *et al.* (1994) MRT | 3 | MRT participants had a lower rate of reincarceration (33.1%) than the control group (48.9%), had been re-arrested (65.5%) less than the control group (77.8%), and received fewer mean additional days of sentence (M = 737) than the control group (M = 948) |
| Burnett (1997) MRT | 2 | MRT participants had fewer re-arrests (10%) than control group (20%) and lower reincarceration rates (0%) than control group (10%) |
| Krueger (1997) MRT Study 1 | 2 | MRT participants had fewer re-arrests (11%) than control group (51%) |
| Study 2 | | MRT participants had fewer re-arrests (45%) than control group (67%) |
| Study 3 | | MRT participants had fewer re-arrests (62%) than control group (95%) |
| Little *et al.* (1991a) MRT | 2 | MRT participants had fewer arrests per offender (M = 1.6) than the control group (M = 1.8), fewer arrests for any crime (61%) than control group (70%), and lower reincarceration rates (24.3%) than the control group (36.6%) |

| Study | Scientific methods score | Findings |
|---|---|---|
| Little *et al.* (1991b) MRT | 2 | MRT participants had more re-arrests for DWI (18.3%) than control group (16.9%) and fewer re-arrests for any crime (45.2%) than control group (61.5%). Of a subset who participated in MRT and aftercare (n = 24), fewer were re-arrested for DWI (16.7%) than control group (16.9%), and fewer were re-arrested for any crime (45.8%) than control group (61.5%) |
| Little *et al.* (1990) MRT | 2 | MRT participants had fewer DWI or DWI re-arrests (10.4%) than control group (15.4%), fewer re-arrests other than DWI (31.3%) than control group (36.9%), fewer arrests for any crime (39.1%) than control group (78.5%), a lower rate of reincarceration (13.9%) than control group (21.5%), and had fewer days of additional jail days (M = 17.7) than the control group (M = 20.3) |
| Little and Robinson (1989a) MRT | 2 | MRT participants had a lower rate of reincarceration (7.8%) than control group (17%) |
| Little and Robinson (1989c) MRT | 2 | MRT participants had fewer re-arrests for any crime (20%) than control group (27.6%) and fewer re-arrests for alcohol-related charges (8.7%) than control group (10.8%) |
| Porporino and Robinson (1995) R&R | 4 | R&R participants had more reconvictions (15%) than control group (14%), fewer readmissions (32%) than control group (37%); among low-risk offenders, R&R participants had fewer reconvictions (7%) than control group (12%) and fewer readmissions (21%) than control group (33%); among high-risk offenders, R&R participants had more reconvictions (21%) than control group (14%) and fewer readmissions (42%) than control group (41%) |
| Ross *et al.* (1988) R&R | 4 | R&R group had fewer reconvictions (18.1%) than either the group receiving life skills training (47.5%) or the control group (69.5%), and a lower rate of reincarcerations (0%) than either the life skills group (11%) or the control group (30%) |
| Robinson (1995) R&R | 3 | R&R completers had fewer readmissions (44.5%) and fewer reconvictions (19.7%) than the control group (50.1%, 24.8%) and fewer readmissions (30.6%) and reconvictions (6.4%) than the control group (50.1%, 24.8%); among institutionally-based programs, R&R completers had fewer readmissions (45.9%), but more reconvictions (28.8%) than the control group (50.1%, 24.8%); among violent offenders, R&R completers had fewer reconvictions (21.2%) than the control group (32.8%); among sex offenders, R&R completers had fewer |

*Table 9.7* Continued

| Study | Scientific methods score | Findings |
|---|---|---|
| | | reconvictions (8.2%) than the control group (19.6%); among drug offenders, R&R completers had fewer reconvictions (22.8%) than the control group (36.8%); among nonviolent property offenders, R&R completers had fewer reconvictions (31%) than the control group (33%); among robbery offenders, R&R completers had fewer reconvictions (27%) than the control group (30%) |
| Raynor and Vanstone (1996) R&R | 3 | After 12 months, R&R participants had fewer reconvictions overall (44%) and fewer reconvictions for serious offenses (18%) than control group (49%, 21%); after 24 months, R&R participants had the same number of reconvictions (65%) but more serious offenses (27%) than controls (65%, 25%); upon reconviction, more R&R participants received a prison term (20%) than controls (15%) |
| Johnson and Hunter (1995) R&R | 3 | Drug program participants receiving R&R had fewer revocations (26%) than participants who did not have R&R (29%) and regular probationers (42%); among high-risk offenders, R&R drug treatment participants had fewer revocations (14%) than drug treatment participants with no R&R (35%) and regular probationers (75%) |
| Knott (1995) R&R | 3 | R&R participants had more reconvictions (44%) than controls (40%) and higher reincarceration rates (37%) than controls (27%); R&R completers had lower reconviction rates (35%) than drop-outs, and fewer violent offense reconvictions (13%) than program drop-outs (26%) |
| Porporino *et al.* (1991) R&R | 3 | Fewer R&R participants were readmitted to an institution (45%) than the control group (52.1%), fewer had readmissions with new convictions (20%) than control group (30.4%) and more had readmissions with no new convictions (25.0%) than control group (21.7%) |
| Robinson *et al.* (1991) R&R | 3 | R&R participants had fewer readmissions (20%) than controls (30.4%); among high-risk subjects, R&R participants had fewer readmissions with new convictions (18%) than control group (42%); among low-risk subjects, R&R participants had more readmissions with new convictions (16%) than control group (0%) |

Note
M = mean average.

the studies). At least five studies, of sufficiently rigorous scientific methodology, have found significantly lower recidivism rates between MRT participants and comparison groups on at least some measures of recidivism (Little *et al.*, 1996, 1995a, 1995b; Little, Robinson and Burnette, 1994, 1993a, 1993b).

### Reasoning and Rehabilitation

In an examination of correctional rehabilitation programs, Ross and Fabiano (1985) determined that successful programs shared one factor: the inclusion of an offender's cognitions, thoughts and attitudes as a target for change. Ross and Fabiano (1985) also found that the development of certain cognitive skills, including the ability to identify consequences of behavior, problem-solving, and ability to use means-ends reasoning, is delayed in many offenders. In response to this research, Reasoning and Rehabilitation (R&R) was developed as an educational, skills-based intervention for high-risk offenders (Ross and Fabiano, 1985).

Reasoning and Rehabilitation programs are effective in reducing the recidivism of offenders. At least two studies, using reasonably rigorous scientific methods, found significant differences in recidivism between R&R participants and control groups. In the majority of the eight studies, and on the majority of the different measures of recidivism, the R&R participants had lower recidivism than the comparison groups. Thus, according to our criteria, R&R is effective.

## Sex offender treatment

Meta-analyses and literature reviews have led to mixed conclusions regarding the effectiveness of treatment for sex offenders (Furby, Weinrott and Blackshaw, 1989; Hall, 1995; Quinsey *et al.*, 1993; Marshall, Jones *et al.*, 1991). In 1995, Hall conducted a meta-analysis of twelve sex offender treatment studies comparing treated and untreated offenders. The study found that the treated sex offenders had fewer sexual re-arrests (9 percent) than the sex offenders in the control group (i.e. the group not receiving treatment; 12 percent). In reviews of the literature, Marshall, Jones *et al.* (1991) and Blanchette (1996) also concluded that sex offender treatment was effective. In contrast to the positive treatment effects mentioned above, Furby, Weinrott and Blackshaw (1989), in a literature review, and Quinsey *et al.* (1993), in a meta-analysis, argue that there is no convincing evidence that treatment reduces future sexual deviance.

According to our assessment of the research, non-prison-based sex offender treatment programs using cognitive-behavioral treatment methods are effective in reducing the sexual offense recidivism of sex offenders. At least two studies, judged to be of scientific merit, demonstrated a significant reduction in recidivism for those who participated in the programs (see Table 9.8): Marshall and Barbaree's (1988) study of child molesters and Marshall, Eccles and Barbaree's (1991) study of exhibitionists. A third study, also of sufficient scientific merit, found child molesters and adult rapists who participated in the cognitive-behavioral treatment had lower recidivism in comparison to the control groups, however this difference was not statistically significant (Marques, Day and West, 1994).

Prison-based sex offender treatment programs using cognitive-behavioral treatment are promising methods for reducing sex offense recidivism. We identified two studies that were assessed as using sufficiently rigorous scientific methodology: Hanson, Steffy and Gauthier's (1993) study of child molesters and Nicholaichuk and colleagues' (1995) study of high-risk sex offenders. Hanson, Steffy and Gauthier (1993) did not find any significant differences between the groups. In contrast, Nicholaichuk *et al.* (1995) found that sex offenders had significantly fewer sex offense reconvictions, and reconvictions leading to a return to prison, than comparison groups. The program did not appear to have an impact on non-sexual recidivism. We identified six other studies of prison-based sex offender treatment programs but they were assessed as having relatively low scientific merit (see Table 9.8). The results did consistently show that the treated groups had lower levels of recidivism; however, because the scientific merit is so low, we are cautious about giving the results much weight in the decision about effectiveness.

There are too few studies focusing on particular types of sex offenders (e.g. exhibitionists, child molesters, adult rapists and high-risk sex offenders) to enable us to draw conclusions about the effectiveness of the programs for different types of sex offenders.

## Anger/stress management, victim awareness and life skills training

Three treatment programs that are relatively new are anger management, victim awareness and life skills training. The following sections review the literature on these three programs.

### Anger/stress management

Anger management programs seek to reduce the criminal behavior of offenders by teaching them to become more aware of the causes of their anger and to use various techniques to control their anger. Anger management programs are often one component of larger, more comprehensive treatment programs that deal with related issues such as sex roles and non-violence education (Gondolf, 1993). While these programs are used with a wide variety of offenders, the program seems to be most frequently used with domestic abusers and violent offenders. Very little evaluation research is available on anger/stress management programs, a fact that has been pointed out by other authors (Serin, 1994; Hughes, 1993; Eisikovits and Edleson, 1989). We located two studies (see Table 9.9) examining the effectiveness of anger/stress management programs, but our assessment of the scientific methodology indicated that they did not have an adequate level of rigor to permit us to draw conclusions about the effectiveness of the programs (no study was assessed at higher than level 2 on the scale). Thus, while there were some significant differences showing less recidivism for the treated groups than the comparisons, we do not believe that the designs permit us to draw any conclusions about the effectiveness of the programs.

*Table 9.8* Prison-based and non-prison based sex offender treatment

| Study | Scientific methods score | Findings |
| --- | --- | --- |
| Hanson *et al.* (1993) Prison-based | 4 | Child molesters in cognitive-behavioral treatment had fewer reconvictions for sexual, violent, or both crimes (44%) than offenders who had previously completed the same treatment program (48%), but not compared to offenders who were sentenced to the same institution at the same time as the treatment group, but did not participate in treatment (33%) |
| Nicholaichuk *et al.* (1995) Prison-based | 4 | High-risk sex offenders in cognitive-behavioral treatment had fewer sex offense reconvictions (14.5%) than controls (33.2%), fewer non-sex offense reconvictions (32.1%) than non-participants (35.0%), fewer sex offense reconvictions that resulted in a return to federal prison (6.1%) than program non-participants (20.5%), and more non-sexual convictions that resulted in a return to federal prison (7.8%) than non-participants (7.1%) |
| Oregon Department of Corrections (1994) Prison-based | 2 | Participants in intensive residential correctional treatment (6%) and those in outpatient correctional treatment (7%) had fewer reincarcerations than nonparticipants |
| Song and Lieb (1995) Prison-based Study 1 | 2 | Sex offenders in a community-based treatment program had fewer sexual re-arrests (11%) than eligible offenders (14%), and ineligible offenders (31%); they had fewer violent re-arrests (2%) than eligible offenders (13%), and ineligible offenders (12%); and they had fewer other felony re-arrests (7%) than eligible offenders (25%) and ineligible offenders (32%) |
| Study 2 | 2 | Sex offenders in prison-based treatment had fewer sexual re-arrests (11%) than non-participants (12%), fewer violent re-arrests (1%) than offenders not participating in the treatment program (3%), and fewer other felony re-arrests (5%) than offenders not participating in the treatment program (6%) |
| Huot (1997) Prison-based | 2 | Sex offenders who completed the prison-based treatment program had fewer sexual offense re-arrests (12%), person offense re-arrests (6%), and any other offense re-arrest (11%) than the offenders who never entered treatment (17%, 15%, 17%, respectively), or who dropped out of treatment (26%, 11%, 11%, respectively) |
| Alaska Department of Corrections (1996) Prison-based | 2 | Sex offenders in correctional center treatment had fewer re-arrests (M = 4.4) than the treatment-motivated control group (M = 4.9), the unmotivated sex offender control group (M = 4.7), and the non-sex offender control group (M = 7.0) |
| Gordon and Nicholaichuk (1996) | 2 | Sex offenders in a cognitive-behavioral treatment program had fewer |

| Study | Scientific methods score | Findings |
|---|---|---|
| Prison-based | | reconvictions for a sexual offense (4.7%) than the control group (6.2%) and fewer non-sexual reconvictions (7.8%) than the control group (13.6%); high-risk sex offenders had fewer of sexual reconvictions (6.0%) than the high-risk control group (14.6%) and fewer non-sexual reconvictions (8.6%) than the high-risk control group (14.6%) |
| Marques *et al.* (1994) Non-prison based | 4 | Child molesters and adult rapists in a cognitive-behavioral treatment program had fewer sexual re-arrests (8.3%) than offenders in the volunteer control group (13.4%), and the non-volunteer control group (12.5%); child molesters and adult rapists in cognitive-behavioral treatment had fewer other violent offenses (8.3%) than the volunteer control group (17.5%), and the non-volunteer control group (9.4%) |
| Marshall and Barbaree (1988) Non-prison based | 4 | Fewer child molesters in cognitive-behavior treatment were re-arrested or self-reported any sexual offenses (13.2%, M = 1.44) than the non-treatment comparisons (34.5%, M = 1.6 sexual reoffenses) |
| Marshall *et al.* (1991) Non-prison based Study 1 Study 2 | 3 | Exhibitionists reconvicted or charged with a sexual offense less (39.1%) than untreated exhibitionists (57.1%) Exhibitionists were reconvicted or charged with a sexual offense less (23.6%) than the untreated exhibitionists (57.1%) |
| Rice *et al.* (1991) | 2 | Child molesters in a behavioral treatment program had a higher proportion of sexual convictions (38%) than offenders not participating in the treatment program (31%) |

Note
M = mean average.

### Victim awareness

Victim awareness programs are a unique way of attempting to change offenders' perception of their victims as people, to understand the full impact of their actions on others and assist offenders in developing empathy (Shinar and Compton, 1995; MADD, 1998). Only Shinar and Compton's (1995) study of a victim awareness program reached a level 3 on the scale of scientific methods (see Table 9.9). In this study, none of the comparisons reached statistical significance nor was the direction of the differences between the treated group and the comparisons consistent. The only other studies we could locate were judged to be of low scientific rigor to provide the basis for drawing conclusions (Stutz, 1994; Shinar and Compton, 1995). Thus, at this

*Table 9.9* Anger/stress management, victim awareness and life skills training

| Study | Scientific methods score | Findings |
|---|---|---|
| Faulkner *et al.* (1992) Anger/Stress Study 1 | 2 | Subjects completing treatment scored lower at post-treatment on the Violent Behavior Inventory for the Direct Violence Scale and for the Severe Violence Scale; spouses reported lower scores for subject at post-treatment on both scales |
| Study 2 | 2 | Subjects completing treatment scored lower at post-treatment on the Violent Behavior Inventory Direct Violence Scale and on the Severe Violence Scale; spouses reported lower scores for subjects at post-treatment on both scales |
| Marquis *et al.* (1996) Anger/Stress Sample 1 | 2 | Offenders who completed substance use treatment and anger management treatment had less recidivism (34%) than those who did not receive any treatment (59%) |
| Sample 2 | 2 | Offenders who received anger management treatment only had less recidivism (33%) than those who did not receive any treatment (60%); offenders receiving a combination of substance use and anger management had less recidivism (36%) than those who did not receive any treatment (60%) |
| Shinar and Compton (1995) Victim Awareness California Study | 3 | Victim impact panel (VIP) treatment group (13.5%) had more reoffending for all DWI incidents than the control group (13.4%), more reckless driving or hit and run offenses (1.5%) than the control group (1.2%), fewer DWI incidents (5.9%) within one year after treatment than the control group (6.9%), more DWI or reckless crashes (2.3%) than the control group (1.5%), more drinking/drug crashes (3.5%) than the control group (3.2%); VIP completers had fewer misdemeanor DWIs (11.3%) than the control group (12%) and fewer licenses were suspended or revoked (3.4%) than the control group (5%) |
| Oregon Study | 3 | Offenders treated in the victim impact panel (VIP) had fewer moving violations and crashes (30.1%) than the control group (35%), and fewer DWI violations and crashes (M = .1267) than the control group (M = .1778) |
| Stutz (1994) Victim Awareness | 2 | Offenders who completed the victim awareness education program had less reoffending (9.3%) than offenders who did not complete the treatment (37.3%) |
| Melton and Pennell (1998) Life Skills Training | 4 | Life skills participants had fewer re-arrests (M = .34) after program participation than before the program (M = .89), fewer re-arrests (M = .34) than the control group (M = .37), fewer reconvictions (M = .84) after program participation than before (M = 1.8), and more reconvictions (M = .84) than the control group (M = .79) |
| Ross *et al.* (1988) Life Skills Training | 4 | Life skills participants were reconvicted more following treatment (47.5%) than the cognitive skills group (18.1%), had fewer |

| Study | Scientific methods score | Findings |
|---|---|---|
| | | reconvictions (47.5%) than the probation only group (69.5%), received more sentences of imprisonment (11%) than the cognitive skills group (0%), and received fewer imprisonment sentences (11%) than the probation only group (30%) |
| Miller (1997) Life Skills Training | 3 | Life skills participants from the first stage of the program had fewer re-arrests (19.1%) than the control group (27.1%), and fewer reconvictions and pending charges (21.5%) than the control group (26.8%), fewer pending charges or reconvictions for violent offenses (5.5%) than the control group (5.4%) |
| Miller (1995) Life Skills Training | 3 | Life skills participants had fewer re-arrests (8.2%) than the control group (16.7%) |
| Austin (1997) Life Skills Training | 2 | Fewer life skills graduates were recommitted to Dauphin County Prison (DCP) (44%) than the control group (49%), and of those returned to DCP, fewer life skills graduates were returned for a new offense (22.6%) than the control group (35.8%) |

Note
M = mean average.

point, we do not know how effective victim awareness programs are in reducing recidivism.

### Life skills

Offenders often find themselves challenged by the tasks associated with daily life. Life skills training programs were created to help offenders overcome such challenges. Some of the common components of life skills programs include: budgeting, interpersonal relationships, conflict resolution, taxes and credit, job seeking skills, cultural diversity, anger and stress management, decision making and goal setting.

We identified five evaluation studies of life skills programs that were of sufficient methodological rigor to warrant a review (see Table 9.9). There is insufficient evidence to draw conclusions about the effectiveness of life skills training programs. Studies by Melton and Pennell (1998) and Ross, Fabiano and Ewles (1988) were relatively strong evaluations rated at level 4 on the Scientific Methods Scale, but these higher quality studies do not find consistent evidence of effectiveness of life skills programs in reducing recidivism. No studies have reported significant differences in recidivism rates between participants and control groups. Also, the direction of the effects have differed. At times, the life skills group has had lower recidivism rates, while at other times the rate is higher. Variations were also noted by type of recidivism measure studied (e.g. Melton and Pennell, 1998; Miller, 1997) or in the type of treatment the comparison group receives (cognitive skills or probation in Ross, Fabiano and Ewles, 1988).

## Drug-involved offenders

Advocates of treatment and rehabilitation have perhaps made the strongest arguments in favor of increased treatment for substance using offenders. The need for treatment is demonstrated by the large body of research indicating the relationship between criminal activity and use of alcohol and other drugs (Chaiken, 1986; Chaiken and Chaiken, 1982; Inciardi, 1979; Johnson and Wish, 1986; Nurco, Hanlon and Kinlock, 1990; Speckart and Anglin, 1986). Furthermore, the National Institute of Justice's (NIJ) Drug Use Forecasting (DUF) program consistently finds high rates of illicit drug use among arrestees in the 24 participating cities. In 1995, between 47 and 78 percent of the men and 44 to 85 percent of the women tested positive for use of illegal drugs. Documentation of this high level of use and the strong association between drug use and crime clearly indicates the critical need for treatment for these offenders.

Despite the fact that many drug-involved offenders are not treated while they are under the control of the criminal justice system, a growing body of research indicates that treatment for substance-involved offenders can effectively reduce substance use and criminal recidivism (Gerstein and Harwood, 1992). Effectiveness of drug treatment is directly related to the length of time an individual remains in treatment. This is true for various treatment modalities. Furthermore, the treatment is effective whether the offender enters voluntarily or under some form of coercion (Anglin and Hser, 1990; Anglin and Maughn, 1992a; Falkin, Wexler and Lipton, 1992; Leukefeld and Tims, 1992; Travis *et al.*, 1996). From this perspective, the criminal justice system presents an ideal opportunity to require offenders to participate and remain in treatment.

### Treatment in prison

Some of the most promising evaluations of drug treatment for criminal justice have focused on the effectiveness of prison-based therapeutic communities (TCs) that operate as 24-hour live-in facilities within the prison. We examined evaluations of five such programs (Wexler, Falkin and Lipton, 1992; Martin, Butzin and Inciardi, 1995; Wexler *et al.*, 1995; Field, 1989; Eisenberg and Fabelo, 1996). The studies were judged to be of sufficient rigor to draw conclusions about the effectiveness of the treatment programs (see Table 9.10). In all studies, the researchers found that the graduates of the programs had lower recidivism rates than those who spent less time in the programs. Thus, we conclude that prison-based TCs are effective in reducing the recidivism of offenders. However, drop-outs from treatment present a major problem in terms of both evaluating the effectiveness of the programs and in determining how successful the program will be.

*Table 9.10* In-prison therapeutic communities (TC), drug treatment and urine testing, community-based programs and acupuncture in community-based treatments for drug-involved offenders

| Study | Scientific methods score | Findings |
|---|---|---|
| Wexler *et al.* (1992) TC | 4 | Male participants in TC had fewer re-arrests (27%) compared to milieu (35%), counseling (40%), no treatment (41%) and all groups combined; female participants in TC had fewer re-arrests (18%) compared to counseling group (29%), no treatment (24%) and both groups combined |
| Martin *et al.* (1995) TC | 3 | Combined KEY-CREST (3%) had fewer re-arrests than comparison group; KEY (19%) had fewer re-arrests than comparison group (29%) |
| Wexler *et al.* (1995) TC | 3 | Fewer treatment (Amity TC) plus aftercare (Vista) participants (26%) returned to prison than control group (63%) than treatment drop-outs (50%), and treatment only (43%) |
| Field (1989) TC | 2 | Graduates of Cornerstone program were less likely to be arrested (63%) than those who were in the program for less than 60 days (92%), between 2–6 months (88%), and more than 6 months (79%) and less likely to be convicted (49%) than those who were in the program for less than 60 days (89%), between 2–6 months (76%), and more than 6 months (72%) and less likely to be reincarcerated (26%) than those who were in the program for less than 60 days (85%), between 2–6 months (67%), and more than 6 months (63%) |
| Eisenberg and Fabelo (1996) TC | 2 | Texas Initiative graduates had fewer re-arrests (13%) than non-completers (31%) and than comparison group (29%), and they had fewer reincarcerations (7%) than non-completers (19%) and than comparison group (19%) |
| Taxman and Spinner (1996) Treatment with urine testing | 5 | Treatment with urinalysis reduced rates of new arrests (55.1%) compared to the no-treatment condition (68.1%) |
| Nurco *et al.* (1995) Treatment with urine testing | 3 | Treatment with urinalysis had fewer revocations (48%) than intensive urine monitoring (50%) and routine supervision (56%) |
| Hepburn and Albonetti (1994) Treatment with urine testing | 2 | No differences in revocations when treatment with urinalysis was compared to two urinalysis only conditions |
| Nemes, Wish and Messina (1998) Community-based | 5 | Clients who attended the standard program had lower self-reported and official arrests, self-reported and official imprisonment, and longer average time until arrest after discharge than clients who attended the enhanced program |
| Rhodes and Gross (1997) Community-based | 5 | At 3-months, substance use case management clients had more self-reported criminal behavior in Washington, DC (19%) and Portland (31%) than the control group (DC = 15%; Portland = 29%), but less than the referral group (DC = 20%; Portland = 33%) and they were less likely to be jailed in Washington, DC (15%) than those in the control (20%) and referral groups (20%); Portland clients were more likely to be jailed (26%) than the control group (24%), but less likely to be jailed than the referral group (27%). At 6 months, substance use case management clients had less self-reported criminal behavior in Washington, DC |

*Table 9.10* Continued

| Study | Scientific methods score | Findings |
|-------|--------------------------|----------|
| | | (10%) and Portland (22%) than those in the control group (DC = 15%; Portland = 27%) and those in the referral group (DC = 17%; Portland = 26%) and they were less likely to be jailed in Washington, DC (18%) and Portland (23%) than those in the control (DC = 23%, Portland = 27%) and referral groups (DC = 22%, Portland = 27%). At 3 months and 6 months, substance use case management clients were less likely to have their parole revoked in Washington, DC (3 month = 12%, 6 month = 18%) than those in the control groups (3 month = 15%, 6 month = 21%) and referral groups (3 month = 17%, 6 month = 27%) |
| Petersilia and Turner (1992) Community-based | 5 | Drug offenders under intensive supervision were more likely to be arrested in Seattle (46.1%), Atlanta (11.5%), Santa Fe (48.3%), Macon, GA (42.3%) and Winchester, VA (28.9%) than those on routine parole/probation in Seattle (35.7%), Atlanta (4.2%), Santa Fe (27.6%), Macon (37.5%) and Winchester (12%) but ISP clients were less likely to be arrested in Des Moines (23.7%) and Waycross, GA (12.5%) than those on routine parole/probation in Des Moines (28.7%) and Waycross (15.4%). Drug offenders under intensive supervision were more likely to commit technical violations in Seattle (33.7%), Des Moines (39%), Atlanta (65.4%), Waycross (25%) and Winchester (42.9%) than those on routine parole/probation in Seattle (25%), Des Moines (33.9%), Atlanta (45.8), Waycross (15.4%) and Winchester (20%) but ISP clients had less technical violations in Santa Fe (24.1%) and Macon (57.7%) than those on routine parole/probation in Santa Fe (34.5%) and Macon (62.5%) |
| Anglin *et al.* (1996) Community-based | 4 | Clients who participated in the TASC programs in Birmingham, Canton, Chicago and Portland had higher average numbers of incarceration days than the control group participants but clients participating in TASC programs in Orlando had a lower average number of incarceration days than those in the control group. Clients who participated in the TASC programs in Birmingham, Chicago and Orlando had higher average numbers of property crimes than those in the control groups but participants of TASC programs in Canton and Portland had lower average number of property crimes than those in the control group. Clients who participated in the TASC programs in Canton, Orlando and Portland were more likely to be arrested than those in the control groups but participants of TASC programs in Birmingham and Chicago were less likely to be arrested than those in the control groups. Clients who participated in the TASC programs in Birmingham, Orlando and Portland were more likely to have their parole revoked than those in the control groups but participants of TASC programs in Canton and Chicago were less likely to have their parole revoked than those in the control groups |

| Study | Scientific methods score | Findings |
|---|---|---|
| Martin *et al.* (1995) Community-based | 3 | Participants in prison and outpatient programs were less likely to be arrested (4%) than those in no-treatment (29%). Participants in prison and outpatient programs were less likely to be arrested (4%) than those in prison only treatment (19%). Participants in prison and outpatient programs were less likely to be arrested (4%) than those in outpatient only treatment (17%) |
| Prendergast *et al.* (1996) Community-based | 3 | Women participating in prison and outpatient programs (31.6%) had fewer custody returns than non-participants (72.8%). Women participating in prison and outpatient programs (31.6%) had fewer custody returns than those in prison program only (47.8%) |
| Wexler *et al.* (1995) Community-based | 3 | Participants of the in-prison and aftercare treatment had lower rates of reincarceration (26.2%) than those who received no treatment (63%), dropped out of the program (50%) and participated in the prison treatment only (42.9%) |
| Finigan (1996) Community-based | 2 | Treatment completers of the outpatient drug and alcohol treatment program were less likely to be arrested (43%) than noncompleters (66%), less likely to be convicted (16%) than noncompleters (29%), less likely to be incarcerated (6%) than noncompleters (12%), and they had lower average incarceration days (927 days per 100 clients) than noncompleters (2,215 days per 100 clients) |
| Hiller *et al.* (1996) Community-based | 2 | Completers of the prison and outpatient components of the Step Down program were less likely to be arrested (5%) than those who did not (7%) |
| Oregon Department of Corrections (1994) Community-based | 2 | Fewer clients who participated in outpatient treatment were returned to prison than eligible non-participating comparisons |
| Van Stelle *et al.* (1995) Community-based | 2 | Chemical dependency program completers had fewer re-arrests (43%) than noncompleters (74%), fewer reconvictions (42%) than noncompleters (70%), and received shorter jail sentences (M = 398 days) than noncompleters (M = 605 days) |
| Vito *et al.* (1993) Community-based | 2 | Program completers (3.8%) had lower reincarceration rates than those who did not (19.9%) |
| Martin *et al.* (1995) Community-based | 2 | Treatment completers were less likely to recidivate (arrested and reincarcerated) than those who did not |
| Latessa and Moon (1992) Acupuncture | 5 | Participants in a chemical dependency program with an acupuncture component were more likely to be arrested (20%) than those in the control group (18%), less likely to be convicted (15%) than those in the control group (16%), and more likely to have probation revoked due to technical violation (70%) than those in the control group (61%) |

Note
M = mean average.

## Outpatient drug treatment

Community-based outpatient drug treatment programs began in the 1970s, specifically designed for juvenile drug users. More programs have been implemented in the 1980s and 1990s, due to the more abundant research on the crime–drug use relationship, as well as the evidence that they are a less expensive alternative to incarceration (Anglin and Hser, 1990; Anglin and Maughn, 1992b; Anglin et al., 1996). Outpatient drug treatment programs vary widely in terms of their approach to treatment. Some outpatient-type programs are offered to inmates in prison. These programs are non-residential; inmates attend substance abuse treatment sessions but are housed with the general population.

Programs that combine in-prison therapeutic communities with follow-up community treatment appear to be effective in reducing recidivism. Prendergast, Wellisch and Wong (1996), Wexler et al. (1995), and Martin, Butzin and Inciardi (1995) found that those who participated in both in-prison and community treatment had lower recidivism rates than some or all of the comparison groups. It is not possible to determine whether this is because the in-prison and follow-up group spent a longer period of time in treatment or because the combination of in-prison and follow-up community treatment was particularly effective.

Increased referral, monitoring and management in the community is not effective. The well designed studies of intensive supervision by Petersilia and Turner (1992), of TASC programs by Anglin et al. (1996), and of TASC-like case management programs by Rhodes and Gross (1997) demonstrated that these methods were not effective in reducing recidivism. However, Rhodes and Gross (1997) found inconsistent evidence of effectiveness of a TASC-like program in reducing recidivism. The varying quality and quantity of treatment received may be responsible for this inconsistency.

Additionally, we do not know if community-based outpatient treatment alone (without an additional in-prison phase) is effective. Several studies were identified but they employed such weak research methodology that we could not draw conclusions about the effectiveness of the outpatient programs. A particular problem with this research is the comparison of dropouts with completers. One study found acupuncture provided within a community-based outpatient treatment program was not effective in reducing recidivism (Latessa and Moon, 1992).

## Urine testing

There are many drug testing technologies including urinalysis, hair assays, and other emerging technologies, such as saliva tests and sweat patches (Travis et al., 1996). These technologies are viewed as an important component of criminal justice programming for drug-involved offenders because they provide objective evidence of drug use independent of self-reports. While the new technologies hold great promise for overcoming some of the limitations of urinalysis, at this time urinalysis is the most commonly used testing technology.

Evaluations of the efficacy of such use of urine testing show mixed results (Travis *et al.*, 1996). While use of illegal drugs appears to be associated with criminal activity, there is little evidence that urine testing will reduce drug use and associated criminal activity. Offenders on probation or parole in the community are often required to submit to urine tests. Deschenes *et al.* (1996) evaluated the effect of three levels of urine testing on recidivism rates for drug offenders on probation (no testing, random testing and frequent testing). The authors conclude that increased testing frequency does not affect arrest or conviction rates. They suggest that increased testing does serve to identify sooner, rather than later, offenders "who continue to use drugs while on probation."

## Combining rehabilitation and restraint

Some programs have begun to combine components of community restraints or challenge programs with rehabilitation. As previously reported, there is some evidence, not yet fully tested, suggesting that ISP programs that combine surveillance and treatment may be successful in reducing the recidivism of offenders. Similarly, correctional boot camps that combine the military aspects of the camps with rehabilitation and aftercare show some promise for reducing recidivism. Programs combining urine testing and treatment and the relatively new drug courts are examples of programs designed to combine restraints with rehabilitation. The research examining the crime prevention effectiveness of such programs is described in the following sections.

### Urine testing and drug treatment

Drug testing in combination with drug treatment can be useful as a method of monitoring progress in treatment and holding offenders accountable for treatment participation. The question is whether such testing can reduce the criminal activities of offenders while they are in treatment. Four studies were identified that used testing and treatment interventions for offenders in the community (see Table 9.10). Three of these studies found no significant differences between those with urine monitoring and comparison groups (Nurco, Hanlon, Bateman and Kinlock, 1995; Hepburn and Albonetti, 1994; Anglin *et al.*, 1996). The only study that found significant differences between those who were urine tested and others was the study by Taxman and Spinner (1996). They used a random assignment study to compare a jail-based treatment program using TASC (Treatment Alternatives to Street Crime). Approximately 80 percent of the offenders underwent drug testing while they were in community treatment programs. The experimental group who received jail-based treatment as well as follow-up treatment and urine monitoring in the community had fewer re-arrests (55 percent) than comparison groups (68 percent). Overall, of the four programs only the jail-based treatment programs showed a significant impact on re-arrests. Similar to the finding from the prison-based TCs followed by community treatment, we cannot disentangle the effects of the jail-based treatment followed by community treatment and urine monitoring to identify the specific components of the program that were effective. We can say that this combination is more effective than urine testing alone.

### Drug courts

Faced with the enormous growth and impact of drug-related criminal case-loads in most jurisdictions across the United States, many court systems have searched for alternatives to traditional methods of processing the drug-involved offenders. One solution has been drug courts. Earlier versions of drug courts were designed to rapidly process offenders through the system. However, the recently developed drug courts are treatment-oriented courts that seek to bring substance use treatment to bear on the problems of drug-involved felony defendants in a diversionary, alternative processing approach. Drug use is monitored through urine testing and the results are reported to the court. Frequently the courts emphasize individual account-ability through a system of rewards and graduated sanctions for misbehavior.

The relatively recent development of these programs means there has been little time for outcome evaluations (see Table 9.11). Harrell and Cavanagh (1996) are studying the DC Superior Court Drug Intervention Program; however, recidivism data are not yet available from this study. Gott-fredson, Coblentz and Harmon (1996) examined the Baltimore City Drug Treatment Court Program. While the numbers are quite small, the results suggest that the program may have very different impacts depending upon the court and characteristics of the offenders involved. Males in the circuit and district courts had fewer arrests and convictions than their comparison groups when their criminal risk was controlled in the statistical analysis. On the other hand, women in these two drug courts and cases that entered as probation violators had fewer new arrests and convictions than their comparisons.

*Table 9.11* Drug courts

| Study | Scientific methods score | Findings |
|---|---|---|
| Goldkamp (1994) | 2 | Fewer Miami Drug Court participants were re-arrested (33%) than comparisons (52%), more Miami Drug Court group failed to appear (52%) than comparisons (9%) |
| Deschenes *et al.* (1996) | 4 | Fewer Drug Court participants were re-arrested than probationers, fewer Drug Court arrestees were sentenced to prison (9%) compared to probationer arrestees (23%) |
| Gottfredson *et al.* (1996) | 3 | When seriousness was statistically controlled, male drug court participants had fewer re-arrests and fewer reconvictions than comparison; female drug court participants had fewer re-arrests and fewer convictions |

Goldkamp (1994) completed a study of the original Miami Drug Treatment Court in Dade County. While the results demonstrated a lower re-arrest rate for participants in the drug court, there were several design problems with the study making it difficult to definitely conclude that the effect can be attributed to the drug court. In particular, the groups were not randomly assigned, and furthermore, the failure-to-report rates differed tremendously between the drug court participants (55 percent) and the comparisons (9 percent).

Unlike many drug courts the Maricopa County (Arizona) Drug Court is a post-adjudication program for probationers with a first-time felony conviction for drug possession. Participants are required to participate in an outpatient comprehensive drug treatment program and their progress is monitored by the judge. In a random assignment study of this program, Deschenes *et al.* (1996) found drug court participants had fewer re-arrests (nonsignificant) and fewer incarcerations (significant) in comparison to the control group offenders.

In contrast to many of the other intermediate sanctions, drug courts attempt to combine increased surveillance with treatment. The court's responsibility for oversight of the offender, the treatment programs and the supervising agents also means that all involved can be held accountable for outcomes. There is yet little research to examine how effective the programs are in reducing crime, but the early results appear hopeful.

## Summary and recommendations

It is obvious from this review of the research on crime prevention in the criminal justice system that no one strategy is appropriate for all offenders and all situations. Careful system planning is required to maximize the crime prevention potential of these different strategies. Shown in Table 9.12 are some of the issues that remain unresolved in the research on these strategies. What has not been addressed in this review of the scientific evidence supporting these strategies is the differential impacts of the strategies. For example, important in any consideration of the combination of incapacitation and deterrence strategies is the effect these policies have had on the minority community (Tonry, 1995) and the unintended effect of incarceration on inmates' families (Clear, 1996). Similarly, types of rehabilitation programs may be more effective with some offenders than others. Differences in gender, mental illness or risk level, for instance, may be associated with program effectiveness.

Despite the fact that many such topics have had to be omitted due to time and length constraints, some conclusions can be offered regarding the crime prevention effects of the different criminal justice strategies reviewed.

### *What works?*

The research examined herein provides evidence that the following strategies are effective in reducing crime in the community:

• rehabilitation programs with particular characteristics;

*Table 9.12* Different strategies for preventing crime by the courts and corrections showing issues unresolved by the research

**Crime prevention by the courts and corrections**

| | *Incapacitation* | *Deterrence* | *Rehabilitation* | *Community restraints* | *Structure, discipline and challenge* | *Combining restraints and rehabilitation* |
|---|---|---|---|---|---|---|
| **Unresolved issues** | Limited ability to predict future high risk offenders | What types of deterrents (e.g. day fines) are effective with what types of offenders (e.g. DWI)? | Retaining offenders in treatment? | How to combine with treatment? | Do such programs enhance or conversely reduce the effectiveness of treatment? | How to provide coercion? |
| | Financial costs and increases in imprisonment rates | | How to insure well-implemented intensive rehabilitation programs | Does increased surveillance reduce criminal activities? | What components are associated with success or failure? | How to insure well-implemented rehabilitation program? |
| | Diminishing returns with increased incarceration rates | | Most effective targets (attitudes, values, employment) for change | Do violations of conditions of supervision "signal" new criminal activity? | | How to coordinate treatment and surveillance to maximize the effectiveness of each? |
| | Adequacy of estimates of length of criminal career and rates of offending unknown | | Most effective service delivery methods for change | | | |
| | Negative impact on minorities | | | | | |
| | Unintended consequences | | | | | |
| | Increased use may decrease deterrent effects | | | | | |
| | Self-reported crime rates of those monitored in the community | | | | | |

- prison-based therapeutic community treatment of drug-involved offenders;
- in-prison therapeutic communities with follow-up community treatment;
- cognitive behavioral therapy: Moral Reconation Therapy and Reasoning and Rehabilitation;
- non-prison based sex offender treatment programs;
- vocational education programs;
- multi-component correctional industry programs;
- community employment programs;
- incapacitating offenders who continue to commit crimes at high rates.

There is now substantial evidence that rehabilitation programs work. There is a body of research supporting the conclusion that some treatment programs work with at least some offenders in some situations. Effective rehabilitation programs:

- are structured and focused, use multiple treatment components, focus on developing skills (social skills, academic and employment skills), and use behavioral (including cognitive-behavioral) methods (with reinforcements for clearly identified, overt behaviors as opposed to non-directive counseling focusing on insight, self esteem or disclosure); and,
- provide for substantial, meaningful contact between the treatment personnel and the participant.

The best treatment programs reduced recidivism by as much as 10 to 20 percentage points.

However, in order to be effective, treatment must follow some important principles. Programs must be designed to address the characteristics of the offenders that can be changed and that are associated with the individual's criminal activities. Furthermore, the treatment provided to offenders must be of sufficient integrity to insure that what is delivered is consistent with the planned design.

The research demonstrates that drug treatment is effective in reducing the criminal activities of offenders. The current examination of prison-based therapeutic community treatment for drug-involved offenders demonstrates that these programs are an effective method of providing prison-based treatment. The TCs programs that are followed by community treatment are also effective. These intensive, behaviorally-based programs target offenders' drug use, a behavior that is clearly associated with criminal activities.

Incapacitating offenders who will continue to commit crimes at a high rate and who are not at the end of their criminal careers is effective in reducing crimes in the community. Studies investigating the effectiveness of these incapacitation techniques show there are advantages in locking up the high-rate career criminals who commit serious crimes. The difficulty is in identifying who these high-rate offenders are, and the diminishing return on invested dollars with the increased incarceration rates. It is clear that the most serious offenders such as serial rapists should be incapacitated. However, locking up those who are not high-rate, serious offenders or those who are at the end of their criminal careers is extremely expensive.

Studies demonstrate little evidence that continuing the policies of the past several decades of increasing use of incarceration will have a major impact on reducing crimes at this time. As incarceration rates grow there appear to be diminished returns (e.g. reduced impact on crime rates) because lower-rate offenders are being locked up. It may also be counterproductive by limiting the deterrent effect of prison because people have less fear of incarceration. The impact on minority communities has been disastrous. An additional difficulty with the strategy is that, at this point in time, we cannot intelligently make the distinction between those who will commit serious crimes in the future and those who will not.

## What's promising?

There are, however, some promising signs. Several strategies have been shown in only one study to reduce recidivism of offenders so we classify these as promising. The following are promising programs:

- drug courts combining both rehabilitation and criminal justice control;
- fines;
- juvenile aftercare;
- drug treatment combined with urine testing;
- prison-based sex offender treatment;
- adult basic education;
- transitional programs providing individualized employment preparation and services for high-risk offenders.

## What does not work?

Studies of poorly implemented rehabilitation programs given to low-risk offenders using vague behavioral targets were not effective in reducing crime. Nor were programs that emphasized characteristics such as discipline, structure, challenge and self-esteem that are not directly associated with the offender's criminal behavior. Programs and interventions that did not reduce the recidivism of offenders were:

- specific deterrence interventions, such as shock probation and Scared Straight;
- rehabilitation programs that use vague, nondirective, unstructured counseling;
- intensive Supervised Probation or parole (ISP);
- home confinement;
- community residential programs;
- urine testing;
- increased referral, monitoring and management in the community;
- correctional boot camps using the old-style military model;
- juvenile wilderness programs.

Community restraints without programming and services were not effective in reducing the recidivism rates of offenders. There is now an extensive body of research examining the crime prevention effects of community sanctions designed to restrain offenders while they are in the community. The studies are scientifically rigorous, so it is possible to draw conclusions about the effectiveness of these efforts. Evaluations of these programs have focused on the impact of increased control. The results have been discouraging because there are usually no differences between those in the intermediate sanctions and the comparison groups. In fact, in many cases the group receiving the intermediate sanction has had more technical violations. It is important to note that, while these sanctions may not reduce recidivism, they do not do any worse than other forms of "management as usual" and they may have other advantages when compared to incarceration, such as reduced costs. Therefore, they may compare favorably with other sanctions on grounds other than recidivism.

Other programs that were not shown to be effective (again, if they were not combined with rehabilitation) are those emphasizing structure, discipline and challenge. As with the research examining community restraints, there are a reasonable number of scientifically credible studies that have been completed, so conclusions about the effects of the programs are clear. It is unclear why these programs have failed to show crime reduction effects. Possibly individuals in the programs spend more time in the physical challenge activities and not in therapeutic activities that would more directly address the problems they have that are associated with their criminal activities. Another possibility is that the programs are group-oriented and do not offer enough individualized programming to address specific difficulties of the individual participants.

Deterrence programs that increase the punitive impact of the sentence, such as Scared Straight or shock probation, do not reduce crime. Reviews of the literature on these programs as well as the meta-analyses of rehabilitation continually show that these programs are not effective in preventing crime. In fact, some research suggests that such programs are associated with increases in the later criminal activities of the participants (see the meta-analysis by Lipsey, 1992).

### What we do not know

There is not enough research to draw conclusions about the effectiveness of many programs and interventions:

- intensive supervision programs combining restraints with treatment;
- boot camp programs combining structure with treatment;
- day reporting programs combining accountability with treatment;
- substance use treatment programs receiving referred offenders;
- acupuncture within outpatient substance use treatment programs;
- anger/stress management programs;
- victim awareness programs;
- community vocational training programs;
- success of programs with different types of sex offenders;
- life skills training programs;
- work ethics, in-prison work programs, halfway houses with enhanced services.

We do not know whether rehabilitation combined with ISP or with boot camps will be effective in reducing the recidivism of offenders because the research has been exploratory in nature, and has been a level 1 or 2 on the Scientific Methods Scale. Research examining these programs reveals that these combinations may be effective in preventing the criminal activities of offenders. The exploratory follow-up studies of ISP have investigated the differences in recidivism that can be attributed to treatment. The results from these investigations suggest that rehabilitation programs combined with community restraint programs may be effective in reducing recidivism. Similarly, the research from the discipline, structure and challenge programs suggests that combining these programs with rehabilitation may effectively reduce the later criminal behavior of participants. The idea of combining control and rehabilitation is also supported by the drug treatment research revealing that substance using offenders who are coerced into treatment stay in treatment longer and they do as well as others who were not coerced.

From this perspective, intensive supervision programs and correctional boot camps may be effective in reducing recidivism if the programs incorporate treatment programs that follow the principles of effective rehabilitation. The question is how to combine the programs so that the integrity of the treatment program is not lost. Those responsible for the control and surveillance and those responsible for providing the treatment will have to be held accountable for the component of the program they are expected to deliver. Furthermore, there will have to be close coordination between the groups to insure a close working relationship between the treatment and control providers.

Day reporting programs also hold potential for combining the treatment and community control of offenders. However, to date there are no studies showing whether these are effective. Furthermore, there is a possibility that the programs will emphasize the control and surveillance aspects of the program and not the combination of treatment and control.

Future research needs to focus on determining whether offenders who are at different stages in the change process would benefit from different types of programs. In addition, research should focus on methods of keeping offenders in the programs, once they have decided to enter.

### Improving effectiveness through research

The development of more effective crime prevention in the courts and corrections would be improved if the following steps were taken.

> Require (and provide the substantial financial investment to enable) rigorous evaluation using experimental designs of rehabilitation models that are guided by the principles of effective programs revealed in meta-analyses.

While there appear to be an enormous number of studies examining the effectiveness of rehabilitation, researchers completing reviews of the literature and meta-analyses report that there are a relatively limited number of studies that use a scientifically adequate methodology. As a result, it is impossible to draw unequivocal conclusions about the effectiveness of the programs, for whom they are effective, and the components, intensity and length required to be effective. Ways to encourage partnerships between universities and local, state and federal agencies should be identified and supported. These must solve the problems related to the failure of universities to encourage and support social scientists doing applied research. One possible model for increasing the interaction between local and state agencies is the extension agent concept adapted from colleges of agriculture (MacKenzie, 1998).

> Support the development of a methodology to study the therapeutic integrity (implementation, staff training and treatment modality) of rehabilitation to insure that programs can be held accountable for implementing programs that are effective in reducing recidivism.

Many times the evaluation of programs is unsuccessful because the program is not implemented as designed or is designed so poorly that it would reasonably be expected to have an impact on the individual participants. More research needs to be completed to identify methods to hold rehabilitation programs accountable for the treatment and services delivered.

> Provide funding for research test-sites that enable researchers to be intimately involved in the design and implementation of programs.

The US Congress has earmarked funds for programs like prison construction, drug courts and boot camp prisons. For some of the programs, jurisdictions receiving funding have been required to agree to participate in an evaluation. This arrangement between research and program money causes some difficulties that require researchers to play "catch-up" in trying to design the research and obtain agreements from sites. Many programs would benefit greatly if the researchers were involved from the beginning and the money was tied to the requirement that sites would participate in studies. Such test-site research would insure close cooperation between the programs and the research. This is a particular concern with the funding for programs like boot camps, day reporting programs and drug courts, because they rapidly spread throughout the nation before their effectiveness had been examined.

> Research examining intermediate sanctions, alternative punishments or correctional options should be carefully designed to address the questions that are still unanswered by the research.

These programs are not effective in reducing the recidivism rates of offenders as measured by official records. Self-report measures of criminal activities may reveal that the crime rates are reduced for offenders in such alternatives but that the increased attention to offenders means their misbehavior is more apt to be detected. Furthermore, research should examine whether combining these options with rehabilitation is successful in reducing criminal activity.

More research is needed on the programs identified as promising in this report: drug courts, day fines, juvenile aftercare and drug treatment combined with urine testing.

In summary, what is clear from this chapter is that none of these strategies should be eliminated as an option. In particular situations, each strategy has some support for successfully reducing crime in the community. What will be important is a strategic plan defining who should be incapacitated, who should be rehabilitated, who can be deterred, and how to combine restraint and rehabilitation to effectively reduce crime. Important in this plan will be measures to insure that each program is held accountable for the expected outcome. The question is whether we can reduce the future criminal activities of offenders by holding the individual accountable for his or her own behavior, the treatment program accountable for outcomes and the criminal justice system for sanctioning offenders who do not comply with requirements. Equally as important are questions addressing the differential impacts of programs for individuals who differ in characteristics such as gender, home community (urban/rural), race/ethnicity and age. The argument is not which of these different strategies of crime prevention should be used, but when and where the effect of each strategy can be used to maximize crime prevention in the community.

Support research on incapacitation.

Large-scale research studies examining the effects of increasing the capacity of prisons are needed to determine the effects of incapacitation strategies. There has been little rigorous research examining the impact of incapacitation strategies. This is evident in a recent study of research articles published on the topic of deterrence, rehabilitation and incapacitation. Zimring and Hawkins (1995) examined the titles of articles found in the Social Scisearch (SOSCISCH) system. From 1980 until 1989, over 4,000 studies had rehabilitation/recidivism in the title, 610 had deterrence but only 45 had incapacitation/preventive detention. Self-report studies of the criminal activities of offenders are needed to determine crime rates after arrest or when offenders are serving time on probation, parole or in some alternative sanction in the community (see e.g. MacKenzie *et al.*, 1999).

## Notes

1  Earlier versions of the assessments in this chapter were included in the following reports: *Preventing Crime: What Works, What Doesn't, What's Promising* (Sherman *et al.*, 1997), submitted to the National Institute of Justice, US Department of Justice, and *What Works in Corrections? An examination of the effectiveness of the type of rehabilitation programs offered by Washington State Department of Corrections* (MacKenzie and Hickman, 1998), a report to the State of Washington Legislature Joint Audit and Review Committee.

2  It should be noted that this research made use of a complex statistical model with reasonable estimates of the relevant factors completed by a respected group of researchers. Although there is still debate about the estimates used in the statistical models, it is important to distinguish the predictions from unscientific esti-

mates given in some policy debates. For example, Zimring and Hawkins (1995) describe one unscientific estimate that would have produced a $300 billion savings in the cost of crimes prevented; as noted by Zimring and Hawkins, this unreasonable estimate is greater than the federal deficit or the national defense budget.

3 Note that this is the proportion of all the studies reviewed that show positive and significant reductions in recidivism when the treatment group is compared to the control group.

4 While this analysis included both adult and juvenile treatment programs, the majority of the studies dealt with juvenile programs.

5 This was a more extensive analysis than previous meta-analyses that had focused on delinquents in residential programs (Garrett, 1985), at-risk juveniles (Kaufman, 1985) and treatment of adjudicated delinquents (Gottschalk *et al.*, 1987; Whitehead and Lab, 1989). While the conclusions from these analyses differed, all yielded a positive mean effect of about the same order of magnitude (1/4 to 1/3 of a standard deviation superiority for the treatment group outcome compared with the control group outcome). See also the discussion of the Andrews *et al.* (1990) meta-analysis above.

# References

Adams, K., Bennett, T., Flanagan, T.J., Marquart, J., Cuvelier, S., Fritsch, E.J., Gerber, J., Longmire, D. and Burton, V. (1994) A large-scale multidimensional test of the effect of prison education programs on offender behavior. *The Prison Journal*, 74, 433–9.

Alaska Department of Corrections (1996) *Sex offender treatment program: Initial recidivism study*. Alaska Justice Statistical Analysis Unit Justice Center. Anchorage: University of Alaska Anchorage.

Allen, H.E., Seiter, R.P., Carlson, E.W., Bowman, H.H. Grandfield, J.J. and Beran, N.J. (1976) National Evaluation Program Phase I: Residential inmate aftercare, the state of the art summary. Columbus, OH: Ohio State University, Program for the Study of Crime and Delinquency.

Anderson, S.V. (1995a) *Evaluation of the impact of participation in Ohio penal industries on recidivism*. Ohio Department of Rehabilitation and Correction, Office of Management Information Systems.

Anderson, S.V. (1995b) *Evaluation of the impact of correctional education programs on recidivism*. Ohio Department of Rehabilitation and Correction.

Andrews, D.A. and Bonta, J. (1994) *The psychology of criminal conduct*. Cincinnati, OH: Anderson Publishing Co.

Andrews, D.A., Bonta, J. and Hoge, I. (1990) Classification for effective rehabilitation: Rediscovering psychology. *Criminal Justice and Behavior*, 17, 19–52.

Andrews, D.A., Zinger, I., Hoge, R.D., Bonta, J., Gendreau, P. and Cullen, F.T. (1990) Does correctional treatment work? A clinically-relevant and psychologically-informed meta-analysis. *Criminology*, 28, 369–404.

Anglin, M.D. and Hser, Y.I. (1990) Treatment of drug abuse. In M. Tonry and J.Q. Wilson (eds), *Drugs and crime*. Chicago, IL: University of Chicago Press.

Anglin, M.D, Longshore, D., Turner, S., McBride, D., Inciardi, J. and Pendergast, M. (1996) Studies of functioning and effectiveness of Treatment Alternatives to Street Crime (TASC) programs: Final report. Washington, DC: National Institute on Drug Abuse.

Anglin, M.D. and Maughn, T.H. (1992a) Overturning myths about coerced drug treatment. *California Psychologist*, 14, 20–2.

Anglin, M.D. and Maughn, T.H. (1992b) Ensuring success in interventions with drug-using offenders. *Annals of the American Academy of Political and Social Science*, 521, 66–90.

Arbuthnot, J. and Gordon, D.A. (1988) Crime and cognition: Community applications of sociomoral reasoning development. *Criminal Justice and Behavior*, 15, 379–93.

Armstrong, T. (1988) National survey of juvenile intensive probation supervision: Parts 1 and 2. *Criminal Justice Abstracts*, 20(2,3), 342–8, 497–523.

Austin, J. and Hardyman, P. (1991) The use of early parole with electronic monitoring to control prison crowding: Evaluation of the Oklahoma Department of Corrections pre-parole supervised release with electronic monitoring. Unpublished report to the National Institute of Justice.

Austin, T. (1997) *Life skills for inmates: An evaluation of Dauphin County prison's LASER Program*. Unpublished paper. Shippensburg University, Shippensburg, PA.

Bailey, Walter C. (1966) Correctional outcome: An evaluation of 100 reports. *Journal of Criminal Law and Criminology and Police Science*, 57(2), 153–60.

Baker, S. and Sadd, S. (1979) *The court employment project evaluation, final report*. Vera Institute of Justice: New York, NY.

Barton, W.H. and Butts, J.A. (1990) Viable options: Intensive supervision programs for juvenile delinquents. *Crime and Delinquency*, 36(2), 238–56.

Baumer, T.L., Maxfield, M.G. and Mendelsohn, R.I. (1993) A comparative analysis of three electronically monitored home detention programs. *Justice Quarterly*, 10, 121–42.

Baumer, T.L. and Mendelsohn, R.I. (1991) Comparing methods of monitoring home detention: The results of a field experiment. Paper presented at the meeting of the American Society of Criminology, San Francisco.

Baumer, T.L. and Mendelsohn, R.I. (1992) Electronically monitored home confinement: Does it work? In J.M. Byrne, A.J. Lurigio and J. Petersilia (eds), *Smart sentencing: The emergence of intermediate sanctions*. Newbury Park, CA: Sage.

Beck, A. and Klein-Saffran, J. (1989) Community control project. (Report No. 44.) Washington, DC: United States Parole Commission.

Benekos, P.J. and Merlo, Alida V. (1996) Three strikes and you're out: The political sentencing game. In J.W. Marquart and J.R. Sorensen (eds), *Correctional contexts: Contemporary and classical readings*. Los Angeles, CA: Roxbury Pub. Co.

BJS (Bureau of Justice Statistics) (1995) *The nation's correctional population tops 5 million*. Washington, DC: US Department of Justice Bureau of Justice Statistics.

BJS (Bureau of Justice Statistics) (1996) *Prison and jail inmates, 1995*. Washington, DC: Bureau of Justice Statistics Bulletin.

Blanchette, K. (1996) *Sex offender assessment, treatment, and recidivism: A literature review*. Ottawa, Canada: Correctional Service Canada.

Bloom, H., Orr, L.L., Cave, G., Bell, S.H., Doolittle, F. and Lin, W. (1994) *The national JTPA study: Overview of impacts, benefits, and costs of title IIA*. ABT Associates: Cambridge, MA.

Blumstein, A. and Cohen, J. (1973) A theory of the stability of punishment. *Journal of Criminal Law and Criminology*, 64, 198–206.

Blumstein, A. and Cohen, J. (1979) Estimation of individual crime rates from arrest records. *Journal of Criminal Law and Criminology*, 70, 561–85.

Blumstein, A., Cohen, J., Roth, J.A. and Visher, C.A. (eds) (1986) *Criminal careers and "career criminals."* Washington, DC: National Academy Press.

Bottcher, J., Isorena, T. and Belnas, M. (1996) *Lead: A boot camp and intensive parole program: An impact evaluation: Second year findings*. State of California, Department of the Youth Authority, Research Division.

Boudouris, J. (1985) *Recidivism and rehabilitation.* Iowa Department of Corrections. Des Moines, IA.

Boudouris, J. and Turnbull, B.W. (1985) Shock probation in Iowa. *Journal of Offender Counseling Services and Rehabilitation,* 9, 53–67.

Buckner, J.C. and Chesney-Lind, M. (1983) Dramatic cures for juvenile crime: An evaluation of a prison-run delinquency prevention program. *Criminal Justice and Behavior,* 10, 227–47.

Burnett, W.L. (1997) Treating post-incarcerated offenders with Moral Reconation Therapy®: A one-year recidivism study. *Cognitive-Behavioral Treatment Review,* 6(2), 2.

Butts, J.A., Snyder, H.N. and Finnegan, T.A. (1994) *Juvenile court statistics 1992.* Washington DC, US Department of Justice, Office of Juvenile Justice and Delinquency Prevention.

Byrne, J.M. and Kelly, L.M. (1989) *Restructuring probation as an intermediate sanction: An evaluation of the Massachusetts intensive probation supervision program: Final report to the National Institute of Justice.* Lowell, MA: University of Lowell, Department of Criminal Justice.

Byrne, J.M., Lurigio, A.J. and Petersilia, J. (eds) (1992) *Smart sentencing: The emergence of intermediate sanctions.* Newbury Park, CA: Sage Publications.

Campbell, J. (1996) McNeil Island work ethic camp: Innovations in boot camp reform. In *Juvenile and adult boot camps,* pp. 185–99. American Correctional Association: Lanham, MD.

Casale, Silvia G. and Hillsman, S.T. (1986) The enforcement of fines as criminal sanctions: The English experience and its relevance to American practice. New York: Vera Institute of Justice.

Castellano, T.C. and Soderstrom, I.R. (1992) Therapeutic wilderness programs and juvenile recidivism: A program evaluation. *Journal of Offender Rehabilitation,* 17(3/4), 19–46.

Chaiken, M.R. (1986) Crime rates and substance abuse among types of offenders. In B.D. Johnson and E. Wish (eds), *Crime rates among drug-abusing offenders.* Final report to the National Institute of Justice. New York: Narcotic and Drug Research, Inc.

Chaiken, M.R. and Chaiken, J.M. (1982) *Varieties of criminal behavior.* Santa Monica, CA: RAND Corp.

Clark, P., Hartter, S. and Ford, E. (1992) *An experiment in employment of offenders.* Paper presented at the Annual Meeting of the American Society of Criminology. New Orleans, Louisiana.

Clarke, S.H. (1974) Getting 'em out of circulation: Does incarceration of juvenile offenders reduce crime? *Journal of Criminal Law and Criminology,* 65(4), 528–35.

Clear, T.R. (1996) *The unintended consequences of incarceration.* Paper presented at the NIJ workshop on corrections research, Feb. 14–15.

Cohen, J. (1983) Incapacitation as a strategy for crime control: Possibilities and pitfalls. In M. Tonry and N. Morris (eds), *Crime and justice, an annual review of research.* Chicago: University of Chicago Press.

Cohen, J. (1984) Selective incapacitation: An assessment. *University of Illinois Law Review,* 2, 253–90.

Cohen, J. and Canela-Cacho, Jose, A. (1994) Incarceration and violent crime. In Albert J. Reiss, Jr. and Jeffery A. Roth (eds), *Understanding and preventing violence: Consequence and control.* Vol. 4. Washington, DC: National Academy of Sciences.

Cole, G., Mahoney, B., Thornton, M. and Hanson, R.A. (1987) The practice and attitudes of trial court judges regarding fines as a criminal sanction. Final report submitted to the National Institute of Justice, US Department of Justice, Washington, DC.

Correctional Industries Association (personal communication, January, 1998.).

Cullen, F.T. and Gendreau, P. (1989) The effectiveness of correctional rehabilitation: Reconsidering the 'Nothing Works' debate. In L. Goodstein and D. Mackenzie (eds), *The American prison: Issues in research and policy*. NY: Plenum Press.

Cullen, F.T. and Gilbert, K.E. (1982) *Reaffirming rehabilitation*. Cincinnati, OH: Anderson Publishing Co.

Cullen, F.T., Wright, J.P. and Applegate, B.K. (1996) Control in the community: The limits of reform? In A.T. Harland (ed.), *Choosing correctional options that work: Defining the demand and evaluating the supply*. Thousand Oaks, CA: Sage Publications Company.

Deschenes, E.P., Greenwood, P. and Marshall, G. (1996) *The Nokomis challenge program evaluation*. Santa Monica, CA: RAND Corp.

Deschenes, E.P., Turner, S., Greenwood, P. and Chiesa, J. (1996) *An experimental evaluation of drug testing and treatment interventions for probationers in Maricopa County, Arizona*. RAND Corp.

Deschenes, E.P., Turner, S. and Petersilia, J. (1995) *Intensive community supervision in Minnesota: A dual experiment in prison diversion and enhanced supervised release*. Final report to The National Institute of Justice, Washington, DC.

Downes, E.A., Monaco, K.R. and Schreiber, S.O. (1995) Evaluating the effects of vocational education on inmates: A research model and preliminary results. *The Yearbook of Correctional Education*, 249–62.

English, K. and Mande, M.J. (1992) Measuring from many of the studies about the effectiveness of the programs on crime rates of prisoners. Denver: Colorado Department of Public Safety, Division of Criminal Justice, Office of Research and Statistics.

Eisenberg, M. and Fabelo, T. (1996) Evaluation of the Texas correctional substance abuse treatment initiative: The impact of policy research. *Crime and Delinquency*, 42(2), 296–308.

Eisikovits, Z.C. and Edleson, J.L. (1989) Intervening with men who batter: A critical review of the literature. *Social Service Review*, 385–413.

Elrod, H.P. and Minor, K.I. (1992) Second wave evaluation of a multi-faceted intervention for juvenile court probationers. *International Journal of Offender Therapy and Comparative Criminology*, 36(3), 247–62.

Erwin, B. (1986) Turning up the heat on probationers in Georgia. *Federal Probation*, 50, 17–29.

Fabelo, T. (1992) *Evaluation of the reading to reduce recidivism program*. Texas Criminal Justice Policy Council: Austin, TX.

Falkin, G.P., Wexler, H.K. and Lipton, D.S. (1992) Drug treatment in state prisons. In D.R. Gerstein and H.J. Harwood (eds), *Treating drug problems* (Vol. II, pp. 89–132). Washington, DC: National Academy Press.

Fallen, D.L., Apperson, C.G., Hall-Milligan, J. and Aos, S. (1981) Report: Intensive parole supervision. Washington, DC: Department of Social and Health Services.

Faulkner, K., Stoltenberg, C.D., Cogen, R., Nolder, M. and Shooter, E. (1992) Cognitive-behavioral group treatment for male spouse abusers. *Journal of Family Violence*, 7, 37–55.

Field, G. (1989) The effects of intensive treatment on reducing the criminal recidivism of addicted offenders. *Federal Probation*, 53, 51–6.

Finckenauer, James O. (1982) *Scared straight and the panacea phenomenon*. Englewood Cliffs, NJ: Prentice-Hall.

Finigan, M. (1996) *Societal outcomes and cost savings of drug and alcohol treatment in the state of Oregon*. Report prepared for Office of Alcohol and Drug Abuse Programs, Oregon Department of Human Resources, and Governor's Council on Alcohol and Drug Abuse Programs.

Flanagan, T.J., Thornberry, T.P., Maguire, K. and McGarrell, E. (1988) *The effect of prison industry employment on offender behavior: Report of the prison industry research project.* Albany, NY: Hindelang Criminal Justice Research Center.

Florida Department of Corrections (1990) *Florida executive summary: Boot camp: A 25 month review.* Talahassee, FL: Florida Department of Corrections.

Flowers, G.T., Carr, T.S. and Ruback, R.B. (1991) *Special alternative incarceration evaluation.* Atlanta, GA: Georgia Department of Corrections.

Furby, L., Weinrott, M.R. and Blackshaw, L. (1989) Sex offender recidivism: A review. *Psychological Bulletin*, 105, 3–30.

Garrett, C. (1985) Effects of residential treatment on adjudicated delinquents: A meta-analysis. *Journal of Research in Crime and Delinquency*, 22, 287–308.

Gendreau, P. (1981) Treatment in corrections: Martinson was wrong. *Canadian Psychology*, 22, 332–8.

Gendreau, P. and Ross, R.R. (1979) Effective correctional treatment: Bibliotherapy for cynics. *Crime and Delinquency*, 25, 463–89.

Gendreau, P. and Ross, R.R. (1981) Offender rehabilitation: The appeal of success. *Federal Probation*, 45, 45–8.

Gendreau, P. and Ross, R.R. (1987) Revivification of rehabilitation: Evidence from the 1980's. *Justice Quarterly*, 4, 349–407.

Gerstein, D.R. and Harwood, H.J. (eds) (1992) *Treating drug problems.* Washington, DC: National Academy Press.

Glaser, D. and Gordon, M.A. (1988) Use and effectiveness of fines, jail, and probation. Los Angeles: University of Southern California, Social Science Research Institute.

Goldkamp, J.S. (1994) Miami's treatment drug court for felony defendants: Some implications of assessment findings., *The Prison Journal*, 73(2), 110–66.

Gondolf, E.W. (1993) Male batterers. In R.L. Hampton *et al.* (eds), *Family violence: Prevention and treatment.* Newbury Park, CA: Sage, 230–57.

Gordon, M.A. and Glaser, D. (1991) The use and effects of financial penalties in municipal courts. *Criminology*, 29(4), 651–76.

Gordon, A. and Nicholaichuk, T. (1996) *Applying the risk principle to sex offender treatment.* Forum on Corrections Research Home Page: Managing Sex Offenders. <http://198.103.98.138/crd/forum/e082/e0821.htm>

Gottfredson, D.C. and Barton, W.H. (1993) Deinstitutionalization of juvenile offenders. *Criminology*, 31(4), 591–611.

Gottfredson, D.M., Coblentz, K. and Harmon, M.A. (1996) A short term outcome evaluation of the Baltimore city drug treatment court program. College Park, MD: Department of Criminology and Criminal Justice, University of Maryland.

Gottfredson, M.R. (1979) Parole guidelines and reduction of sentence disparity. *Journal of Research in Crime and Delinquency*, 16, 218–31.

Gottfredson, S.D. and Gottfredson, D.M. (1994) Behavioral prediction and the problem of incapacitation. *Criminology*, 32, 441–74.

Gottschalk, R., Davidson, W., Mayer, J. and Gensheimer, L. (1987) Behavioral approaches with juvenile offenders: A meta-analysis of long-term treatment efficacy. In E. Morris and C. Braukmann (eds), *Behavioral approaches to crime and delinquency: A handbook of application, research, and concepts.* New York: Plenum Press.

Greenberg, David F. (1975) The incapacitative effects of imprisonment: Some estimates. *Law and Society*, 9(4), 541–86.

Greenwood, P.W., with Allan Abrahamse (1982) *Selective incapacitation.* Santa Monica, CA: RAND Corp.

Greenwood, P.W., Deschenes, E.P. and Adams, J. (1993) *Chronic juvenile offenders: Final results from the Skillman aftercare experiment.* Santa Monica, CA: RAND Corp.

Greenwood, P.W., Rydell, C.P., Abrahamse, A.F., Caulkins, J.P., Chiesa, J., Model, P.E. and Klein, S.P. (1994) *Three strikes and you're out: Estimated benefits and costs of California's new mandatory sentencing law*. Santa Monica, CA: RAND Corp.

Greenwood, P. and Turner, S. (1987) *The VisionQuest program: An evaluation*. Santa Monica, CA: RAND Corp.

Greenwood, P.W. and Turner, S. (1993) Evaluation of the Paint Creek Youth Center: A residential program for serious delinquents. *Criminology*, 31(2), 263–79.

Greenwood, P and Zimring, F.E. (1985) *One more chance: The pursuit of promising intervention strategies for chronic juvenile offenders*. Santa Monica, CA: Sage Publications.

Hall, G. (1995) Sexual offender recidivism revisited: A meta-analysis of recent treatment studies. *Journal of Consulting and Clinical Psychology*, 63, 802–9.

Halleck, S. and Witte, A.E. (1977) Is rehabilitation dead? *Crime and Delinquency*, 372–82.

Hanson, R.K., Steffy, R.A. and Gauthier, R. (1993) Long-term recidivism of child molesters. *Journal of Consulting and Clinical Psychology*, 61, 646–52.

Harer, M.D. (1995a) Recidivism among federal prisoners released in 1987. *Journal of Correctional Education*, 46, 98–127.

Harer, M.D. (1995b) *Prison education program participation and recidivism: A test of the normalization hypothesis*. Federal Bureau of Prisons, Office of Research and Evaluation: Washington, DC.

Harland, A.T. (ed.) (1996) *Choosing correctional options that work: Defining the demand and evaluating the supply*. Thousand Oaks, CA: Sage Publications.

Harrell, A. and Cavanagh, S. (1996) Preliminary results from the evaluation of the DC Superior Court Drug Intervention Program for Drug Felony Defendants. Unpublished manuscript presented at the National Institute of Justice Research in Progress Seminar (July). Washington, DC.

Hartmann, D.J., Friday, P.C. and Minor, K.I. (1994) Residential probation: A seven-year follow-up of halfway house discharges. *Journal of Criminal Justice*, 22(6), 503–15.

Hepburn, J.R. and Albonetti, C.A. (1994) Recidivism among drug offenders: A survival analysis of the effects of offender characteristics, type of offense, and two types of intervention. *Journal of Quantitative Criminology*, 10(2), 159–79.

Hiller, M.L., Knight, K., Devereux, J. and Hathcoat, M. (1996) Post-treatment for substance-abusing probationers mandated to residential treatment. *Journal of Psychoactive Drugs*, 28, 291–6.

Hillsman, S.T. (1990) Fines and day fines. In M. Tonry and N. Morris (eds), *Crime and justice: A review of research*. Vol. 12. Chicago, IL: University of Chicago Press.

Hillsman, S.T. and Green, J.A. (1987) *Improving the use and administration of criminal fines: A report of the Richmond county, New York, criminal court day-fine planning project*. New York: Vera Institute of Justice.

Hillsman, S.T. and Green, J.A. (1988) Improving the use and administration of monetary penalties in criminal cases: An experiment to apply means based fining concepts and practices to the Superior Court of Maricopa County, Arizona. New York: Vera Institute of Justice.

Hillsman, S.T., Joyace L. Sichel and Mahoney, B. (1984) *Fines in sentencing: A study of the use of the fine as a criminal sanction*. New York: Vera Institute of Justice.

Horney, J. and Marshall, Haen I. (1991) Measuring lambda through self-reports. *Criminology*, 29(3), 471–95.

Hughes, G.V. (1993) Anger management program outcomes. *Forum on Corrections Research*, 5, 5–9.

Huot, S. (1997) *Sex offender treatment and recidivism*. Minnesota Department of Corrections. A Research Summary.

Inciardi, J.A. (1979) Heroin use and street crime. *Crime and Delinquency*, 25, 335–46.

Johnson, Bruce D. and Wish, Eric D. (1986) The impact of substance abuse on criminal careers. In Alfred Blumstein, Jacqueline Cohen, Jeffrey A. Roth and Christy Visher (eds), *Criminal careers and "career criminals."* Vol. 2. Washington, DC: National Academy Press.

Johnson, G. and Hunter, R.M. (1995) Evaluation of the Specialized Drug Offender Program. In Ross, R.R. and Ross, B. (eds) *Thinking straight.* Ottawa: Cognitive Center.

Jolin, A. and Stipack, B. (1991) Clackamas County community corrections intensive drug program: Program evaluation report. Portland, OR: Portland State University, Department of Administration of Justice.

Kaufman, D. (1985) *Substance abuse and family therapy.* Orlando, FL: Grune and Stratton.

Kirby, B.C. (1954) Measuring effects of treatment of criminals and delinquents. *Sociology and Social Research*, 38, 368–74.

Knott, C. (1995) The STOP programme: Reasoning and rehabilitation in a British setting. In McGuire, J. (ed.), *What works: Reducing reoffending: Guidelines from research and practice.* John Wiley and Sons Ltd.

Krisberg, B., Rodriguez, O., Baake, A., Neuenfeldt, D. and Steele, P. (1989) *Demonstration of post-adjudication non-residential intensive supervision programs: Assessment report.* San Francisco: National Council on Crime and Delinquency.

Krueger, S. (1997) Five-year recidivism study of MRT®-treated offenders in a county jail. *Cognitive-Behavioral Treatment Review*, 6, 3.

Lab, S.P. and Whitehead, J.T. (1988) An analysis of juvenile correctional treatment. *Crime and Delinquency*, 34, 60–83.

Land, K.C., McCall, P.L. and Williams, J.R. (1990) Something that works in juvenile justice: An evaluation of the North Carolina court counselors' intensive protective supervision randomized experimental project, 1987–1989. *Evaluation Review*, 14(6), 574–606.

Latessa, E.J. (1991) A preliminary evaluation of the Cuyahoga County adult probation department's intensive supervision groups. Unpublished manuscript. Cincinnati, OH: University of Cincinnati.

Latessa, E.J. (1992) Intensive supervision and case management classification: An evaluation. Unpublished manuscript. Cincinnati, OH: University of Cincinnati.

Latessa, E.J. (1993a) An evaluation of the Lucas County adult probation department's IDU and high risk groups. Unpublished manuscript. Cincinnati, OH: University of Cincinnati.

Latessa, E.J. (1993b) Profile of the special units of the Lucas County adult probation department. Unpublished manuscript. Cincinnati, OH: University of Cincinnati.

Latessa, E.J. and Allen, H.E. (1982) Halfway houses and parole: A national assessment. *Journal of Criminal Justice*, 10(2), 153–63.

Latessa, E.J. and Moon, M.M. (1992) The effectiveness of acupuncture in an outpatient drug treatment program. *Journal of Contemporary Justice*, 8(4), 317–31.

Latessa, E.J. and Travis, L.F. III. (1991) Halfway house or probation: A comparison of alternative dispositions. *Journal of Crime and Justice*, 14(1), 58–75.

Lattimore, P.K., Witte, A.D. and Baker, J.R. (1990) Experimental assessment of the effect of vocational training on youthful property offenders. *Evaluation Review*, 14(2), 115–33.

Leukefeld, C.G. and Tims, F.M. (eds) (1992) *Drug abuse treatment in prisons and jails.* National Institute of Drug Abuse, Research Monograph Series, No. 18. Washington, DC: US Government Printing Office.

Lewis, R.V. (1983) Scared straight-California style: Evaluation of the San Quentin squire program. *Criminal Justice and Behavior*, 10, 209–26.

Lipsey, M. (1992) Juvenile delinquency treatment: A meta-analytic inquiry into the variability of effects. In T. Cook *et al.* (eds), *Meta-analysis for explanation: A casebook*. New York, NY: Russell Sage Foundation.

Lipton, D. and Pearson, F.S. (1996) *The CDATE Project: Reviewing research on the effectiveness of treatment programs for adult and juvenile offenders*. Paper presented at the Annual Meeting of the American Society of Criminology, Chicago, IL.

Little, G.L. and Robinson, K.D. (1988) Moral reconation therapy: A systematic step-by-step treatment system for treatment resistant clients. *Psychological Reports*, 62, 135–51.

Little, G.L. and Robinson, K.D. (1989a) Effects of moral reconation therapy upon moral reasoning, life purpose, and recidivism among drug and alcohol offender. *Psychological Reports*, 64, 83–90.

Little, G.L. and Robinson, K.D. (1989b) Relationship of DWI recidivism to moral reasoning, sensation seeking, and MacAndrew alcoholism scores. *Psychological Reports*, 65, 1171–4.

Little, G.L. and Robinson, K.D. (1989c) Treating drunk drivers with moral reconation therapy: A one-year recidivism report. *Psychological Reports*, 64, 960–2.

Little, G.L., Robinson, K.D. and Burnette, K.D. (1990) Treating drunk drivers with moral reconation therapy: A two-year follow-up. *Psychological Reports*, 66, 1379–87.

Little, G.L., Robinson, K.D. and Burnette, K.D. (1991a) Treating drug offenders with moral reconation therapy: A three-year recidivism report. *Psychological Reports*, 69, 1151–4.

Little, G.L., Robinson, K.D. and Burnette, K.D. (1991b) Treating drunk drivers with moral reconation therapy: A three-year report. *Psychological Reports*, 69, 953–4.

Little, G.L., Robinson, K.D. and Burnette, K.D. (1993a) 42 month alcohol treatment data: Multiple DWI offenders treated with MRT show lower recidivism rates. *Cognitive-Behavioral Treatment Review*, 2(3), 5.

Little, G.L., Robinson, K.D. and Burnette, K.D. (1993b) Cognitive behavioral treatment of felony drug offenders: A five-year recidivism report. *Psychological Reports*, 73, 1089–90.

Little, G.L., Robinson, K.D. and Burnette, K.D. (1994) Treating offenders with cognitive-behavioral therapy: Five-year recidivism outcome data on MRT. *Cognitive-Behavioral Treatment Review*, 3(2–3), 1–3.

Little, G.L., Robinson, K.D., Burnette, K.D. and Swan, S. (1995a) Seven-year recidivism of felony offenders treated with MRT. *Cognitive-Behavioral Treatment Review*, 4(3), 6.

Little, G.L., Robinson, K.D., Burnette, K.D. and Swan, S. (1995b) Six-year MRT recidivism data on felons and DWI offenders: Treated offenders show significantly lower reincarceration. *Cognitive-Behavioral Treatment Review*, 4(1), 1, 4–5.

Little, G.L., Robinson, K.D., Burnette, K.D. and Swan, E.S. (1996) Review of outcome data with MRT: Seven year recidivism results. *Cognitive-Behavioral Treatment Review*, 5(1), 1–7.

Logan, C. (1972) Evaluation research in crime and delinquency: A reappraisal. *Journal of Criminal Law Criminology and Police Science*, 63, 378–87.

Lurigio, A.J. and Petersilia, J. (1992) The emergence of intensive probation supervision programs in the United States. In J.M. Byrne, A.J. Lurigio and J. Petersilia (eds) *Smart sentencing: The emergence of intermediate sanctions* (pp. 18–41). Newbury Park, CA: Sage Publications.

MacKenzie, D.L. (1990) Boot camp prisons: Components, evaluations, and empirical issues. *Federal Probation*, 54(3), 44–52.

MacKenzie, D.L. (1998) Using the US Land-Grant University system as a model to attack this nation's crime problem. *The Criminologist*, 23(2), 1–4.

MacKenzie, D.L., Brame, R., MacDowall, D. and Souryal, C. (1995) Boot camp prisons and recidivism in eight states. *Criminology*, 33(3), 327–58.

MacKenzie, D.L., Browning, K., Skroban, S. and Smith, D. (1999) The impact of probation on the criminal activities of offenders. *Journal of Research in Crime and Delinquency*, 36, 423–53.

MacKenzie, D.L. and Hickman, L. (1998) *What works in Corrections?* Unpublished report to the State of Washington Legislature Joint Audit and Review Committee. College Park, MD: Department of Criminology and Criminal Justice, University of Maryland.

MacKenzie, D.L. and Parent, D.G. (1991) Shock incarceration and prison crowding in Louisiana. *Journal of Criminal Justice*, 19, 225–37.

MacKenzie, D.L. and Shaw, J.W. (1993) The impact of shock incarceration on technical violations and new criminal activities. *Justice Quarterly*, 10, 463–87.

MacKenzie, D.L., Shaw, J.W. and Gowdy, V. (1993) *An evaluation of shock incarceration in Louisiana*. Washington, DC: National Institute of Justice.

MADD (1998) Minnesota MADD Homepage: Victim Impact Panels. <http://www.mtn.org/maddmn/Vicimp>

Maguire, K.E., Flanagan, T.J. and Thornberry, T.P. (1988) Prison labor and recidivism. *Journal of Quantitative Criminology*, 4(1), 3–18.

Mahoney, M.J. and Lyddon, W.J. (1988) Recent developments in cognitive approaches to counseling and psychotherapy. *The Counseling Psychologist*, 16, 190–234.

Marques, J.K., Day, D.M. and West, M. (1994) Effects of cognitive-behavioral treatment on sex offender recidivism. *Criminal Justice and Behavior*, 21, 28–34.

Marques, K.H. and Ebener, P.A. (1981) *Quality of prisoner self-reports: Arrest and conviction response errors*. Santa Monica, CA: RAND Corporation.

Marquis, H.A., Bourgon, G.A., Armstrong, B. and Pfaff, J. (1996) Reducing recidivism through institutional treatment. *Forum on Correctional Research*, 8, 3–5.

Marshall, W.L. and Barbaree, H.E. (1988) The long-term evaluation of a behavioral treatment program for child molesters. *Behavior Research and Therapy*, 26, 499–511.

Marshall, W.L., Eccles, A. and Barbaree, H.E. (1991) The treatment of exhibitionists: A focus on sexual deviance versus cognitive and relationship features. *Behavior Research and Therapy*, 29, 129–35.

Marshall, W.L., Jones, R., Ward, T., Johnston, P. and Barbaree, H.E. (1991) Treatment outcome with sex offenders. *Clinical Psychology Review*, 11, 465–85.

Martin, S.S., Butzin, C.A. and Inciardi, J. (1995) Assessment of a multistage therapeutic community for drug involved offenders. *Journal of Psychoactive Drugs*, 27(1), 109–16.

Martinson, R. (1974) What works? Questions and answers about prison reform. *The Public Interest*, 10, 22–54.

McGee, C. (1997) *The positive impact of corrections education on recidivism and employment*. Illinois Department of Corrections School District 428.

Melton, R. and Pennell, S. (1998) *Staying out successfully: An evaluation of an in-custody life skills training program*. San Diego Association of Governments.

Menon, R., Blakely, C., Carmichael, D. and Silver, L. (1992) *An evaluation of project RIO outcomes: An evaluative report*. College Station, TX: Public Policy Resources Laboratory.

Milkman, R.H. (1985) *Employment services for ex-offenders field test: Detailed research results*. McLean, VA: Lazar Institute.

Miller, M. (1995) The Delaware life skills program: Evaluation report, August 1995.

*Cognitive-Behavioral Treatment Review*, 4(3), 1–4.

Miller, M. (1997) *Evaluation of the life skills program*. Division of Correctional Education, Delaware State Department of Corrections.

Minor, K.I. and Elrod, H.P. (1990) The effects of a multi-faceted intervention on the offense activities of juvenile probationers. *Journal of Offender Counseling, Service and Rehabilitation*, 1(2), 87–108.

Minor, K.I. and Elrod, P. (1994) The effects of a probation intervention on juvenile offenders self-concepts, loci of control, and perceptions of juvenile justice. *Youth and Society*, 25(4), 490–511.

Miranne, A.C. and Geerken, M.R. (1991) The New Orleans inmate survey: A test of Greenwood's predictive scale. *Criminology*, 29(3), 497–518.

Mitchell, C.J.Z. and Butter, C. (1986) Intensive supervision/early release parole. Utah Department of Corrections.

Molof, M. (1991) Study of the intensive probation supervision for multiple DUI offenders in Linn County, Oregon. Linn County, OR: Integrated Research Services.

Moon, M.M. and Latessa, E.J. (1993) The effectiveness of an outpatient drug treatment program on felony probationers. Paper presented at the annual meeting of the Academy of Criminal Justice Sciences, Kansas City.

National Council on Crime and Delinquency (1991) *Evaluation of the Florida community control program*. San Francisco, CA: Author.

Nemes, S., Wish, E. and Messina, N. (1998) *The District of Columbia Treatment Initiative (DCI)*. Center for Substance Abuse Research. University of Maryland, College Park, MD.

Nicholaichuk, T., Gordon, A., Andre, G. and Gu, D. (1995) *Long-term outcome of the Clearwater Sex Offender Treatment*. Presented to the 14th Annual Conference of the Association for the Treatment of Sexual Abusers: New Orleans, LA.

Nurco, D., Hanlon, T. and Kinlock, T. (1990) *Offenders, drugs and treatment*. Washington, DC: United States Department of Justice.

Nurco, D.N., Hanlon, T.E., Bateman, R.W. and Kinlock, T.W. (1995) Drug abuse treatment in the context of correctional surveillance. *Journal of Substance Abuse Treatment*, 12(1), 19–27.

NYDCS and NYDP (New York Department of Correctional Services and New York Division of Parole) (1992) The fourth annual report to the legislature on shock incarceration and shock parole supervision. Albany, NY: Department of Correctional Services and Division of Parole.

NYDCS and NYDP (New York Department of Correctional Services and New York Division of Parole) (1993) The fifth annual report to the legislature on shock incarceration and shock parole supervision. Albany, NY: Department of Correctional Services and Division of Parole.

NYDCS (New York State Department of Correctional Services) (1992) *Overview of Department follow-up research on return rates of participants in major programs: 1992*. Albany, NY: Author.

Ohio Department of Rehabilitation and Corrections (1995) *Evaluation of the impact of correctional education programs on recidivism*. Dept. of Rehabilitation and Correction.

Oregon Department of Corrections (1994) *Comparison of outcomes and costs of residential and outpatient treatment programs for inmates: CTP and CTS evaluation of outcomes and cost*. Executive Summary, Oregon Department of Corrections: Salem, OR.

Palmer, T. (1975) Martinson revisited. *Journal of Research in Crime and Delinquency*, 12, 133–52.

Palmer, T. (1983) The "effectiveness" issue today: An overview. *Federal Probation*, 46, 3–10.

Parent, D.G., Byrne, J., Tsarfaty, V., Valdae, L. and Esselman, J. (1995) *Day reporting centers.* Vol, 1 and 2. Washington, DC: National Institute of Justice.

Pearson, F.S. (1987) *Research on New Jersey's intensive supervision program.* Washington, DC: US Department of Justice, National Institute of Justice.

Peters, M. (1996a) *Evaluation of the impact of boot camps for juvenile offenders: Denver interim report.* Washington, DC: US Department of Justice, Office of Juvenile Justice and Delinquency Prevention.

Peters, M. (1996b) *Evaluation of the impact of boot camps for juvenile offenders: Cleveland interim report.* Washington, DC: US Department of Justice, Office of Juvenile Justice and Delinquency Prevention.

Peters, M. (1996c) *Evaluation of the impact of boot camps for juvenile offenders: Mobile interim report.* Washington, DC: US Department of Justice, Office of Juvenile Justice and Delinquency Prevention.

Petersilia, J. and Greenwood, Peter W. (1978) Mandatory prison sentences: Their projected effects on crime and prison populations. *Journal of Criminal Law and Criminology*, 69, 604–15.

Petersilia, J. and Turner, S. (1992) Intensive supervision programs for drug offenders. In Byrne, J.M., Lurigio, A.J. and Petersilia, J. (eds), *Smart sentencing: The emergence of intermediate sanctions* (pp. 18–37). Newbury Park: Sage Publications.

Petersilia, J. and Turner, S. (1993a) Intensive probation and parole. In *Crime and justice: A review of research, Vol. 19* (pp. 281–335). Chicago, IL: University of Chicago Press.

Petersilia, J. and Turner, S. (1993b) *Evaluating intensive supervision probation/parole: Results of a nationwide experiment.* Washington, DC: National Institute of Justice.

Peterson, M.A. and Braiker, H.B. (1980) *Doing crime: A survey of California prison inmates,* Report R-2200-DOJ. Santa Monica, CA: RAND Corporation.

Peterson, M.A. and Braiker, H.B., with Polich, S.M. (1981) *Who commits crimes: A survey of prison inmates.* Cambridge, MA: Oelgeschlager, Gunn and Hain.

Peterson, M., Chaiken, J., Ebener, P. and Honig, P. (1982) *Survey of prison and jail inmates: Background and methods.* Santa Monica, CA: RAND Corporation.

Peterson, M.A., Greenwood, P.W. and Lavin, M. (1977) *Criminal careers of habitual felons.* Santa Monica, CA: RAND Corporation.

Piehl, A.M. (1995) *Learning while doing time: Prison education and recidivism among Wisconsin males.* Princeton University.

Porporino, F.J., Fabiano, E.A. and Robinson, D. (1991) *Focusing on successful reintegration: Cognitive skills training for offenders, R-19.* Research and Statistics Branch, The Correctional Service of Canada.

Porporino, F.J. and Robinson, D. (1995) An evaluation of the Reasoning and Rehabilitation program with Canadian federal offenders. In Ross, R.R. and Ross, B. (eds), *Thinking straight.* Ottawa: Cognitive Center.

Prendergast, M.L., Wellisch, J. and Wong, M.M. (1996) Residential treatment for women parolees following prison-based drug treatment: Treatment experiences, needs, and service outcomes. *The Prison Journal*, 76, 253–74.

Quinsey, V., Harris, G., Rice, M. and Lalumiere, M. (1993) Assessing treatment efficacy in outcome studies of sex offenders. *Sex Offender Treatment*, 8(4), 512–23.

Ramsey, C. (1988) *The value of receiving a general education development certificate while incarcerated in the South Carolina Department of Corrections on the rate of recidivism.* South Carolina Department of Corrections.

Raynor, P. and Vanstone, M. (1996) Reasoning and rehabilitation in Britain: The results of the Straight Thinking on Probation (STOP) programme. *International Journal of Offender Therapy and Comparative Criminology*, 40, 272–84.

Renzema, M. (1992) Home confinement programs: Development, implementation, and impact. In J.M. Byrne, A.J. Lurigio and J. Petersilia (eds). *Smart sentencing: The emergence of intermediate sanctions*. Newbury Park, CA: Sage Publications.

Rhodes, W. and Gross, M. (1997) *Case management reduces drug use and criminality among drug-involved arrestees: An experimental study of an HIV prevention intervention*. A final summary report presented to the National Institute of Justice and the National Institute on Drug Abuse.

Rice, M.E., Quinsey, V.L. and Harris, G.T. (1991) Sexual recidivism among child molesters released from a maximum security psychiatric institution. *Journal of Counseling and Clinical Psychology*, 29, 381–6.

Robinson, D. (1995) *The impact of cognitive skills training on post-release recidivism among Canadian Federal offenders*. Research Report, Correctional Research and Development, Correctional Service of Canada.

Robinson, D., Grossman, M. and Porporino, F. (1991) *Effectiveness of the cognitive skills training program: From pilot to national implementation, B-07*. The Research and Statistics Branch, Correctional Service of Canada.

Ross, R.R. and Fabiano, E.A. (1985) *Time to think: A cognitive model of delinquency prevention and offender rehabilitation*. Johnson City, TN: Institute of Social Sciences and Arts.

Ross, R.R., Fabiano, E.A. and Ewles, C.D. (1988) Reasoning and rehabilitation. *International Journal of Offender Therapy and Comparative Criminology*, 32, 29–36.

Ryan, T.P. (1997) *A comparison of recidivism rates for Operation Outward Reach (OOR) participants and control groups of non-participants for the years 1990 through 1994. Program evaluation report*. Operation Outward Reach, Inc., Youngwood, PA.

Saylor, W.G. and Gaes, G.G. (1996) *PREP: Training inmates through industrial work participation and vocational and apprenticeship instruction*. US Federal Bureau of Prisons, Washington, DC.

Schumacker, R.E., Anderson, D.B. and Anderson, S.L. (1990) Vocational and academic indicators of parole success. *Journal of Correctional Education*, 41, 8–12.

Siegal, G.R. and Basta, J. (1997) *The effect of literacy and general education development programs on adult probationers*. Adult Probation Department of the Superior Court of Pima County: Pima, AZ.

Serin, R. (1994) *Treating violent offenders: A review of current practices*. Correctional Research and Development: Ontario, Canada.

Sherman, L.W., Gottfredson, D., MacKenzie, D.L., Eck, J., Reuter, P. and Bushway, S. (1997) *Preventing crime: What works, what doesn't, what's promising*. National Institute of Justice: Washington, D.C.

Shinar, D. and Compton, R.P. (1995) Victim impact panels: Their impact on DWI recidivism. *Alcohol, Drugs and Driving*, 11, 73–87.

Smykla, J.O. and Selke, W.L. (eds) (1995) *Intermediate sanctions: Sentencing in the 1990s*. Cincinnati, OH: Anderson Publishing Co.

Sontheimer, H. and Goodstein, L. (1993) Evaluation of juvenile intensive aftercare probation: Aftercare versus system response effects. *Justice Quarterly*, 10, 197–227.

Song, L. and Leib, R. (1995) *The Twin Rivers Sex Offenders Treatment Program: Recidivism rates*. Washington State Sex Offenders: Overview of Recidivism Studies. Washington State Institute for Public Policy: Olympia, WA.

Speckart, G. and Anglin, D.M. (1986) Narcotics and crime: A causal modeling approach. *Journal of Quantitative Criminology*, 2, 3–28.

Spelman, W. (1994) *Criminal incapacitation*. New York: Plenum Press.

Stutz, W.A. (1994) *Victim awareness educational program evaluation*. Washington State Department of Corrections, Division of Community Corrections, Victim Awareness Unit.

Taxman, F.S. and Spinner, D.L. (1996) The jail addiction services (JAS) project in Montgomery County, Maryland: Overview of results from a 24 month follow-up study. Unpublished Manuscript, University of Maryland, College Park, MD.

Texas Department of Criminal Justice (1991) Shock incarceration in Texas: Special incarceration program. Austin, TX: Author.

Texas Youth Commission (1993) *The relationship between GED attainment and recidivism.* Texas Department of Research and Planning.

Tonry, M. (1995) *Malign neglect: Race, crime, and punishment in America.* New York: Oxford University Press.

Tonry, M. and Lynch, M. (1996) Intermediate sanctions. In M. Tonry (ed.), *Crime and justice: A review of research,* Vol. 20. Chicago, IL: The University of Chicago Press.

Travis, J., Wetherington, C., Feucht, T.E. and Visher, C. (1996) *Drug involved offenders in the criminal justice system.* Washington, DC: National Institute of Justice, Working Paper – 96–02.

Turner, S. and Petersilia, J. (1996) Work release in Washington: Effects on recidivism and corrections costs. *Prison Journal,* 76(2), 138–64.

Uggen, C. (1997) *Age, employment and the duration structure of recidivism: Estimating the "true effect" of work on crime.* Paper delivered at the 1997 American Society of Criminology meeting. San Diego, CA.

Van Dine, Stephan, Conrad, John P. and Dinitz, Simon (1977) The incapacitation of dangerous offender: A statistical experiment. *Journal of Research in Crime and Delinquency,* 14, 22–35.

Van Stelle, K.R., Lidbury, J.R. and Moberg, D.P. (1995) *Final evaluation report, Specialized Training and Employment Project (STEP).* Madison, WI: University of Wisconsin Medical School, Center for Health Policy and Program Evaluation.

Van Voorhis, P. (1987) Correctional effectiveness: The high cost of ignoring success. *Federal Probation,* 51(1), 56–62.

Visher, C.A. (1987) Incapacitation and crime control: Does a "lock 'em up" strategy reduce crime? *Justice Quarterly,* 4(4), 513–43.

Vito, G. (1984) Developments in shock probation: A review of research findings and policy implications. *Federal Probation,* 48, 22–7.

Vito, G. and Allen, H.E. (1981) Shock probation in Ohio: A comparison of outcomes. *International Journal of Offender Therapy and Comparative Criminology,* 25(1), 70–5.

Vito, G., Wilson, D. and Holmes, S. (1993) Drug testing in community corrections: Results from a four-year program. *The Prison Journal,* 73, 343–54.

Von Hirsch, Andrew and Gottfredson, D. (1984) Selective incapacitation: Some queries on research design and equity. *New York University Review of Law and Social Change,* 12(1), 11–51.

Walsh, A. (1985) An evaluation of the effects of adult basic education on rearrest rates among probationers. *Journal of Offender Counseling, Services, and Rehabilitation,* 9, 69–76.

Washington State Department of Corrections (1995) *Work ethic camp: One year after (1993–1994). Program report.* Washington State Department of Corrections.

Weibush, R.G. (1993) Juvenile intensive supervision: The impact on felony offenders diverted from institutional placement. *Crime and Delinquency,* 39(1), 68–89.

Wexler, H.K., Falkin, G.P. and Lipton, D.S. (1992) Outcome evaluation of a prison therapeutic community for substance abuse treatment. *Criminal Justice and Behavior,* 17(1), 71.

Wexler, H.K., Graham, W.F., Koronowski, R. and Lowe, L. (1995) Evaluation of Amity in-prison and post-release substance abuse treatment programs. Washington, DC: National Institute of Drug Abuse.

Whitehead, J.T. and Lab, S.P. (1989) A meta-analysis of juvenile correctional treatment. *Journal of Research in Crime and Delinquency*, 26, 276–95.

Wolfgang, M.E., Figlio, R.M. and Sellin, T. (1972) *Delinquency in a birth cohort*. Chicago, IL: University of Chicago Press.

Worzella, D. (1992) The Milwaukee Municipal Court day-fine project. In D.C. McDonald, J. Green and C. Worzella (eds), *Day fines in American courts: The Staten Island and Milwaukee experiments*. Issues and Practices in Criminal Justice, National Institute of Justice, Washington, DC: 61–76.

Zedlewski, Edwin M. (1987) *Making confinement decisions*. Washington, DC: US Department of Justice.

Zimring, F.E. and Hawkins, Gordon (1995) *Incapacitation: Penal confinement and the restraint of crime*. New York: Oxford University Press.

# 10 Conclusion

## What works, what doesn't, what's promising, and future directions

*Brandon C. Welsh and David P. Farrington*

The main aims of this chapter are to summarize the findings on what works, what does not work, what is promising and what is unknown in preventing crime in seven institutional settings in which crime prevention takes place, and to bring together the main conclusions of the book. We hope that this book has made progress towards the evidence-based ideal, where conclusions about crime prevention effectiveness based on the highest quality science are used by policymakers as the basis of local, state and national policies on preventing crime.

As noted in Chapter 1, the "bottom line" of this book is what works, what does not work and what is promising in preventing crime. (For the criteria to classify programs into these 3 categories and the category "what is unknown," see Chapter 2.) Overall, 29 programs worked, 25 programs did not work, and 28 programs were promising in preventing crime. As many as 68 programs were of unknown effectiveness.

Before turning to a discussion of findings on the effectiveness of crime prevention, it is important to draw attention to program cross-over or overlap; that is, those programs that were reviewed in multiple institutional settings. Of the 675 programs reviewed in this book (in Chapters 3 to 9), 13 or 2 percent were reviewed in more than one setting. Table 10.1 lists those programs that were reviewed in multiple settings. With the exception of the Quantum Opportunities Program (Hahn, 1999), which was reviewed in three different settings (schools, communities and labor markets), the other twelve programs were reviewed in no more than two settings. Most of the overlap was between labor markets and courts/corrections, with eight of the same programs reviewed in these two settings.[1]

Many more of the programs reviewed in the seven settings could have been reviewed in more than one setting. This is because crime prevention programs are often multi-modal, targeting risk factors in multiple domains; few crime prevention programs can actually be classified as "true" single domain programs. Multi-modal programs are more effective than those based on a single modality (Wasserman and Miller, 1998). However, for most programs there is either some specification by the study authors about what domain is most important, or it is clear from a reading of the report on the program what interventions specific to domains (e.g. family-based, school-based) are more important. The present authors used this information in deciding in which setting a program should be placed in this book. Meetings and correspondence by the authors also facilitated these decisions.

*Table 10.1* Programs reviewed in multiple settings

| Program author and name | Families (N = 34) | Schools (N = 178) | Communities (N = 29) | Labor markets (N = 53) | Places (N = 109) | Police (N = 136) | Courts and corrections (N = 150) |
|---|---|---|---|---|---|---|---|
| Hawkins et al. (1999), Seattle Social Development Project | X | X | | | | | |
| Tremblay et al. (1995), Montreal Longitudinal-Experimental Study | X | X | | | | | |
| Hahn (1999), Quantum Opportunities Program | | X | X | | | | |
| Greenwood and Turner (1993), Paint Creek Youth Center | | | | X | | | X |
| Lattimore et al. (1990), Vocational Delivery System | | | | X | | | |
| Adams et al. (1994), PERP | | | | X | | | X |
| Hartmann et al. (1994), KPEP | | | | X | | | X |
| Maguire et al. (1988), PIRP | | | | X | | | X |
| Menon et al. (1992), Project RIO | | | | X | | | X |
| Saylor and Gaes (1996), PREP | | | | | | | X |
| Van Stelle et al. (1995), STEP | | | | | | | X |
| Kennedy et al. (1996), Boston Gun Project | | | X | | | X | |
| Hope (1994), St. Louis Drug Market Project | | | | | X | X | |

Notes

X = program reviewed: KPEP = Kalamazoo Probation Enhancement Project; PERP = Prison Education Research Project; PIRP = Prison Industry Research Project; PREP = Post Release Employment Program; RIO = Re-Integration of Offenders; STEP = Specialized Training and Employment Project.

**What works**

Across the seven settings, 29 programs were found to be of proven effectiveness in preventing crime or related problem behaviors. Table 10.2 lists, by institutional setting, these programs. With the exception of communities, each setting identified at least two programs that were effective in preventing crime. Those settings with the highest number of effective programs were courts/corrections with nine, followed by schools with seven. For both labor markets and places, two programs were found to be effective in preventing crime: job training for older male ex-offenders no longer under criminal justice supervision and intensive residential training programs for at-risk youth (Job Corps); and nuisance abatement and improved street lighting in open public places, respectively. The four family programs found to be effective were not limited to one stage of the life course, but ranged from early childhood (home visitation services for newborns/toddlers and mothers), to middle childhood (school-based child training plus day care/preschool and school-based child training plus parent training), to late adolescence (multisystemic therapy).

In the schools setting, program effectiveness was assessed for crime and three related problem behaviors: alcohol or other drug use, antisocial behavior, and drop-out/truancy. (These outcomes were also examined in the school setting for the categories of what does not work, what is promising and what is unknown; see below.) The program of school and discipline management, for example, was found to be effective for the outcomes of crime, alcohol or other drug use, and antisocial behavior, but not for drop-out/truancy. Of the seven school programs that were effective in preventing one or more of these four problem behaviors, three were effective in preventing crime: (1) school and discipline management, (2) interventions to establish norms or expectations for behavior, and (3) self-control or social competency instruction using cognitive-behavioral or behavioral instruction methods.

Five measures by police agencies were found to be effective in preventing crime: (1) increased directed patrols in street-corner hot spots of crime; (2) proactive arrests of serious repeat offenders; (3) proactive drunk driving arrests; (4) arrests for domestic assault for employed suspects; and (5) problem-oriented policing.

Of the nine programs found to be effective in preventing crime in the courts/corrections setting, all were corrections-based programs, delivered in the community, an institutional facility, or some combination of the two. Some of the effective institution-based programs included: rehabilitation, prison-based therapeutic community treatment of drug-involved offenders, and incapacitating offenders who continue to commit crimes at high rates.

**What does not work**

Twenty-five programs were found to be ineffective in preventing crime or related problem behaviors across the seven institutional settings. Table 10.3 lists, by institutional setting, these programs. With the exception of places, each of the settings had at least one program that was ineffective in preventing

Table 10.2 What works in preventing crime

| Families | Schools | Communities | Labor markets | Places | Police | Courts and corrections |
|---|---|---|---|---|---|---|
| 1. Home visitation | 1. School and discipline management (crime, AOD, ASB) | No programs were found with evidence of proven effectiveness | 1. Ex-offender job training for older males no longer under criminal justice supervision | 1. Nuisance abatement (crime, street-corner hot spots of crime) | 1. Increased directed patrols in street-corner hot spots of crime | 1. Rehabilitation with particular characteristics (e.g. target specific problems of offenders, intensive treatment) |
| 2. Parent education plus day care/preschool | 2. Interventions to establish norms or expectations for behavior (crime, AOD, ASB) | | 2. Intensive, residential training programs for at-risk youth (Job Corps) | 2. Improved street lighting in open public places | 2. Proactive arrests of serious repeat offenders | 2. Prison-based therapeutic community treatment of drug-involved offenders |
| 3. School-based child training plus parent training | 3. Classroom or instructional management (AOD, DO/T) | | | | 3. Proactive drunk driving arrests | 3. In-prison therapeutic communities with follow-up community treatment |
| 4. Multisystemic therapy | 4. Reorganization of grades or schools (ASB, DO/T) | | | | 4. Arrests of employed suspects for domestic assault | 4. Cognitive behavioral therapy: moral reconation therapy and reasoning and rehabilitation |
| | 5. Self-control or social competency instruction using cognitive- | | | | 5. Problem-oriented policing | 5. Non-prison-based sex offender treatment |

behavioral or
behavioral
instruction methods
(crime, AOD, ASB,
DO/T)
6. Cognitive
behavioral,
behavioral
modeling, or
behavior
modification (ASB,
DO/T)
7. Mentoring,
tutoring and work
study (ASB, DO/T)

6. Vocational
education for
adult offenders
and juvenile
delinquents

7. Multi-
component
correctional
industry
programs
8. Community
employment
9. Incapacitating
offenders who
continue to
commit crimes at
high rates

Notes
AOD = alcohol or other drug use; ASB = antisocial behavior; DO/T = drop-out/truancy.

*Table 10.3* What does not work in preventing crime

| Families | Schools | Communities | Labor markets | Places | Police | Courts and corrections |
|---|---|---|---|---|---|---|
| 1. Home/ community parent training | 1. Self-control or social competency instruction using cognitive behavioral or behavioral instruction methods (ASB, DO/T) | 1. Gun buy-back campaigns (criminal gun-related deaths and injuries) | 1. Summer job or subsidized work programs for at-risk youth | No programs were found with evidence of proven ineffectiveness | 1. Neighborhood block watch | 1. Specific deterrence interventions such as shock probation and Scared Straight |
| | 2. Other instructional programs (i.e. do not focus on social competency or do not make use of cognitive-behavioral teaching methods (crime, DO/T) | 2. Short-term, nonresidential training programs for at-risk youth | | | 2. Arrests of some juveniles for minor offenses | 2. Rehabilitation programs that use non-directive, unstructured counseling |
| | 3. Counseling, social work, and other therapeutic interventions (ASB, DO/T) | | 3. Diversion from court to job training for adult offenders as a condition of case dismissal | | 3. Arrests of unemployed suspects for domestic assault | 3. Intensive supervised probation or parole |
| | 4. Mentoring, tutoring and work study (AOD) | | | | 4. Drug market arrests | 4. Home confinement |
| | 5. Recreation, community service, enrichment and leisure activities (AOD) | | | | 5. Community policing with no clear crime-risk factor focus | 5. Community residential programs |

6. Adding extra
police to cities,
regardless of
assignment or
activity

6. Urine testing

7. Increased
referral,
monitoring and
management in
the community

8. Correctional
boot camps
using the old-
style military
model

9. Juvenile
wilderness
programs

Notes

AOD = alcohol or other drug use; ASB = antisocial behavior; DO/T = drop-out/truancy.

crime. The highest number of ineffective programs were found in courts/corrections (nine), police (six), schools (five) and labor markets (three). In each of the families and communities settings, one program was found to be ineffective: home/community parent training and gun buy-back campaigns, respectively.

Of the five ineffective school-based programs, only one was ineffective in preventing crime; the others were unsuccessful in preventing one or more of the related problem behaviors of alcohol or other drug use, antisocial behavior, or drop-out/truancy. The three labor market programs that were found to be ineffective were quite diverse: summer job or subsidized work programs for at-risk youth, short-term nonresidential training programs for at-risk youth and diversion from court to job training for adult offenders as a condition of case dismissal. Equally diverse were those programs found to be ineffective in the police setting (e.g. neighborhood block watch, arrests of unemployed suspects for domestic assault, drug market arrests), and in the courts/corrections setting, some of which include: specific deterrence interventions (e.g. shock probation, Scared Straight), home confinement, community residential programs, correctional boot camps using the old-style military model and juvenile wilderness programs.

## What is promising

A total of 28 programs were identified as promising in preventing crime or related problem behaviors; that is, they were promising enough to merit further replication and evaluation. Table 10.4 lists, by institutional setting, those programs found to be promising. For each setting, at least one program was found to be promising, with the families setting having only one promising program: clinic-based child training plus parent training. The schools, communities and labor markets settings had the next fewest number of promising programs at three apiece, while the places and courts/corrections settings had the highest number of promising programs at seven each.

Of the four promising police programs two involved community policing orientation: community policing with community participation in setting priorities for the police and community policing focused on improving police legitimacy. The other two were: police traffic enforcement patrols against illegally carried handguns and warrants for arrest of absent suspects when police respond to domestic violence.

Of the seven promising courts/corrections programs two were court-based: fines and drug courts combining both rehabilitation and criminal justice controls. Among the five promising programs that were corrections-based, three were aimed to reintegrate offenders into the community (juvenile aftercare, drug treatment combined with urine testing, and transitional programs providing individualized employment preparation and services for high-risk offenders) and two were aimed to prepare offenders for eventual reintegration into the community, but in an institutional setting (prison-based sex offender treatment and adult basic education).

Of the three programs in the labor markets setting, one showed promise in preventing crime (prison-based vocational education programs for adults), while the other two showed promise in preventing crime risk factors such as high school drop-out or unemployment; dispersing inner-city public housing residents to scattered-site suburban public housing and enterprise zones with tax break incentives in areas of extremely high unemployment. Two of the promising school-based programs were targeted at crime (class-room or instructional management and reorganization of grades or classes), while the third was targeted at drop-out/truancy (recreation, community service, enrichment and leisure activities).

Crime outcomes were the exclusive focus of both the community- and place-based programs. The three promising community programs of gang intervention, mentoring and after-school recreation applied to all crime types, while the seven promising place-based programs were specific to particular crime types; for example, metal detectors in airports and guards or sky marshals on airplanes (hijackings), store redesign (shoplifting), and improved training and management of bar staff (drinking-related offenses).

## What is unknown

Across the seven settings, 68 programs were found to be of unknown effec-tiveness. Table 10.5 lists, by institutional setting, those programs for which there is not enough research to draw conclusions about effectiveness. Across the seven settings, there was a great amount of variability in the number of programs found to be of unknown effectiveness, ranging from none for families to 31 for places.

As shown in Table 10.5, the 31 place-based programs have been divided among seven categories: residences, commercial stores, commercial banking and money handling outlets, public transport, parking lots, open public spaces and public facilities. Of these seven places, commercial stores accounted for the largest number (ten) of programs of unknown effective-ness and public facilities accounted for the fewest (two). Multiple outcomes were again measured for the school-based programs. Of the nine school-based programs of unknown effectiveness, five assessed crime, three assessed antisocial behavior, four assessed alcohol or other drug use, and two assessed drop-out/truancy (five programs had multiple outcomes).

Although absent from the title of this chapter and given less attention throughout this volume than the other three categories, the category of unknown effectiveness is nevertheless very important. For instance, many criminal justice programs become popular in the media, with the public and policymakers, and are rapidly spread throughout the US without evidence of effectiveness (see Petrosino, Turpin-Petrosino and Finckenauer, 2000). At best, this may waste money on ineffective programs; at worst, these programs could increase crime.

## Implications for policy

The findings of this book suggest that we do know a fair amount about the "bottom line" of preventing crime; that is, what works, what does not work and what is promising. Unfortunately, the effectiveness of many other pro-grams is unknown. The findings of this book also suggest three broad-based courses of action.

Table 10.4 What is promising in preventing crime

| Families | Schools | Communities | Labor markets | Places | Police | Courts and corrections |
|---|---|---|---|---|---|---|
| 1. Clinic-based child training plus parent training | 1. Classroom or instructional management (crime) | 1. Gang intervention focused on reducing cohesion among juvenile gangs and individual gang members | 1. Prison-based vocational education programs for adults | 1. Multiple clerks in already robbed convenience stores against illegally carried handguns (robberies) | 1. Police traffic enforcement patrols against illegally carried handguns | 1. Drug courts combining both rehabilitation and criminal justice control |
| | 2. Reorganization of grades or classes (crime, AOD) | 2. Community-based mentoring | 2. Dispersing inner-city public housing residents to scattered-site suburban public housing (e.g. high school drop-out, parental unemployment) | 2. Improved training and management of bar staff (drinking-related offenses) | 2. Community policing with community participation in priority setting | 2. Fines |
| | 3. Recreation, community service, enrichment and leisure activities (DO/T) | 3. After-school recreation | 3. Enterprise zones with tax-break incentives in areas of extremely high unemployment (adult unemployment) | 3. Metal detectors in airports (hijackings) | 3. Community policing focused on improving police legitimacy | 3. Juvenile aftercare |
| | | | | 4. Guards (sky marshals) on airplanes (hijackings) | 4. Warrants for arrest of suspect absent when police respond to domestic violence | 4. Drug treatment combined with urine testing |
| | | | | 5. Street closures (various offenses) | | 5. Prison-based sex offender treatment |

6. Target hardening (theft, vandalism)

7. Store redesign (shoplifting)

6. Adult basic education

7. Transitional programs providing individualized employment preparation and services for high-risk offenders

Notes

AOD = alcohol or other drug use; ASB = antisocial behavior; DO/T = drop-out/truancy.

Table 10.5 What is unknown in preventing crime

| Families | Schools[a] | Communities | Labor markets | Places | Police | Courts and corrections |
|---|---|---|---|---|---|---|
| No programs were found to be of unknown effectiveness | 1. School and discipline management (DO/T) | 1. Community mobilization | 1. Criminal justice-based programs for juvenile offenders | 1–6. Residences: target hardening, restricting movement, guards, CCTV, cocoon watch, property marking | 1. Police recreation activities with juveniles | 1. Intensive supervision combining restraints with treatment |
| | 2. Interventions to establish norms or expectations for behavior (DO/T) | 2. Gang membership prevention | 2. Post-release transitional assistance for offenders | 7–16. Commercial stores: EAS, CCTV, target hardening, frequent inventory counts, prohibiting offenders, electronic monitoring, ink tags, guards, cameras, restricting movement | 2. Various new police technologies (e.g. in-car computer terminals) | 2. Boot camps combining structure with treatment |
| | 3. Classroom or instructional management (ASB) | | 3. Reverse commuting (e.g. providing transportation to place of work) | 17–19. Commercial banking and money handling; cameras, target hardening, guards | 3. Multi-jurisdictional task forces to address different crime problems | 3. Day reporting programs combining accountability with treatment |
| | 4. Self-control or social competency instruction without cognitive-behavioral or behavioral instruction methods (crime, AOD) | | 4. Wage subsidies | 20–3. Public transportation: removing targets, rapid cleanup, design, informal watching | 4. Police equipment problems (e.g. what effect computers in police cars have on crime) | 4. Substance use treatment programs for referred offenders |
| | 5. Other instructional programs (i.e. do | | 5. Bonding programs (compensation for | 24–6. Parking lots: CCTV, guards, restricting | 5. Police strategies against gangs | 5. Acupuncture within outpatient substance use |

not focus on social competency or make use of cognitive-behavioral teaching methods) (AOD, ASB)

6. Cognitive-behavioral, behavioral modeling, or behavior modification (crime, AOD)

7. Counseling, social work and other therapeutic interventions (crime, AOD)

8. Mentoring, tutoring and work study (crime)

9. Recreation, community service, enrichment and leisure activities (crime, ASB)

employers hiring workers with a criminal record)

6. Community development through the Community Development Block Grant Program

7. School-to-work programs funded by the School-to-Work Opportunities Act

8. Weed and seed (i.e. removing criminogenic influences and increasing investment in communities or individuals)

movement

27–9. Open public spaces: CCTV, prohibiting offenders, controlling drinking

30–1. Public facilities: removing targets, signs

treatment programs

6. Various policing strategies of domestic violence (e.g. police training)

7. Federal support for juvenile curfew enforcement

treatment programs

6. Anger/stress management

7. Victim awareness

8. Community vocational training

9. Success of (all types of) programs with different types of sex offenders

10. Life skills training

11. Work ethics, in-prison work programs, halfway houses with enhanced services

Notes

a Programs were of unknown or mixed effectiveness.

AOD = alcohol or other drug use; ASB = antisocial behavior; DO/T = drop-out/truancy; CCTV = closed circuit television; EAS = electronic article surveillance.

First, governments (and industry in the case of privately funded programs) need to increase resources devoted to those programs with demonstrated effectiveness in preventing crime. Six of the seven settings (except communities) have at least one program type with evidence of proven effectiveness in preventing crime. Importantly, Table 10.2 may be seen as a menu from which policymakers can choose programs to match government priorities and funding capabilities. Less is known about potential interaction effects from implementing effective programs in different settings at the same time, but because these settings represent the major areas that can influence crime and offending there may be a great deal of benefit from implementing effective programs in all of the six settings.

Second, governments need to stop funding those programs with proven evidence of ineffectiveness. These programs are either making no difference to crime and offending rates or are producing harmful results. Action to end programs with harmful effects should be a top priority. The need for immediate action to stop the funding of crime prevention programs with evidence of proven ineffectiveness is reinforced by the likelihood that the tax-paying public would be annoyed to discover how their taxes are being wasted.

Third, governments should begin further testing of those programs with promising evidence of effectiveness in preventing crime. In many ways, some of these programs may mark the next generation of effective crime prevention programs and policies. Importantly, as we discuss below, only the most rigorous research should be used to evaluate the impact of these programs on crime and offending: experimental and quasi-experimental designs (Cook and Campbell, 1979).

## Towards evidence-based crime prevention

Arguably, all public services share a common interest: the most convincing scientific evidence should be used in the development of public policy and practice. It is, of course, a well-known fact that having convincing research evidence and having it influence policy and practice are two very different matters.

In criminology and criminal justice, discussions about implementing new crime prevention programs, expanding existing ones, or putting an end to ineffective or harmful ones, political and policy considerations are dominant. In fact, it is all too common that the strength of the programmatic evidence under consideration for developing policy becomes secondary to the political considerations of the day.

Some of these considerations are important. Other government priorities, such as military defense spending, environmental protection and lower costs of prescription drugs for seniors, are competing for scarce public resources. National polls may show that the public are more concerned with matters of public policy other than crime prevention or community safety.

Political considerations that are unique to crime prevention include the perception by politicians that they are being "soft" on crime by supporting non-criminal justice crime prevention efforts, and the short time horizons of politicians (Tonry and Farrington, 1995), which makes programs that only show results in the longer-run less appealing to politicians who are trying to get elected every few years.

Political considerations can have a wide range of implications, from the disappointing effect of dismissing strong evidence of the effectiveness of a program to the disastrous effect of ignoring strong evidence of the harmful results of a program. Examples of these effects in criminology and criminal justice are all too common. Another implication of political barriers to evidence-based crime prevention is that the research evidence may not be used in the country in which it was produced, not to mention commissioned by and paid for. As noted in Chapter 1, this applied to this book's predecessor (Sherman *et al.*, 1997). Despite the report by Sherman and his colleagues being the subject of four US Congressional hearings and the authors being invited on numerous occasions to brief policymakers and other criminal justice leaders throughout the US (as well as internationally), the report's largest impact was on British crime prevention policy.

How to overcome some of the misconceived political barriers and get more of what works in preventing crime into policy and practice is by no means an easy task, but fortunately it has received some attention in criminology and criminal justice (e.g. Cullen, 2002), public management (e.g. Nutley and Davies, 2000; Nutley, Davies and Tilley, 2000), public health care (Millenson, 1997; Halladay and Bero, 2000) and evaluation science (e.g. Weiss, 1998), to name a few of the academic disciplines that have been investigating this important issue.

Efforts to work closer and more constructively with policymakers, practitioners and politicians must be a top priority in advancing an evidence-based approach to preventing crime. As important as these efforts are, they need to be supported by a program of research of new crime prevention experiments and quasi-experiments. Here, it will be important to act on the findings of this book, by increasing the use of those programs with demonstrated effectiveness in preventing crime, and further testing of those programs with promising evidence of effectiveness in preventing crime.

These new crime prevention experiments and quasi-experiments should have large samples, long follow-up periods and follow-up interviews. Long-term follow-ups are needed to assess how long effects persist after the intervention ended. Long follow-ups are a rarity in criminological interventions and should be a top priority of funding agencies.

Research is needed to identify the active ingredients of successful (and promising) crime prevention programs. Many programs are multi-modal, making it difficult to isolate the independent effects of different components. Future experiments are needed that attempt to disentangle the effects of different elements of the most successful programs. It is also important that programs include, as part of the original research design, provision for an economic analysis, either a cost–benefit or cost-effectiveness analysis, to allow for an assessment of the economic efficiency of the program.

We are very happy to reach optimistic conclusions. A great deal is known about effective programs to prevent crime. Communities should invest in wide-ranging multi-modal programs including such elements as home visitation of pregnant women, parent education, child skills training, school and discipline management, job training for ex-offenders, improved street lighting, police patrols targeting hots spots of crime, proactive arrests of serious repeat offenders, and cognitive-behavioral therapy in institutions. The time is ripe to mount both national and local crime prevention strategies based on the findings in this book.

## Note

1    The findings from these two assessments are quite similar with one exception. Chapter 6 on labor markets assessed vocation education for adults as promising. In Chapter 9 on corrections, MacKenzie combines evaluations of vocation education for adults and juveniles and concludes that the programs are effective.

## References

Adams, K., Bennett, T., Flanagan, T.J., Marquart, J., Cuvelier, S., Fritsch, E.J., Longmire, D. and Burton, V. (1994) A large-scale multidimensional test of the effect of prison education programs on offender behavior. *The Prison Journal*, 74, 433–49.

Cook, T.D. and Campbell, D.T. (1979) *Quasi-experimentation: Design and analysis issues for field settings*. Chicago, IL: Rand McNally.

Cullen, F.T. (2002) Rehabilitation and treatment programs. In J.Q. Wilson and J. Petersilia (eds), *Crime: Public policies for crime control*. Oakland, CA: Institute of Contemporary Studies Press, 253–89.

Greenwood, P.W. and Turner, S. (1993) Evaluation of the Paint Creek Youth Center: A residential program for serious delinquents. *Criminology*, 31, 263–79.

Hahn, A. (1999) Extending the time of learning. In D.J. Besharov (ed.), *America's disconnected youth: Toward a preventive strategy*. Washington, DC: Child Welfare League of America Press, 233–65.

Halladay, M. and Bero, L. (2000) Implementing evidence-based practice in health care. *Public Money and Management*, 20, 43–50.

Hartmann, D.J., Friday, P.C. and Minor, K.I. (1994) Residential probation: A seven-year follow-up of halfway house discharges. *Journal of Criminal Justice*, 22, 503–15.

Hawkins, J.D., Catalano, R.F., Kosterman, R., Abbott, R. and Hill, K.G. (1999) Preventing adolescent health-risk behaviors by strengthening protection during childhood. *Archives of Pediatrics and Adolescent Medicine*, 153, 226–34.

Hope, T. (1994) Problem-oriented policing and drug market locations: Three case studies. In R.V. Clarke (ed.), *Crime prevention studies: Vol. 2*. Monsey, NY: Criminal Justice Press, 5–32.

Kennedy, D.M., Piehl, A.M. and Braga, A.A. (1996) Youth violence in Boston: Gun markets, serious youth offenders, and a use-reduction strategy. *Law and Contemporary Problems*, 59, 147–96.

Lattimore, P.K., Witte, A.D. and Baker, J.R. (1990) Experimental assessment of the effect of vocational training on youthful property offenders. *Evaluation Review*, 14, 115–33.

Maguire, K.E., Flanagan, T.J. and Thornberry, T.P. (1988) Prison labor and recidivism. *Journal of Quantitative Criminology*, 4, 3–18.

Menon, R., Blakely, C., Carmichael, D. and Silver, L. (1992) *An evaluation of Project RIO outcomes: An evaluative report*. College Station, TX: Public Policy Resources Laboratory.

Millenson, M.L. (1997) *Demanding medical excellence: Doctors and accountability in the information age*. Chicago, IL: University of Chicago Press.

Nutley, S. and Davies, H.T.O. (2000) Making a reality of evidence-based practice: Some lessons from the diffusion of innovations. *Public Money and Management*, 20, 35–42.

Nutley, S., Davies, H.T.O. and Tilley, N. (2000) Editorial: Getting research into practice. *Public Money and Management*, 20, 3–6.

Petrosino, A., Turpin-Petrosino, C. and Finckenauer, J.O. (2000) Well-meaning programs can have harmful effects! Lessons from experiments of programs such as Scared Straight. *Crime and Delinquency*, 46, 354–79.

Saylor, W.G. and Gaes, G.G. (1996) *PREP: Training inmates through industrial work participation and vocational and apprenticeship instruction*. Washington, DC: US Federal Bureau of Prisons.

Sherman, L.W., Gottfredson, D.C., MacKenzie, D.L., Eck, J., Reuter, P. and Bushway, S.D. (1997) *Preventing crime: What works, what doesn't, what's promising*. Washington, DC: National Institute of Justice, US Department of Justice.

Tonry, M. and Farrington, D.P. (1995) Strategic approaches to crime prevention. In M. Tonry and D.P. Farrington (eds), *Building a safer society: Strategic approaches to crime prevention. Vol. 19: Crime and justice: A review of research*. Chicago, IL: University of Chicago Press, 1–20.

Tremblay, R.E., Pagani-Kurtz, L, Mâsse, L.C., Vitaro, F. and Pihl, R.O. (1995) A bimodal preventive intervention for disruptive kindergarten boys: Its impact through mid-adolescence. *Journal of Consulting and Clinical Psychology*, 63, 560–8.

Van Stelle, K.R., Lidbury, J.R. and Moberg, D.P. (1995) *Final evaluation report: Specialized Training and Employment Project (STEP)*. Madison, WI: University of Wisconsin Medical School, Center for Health Policy and Program Evaluation.

Wasserman, G.A. and Miller, L.S. (1998) The prevention of serious and violent juvenile offending. In R. Loeber and D.P. Farrington (eds), *Serious and violent juvenile offenders: Risk factors and successful interventions*. Thousand Oaks, CA: Sage, 197–247.

Weiss, C.H. (1998) Have we learned anything new about the use of evaluation? *American Journal of Evaluation*, 19, 21–33.

# Index

Note: page numbers in *italics* refer to tables or figures